Social and Personality Assessment of School-Aged Children

Developing Interventions for Educational and Clinical Use

Edited by
Janet F. Carlson
State University of New York at Oswego

Betsy B. Waterman
State University of New York at Oswego

Allyn and Bacon

Boston London Toronto Sydney Tokyo Singapore

Executive Editor: *Rebecca Pascal*
Editorial Assistant: *Kate Edwards*
Editorial Production Administrator: *Bryan Woodhouse*
Editorial Production Service: *Chestnut Hill Enterprises, Inc.*
Composition and Prepress Buyer: *Linda Cox*
Manufacturing Buyer: *Joanne Sweeney*
Cover Administrator: *Kristina Mose-Libon*
Electronic Composition: *Modern Graphics*

Library of Congress Cataloging-in-Publication Data

Social and personality assessment of school-aged children : developing interventions for educational and clinical use / edited by Janet F. Carlson, Betsy B. Waterman.
    p. cm.
Includes bibliographical references and index.
ISBN 0-205-32592-0
   1. Psychological tests for children.   2. Personality tests for children.   3. Child
psychotherapy.   I. Carlson, Janet.   II. Waterman, Betsy B.

BF722.3 .S62 2002
155.4'1--dc21

    2001053768

Printed in the United States of America

10   9   8   7   6   5   4   3   2   1   RRD-VA   06   05   04   03   02   01

Contents

PART TWO • *Foundations for Social and Personality Assessment*

4 *Functional Behavioral Assessment*   64

James L. McDougal and Sandra M. Chafouleas

5 *Use of Direct Assessment Techniques with School-Aged Children*   85

Sandra M. Chafouleas and Ronald Dumont

6 *Neuropsychological Assessment with School-Aged Children*   105

Lawrence J. Lewandowski and Jeremie R. Barlow

PART FOUR · *Developing Interventions*

Contributors

ACHILLES N. BARDOS is Professor of School Psychology and Coordinator of the External Degree Program at the University of Northern Colorado. Dr. Bardos's teaching and research interests include psychoeducational assessment, program evaluation, and computer applications in psychology. He has coauthored the *Draw A Person: Screening Procedure for Emotional Disturbance* (1991) and the *General Ability Measure for Adults* (1997) with Jack Naglieri.

JEREMIE RENTAS BARLOW is a doctoral student in the school psychology program at Syracuse University. She received her B.S. in psychology from Fordham University and her M.S. in psychology from Syracuse University. She currently works as a school psychologist in Louisville, Kentucky, where she is completing her doctoral work.

BRUCE A. BRACKEN is a Professor at The College of William & Mary. He obtained his M.A. and Ph.D. at the University of Georgia in 1979. Dr. Bracken has published several tests, including the *Universal Nonverbal Intelligence Test, Bracken Basic Concept Scale—Revised, Multidimensional Self-Concept Scale*, and the *Assessment of Interpersonal Relations*. He coedits the *Journal of Psychoeducational Assessment* and sits on several psychological journal editorial boards. He edited the texts *Psychoeducational Assessment of Preschool Children* (3rd ed.) and the *Handbook of Self-Concept*, and he authored the *Bracken Concept Development Program* and coauthored the *Essentials of Nonverbal Assessment*. Dr. Bracken recently chaired the APA Committee on Psychological Testing and Assessment, and currently is President-Elect of the International Test Commission. He is a Diplomate in the American Board of Psychological Assessment and a Fellow in the APA, and currently sits on a National Academies of Science panel on disability diagnosis.

JANET F. CARLSON is a Professor in the Counseling and Psychological Services Department at the State University of New York at Oswego. She earned her M.A. and Ph.D. in clinical psychology from Fordham University. She is a licensed psychologist and certified school psychologist in New York State, has held full-time teaching positions and has taught numerous courses including several related to assessment, diagnosis, and personality at Fordham University, Fairfield University, Le Moyne College, and SUNY at Oswego. Her publications and presentations have included such topics as computer-based test interpretation, effective teaching, childhood depression, and a number of test reviews. Before teaching, Dr. Carlson worked as a psychologist in clinical and school settings. Since beginning her teaching career, she has served as a consultant to school systems, including the New York City Board of Education's Office of Research, Evaluation, and Assessment.

JEANETT CASTELLANOS, Ph.D., is a Lecturer at the University of California-Irvine in both the departments of Social Science and Chicano Studies. She is also a consultant for Pacific Opinions: An Independent Research Group, and has worked with community agencies to enhance services provided to the diverse populations of Southern California. Her research interests include cultural competency, the underutilization of psychotherapy among minorities, and coping strategies leading to resilience among ethnic minority clients.

JAY CERIO, Ph.D., is a Professor of School Psychology at Alfred University in Western New York State, with more than 25 years of experience as a practitioner of play therapy and family therapy in school and agency settings. He has authored numerous articles on these subjects and one text, *Play*

Therapy: A Do-It-Yourself Guide for Practitioners. He is a frequent presenter on play therapy and family therapy techniques at regional and national conferences.

SANDRA M. CHAFOULEAS is currently an Assistant Professor with the School Psychology program at the University of Connecticut. Previously, Dr. Chafouleas directed the School Psychology program at the State University of New York at Plattsburgh. In both positions, she provided training in behavioral assessment and intervention to future and practicing school psychologists. She also has taught courses in academic and intellectual assessment, ethics, and the roles and functions of school psychologists. Dr. Chafouleas's primary area of research interest involves the prevention of reading difficulties, and the applicability of empirically based strategies to the classroom. Her research efforts to date have focused on identifying accurate and efficient measures of early literacy assessment and intervention. Prior to becoming a university trainer, Dr. Chafouleas worked in a variety of settings as a school psychologist and school administrator with children with behavior disorders.

HARRIET C. COBB is a Professor of Psychology on the faculty of the Psy.D. program in Combined Clinical, School, and Counseling Psychology at James Madison University (JMU). She practiced as a school psychologist for eight years prior to her appointment at JMU, where she teaches courses in psychotherapy, school-based assessment and interventions, and consultation and supervision. Harriet has maintained a part-time clinical practice for the past 20 years, working with children, adults, and families. Her recent publications have included book chapters on the topics of therapy with disabled children, cultural responsiveness in therapy, and graduate training issues.

SCOTT L. CONE received his Ph.D. from Fordham University. He has worked with children and adolescents for 15 years as a child-care worker, counselor, and psychologist, primarily with adolescents in residential care. His experiences also include work in outpatient and school settings. Currently, Dr. Cone serves as the Director of Clinical Services at Edwin Gould Academy in Rockland County, New York, a coeducational residential treatment center serving inner-city youth from the foster care and juvenile justice systems. As the only New York State Special Act Public School coordinated with a child-care agency under one mission, one strategic plan, and one administration, Edwin Gould Academy was named a 1998 winner of the prestigious Innovations in American Government Award, a program of the Ford Foundation and Harvard University.

THOMAS P. CUSHMAN, Ph.D., is a certified school psychologist and a licensed psychologist. He has provided psychological services to children, adolescents, parents, teachers, and school administrators for over 25 years on a full- or part-time basis. Dr. Cushman is an Associate Professor and past chair of the Department of Counseling and Psychological Services at the State University of New York at Oswego. He is currently the Assistant Editor of *The NASP Communiqué*, and is on the editorial review board of the *Person Centered Journal*. Dr. Cushman has published a number of articles on the various sources of inattention with Dr. Thomas B. Johnson and he is a frequent speaker on the topic.

RONALD DUMONT is currently an Associate Professor of Psychology at Fairleigh Dickinson University in Teaneck, New Jersey, and Director of the master's and doctoral programs in School Psychology. Previously he directed the School Psychology program at the State University of New York at Plattsburgh. He was a practicing school psychologist for 20 years, and Director of Psychological Services for the Hudson-Litchfield, New Hampshire school districts. Dr. Dumont has published numerous journal articles and has coauthored, with John Willis, a *Guide to the Identification of Learning Disabilities*. He was senior author and computer programmer for the *Differential Ability Scales Scoring Assistant*, published by the Psychological Corporation. He is a contributing editor on assessment for *The NASP Communiqué*, and serves on the editorial boards of *Psychology in the Schools* and the *Journal of Psychoeducational Assessment*. His research interests include cognitive assessment, learning disabilities, emotional disorders, and test reviews.

NANCY J. EVANGELISTA, Ph.D., is an Assistant Professor in the Division of School Psychology at Alfred University. She earned her master's and doctoral degrees in school psychology at Syracuse University. Her teaching and research interests focus on developmental and behavioral disorders in early childhood, cognitive assessment, and supervision of psychological services. Prior to her academic appointment, she was the senior psychologist at the Developmental Evaluation Center, a regional clinic operated by the State University of New York Health Sciences Center in Syracuse. She holds a teaching degree in Special Education from

Western Michigan University and has worked in Head Start and preschool special education programs. Active in professional organizations, Dr. Evangelista is the President-Elect of the New York Association of School Psychologists and Treasurer of the School Psychology Educators' Council of New York.

SENAIDA FERNANDEZ is currently a doctoral student in clinical psychology at the San Diego State University/University of California at San Diego Joint Doctoral Program in Clinical Psychology. Her research interests include the mental health of women of color, body image concerns among women from diverse ethnic backgrounds, and issues related to the psychological assessment of women of color. She has authored a number of presentations on the mental health of women and has presented her research findings at numerous national conferences.

BARBARA A. FISCHETTI, D.Ed., is the Coordinator of Psychological Services and a school psychologist for the Westport, Connecticut Public Schools. She is a licensed psychologist, certified school psychologist, and certified MBTI/MMTIC trainer. She has served as an adjunct professor at Fairfield University and Western Connecticut State University. Additionally, Dr. Fischetti has provided numerous workshops on type theory to educational and nonprofit institutions. Dr. Fischetti is the past president of the Connecticut Association of School Psychologists and the state delegate to the National Association of School Psychologists.

SHERRI L. GALLAGHER is a doctoral student in school psychology at the University of Northern Colorado. Previously, she was employed as a School Psychologist in the Baltimore City Public School System. She received her Master of Science degree in clinical psychology at Loyola College in Maryland. Her research interests include prevention, early intervention, health psychology, and prosocial behavior.

KURT F. GEISINGER, Ph.D., is Vice President for Academic Affairs and Professor of Psychology at the University of St. Thomas in Houston, Texas. He has held administrative and faculty appointments previously at Le Moyne College, the State University of New York at Oswego, and Fordham University. At Fordham, he chaired the Psychology Department and directed the doctoral program in Psychometrics. Among his publications, he coauthored *Test Interpretation for*

Members of Diverse Groups, edited *Psychological Testing of Hispanics*, and coedited *Test Interpretation and Diversity: Achieving Equity in Psychological Assessment*. His professional service includes membership on the APA's Committee on Psychological Testing and Assessment, and cochairing the Joint Committee on Testing Practices (1993–1997). He currently serves as consulting editor for the *International Journal of Testing* and *Educational Research Quarterly*. He has served on numerous editorial boards previously, and as an expert witness in legal cases concerning proper test use. A fellow of the APA, his specialties include psychometrics, test construction, testing language minorities and individuals with disabilities, and test translation.

JANE S. HALONEN is Professor and Director of the School of Psychology at James Madison University in Harrisonburg, Virginia. Her scholarship in critical thinking and faculty development has been enriched by many opportunities to serve as a consultant and reviewer in psychology programs across the country. Jane was a private practitioner in Milwaukee for 12 years coincident with her teaching career at Alverno College before moving to James Madison University. In her practice, she specialized in working with children and families, particularly around issues of loss. Jane is the winner of the 2000 American Psychological Foundation Award for Distinguished Teaching and was designated the Harry Kirke Wolfe Lecturer on Teaching for the 2001 APA convention in San Francisco. Her textbooks include *Psychology: Contexts, Science, and Applications* (McGraw-Hill) and *Your Guide to College Success* (Wadsworth), both coauthored with John Santrock, and *The Critical Thinking Companion for Introductory Psychology* (Worth) with coauthor Cynthia Gray.

VIRGINIA SMITH HARVEY, Ph.D., is an Associate Professor in the School Psychology program at the University of Massachusetts-Boston. She was a practicing school psychologist for 18 years, and supervised school psychology interns and school psychologists throughout those years. During her eight years as a university professor, she has supervised practicum, intern, and postgraduate students. She has researched the functioning of school psychologists, and has published articles on improving the readability of psychological reports and providing a system of care for students through interagency collaboration. Dr. Harvey is also the author of *Effective Supervision of School Psychologists*.

JOHN R. HOLMBERG, Psy.D., is a Senior Professional Research Assistant coordinating research projects at the Prevention Research Center for Family and Child Health of the University of Colorado Health Sciences Center. He pursued his undergraduate studies in psychology at the University of Colorado at Boulder, and his graduate studies in clinical psychology were completed through the Doctor of Psychology program at Baylor University. He also completed a Clinical Fellowship at the Child Study Center of the Yale University School of Medicine. His research interests include child development, the study and reduction of risk factors associated with child and adolescent psychopathology, learning disabilities and child assessment techniques, trauma and exposure to violence, therapy with children and families, and clinical applications of play, as well as community-based intervention programs.

LAWRENCE J. LEWANDOWSKI is a Professor of Psychology and a Meredith Professor of Teaching Excellence at Syracuse University. He is the former director of the School Psychology program. Professor Lewandowski serves on the editorial boards of the *Journal of Learning Disabilities* and the *Journal of Psychoeducational Assessment*, and is an associate editor for the *ADHD Report*. He serves as a consultant to the National Board of Medical Examiners and several state boards of Law Examiners as an expert in the area of learning disabilities. He has published over 70 articles, chapters, and books on the topics of learning disabilities and neuropsychology. He is licensed as a psychologist in New York State and has held certification in school psychology in several states.

JAMES L. MCDOUGAL is currently the Mental Health Coordinator for the Syracuse City School District. In this capacity he provides academic, behavioral, and mental health consultation to over 40 schools and programs. Dr. McDougal developed the nationally recognized Behavior Consultation Team Program that was listed among exemplary mental health programs cited by the National Association of School Psychologists. He was instrumental in the development and implementation of the School-Based Intervention Team program, selected by the New York State Education Department for inclusion in their Instructional Support Team Training Manual. He is an adjunct instructor for Le Moyne College's Education Department and conducts presentations and workshops for school personnel and parent groups. His

recent emphasis is on developing behavior assessment and intervention techniques that are effective and feasible for use in the public school setting and on the creation of safe school environments, topics on which he provides private consultation services.

NATALIE POLITIKOS is a practicing School Psychologist in the Poudre School District in Fort Collins, Colorado and an adjunct faculty member of the School Psychology Program at the University of Northern Colorado. She teaches courses in psychological testing and measurement, intellectual and cognitive assessment, and computer applications to psychology. Dr. Politikos's research interests are in the areas of cross-cultural psychology, assessment, human figure drawings, and neuropsychology.

GERALD PORTER is a school psychologist and an Associate Professor in the Department of Counseling and Psychological Services at The State University of New York at Oswego, where he also serves as Assistant Dean in the School of Education. Before coming to academia, Dr. Porter worked as a psychologist with the New York State Department of Correctional Services and the Division for Youth. He served as a policy analyst with the New York Job Training Partnership Council and the New York State Department of Education. Dr. Porter's research interests include community-based service delivery, economic equity issues in education and mental health; as well as the social construction of race and gender and its implications in education.

RONA PRELI, Ph.D., is an Associate Professor and the Department Chairperson of the Masters in Marriage and Family Therapy program at Fairfield University in Fairfield, Connecticut. She is a licensed, practicing marriage and family therapist and supervisor. Dr. Preli has held several state and national positions. Currently, she is the President-Elect of the Connecticut Association for Marriage and Family Therapy, a Commissioner for the Commission on Accreditation for Marriage and Family Therapy Education, and serves on the editorial board for *The Journal of Marriage and Family Therapy*. Her primary research is in the area of multicultural issues in training and supervision.

ROBERTO J. VÉLASQUEZ is an Associate Professor in the San Diego State University–University of California at San Diego Joint Doctoral Program in Clinical Psychology, and maintains a private practice in assessment psychology. He obtained his Ph.D. in Counseling Psychology in 1986 from Arizona State University. His research interests include the valid evaluation of bilingual–bicultural people in mental health settings, the mental health status and adjustment of Cuban and Vietnamese refugees, forensic evaluation of culturally diverse children, and use of the MMPI-2 with U.S. minorities, most notably Latinos. Presently, Dr. Vélasquez is editing two books for publication in 2002, *The Handbook of Chicana and Chicano Psychology* and *The Handbook of Latino MMPI-2/MMPI-A Research and Application.* He serves on the Committee on Psychological Testing and Assessment for the American Psychological Association.

LAWRENCE A. VITULANO, Ph.D., received his undergraduate degree from Georgetown University and his Ph.D. in clinical psychology from Catholic University. He is currently Associate Clinical Professor of Child and Adolescent Psychology at the Child Study Center of the Yale School of Medicine in New Haven, Connecticut and was a former chief child psychologist for the Connecticut Department of Children and Families. His major areas of interest include effective short-term treatment, obsessive-compulsive disorder, trichotillomania, hypnosis, chronic disease, child abuse, and violence and trauma. Dr. Vitulano has lectured throughout the world, including Italy, the Vatican, and Croatia. He has published extensively and currently is involved in training police in Europe and the United States to intervene more effectively on behalf of children who are the victims of violence.

JOHN D. WASSERMAN is an Associate Professor at George Mason University in Fairfax, Virginia. He obtained his Ph.D. in 1990 in clinical psychology from the University of Miami, and completed a two-year fellowship in clinical neuropsychology at Louisiana State University and Tulane University Medical Centers. Dr. Wasserman is a licensed psychologist and directed a pediatric neuropsychology service at Children's Hospital in New Orleans before entering academia. The author of over 50 papers and professional presentations, he also coauthored the book, *Essentials of Nonverbal Assessment.* He serves on the editorial board of the *Journal of Psychoeducational Assessment.* For nearly a decade, he worked in the test development industry as Director of Psychological Assessments at Riverside Publishing and as a Project Director at the Psychological Corporation. In 1999, he chaired the Clinical Division of the Association of Test Publishers and served as a member of the APA committee to implement the recommendations of the Psychological Assessments Work Group.

BETSY B. WATERMAN is Professor and Chair of the Counseling and Psychological Services Department at The State University of New York at Oswego, where she teaches in a graduate program that trains school psychologists and counselors. She is also an active researcher in the area of learning problems, reading, memory, and early childhood. Betsy earned her Ph.D. in School Psychology from Syracuse University, and is a licensed psychologist. She has a background in special education and taught students with emotional disabilities prior to her work as a school psychologist and college professor. She worked as part of a preschool assessment team for several years and currently is a mental health consultant to Head Start in Oswego County. Betsy is a regular presenter on a variety of topics internationally, nationally, and regionally.

Preface

The major focus of *Social and Personality Assessment of School-Aged Children* concerns the development of assessment processes that lead to appropriate and effective interventions for a range of social and personal difficulties experienced by school-aged children (e.g., attention, social problems) in a variety of contexts (e.g., home, school, ethnically and culturally diverse communities). Its emphasis is grounded in the belief that effective interventions rely on assessment processes that move well beyond classification and diagnosis. Ideally, this volume will help assessment professionals arrive at comprehensive understandings of behaviors that interfere with children's social and personal growth, the contexts in which these behaviors develop, the events or situations that maintain the behaviors, and the range of possible means by which to effect change.

The audience for this professional book includes practicing school and clinical psychologists who work with school-aged children as well as faculty who train school and clinical psychologists. The book provides foundational material (e.g., measurement issues, overviews of basic techniques) that is critical for those still in training and serves as a good refresher for those already in practice. The more advanced and practical material that makes up the bulk of the book is an invaluable resource for the clinician and for the student as they move beyond the classroom into actual practice. The comprehensive nature of this professional book makes it an important acquisition for college and university libraries and agencies, as well as individual practitioners in school and agency settings.

As a text, the volume's primary use likely will occur in graduate-level school and clinical psychology classes in the area of personality or social assessment. It also is appropriate for use in courses that highlight the development of interventions for school-aged children. Such courses are typically required in both school and clinical psychology training programs. In fact, the original inspiration for this work was in response to a frustrating search for a text to use for training school psychologists in personality assessment. The few texts that were found seemed to be almost exclusively clinically focused and included few interventions that would retain their relevance in a school setting. As editors, we worked assiduously to bridge the oft-observed gap between clinical and educational (i.e., school) psychological domains. Especially when working with school-aged children, we do not see advantages in regarding these realms as separate and nonoverlapping. We worked closely with our contributing authors to retain a focus on children's difficulties, ways of understanding their problems, and ways of diminishing their problems, in order to maintain a balance between clinical "diagnostic" approaches and school-based "classification" systems.

This book is predicated on the belief that the current tendency toward the identification of symptoms and classification of disorders does a disservice to school-aged children, as does the tendency to view school and clinical realms as nonoverlapping. Bridging these two domains gives greater emphasis to the development of appropriate interventions for children of school-age who struggle with social problems, personal adjustment issues, or behavioral difficulties. Chapter authors frame problematic behaviors demonstrated by children in terms of problem assessment and problem resolution. Interpretive strategies are aimed at the generation and testing of hypotheses, with due consideration to the context within which assessment data have been collected. Intervention strategies stress the development of interventions whose effectiveness extends beyond the school setting.

Several features set this volume apart from others in the field. One of our sustaining goals, noted above, was bridging the arenas of school and clinical practice. With discussions centered on problem recognition, understanding, and amelioration, the volume makes a strong connection between assessment practices themselves and the formulation of interventions. Another common thread that runs throughout the volume concerns diversity and its implications for conducting assessments, understanding or interpreting findings, and planning interventions. Finally, we have included assessment-related topics that add considerable breadth in such areas as functional behavioral assessment, information-processing perspectives, neuropsychological assessment, computer-based interpretation practices, assessment of family functioning, and discussion of assessment, interpretation, and interventions in early childhood.

The book has five major sections. The first, an introductory section, provides the conceptual framework for the remainder of the book. It establishes the content to be covered and creates an organizational scheme for the reader. It specifies the populations and contexts that are the subject matter of the book, describes critical considerations in the selection of measures, and summarizes the major difficulties exhibited by school-aged children in social and personal functioning.

The second section covers assessment issues directly with something of a "how-to" orientation. Chapter authors address various types of assessment, instruments, and procedures that are recommended to ascertain a child's level of functioning in relevant domains.

The third section addresses interpretive issues, using the theme of "problem assessment" versus the more typical "symptom listing" or "classification" approaches. In this section, chapter authors provide insight about how to interpret test results in a comprehensive manner that focuses on understanding the problems a child may experience, rather than (merely) accounting for symptoms a child may evidence. Thus, the focus is on understanding problem behaviors in the context of both the individual child and his or her place in the world, and developing and testing hypotheses suggested by the data. The closing chapter in this section concerns effective report writing and serves as a bridge between the interpretive elements of the assessment process and the formulation of effective interventions that are at the heart of the next section.

The fourth major section has a decidedly practical orientation, as its content addresses the formulation of appropriate interventions for use with school-aged children in educational and clinical settings. Chapter authors offer strategies for developing interventions that have applicability, in and out of school, for children with special needs, while keeping in mind the full context of the child's inner and outer worlds.

The fifth section anticipates future issues concerning assessment and intervention processes used with children in social and personal areas and contexts. For example, the challenges posed by our expanding population and increasing diversity and those prompted by the ready availability of computer technology with applications in the assessment domain are addressed. In the final chapter, the authors present a multifaceted, futuristic view of assessment and assessment practices and challenges.

We are indebted to a substantial number of individuals who, in various ways, gave of themselves to help us complete this work. In addition to our contributing authors, we are especially grateful for the assistance we received from Jeremy Waterman, Wayne Weiten, Rebecca Pascal, Myrna Breskin, Renata Cary, Mandy Morrell, Whitney Brown, Vicki Parsnow, and Deborah Sawyer. We also wish to thank Jane Halonen for her insightful comments about the book, generally, and several chapters in particular. Further, we are deeply appreciative of Kurt Geisinger, who not only contributed a swell chapter for our "Future Directions" section, but also provided expert guidance, good humor, and ceaseless personal support through the various rough spots.

A surprising number of events related to the creation of this work proceeded more or less as expected. In fact, we would change only one major event that took place during the book's development, which was both unexpected and—ultimately—unavoidable. Nothing would give us greater joy than to be able to share this finished work in person with one of our most stalwart supporters, Gary S. Waterman, whose untimely passing preceded our completion of this project. Posthumously, we express our gratitude and love to him for his incredible patience, untiring encouragement, lighthearted humor, and enduring spirit.

1

Domains and Contexts of Social and Personality Assessment

Betsy B. Waterman and

Janet F. Carlson

Observing behavior in a consistent manner and distilling its meaning accurately are ambitious goals, but unless the understanding of behavior can propel corrective actions in the form of interventions, the purpose of these tasks will be less than complete. In the context of working with school-aged children, it can be difficult to separate the tasks of problem recognition, instrument selection, data collection, data interpretation, designing interventions, communicating findings, and evaluating outcomes. Yet, it is essential to understand these assessment components individually, and then to strive to understand them as they interface with one another, as we have done in this volume. Throughout this introductory chapter, we make specific references to several chapters in this volume as a matter of convenience for the reader who wishes to explore the topic under discussion more completely and immediately. Even chapters not mentioned specifically in this chapter, however, are germane to the objectives of the book as described herein.

As reviewed in Chapter 3, children demonstrate a wide variety of difficulties that may necessitate closer attention and intervention. Behavior that is potentially problematic in a child's social or personal domain of functioning may be assessed by an enormous number of instruments and methods. Many other books address the wide variety of specific tests and applications of measures that may be put to this purpose (e.g., Anastasi & Urbina, 1997; Cohen & Swerdlik, 1999; Hopkins, 1998; Thorndike, 1997). Our intention in this chapter is to frame a different purpose than that seen in these other useful volumes. The themes we articulate are echoed in individual chapters. Specifically, this current chapter describes the assessment realms and contextual considerations that form the subject matter of the remainder of the book. Issues that accompany the development of social and personal assessment questions, the collection and interpretation of relevant data, and the enumeration of appropriate interventions for use with school-aged children structure this chapter and frame the discussions that follow in subsequent chapters.

Broadly speaking, the goal of assessment is to foster effective decision making (Meehl, 1973) in order to intervene in ways that bring about optimal functioning by addressing problem behaviors expeditiously and as completely as possible. Assessment of social and personal functioning among school-age children can serve a number of important purposes, including screening and identification, classification and eligibility for special education determination, diagnosis, development of intervention strategies, and evaluation of treatment effectiveness. Attention to individual needs of a particular child is paramount and must include thorough consideration of factors within the child's internal and external environments. Therefore, physiology and information processing, as well as belief systems emanating from the child's view of self, coupled with his or her actual interpersonal skills, must be prime components of social and personal assessment. Equally important, however, are considerations of external factors such as cultural influences, developmental issues and expectations, familial structure and functioning, community and school influences, and, perhaps, other concerns. Without consideration of both the child's internal and external environments, "optimal functioning" is difficult to discern, and effective interventions that work within some cultures or some kinds of families or some communities or at some age levels may not work for the individual child the psychologist has in mind.

Sound Decision Making Depends on Sound Theoretical Bases

The questions one asks about the social and personal aspects of a child's life need to be well grounded in an established, well-researched theoretical base. The complex nature of social and personal development may make the delineation of constructs associated with social and personal assessment difficult. Some writers suggest that personality assessment is so fraught with problems that it should be abandoned. Most psychologists, however, disagree more about the methods or instruments to be used in social and personal assessment and the means by which to interpret resultant data than whether or not to perform these types of assessment. To ignore social and personal domains of a child's functioning would clearly diminish one's understanding of the individual child and his or her struggles in these areas.

One theoretical argument among the early personality theorists involved the type of approach that should be applied in the study of social and personal development. Allport (1937) suggested two means by which personality could be considered: nomothetic and idiographic. The nomological network originally proposed by Cronbach and Meehl (1955) linked the theoretical and observable realms in much the same way seen in other sciences. According to this view, the *nomological network* should relate observable, measurable properties to each other, relate different theoretical constructs to each other, and relate theoretical constructs to observable properties.

The nomological approach searches for the prevailing traits or motives that might influence a person's behavior. This perspective supports the use of objective instruments that allow for decisions made on the basis of statistical predictions stemming from laws that guide people in general.

Not surprisingly, there were a number of personality theorists and practitioners who believed the human condition could not always be captured adequately in observable, objective ways. These theorists proposed the *idiographic* point of view for studying and assessing social and personal data, wherein the patterns or laws that guide an individual's behavior are gathered. Proponents of this viewpoint argue for gathering and reviewing individual data, including qualitative information, and for making inferences about individuals primarily on clinical judgment derived from their own clinical expertise.

Although the foregoing controversy continues to some extent today, most practitioners and theorists value both types of data in the study and assessment of social and personal functioning. Nomothetic data provide a link to theoretical and philosophical foundations and the understanding of how certain groups of people may behave in given situations. Idiographic data provide information about how a specific person is likely to respond in a specific situation (Bem, 1983).

A second area of theoretical dispute relates to the understanding and measurement of traits. The belief held by some personality theorists is that basic, consistent characteristics (i.e., traits) that impel certain behaviors can be identified (Goldberg, 1992). Tupes and Christal (1961), and, more recently, McCrae and Costa (McCrae & Costa, 1994; McCrae et al., 2000), for instance, suggested that five bipolar traits could be identified that were stable within an individual across the dimensions of time and situation. The five factors relate to surgency (extraversion), agreeableness, conscientiousness, emotional stability, and culture, intellect, openness, or sophistication. Although considerable research supports the viability of these factors, even across many cultures (McCrae & Costa, 1997), very little extant research has involved children or adolescents (Kamphaus & Frick, 1996).

Other personality theorists reject the notion of enduring characteristics that can be measured in any meaningful way (Barnett & Zucker, 1990; Cantor, 1981; Mischel, 1981). As Barnett and Zucker state, instruments designed to measure "generalized characteristics" are costly and time-consuming to produce, may have limited utility in a practical sense, and result in high error rates when applied on an individual basis. Mischel and Cantor both emphasize the importance of studying social and personal variables in natural situations such as within the school, family, and other social systems.

Similarly, Macmann et al. (1996) suggest that assessments should go well beyond diagnoses. These authors encourage the placement of assessment processes within a "decision-making" context. They emphasize that diagnostic problem solving should be shared among several active participants with the design and implementation of appropriate, effective interventions as the outcome. In a related vein, Kratochwill and McGivern (1996) stress the need to evaluate the treatment utility of methodologies used to assess behaviors of various kinds. They emphasize the importance of treatment outcome over the mere selection, formulation, or monitoring of treatment, because evidence of some positive outcome attributable to the treatment is essential in order to document its effectiveness.

There are a number of broader theoretical perspectives from which social and personal development have been explained and studied. It is important to understand how differing theoretical approaches to assessment may affect the interpretation of behavior and the interventions designed. Behaviorism, for example, places importance on behavioral change and on the interventions utilized to achieve such change. An outgrowth of behaviorism is social cognitive theory, an approach that was influenced greatly by the work of Bandura (e.g., 1977, 1978, 1986, 1993, 1997). Social cognitive theory integrates cognition, language, personality development, assessment, and behavior modification (Barnett & Zucker, 1990). Like behaviorism, the emphasis in social cognitive theory is on behavioral change. The constructs of "self-system," self-regulation, self-efficacy, and life events are highlighted as a part of this theory. Self-system differs from self-concept in that it is less traitlike in nature and, as Barnett and Zucker have suggested, may better "address the variation in self-reactions and the manner in which self-percepts regulate behavior" (p. 11). Self-regulatory processes, according to Bandura (1978), involve a person's ability to observe, judge, and monitor the self, and are associated with one's beliefs or fantasies.

Developmental psychology is another perspective important to the understanding of social and personal assessment, as discussed more fully in Chapter 12. Early developmental theorists suggested that social and emotional skills, attitudes, and characteristics develop in predictable stages as children grow. Although developmentalists initially believed that most personality characteristics were reasonably stable by age 6, it is now believed that social and personal development occurs across the life span. Issues of development are important in understanding the reliability and validity of children's and adolescents' self-reports (Bruck, Ceci, & Hembrooke, 1998; Smith, Pelham, Gnagy, Molina, & Evans, 2000), the adjustment to such events as divorce or remarriage, the impact of poverty on child development (Frisby, 1998b; McLoyd, 1998), the power of early intervention, the development of resilience among children (Henderson & Milstein, 1996), and the differing manifestation of symptoms across the age span. Developmental level is equally important in the formulation of effective interventions for school-aged children, a point that is amplified by Cerio, in Chapter 18, through his discussion of play therapy interventions.

Systems approaches to understanding social and personal development suggest that the context (e.g., family, school, community) in which a child functions influences his or her social and personal development. These approaches highlight the interconnectedness of the family system and assessment examines the interactions, patterns, and sequences that exist among family members. From a systems perspective, assessment requires an understanding of the child from a broad, ecological view and interventions should be considered that change how the system operates more so than the child. Consistent with these perspectives, Cone, in Chapter 16, and Porter and Vitulano, in Chapter 17, offer a number of intervention models and approaches.

Finally, information-processing perspectives, although often overlooked in the area of social and personal assessment, provide a framework for understanding the ways children absorb, process, and act on social information. Children who misinterpret social events or struggle to hold information in memory while generating and executing plans of action are at risk for developing poorer social strategies, experiencing a lowered sense of self-efficacy, and engaging in a greater number of inappropriate social behaviors. In Chapter 8, Waterman presents compelling evidence for the contributions of information-processing perspectives in understanding the social and personal functioning of children as observed in the assessment process.

Sound Decision Making Depends on Sound Instruments and Test Administration Practices

If practitioners are to make sound decisions based on the assessment information they gather, then it is essential to use instruments that measure what they are intended to measure consistently, accurately, and efficiently. Although one may assume that readers will have had prior training in the area of measurement, a brief review of the psychometric concepts central to measurement follows below. In Chapter 2, Wasserman and Bracken provide extensive coverage and discussion of psychometric and pragmatic concerns as they bear on the selection of appropriate instruments.

Two basic concerns with regard to measurement, validity and reliability long have been the primary criteria by which test users evaluate tests and ascertain their appropriateness for use in particular contexts (Eyde et al., 1993). Despite some rather recent shifts in emphasis (see Geisinger, 2000), the central concerns of test users continue to involve the extent to which test results are consistent and the inferences drawn are accurate. Accurate inferences drawn from dependable test results will lead to the most effective interventions for the largest proportion of test takers.

Validity

Validity does not exist in an absolute sense, and must be viewed in the context of the use to which a test is put. A test that is valid when used in one context or for a specific purpose may be considerably less valid or not at all valid when used in another context, such as a different culture (Geisinger, 1994). Validity of instruments, therefore, must be appraised in a context-dependent manner. Traditionally, discussions of test validity include coverage of content, criterion-related validity, and construct validity.

Content validity refers to the degree to which a test's content covers a representative sample of the behavior domain of interest. At issue are whether the entire content has been sampled and whether the sampling is in proper proportion. In the case of childhood depression, for example, one would expect a measure intended to assess the level of depression to include an evaluation of mood, cognitions, physical state, and motivational features. An instrument that tapped only a child's mood would be lacking in terms of its content validity. Building a case for content validity may involve the use of experts who review the test's content and test specifications as presented in the test manual, as well as various empirical checks such as those concerning the degree to which speed is a factor or the extent to which items reflect substantial age or grade gains.

Criterion-related validity concerns the degree of relationship between a new, targeted test and an established test that purport to measure the same construct. Generally, criterion-related validity is established by the administration of the targeted test and an existing measure followed by determination of the correlation coefficient that characterizes performance on both measures. The instruments are administered to the same population, either at the same point in time—a process that establishes concurrent validity, or separated by a specific interval of time—a process used to establish predictive validity. In either case, the size of the coefficient is directly proportional to the magnitude of the association between the two measures. High positive correlation coefficients indicate that the targeted test measures the same construct as effectively as the established test and signify a high level of criterion-related validity.

Many psychometricians now view *construct validity* as the superordinate form of test validity (Geisinger, 1992; Messick, 1989). "The construct validity of a test is the extent to which the test may be said to measure a theoretical construct or trait" (Anastasi & Urbina, 1997, p. 126). More so than other forms of test validity, "construct validation has focused attention on the role of psychological theory in test construction and on the need to formulate hypotheses that can be proved or disproved in the validation process" (p. 126). Evidence for the existence of a construct is amassed gradually and stems from many sources, each of which adds something to the understanding of the particular trait under consideration. Developmental changes in raw scores on a test of communication skills, for example, are expected because communication skills are thought to grow as a child matures. A test of communication skills whose raw scores increase progressively with age would be consistent with the nature of the construct, as theorized, and this evidence could be used to bolster the construct validity of such an instrument.

Tests that function well to assess a particular construct when used with a group of test takers who resemble the normative sample may function considerably less well when applied in a different context. "When standardized personality . . . tests are evaluated for construct equivalence across groups, many researchers have discovered instances in which language differences (and the cultural traits associated with them) are crucial factors that make construct equivalence difficult" (Frisby, 1998a, p. 68). As noted previously, validity is a context-dependent feature of tests, as is readily apparent when one considers using tests in cross-cultural situations.

Reliability

Reliability refers to the degree to which testing outcomes are stable and consistent across time, test forms, scorers, and test content. Essentially, reliability measures the degree to which an instrument is free from systematic error. Tests used to render crucial decisions about an individual test taker, such as classification or diagnostic determinations, must be highly reliable. Many experts recommend that such tests demonstrate reliability coefficients at the .90 level or better (e.g., Guilford, 1956; Nunnally, 1978; Salvia & Ysseldyke, 1988). Those used in more benign applications, such as research or screening, generally are held to a less rigorous standard.

Historically, reliability coefficients have been used to evaluate test-retest, alternate forms, interrater, and internal consistency reliabilities by quantifying the extent to which test scores are stable. In all types of reliability, a correlation coefficient is used to represent the strength of the relationship, where higher values denote greater dependability. In the next chapter, Wasserman and Bracken amplify this discussion and offer specific recommendations concerning the selection of appropriate tests.

Test-retest reliability concerns psychologists who administer tests because they need to ascertain that the same test results would occur again were a particular test administered a second time. Random day-to-day fluctuations in the state of the test taker or the testing conditions should not influence the test outcome unduly unless, of course, the test itself is not a dependable indicator of the attribute under study. In many school and clinical applications, instruments with high test-retest reliability are extremely helpful in determining whether an observed change in a specific ability or attribute represents an actual improvement or worsening of a particular condition. For example, it would be essential to distinguish whether or not an improved score on a measure of childhood depression represents an actual reduction of symptoms, especially if the apparently improved score followed a period of intensive intervention.

For measures that offer more than one form of a test, it is important that the various forms of the test produce comparable outcomes; the extent to which they do so is a function of the test's *alternate-form reliability*. The correspondence of scores across two forms of an instrument is quantified by a correlation coefficient. The development of truly equivalent test forms is a costly undertaking, a reality that may preclude the development of more than one form of a test. Some instruments used in the assessment of social and personal attributes, however, are quite brief and many are completed via self-report, making them highly susceptible to practice effects or even memory effects. Therefore, in the realm of social and personal assessment, it would be helpful to have more instruments in more than one form, as this could make outcome evaluation feasible and more robust.

Just as forms of a test must yield comparable results, individual scorers also should produce similar outcomes. That is, the individual who scores an instrument should not influence the actual scoring process or the actual score obtained by a particular test taker. The extent of the agreement in scores produced by two different scorers across a sample of tests provides an indication of the test's *interscorer* or *interrater reliability*, as represented by a correlation coefficient. Of particular concern in this regard are tests that leave much room for judgment or subjectivity in the scoring process, as often has been the case for projective techniques, tests of creativity or divergent thinking, and other clinical instruments.

Internal consistency reliability is used to indicate a test's consistency across its content by evaluating scores derived from half the test items with scores obtained using the other half. This type of reliability serves to assess interitem consistency within a given instrument. Several techniques have been developed for splitting the items of a test in order to determine interitem consistency, including splitting odd- and even-numbered items, applying Kuder-Richardson formula 20 for dichotomously scored items (Kuder & Richardson, 1937), or computing coefficient alpha for items that are multiply scored (Cronbach, 1951). In particular, coefficient alpha is a useful consideration in many social and personality measures because it helps to establish the consistency of test content when the items are multiply scored and when the test content itself must be heterogeneous in order to capture a complex construct such as personality.

In any testing application, it is essential to know "the limits of confidence that an examiner can have in any one test score" (Hammill, Brown, & Bryant, 1989, p. 10). A test's *standard error of measurement* (SEM) is used to establish these confidence limits, and is determined using reliability coefficients. The relationship between a test's reliability and its SEM is such that highly reliable tests yield relatively small SEMs. In common vernacular, a test's SEM represents the "give or take" element that accompanies a test score, as one allows for less than perfect reliability for any given measure.

"Bias is a lack of similarity of psychological meaning of test scores across cultural groups" (Van de Vijver, 2000, p. 88). Regardless of the psychometric evidence for a particular assessment instrument, therefore, due consideration must be given to how the test or its individual items functions in practice when used with diverse groups of test takers. Bias in testing and assessment arises from many sources. Some aspects of bias can be identified either statistically (via item bias analyses) or through the use of experts (e.g., by bias review panels) during the test development process. These kinds of bias detection efforts constitute important steps in the development of sound instruments. However, it is essential to monitor published tests and to ascertain whether test outcomes vary across groups that are not believed to differ from one another on the construct evaluated. One must be mindful especially of the potential positive or negative costs that may occur as a result of the decisions prompted by the assessment. Thus, although attention to statistical indications of bias is necessary, it is not sufficient to ensure that assessment processes—as applied in practice—will be free from bias. For these reasons, elimination of bias may be theoretically possible from a technical standpoint, but it is essentially impossible from a practical point of view. As Moreland (1996) observed, the absence of psychometric bias does not assure accuracy in the assessment of social and emotional functioning. The minimization of bias and its potential negative effects on decision making, however, is a critical and ongoing goal of assessment and "there is general consensus that consideration of bias is critical to sound testing practice" (American Educational Research Association, American Psychological Association, & National Council on Measurement in Education, 1999, p. 74). In Chapter 2, Wasserman and Bracken frame this discussion in an alternative—but not contradictory—manner. They link the more molar concerns to the concept of "test score fairness" and the more molecular issues to the narrower concept of "test score bias," and make specific connections to both psychometric and pragmatic considerations. Their expanded coverage of statistical remedies or safeguards offers solid recommendations for test users to consider (and for test developers to follow).

Bias associated with the assessment of individuals from differing cultural or ethnic backgrounds may be reduced in several ways. Van de Vijver (2000) described a number of types of bias that are most germane to personality assessment using projective techniques, and offered specific remedies for each. In addition, the Office of Ethnic Minority Affairs (OEMA) of the American Psychological Association (1993) provided numerous guidelines for psychologists who provide services to members of diverse populations. Many of the guidelines are directly applicable to the assessment process. Among the responsibilities noted by OEMA is a call for self-awareness on the part of psychologists concerning the potential impact of their own backgrounds on the development of biases, and a call for ongoing training of psychologists in areas relevant to cultural issues. Respect for systems and religious customs associated with different cultures and an effort to use the language preferred by the test taker also are important practices for psychologists conducting an assessment to follow. It is vital to recognize the pervasive effects ethnic and cultural factors may exert on behavior during testing (Nuttall, De Leon, & Valle, 1990). The effects may be evident in a test taker's actual behavior and performance, as well as in a test giver's interpretation of test session behavior and obtained scores (Carlson, 1998; Dana, 1993; Glutting, Oakland, & McDermott, 1989; Miller-Jones, 1989). The influences of language and culture are not easily separable, as the two are intertwined. The *Standards for Educational and Psychological Testing* (American Educational Research Association et al., 1999) caution that linguistic behavior often reflects cultural values as when, for example, verbosity may be regarded by some cultures as rude and this cultural value may undermine test performance for a child evaluated according to the mores of a culture that values verbosity differently (p. 97).

Sound Decision Making Requires Cultural Competence and Knowledge of Diverse Groups

Sedlacek and Kim (1995) summarized several ways in which assessment practices may introduce difficulties when used in multicultural applications. Among the issues discussed were the mistaken assumption that making a diagnosis automatically solves problems, the use of measures normed on White populations with non-White test takers, failure to consider adequately the role of culture during the test development process, and failure to consider the practical outcomes that occur as a result of the assessment. In a discussion of assessment practices with Native Americans, Thomason (1999) highlighted the importance of using multiple methods in gathering assessment information. These methods include interviews with the client, family and friends, review of records, real-life observations, and the use of appropriately normed instruments. Some of the more general issues of multicultural assessment discussed by Thomason involved language differences, the test taker's reading level, the level of trust or mistrust the test taker holds concerning all aspects of the assessment process and related personnel, the amount of similarity between the test taker and the test giver, the level of the test taker's acculturation, whether the test has been translated from another language, and potential bias in standardized tests.

Certainly, testing should be conducted in the primary language of the child or adolescent being evaluated (e.g., OEMA, 1993). However, the dearth of psychometrically sound instruments available in languages other than English prompted some writers to view such directives as "hollow" (e.g., Figueroa, 1990). Compounding the problem is the rapid expansion of the population of school-age children who enter public schools each year without complete English proficiency (Sandoval, 1998a), a pattern that is expected to continue well into the future (see Geisinger's discussion of these demographic trends in Chapter 20 of this volume). About 1 in 7 school-age children speak a language other than English at home, and demographers project that this level of diversity will continue to expand over the coming decades. Even when both the test taker and test giver speak the same language, cultural, ethnic, socioeconomic, or geographic differences may create misunderstandings that lead to inaccurate inferences and the development of ineffective interventions. Unfortunately, it remains unclear how language used during an assessment affects test outcomes; considerable contradictory findings led Lopez (2000, p. 678) to conclude simply, "language matters, perhaps in more than one way." In the interest of establishing or preserving rapport when testing linguistically diverse or culturally diverse children, examiners may depart from standardized test administration practices (Leichtman, 1995). If these departures are severe, they may undermine test validity and, ultimately, the decisions emanating from the test results (Geisinger & Carlson, 1995).

Several authors have offered suggestions to improve multicultural assessment (e.g. Dana, 1993; Frisby, 1998a; Lopez, 2000; Nuttall et al. 1990; Sedlacek & Kim, 1995). For example, Sedlacek and Kim encourage those who develop multicultural measures to move beyond labels and focus on the empirical or operational definitions of groups. They further encourage test developers to include cultural factors very early in the test development process, and stress the importance of using guidance from people with expertise in quantitative areas as well as from those knowledgeable about multicultural issues. Measures specifically designed for use with certain groups should be identified. Clearly, there is great need for ongoing research concerning the validity and reliability of instruments used to evaluate specific culturally distinct groups. In Chapter 20, Geisinger offers suggestions for meeting future assessment demands without compromising the soundness of tests.

Members of diverse groups may not be seen routinely by clinicians charged with assessing such individuals, in part because they simply are less numerous than other groups and, in part, because of other selection factors (Sandoval, 1998b). The clinician often renders decisions about individuals based on limited experience drawn from his or her interactions with select members of a particular group. Essentially, this reality is analogous to having a sample size that is too small to be representative, a situation that severely restricts generalizability, that is, external validity. Among other concerns related to test interpretation in a multicultural context, Sandoval discusses confirmatory bias. This kind of bias stems from the "tendency to confirm existing cognitive schemas" (p. 32), wherein test givers may attend to data that confirm preexisting beliefs about members of particular groups, while ignoring data that fail to offer such confirmation. In the context of multicultural assessment, then, test givers may give greater weight to test findings or interpretations that fit with their established belief systems about groups of individuals, regardless of the existence of contradictory evidence. In Chapter 11, Vélascuez, Castellanos, and Fernandez discuss cultural considerations from the vantage point of the individual practitioner assessing an individual Latino child and offer guidance for examiners working with children from diverse cultures.

In the determination of effective interventions, it is imperative for psychologists to consider the diverse socioeconomic and political factors experienced by members of particular cultures. These factors can influence directly the number and type of social experiences a child has, his or her social status, and the belief systems the child builds, all of which affect the child's development, socially and personally. Language, cultural and ethnic background, a child's motivation toward tests, his or her understanding of the purpose of the tests and level of test sophistication, and his or her attitude toward the procedures used and the individual examiner are influenced by socioeconomic and political status. Often, these influences have been in place for many years, which makes it difficult to isolate cause and effect in an effort to quantify their impact on test outcomes. Even without hard data, however, these factors must be considered in every aspect of the assessment process, from referral to instrument selection, test administration, interpretation of data, and placement or treatment recommendations. It also is important to recognize that these forces may influence the types of interventions that may be available and acceptable to certain groups, as well as the access certain groups have to them, a point reiterated in Chapter 4 concerning functional assessments, and in Chapter 5 in the authors' discussion of direct assessment techniques.

Lee (1998) defined *worldview* as the perceptions of human experience that one comes to have over time and across situations that contribute to the extremely diverse ways that people conceptualize and perceive their world. Ultimately, it becomes essential to include the test taker's worldview in making decisions about him or her. Dana (1993) suggested that these "culturally specific cognitions" serve to organize and "make sense of life experiences that might otherwise be construed as chaotic, random, and meaningless" (p. 9). Effective interventions will build on these culturally specific, organizing cognitions or, at least, will not contradict them.

Sound Decision Making Requires an Understanding of Physiological Bases for Social and Personal Development

Physiology is at the base of all social and personal functioning. There are at least three general areas in which physiology plays a role in social and emotional development. First, all social and emotional activity is centered in the brain. Areas of the brain are especially adapted to process, remember, and retrieve social information. Brain function also is associated with problem solving and decision making. Recent technological advances, such as functional magnetic resonance imaging (MRI), have allowed scientists to map brain areas according to function (Bandettini, Jesmanowicz, Wong, & Hyde, 1993; McCarthy et al., 1994). For example, researchers recently found that the prefrontal cortex appears to be the area involved in working memory function, that is, where information is maintained so that it can be acted on (National Coordination Office for Computing, Information, and Communication, 1998). Other areas, such as Broca's and Wernicke's areas, have long been associated with language function and, through magnetoencephalography (MEG), have been confirmed as language function areas (Binder, Rao & Hammeke, 1994). Although techniques such as functional MRI seldom are used as part of a child's social and personal assessment, it is important to remember that all functioning has, at its roots, a neurological base. Lewandowski and Barlow further examine these aspects of assessment in Chapter 6.

Second, a child's social and personal development is dependent, in part, on a number of unique biologically driven factors. As Bye and Jussim (1993) note, each child possesses an individual and unique temperament, arousal system, level of stamina, attention span, and hearing and visual systems. A child's ability to hear or see adequately can influence the amount of social information available to the child as well as the child's ability to use such information (i.e., social performance). Mental health problems, such as depression, obsessive-compulsive disorders, or pervasive developmental disorders, also are associated with physiological aspects of the individual and impact the child's social and emotional behaviors.

Third, Maslow (1973, 1987), Glasser (1998), and other theorists highlighted physiological factors in their models for understanding motivation and the acquisition of emotions, attitudes, and interpersonal skills. Maslow's famous hierarchy, in which physiological needs must be met before the individual can move to meeting higher level needs, explains why a child who is hungry or tired expends energy to have these needs met first, even if doing so may interfere with pursuing connections with others. Similarly, Glasser included physiological needs among those that must be met in order for a child to engage in learning.

Sound Decision Making Requires an Understanding of External Factors

A child's sense of self-worth and self-efficacy are influenced by the contexts in which he or she lives and functions including family, school, and community. The interactions that children have with individuals or groups within these contexts exert important influences on the development of self-worth and self-efficacy. Pajares (1996) further suggests that self-efficacy affects a child's learning indirectly, as it results in differences in levels of persistence in the face of failure and in the child's willingness to engage in a difficult task. Despite the inherent difficulties in measuring or assessing environmental factors in a child's life, it continues to be an essential area for evaluation. Assessment of the major systems in which the child functions, including family, school, and community should be undertaken if one aspires to design interventions that will retain their effectiveness across a variety of contexts.

Moos (1986) suggests three general areas of family assessment: relationship dimensions, such as the support available within a family system; personal growth dimensions, such as the opportunities for learning appropriate effective models for making decisions or involvement in social or political activities; and system maintenance dimensions, such as the rules on which family functioning is based. Assessment of these dimensions is important as the examiner seeks to contextualize the child's experiences. Barnett and Zucker (1990) have proposed a model for family assessment based on an analysis of Laosa and Sigel's (1982) earlier work in the area of learning and mediational contexts. These authors suggest two primary areas for family assessment: "family realities" and the child's personal and social learning experiences. Assessment of family realities, according to Barnett and Zucker (1990), includes the determination of such factors as the number of family members, roles within the family, level of parental stress, available supports, and parental coping strategies. The child's personal and social learning experiences often relate to such factors as a parent's level of anger control, discipline techniques, and family recreational activities. In Chapter 10, Preli discusses the role of family systems in the development, maintenance, and remediation of social and personal difficulties among children.

The school environment also is an important area for assessment. Teacher, instructional, and physical aspects of the classroom all can impact a child's academic and social and emotional growth. Teacher style, methods of child and classroom management, amount and timing of feedback, and amount of teacher flexibility all have been found to influence the child's sense of self. The match between teaching (or parenting) style and a student's learning style can impact the interpersonal connections that the child establishes. Research also suggests that teacher expectations can influence both the way the teacher responds and evaluates the child and the child's own sense of competence (Mercer & Mercer, 1998). A wide range of information about teacher, instructional, and physical aspects of the classroom, then, is essential as the practitioner attempts to develop meaningful interventions, as described more fully in Chapter 9 by Fischetti.

Community environments are important considerations, especially in the development of effective interventions. Assessment of the resources available, the methods and the effectiveness and content of communication within the community, opportunities for involvement within the community, socioeconomic and sociopolitical factors, and the match between the home culture and the community culture are relevant to a child's social and emotional development. Bandura (1993) suggested that communities may differ in the ways they view their own ability to change. Their beliefs, according to Bandura, influence the level of active involvement in change processes, such that a child whose community does not view itself as having sufficient collective power to effect change may see him- or herself as incapable of effecting change in his or her own life. Ideas for understanding challenges and instituting changes at the community level are presented by Cone in Chapter 16 and Porter and Vitulano in Chapter 17.

Conclusion

The foregoing pages outline concerns that assessment professionals share with regard to school-aged children and their social and personal functioning. When children encounter difficulties in these domains, optimal performance in these and related areas may suffer, and psychologists charged with assessing such individuals must strive to gather accurate and meaningful data, understand these data within the individual child's context, and develop strategies that address the child's difficulties most effectively.

Psychologists involved in the assessment of children's social and personal domains of functioning represent several specialties within the discipline of psychology. Many clinical and school psychologists have a keen interest in these types of assessment, given their frequent involvement in individual decision making such as diagnosis and treatment planning, or educational classification and service needs determinations. Although we recognize inherent differences in training, orientation, and terminology within psychological specialties, we also find much common ground. When psychological professionals use assessment techniques in an effort to illuminate and rectify social and personal difficulties that children experience, they are more alike than different, despite certain variations in nomenclature, experiences, or beliefs.

Throughout this volume, we strove to keep the child and the problems he or she may experience in the social and personal domains as central concerns, and attempted to avoid aligning the book's content categorically with any particular specialty. Our contributing authors represent educators and practitioners from clinical and school psychological settings and institutions. We encouraged them to use language that is more inclusive than exclusive in an effort to avoid false dichotomies. Our goal is, as it has been from the beginning of this project, to focus on the difficulties children experience, to understand these difficulties more completely, and to seek remedies to these difficulties that will improve the lives of children in some way.

References

Allport, G. W. (1937). *Personality: A psychological interpretation.* New York: Holt.

American Educational Research Association, American Psychological Association, Council on Measurement in Education. (1999). *Standards for educational and psychological testing.* Washington, DC: American Educational Research Association.

Anastasi, A., & Urbina, S. (1997). *Psychological testing* (7th ed.). Upper Saddle River, NJ: Prentice-Hall.

Bandettini, P. A., Jesmanowicz, A., Wong, E. C., & Hyde, J. S. (1993). Processing strategies for time-course data sets in functional MRI of the human brain. *Magnetic Resonance Medical, 30,* 161–173.

Bandura, A. (1969). *Principles of behavior modification.* New York: Holt, Rinehart & Winston.

Bandura, A. (1977). *Social learning theory.* Englewood Cliffs, NJ: Prentice-Hall.

Bandura, A. (1978). The self-system in reciprocal determinism. *American Psychologist, 33,* 344–358.

Bandura, A. (1986). *Social foundations of thought and action: A social cognitive theory.* Englewood Cliffs, NJ: Prentice-Hall.

Bandura, A. (1993). Perceived self-efficacy in cognitive development and functioning. *Educational Psychologist, 28,* 117–148.

Bandura, A. (1997). *Self-efficacy: The exercise of control.* New York: Freeman.

Barnett, D. W., & Zucker K. B. (1990). *The personal and social assessment of children: An analysis of current status and professional practice issues.* Boston: Allyn and Bacon.

Bem, D. (1983). Constructing a theory of triple typology: Some (second) thoughts on nomothetic and idiographic approaches to personality. *Journal of Personality, 51,* 566–577.

Binder, J. R., Rao, S. M., & Hammeke, T. A. (1994). Functional magnetic resonance imaging of human auditory cortex. *Neurology, 35,* 662–671.

Bruck, M., Ceci, S. J., & Hembrooke, H. (1998). Reliability and credibility of young children's reports: From research to policy and practice. *American Psychologist, 53,* 136–151.

Bye, L., & Jussim, L. (1993). A proposed model for the acquisition of social knowledge and social competence. *Psychology in the Schools, 30,* 141–161.

Cantor, N. (1981). A cognitive-social approach to personality. In N. Cantor & J. F. Kihlstrom (Eds.), *Personality, cognition, and social interaction* (pp. 23–44). Hillsdale, NJ: Erlbaum.

Carlson, J. F. (1998). A psychometric view of those who administer standardized tests: Are test givers instruments too? *Educational Research Quarterly, 22,* 58–71.

Cohen, R. J., & Swerdlik, M. E. (1999). *Psychological testing and assessment: An introduction to tests and measurement* (4th ed.). Mountain View, CA: Mayfield.

Cronbach, L. J. (1951). Coefficient alpha and the internal structure of tests. *Psychometrika, 16,* 297–334.

Cronbach, L. J., & Meehl, P. E. (1955). Construct validity in psychological tests. *Psychological Bulletin, 52,* 281–302.

Dana, R. H. (1993). *Multicultural assessment perspectives for professional psychology.* Boston: Allyn and Bacon.

Eyde, L. D. , Robertson, G. J., Krug, S. E., Moreland, K. L., Robertson, A. G., Shewan, C., M., Harrison, P. L., Porch, B. E., Hammer, A. L., & Primoff, E. S. (1993). *Responsible test use: Case studies for assessing human behavior.* Washington, DC: American Psychological Association.

Figueroa, R. A. (1990). Best practices in the assessment of bilingual children. In A. Thomas & J. Grimes (Eds.), *Best practices in school psychology-II* (pp. 93–106). Washington, DC: National Association of School Psychologists.

Frisby, C. L. (1998a). Culture and cultural differences. In J. Sandoval, C. L. Frisby, K. F. Geisinger, J. D. Scheuneman, & J. R. Grenier (Eds.), *Test interpretation and diversity* (pp. 51–73). Washington, DC: American Psychological Association.

Frisby, C. L. (1998b). Poverty and socioeconomic status. In J. Sandoval, C. L. Frisby, K. F. Geisinger, J. D. Scheuneman, & J. R. Grenier (Eds.), *Test interpretation and diversity* (pp. 241–270). Washington, DC: American Psychological Association.

Geisinger, K. F. (1992). The metamorphosis in test validation. *Educational Psychology, 27,* 197–222.

Geisinger, K. F. (1994). Cross-cultural normative assessment: Translation and adaptation issues influencing the normative interpretation of assessment instruments. *Psychological Assessment, 6,* 304–312.

Geisinger, K. F. (2000). Psychological testing at the end of the millennium: A brief historical review. *Professional Psychology: Research and Practice, 31,* 117–118.

Geisinger, K. F., & Carlson, J. F. (1995). Standards and standardization. In J. N. Butcher (Ed.), *Clinical personality assessment: Practical approaches* (pp. 211–223). New York: Oxford University Press.

Glasser W. (1998). *Choice theory: A new psychology of personal freedom.* London: HarperCollins.

Glutting, J. J., Oakland, T., & McDermott, P. A. (1989). Observing child behavior during testing: Constructs, validity, and situational generality. *Journal of School Psychology, 27,* 155–164.

Goldberg, L. R. (1992). The development of markers for the big-five factor structure. *Psychological Assessment, 4,* 26–42.

Guilford, J. P. (1956). *Fundamental statistics in psychology and education* (3rd ed.). New York: McGraw-Hill.

Hammill, D. D., Brown, L., & Bryant, B. R. (1989). *A consumer's guide to tests in print.* Austin, TX: PRO-ED.

Henderson, N., & Milstein, M. M. (1996). *Resiliency in schools: Making it happen for students and educators.* Thousand Oaks, CA: Corwin Press.

Hopkins, K. D. (1998). *Educational and psychological measurement and evaluation* (8th ed.). Boston: Allyn and Bacon.

Kamphaus, R. W., & Frick, P. J. (1996). *Clinical assessment of child and adolescent personality and behavior.* Boston: Allyn and Bacon.

Kratochwill, T. R., & McGivern, J. E. (1996). Clinical diagnosis, behavioral assessment, and functional analysis: Examining the connection between assessment and intervention. *School Psychology Review, 25,* 342–355.

Kuder, G. F., & Richardson, M. W. (1937). The theory of estimation of test reliability. *Psychometrika, 2,* 151–160.

Laosa, L. M., & Sigel, I. E. (1982). *Families as learning environments for children.* New York: Plenum Press.

Lee, C. C. (1998). *Assessing diverse populations.* Paper presented at the ERIC Clearinghouse on counseling and student services conference: Assessment '98. Washington, DC: U. S. Department of Education. Office of Educational Research and Improvement.

Leichtman, M. (1995). Behavioral observations. In J. N. Butcher (Ed.), *Clinical personality assessment: Practical approaches* (pp. 251–266). New York: Oxford University Press.

Lopez, S. R. (2000). Teaching culturally informed psychological assessment. In R. H. Dana (Ed.), *Handbook of cross-cultural and multicultural personality assessment* (pp. 669–687). Mahwah, NJ: Erlbaum.

Macmann, G. M., Barnett, D. W., Allen, S. J., Bramlett, R. K., Hall, J. D., & Ehrhardt, K. E. (1996). Problem solving and intervention design: Guidelines for the evaluation of technical adequacy. *School Psychology Quarterly, 11,* 137–148.

Maslow, A. H. (1973). Theory of human motivation. In R. J. Lowry (Ed.), *Dominance, self-esteem, self-actualization: Germinal papers of A. H. Maslow*. Monterey, CA: Brooks/Cole.

Maslow, A. H. (1987). *Motivation and personality* (3rd ed.). New York: Harper & Row.

McCarthy, G., Blamire, A. M., Puce, A., Nobre, A. C., Bloch, G., Hyder, F., Goldman-Rakie, P., & Shulman, R. G. (1994). Functional magnetic resonance imaging of human prefrontal cortex activation during a spatial working memory task. *Proceedings of the National Academy of Science, 91,* 5187–5191.

McCrae, R. R., & Costa, P. T., Jr. (1994). The stability of personality: Observation and evaluations. *Current Directions in Psychological Science, 3,* 173–175.

McCrae, R. R., & Costa, P. T., Jr. (1997). Personality trait structure as a human universal. *American Psychologist, 52,* 509–516.

McCrae, R. R., Costa, P. T., Jr., Ostendorf, F., Angleitner, A., Hrebickova, M., Avia, M. D., Sanz, J., Sanchez-Bernardos, M. L., Kusdil, M. E., Woodfield, R., Saunders, P. R., & Smith, P. B. (2000). Nature over nurture: Temperament, personality, and life span development. *Journal of Personality and Social Psychology, 78,* 173–186.

McLoyd, V. C. (1998). Socioeconomic disadvantage and child development. *American Psychologist, 53,* 185–204.

Meehl, P. E. (1973). *Psychodiagnosis: Selected papers.* Minneapolis, MN: University of Minnesota Press.

Mercer, C. D., & Mercer, A. R. (1998). *Teaching students with learning problems* (5th ed.). Upper Saddle River, NJ: Prentice-Hall.

Messick, S. (1989). Validity. In R. L. Linn (Ed.), *Educational measurement* (3rd ed., pp. 13–103). New York: American Council on Education/Macmillan.

Miller-Jones, D. (1989). Culture and testing. *American Psychologist, 44,* 360–366.

Mischel, W. (1981). A cognitive-social learning approach to assessment. In T. V. Luzzi, C. R. Glass, & M. Genest (Eds.), *Cognitive assessment* (pp. 479–599). New York: Guilford Press.

Moos, R. H. (1986). *Family Environment Scale manual.* Palo Alto, CA: Consulting Psychologists Press.

Moreland, K. L. (1996). Persistent issues in multicultural assessment of social and emotional functioning. In L. A. Suzuki, P. J. Meller, & J. G. Ponterotto (Eds.), *Handbook of multicultural assessment: Clinical, psychological, and educational applications* (pp. 51–76). San Francisco: Jossey-Bass.

National Coordination Office for Computing, Information, and Communication. (1998). *Technologies for the 21st century: Human brain mapping* [On-line] Available: http://www.ccic.gov/pubs/blue98/brain_mapping.html

Nunnally, J. S. (1978). *Psychometric theory.* New York: McGraw-Hill.

Nuttall, E. V., De Leon, B., & Valle, M. (1990). Best practices in considering culture factors. In A. Thomas & J. Grimes (Eds.), *Best practices in school psychology-II* (pp. 219–233). Washington, DC: National Association of School Psychologists.

Office of Ethnic Minority Affairs. (1993). Guidelines for providers of psychological services to ethnic, linguistic, and culturally diverse populations. *American Psychologist, 48,* 45–48.

Pajares, F. (1996). Self-efficacy beliefs in academic settings. *Review of Educational Research, 66,* 543–578.

Salvia, J., & Ysseldyke, J. E. (1988). *Assessment in special and remedial education* (4th ed.). Boston: Houghton Mifflin.

Sandoval, J. (1998a). Critical thinking in test interpretation. In J. Sandoval, C. L. Frisby, K. F. Geisinger, J. D. Scheuneman, & J. R. Grenier (Eds.), *Test interpretation and diversity* (pp. 31–49). Washington, DC: American Psychological Association.

Sandoval, J. (1998b). Testing in a changing world: An introduction. In J. Sandoval, C. L. Frisby, K. F. Geisinger, J. D. Scheuneman, & J. R. Grenier (Eds.), *Test interpretation and diversity* (pp. 3–16). Washington DC: American Psychological Association.

Sedlacek, W. E., & Kim, S. H. (1995). *Multicultural assessment.* Greensboro, NC: ERIC Clearinghouse on Counseling and Student Services.

Smith, B. H., Pelham, W. E., Jr., Gnagy, E., Molina, B., & Evans, S. (2000). The reliability, validity, and unique contributions of self-report by adolescents receiving treatment for attention-deficit/hyperactivity disorder. *Journal of Consulting and Clinical Psychology, 68,* 489–499.

Thomason, T. C. (1999). *Psychological and vocational assessment of Native Americans.* Greensboro, NC: ERIC Clearinghouse on Counseling and Student Services.

Thorndike, R. M. (1997). *Measurement and evaluation in psychology and education* (6th ed.). Upper Saddle River, NJ: Prentice-Hall.

Tupes, E. C., & Christal, R. E. (1961). *Recurrent personality factors based on trait ratings.* (Technical Report ASD-TR-61–97). Lackland Air Force Base, TX: U. S. Air Force.

Van de Vijver, F. (2000). The nature of bias. In R. H. Dana (Ed.), *Handbook of cross-cultural and multicultural personality assessment* (pp. 87–106). Mahwah, NJ: Erlbaum.

2

Selecting Appropriate Tests: Psychometric and Pragmatic Considerations

John D. Wasserman and

Bruce A. Bracken

When Binet and Simon (1905, 1916) published their pioneering intelligence scale in *L'Année Psychologique*, their objective was to identify and adequately serve intellectually retarded children in French schools. Their scale was intended to be objective, precise, and practical, and in successive revisions they attempted to address its technical limitations. Most importantly, they were aware that assessment was not about *the measure itself*, but rather about the purpose of the measurement and the examinee to be tested.

In the century since, psychological tests have proliferated and now provide consumers with many choices and decisions. The complexity of current instruments and the limited number of sound test reviews make it difficult for consumers to compare the salient features of available instruments. As a result, decisions about test use are often based on personal experiences with specific tests (Reynolds, 1979; Reynolds & Sundberg, 1976; Wade & Baker, 1977), including pragmatics and usefulness. Results of a national survey of school psychologists (Chattin & Bracken, 1989) emphasized the importance of practicality in test selection: "Psychologists seem to desire tests that are theoretically and practically sound. They appear not to shy away from psychometric tradition; they prefer a test that has a practical theory . . . , yields ample information . . . [that is] intuitively important in the classroom, is viewed as diagnostically useful, is reasonably easy to administer and interpret, and is well organized" (p. 128).

In this chapter, psychometric accountability is a central theme, and a rational approach to evaluating the technical adequacy of tests is presented. Emphasis is placed on applied and pragmatic aspects of test selection and consequent implications for decision making. Our focus is broadened beyond traditional test-centered psychometric issues to include the applications, consequences, and purposes for which personality and other psychological tests are used (*application-centered psychometrics*). Building on the standards originally proposed for preschool cognitive instruments (Bracken, 1987), criteria are proposed to address instrument quality within the domains of academic, adaptive, characterological, cognitive, emotional, neuropsychological, and psychosocial functioning. Minimal levels of technical adequacy are proposed, and some technical qualities that are more ideal or aspirational in nature are suggested. These evaluative guidelines include more specificity than and extend the *Standards for Educational and Psychological Testing* (American Educational Research Association [AERA], American Psychological Association, & National Council on Measurement in Education, 1999) and build on the advice proffered by such authorities as Cattell (1986a), Cicchetti (1994), Nunnally and Bernstein (1994), and Anastasi and Urbina (1997). The proposed guidelines are intended to aid test selection rather than merely create a rigid framework for test evaluation. Just as decisions in test development should be made according to the purposes for which tests will be used, a professional's selection of tests should be based on the context in which the test is or will be used.

Early Tests and Their Limitations

As recently as a few decades ago, there were several commonly used psychoeducational and personality instruments that would now appear shockingly deficient in most aspects of technical adequacy. For example, many instruments developed during the 1940s, 1950s, and 1960s were regionally normed and included normative samples that were entirely White (e.g., *Peabody Picture Vocabulary Test, PPVT; Minnesota Multiphasic Personality Inventory, MMPI; Vineland Social Maturity Scale*). In addition, the stimulus materials included in this generation of tests typically were devoid of social sensitivity. The *PPVT*, for example, was normed on slightly more than 4,000 White individuals from Nashville, Tennessee. Its artwork depicted blatant sex-role and racial stereotyping: pictures of women hosting tea parties, changing diapers, and cleaning the house, while men were depicted as scientists, judges, and businessmen. People of color were pictured only twice in the test: an African American train station porter and a native carrying a spear. The original *MMPI* was normed on a group of 724 Minnesota White adults who were, for the most part, relatives of patients or visitors at the University of Minnesota Hospitals. It contained self-report items referring to culture-specific games ("drop-the-handkerchief"), literature (*Alice in Wonderland*), and religious beliefs (the "second coming of Christ"). Fortunately, these tests have been revised and have improved considerably in more recent editions, demonstrating more defensible normative samples and increased awareness of issues related to stereotyping and fairness. Unfortunately, many personality tests remain in use that have inadequate norms (e.g., *Draw a Man, House-Tree-Person, Kinetic Family Drawings*, various sentence completion blanks) or include stimulus artwork that depicts only Caucasian characters (e.g., *Thematic Apperception Test*).

Sampling, Scaling, and Normative Standards

The adequacy of normative samples is central to norm-referenced testing. The quality of a test's norms is dependent on several factors. As long ago as 1949, Cronbach summarized these issue: "(1) Are the norms based on a sufficiently large group? (2) Is the standard group representative? (3) Does the standard group resemble the persons with whom we wish to compare our subject?" (pp. 75–76). Despite the clarity of Cronbach's questions, there are still no objective criteria for determining the adequacy of test norms. In this section, several guidelines for sampling, scaling, and norming are provided.

Samples should be appropriate for intended test applications.   The primary goal of normative sampling is to accurately represent the population, and the first issue associated with sample selection is accurately defining the population. Most U.S. test norms consist of full-range representative samples of the U.S. population because the goal of the norm-referenced tests is to identify the degree to which an individual deviates from normative expectations. In these norms, sampling plans consider all potential examinees who are testable in an effort to reflect the entire distribution of the construct being measured.

Despite the goal of accurately representing the population, some test developers use a truncated sampling approach in which individuals with impairments and other special needs, who would presumably score in the lower end of the distribution, are systematically excluded from the normative test sample (McFadden, 1996). Truncated sampling is usually conducted with the objective of enhancing the discriminability of the test in the identification of disordered and "normal" individuals. By developing norms only on nondisordered participants, it is thought that identification of clinically disordered examinees will be enhanced. However, truncated sampling may violate the statistical assumptions of normality, thus lowering the relative percentile rankings of many members of the sample and, consequently, identifying a larger number of *false positive* errors in classification decisions. Test results generated through full-range sampling and truncated sampling are not comparable (i.e., individual percentile ranks will not have equivalent meanings across these two sampling approaches).

Conversely, there are instances when samples are selected exclusively from populations of individuals with educationally or clinically diagnosed conditions (e.g., conduct disorders, learning disabilities). As best practice, Hollon and Flick (1988) recommend that, when test norms are developed for special populations, the norms still should be based on unscreened, demographically representative samples. Millon, Davis, and Millon (1997) note that tests normed on special populations may require use of base-rate scores rather than traditional standard scores, because assumptions of a normal distribution of scores often cannot be met within clinical populations.

Normative samples should be sufficiently large.   Normative samples should be sufficiently large to provide stable parameter estimates of identified populations, reduce sampling error to acceptable levels, and permit appropriate statistical analyses.

For large-scale group administered tests, standardization programs often involve 10,000 to 20,000 students per grade. In contrast, samples of 100 to 200 participants per grade or age level are frequently employed with individually administered tests.

Consider an illustration of sample size requirements using probability sampling, with the goal of obtaining a sample mean that is within ±2 percent of the population mean, with 95% confidence. To achieve reduced sampling error to this degree, a standardization sample of 2,400 for one stratification level would be necessary. Compare this sample size to the average of 100 to 200 participants per stratification level in most psychological tests. Unfortunately, increasing sample size results in corresponding decreases in sampling error only to a point. Cattell (1986b) notes that diminishing returns quickly occur when sample sizes are increased in an effort to reduce sampling error.

Another consideration when determining acceptable sample size is whether various univariate and multivariate statistics (e.g., differential item functioning) can reasonably be conducted on data from the standardization sample. Test developers frequently oversample minority participants to create sample sizes for these groups that are sufficiently large to permit bias analyses. Studies of factor structure and test reliability also require larger than typical samples to enhance the generalizability of conclusions, especially for low-incidence population groups (e.g., deaf, Native Americans). As with statistical analyses in general, minimal acceptable sample sizes should be based on practical considerations such as desired alpha level, known strength of relationships, and desired statistical power.

Normative samples should reflect appropriate demographic stratifications.
Psychological tests generally include the following demographic stratification variables: age, grade level, sex, ethnic origin, race, geographic region, metropolitan–nonmetropolitan residence, and socioeconomic status. Identifying and selecting variables for stratification is influenced by the extent to which the variables are known to capture variability in the construct that is related to documented or suspected differences among groups (e.g., gender or age differences). When a stratification variable shows little test score variability across levels, the breadth of the stratification levels may be widened or the stratification variable may be removed altogether. For example, there is little evidence of a developmental age progression during the early school years in self-concept, and, accordingly, self-concept scales usually have wide age-level norms (Bracken, 1992; Bracken, 1996; Crain & Bracken, 1994; Wylie, 1979, 1989). Stratification and selection of participants based on redundant variables also should be avoided. Thus, there is no need to stratify by age *and* grade on most tests because grade is largely redundant with age in personal and social development. However, there are some psychosocial constructs (e.g., interpersonal relations) that require combined norms based on both gender and age because of developmental gender differences that increase throughout childhood and adolescence (Bracken, 1993; Bracken & Crain, 1994).

Many tests include students with psychological disorders, disabling conditions, and educational exceptionalities in their normative samples. Inclusion of such individuals is based on the logic that the intended function of the normative sample (and test) is to serve a comprehensive group of children rather than only children without known pathologies, deficits, or gifts (Elliott, 1990). If the test is intended to serve individuals with psychiatric diagnoses, disabling conditions, or exceptionalities, it should include proportionate representation of these populations in the normative sample.

Sampling should be representative and precise.   The accuracy and precision of a stratified sample is most readily determined by the degree to which the sample matches the sampling plan. The degree to which the composition of an acquired sample reflects census proportions should be assessed through examination of not only single demographic characteristics (e.g., gender) but by examining combined demographic sampling cells (e.g., geographic region by race/ethnicity by parent education). It is at these smaller, more unique cells that sampling plans typically fail by the greatest degree.

The importance of accurate representation has been shown in research on the *MMPI-2*. Based on the overrepresentation of individuals with post-college education at the expense of individuals with a high school education or less in the *MMPI-2* normative sample, Schinka and LaLone (1997) selected a more representative census-matched subsample from the larger standardization sample. They then compared normative *T* scores on *MMPI-2* scales and found meaningful differences on one scale, providing evidence that nonrepresentative samples may distort some scale norms. In this instance, misleading interpretations could be made artifactually on the basis of nonrepresentative norms.

We recommend that test developers provide tables in test manuals to show the composition of the standardization sample across all stratification criteria (e.g., percentages by age by race by parent education). The advantage of maintaining this level of stringency is to ensure that important demographic variables are distributed proportionately across other stratifying variables according to census proportions. Some test developers only report sampling "on the margins" to reveal distribution of the sample for each individual demographic variable. Such reporting runs the risk of concealing important descriptive information (e.g., that low socioeconomic status was concentrated primarily within minority groups in the sample). The more the sample deviates from being nationally representative, even in the smaller unique cells, the greater the degree of sampling error.

All statistical transformations used to develop interpretive scores should be reported.   Because raw scores have minimal interpretable value, raw scores should be transformed into more easily interpreted metrics. The statistical procedures by which raw scores are transformed should be clearly documented in the test manual. Test manuals should also delineate the procedures used to calibrate item difficulties (or the amount of the latent trait being measured), make raw score to norm-referenced score transformations, and smooth irregularities in score distributions. This documentation should include any normalization of test scores and the need for linear or nonlinear transformations of the raw score scale.

One issue in raw score to standard score transformations is deciding whether to manipulate the composition of the standardization sample through sample weighting.

Weighting generally is not necessary with most psychological tests unless the goals of the sampling plan have not been adequately met. When specific demographic groups have been undersampled, score weighting is sometimes used to "correct" for this slight; however, weighting scores often increases sampling error because a smaller than desired sample is used to represent the entire population.

Standardization examiners and procedures should be clearly described. Procedures to recruit, qualify, train, and provide feedback to standardization examiners should be carefully described in test manuals. Also, quality assurance procedures intended to correct invalid administration procedures and to identify invalid test protocols should be detailed. Ideally, standardization examiners should resemble those professionals who will eventually use the test, and examiners should have prior formal training in psychological assessments that are similar to the test undergoing standardization. Use of *Test User Qualifications: A Data-Based Approach to Promoting Good Test Use* (Joint Committee on Testing Practices, 2000) constitutes an appropriate standard for test standardization examiners as well as test users. Because of the high costs of test standardization, some test development projects hire examiners who ordinarily would not be considered qualified to administer the test once it is published. The overall effect of this practice is unknown, but employing unqualified examiners likely qualitatively diminishes many aspects of the testing process (e.g., rapport building, pacing, responding to examinee's frustrations) that may be offered by qualified professionals.

Test manuals also should carefully describe the standardized test conditions under which the test norms were established. Changes in artwork and stimulus materials, instructions, and test sequence after standardization should be described in the test manual. For example, the *Comprehensive Test of Nonverbal Intelligence* (*CTONI;* Hammill, Pearson, & Wiederholt, 1996), allows for either pantomimed or oral test administration; however, the *CTONI* Examiner's Manual does not indicate the condition (i.e., pantomime or oral administration) under which the test was normed. Exner (1993) has described how even small changes in standardized administration may significantly affect responses on the *Rorschach inkblot* technique. Even traditional assumptions about the local independence of test items and procedures from effects of changes in administration sequence is undergoing reevaluation (Zhu & Tulsky, in press), suggesting that, in many cases, the standardization item and procedure testing sequence must be retained in the final published test.

The standardization sample should be 10 or fewer years old. Investigations in the last two decades have shown that normative scores change systematically over time on cognitive tests. For example, when an individual's intelligence test performance is referenced to outdated norms rather than to current ones, the obtained IQ will be inflated (Wechsler, 1997).

The rise in cognitive and intellectual test scores for at least three generations has been termed the *Flynn effect* (Herrnstein & Murray, 1994). Based on findings reported initially in 1984, the Flynn effect describes a robust finding of massive IQ gains over time and across nations (Flynn, 1984, 1987, 1994, 1999). For intelligence tests, the rate of gain is about .3 IQ points per year (3 points per decade), roughly uniform over time and similar for all ages (Flynn, 1999). The Flynn effect appears to occur as early as infancy (Bayley, 1993; Campbell, Siegel, Parr, & Ramey, 1986) and continues throughout childhood and adolescence. Chan, Drasgow, and Sawin (1999) have demonstrated that a variety of cognitive abilities, especially those involving more semantically-laden content and procedures, tend to be most susceptible to changes over time.

In the area of personality assessment, similar reports of systematic generational change have been reported for behavior rating scales and personality measures. Restandardizations of tests of personality and psychopathology suggest population-based generational increases in behavioral maladjustment. For example, the *MMPI-2* produces lower normative *T*-score values than the *MMPI* when administered to the same sample (Blake et al., 1992; Harrell, Honaker, & Parnell, 1992; Litz et al., 1991; Ward, 1991), suggesting that the original *MMPI* norms were derived from samples with less mean psychopathology than contemporary samples. Similarly, parent and teacher reports on the Achenbach system of empirically-based assessments show increased numbers of behavior problems and lower competence scores in the general population of children and adolescents from 1976 to 1989 (Achenbach & Howell, 1993).

Given the verity of these generational changes in psychological test norms, we recommend that tests undergo normative updates, restandardizations, or revisions at time intervals corresponding to the time expected to produce one standard error of measurement (SE_M) of change. For example, given a *WISC-III* FSIQ SE_M of 3.20, one could expect about ten to eleven years before the test's norms would "soften" to the magnitude of one SE_M. The test revision cycle for tests of social and emotional functioning will vary according to the amount of normative change occurring over time. Unfortunately, change in personality constructs over time has not been as widely studied as population changes in intelligence over periods of time. The failure to study these changes systematically has contributed to the longevity of some personality tests well beyond a reasonable lifespan.

Comparing an individual to an outdated rather than current normative sample introduces systematic error into the identification process and diminishes the accuracy of the test. Most importantly, failure to use current norms may result in the systematic denial of services (e.g., for serious emotional disturbance) to sizeable numbers of children and adolescents who otherwise would have been identified as eligible to receive psychological and special education services. Professional psychological organizations (e.g., American Psychological Association, National Association of School Psychologists) and the joint *Standards for Psychological and Educational Testing* (AERA et al., 1999) all admonish psychologists to use instruments with up-to-date norms.

Norms should reflect adequate item change or difficulty gradients.   *Item gradients* reflect the degree to which standard scores change as a function of success or failure on a single item (Bracken, 1987). The larger the resulting standard score difference in relation to a change in a single raw score, the less sensitive, discriminating, and effective the test is. In order for a test to have adequate sensitivity, it must have adequate item density across the ability range. Bracken (1987; see also Bracken & McCallum, 1998) suggested that item gradients should not be so steep that a single item passed or failed would result in a standard score change of more than one-third standard deviation (0.33 *SD*).

Similarly, norm tables should be sufficiently sensitive that an identical raw score entered into two adjacent age tables should not produce changes of more than one-third standard deviation in standard scores. For example, on the Personal-Social Domain (Expression of Feelings/Affect subtest) of the *Battelle Developmental Inventory* (Newborg, Stock, Wnek, Guidubaldi, & Svinicki, 1984), a child who is 6 years, 11 months old and who earned a raw score of 5 would have a corresponding percentile rank of 2. Raw scores of 6, 7, and 8, would result in subsequent percentile ranks of 47, 53, and 73, respectively. Converted to standard scores, these four items range in standard score equivalents (with a mean of 100 and standard deviation of 15) from 68 to 109, or a spread of standard scores of approximately 3 standard deviations. Such an item gradient is excessively steep and yields very little useful information, especially when one establishes a confidence interval around any of these four raw scores.

Norms should have adequate floors and ceilings.   When tests are used to identify exceptional children, it is important that the tests have sufficient discriminating power at the extreme ends of the distributions for accurate diagnoses. Ability tests should have floors sufficiently strong to differentiate the extreme lowest 3% of the population from the top 97% (Bracken, 1987, 1988; Bracken & McCallum, 1998). Conversely, tests should have ceilings that are sufficiently high to differentiate the extreme upper 3% from the lower 97%. The adequacy of test floors and ceilings is as relevant for the assessment of behavior problems, personality, and psychopathology as it is for assessment of cognitive and intellectual ability. Tests with inadequate floors or ceilings are inappropriate for assessing children suspected of severe psychopathology or superior social and educational competencies. At the same time, floors and ceilings should be relevant to actual practice. The *Woodcock-Johnson Tests of Cognitive Abilities*, (Woodcock, McGrew, & Mather, 2001) and the *Scales of Independent Behavior-Revised* (Bruininks, Woodcock, Weatherman, & Hill, 1996) yield standard scores as low as zero, and we know of no professionals in the fields of learning, cognition, or adaptive behavior who would identify a conscious individual as having zero intelligence or functional adaptation.

Evidence of Test Score Validity

As noted in Chapter 1, the validity of a test is described by the extent to which test scores exclusively measure their targeted construct(s), as well as the extent to which test scores may be meaningfully used to guide decision making. The emphasis on the meaning and application of test results represents a "metamorphosis" in understanding test validation, in which emphasis is shifting from test-centered validity to application-centered validity and in which all forms of validity are seen as contributing ultimately to construct validity (Geisinger, 1992a; Guion, 1977). In general, increasing emphasis is being placed on the extent to which test scores serve their intended purposes and applications (e.g., Messick, 1995).

Construct validity can be supported with two broad classes of evidence: *internal* and *external*, which parallel the classes of threat to validity of research designs (Campbell & Stanley, 1963; Cook & Campbell, 1979). Internal evidence for construct validity includes aspects intrinsic to the measure itself, including substantive validation (i.e., content validity, face validity, and theoretical–substantive validity) and structural validation (analysis of factor composition and scale properties). External evidence for construct validity includes convergent and discriminant validation, criterion-related validation, consequential validation, and demonstration of generalizability of score properties and interpretations. Although scholars have described test-related validity in many different ways and with varying terminology, this simplified taxonomy represents a distillation of concepts described by Loevinger (1957), Jackson (1971), Millon, Davis, and Millon (1997), Messick (1995), and Anastasi and Urbina (1997), among others.

Internal Evidence of Test Validity

Internal sources of validity may include procedures to examine systematically the characteristics of a test, especially its content, assessment methods, structure, and theoretical underpinnings. In this section, several criteria for test selection are described as they relate to internal validity, including face validity, content validity, theory-based validity, and structural validity.

The test should appear as a credible measure of the targeted construct.   *Face validity* refers to the degree to which test items may be judged on examination to appropriately measure the targeted construct and objectives. Although not considered a source of validity in a technical sense, because it deals with what a test *looks like* it measures as distinguished from what it *actually* measures (Anastasi & Urbina, 1997), face validity has been shown to be related to examinee motivation and effort, as well as social desirability biases, labeling, and fairness (Bornstein, 1996). Examinees are commonly thought to be most cooperative when test content is commensurate with their understanding about the purpose of the assessment. Tests with items that are empirically keyed and not entirely face valid (e.g., *Personality Inventory for Children-Revised, PIC-R*) sometimes are met with resistance by examinees who perceive test items as not relevant or sensitive to the presenting complaints or reason for referral (e.g., adults or older adolescents who are asked to complete projective drawing tasks or sentence completion blanks). Examinees who are motivated to misrepresent themselves or their level of adjustment may find it easier to fake or intentionally distort their performance on tests that have greater face validity.

The test should representatively sample its targeted construct(s).   *Content validity* is the degree to which elements of a test, including individual items, response formats, and instructions, are relevant to and representative of varying facets of the targeted construct (Haynes, Richard, & Kubany, 1995). Phrased differently, content validity can be described as the degree to which a test adequately samples the domains of interest. That is, a depression scale should sample content associated with mood, ideation, hedonics, and psychomotor and other vegetative symptoms. Content validity varies with the purpose of the test and the nature of the inferences that may be drawn from test scores (Messick, 1993).

Multiple methods and quantitative and qualitative procedures involving people from the targeted population and expert judges may be used to establish content validity. Haynes et al. (1995) compiled a series of procedures by which content validity may be ascertained. Hopkins and Antes (1978) also recommended that test authors develop a table of specifications in which the facets and dimensions of the construct are listed alongside the number and identity of items assessing each facet.

In general, tests that contain more homogeneous item content tend to yield higher reliabilities than tests with heterogeneous item content, at the potential cost of generalizability and validity. In contrast, tests with more heterogeneous items sampling more facets of the construct may demonstrate higher predictive validity at the cost of scale reliability. There is a trade-off between the (in)adequacy of content sampling and scale unidimensionality, and both characteristics of the scale should be optimized to maximize construct validity. Clinical inferences made from tests with inadequate content validity may be suspect, even when other indices of validity are satisfactory (Haynes et al., 1995).

The content and structure of the test should be theoretically based.   The formulation of test items and procedures based on and consistent with a theory has been termed *substantive validity* (Loevinger, 1957) and is closely related to content validity. As a maturing science, psychology has produced rich and cohesive theories of behavior and cognition, theories that have shaped the development of new tests and assessment practices such as the *Millon Adolescent Clinical Inventory* (Millon & Davis, 1993), the *Cognitive Assessment System* (Naglieri & Das, 1997), and the *Assessment of Interpersonal Relations* (Bracken, 1993).

Theories are distinguished by their capacity to conceptualize categories and constructs, logically explain relations between elements, predict undetermined parameters, and explain findings that would be anomalous within another theory (e.g., Kuhn, 1970). According to Meehl (1978), theoretical systems consist of related assertions, shared terms, and coordinated propositions that provide fertile grounds for deducing and deriving new empirical and clinical observations.

An ideal standard for a psychological test is that it is based on an underlying theory. Crocker and Algina (1986) suggest, "psychological measurement, even though it is based on observable responses, would have little meaning or usefulness unless it could be interpreted in light of the underlying theoretical construct" (p. 7). In terms of theory-based test development, personality assessment has taken a leading role (e.g., the "Big Five" broad orthogonal factors of personality and Millon's "three polarity" bioevolutionary theory), while theoretical advances in cognitive–intellectual and adaptive behavior assessment have lagged behind. In describing best practices for the measurement of personality some three decades ago, Loevinger (1972) commented, "Theory has always been the mark of a mature science. The time is overdue for psychology, in general, and personality measurement, in particular, to come of age" (p. 56). It appears that these theoretical advances in some areas of psychosocial assessment have been forthcoming, but not all areas of personality assessment have advanced equally.

Composite test indices should correspond to the results of exploratory factor analyses. Exploratory factor analyses allow for empirical derivation of the natural structure of an instrument, often without *a priori* expectations, and are best interpreted according to the "psychological meaningfulness" of the dimensions or factors that emerge (e.g., Gorsuch, 1983). This criterion refers to the degree to which factor-analytic results match the composite scales or subscales of the test. Factor analyses are often used to determine the subtest composition of test composite scales or subscales (Floyd & Widaman, 1995), and some new instruments have been criticized for this mismatch (e.g., Keith & Kranzler, 1999; Stinnett, Coombs, Oehler-Stinnett, Fuqua, & Palmer, 1999), even when there is a theoretical and clinical rationale for scale composition.

Exploratory factor analyses provide a methodology by which the underlying dimensions assessed by a test may be separated or summarized. Floyd and Widaman (1995) suggest that exploratory factor analyses for clinical assessment instruments should routinely report principal component analysis or common factor analysis, initial communality estimates, the method of factor extraction, the criteria for retaining factors, the eigenvalues and the percentage of variance accounted for by the unrotated factors, the rotation method and rationale, all rotated factor loadings, factor intercorrelations, and the variance explained by the factors after rotation.

Competing models or theories should be tested with confirmatory factor analyses. Confirmatory factor analyses evaluate the congruence of the test data with an *a priori* theoretical model, as well as measure the relative fit of competing models. Confirmatory analyses provide evidence that the proposed factor structure of a test explains its underlying dimensions better than alternative hypothetical structures. Floyd and Widaman (1995) recommend that confirmatory factor analyses should report proposed model(s), number and composition of factors, orthogonal versus correlated factors, secondary loadings, correlated error terms, other model constraints (fixed and free parameters), method of estimation, goodness of fit, overall fit, relative fit, parsimony, any model modification to improve model fit to data, factor loadings and standard errors, communality (or squared correlations of observed variables with the factors), and factor correlations and standard errors with statistical significance. Comprehensive treatment and inclusion of such information allows test users to better understand the extent to which the test fits its proposed model or other competing models.

External Evidence of Test Validity

Evidence of test validity extends beyond analysis of the internal qualities of a test to include the extent to which the test relates to external variables in differing populations. Tests should be validated with regard to the purposes for which they are given and the consequences of their use. In this section, external classes of evidence for test construct validity are described, including criterion-related validity, consequential validity, and generalizability, as well as specialized forms of validity within these categories.

Tests should demonstrate convergent and discriminant validity evidence.
Evidence of test validity may also be accumulated through the study of relationships between test scores and variables external to the test. As suggested originally by Campbell and Fiske (1959), test scores should be related to other measures of the same psychological construct (*convergent* evidence of validity) and comparatively unrelated to measures of different psychological constructs (*discriminant* evidence of validity). For example, two measures of trait anxiety should correlate to a higher degree than the two anxiety scales would correlate with measures of extraversion or agreeableness.

Evidence of validity includes criterion scores that are obtained at about the same time (*concurrent* evidence of validity) or criterion scores that are obtained at some future date (*predictive* evidence of validity). For example, infant and preschool behavior rating scales have a primary goal of predicting behavioral difficulties before the child's clinical picture is complicated by social and educational developments associated with beginning school. Such prediction permits guidance as to the nature of any necessary early behavioral interventions. As appropriate, tests should demonstrate concurrent and predictive validity, depending on their intended use (e.g., diagnosis, prediction).

Test scores should demonstrate ecological validity. The emphasis on understanding the functional implications of test findings has been termed *ecological validity* (Neisser, 1978). Banaji and Crowder (1989) suggested that "if research is scientifically sound it is better to use ecologically lifelike rather than contrived methods" (p. 1188). In essence, ecological validity is intended to relate test performance to various aspects of person–environment functioning in everyday life, including identification of both competencies and deficits in social and educational adjustment. Test developers should show the ecological relevance of the constructs a test purports to measure, as well as the utility of the test for predicting everyday functional limitations for remediation. In contrast, tests based on laboratory-like procedures with little or no discernible relevance to real life may be said to have little ecological validity.

Tests may be built on a theoretical foundation that is ecologically relevant. The *Multidimensional Self Concept Scale* (Bracken, 1992), for example, was based on an ecological theory that proposes that children's self-concepts are differentially influenced by the contexts in which they developed (e.g., family, academic, social) and that remediation of children's specific domain-specific self-concepts also should be context-dependent.

An illustration of externally predictive and ecologically relevant test correlates was provided by Achenbach and his colleagues (1995), who found a correlation of .58 between scores on a delinquent behavior syndrome scale averaged over parent, teacher, and self-rating forms and subsequent police contacts and substance abuse. Tests are intended to predict real-life behaviors, and ecological validity can enhance predictive capability.

Tests should demonstrate the extent to which they meaningfully guide decision making.   Assessments frequently are conducted to enhance diagnosis and treatment planning. Tests should never be the sole determinant in diagnosis or decision making, but their utility in both arenas should be validated. Decision theory is a process involving calculations of decision making accuracy in comparison to the base rate occurrence of an event or diagnosis in a given population. Decision theory has been applied to psychological tests (Cronbach & Gleser, 1965) and other high-stakes diagnostic tests (Swets, 1992), and is useful for identifying the extent to which tests improve clinical or educational decision making.

The method of contrasted groups (Anastasi, 1982) is a commonly used methodology for validating psychological tests. In this methodology, the test performances of two samples known to be different on the criterion of interest are compared. For example, a scale purporting to assess attentional processes may be validated by showing large differences between a sample of children diagnosed with attention-deficit/hyperactivity disorder and a demographically matched sample drawn from the normative standardization group. Decision-making classification accuracy can be determined by developing cut scores or rules to differentiate the groups, so long as the rules show adequate sensitivity, specificity, positive predictive power, and negative predictive power.

Tests should identify intervention needs.   *Treatment utility* (Hayes, Nelson, & Jarrett, 1987) and *rehabilitation-referenced assessment* (Heinrichs, 1990) refer to the utility of assessment on treatment outcome (i.e., the selection and implementation of interventions and treatments that will benefit the examinee). The origins of treatment utility as it relates to test scores can be traced to the concept of aptitude by treatment interactions originally proposed by Cronbach (1957). In clinical and educational settings, the *raison d'être* for assessment is to describe, classify, and intervene to help a child (Hayes et al., 1987). The belief that children with certain developmental characteristics need specialized and individualized educational programs of instruction is a foundation of special education (Cole, Dale, Mills, & Jenkins, 1993). Treatment validity is the extent to which test-based inferences or statements benefit the patient, the client, or the user in some way by leading directly to a systematic intervention (Heinrichs, 1990). Unfortunately, reviews of current individually administered tests of learning and behavior problems in school psychology (e.g., social skills) suggest that most tests thus far have limited treatment utility (Reschly, 1997).

Tests should provide evidence of consequential validity.   A form of validity that emphasizes the intended and unintended societal impact of test results on individuals and groups is known as *consequential validity.* Consequential validity evaluates the utility of score interpretation as a basis for action, as well as the actual and potential consequences of test use (Messick, 1989). While adding value implications and social consequences to the validation process may further burden test developers, Messick (1995) argues that some values are intrinsic to the purpose and applications of psychological tests, and examination of the consequences of test use as a trigger to social and educational actions is a necessary element of validating tests.

As the social consequences of test use and interpretation are ascertained, the development and determinants of the consequences need to be explored. A measure with unintended negative side effects calls for the examination of alternative measures and assessment counterproposals. Consequential validity is especially relevant to issues of bias, fairness, and distributive justice.

Evidence of test score validity should be shown to generalize across the populations for which the test is intended.　　The accumulation of external evidence of test validity becomes most important when test results may be generalized across contexts, situations, and populations, and when the consequences of testing reach beyond the test's original intent. According to Messick (1995), "The issue of generalizability of score inferences across tasks and contexts goes to the very heart of score meaning. Indeed, setting the boundaries of score meaning is precisely what generalizability evidence is meant to address" (p. 745).

Hunter and Schmidt (1990; Hunter, Schmidt, & Jackson, 1982; Schmidt & Hunter, 1977) developed a methodology of validity generalization, a form of meta-analysis, that analyzes the extent to which variation in test validity across studies is due to sampling error or other sources of error such as imperfect reliability, imperfect construct validity, range restriction, or artificial dichotomization. Once incongruent or conflictual findings across studies can be explained in terms of sources of error, meta-analysis enables theory to be tested, generalized, and quantitatively extended.

Evidence of Test Score Reliability

The *reliability* of test scores refers to the reproducibility (*precision, consistency, and repeatability*) of test results, or the degree to which test scores are free from measurement error. Measurement precision can be enhanced and error reduced by making test elements internally consistent, temporally stable, accurately understood, and convergently scored by different examiners and scorers. In this section, multiple methods of demonstrating the reliability of psychological tests are presented. These methods include procedures from classical test theory as well as from item response theory. Reliability may be evaluated only in the context of test use (Nunnally & Bernstein, 1994).

Internal consistency should be $\geq .90$ for high-stakes tests; $\geq .80$ for lower-stakes tests. The internal consistency of a test informs us about the uniformity and coherence of test content (i.e., items) and is a prerequisite to precise measurement. In classical test theory, reliability is based on the assumption that measurement error is distributed normally and equally for all score levels. By contrast, item response theory posits that reliability differs between individuals with different response patterns and levels of ability but generalizes across populations (Embretson & Hershberger, 1999).

The statistic used to determine internal consistency is usually *coefficient alpha* or split-half reliability. Several psychometricians (e.g., Bracken, 1987; Clark & Watson,

1995; Nunnally & Bernstein, 1994) have recommended that minimal levels of internal consistency should average across ages at or above .80 or .90, depending on the nature and applications of the test scale (low-stakes and high-stakes applications, respectively). In a review of 13 preschool third-party social–emotional scales, Bracken, Keith, and Walker (1994) reported that, although most instruments studied demonstrated total test reliability ≥ .90, subtest and scale reliabilities often fell far short of desired levels for clinical use.

Overconcern with internal consistency beyond this minimal level can be counterproductive, however, because increases in internal consistency may occur at the expense of validity known as the *attenuation paradox*, Clark and Watson (1995) conclude that "[m]aximizing internal consistency almost invariably produces a scale that is quite narrow in content; if the scale is narrower than the target construct, its validity is compromised" (pp. 316–317).

Following Nunnally's (1978) original standards, Bracken (1987; Bracken & McCallum, 1998) recommended that total test or total scale internal consistency of high-stakes tests (e.g., intelligence tests) should equal or exceed .90 when averaged across the age levels. Cicchetti and Sparrow (1990) suggested that internal consistency below .70 is unacceptable for clinical applications; between .70 and .79 reliability is fair; reliability is good when it is between .80 and .89; and .90 and above reliability is excellent. Bracken (1987; Bracken & McCallum, 1998) further recommended that median internal consistency at the subtest or subscale level (low-stakes applications) should average across ages at $r \geq .80$. Cicchetti (1994) noted that, for example, from infancy through the preschool years, the *Vineland Adaptive Behavior Scales* consistently yield coefficient alphas within the desirable range, with coefficient alphas ranging between .89 and .94 for Communication; between .86 and .92 for Daily Living Skills; between .82 and .94 for Socialization; between .74 and .95 for Motor Skills, and between .96 and .98 for the Vineland Adaptive Behavior Composite.

Local reliability estimates should be reported.   Local reliability refers to measurement precision at specified levels or ranges of scores, and has special value as a guide for selecting appropriate tests for individuals. For example, a test with high local reliability at low ability levels may be more appropriate than other tests for the assessment of children who are mildly mentally retarded.

As an illustration, the *Universal Nonverbal Intelligence Test (UNIT;* Bracken & McCallum, 1998) presents local reliabilities from a classical test theory orientation. A common cut score for classifying individuals as mentally retarded is a Full Scale IQ equal to or less than 70. To investigate *UNIT* reliability near this cut point, coefficient alpha reliabilities were calculated for Full Scale IQs between −1.33 and −2.66 standard deviations from the normative mean. Reliabilities were corrected for restriction in range, and results showed that composite IQs exceeded the .90 suggested criterion. That is, the *UNIT* is sufficiently reliable at this range to reliably identify mentally retarded levels of functioning. Item response theory permits the determination of local standard error at every level of performance, thereby determining whether a test is more accurate for some members of a group (e.g., high-functioning individuals) than for others (Daniel, 1999). Using item response theory, tests such as the *Scales of*

Independent Behavior-Revised (SIB-R; Bruininks et al., 1996) report local standard errors for every score, and Elliott (1990) converts local standard errors to local reliabilities for the *Differential Ability Scales.* Additional methodologies also exist for estimating local scale reliabilities using item response theory (Kolen, Zeng, & Hanson, 1996; Samejima, 1994).

Total test stability coefficients should be ≥.90 for high-stakes tests, ≥.80 for lower-stakes tests. Test scores must be reasonably stable to have practical utility for making clinical and educational decisions and to be predictive of future performance. Stability is typically estimated through use of test-retest score stability coefficients, which can be calculated by correlating test performance at two points in time. Bracken (1987; Bracken & McCallum, 1998) suggest that the total test stability coefficient should be greater than or equal to .90 for high-stakes tests over a relatively short time interval (e.g., 2 to 6 weeks); .80 for lower-stakes tests. Test-retest reliability is a measure of construct stability, but its interpretation in clinical contexts can be influenced by several factors (e.g., deleterious effects of degenerative disorders, successful therapeutic interventions, spontaneous improvement in individuals recovering from traumatic brain injury). For example, personality tests measuring enduring trait-based constructs (e.g., trait anxiety) should be expected to have higher stability coefficients than measures of transient emotional states (e.g., state anxiety).

Test score reliability should generalize across populations. *Reliability generalization* is a meta-analytic methodology to investigate the reliability of scores across studies and samples (Vacha-Haase, 1998). An extension of validity generalization (Hunter & Schmidt, 1990; Schmidt & Hunter, 1977), reliability generalization investigates the stability of reliability coefficients across samples and studies. In order to demonstrate measurement precision for the populations for which a test is intended, the test should show comparable levels of reliability across various demographic subsets of the population, as well as salient clinical and exceptional populations.

Evidence of Test Score Fairness

In this section, methodologies are described by which evidence of test score fairness may be accumulated. Fairness has not been considered historically as a leading criterion by which test selection decisions are made, but recent court decisions have elevated its level of importance. Tiedeman (1978) notes that, "Test equity seems to be emerging as a criterion for test use on a par with the concepts of reliability and validity" (p. xxviii).

 For the purposes of clarity, we offer the following definitions. We consider *fairness* to refer in a global way to the extent to which test scores are (a) statistically shown to be free from evidence of psychometric bias, (b) comparably reliable and valid across demographic groups, and (c) equitably applied and equally predictive in real-life consequences and pragmatic impact. Fairness is a concept that transcends psychometrics and includes the philosophic, legal, or practical considerations used to formulate policy.

Test score fairness also may be conceptualized as a part of validity generalization, placing emphasis on determination of whether test scores mean the same things across situations and samples. According to Jensen (1980), fairness refers "to the ways in which test scores (whether of biased or unbiased tests) are used in any selection situation" (p. 376). Willingham (1999) suggests that evidence of test fairness should be accumulated at every stage during and following test development.

Test score bias has been defined in more narrow, circumscribed statistical terms. We consider bias to refer to elements of a test and its usage that are construct irrelevant *and* that yield systematic errors related to specific demographic group membership. Test score bias results in differential performance for individuals of the same ability or proficiency but from different ethnic, sex, cultural, or religious groups (Hambleton & Rodgers, 1995). Test bias has also been described as "a kind of invalidity that harms one group more than another" (Shepard, Camilli, & Averill, 1981, p. 318). The concept of bias overlaps with fairness but is not identical; tests that do not show evidence of bias can still be used unfairly.

This section considers both internal and external evidence of test score fairness. The internal/external dichotomy is convenient to differentiate between methodologies that do or do not use an external criterion (Camilli & Shepard, 1994). Fairness may be sought through a multimethod approach including review of test content and assessment procedures for potential bias by a multicultural bias and sensitivity panel; statistical analyses of differential item and test functioning to minimize internal test characteristics that should be expected to be comparable across groups; and external criterion analyses to determine whether a test has comparable prediction of performance and impact across groups.

Consistent with the emphasis in this chapter on application-centered psychometrics in addition to test-centered psychometrics, Sue (1999) suggests that issues of test fairness can be addressed through demonstration of external validity to explicitly specify the population groups to which test findings are applicable, while maintaining strong standards for demonstration of internal validity. Camilli and Shepard (1994) concur about the importance of external validation across groups: "Item bias procedures, internal to a test, cannot address larger issues of test bias and fair test use" (p. 153).

Internal Evidence of Test Fairness

The *internal* features of a test related to fairness generally include the test's theoretical underpinnings, item content and format, differential item and test functioning, measurement precision, and factorial structure. The two best-known procedures for evaluating test fairness include expert reviews of item bias and analysis of differential item functioning. These and several additional sources of evidence of test fairness are discussed in this section.

Theoretical underpinnings of a test related to fairness should be presented.   The theory on which a test is built may have an inherent sensitivity to issues of fairness and should be fully discussed in the test manual. For example, tests that place a premium on speeded responses may place minority groups whose cultures do not value speed at a disadvantage. Some clinicians may interpret slowed response times in personality testing as an indication of guardedness or defensiveness; however, such an interpretation may not be appropriate with Hispanic examinees from cultures in which time is considered a less salient concept (e.g., Scheuneman & Oakland, 1998). Individuals who are not native speakers of English may be disadvantaged by English-language test directions and procedures (e.g., Bracken & McCallum, 1998; Duran, 1989; Geisinger, 1992b; Oakland & Parmelee, 1985). In addition, performance on measures that require crystallized ability and knowledge, even if only to understand task instructions, may be inextricably linked to culture (e.g., Carroll, 1993) and, accordingly, may show differential performance across otherwise equally able groups.

Item content and procedures should undergo multicultural bias and sensitivity reviews. The use of multicultural reviewers to examine the type, content, and format of test items for potential bias is a common practice among publishers of psychological tests, usually with the goals of (a) identifying offensive or controversial material, (b) identifying unfair material, and (c) remaining sensitive to population diversity. Among the considerations of such reviewers are language usage, ethnocentrism, minority-group representation, and minority-group portrayals in the test materials (Sireci & Geisinger, 1998). Representative questions to be included as part of item bias reviews are available from Hambleton and Rodgers (1995).

We recommend that all tests present items in a gender-, culture-, age-, and race-neutral manner. Stimulus artwork should depict people, regardless of gender, age, race and cultural backgrounds performing similar or equivalent roles and activities. Artwork that portrays negative facial expressions (e.g., anger, fear, boredom), physical limitations (e.g., eyeglasses, hearing aids, use of crutches), styles and manner of dress or expressed socioeconomic status, and disabling conditions (e.g., being wheelchair-bound) should be distributed evenly across individuals of differing genders, races, and ages. Stereotyping of any sort in stimulus materials for tests should be avoided.

Items should be analyzed for differential item functioning. *Differential item functioning* (DIF) refers to a family of statistical procedures aimed at determining whether test items display different statistical properties in different group settings after controlling for differences in the abilities of the comparison groups (Angoff, 1993). The most popular DIF procedure is the Mantel-Haenszel technique (Holland & Thayer, 1988), which assesses similarities in item functioning across various demographic groups of comparable ability. Items with properties that disadvantage one group over another are considered for deletion from the test.

McAllister (1993) observes that the testing profession has embraced DIF as the preferred method for detecting potential item bias and enhancing the development of fair tests. However, Camilli and Shepard (1994) caution: "DIF statistics rely on an internal criterion; therefore, it is impossible to escape their inherent circularity. DIF statistics cannot detect constant bias, nor can they get outside a test to evaluate the relative validity and group impact of other ways of measuring the same construct" (p. 155).

DIF has been extended by Shealy and Stout (1993) to a test score-based level of analysis known as *differential test functioning* (*DTF*; also known as *multiple item DIF*). DTF statistics are derived from the aggregated influence of DIF for two or more items considered simultaneously. DTF is important because some tests produce a small and common number of off-setting items that are identified as biased against both comparison groups (e.g., males and females). Because the number of biased items are offsetting, the overall effects on DTF are minimal.

Factor structure and scale reliabilities should be invariant across groups. The examination of comparable reliability and validity across separate demographic groups should be conducted. Jensen (1980) notes that, if test reliability and validity coefficients differ significantly for designated subgroups of interest, then "it is clear that the test scores are not equally [reliable or valid] measures for both groups" (p. 430).

The demonstration of factorial invariance across sex, racial, and ethnic groups for which a test may be used constitutes another way to establish the fairness of the measure. In this instance, factor analysis shows that the test assesses the same fundamental constructs across groups, and analyses are conducted separately for different demographic groups and compared. In a review of exploratory and confirmatory factor analyses, Floyd and Widaman (1995) suggest that, "Increasing recognition of cultural, developmental, and contextual influences on psychological constructs has raised interest in demonstrating measurement invariance before assuming that measures are equivalent across groups" (p. 296). Meredith (1993) has further asserted that strict *factorial invariance* is required for test fairness and equity to exist.

The Achenbach system of empirically-based assessments, including the *Child Behavior Checklist (CBCL)*, *Teacher's Report Form (TRF)*, and *Youth Self Report (YSR)*, offers one of the best available examples of factorial invariance across cultures. In the U.S. standardizations, eight cross-informant syndrome constructs for males and females have been identified across the parent, teacher, and self-report forms through item-level factor analyses: withdrawn, somatic complaints, anxious/depressed, social problems, thought problems, attention problems, delinquent behavior, and aggressive behavior (e.g., Achenbach, 1993). The cross-cultural invariance of the factor-derived syndromes has been supported by confirmatory factor analyses of *CBCL*, *TRF*, and *YSR* ratings of several thousand clinically referred Dutch children (De Groot, Koot, & Verhulst, 1994, 1996). Extension of this methodology to various racial and ethnic subgroups will further establish the structural consistency of the Achenbach system.

The demonstration of comparable internal reliabilities across sex, racial, and ethnic samples has been studied in some recent generation intelligence tests (e.g., Bracken & McCallum, 1998; Matazow, Kamphaus, Stanton, & Reynolds, 1991; Vance & Gaynor, 1976; Zhu, Chen, & Tulsky, 1999). Geisinger (1998) notes that, "subgroup-specific reliability analysis may be especially appropriate when the reliability of a test has been justified on the basis of internal consistency reliability procedures (e.g., coefficient alpha). Such analysis should be repeated in the group of special test takers because the meaning and difficulty of some components of the test may change over groups, especially over some cultural, linguistic, and disability groups" (p. 25).

External Evidence of Test Fairness

The *external* features of test fairness involve the examination of relations between test scores and external criteria, and include the concepts of equal prediction and comparable consequential impact. External evidence of fairness has been traditionally applied to personnel selection and educational placement for children with disabling conditions, but it also has relevance for measures of social and emotional functioning such as special education placement for serious emotional disturbance (Wood, Johnson, & Jenkins, 1986). Most studies examining test bias tend to rely solely on methodologies such as DIF, while neglecting to examine external criterion-based studies. To focus solely on internal criteria may not capture the presence of bias (Shepard et al., 1981).

Test scores should be comparably predictive across groups.   The demonstration of equivalent predictive validity across demographic groups constitutes an important source of fairness that is related to validity generalization. This methodology, which has been most frequently utilized with cognitive measures, but which has equal application with personal and social measures, investigates whether a test predicts relevant external criteria comparably for different demographic groups.

Cleary (1968) suggests a procedure that compares predictive validity by using multiple regression to regress the predictor variable and relevant demographic characteristics against the external criterion measure. Cleary notes that test bias exists when criterion scores predicted from a common regression line are consistently too high or too low for members of one subgroup. A test is also considered to be biased if the regression slopes differ significantly between the compared demographic groups. It is important to note that this methodology assumes adequate levels of reliability for both the predictor and criterion variables. This procedure has several limitations that have been described by Thorndike (1971) and summarized by Camilli and Shepard (1994).

Test scores should produce minimal adverse impact and selection bias outcomes.   A second form of bias detection addresses the limitations of predictive bias methodologies. Thorndike (1971) noted that group mean score differences on a predictor variable can still yield equal prediction to a criterion, even while resulting in disproportionate impact against one or another demographic group. He suggested a model for fair selection based on predictions that require different test cut scores be chosen so that members of each group are selected in proportion to their success on the criterion. Such consequential aspects of test bias are commonly referred to as indicators of *selection bias* (Jencks, 1998). When test scores produce adverse, disparate, or disproportionate impact for one group over another, even when that impact is construct relevant, test users should consider the societal and legal implications of such selection bias.

Selection bias stems secondarily from the presence of moderate to large group mean score differences that do not in themselves meet criteria for psychometric bias, insofar as the differences may represent genuine group differences in the construct being assessed. As McAllister (1993) has observed: "In the testing community, differences in correct answer rates, total scores, and so on do not mean bias. In the political realm, the exact opposite perception is found; differences mean bias" (p. 394).

Federal mandates and court rulings have frequently indicated that adverse, disparate, or disproportionate impact in selection decisions based on psychological test scores constitutes evidence of unlawful discrimination. The 1991 Civil Rights Act, Section 9, specifically and explicitly prohibits any discriminatory use of test scores for minority groups. Since enactment of the Civil Rights Act of 1964, demonstration of *adverse impact* has been treated in legal settings as prima facie evidence of test bias. Adverse impact occurs when group test score differences have systematic effects on decision making that disproportionately disadvantage members of minority groups. The U. S. Supreme Court held in 1988 that statistical selection ratios can constitute sufficient evidence of adverse impact. Disproportionate impact due to psychological tests also has been alleged from evidence of overrepresented minority schoolchildren in special education classes in prominent rulings related to mental retardation (e.g., *Larry P. v. Riles*, 1979, 1984) and serious emotional disturbance (e.g., *Lora v. Board of Education of the City of New York*, 1978).

In conclusion, test items may be free of evidence of demonstrable psychometric bias, but significant group mean score differences among racial and ethnic groups may still exist and contribute to selection bias. Jencks and Phillips (1998) stress that the test score gap is the single most important obstacle to achieving racial balance and social equity. Tests that demonstrate a relative absence of group mean score differences for demographically matched samples will likely minimize selection bias and increase the equitable use of tests across different groups. Newer generation personality tests have examined mean score differences between various demographic groups (e.g., age, race, gender) and factored such differences into norm development and the consideration of potential outcomes (e.g., Bracken, 1992, 1993).

Conclusion

In this chapter, we have described psychometric and pragmatic guidelines for selecting appropriate tests. Both traditional and newer developments in the assessment of psychometric adequacy have been discussed. Illustrative examples have been presented for measures related to social and personal assessment, but the guidelines may be equally applied to tests of cognitive ability, functional adaptation, and neuropsychological functioning. An emphasis has been placed on application-centered psychometrics, such as treatment utility, in addition to test-centered psychometrics. Most importantly, these criteria should be applied according to the context in which the test is being utilized.

Test development remains an art, with the science behind building good tests growing quickly. Decisions about using a test should include consideration as to the qualities of the instrument, but the interests of the child should remain paramount at all times. As we remind our graduate students, the process of psychological assessment is not about the test; it is about the child.

References

Achenbach, T. M. (1993). *Empirically based taxonomy: How to use syndromes and profile types derived from the CBCL/4-18, TRF, and YSR.* Burlington, VT: University of Vermont Department of Psychiatry.

Achenbach, T. M., & Howell, C. T. (1993). Are American children's problems getting worse? A 13-year comparison. *Journal of the American Academy of Child and Adolescent Psychiatry, 32,* 1145–1154.

Achenbach, T. M., Howell, C. T., McConaughy, S. H., & Stanger, C. (1995). Six-year predictors of problems in a national sample of children and youth: II. Signs of disturbance. *Journal of the American Academy of Child and Adolescent Psychiatry, 34,* 488–498.

American Educational Research Association, American Psychological Association, & National Council on Measurement in Education. (1999). *Standards for educational and psychological testing.* Washington, DC: American Educational Research Association.

Anastasi, A. (1982). *Psychological testing* (5th ed.). New York: Macmillan.

Anastasi, A., & Urbina, S. (1997). *Psychological testing* (7th ed.). Upper Saddle River, NJ: Prentice-Hall.

Angoff, W. H. (1993). Perspectives on differential item functioning methodology. In P. W. Holland & H. Wainer (Eds.), *Differential item functioning* (pp. 3–24). Hillsdale, NJ: Erlbaum.

Banaji, M. R., & Crowder, R. C. (1989). The bankruptcy of everyday memory. *American Psychologist, 44,* 1185–1193.

Bayley, N. (1993). *Bayley Scales of Infant Development second edition manual.* San Antonio, TX: The Psychological Corporation.

Binet, A., & Simon, T. (1916). New methods for the diagnosis of the intellectual level of subnormals. In E. S. Kite (Trans.), *The development of intelligence in children* (pp. 37-90). Baltimore: Williams and Wilkins. (Original work published 1905)

Blake, D. D., Penk, W. E., Mori, D. L., Kleespies, P. M., Walsh, S. S., & Keane, T. M. (1992). Validity and clinical scale comparison between the MMPI and MMPI-2 with psychiatric inpatients. *Psychological Reports, 70,* 323-332.

Bornstein, R. F. (1996). Face validity in psychological assessment: Implications for a unified model of validity. *American Psychologist, 51,* 983-984.

Bracken, B. A. (1987). Limitations of preschool instruments and standards for minimal levels of technical adequacy. *Journal of Psychoeducational Assessment, 4,* 313–326.

Bracken, B. A. (1988). Ten psychometric reasons why similar tests produce dissimilar results. *Journal of School Psychology, 26,* 155–166.

Bracken, B. A. (1992). *Multidimensional Self Concept Scale.* Austin, TX: PRO-ED.

Bracken, B. A. (1993). *Assessment of Interpersonal Relations.* Austin, TX: PRO-ED.

Bracken, B. A. (Ed.). (1996). *Handbook of self-concept: Developmental, social, and clinical considerations.* New York: Wiley.

Bracken, B. A., & Crain, M. R. (1994). Children's and adolescents' interpersonal relations: Do age, race, and gender define normalcy? *Journal of Psychoeducational Assessment, 12,* 14–32.

Bracken, B. A., Keith, L. K., & Walker, K. C. (1994). Assessment of preschool behavior and social–emotional functioning: A review of thirteen third-party instruments. *Assessment in Rehabilitation and Exceptionality, 1,* 331–346.

Bracken, B. A., & McCallum, R. S. (1998). *Universal Nonverbal Intelligence Test examiner's manual.* Itasca, IL: Riverside.

Bruininks, R. H., Woodcock, R. W., Weatherman, R. F., & Hill, B. K. (1996). *Scales of Independent Behavior-Revised comprehensive manual.* Itasca, IL: Riverside.

Camilli, G., & Shepard, L.A. (1994). *Methods for identifying biased test items* (Vol. 4). Thousand Oaks, CA: Sage.

Campbell, D. T., & Fiske, D. W. (1959). Convergent and discriminant validation by the multitrait–multimethod matrix. *Psychological Bulletin, 56,* 81–105.

Campbell, D. T., & Stanley, J. C. (1963). *Experimental and quasi-experimental designs for research.* Chicago: Rand McNally.

Campbell, S. K., Siegel, E., Parr, C. A., & Ramey, C. T. (1986). Evidence for the need to renorm the Bayley Scales of Infant Development based on the performance of a population-based sample of 12-month-old infants. *Topics in Early Childhood Special Education, 6,* 83–96.

Carroll, J. B. (1993). *Human cognitive abilities: A survey of factor-analytic studies.* New York: Cambridge University Press.

Cattell, R. B. (1986a). Scales and the meaning of standardized scores. In R. B. Cattell & R. C. Johnson (Eds.), *Functional psychological testing: Principles and instruments* (pp. 79–104). New York: Brunner/Mazel.

Cattell, R. B. (1986b). The psychometric properties of tests: Consistency, validity, and efficiency. In R. B. Cattell & R. C. Johnson (Eds.), *Functional psychological testing: Principles and instruments* (pp. 54–78). New York: Brunner/Mazel.

Chan, K., Drasgow, F., & Sawin, L. L. (1999). What is the shelf life of a test? The effect of time on the psychometrics of a cognitive ability test battery. *Journal of Applied Psychology, 84,* 610–619.

Chattin, S. H., & Bracken, B. A. (1989). School psychologists' evaluation of the K-ABC, McCarthy Scales, Stanford-Binet IV, and WISC-R. *Journal of Psychoeducational Assessment, 7,* 112–130.

Cicchetti, D. V. (1994). Guidelines, criteria, and rules of thumb for evaluating normed and standardized assessment instruments in psychology. *Psychological Assessment, 6,* 284–290.

Cicchetti, D. V., & Sparrow, S. S. (1990). *Assessment of adaptive behavior in young psychology: A handbook* (pp. 173–196). New York: Pergamon Press.

Clark, L. A., & Watson, D. (1995). Constructing validity: Basic issues in objective scale development. *Psychological Assessment, 7,* 309–319.

Cleary, T. A. (1968). Test bias: Prediction of grades for Negro and White students in integrated colleges. *Journal of Educational Measurement, 5,* 115–124.

Cole, K. N., Dale, P. S., Mills, P. E., & Jenkins, J. R. (1993). Interaction between early intervention curricula and student characteristics. *Exceptional Children, 60,* 17–28.

Cook, T. D., & Campbell, D. T. (1979). *Quasi-experimentation: Design and analysis issues for field settings.* Chicago: Rand McNally.

Crain, M. R., & Bracken, B. A. (1994). Age, race, and gender differences in child and adolescent self-concept: Evidence from a behavioral-acquisition, context-dependent model. *School Psychology Review, 23,* 496–511.

Crocker, L., & Algina, J. (1986). *Introduction to classical and modern test theory.* New York: Holt, Rinehart and Winston.

Cronbach, L. J. (1949). *Essentials of psychological testing.* New York: Harper & Brothers.

Cronbach, L. J. (1957). The two disciplines of scientific psychology. *American Psychologist, 12,* 671–684.

Cronbach, L. J., & Gleser, G. C. (1965). *Psychological tests and personnel decisions.* Urbana, IL: University of Illinois Press.

Daniel, M. H. (1999). Behind the scenes: Using new measurement methods on the DAS and KAIT. In S. E. Embretson & S. L. Hershberger (Eds.), *The new rules of measurement: What every psychologist and educator should know* (pp. 37–63). Mahwah, NJ: Erlbaum.

De Groot, A., Koot, H. M., & Verhulst, F. C. (1994). Cross-cultural generalizability of the Child Behavior Checklist cross-informant syndromes. *Psychological Assessment, 6,* 225–230.

De Groot, A., Koot, H. M., & Verhulst, F. C. (1996). Cross-cultural generalizability of the Youth Self-Report and Teacher's Report Form cross-informant syndromes. *Journal of Abnormal Child Psychology, 24,* 651–664.

Dorans, N. J., & Holland, P. W. (1993). DIF detection and description: Mantel-Haenszel and standardization. In P. W. Holland & H. Wainer (Eds.), *Differential item functioning* (pp. 35–66). Hillsdale, NJ: Erlbaum.

Duran, R. P. (1989). Testing of linguistic minorities. In R. L. Linn (Ed.), *Educational measurement* (3rd ed., pp. 573–588). New York: Macmillan.

Elliott, C. D. (1990). *Differential Ability Scales: Introductory and technical handbook.* San Antonio, TX: The Psychological Corporation.

Embretson, S. E., & Hershberger, S. L. (Eds.). (1999). *The new rules of measurement: What every psychologist and educator should know.* Mahwah, NJ: Erlbaum.

Exner, J. E. (1993). *The Rorschach: A comprehensive system. Volume 1: Basic foundations* (3rd ed.). New York: Wiley.

Floyd, F. J., & Widaman, K. F. (1995). Factor analysis in the development and refinement of clinical assessment instruments. *Psychological Assessment, 7,* 286–299.

Flynn, J. R. (1984). The mean IQ of Americans: Massive gains 1932 to 1978. *Psychological Bulletin, 95,* 29–51.

Flynn, J. R. (1987). Massive IQ gains in 14 nations: What IQ tests really measure. *Psychological Bulletin, 101,* 171–191.

Flynn, J. R. (1994). IQ gains over time. In R. J. Sternberg (Ed.), *The encyclopedia of human intelligence* (pp. 617–623). New York: Macmillan.

Flynn, J. R. (1999). Searching for justice: The discovery of IQ gains over time. *American Psychologist, 54,* 5–20.

Geisinger, K. F. (1992a). The metamorphosis of test validation. *Educational Psychologist, 27,* 197–222.

Geisinger, K. F. (Ed.). (1992b). *Psychological testing of Hispanics.* Washington, DC: American Psychological Association.

Geisinger, K. F. (1998). Psychometric issues in test interpretation. In J. Sandoval, C. L. Frisby, K. F. Geisinger, J. D. Scheuneman, & J. R. Grenier (Eds.), *Test interpretation and diversity: Achieving equity in assessment* (pp. 17–30). Washington, DC: American Psychological Association.

Gorsuch, R. L. (1983). *Factor analysis* (2nd ed.). Hillsdale, NJ: Erlbaum.

Guion, R. M. (1977). Content validity—The source of my discontent. *Applied Psychological Measurement, 1*, 1–10.

Hambleton, R., & Rodgers, J. H. (1995). Item bias review. (ERIC Clearinghouse on Assessment and Evaluation, EDO-TM-95-9). Washington, DC: The Catholic University of America Department of Education.

Hammill, D. D., Pearson, N. A., & Wiederholt, J. L. (1996). *Comprehensive Test of Nonverbal Intelligence.* Austin, TX: PRO-ED.

Harrell, T. H., Honaker, L. M., & Parnell, T. (1992). Equivalence of the MMPI-2 with the MMPI in psychiatric patients. *Psychological Assessment, 4*, 460–465.

Hayes, S. C., Nelson, R. O., & Jarrett, R. B. (1987). The treatment utility of assessment: A functional approach to evaluating assessment quality. *American Psychologist, 42*, 963–974.

Haynes, S. N., Richard, D. C. S., & Kubany, E. S. (1995). Content validity in psychological assessment: A functional approach to concepts and methods. *Psychological Assessment, 7*, 238–247.

Heinrichs, R.W. (1990). Current and emergent applications of neuropsychological assessment problems of validity and utility. *Professional Psychology: Research and Practice, 21*, 171–176.

Herrnstein, R. J., & Murray, C. (1994). *The bell curve: Intelligence and class in American life.* New York: Free Press.

Holland, P. W., & Thayer, D. T. (1988). Differential item functioning and the Mantel-Haenszel procedure. In H. Wainer & H. I. Braun (Eds.), *Test validity* (pp. 129–145). Hillsdale, NJ: Erlbaum.

Hollon, S. D., & Flick, S. N. (1988). On the meaning and methods of clinical significance. *Behavioral Assessment, 10*, 197–206.

Hopkins, C. D., & Antes, R. L. (1978). *Classroom measurement and evaluation.* Itasca, IL: F. E. Peacock.

Hunter, J. E., & Schmidt, F. L. (1990). *Methods of meta-analysis: Correcting error and bias in research findings.* Newbury Park, CA: Sage.

Hunter, J. E., Schmidt, F. L., & Jackson, C. B. (1982). *Advanced meta-analysis: Quantitative methods of cumulating research findings across studies.* San Francisco: Sage.

Jackson, D. N. (1971). A sequential system for personality scale development. In C. D. Spielberger (Ed.), *Current topics in clinical and community psychology* (Vol. 2, pp. 61–92). New York: Academic Press.

Jencks, C. (1998). Racial bias in testing. In C. Jencks & M. Phillips (Eds.), *The Black–White test score gap* (pp. 55–85). Washington, DC: Brookings Institute.

Jencks, C., & Phillips, M. (Eds.). (1998). *The Black–White test score gap.* Washington, DC: Brookings Institute.

Jensen, A. R. (1980). *Bias in mental testing.* New York: Free Press.

Joint Committee on Testing Practices. (2000). *Test user qualifications: A data-based approach to promoting good test use.* Washington, DC: American Psychological Association.

Keith, T. Z., & Kranzler, J. H. (1999). The absence of structural fidelity precludes construct validity: Rejoinder to Naglieri on what the Cognitive Assessment System does and does not measure. *School Psychology Review, 28*, 303–321.

Kuhn, T. (1970). *The structure of scientific revolutions* (2nd ed.). Chicago: University of Chicago Press.

Kolen, M. J., Zeng, L., & Hanson, B. A. (1996). Conditional standard errors of measurement for scale scores using IRT. *Journal of Educational Measurement, 33*, 129–140.

Larry P. v. Riles, No. C-71-2270 RFP (1979), and No. 80-4027 DC No. CV 71-2270, United States Court of Appeals for the Ninth Circuit (1984).

Litz, B. T., Penk, W. E., Walsh, S., Hyer, L., Blake, D. D., Marz, B., Keane, T. M., & Bitman, D. (1991). Similarities and differences between the Minnesota Multiphasic Personality Inventory (MMPI) and MMPI-2. *Journal of Personality Assessment, 57*, 238–254.

Loevinger, J. (1957). Objective tests as instruments of psychological theory [Monograph]. *Psychological Reports, 3*, 635–694.

Loevinger, J. (1972). Some limitations of objective personality tests. In J. N. Butcher (Ed.), *Objective personality assessment* (pp. 45-58). New York: Academic Press.

Lora v. Board of Education of the City of New York, 456 Supp 1211 (E.D.N.Y. 1978). Vacated and remanded or reworded 623 F. 2nd 248 or 298 2nd Cir. (1980).

Matazow, G. S., Kamphaus, R. W., Stanton, H. C., & Reynolds, C. R. (1991). Reliability of the Kaufman Assessment Battery for Children for Black and White students. *Journal of School Psychology, 29*, 37–41.

McAllister, P. H. (1993). Testing, DIF, and public policy. In P. W. Holland & H. Wainer (Eds.), *Differential item functioning* (pp. 389–396). Hillsdale, NJ: Erlbaum.

McFadden, T. U. (1996). Creating language impairments in typically achieving children: The pitfalls of "normal" normative sampling. *Language, Speech, and Hearing Services in Schools, 27,* 3–9.

Meehl, P. E. (1978). Theoretical risks and tabular asterisks: Sir Karl, Sir Ronald, and the slow progress of soft psychology. *Journal of Consulting and Clinical Psychology, 46,* 806–834.

Meredith, W. (1993). Measurement invariance, factor analysis and factorial invariance. *Psychometrika, 58,* 525–543.

Messick, S. (1989). Meaning and values in test validation: The science and ethics of assessment. *Educational Researcher, 18,* 5–11.

Messick, S. (1993). Validity. In R. L. Linn (Ed.), *Educational measurement* (2nd ed., pp. 13–104). Phoenix, AZ: American Council on Education and Oryx Press.

Messick, S. (1995). Validity of psychological assessment: Validation of inferences from persons' reponses and performances as scientific inquiry into score meaning. *American Psychologist, 50,* 741–749.

Millon, T., & Davis, R. D. (1993). The Millon Adolescent Personality Inventory and the Millon Adolescent Clinical Inventory. *Journal of Counseling and Development, 71,* 570–574.

Millon, T., Davis, R., & Millon, C. (1997). *MCMI-III: Millon Clinical Multiaxial Inventory-III manual* (3rd ed.). Minneapolis, MN: National Computer Systems.

Naglieri, J. A., & Das, J. P. (1997). *Das-Naglieri Cognitive Assessment System interpretive handbook.* Itasca, IL: Riverside.

Neisser, U. (1978). Memory: What are the important questions? In M. M. Gruneberg, P. E. Morris, & R. N. Sykes (Eds.), *Practical aspects of memory* (pp. 3–24). London: Academic Press.

Newborg, J., Stock, J. R., Wnek, L., Guidubaldi, J., & Svinicki, J. (1984). *Battelle Developmental Inventory.* Itasca, IL: Riverside.

Nunnally, J. C. (1978). *Psychometric theory.* New York: McGraw-Hill.

Nunnally, J. C., & Bernstein, I. H. (1994). *Psychometric theory* (3rd ed.). New York: McGraw-Hill.

Oakland, T., & Parmelee, R. (1985). Mental measurement of minority-group children. In B. B. Wolman (Ed.), *Handbook of intelligence: Theories, measurements, and applications* (pp. 699–736). New York: Wiley.

Reschly, D. J. (1997). Utility of individual ability measures and public policy choices for the 21st century. *School Psychology Review, 26,* 234–241.

Reynolds, W. M. (1979). Psychological tests: Clinical usage versus psychometric quality. *Professional Psychology: Research and Practice, 10,* 324–329.

Reynolds, W. M., & Sundberg, N. D. (1976). Recent research trends in testing. *Journal of Personality Assessment, 40,* 228–233.

Samejima, F. (1994). Estimation of reliability coefficients using the test information function and its modifications. *Applied Psychological Measurement, 18,* 229–244.

Scheuneman, J. D., & Oakland, T. (1998). High-stakes testing in education. In J. Sandoval, C. L. Frisby, K. F. Geisinger, J. D. Scheuneman, & J. R. Grenier (Eds.), *Test interpretation and diversity: Achieving equity in assessment* (pp. 77–103). Washington, DC: American Psychological Association.

Schinka, J. A., & LaLone, L. (1997). MMPI-2 norms comparisons with a census-matched subsample. *Psychological Assessment, 9,* 307–311.

Schmidt, F. L., & Hunter, J. E. (1977). Development of a general solution to the problem of validity generalization. *Journal of Applied Psychology, 62,* 529–540.

Shealy, R., & Stout, W. F. (1993). A model-based standardization approach that separates true bias/DIF from group differences and detects test bias/DTF as well as item bias/DIF. *Psychometrika, 58,* 159–194.

Shepard, L., Camilli, G., & Averill, M. (1981). Comparison of procedures for detecting test-item bias with both internal and external ability criteria. *Journal of Educational Statistics, 6,* 317–375.

Sireci, S. G., & Geisinger, K. F. (1998). Equity issues in employment testing. In J. Sandoval, C. L. Frisby, K. F. Geisinger, J. D. Scheuneman, & J. R. Grenier (Eds.), *Test interpretation and diversity: Achieving equity in assessment* (pp. 105–140). Washington, DC: American Psychological Association.

Stinnett, T. A., Coombs, W. T., Oehler-Stinnett, J., Fuqua, D. R., & Palmer, L. S. (1999, August). *NEPSY structure: Straw, stick, or brick house?* Paper presented at the Annual Convention of the American Psychological Association, Boston, MA.

Sue, S. (1999). Science, ethnicity, and bias: Where have we gone wrong? *American Psychologist, 54,* 1070–1077.

Swets, J. A. (1992). The science of choosing the right decision threshold in high-stakes diagnostics. *American Psychologist, 47,* 522–532.

Thorndike, R. L. (1971). Concepts of culture-fairness. *Journal of Educational Measurement, 8,* 63–70.

Tiedeman, D. V. (1978). Assessment of Career Development In O. K. Buros (Ed.), *The eighth mental measurements yearbook* (pp. 1542–1454). Highland Park, NJ: Gryphon Press.

Uniform guidelines on employee selection procedures. (1978). *Federal Register, 43,* 38296-38309.

Vacha-Haase, T. (1998). Reliability generalization: Exploring variance in measurement error affecting score reliability across studies. *Educational and Psychological Measurement, 58,* 6–20.

Vance, H. B., & Gaynor, P. E. (1976). A note on cultural difference as reflected in the Wechsler Intelligence Scale for Children. *Journal of Genetic Psychology, 129,* 171–172.

Wade, T. C., & Baker, T. B. (1977). Opinions and use of psychological tests: A survey of clinical psychologists. *American Psychologist, 32,* 874–882.

Ward, C. L. (1991). A comparison of T scores from the MMPI and the MMPI-2. *Psychological Assessment, 3,* 688–690.

Wechsler, D. (1997). *WAIS-III WMS-III technical manual.* San Antonio, TX: The Psychological Corporation.

Willingham, W. W. (1999). A systematic view of test fairness. In S. J. Messick (Ed.), *Assessment in higher education: Issues of access, quality, student development, and public policy* (pp. 213–242). Mahwah, NJ: Erlbaum.

Wood, F. H., Johnson, J. L., & Jenkins, J. R. (1986). The Lora case: Nonbiased referral, assessment, and placement procedures. *Exceptional Children, 52,* 323–331.

Woodcock, R. W., McGrew, K. S., & Mather, N. (2001). *Woodcock-Johnson III Tests of Cognitive Abilities.* Itasca, IL: Riverside.

Wylie, R. C. (1979). *The self-concept: Vol. 2. Theory and research on selected topics (Rev. ed.).* Lincoln, NE: University of Nebraska Press.

Wylie, R. C. (1989). *Measures of self-concept.* Lincoln, NE: University of Nebraska Press.

Zhu, J., Chen, H., & Tulsky, D. (1999, April). *WISC-III reliability data for special clinical groups.* Paper presented at the Annual Convention of the National Association of School Psychologists, Las Vegas, NV.

Zhu, J., & Tulsky, D. S. (in press). Co-norming the WAIS-III and WMS-III: Is there a test-order effect on IQ and memory scores? *The Clinical Neuropsychologist.*

3

Common Disorders and Difficulties Seen among School-aged Children

Lawrence A. Vitulano,

Janet F. Carlson, and

John R. Holmberg

An overview of the history of child and adolescent psychology reveals astonishing changes in our understanding of childhood psychopathology (Lewis & Vitulano, 1989). The predominant perspective has moved from primarily descriptive through social, psychological, and biological theories of etiology to more recent developmental and interactional models that attempt to explain complicated, disruptive, even delinquent or criminal patterns of behavior in childhood. These changes were sometimes precipitated by the genius of new conceptual approaches or development of technological advances, or simply were shaped by prevailing economic and social climates.

With time, a number of earlier approaches decreased in popularity in support of a more developmental bias that considers both the age and stage of the child. Symptoms are currently understood in the context of often normal fluctuations in patterns of development by children who, nevertheless, adhere to predictable sequences of emotional and intellectual development. Perhaps the most current understanding of child psychopathology is best described as a multiple interactional perspective, which appreciates all of the previous contributory models and integrates them into an interactive model. One example of this approach is the advent of innovative community intervention programs that utilize several levels of theoretical and systemic interventions in order to help children with multiple disabilities and their families in the community with such problems as adjustment to psychiatric hospital discharge and chronic and acute exposure to violence (Vitulano, Holmberg, & Vitulano, in press).

Several considerations affecting the selection of measures appropriate for personality and social assessment of children were discussed in Chapter 2. In the present chapter, we address some of the most frequently encountered disorders of childhood along with selected assessment and intervention techniques that can be helpful in understanding personality and social aspects and difficulties experienced by children. In our opinion, it is useful to include assessment of cognitive and academic functioning whenever possible, as these abilities often illuminate other aspects of functioning, including personality and patterns of difficulties. During assessment of cognitive or academic abilities, for example, testing professionals may detect motivational issues or attention difficulties that themselves warrant closer scrutiny.

The most frequently used classification system for psychiatric diagnosis of children in the Unites States is the *Diagnostic and Statistical Manual of Mental Disorders (DSM-IV;* American Psychiatric Association, 1994). Although this system comes under frequent criticism for its shortcomings, it nevertheless provides a common language and reference point for research and practice. The *DSM-IV* is an operationalized system of classification that is intended to be symptom-based, thereby reducing subjectivity and allowing for more reliable diagnoses in comparison to earlier versions of the system. However, individuals who meet many, but not all, of the specified criteria often are grouped somewhat amorphously under broad residual categories of "Not Otherwise Specified." These nonspecific classifications are considerably less helpful in understanding the nature of an individual child's struggles. In addition, this system does not account for the inner life of the child or the child's family context. Finally, when an individual's symptoms satisfy the diagnostic criteria for more than one disorder, both diagnoses are rendered and treated as completely separate disorders. This practice stands in opposition to the common clinical observation of individuals who experience, for example, a combination of both anxiety and depression in the context of their problems.

Practitioners must strive to understand the children with whom they work from the vantage point of the problems or difficulties experienced within their current contexts, rather than solely from the perspective of their diagnostic or classification label. When used prudently, taxonomic systems may expedite procedural matters, offer therapeutic value, and establish a child's eligibility for specialized support services in educational or clinical settings. Ultimately, these may improve the child's situation. Classification and placement, however, seldom are sufficient and specific interventions tailored to an individual child's particular set of symptoms and functions of behavior are essential.

In the following sections, we describe briefly a number of childhood disorders that occur with some degree of frequency among school-aged children and that have a primary impact on personality and social aspects of functioning. Thus, we do not include discussions related to cognitive abilities or learning disorders specifically in this chapter, as the major effects of these difficulties center in functional domains that appear largely outside of personality, per se. That is not to say that these distinctions are clear-cut, however, as demonstrated in Chapter 8 of this volume, where Waterman suggests and describes a possible link between learning difficulties and features of personality predicated on an information-processing model. Despite the pervasive personal and social costs of disturbances in reality contact (e.g., as in childhood-onset schizophrenia), the extraordinarily low prevalence rates of these most perplexing disorders (Doll, 1996) and space limitations of this volume do not permit coverage of these low base-rate phenomena. We restrict our coverage to the most prominent areas of difficulty experienced by children and adolescents, namely stress reactions and adjustment, substance use problems, suicide and risk of harm, depression, excessive anxiety, attention difficulties, behavioral problems, and impaired social functioning, consistent with epidemiological findings reviewed by Doll (1996) concerning the most prevalent psychiatric disorders reported in children and youth. The coverage herein is intended to acquaint readers with or remind readers of the most often encountered kinds of difficulties experienced by this age group, and to emphasize the most salient assessment and intervention concerns in each category.

Reaction and Adjustment to Stressors

For children and adolescents, life represents a continuity of experience amidst frequent changes internal and external, large and small, that typically are integrated into their overall experience without undue complications. Beyond these normative experiences, there are a range of life events that cause a disruption in this ordinarily smooth integration of the ebb and flow of life and development. When a child experiences stress through life events, changes, or a series of changes to such an extent that there is significant impairment in functioning or the reaction becomes truly disabling, he or she is likely experiencing an adjustment reaction.

Most often, problems related to adjustment become evident as a child's family and other significant adults are consistently impressed by a marked change in functioning after a particular stressful event. The form of the behavior or symptom can vary greatly but the function is typically an expression of the distress experienced as a result of the change. Subclinical or briefly evident clusters of symptoms and behaviors that would otherwise suggest the presence of a depressive, anxiety, or conduct disorder commonly are associated with this type of difficulty. Often, children experience a mix of mood and behavioral difficulties following the stressor. A helpful heuristic in the conceptualization of an adjustment reaction is understanding that the behavior change represents the child's attempt to find expression for the distress experienced in the face of confusion, disillusionment, and lack of control experienced when the life change cannot be integrated simply into his or her experience base. Thus, the hallmark sign of this type of difficulty is the marked change in behavior or emergence of new symptoms following an identifiable stressful event. A second key feature of this type of difficulty is that, after the initial stress has ended, maladaptive behaviors subside and normal functioning resumes within a relatively brief period of time, up to, perhaps, a few months.

Typical examples of adjustment difficulties include family events such as major occupational or health changes for the child's parents, changes in primary residence, birth of a sibling, emancipation of an adolescent in the family, and divorce or remarriage of one's parent(s). Other examples would include the child experiencing a life change, such as changing schools or change in his or her health or experiencing a frightening event, such as a burglary, fire, or automobile accident. All these events are relatively common in our society and may or may not be overwhelming for a child, but each certainly represents a need for substantial adjustment. A normal period of mourning following the death of a loved one ordinarily is not viewed as this type of difficulty unless the disruption extends well beyond what would be expected.

In assessing the presence of an adjustment problem, interviewing techniques (such as those described in Chapter 5 of this volume) are likely the most common, efficient, and effective. The evaluator will be most effective if interviews with caregivers and other significant adults occur prior to meeting with the child. Information regarding the significant adults' observations of the child's levels of adaptive functioning before and after the event, as well as identifying the ways that the difficulties appear to be expressed in new symptoms and behaviors, are essential pieces of data. When meeting with the child, drawing often is used as part of, or instead of, traditional semistructured interviews (refer to Chapter 7 of this volume for an expanded discussion of drawing techniques). Many times, initial drawings represent especially happy, harmonious, or wished-for scenes. As trust develops, subsequent drawings may begin to reveal themes and scenes that reflect the significant event or change or the child's experience of the change. Knowledge gained from the child's significant others regarding the sociocultural or religious meaning of the change for the family and for the child also will be important to include in one's conceptual formulation. For example, a preoperational child (i.e., one between the ages of 3 and 7) whose parents are divorcing due to parental infidelity may struggle to align the parent's behaviors with the spiritual teachings that the parent had earlier supported, bringing into question all that the parent had previously taught and said, including his or her love for the child.

Because adjustment problems may remit with little or no intervention within a few months of the event, recommendations following an assessment generally include monitoring and follow-up, parent guidance, and short-term supportive individual or family interventions. Minimizing further disruption or feelings of stigmatization is important in treating adjustment reactions. Thus, finding ways to make interventions part of the regular family routine and to embed them within the child's activities at school may be most helpful.

Substance Use, Abuse, and Addiction

Alcohol and drug abuse are among the most widespread and persistent mental health problems facing us today as children begin drinking and using drugs at younger and younger ages. Based on 1999 reports from the National Institute on Drug Abuse, 10 million teenagers drank last month, half as "binge drinkers" having had five or more drinks in a row. Additionally, 50% have used marijuana within the last 30 days. Nationally, the typical pattern of alcohol use begins at 13 years of age; marijuana use begins around 14 years. Problems of substance abuse can involve difficulties that result either from the intoxicating effects of the substance or from dependence after an individual develops tolerance for a substance or experiences withdrawal when abstinence is attempted. Several severe reactions to alcoholism include intoxication, withdrawal delirium, chronic alcohol hallucinations, and dementia. In general, alcoholism is defined as dependence that interferes with life adjustment and keeps someone from attaining his or her potential economically, socially, or emotionally. Although the data are not yet conclusive, a number of etiological factors are considered influential, including inherited genetic vulnerability, biological sensitivity, and psychological susceptibility to alcoholism. Peer pressure, parental role-modeling, and environmental stressors also comprise significant contributory factors in the development of alcohol abuse disorders.

Drug abuse disorders involve dependence on opiates (heroin and other narcotics), sedatives, stimulants (including cocaine), hallucinogens, anti-anxiety drugs (Valium, Zanax, and others), and marijuana. Caffeine and nicotine addictions also are included in this category of addictions. Drug abuse and addiction are most common during adolescence and young adulthood, although they may develop at any age. Dependence can be either primarily physical or psychological in nature. Contributing factors include the influence of a peer group, the availability of drugs along with the existence of a drug culture, and the tendency to view and use drugs to curb tension and relieve pain.

Given the very strong association between substance abuse and suicide, effective treatments are urgently needed (e.g., Forman & Kalafat, 1998), yet the treatment of children and adolescents who abuse substances remains quite challenging. Prognosis depends on the chronicity of the problem, motivation for change, and the immediate availability of social supports both in the family and within the community. It is often necessary to remove the individual from the community drug culture for a period of residential treatment. Such programs of quality are increasingly difficult to locate and fund, especially for preadolescents or those with a less established pattern of chronic abuse, but they are, nevertheless, extremely valuable to the addicted abuser. After intensive inpatient treatment, follow-up care is essential and should include supportive group therapy, relapse prevention training, individual counseling as indicated, and some form of peer support group, such as Alcoholics Anonymous or Narcotics Anonymous.

Suicide and Risk of Harm

Suicides, suicide attempts, and suicidal ideation occur among young people at alarmingly high rates, despite the belief of many that suicide data grossly underestimate reality (e.g., Davis & Sandoval, 1991). It has been difficult to conduct large-scale survey research using school-aged children to ascertain their history of suicide attempts and their thoughts about suicide. School districts and parents often oppose such inquiries, fearing that the questions themselves will cause children to contemplate suicidal actions that they otherwise would not. Epidemiological research in this area generally regards "adolescence" as including the ages from 15 to 24, in part because the rate of suicide among younger children is extraordinarily low, at least in terms of what appears on a death certificate (Davis & Sandoval, 1991). Data from older adolescents frequently derive from college samples, which may not mirror the noncollege population or the younger school-aged population—or perhaps they do. In view of the paucity of information directly related to younger children, it seems reasonable to consider incidence and prevalence data from slightly older age groups, if only to gain a foothold on the likely scope of the problem among children of still younger ages.

Berman and Jobes (1991) cited a threefold increase in suicide rates among young people between the ages of 15 to 24 from 1957 to 1987. Disaggregating data for the narrower, more school-aged cohort, Davis and Sandoval (1991) reported a dramatic 73% increase in death rates from suicide among 15- to 19-year-olds, across the 16–year period extending from 1970 to 1986. A more recent study, using 18- to 24–year-old college students who provided data in 1995 (Brener, Hassan, & Barrios, 1999) and were demographically similar to the general population, revealed that 1 in 10 respondents (10%) reported that they had considered suicide seriously within the last year. From the same group, 7% had made a suicide plan and 2% had made an attempt. Among those who made an attempt, one fifth required medical attention. Freshmen and sophomores were most likely to have contemplated suicide, as were students who identified themselves as non-White. Brener et al. noted that their data comprised the first prevalence study of suicidal ideation in a nationally representative sample and that their findings were similar to at least two other studies that used convenience samples. By any standard, these indicators require serious consideration and planful action on the part of mental health care professionals.

Most children who undergo assessment of personal and social functioning will be evaluated for risk of self-injury or suicide as well, most notably when concerns center around potential substance use disorders, mood disorders, and conduct disorders, as these problems often co-occur. It is important to assess as accurately as possible individuals who truly are at risk for suicide, as well as those who truly are not at risk. These individuals comprise *true positives* and *true negatives*, respectively, and an assessment process that maximizes these identifications facilitates the effective use of intervention strategies by making it possible to treat those who need treatment and avoid treating those who do not need treatment.

Individuals not at risk who are erroneously identified as at risk constitute *false positives*, while those at risk but erroneously identified as not at risk constitute *false negatives*. Both types of errors are costly. In the former instance, individuals wrongly believed to be at risk receive treatment unnecessarily, and may generate unnecessary expenses in terms of financial and personnel resources as well as time. In the latter instance, individuals who truly are at risk are missed, and do not receive the treatment they need. In the case of assessment of suicide risk, "missing" such individuals may mean the difference between life and death.

Berman and Jobes (1991) suggest the use of multifocal assessment in an effort to increase the fidelity of the assessment process. They stress the importance of evaluating imminent risk, lethality and intent, as well as other factors that collectively provide a context for a more complete understanding of the risk of suicide and prognosis under particular circumstances. In assessing *imminent risk*, Berman and Jobes emphasize the importance of heeding signals often sent by adolescents contemplating suicide, such as may be evident indirectly in their writing or artwork in which themes of death, dying, suicide, or the afterlife prevail. It is especially important to assess further in these instances and to ascertain whether a plan exists and whether there has been any rehearsal behavior, such as accumulating pills. The assessment of lethality and intent also are important considerations in that these factors establish the extent to which a person poses a danger to him- or herself. *Lethality* refers to the expected consequence of a particular planned action, and generally is taken to describe or quantify the likelihood that death will follow. One reason for higher rates of suicide completion among boys and men, as compared to girls and women, is that they choose methods with higher lethality (e.g., use of firearms) that leave less room for rescue efforts than methods with lower lethality (e.g., ingestion of pills). Although suicide attempts are considerably higher among female adolescents, for example, suicide completions are 8 times more likely among male adolescents (Martinez, 2000). *Intent* refers to the "purpose or goal of the self-harm behavior" (Berman & Jobes, 1991, pp. 138–139), and often goes to the alleviation of some form of pain or distress.

The act of suicide itself is the ultimate final act and recovery is, flatly, impossible. The impact is especially traumatic for "survivors" of the suicide. *Survivors* are those left behind, generally including individual family members, friends, associates, and classmates of suicide completers. Capuzzi and Golden (1988) estimate that, on average, 6 to 10 people experience long-term negative effects for each adolescent suicide or attempt, although the circle may well expand to include entire communities or school districts, depending on the particular circumstances surrounding the suicide. More than any other disturbance or sign thereof, suicide leaves in its wake survivors who ask innumerable and wrenching questions of themselves: Why didn't I see this coming? Why didn't I do something? These kinds of questions must not be dismissed as idle musings, given that "[e]xposure to another's suicide may be considered an accelerating risk factor among those already predisposed to be at risk" (Berman & Jobes, 1991, p. 101). Although beyond the scope of this chapter, many resources on adolescent suicide include considerable coverage of postsuicide intervention, which has come to be called *postvention*, in addition to prevention efforts (e.g., Berman & Jobes, 1991; Capuzzi & Golden, 1988; Davis & Sandoval, 1991; Poland, 1989; Sandoval & Brock, 1996).

Depression and Related Mood Disturbances

There is growing recognition that disorders of mood occur among school-aged children with striking regularity, a shift that followed decades of clinical lore suggesting that children were not emotionally mature enough or psychologically sophisticated enough to experience serious mood disturbances. Although practitioners today generally hold that children and adolescents may meet the criteria for any of the various mood disorders, most interest in this area has centered on depression and related disturbances in mood state, such as dysthymic disorder. Epidemiological studies of bipolar disorders in young children are virtually nonexistent. In part, the interest in depression among children and adolescents may stem from the suggestion that "untreated depression is the number one cause of suicide" (Martinez, 2000, p. 18).

Recent prevalence rates indicate that between about 2% and 9% of children and adolescents meet the criteria for major depressive episode (Goodyer, 1995; Harrington, 1993). Up until mid- to late-adolescence, the frequency rate among boys and girls is approximately equal. Thereafter, gender differences begin to emerge in a pattern that ultimately establishes that seen among adults, wherein twice as many women as men are affected (APA, 1994; Compas et al., 1997; Martinez, 2000). As well, first-degree biological relatives are up to 3 times more likely to demonstrate depression than the general population.

Several patterns observed among adults are seen as well among children, with the course of depression demonstrating rates of relapse and recurrence that are comparable to adult sufferers, at least for adolescents (APA, 1994; Callahan, Panichelli-Mindel, & Kendall, 1996). Children, it seems, demonstrate a lower rate of recurrence than older individuals, perhaps because their bodies do not produce the hormones that have been implicated in adolescent and adult courses (Martinez, 2000). One particularly worrisome difference between adult depressives and children is that children do not often self-refer and—perhaps because society remains somewhat reluctant to acknowledge depression among children—their problems may escape notice by significant others in their lives, in part due to the disorder's heterogeneity of causes and symptoms (Goodyer, 1995). Briefly stated, a diagnosis of major depressive disorder in children requires a persistent depressed mood or anhedonia for a period of at least 2 weeks. The individual often evidences a diminished interest in previously pleasurable activities. Physical symptoms, such as insomnia or hypersomnia, fatigue or general malaise, or changes in appetite or weight, also may characterize the disorder. Frequently, a negative view of the self is apparent through the individual's statements about his or her lack of worth, sense of guilt, and view of the future.

Although the areas of functioning affected by depression in children are similar to those affected among depressed adults (i.e., emotional, cognitive, motivational, somatic/physical domains), the demands of the educational setting may act to mask some of the classic symptoms of depression. As children progress in school, there tends to be greater emphasis on academic subjects and considerably less attention to personal or social functions. It is not uncommon in kindergarten screenings, for instance, to assess a child's ability to wait, take turns, and share toys appropriately. Children are grouped into classes that are much larger than even the largest family in all but very rare instances, with social demands that are beyond what they have experienced to date. A child who evidences a sad mood because of a depressive disorder very well may be mistaken for one who simply is having difficulty making the transition to school. Although dysphoric mood is considered a hallmark symptom of depression, it is also nonspecific; as such, it accompanies many other disorders and, in this case, also occurs in everyday life as part of the normal variation of mood, which is expected to show transitory negative and positive feelings alternating in a fairly balanced manner.

Another hallmark symptom, anhedonia, is more specific to depression than dysphoria, but in a school context it may be easily misconstrued as attention seeking, or may be attributed wrongly to social inhibition, shyness, or any number of other things seen commonly among young schoolchildren. In a classroom full of 25 youngsters, a disorder whose symptom picture varies considerably from case to case, but generally appears as a rather quiet, unobtrusive constellation of behaviors, is easily overlooked. Another complication in attempting to recognize depression among children relates to the co-occurrence of childhood depression and several other disorders, including anxiety (Kendall, Kortlander, Chansky, & Brady, 1992; Kovacs, Gatsonis, Paulauskas, & Richards, 1989; Strauss, Last, Hersen, & Kazdin, 1988), substance use disorders (Greenbaum, Prange, Friedman, & Silver, 1991), personality disorders (Grilo, Walker, Becker, Edell, & McGlashan, 1997), and perhaps others.

Risk factors for depressive disorders are not uniformly demonstrated in empirical studies. Among adults, prevalence rates appear unrelated to socioeconomic status or marital status (APA, 1994). Similarly, some investigations concerning children or adolescents failed to demonstrate group differences on factors including socioeconomic status (e.g., Grilo et al., 1997). Several studies involving children, however, indicated that a disproportionate number of children and adolescents referred for mental health reasons had experienced early loss of one or both parents (Seligman, Gleser, Rauh, & Harris, 1974). The effects noted were more pronounced for children who sustained the loss between the ages of 3 and 6 and between 12 and 15 years. With specific reference to depression, Caplan and Douglas (1969) noted that fully half of the depressed school-age children in their study had experienced parental loss prior to the age of 8, compared to fewer than one quarter of same-age nondepressed children. Other studies have shown an increased occurrence of depression among children from households in which there is some aspect of family dysfunction (Harrington, 1993) and from low-income families (e.g., Kandel & Davies, 1982; Kaplan, Hong, & Weinhold, 1984). Environmental factors also appear to play a role as noted by Fitzpatrick's (1993) work that demonstrated the differential effects of violence on the development of depression among females. Specifically, Fitzpatrick found that being a female victim of violence increased the odds of developing depression, whereas being an older witness to violence actually buffered against the development of depression.

Goodyer (1995) noted that children developed anxious or depressed disorders at exponentially higher rates as family adversities accumulated, demonstrating that the relationship between adverse environmental factors and the appearance of childhood disorders is not merely additive but multiplicative. Still, Goodyer explained that these relationships are not absolute, noting a striking feature in "the lack of any clear specific associations between any one pattern of social adversities and the subsequent onset of major depression . . . [O]nset of major depression *or* anxiety may occur as a consequence of a range of recent life events and difficulties" (p. 190).

In assessing mood, it is vital to consider more than the *DSM-IV* diagnostic criteria, which in fact are the same criteria used for adults. Although it is generally true that similar symptom pictures characterize depressive disorders in children and adults, research has illuminated some important differences not specified in the *DSM-IV* criteria (Callahan et al., 1996). For example, hopelessness is a strong indicator of depression in children, as illustrated by the findings of Goodyer and Cooper (1993), who found that the presence of hopelessness was 100% predictive of depression in a sample of 11- and 12-year-olds.

It also is essential to view the child in his or her context and to gather information from a variety of sources familiar with the child over a sustained period of time. As noted in the previous discussion of adjustment disorders, many indicators of depression depend on comparative judgments wherein a child's current state must be evaluated for change from a previous state. For example, an examiner might need to ascertain from relevant sources whether the child has lost interest in something he or she used to value highly or whether there has been a change in appetite or sleeping patterns. Thus, one must ask the child and relevant third parties to report not only the child's current state, but whether or not this state represents a change from an earlier one. Instruments that screen for depression in children (e.g., *Children's Depression Inventory*, Kovacs, 1992; *Reynolds Adolescent Depression Scale*, Reynolds, 1987) may be useful for larger scale screenings, such as those that occur as part of a district-wide screening program, to help identify at-risk children.

Overall, efforts to treat depression in adolescents and children have involved an eclectic mix of orientations and intervention strategies with, perhaps, interventions aimed at cognitive distortions and those involving families being somewhat more prominent. Very little empirical evidence has been amassed concerning the treatment of depression in children, per se, as the majority of the research in this area has involved adolescents. With regard to adolescents, findings to date support the efficacy of cognitive–behavioral therapy generally (e.g., Reinecke, Ryan, & DuBois, 1998), and some have found this approach to be more efficacious than other specific approaches (Brent et al., 1997). Even in these studies, however, a large proportion of the variance remains unaccounted for, lending support to the concept that nonspecific factors, such as treatment consistency and therapeutic empathy, account for more improvement than specific actions of any particular brand of treatment (Kolko, Brent, Baugher, Bridge, & Birmaher, 2000). Results of other research prompted the researchers (Ostrander, Weinfurt, & Nay, 1998) to suggest that treatment approaches be adjusted as a function of the child's age, noting that younger children need their supportive relationships bolstered to a greater extent than adolescents, who seem to profit from interventions consistent with a more purely cognitive bent.

Difficulties Stemming from Excessive Anxiety

Anxiety and avoidant behavior are the hallmarks of a loosely coupled group of disorders termed *anxiety disorders.* Although fears and anxieties are common and transitory throughout childhood (Lapouse & Monk, 1959), more severe and persistent patterns of behavior require professional attention. Generalized anxiety disorders are characterized by chronic excessive worry not ascribable to any specific object or situation. Children with this disorder often are restless, easily fatigued, irritable, tense, and have problems concentrating and sleeping. No matter how well things seem to be going on the outside, these children seem to be worried and anxious constantly.

Thorough assessment of childhood anxiety should include a comprehensive evaluation of the three-channel response system of subjective feelings and thoughts, behavioral avoidance, and physiological activity (Graziano, DeGiovanni, & Garcia,

1979). This wide-spectrum approach to assessment facilitates treatment planning and enhances outcomes by promoting the use of treatments specifically targeted for a particular kind of difficulty. For example, an avoidant child would most likely benefit from reinforced practice (i.e., motor channel), while an overly worried child might utilize self-control strategies (i.e., cognitive channel), and a physically symptomatic child probably would improve after relaxation training. Generalized anxiety disorders are relatively common disorders among children that can respond favorably to cognitive behavioral and family interventions. Children need to be taught behavioral competencies and adaptive behaviors while their environments are modified in order to reinforce more adaptive patterns of responses.

Post-traumatic stress disorder is a pattern of response to a severe traumatic event or chronic exposure to such conditions or events. Often the child's responses include persistent reexperiences (nightmares or flashbacks), avoidance of reminders or triggers of the trauma, increased worry and tension, impaired concentration and memory, and potential symptoms of depression. Treatment that is immediate and supportive is most efficacious. However, long-term symptoms may not become evident to others until well after the trauma has subsided, in which case symptomatic relief along with insight-oriented and behavioral exposure treatments may be indicated. When it is believed that extreme or prolonged stress may affect a child, stress prevention or reduction techniques may be helpful. It is sometimes possible to inoculate a child by providing information about likely stressors ahead of time and developing effective means to cope with them when they do occur.

Obsessive-compulsive disorder refers to the occurrence of unwanted and intrusive thoughts that are usually accompanied by compulsive rituals designed to neutralize the thoughts or prevent some dreaded event or situation. For example, compulsive hand washers try to avoid contamination and compulsive checkers attempt to prevent a feared event, such as fires from stoves left on or burglaries due to unlocked doors and windows. Although most children experience minor worries, such as finishing homework or locking doors, in obsessive-compulsive disorder the thoughts and behaviors are so persistent and intrusive that they often interfere substantially with optimal functioning.

The most effective treatment for obsessive compulsive disorder is exposure and response prevention (Steketee & Foa, 1985). Rather than allowing the child to perform rituals that only temporarily reduce anxiety and need to be repeated incessantly, the behavioral treatment teaches children to tolerate anxiety and learn how to prevent unwanted patterns of responding. The child first develops a hierarchy of upsetting stimuli and then is exposed to moderately highly arousing stimuli first in guided fantasy (*in vitro*) and then directly (*in vivo*). Throughout the treatment the individual is encouraged to stop responding with useless rituals until the anxiety subsides on its own and the child regains behavioral control. Although obsessive-compulsive disorder rarely remits completely, most individuals will improve enough to continue with their social and emotional development more adaptively. In the most severe cases, medication may be indicated.

Finally, tics are localized intermittent but persistent muscle twitches including eye blinking, mouth movements, lip licking, neck and shoulder shrugging, throat clearing, and sniffing, among other movements. Sometimes children are aware of their tics, but more often these actions are involuntary and only noticed by the child in social situations where they may be the cause of criticism or ridicule. Tourette's syndrome involves multiple motor tics and at least one vocal tic. This tic disorder may be more severe and include copralalia, "a complex vocal tic involving the uttering of obscenities" (APA, 1994, p. 102). Tic disorders generally are more common in males and may respond to relaxation training, stress management, or medication together with school consultation to help with adjustment problems, educate peers and teachers, and provide classroom management strategies.

Disrupted Attention and Problems with Inattention

Of all the children and adolescents referred for assessment of emotional and behavioral disturbances, one of the most common sets of difficulties involves distraction, inattention, and poor concentration. Often, but far from always, difficulties with inattention are accompanied by impaired impulse control, excessive unfocused energy, and frenetic activity. Large epidemiological studies typically found prevalence rates for significant problems with inattention in about 5% of children (APA, 1994), with almost half of these cases meeting *DSM-IV* diagnostic criteria for attention deficit disorder (Doll, 1996). In child psychiatric clinics, as many as 50% of the children served have impaired attention as a primary reason for evaluation and treatment (Cantwell, 1996). As amplified in Chapter 15, important gender differences exist, with male greater than female frequency ratios ranging from 4:1 to 9:1, depending on context, age, and population (general vs. clinical; APA, 1994). Some studies found that gender difference ratios significantly decrease when the behavioral disturbance under consideration related primarily to inattention without associated impulsivity or hyperactivity (Wolraich, Hannah, Pinnock, Baumgaertel, & Brown, 1996). Although some studies found greater percentages of people with attention difficulties among minority and low socioeconomic groups, these differences typically became nonsignificant when other than single-teacher behavior ratings were used to identify the problem (Barkley, 1997).

A sophisticated system of cognitive filters has evolved to help us identify and emphasize important incoming information and reduce focus on trivial matters. This system requires a great number of switching and gating mechanisms that are highly interrelated and coordinated as executive functions, all of which create a nearly universal experience that is highly difficult and elusive to operationalize and research. High prevalence rates for problems with inattention also likely relate to the vulnerability for disrupting key neuropsychological functions related to attention, focus, and concentration, a point considered more fully in Chapter 6. A wide range of injuries, illnesses, delays, and difficulties can result in problems with inattention, many of which look alike initially despite stemming from vastly different causes. In diagnostic sessions, evaluators are likely to see a large number of children with attention problems, but many will not be found to have attention deficits as a primary difficulty.

Rather, the child's attention problems likely relate to the notion that attention difficulties represent and emerge as a final common symptom or outcome from a range of potential insults, difficulties, and causes.

As many as 66% of children who have difficulties in the three primary domains of attention, impulsivity, and activity have other, comorbid, difficulties as well (Barkley, 1998). Attention and executive functioning systems are vulnerable to a range of difficulties. Some of the most common comorbid difficulties are discussed in Cushman's Chapter 15. It also is important to note that attention deficits associated with, but not primary in, the diagnosis occur in impaired cognitive functioning, head injuries, illnesses that impact the brain, social disabilities such as autism, and psychotic and dissociative disorders. The difficult task for assessment professionals is to determine whether the attention-related difficulties are causing, caused by, or merely exacerbating the associated difficulties. The evaluation also must rule out physical toxins (e.g., lead, drug use, cocaine, or alcohol toxicity in utero), injuries (especially head trauma), and everyday events (e.g., fatigue, hunger, pain, and acute distress) as potential causes for the attention problems.

In assessing the presence of problems related to inattention, impulsivity, and hyperactivity, comprehensive evaluation is key. Although most clinicians are capable of doing the majority of the work in a thorough assessment, evaluators who have not been trained in neuropsychological assessment may need a consultation or to refer aspects of the evaluation to a neuropsychologist. The components of an evaluation for attention problems should include: (a) a full parent interview, family and developmental history, and assessment of the child's adaptive or independence skill development; (b) developmentally appropriate diagnostic interviews with the child; (c) use of both broad-spectrum and specific behavior checklists, completed by the child and at least two informants within each of the child's main social contexts, including home, school, and after-school programs; (d) thorough medical evaluation and neurological screening; (e) appropriate cognitive and achievement testing; (f) social–emotional testing; (g) neuropsychological assessment of the child's executive functions; and (h) adjunct assessments based on specific identified areas of difficulty as indicated (e.g., speech/language, gross or fine motor). It is vital to assess the duration of the child's difficulties in the context of his or her developmental profile and across his or her varied social contexts. By doing so, clinicians not only can arrive at a useful conceptualization of the present problem or problems but also can identify factors that led to more adaptive functioning at other times and avoid interventions that were not effective for that child in the past.

Intervention recommendations must be broadly based due to the complex nature of the difficulties, multiple related causal factors, and numerous related problems spawned by attention difficulties. Most interventions attempt to provide coordinated efforts that include: (a) behavior management plans implemented both at school and in the home, (b) classroom assignment to classes with smaller student-to-teacher ratios and greater structure in the expectations and routines of the class, (c) parent guidance (even as learned in the home) related to specific behavior management skills and refining the behavior modification plans, (d) medication evaluation and trials, (e) therapeutic groups focused on social skills development, and (f) individual therapy focused on developing skills for stress management, gratification delay, and improved social interactions as well as dealing with self-confidence issues and frustration experienced as a result of these difficulties.

Behavioral Disturbances

Disturbances in behavior or conduct disorders include a broad range of disturbances in which a child or adolescent engages persistently in aggressive activities without regard for social norms or rules of conduct. The progression to more serious antisocial behavior appears to start at a young age and to be influenced by genetic vulnerabilities, environmental exposure, and family factors. A history of accidents, injuries, and illnesses that affect central nervous system functioning commonly are found in behaviorally disordered youngsters (Lewis, 1996). Lower levels of intelligence, especially in verbal areas, and learning problems frequently are evident in these troubled children as well. However, the bulk of the evidence suggests socioeconomic disadvantages, peer group influences, and deficiencies in parenting are the most important contributing factors. Aggressive children often come from resource-poor communities and have experienced a high degree of peer rejection along with increased associations with other aggressive peers. Parents and teachers of aggressive children tend to be harsher and more aggressive themselves. Consequently, such children may become alienated, isolated, and turn to deviant peer groups and gangs for companionship (Coie & Lenox, 1994). Somewhat ironically, these peer group members often act to reinforce antisocial tendencies, a reality that has been turned around and used effectively in peer group interventions, such as those described by Cone in Chapter 16 of this volume.

Although many treatments for aggressive children have proven unsuccessful, at least two types of behavioral treatment appear to hold considerable promise, having demonstrated positive results: problem-solving skills training (PSST) and parent training (Vitulano & Tebes, 1996). PSST typically consists of 20–25 sessions of active behavioral rehearsal, role-playing, and modeling along with corrective feedback and social reinforcement. It provides training in problem-solving skills such as generating solutions, consequential thinking, and perspective taking. Parent training, as most popularly developed by Patterson and his colleagues (Patterson 1975, 1982; Patterson, Reid, & Dishion, 1991), provides the opportunity for parents to learn the basic principles and techniques of effective parenting and how to apply these methods with their child. As part of this training, parents are taught to set clear goals, observe and record their child's behaviors, and provide rewards and positive criticism. Without effective intervention, the aggressive child is more likely to continue and even escalate his or her behaviors.

Impaired Social Functioning

The capacity for social relatedness is a central organizing feature of existence for human beings. Deviations in the primary capacity for normative reciprocal social interactions have a diffuse and profound impact on all aspects of development.

Disturbances described in this section involve impaired capacities for social relatedness and should not be confused with poorly actualized or compromised social skills
such as those associated with impoverished environments, psychiatric problems, or
conduct disturbances. Rather, in the continuum of social disabilities, also called *pervasive developmental disorders* (PDD) or *autism spectrum disorders*, the central feature is
significant impairment in the capacity for normative social interactions. Associated
moderate to profound delays or deviations across many key developmental domains
(e.g., cognition, communication and language, executive functions, play, etc.) often
further complicate the child's social difficulties. Social disability disorders are relatively uncommon, occurring in 5–10 individuals per 10,000, a rate observed consistently across cultures and socioeconomic groups. For the most part, gender
differences exist, with males outnumbering females by a margin of roughly 4:1. Given
the profound impairments that accompany these problems, it is not surprising that
disorders with a primary social disability generally are apparent within the first three
years of life, most often within the first 12 months (Volkmar et al., 1994).

Children with social disabilities often have significant problems with recipro-
cating social communications, maintaining appropriate eye contact, and using voice
inflection to communicate meaning. These children also have difficulties in their use
and perception of nonverbal cues and facial expressions. The ability to appreciate another person's perspective as well as the ability to communicate empathy also are compromised. Poor gross motor coordination and fine-motor control commonly are
associated with PDD, as are attention problems and impulsivity. Attention problems
range from great difficulty with focus and distractibility to intense focus on irrelevant
aspects. Impulsive actions and a low tolerance for frustration also are common.

Nearly all children with a PDD have language development delays or deviations
that negatively impact their ability to communicate effectively and navigate their environment. Examples of the deviations in language use include echolalia (i.e., verbatim repetition of words or phrases), as well as atypical rhythm, intonation, and
volume. PDD-spectrum children frequently make a range of repetitive nonlinguistic
vocal sounds, such as shrieks. The nonlinguistic noises likely represents attempts at
communication but also may serve simply as self-stimulation.

Relationships for socially disabled children are atypical but the quality of their
relationships are often very confusing for clinicians not familiar with assessment of
children on the PDD spectrum. Children with social disabilities can and often do
maintain close proximity to parents, even clinging to parents when anxious, but the
quality and expression of their attachment behaviors are quite different from children
without such difficulties. Typically, children with a PDD seldom seek adult attention,
as demonstrated by their limited to very limited tendency to share gazes with adults
in relation to enjoyment, success in an activity, surprise, or interest in a novel object.
Most often, social impairment is not so severe that there are no attempts at social ref-
erencing, nor is there a complete inability to recognize familiar and nonfamiliar people. In fact, when stereotypies (i.e., flapping, rocking, and spinning) are factored out
in studies of attachment patterns, global attachment problems do not appear to be
pervasive across the full spectrum of PDD children. However, children at the more
severe end of the autism spectrum often exhibit very little social or attachment inter-

action. At school, children with social disabilities are often ostracized from normal social groupings and, typically, are easily identified during classroom observations due to their social oddities, stereotypies, and inability to integrate into group activities.

In addition, play and imagination commonly are impaired in children with social disabilities. PDD-spectrum children experience difficulties in their interest and ability to play with others and also evidence differences in actual play behaviors as well. Socially disabled children do not readily identify or make use of toys in conventional ways. Inscribed model numbers or hinges in figures may be of greater interest and focus than the action figure or doll as a whole representation of a figure or person. Children with these difficulties may choose odd materials to play with, such as empty bottles or spatulas. Although adults may describe the behaviors as play, the free-time behavior of significantly impaired socially disabled children often has less a quality of play than of excessive, almost obsessive, scrutiny. Children with autism often examine, twirl, and manipulate even non-toy objects for hours at a time with a level of intensity that surpasses that normally observed in youngsters. Children at this profound level of difficulty seldom generate or maintain themes, characters, or linked play sequences during play activities.

These types of difficulties often are associated with additional unusual behaviors that further impair social interactions. Examples include extraneous motor movements, repetitive or stereotyped behaviors, narrowly defined interests, and self-injurious behaviors. Some individuals with profound social difficulties do develop atypically advanced skills as well. For example, a child may develop an acute specialization in identifying manufacturers and models of deep-fat fryers or develop a narrow skill to exceptional proficiency (e.g., calendar counting, music performance, or rote memory recall).

Due to the complex developmental profiles and infrequent occurrence of social disabilities in children, consultation from or referrals to professionals with expertise in assessing children on the PDD/autism spectrum is important. The high frequency of cognitive functioning in the low average to mentally retarded range among PDD-spectrum children supports the use of measures that assess cognitive abilities in a thorough manner. However, the language delays demonstrated by these children make the use of verbally loaded cognitive measures problematic. Tests with an emphasis on nonverbal processing and responding (e.g., *Leiter International Performance Scale-Revised*, Roid & Miller, 1997; *Universal Nonverbal Intelligence Test*, Bracken & McCallum, 1998) are often the measures of choice. Some children on the PDD spectrum have sufficiently impaired cognitive development that assessment of cognitive functioning may be best accomplished by developmental rather than intellectual scales (e.g., *Bayley Scales of Infant Development-II*, Bayley, 1993; *Mullen Scales of Early Learning*, Mullen, 1995). Because children on the PDD spectrum often have highly varied development across cognitive domains, approaching the assessment from a neuropsychological or specific brain-function perspective also is important. Differences in cognitive profiles have been an important feature in differentiating diagnoses within the PDD spectrum. For example, both children with high-functioning autism and Asperger's disorder often exhibit significant Verbal–Performance score discrepancies on the *Wechsler Intelligence Scales for Children-III* (Wechsler, 1991), but the differences typically show an inverse pattern by diagnosis. That is, children with Asperger's demonstrate significantly lower Performance compared to Verbal IQ scores, while high-functioning autistic children evidence significantly lower Verbal compared to Performance IQ scores (Volkmar, 1999).

There also exists a range of specialized checklists, interview, and observation measures that have been developed to aid in the assessment of children along the PDD spectrum. Some of the behavior checklists include the *Checklist for Autism in Toddlers* and the *Childhood Autism Rating Scale* (Krug, Arick, Almond, 1980; Schopler, Reichler, & Renner, 1986). Parent interviews include the *Autism Diagnostic Interview-Revised* and the *Parent Interview for Autism* (Lord, Rutter, & LeCouteur, 1994; Stone & Hogan, 1993). Examples of structured observation measures include the *Behavior Observation System* and the *Autism Diagnostic Observation Schedule* (Freeman, Ritvo, & Schroth, 1984; Lord et al., 1989). One of the key domains to assess in PDD-spectrum children is adaptive or functional independence skills. Measures such as the *Vineland Adaptive Behavior* Scales (Sparrow, Balla, & Cicchetti, 1984) or the *Adaptive Behavior Scale of the American Association on Mental Retardation* (Lambert, Ninhira, & Leland, 1993) are well suited to provide criterion-referenced, quantified estimates of a child's development in those skills.

Intervention with children with social disabilities is typically intense, comprehensive, and based on behavioral criteria. In addition to academic learning, instruction and practice in social skills as well as in adaptive behaviors are often integrated into an effective intervention plan. Behavior management strategies may be used to diminish the interference from attention problems and atypical movements or self-stimulation behaviors. Two of the most highly developed research programs that guide intervention for PDD-spectrum children are Schopler and Mesibov's TEACH (Mesibov, 1996) method and the Lovaas approach (Lovaas et al., 1981), but every child's plan should be developed with expert multidisciplinary consultation, as needed.

Conclusion

Recognition of legitimate difficulties experienced by children and adolescents has been somewhat slow to develop. In part, this reluctance may be due to a rather pervasive—though largely unsubstantiated—view, especially of adolescents, that "a healthy adolescent should appear to have a mild case of mental illness" as they routinely are "expected to be extremely moody and depressed one day and excitedly 'high' the next. . . . Explosive conflict with family, friends, and authorities is thought of as commonplace" (Powers, Hauser, & Kilner, 1989, p. 200). Progressively, research and practice have revealed that behaviors or symptoms that bring forth concern when they occur in adults should bring about similar concerns when they occur in children or adolescents. Not only should they prompt concern, they should be evaluated, understood, and—if indicated—treated.

The foregoing sections delineate a number of common difficulties seen among school-aged children that affect their personalities or social relatedness. The discussions within each section frame these problems in terms of relevant assessment and intervention considerations. In some instances, the problematic behaviors would satisfy the diagnostic criteria of *DSM-IV* for a particular mental disorder, yet our intention has been simply to remind testing professionals of the kinds of struggles children and adolescents experience with some degree of regularity, rather than to provide instruction on diagnostics. With this effort, we encourage readers to recognize that "students meeting the *DSM* . . . diagnostic criteria are not the only ones with mental health needs significant enough to require . . . attention" (Doll, 1996, p. 34).

References

American Psychiatric Association. (1994). *Diagnostic and statistical manual of mental disorders* (4th ed.). Washington DC: Author.

Barkley, R. A. (1997). Attention-deficit/hyperactivity disorder. In E. J. Mash & L. G. Terdal (Eds.), *Assessment of childhood disorders* (3rd ed., pp. 71–129). New York: Guilford Press.

Barkley, R. A. (1998). *Attention-deficit hyperactivity disorder: A handbook for diagnosis and treatment* (2nd ed.). New York: Guilford Press.

Bayley, N. (1993). *Bayley Scales of Infant Development* (2nd ed.). San Antonio, TX: The Psychological Corporation.

Berman, A. L., & Jobes, D. A. (1991). *Adolescent suicide: Assessment and intervention*. Washington, DC: American Psychological Association.

Bracken, B. A., & McCallum, R. S. (1998). *Universal Nonverbal Intelligence Test*. Itasca, IL: Riverside.

Brener, N. D., Hassan, S. S., & Barrios, L. C. (1999). Suicidal ideation among college students in the United States. *Journal of Consulting and Clinical Psychology, 67*, 1004–1008.

Brent, D. A., Holder, C., Kolko, D., Birmaher, B., Baugher, M., Roth, C., & Johnson, B. (1997). A clinical psychotherapy trial for adolescent depression comparing cognitive, family, and supportive treatment. *Archives of General Psychiatry, 54*, 877–885,

Callahan, A. A., Panichelli-Mindel, S. M., & Kendall, P. C. (1996). *DSM-IV* and internalizing disorders: Modifications, limitations, and utility. *School Psychology Review, 25*, 297–307.

Cantwell, D. P. (1996). Attention deficit disorder: A review of the past 10 years. *Journal of the American Academy of Child and Adolescent Psychiatry, 35*, 978–987.

Caplan, M., & Douglas, V. (1969). Incidence of parental loss in children with depressed mood. *Journal of Child Psychology and Psychiatry, 10*, 225–232.

Capuzzi, D., & Golden, L. (1988). *Preventing adolescent suicide*. Muncie, IN: Accelerated Development.

Coie, J. D., & Lenox, K. F. (1994). The development of anti-social individuals. In D. C. Fowles, P. Sutker, & S. H. Goodman (Eds.), *Progress in experimental personality and psychopathology research* (pp. 45–72) New York: Springer.

Compas, B. E., Oppedisano, G., Connor, J. K., Gerhardt, C. A., Hinden, B. R., Achenbach, T. M., & Hammen, C. (1997). Gender differences in depressive symptoms in adolescence: Comparison of national samples of clinically referred and nonreferred youths. *Journal of Consulting and Clinical Psychology, 65*, 617–626.

Davis, J. M., & Sandoval, J. (1991). *Suicidal youth: School-based intervention and prevention*. San Francisco: Jossey-Bass.

Doll, B. (1996). Prevalence of psychiatric disorders in children and youth: An agenda for advocacy by school psychology. *School Psychology Quarterly, 11*, 20–47.

Fitzpatrick, K. M. (1993). Exposure to violence and presence of depression among low-income, African-American youth. *Journal of Consulting and Clinical Psychology, 61*, 528–531.

Forman, S. G., & Kalafat, J. (1998). Substance abuse and suicide: Promoting resilience against self-destructive behavior in youth. *School Psychology Review, 27*, 398–406.

Freeman, B. J., Ritvo, E. R., & Schroth, P. C. (1984). Behavioral assessment of the syndrome of autism: Behavior Observation System. *Journal of the American Academy of Child Psychiatry, 23*, 588–594.

Goodyer, I. M. (Ed.). (1995). *The depressed child and adolescent: Developmental and clinical perspectives*. New York: Cambridge University Press.

Goodyer, I. M., & Cooper, P. J. (1993). A community study of depression in adolescent girls. II. The clinical features of identified disorder. *British Journal of Psychiatry, 163*, 374–380.

Graziano, A. M., DeGiovanni, I. S., & Garcia, K. A. (1979). Behavioral treatment of children's fears: A review. *Psychological Bulletin, 86*, 804–830.

Greenbaum, P. E., Dedrick. R. F., Prange, M. E., & Friedman, R. M. (1994). Parent, teacher, and child ratings of problem behaviors of youngsters with serious emotional disturbances. *Psychological Assessment, 6*, 141–148.

Greenbaum, P. E., Prange, M. E., Friedman, R. M., & Silver, S. E. (1991). Substance abuse prevalence and comorbidity with other psychiatric disorders among adolescents with severe emotional disturbances. *Journal of the American Academy of Child Psychiatry, 30*, 575–583.

Grilo, C. M., Walker, M. L., Becker, D. F., Edell, W. S., & McGlashan, T. H. (1997). Personality disorders in adolescents with major depression, substance use disorders, and coexisting major depression and substances use disorders. *Journal of Consulting and Clinical Psychology, 65*, 328–332.

Harrington, R. (1993). *Depressive disorder in childhood and adolescence.* New York: Wiley.

Kandel, D. B., & Davies, M. (1982). Epidemiology of depressive mood in adolescents. *Archives of General Psychiatry, 43*, 255–262.

Kaplan, S. L., Hong, G. K., & Weinhold, C. (1984). Epidemiology of depressive symptomatology in adolescents. *Journal of the American Academy of Child Psychiatry, 23*, 91–98.

Kendall, P. C., Kortlander, E., Chansky, T. E., & Brady, E. U. (1992). Comorbidity of anxiety and depression in youth: Treatment implications. *Journal of Consulting and Clinical Psychology, 60*, 869–880.

Kolko, D. J., Brent, D. A., Baugher, M., Bridge, J., & Birmaher, B. (2000). Cognitive and family therapies for adolescent depression: Treatment specificity, mediation, and moderation. *Journal of Consulting and Clinical Psychology, 68*, 603–614.

Kovacs, M. (1992). *The Children's Depression Inventory.* Tonawanda, NY: Multi-Health Systems.

Kovacs, M., Gatsonis, C., Paulauskas, S. L., & Richards, C. (1989). Depressive disorders in childhood: A longitudinal study of comorbidity with and risk for anxiety disorders. *Archives of General Psychiatry, 46*, 776–782.

Krug, D. A., Arick, J., & Almond, P. (1980). Behavior checklist for identifying severely handicapped individuals with high levels of autistic behavior. *Journal of Child Psychology and Psychiatry, 21*, 221–229.

Lambert, N., Ninhira, K., & Leland, H. (1993). *AAMR Adaptive Behavior Scale-School* (2nd ed.). Austin, TX: PRO-ED.

Lapouse R., & Monk, M. A. (1959). Fears and worries in a representative sample of children. *American Journal of Orthopsychiatry, 29*, 803–813.

Lewis, D. O. (1996). Conduct disorder. In M. Lewis (Ed.), *Child and adolescent psychiatry: A comprehensive textbook* (2nd ed., pp. 564–577). Baltimore: Williams and Wilkins.

Lewis, M., & Vitulano, L. A. (1989). A historical perspective on views of childhood psychopathology. In C. Last & M. Hersen (Eds.), *Handbook of child psychiatric diagnosis* (pp. 3–11). New York: Wiley.

Lord, C., Rutter, M., Goode, S., Heemsbergen, J., Jordan, H., Mawhood, L., & Schopler, E. (1989). Autism Diagnostic Observation Schedule: A standardized observation of communicative and social behaviors. *Journal of Autism and Developmental Disorders, 19*, 185–212.

Lord, C., Rutter, M., & LeCouteur, A. (1994). Autism Diagnostic Interview-Revised: A revised version of a diagnostic interview for caregivers of individuals with possible pervasive developmental disorders. *Journal of Autism and Developmental Disorders, 24*, 659–685.

Lovaas, O. I., Ackerman, A., Alexander, D., Firestone, P., Perkins, M., & Young, D. B. (1981). *Teaching developmentally disabled children.* Baltimore: University Park Press.

Martinez, E. S. (2000, Summer). Emerging from the shadows. *NARSAD Research Newsletter, 12*, 18–19.

Mesibov, G. B. (1996). Division TEACH: A program model for working with autistic people and their families. In M. C. Roberts (Ed.), *Model practices in service delivery in child and family mental health* (pp. 269–291). Hillsdale, NJ: Erlbaum.

Mullen, E. M. (1995). *Mullen Scales of Early Learning-AGS Edition.* Circle Pines, MN: American Guidance Service.

National Institute on Drug Abuse. (1999). 1999 Monitoring the future study, secondary students [On-line]. Available: http://www.ncadd.org/youthalc.html

Ostrander, R., Weinfurt, K. P., & Nay, W. R. (1998). The role of age, family support, and negative cognitions in the prediction of depressive symptoms. *School Psychology Review, 27*, 121–137.

Patterson, G. R. (1975). *Families: Applications of social learning to family life.* Champaign, IL: Research Press.

Patterson, G. R. (1982). *Coercive family process.* Eugene, OR: Castilia.

Patterson, G. R., Reid, J. B., & Dishion, T. J. (1991). *Antisocial boys.* Eugene, OR: Castilia.

Poland, S. (1989). *Suicide intervention in the schools.* New York: Guilford Press.

Powers, S. I., Hauser, S. T., & Kilner, L. A. (1989). Adolescent mental health. *American Psychologist, 44,* 200–208.

Reinecke, M. A., Ryan, N. E., & DuBois, L. (1998). Cognitive–behavioral therapy of depression and depressive symptoms during adolescence: A review and meta-analysis. *Journal of the American Academy of Child and Adolescent Psychiatry, 37,* 26–34.

Reynolds, W. M. (1987). *Reynolds Adolescent Depression Scale.* San Antonio, TX: The Psychological Corporation.

Roid, G. H., & Miller, L. J. (1997). *Leiter International Performance Scale-Revised.* Wood Dale, OK: Stoelting.

Sandoval, J., & Brock, S. E. (1996). The school psychologist's role in suicide prevention. *School Psychology Quarterly, 11,* 169–185.

Schopler, E., Reichler, R. J., & Renner, B. R. (1986). *Childhood Autism Rating Scale.* Los Angeles: Western Psychological Services.

Seligman, R., Gleser, G., Rauh, J., & Harris, L. (1974). The effect of earlier parental loss in adolescence. *Archives of General Psychiatry, 31,* 475–479.

Sparrow, S. S., Balla, D. A., & Cicchetti, D. V. (1984). *Vineland Adaptive Behavior Scales.* Circle Pines, MN: American Guidance Service.

Steketee, G., & Foa, E. B. (1985). Obsessive-compulsive disorder. In D. H. Barlow (Ed.), *Clinical handbook of psychological disorders* (pp. 69–144). New York: Guilford Press.

Stone, W. L., & Hogan, K. L. (1993). A structured parent interview for identifying young children with autism. *Journal of Autism and Developmental Disorders, 23,* 639–652.

Strauss, C. C., Last, C. G., Hersen, M., & Kazdin, A. E. (1988). Association between anxiety and depression in children and adolescents with anxiety disorders. *Journal of Abnormal Child Psychology, 16,* 57–68.

Vitulano, L. A., Holmberg, J. R., & Vitulano, D. S. (in press). Innovative community intervention programs. In T. A. Petti & C. Salguero (Eds.), *Community, child, and adolescent psychiatry: A manual of clinical practice and consultation.* Washington, DC: American Psychiatric Press.

Vitulano, L. A., & Tebes J. K. (1996). Child and adolescent behavior therapy. In M. Lewis (Ed.), *Child and adolescent psychiatry: A comprehensive textbook.* (2nd ed., pp. 815–831). Baltimore: Williams and Wilkins.

Volkmar, F. R. (Ed.). (1999). *Autism and pervasive developmental disorders.* Cambridge, MA: Cambridge University Press.

Volkmar, F. R., Klin, A., Siegel, B., Szatmari, P., Lord, C., Campbell, M., Freeman, B. J., Cicchetti, D. V., Rutter, M., Kline, W., Buitelaar, J., Hattab, Y., Fombonne, E., Fuentes, J., Werry, J., Stone, W., Kerbeshian, J., Hoshino, Y., Bregman, J., Loveland, K., Szymanski, L., & Towban, K. (1994). Field trial for autistic disorder in *DSM-IV. American Journal of Psychiatry, 151,* 1361–1367.

Wechsler, D. (1991). *Wechsler Intelligence Scale for Children-III.* New York: The Psychological Corporation.

Wolraich, M. L., Hannah, J. N., Pinnock, T. Y., Baumgaertel, A., & Brown, J. (1996). Comparison of diagnostic criteria for attention-deficit hyperactivity disorder in a country-wide sample. *Journal of the American Academy of Child and Adolescent Psychiatry, 35,* 319–324.

4

Functional Behavioral Assessment

James L. McDougal and

Sandra M. Chafouleas

Two five-year-olds display tantrum behaviors in separate settings removed by time and space. Both children exhibit similar behaviors, including crying, yelling, throwing objects, and dropping to the floor pounding hands and feet in escalated distress. On the surface, the tantrums look quite similar, but each happened for a different reason. For one child, the tantrum erupted after he was asked to share some toys with the other children. The second child began to tantrum when she was playing alone and no one was attending to her. This added information has important implications for intervening and also preventing future tantrums. The remainder of this chapter presents an assessment procedure shown to assist in understanding, preventing, and intervening with challenging behavior by assessing the function (purpose) it serves for the individual.

The intent of this chapter is to describe the methodology of functional behavioral assessment, which is encompassed within the area of behavioral assessment. *Functional assessment* refers to the procedures used to identify variables in the environment and within the person that maintain a given behavior. That is, functional assessment addresses questions such as: Why does this behavior occur, what factors predict the occurrence and nonoccurrence of a behavior, and what consequences might maintain or reinforce the behavior? Functional assessment information may be collected using a wide range of procedures, including direct observation, interviews, questionnaires, and rating scales. The most stringent and empirically supported procedure available to conduct a functional assessment is *functional analysis*, the systematic manipulation of variables in the individual's environment in order to directly test the impact of these factors on that individual's behavior (Vollmer & Northrup, 1996). The development of the functional assessment process emerged from early research using functional analysis. In his review of the motivation for engaging in self-injurious behavior, Carr (1977) proposed that functional analysis involves first asking why a behavior exists (i.e., what conditions in the environment support the behavior), prior to developing an intervention. Factors influencing behavior are identified by systematically exposing an individual to controlled conditions (e.g., high attention/low attention, hard task/easy task) in which hypothesized reasons for the behavior can be tested. The effects on behavior in each condition can be assessed to decide why it occurs, and then it is possible to effectively manipulate the appropriate condition in order to change behavior.

Following this research on functional analysis, other methods of functional assessment have been developed to aid in the identification of factors that predict the occurrence of specific behaviors. For example, interview procedures and direct observation techniques also can assist in collecting functional assessment information such as identifying the times, activities, and events that predict problem behavior as well as the consequences that reinforce and maintain it. The results of functional assessment can then be used to design effective behavior management procedures through the elimination or reversal of the contingencies maintaining problem behavior, or modification of the situational features of the environment (Martens, Witt, Daly, & Vollmer, 1999). The ultimate goal of the functional assessment process is the selection of those behavioral interventions most likely to be successful for a specific individual in a specific situation, and, subsequently, to determine if the intervention worked to change behavior.

Steps in the Functional Assessment Process

The objectives of functional assessment are to (a) clearly identify and operationally define the problematic behavior; (b) analyze, investigate, and identify the variables in the environment that appear to be related to the occurrence (and nonoccurrence) of the problem behavior and clearly identify its perceived function; (c) develop and refine a functional hypothesis; and (d) identify individual strengths and motivators to be used in the intervention (Horner, 1994; O'Neill et al., 1997). Table 4.1 presents an outline of the functional assessment process, including a summary of the information to be collected during each step in an assessment.

Problem Identification

The first objective in the functional assessment process is to clearly identify the negative behavior(s) in need of remediation. This process involves listing and observing negative behaviors that the individual exhibits as well as identifying classes or sequences of behaviors that frequently occur together (i.e., behavior chains). From this list of behaviors, a limited number of target behaviors are prioritized, based on several factors. Some factors to consider include the likelihood that the behavior will result in physical harm to self or others, the extent to which it interferes with learning or daily functioning, the likelihood that the behavior will become more serious in the future if not modified, and the extent to which it is of concern to educators or care providers (e.g., Demchak, 1993; Meyer & Evans, 1989).

TABLE 4.1   *Applied Functional Behavioral Assessment: Components of the Process*

Step	Components
Identify the Problem	List negative behaviors
	Prioritize list, consider behavior chains, select one or two target behaviors
	Define in observable, measurable terms
	Indicate the frequency, intensity, duration
Investigate the Problem	For each behavior:
	Indicate what occurs before (the triggers, antecedents)
	Indicate the context in which it occurs (concurrent events)
	Indicate the consequences that typically follow
	Rule out academic or behavioral skill deficits/communicative intent
	Identify perceived function
Develop and Refine a Hypothesis or Theory	Develop a theory including triggers or antecedents, setting/concurrent events, the target behavior, the function, and any related skill deficits or communicative intent
	Test the hypothesis using direct monitoring techniques and/or data collected in the applied setting over time
Identify Personal Strengths and Motivators	Positive alternative/competing behaviors
	Persons, places, and times where problem behavior is typically not displayed
	Potential sources of reinforcement (preferred objects, activities, persons, places)

Each target behavior selected must be operationally defined in measurable and observable terms so that an initial baseline measure can be recorded. A behavior is considered operational if specific ideas regarding intervention could be created based on the definition. For example, if we are told that Johnny has a reading disability, it would be difficult to intervene without collecting further information such as his current reading level, reading rate and error patterns, and knowing what is expected of him. On the other hand, if we are told that Susie does not independently initiate social interactions with peers, a number of possible intervention strategies almost immediately come to mind. Along with the specification of the behavior, it can be helpful at this stage to collect tentative information regarding conditions under which the behavior is most likely to occur, and the intensity, frequency and duration of the behavior.

Figure 4.1 provides an example of a functional assessment worksheet designed for use in the school setting. Typically, the information summarized on this form would be gathered by conducting interviews with people having daily contact with the referred child (parent, teachers, paraprofessionals) in conjunction with direct observation of the child in the classroom setting. (See Chapter 5 for a more comprehensive discussion of observational and interview techniques.)

The FBA Worksheet provides an area to record the operational definition of up to two target behaviors as well as the baseline level of each. Next, the consideration of behavior chains is prompted as smaller, less intense behaviors often occur as precursors to larger, more intense episodes. For example, a student may begin to tap a pencil, shuffle the desk, bother a peer, and end up in a confrontation with a peer and the teacher. In this scenario, the behavioral consultant may want to target the occurrence of off-task behavior as well as the more disruptive confrontation behaviors. Therefore, the successful identification of behavioral chains may result in the revision of selected target behaviors.

Issues in Target Behavior Selection. During the functional assessment process, questions arise regarding how to select a target behavior, or how to choose a behavior for intervention when presented with a multitude of problem behaviors. The initial selection comes from the referring source, and, typically, concerns are expressed during an interview with the consultant(s). This interview sets the stage for the rest of the process, and is essential to the success of behavior change. After all, if the behavior is not clearly identified, then it is impossible to specify a goal or determine whether change was evident. Clear specification of a behavior can be difficult to achieve without support for the referring source. In an often-cited study by Lambert (1976), which examined teachers' skill at identifying student problems, results suggested that teacher descriptions of problems were often presented in vague or general terms. One implication of this finding is that a referring source would need support in providing more precise information about behavior(s) before useful interventions could be developed.

Careful use of interviewing tactics such as open-ended and guided questioning will help build rapport with the referring source and begin to sort out the issues of concern. For further information regarding specific interviewing tactics, the reader is referred to consultation literature (see Erchul & Martens, 1997; Meyers, Parsons, & Martin, 1979; Sheridan, Kratochwill & Bergan, 1996). As most consultants have experienced, it is not uncommon for the referring source to mention a plethora of problems during the initial interview. In fact, it would be considered a rarity to find that the target behavior is clearly specified without any discussion. After thorough clarification of the problem areas, it is necessary to select the one or two most problematic behaviors. This determination can be considered somewhat subjective in that the selected problems often are the ones perceived as most problematic for those working with the child. The perceived worth or acceptability of the selected target behaviors is related, perhaps, to the concept presented by Wasserman and Bracken in Chapter 2 as ecological validity. Ecological validity emphasizes the need to use measures that are relevant to the user, fit the context in which they are used, and result in practical change for the child. In part, then, the consultant's job is to listen carefully to what the

Sample Worksheets

Student Name: _____ Date:_____

Referral Source: _____

Prioritize up to **two target behaviors** that most interfere with the child's functioning in the class-room. Assess or directly observe the frequency (how often), intensity (hi, med, lo), and duration of each:

Behavior: Frequency: Intensity: Duration:

_____

_____

_____

_____

> • Identify any observed **behavior chains** (smaller behaviors exhibited prior to larger more intense behaviors).

From the list below indicate the **triggers** (antecedents), **concurrent events**, and **consequences** that occur in the context of the current behavior:

Triggers/Antecedents

__ Lack of social attention
__ Demand/Request
__ Difficult task
__ Transition (task)
__ Transition (setting)
__ Interruption in routine
__ Negative social interaction
__ Consequences imposed for negative behavior
__ Other _____

Setting/Concurrent Events

__ Independent seatwork
__ Group Instruction
__ Crowded setting
__ Unstructured activity
__ Peer attention
__ Adult attention
__ Specific task/subject
_____
__ Other _____

Consequences

__ Behavior ignored
__ Reprimand/Warning
__ Time-out
__ Loss of incentives/privileges
__ Sent to office
__ Communications with home
__ In-School suspension
__ Out-of-School suspension
__ Restraint
__ Other _____

> • Is the problem behavior believed to be **related to**:
>
> **SKILL DEFICITS?**   **COMMUNICATION?**
>
> ☐ **Academic Deficit**   ☐ **Behavioral Deficit**   ☐ **Communicative Intent**
>
> __ work is too hard   __ lacks the expected behavior   __ to request assistance
> __ not enough practice   __ needs practice/modeling   __ to request a break
> __ not enough help   __ requires more structure   __ to indicate a need (i.e., food)
> __ not generalized skill __ can't apply across settings   __ to protest
>   __ to indicate frustration

FIGURE 4.1   *Functional behavioral assessment: Sample worksheet*

What **function(s)** does the identified behavior(s) seem to serve for the child

☐ **Escape**

___ Avoid a demand or request
___ Avoid an acitivy/task (if known)
___ Avoid a person
___ Escape the school
___ Other _____

☐ **Sensory/Perceptual**

___ Automatic sensory stimulation
___ Perceptual reinforcement

☐ **Attention/Control**

___ Gain adult attentin
___ Gain peer attention
___ Get sent to preferred adult
___ Other
_____

☐ **Gain Desired Item**

___ Get desired item/activity
List: _____

Develop Functional Theory (Hypothesis)

When _____ in the context of
　　　　　　　　　　(triggers/antecedents)

_____ the student displays
　　　(settings, activities, concurrent events)

_____ in order to
　　　　　　　　　(problem behavior)

_____
　　　　　　　　　(perceived function)

List Prosocial, Adaptive, and Replacement Behaviors and Roles

What does the student do well? What positive behaviors, activities, and/or roles could replace the problem behaviors and <u>still serve the same function for the student</u>?

_____

_____

When, where, and with whom is problem behavior typically not displayed?

_____

_____

List some potential incentives or motivators for the student.

_____

_____

_____

FIGURE 4.1　　*Continued*

referring teacher or clinic staff has to say, and then help clarify and define what is wanted and needed.

Although this is clearly not an objective process (objective measurement could and should also be incorporated), if the selected behaviors are ecologically valid, gaining acceptance and investment in changing the problem from the referring source is more likely. Selection of target problems may be guided by considering behaviors with the following characteristics (Alessi, 1998):

- behavior that is most distressing to the parent or teacher (by rank order)
- behavior that would be easy to change in order to build skills and confidence
- behavior that is a prerequisite to other problem behaviors (i.e., behavior chain)
- behavior deemed important by the child, or that might most improve the child's life
- behavior that is too far from age norms for that child
- a pair of behaviors in which one can be used to modify the other

Issues related to interviewing tactics, ecological validity, and the prioritization of problem behaviors are important when collecting and refining information during the first (problem identification) stage of the functional assessment process. These considerations inform a process for listing and observing behaviors exhibited by the referred individual and identifying classes or sequences of behaviors that frequently occur together. From this list of behaviors, a limited number of operationally defined target behaviors is prioritized and selected for intervention.

Collecting Baseline Data.   Once the target behavior has been identified, a baseline measure is collected. The baseline represents the level of exhibited behavior prior to intervention and serves as the benchmark against which intervention effects are compared. Typically, behavior is measured along three main dimensions: frequency (the number of times the behavior occurs per minute, hour, etc.), intensity (a general measure of the disruptiveness or dangerousness of the exhibited behavior), and duration (the length of time the exhibited behavior lasts). Baseline levels of behavior are generally collected via direct observation techniques, although some behavior report forms have been developed to collect this information in applied settings. For a detailed review of direct observation techniques, the reader is referred to Chapter 5. In addition, Figure 4.2 provides an example of a self-monitoring form used to collect behavioral data.

Self-monitoring refers to a procedure in which students observe and periodically record their behavior (e.g., Lloyd, Landrum, & Hallahan, 1991; Shapiro, & Cole, 1994). The form illustrated in Figure 4.2 was designed for use with a second-grade student who was referred for noncompliance with teacher requests and physical aggression toward peers. The self-monitoring procedure required the student to rate her behavior at specified intervals across the day (breaks in the schedule), with the teacher periodically checking the accuracy of the student's ratings. In addition to providing a method for recording behavior, self-monitoring procedures are typically used as an intervention component in which incentives are offered based on an agreed upon

Student: _____   Date: _____

Today this is how well I did my personal best by *following directions* and *respecting others*:

Morning Time One_____

      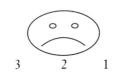

9   8   7   6   5   4   3   2   1

Morning Time Two_____

9   8   7   6   5   4   3   2   1

Morning Time Three_____

   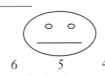   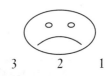

9   8   7   6   5   4   3   2   1

Number of Morning Smiley Faces: _____   Got Morning Incentive: Yes   No

---

Afternoon Time One_____

      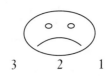

9   8   7   6   5   4   3   2   1

Afternoon Time Two_____

9   8   7   6   5   4   3   2   1

Afternoon Time Three_____

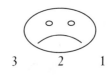

9   8   7   6   5   4   3   2   1

Number of Afternoon Smiley Faces: _____   Got Afternoon Incentive: Yes   No

---

Teacher Comments:

_____

FIGURE 4.2   *Example of self-monitoring*

contingency plan (e.g., 2 out of 3 smiley face ratings per half day with no instances of physical aggression).

Regardless of the data-collection procedure, baseline measures are generally collected across no fewer than three assessment points in order to ensure an accurate reflection of the current level of behavior is obtained. If analysis of the data reveals high variability and inconsistency regarding the level or amount of exhibited behavior, then it is more difficult to determine later if the intervention is working or not because a good comparison is unavailable. Thus, it is typically recommended that more than one baseline data point be established, or that data be collected until some stability appears. Examples of baseline statements of behavior are as follows: (a) Janey engages in tantrums an average of 5 times per week with high intensity and a duration of 10 to 20 minutes; (b) Johnny bangs his head on hard objects an average of 3 times a day with moderate to high intensity for a duration of 5 to 10 minutes or until restrained; and (c) Jackie runs from supervised areas an average of twice a day with low to medium intensity for a duration of 1 to 3 minutes.

The first step of the functional assessment process, problem identification, is complete when there is: (a) a fairly complete listing of the behaviors that the client or student exhibits (b) a prioritization and selection of 1 to 3 target behaviors for further assessment and intervention (c) an operational (measurable, observable) definition of each target behavior and (d) a collection of baseline data that accurately reflect the pre-intervention level of the client's or student's target behavior.

Problem Investigation or Analysis

The problem analysis objective seeks to identify information that would predict the occurrence of selected behaviors. This may include examining factors related to the behavior such as where, when, with whom, and during which task or activity the behavior is most likely to occur. Environmental factors related to the behavior are considered, including antecedent variables that appear to trigger (or predict) behavior, concurrent or settings variables that seem to co-occur with the target behavior, and the identification of consequences that typically follow the behavior. For example, analysis of Jim's swearing may suggest that it occurs most often when he is frustrated with difficult writing tasks. As a consequence for swearing, Jim is typically removed from the task. In addition to observable environmental variables, this analysis may include nonobserved factors that could affect behavior, such as medication regimes, sleep patterns, and nutrition or diet concerns.

In order to complete a comprehensive analysis, each target behavior selected during the problem identification stage must be investigated. The first step in the analysis is the identification of antecedents, setting variables, and consequences that appear to be associated with the occurrence of the identified behavior. Antecedents that predict negative behaviors could include interruptions in routine, specific demands or requests, lack of attention, and transitions from one task or setting to another. Setting variables that might be associated with the occurrence of negative behavior include a high noise level, uncomfortable room temperature, crowded setting, and lack of structure or predictability. In the school setting, reviewing the student's schedule with educators may assist in the identification of activities, tasks, times, settings, or people that appear to predict the occurrence and nonoccurrence of the problem behavior. The typical consequences that might follow negative behavior in the school setting might include a reprimand or redirection, a loss of incentives, removal from the classroom, and suspension. In a clinic setting, consequents of aberrant behavior might include an increase in staff interactions, removal of task demands, and a change in setting. At this stage of the assessment, the goal with respect to consequences is to create a list of those commonly occurring events subsequent to the exhibited behavior. Hypotheses as to why each target behavior occurs (determining the function) are developed later in this stage, and are often based on these identified consequents in the context of additional assessment information.

Next, behavioral and academic skill deficits and the communicative intent of behavior are considered (see Figure 4.3) in order to assess whether the negative behavior is related to a lack of skill (behavioral or academic) or has some communicative value for the individual. For example, a third-grade student reading below grade level might exhibit disruptive and noncompliant behavior when asked to participate in oral reading with the class due to a skill deficit in reading. In this scenario, increasing direct instruction and practice in reading may be a critical part of the intervention. Alternatively, a developmentally delayed child referred for self-injurious behavior (SIB) may use the behavior to communicate frustration. In addition, the child may have learned that SIB results in rapid and long-term removal of task demands. The implications for intervention with this identification of communicative intent may include teaching and reinforcing an alternative method of communicating frustration or requesting a break.

After considering the child's current behavioral, academic, or communicative skills within the context of the setting demands, the clinician further reviews the evidence (observations; interviews; evaluation results from speech and language, academic, or adaptive behavior assessments, etc.) to assess whether or not the referred child has the skills necessary to function productively in the current setting. If not, then the intervention will need to address skill development focused on increasing positive adaptive behaviors (i.e., Koegel, Koegel, Hurley, & Frea, 1992; Risley, 1996), academic skills (see Daly & Martens, 1994; Martens, et al., 1999) or developing functional communicative skills (i.e., Carr & Durand, 1985; Carr et al., 1994; Durand, 1990).

Following the identification of any academic or behavioral skill deficits and the communicative intent of behavior, the assessment moves to the consideration of functional consequences supporting the target behavior. Research over the last few decades has identified three major functional consequences that typically support negative behavior: positive reinforcement, negative reinforcement, and automatic reinforcement (Carr, 1977; Iwata, Dorsey, Slifer, Bauman, & Richman, 1982). Positive reinforcement occurs when exhibiting the target behavior results in an increase in attention (staff, teacher, peer) or access to a preferred activity, item, or area. For example, a student's calling-out behavior during instructional periods may be supported by the peer and teacher attention elicited by this behavior. Alternatively, challenging behavior may be supported by negative reinforcement if the result is the cessation or escape from a nonpreferred or aversive activity, task, or area. For instance, the tantrums of young children may be unwittingly supported by parents' reactions if the child is allowed to prolong bedtime or avoid picking up toys subsequent to aberrant behavior. Lastly, a behavior may be supported by automatic reinforcement based on the sensory

—— RULE OUT ——→   —— RULE OUT ——→   —— RULE OUT ——→

Behavior Functions

"Pay-Off" for Negative Behavior(s)

SKILL DEFICIT

☐ **Behavioral Deficit:**
- Does not know expected behavior
- Not enough practice
- Not enough structure to perform
- Not able to generalize behavior across settings

☐ **Academic Deficit:**
- It is too hard—instructional mismatch
- Not enough practice—needs more time
- Not enough help—needs more support
- Not had to do it that way before—needs to generalize skills

COMMUNICATIVE INTENT

☐ **Communicative Intent:** The child uses negative behavior to communicate needs, desires, and emotions. Target behavior appears intended to:

- Request assistance
- Indicate physiological discomfort
- Request a break
- Indicate frustration
- Request a preferred activity/item
- Other (list) _____

☐ **Attention**
The student finds the social attention from peers or adults gained for misbehavior to be rewarding.

☐ **Gain Desired Item, Activity, Area**
The student uses inappropriate behavior as a strategy to gain access to desired activities, objects or areas.

☐ **Sensory/Perceptual**
Student uses self stimulative, self-injurious, or stereotypic behavior as source of automatic sensory or perceptual reinforcement.

☐ **Escape/Avoidance**
The student uses inappropriate behaviors as a strategy to stop or avoid unpleasant academic or social demands.

Copyright 2000, J. L. McDougal, & S. M. Chafouleas

FIGURE 4.3 *Analyzing behavior problems: Assessment*

or perceptual stimulation the individual receives while engaging in the behavior (i.e., flapping, humming, spinning, head-tapping). In the school setting, the most empirically supported functions of negative classroom behavior are to gain peer or teacher attention (or both), and to escape from academic tasks and activities (Vollmer & Northrup, 1996).

The FBA Worksheet provided in Figure 4.1 and the assessment flow sheet in Figure 4.3 provide illustrations of the analysis process considering behavioral and academic skill deficits, communicative intent of behavior, as well as the major functional consequences supporting negative behavior. As evidenced in the worksheet, the analysis objectives are met after (a) the target behavior has been defined; (b) baseline measures are collected; (c) antecedents, concurrent variables, and typical consequences are identified; (d) existing skill deficits and communicative intent have been assessed; and (e) the primary function of the behavior has been identified. After completing the steps involved in the identification and analysis stages, the clinician is finally ready to develop, test, and revise a functional theory.

Developing and Refining a Functional Theory

The culmination of the problem identification and analysis stages are the development and refinement of a functional theory to explain the referred child's negative behavior. The purpose of the functional theory statement is to summarize the previously collected assessment information in a way that can be easily tested. If a functional theory statement provides an accurate summary, it will allow for the uncomplicated creation of an intervention tailored specifically for the individual and situation that is functionally relevant and optimally effective.

An example of a functional theory statement can be found in Figure 4.1. This statement guides the evaluator in defining the problem behavior, listing the identified antecedents, setting, and concurrent events as well as the hypothesized function. A completed statement could be similar to "When a lack of attention or a setting transition (antecedents) occurs in the context of large group instruction or a crowded setting (concurrent events), the student displays calling-out and other disruptive behaviors (problem behavior) in order to gain attention (function)." This example describes disruptive behavior that is believed to be attention-seeking in nature. If this hypothesis is correct, the student's disruptive and calling-out behavior should be higher during group instruction and transitions, and lower during small group activities and other attention-rich settings. If direct observation and informant information supported this hypothesis, an intervention could provide periodic social attention contingent on the student displaying hand-raising and socially appropriate pleas for attention. In addition, the intervention might be strengthened by adding a brief time-out procedure as a consequence for the student's disruptive behavior (ensuring that the consequence for the disruptive behavior is no longer functional).

Other identified skill deficits and communicative intent related to the negative behavior also can be identified in the functional theory statement, typically adjacent to the statement of the function. One such example is "When oral reading task demands occur in the context of group instruction, the child displays disruptive and noncompliant behavior in order to escape the task, which may be related to an academic deficit in reading." In this example, the recommended intervention would not only focus on increasing the student's persistence during reading tasks, but also may include an instructional component to increase the amount of available academic support or modify the curriculum to the student's academic level.

If the examiner were interested in progressing to a functional analysis procedure, the student or client would be exposed to different conditions to test the impact of various consequence on the target behavior. Given the functional theory hypothesized in the first example (disruptive behavior supported by attention), a functional analysis condition that offered the target student attention for call-outs in the form of teacher redirection and peer responses would be expected to produce increased incidents of disruptive behavior as opposed to a condition in which fewer peers were present and call-outs were ignored. Therefore, the use of high attention/low attention conditions could be used to assess the impact on the student's calling-out behavior in order to validate the functional hypothesis.

Identifying Personal Strengths and Motivations

Once a supportable functional theory has been developed, the remaining assessment task is to identify the positive, prosocial, and adaptive behaviors that the individual displays (or could display with some guidance), as well as the types of experiences, settings, or items that serve to motivate the referred individual. At this point in the process, the examiner (a) attempts to identify a positive replacement behavior (a socially appropriate behavior that could replace the target behavior and serve the same function for the child), (b) looks for settings in which the problem behavior is typically not displayed, and (c) identifies potential sources of reinforcement to be provided contingent on use of the positive replacement behavior. These positively oriented assessment components in the context of the problem identification and analysis serve as the bridge to effective intervention.

For instance, it is determined that a third-grade student referred for disruptive classroom behavior is reinforced by the teacher and peer attention he gains from disrupting the class. One of the student's strengths is in the area of reading and helping others. Therefore, he is enlisted as a kindergarten class assistant who reads books to groups of students during the days he avoids class disruptions. This incentive is functionally relevant (the student gains peer and teacher attention), reinforces prosocial behavior, and builds on the student's identified strengths and motivations.

Linking the Assessment to Intervention

Now that the assessment pieces are completed, it is time to use the information to develop and implement an intervention. The information obtained during each step of the functional assessment process has implications for intervention. For example, the problem identification objective provides the selection and operational definition of the target behaviors that can be accurately measured. The baseline level of target behaviors serves as the benchmark to which future levels of behavior will be compared in order to assess intervention effectiveness. The key to a successful link between assessment and intervention is to have accurate and complete assessment information that can be easily related to intervention. That is, building an intervention should be relatively straightforward and individually tailored based on the information provided through assessment. This link is referred to as *functional* or *conceptual relevance* and involves the identification and promotion of a socially desirable behavior that serves the same function for the individual as the target (i.e., undesirable) behavior (e.g., Carr & Durand, 1985; Erchul & Martens, 1997).

When designing an intervention, Mace, Lalli, and Lalli (1991) have suggested that "The general strategy is to alter the environment so as to minimize the reinforcement for aberrant behavior and, whenever possible, provide reinforcement for adaptive responses to compete with maladaptive behavior" (p. 173). In general, intervention design involves manipulating antecedent and setting variables associated with the target behavior, addressing skill deficits related to the target behavior, promoting socially appropriate alternative or competing behavior, and effectively using the individual's personal strengths and motivations to support more adaptive behavior. Figure 4.4 presents a flowchart with relevant intervention suggestions based on the behavior function. Further exploration of antecedent and setting variable manipulation, skill deficit remediation, and addressing the functions of behaviors is provided below.

Manipulation of Antecedent and Setting Variables

In some situations, the occurrence of problem behavior can be predicted by certain antecedent (trigger) or setting (concurrent) variables. For example, disruptive behavior may be related to a difficult or nonpreferred task (antecedent) or to a loud and crowded cafeteria during lunch (setting). In these instances, altering the predictor variables may help decrease the occurrence of negative behavior. When the antecedent involves a difficult task, the task could be modified to be easier or shorter, or more support and assistance could be offered to the child to complete the task. The example of the loud crowded cafeteria setting could be avoided by offering a smaller, quiet setting for lunch or by offering the student lunch before, after, or in-between crowded lunch periods. Other examples of antecedent manipulation include structuring or limiting transition times, use of errorless teaching procedures (Weeks & Gaylord-Ross, 1981), increasing predictability in the schedule or daily routine, increasing choice of activities, and attending to the student's physiological needs (sleep, hunger, medication side effects). Modifying setting and concurrent events that predict problem behavior might include a change in seating arrangement, reducing noise levels, avoiding or limiting time in settings known to be problematic (e.g., crowded settings), tailoring intervention components to specific settings (e.g., behavior plan for the bus), and providing support (e.g., proximity) during setting transitions. The goal with respect to manipulating antecedent variables and setting events is to structure the individual's environment to reduce the opportunity for problem behavior to occur.

— RULE OUT →

SKILL DEFICIT

☐ **Behavioral Skill Deficit:** The intervention would include teaching, modeling, and reinforcing the desired behavior.

- Teach expected behavior through modeling, practice, and feedback.
- Provide opportunities to practice and receive positive feedback.
- Modify setting to optimize correct performance.
- Provide opportunity for feedback across settings.

☐ **Academic Skill Deficit:** The intervention would include instructional techniques to promote accuracy, fluency, and generalization of skills.

- Too hard? Assess student skills, modify curriculum, ensure instructional match.
- Need more practice? Increase active responding opportunities, use drill and practice techniques and structured teaching tasks.
- Need more assistance? Increase performance feedback. Consider use of response cards, choral tasks, and peer tutors.
- Need to generalize skills? Design applied tasks, promote recognition of when to apply the skill (and when not to), ensure curricular demands to promote skill mastery.

— RULE OUT →

COMMUNICATIVE INTENT

☐ **Functional Communicative Training:** Teach the child specific verbal phrases (or if nonverbal use appropriate communicative cues) to address each of the areas identified in the assessment stage (i.e., solicit adult attention, request assistance, request a break from task, etc.).

Steps to Functional Communication Training

- Instruct in the use of the communicative phrase/cue.
- Differentially reinforce (i.e., with praise, attention, task assistance, a break) the functional communication.
- Ensure that negative behavior is no longer reinforced with a functional consequence (see functions column).

Behavior Functions

"Payoff" for Negative Behavior(s) →

Attention

☐ Teach adaptive behavior/appropriate ways to solicit adult attention. Use praise and opportunities for social attention as reinforcement for adaptive behavior (consider peer tutoring/mentoring, reading to younger students, and enlisting "special" role as potential reinforcers). Also, ignore or decrease attention for negative behavior (e.g., time-out).

Gain Desired Item, Activity, Area

☐ Turn desired item, activity, area, or person into an incentive for positive behavior. Teach adaptive behavior that will result in access to identified reinforcer. Ensure that negative behavior does not result in access to reinforcer.

Sensory/Perceptual

☐ Interrupt automatic reinforcement. Teach alternative/adaptive behavior. Provide incentives offering sensory stimulation (furry item, koosh ball, walkman) as reinforcer to promote positive competing/alternate behaviors.

Escape/Avoidance

☐ Teach student cues to solicit assistance with difficult tasks. Increase support for student to persist and reinforce effort. Look for ways to increase the attractiveness of unpleasant demands. Ensure that negative behavior does not result in avoidance of work demands (e.g., student can make up incomplete assignments during free time or after school).

FIGURE 4.4 *Analyzing behavior problems: Intervention*

Copyright 2000, J. L. McDougal, & S. M. Chafouleas

Addressing Skill Deficits

In many situations, academic and behavioral skill deficits influence the occurrence of problem behaviors. When skill deficits are related to the target behavior, an instructional component is often specified in the intervention plan. For example, Carr and Durand (1985) demonstrated that SIB in developmentally delayed individuals could be successfully diminished by implementing functional communication training procedures. This process involved teaching communicative phrases to replace the negative behavior while allowing the individual to continue to gain attention (i.e., serve the same function). In general, academic skill deficits may be addressed by increasing time spent on instructional material at the student's level or increasing the amount of academic support available to the student (e.g., increased access to a paraprofessional, peer tutor, or small group instruction). Behavioral assessment procedures have been developed and continue to be refined in order to inform academic intervention design (Martens & Kelly, 1993; Martens et. al., 1999). In general, these procedures ensure that an instructional match exists between the student's skills and the curriculum. Instructional procedures are then presented in a hierarchy to sequentially promote accuracy, fluency, and generalization of academic skills (see Daly & Martens, 1994; Haring, Lovitt, Eaton, & Hanson, 1978).

Behavior skill instruction is undertaken when the assessed child is believed to lack the necessary skills to be successful in the current setting. Behavioral skills are generally developed through procedures such as teaching the student the desired behavior, modeling the behavior, and reinforcing displays of the desired behavior. Examples of behavioral skill instruction can be readily observed in virtually every kindergarten classroom as teachers instruct children on appropriate learning behavior ("When the teacher is talking, we keep our eyes to the front, our ears open, and our mouths quiet"), model the behavior, and then wait patiently until the class is quiet before providing praise and continuing instruction. When minor disruption occurs in the class, the wise teacher ignores children who are off-task and instead praises those who exhibit appropriate behavior ("I like the way Johnny and Susie are sitting quietly, looking forward, ready to learn"). Many programs have been developed to promote prosocial skills development (e.g., Goldstein, Sprafkin, Gershaw, & Klein, 1980; Walker, Todis, Holmes, & Horton, 1988), social problem solving (e.g., Camp & Bash, 1981; Shure, 1992), and self-control (Feindler, 1995; Goldstein & Glick, 1987) with-school age children in order to enhance their behavioral skill repertoires.

Addressing the Functions of Behavior

As previously indicated, the goal with respect to behavior intervention planning is to ensure that negative behavior becomes functionally irrelevant while simultaneously promoting more adaptive behavior. Specifically, the intervention alters the consequences of behavior in general through the use of differential reinforcement procedures and extinction procedures. The goal of these procedures is to make problem behaviors irrelevant, inefficient, and ineffective in the settings in which the child is accommodated (O'Neill et al., 1997). Extinction procedures involve withholding the reinforcing consequence of the problem behavior so that performing the behavior is no longer functional. While the negative behavior is extinguished, a more adaptive replacement behavior can be reinforced as well. For example, suppose that a client was suffering from auditory and visual hallucinations. The intensity and duration of the hallucinations appeared to be related to the amount of attention derived from clinic staff. Although the client was involved in pharmacological treatment for psychosis, as an additional intervention clinic staff were asked to ignore the patient's references to hallucinations and instead speak to the client about reality-oriented topics such as family members, upcoming events, and current issues in the news. Thus, reality-based topics began to be reinforced with social attention while the references to hallucinatory subjects were placed on extinction. In this example, the clinic staff would expect a decrease in hallucinatory talk from the client and an increase in reality-based discussion. For more specific intervention ideas related to the identified function of behavior, the reader is again referred to Figure 4.4, to the case study provided at the end of the chapter, or to a basic text on applied behavior analysis (e.g., Wolery, Bailey, & Sugai, 1988).

Criticisms of Functional Assessment and Future Research Directions

Despite the promise of functional assessment, some concerns regarding the use of functional assessment for all problems have arisen. Many of the concerns relate to the potential labor-intensive or cumbersome process. For example, Braden and Kratochwill (1997) discussed three situations in which functional assessment may not be essential, and suggested that it is not always necessary to determine the cause of the behavior. First, they suggested that functional assessment is not essential when the cost (i.e., resources needed, time involved) of the individualized assessment is greater than the treatment. Second, it is not essential when the consequences of delayed problem analysis are minimal. Finally, when a treatment is identified that has high strength or is likely to work with many problem causes, then it may not be necessary to determine the cause of the behavior before implementing treatment. For example, if research indicates that self-monitoring can be an effective intervention for students with attention difficulties, it could be suggested that a self-monitoring intervention be implemented immediately. The literature is currently unclear regarding which behaviors warrant functional assessment and which could be addressed with more general intervention procedures

There are also many empirical questions still to be answered through research in the area of functional assessment (see Heckaman, Conroy, Fox, & Chait, 2000; Nelson, Roberts, Mathur, & Rutherford, 1999). First, to what extent are the functions of an individual's behaviors tied to the environment? In other words, exploration of the similarity or difference in the function of a specific behavior across environments is warranted. Also, within functionally equivalent environments (e.g., a classroom), to what extent are interventions designed for one child able to be generalized (e.g., by the teacher) to other children? Second, are descriptive and informant methods of collecting functional assessment information sufficient to create effective interventions in applied settings and how should decisions be made regarding which cases need a time-intensive functional analysis procedure? These considerations are especially applicable to school settings in which the administrator and teacher may be reluctant to systematically expose the referred student to conditions likely to escalate aggressive and unsafe behavior.

Further, the process whereby functional assessment results are used to design an intervention may be potentially confusing (for discussion, see Horner, 1994). Improved articulation of the procedures used to link assessment results to intervention design is warranted so that specific procedures utilized in research literature can be replicated in applied settings. Finally, the extent to which these procedures are feasible (contextually sound) and technically adequate for effective use by educators and clinic staff is unknown. Current research in this area generally has been conducted by teams using highly trained individuals and external resources to achieve the documented results (see Heckaman et al., 2000). Future research needs to address issues related to professional development and to the feasibility of these procedures in applied settings (Heckaman et al., 2000; Scott & Nelson, 1999).

Conclusion

Despite unanswered questions regarding the use of functional assessment, the current literature base is generally supportive of the use of these procedures to generate interventions that effectively reduce challenging behaviors in both clinic and school settings (e.g., Heckaman et al., 2000; Repp, 1994). Given this, the current chapter describes an assessment process that can lead to effective interventions for a wide range of social and personal difficulties. Further, with respect to intervention-oriented assessment, Martens et al. (1999) have stated that the benefits of functional assessment outweigh the risks, primarily due to ethical responsibilities. For example, it would be unethical to prescribe an intervention that did not work or actually strengthened a problematic behavior. In addition, recent regulations guiding the provision of special education services to school-aged children mandates the use of functional assessment and behavior intervention procedures in certain situations involving the disciplining of students with disabilities, according to conditions specified in IDEA, the Individuals with Disabilities Education Act Amendments of 1997. Thus, while the unanswered questions regarding functional assessment gradually are being answered, familiarity with this assessment process appears warranted. The functional assessment procedures described here appear aptly suited for inclusion in the practitioner's repertoire of assessment practices.

In sum, use of the current process promotes a problem-solving frame of mind regarding assessment that is not only good practice but also is mandated for use with specific students in the educational realm. Further, these assessment procedures have received some empirical support for use in both clinic and school settings. This approach to social and personal assessment is highly desirable given the strong focus on intervention that is tailored to individual needs and settings, and, thus, may be more likely to be beneficial in terms of promoting positive change. The following case study serves to integrate information presented previously and illustrates some of the major considerations in regard to functional behavioral assessment of children.

Case Study

Todd is an eight-year-old child with autism who attends an inclusive third-grade classroom. Todd was referred by his teacher for a functional assessment and behavior intervention plan due to physical aggression exhibited toward the classroom teacher and other adult staff. Although educators had several concerns about Todd, including his occasional noncompliance and refusal to work, physical aggression was selected as the primary target behavior as these incidents most interfered with Todd's potential to be successfully integrated into the classroom.

Through the functional assessment process, Todd's target behavior was defined as "physical aggression toward staff—hitting, kicking, biting, scratching, or hurting adults working with Todd in school." This behavior occurred an average of 2 to 3 times per day, with moderate to high intensity and short duration (1–2 seconds). At times, Todd was off-task and fidgeting prior to the aggressive incidents, but at other times no specific precursor to his behavior could be identified. His aggressive actions occurred most often during a direct instruction period during which he was provided individualized academic instruction. The typical consequence for exhibiting the target behavior was either removal of the task or Todd was sent home for the day. Academic and behavioral skill deficits were ruled out as Todd was generally academically on level and displayed appropriate behavior in other settings. Communicative intent could not be ruled out as the teacher indicated that Todd did not use words to ask for a break or for assistance with his work.

The functional hypothesis generated was, "when academic demands occur in the context of direct instruction activities, the student displays physical aggression toward staff in order to communicate dissatisfaction with instruction and to escape the task." Todd's strengths were identified in the areas of academic skill development and in his general affinity toward completing special jobs around the school (e.g., helping the school secretary copy and collate materials).

Based on this functional theory, observations were conducted during the direct instruction period. The observer found that Todd had no incidents of physical aggression during independent tasks but engaged in two acts of aggression toward the teacher during instructional lessons. The intervention for Todd was threefold. First, functional communication training was conducted with Todd to teach him to say, "I can do it." The teacher was asked to suspend instruction when he made the statement and give him an independent task to complete that would demonstrate mastery of the lesson. Second, when Todd did aggress toward the teacher, she was asked to hold his hands and create some distance between herself and Todd. After the incident, Todd was expected to complete the academic task to ensure that aggressive behaviors were no longer supported by negative reinforcement. Finally, at the end of the direct instruction period, if Todd completed his assigned work and was socially appropriate, he was escorted to the office to complete his favorite school job.

After one week of the intervention, Todd's aggressive acts toward staff had ceased and the teacher found that he was able to complete more work independently. Todd continued as the clerical assistant in the office, and had an overall successful year in school.

References

Alessi, G . J. (1988). Direct observation methods for emotional/behavior problems. In E. S. Shapiro & T. R. Kratochwill (Eds.), *Behavioral assessment in schools: Conceptual foundations and practical applications* (pp. 14–75). New York: Guilford Press.

Braden, J. P., & Kratochwill, T. R. (1997). Treatment utility of assessment: Myths and realities. *School Psychology Review, 26,* 475–485.

Camp, B. W., & Bash, M. A. (1981). *Think aloud.* Champaign, IL: Research Press.

Carr, E. G. (1977). The motivation of self-injurious behavior: A review of some hypotheses. *Psychological Bulletin, 84,* 800–816.

Carr, E. G., & Durand, M. (1985). Reducing problem behaviors through functional communication training. *Journal of Applied Behavioral Analysis, 18,* 111–126.

Carr, E. G., Levin, L., McConnachie, G., Carlson, J. I., Kemp, D. C., & Smith, C. (1994). *Communication-based interventions for problem behavior: A user's guide for producing positive behavior change.* Baltimore, MD: Paul H. Brookes.

Daly, E. J., III, & Martens, B. K. (1994). A comparison of three interventions for increasing oral reading performance: Application of the instructional hierarchy. *Journal of Applied Behavioral Analysis, 27,* 459–469.

Demchak, M. A. (1993). Functional assessment of problem behaviors in applied settings. *Intervention in School and Clinic, 29,* 89–95.

Durand, V. M. (1990). *Severe behavior problems: A functional communication training approach.* New York: Guilford Press.

Dyer, K., Dunlap, G., & Winterling, V. (1990). The effects of choice-making on the serious problem behaviors of students with developmental disabilities. *Journal of Applied Behavioral Analysis, 23,* 515–524.

Erchul, W. P., & Martens, B. K. (1997). *School consultation: Conceptual and empirical bases of practice.* New York: Plenum Press.

Feindler, E. L. (1995). Ideal treatment package for children and adolescents with anger disorders. *Issues in Comprehensive Pediatric Nursing, 18,* 233–260.

Goldstein, A. P., & Glick, B. (1987). *Aggression replacement training: A comprehensive intervention for aggressive youth.* Champaign, IL: Research Press.

Goldstein, A. P., Sprafkin, R. P., Gershaw, N. J., & Klein, P. (1980). *Skillstreaming the adolescent.* Champaign, IL: Research Press.

Haring, N. G., Lovitt, T. C., Eaton, M. D., & Hanson, C. L. (1978). *The fourth R: Research in the classroom.* Columbus, OH: Merrill.

Heckaman, K., Conroy, M., Fox, J., & Chait, A. (2000). Functional assessment-based intervention research on students with or at risk for emotional and behavioral disorders in school settings. *Behavioral Disorders, 25,* 196–210.

Horner, R. E. (1994). Functional assessment: Contributions and future directions. *Journal of Applied Behavioral Analysis, 27,* 401–404.

Individuals with Disabilities Act Amendments of 1997. (Pub. L. No. 105–17), 20 U.S.C. §1400 et seq.

Iwata, B., Dorsey, M., Slifer, K., Bauman, K., & Richman, G. (1982). Toward a functional analysis of self-injury. *Analysis and Intervention in Developmental Disabilities, 2,* 3–20.

Koegel, L. K., Koegel, R. L., Hurley, C., & Frea, W. D. (1992). Improving social skills and disruptive behavior in children with autism through the use of self-management. *Journal of Applied Behavioral Analysis, 25,* 341–353.

Kratochwill, T. R., Sheridan, S. M., Carlson, J., & Lasecki, K. L. (1999). Advances in behavioral assessment. In C. Reynolds & T. Gutkin (Eds.), *Handbook of school psychology* (3rd ed., pp. 350–382). New York: Wiley.

Lambert, N. M. (1976). Children's problems and classroom interventions from the perspective of classroom teachers. *Professional Psychology, 7,* 507–517.

Lloyd, J. W., Landrum, T. J., & Hallahan, D. P. (1991). Self monitoring applications for classroom intervention. In G. Stoner, M. R. Shinn, & H. M. Walker (Eds.), *Interventions for achievement and behavior problems* (pp. 201–214). Silver Spring, MD: National Association of School Psychologists.

Mace, F. C., Lalli, J. S., & Lalli, E. P. (1991). Functional assessment and treatment of aberrant behavior. *Research in Developmental Disabilities, 12,* 155–180.

Martens, B. K., & Kelly, S.Q. (1993). A behavioral analysis of effective teaching. *School Psychology Quarterly, 12,* 33–41.

Martens, B. K., Witt, J. C., Daly, E. J., & Vollmer, T. R. (1999). Behavior analysis: Theory and practice in educational settings. In C. Reynolds & T. Gutkin (Eds.), *Handbook of school psychology* (3rd ed., pp. 638–663). New York: Wiley.

Meyer, L. H., & Evans, I. M. (1989). *Nonaversive intervention for behavior problems: A manual for home and community.* Baltimore, MD: Paul H. Brookes.

Meyers, J., Parsons, R. D., & Martin, R. (1979). *Mental health consultation in the schools.* San Francisco: Jossey-Bass.

Nelson, J. R., Roberts, M. L., Mathur, S., & Rutherford, R. B. (1999). Has public policy exceeded our knowledge base? A review of the functional behavioral assessment literature. *Behavioral Disorders, 24,* 169–179.

New York State Education Department (1998, July). *Guidance on functional assessments for students with disabilities.* Albany, NY: University of the State of New York.

O'Neill, R. E., Horner, R. H., Albin, R. W., Sprague, J. R., Storey, K., & Newton, J. S. (1997). *Functional assessment and program development for problem behavior: A practical handbook* (2nd ed.). Pacific Grove, CA: Brooks/Cole.

Repp, A. (1994). Comments on functional analysis procedures for school-based behavior problems. *Journal of Applied Behavior Analysis, 27,* 409–411.

Risley, T. (1996). Get a life! Positive behavioral intervention for challenging behavior through life arrangement and life coaching. In L. K. Koegel, R. L. Koegel, & G. Dunlap (Eds.), *Positive behavioral support: Including people with difficult behavior in the community* (pp. 425–437). Baltimore, MD: Paul H. Brookes.

Scott, T. M., & Nelson, C. M. (1999). Functional behavioral assessment: Implications for training and staff development. *Behavioral Disorders, 24,* 249–252.

Shapiro, E. S., & Cole, C. L. (1994). *Behavior change in the classroom: Self-management interventions.* New York: Guilford Press.

Sheridan, S. M., Kratochwill, T. R., & Bergan, J. R. (1996). *Conjoint behavioral consultation: A procedural manual.* New York: Plenum Press.

Shure, M. B. (1992). *I can problem solve: An interpersonal cognitive problem-solving program (intermediate elementary grades).* Champaign, IL: Research Press.

Vollmer, T. R., & Northrup, J. (1996). Some implications of functional analysis for school psychologists. *School Psychology Quarterly, 11,* 76–92.

Walker, H. M., Todis, B., Holmes, D., & Horton, G. (1988). *The Walker social skills curriculum: The ACCESS program.* Austin, TX: PRO-ED.

Weeks, M., & Gaylord-Ross, R. (1981). Task difficulty and aberrant behavior in severely handicapped students. *Journal of Applied Behavior Analysis, 14,* 449–463.

West, R. P., & Sloane, H. N. (1986). Teacher presentation rate and point delivery rate. *Behavior Modification, 10,* 267–286.

Wolery, M., Bailey, D. B., & Sugai, G. M. (1988). *Effective teaching: Principles and procedures of applied behavior analysis with exceptional students.* Boston: Allyn and Bacon.

Wolf, M. M. (1978). Social validity: The case for subjective measurement, or how applied behavior analysis is finding its heart. *Journal of Applied Behavior Analysis, 11,* 203–214.

5

Use of Direct Assessment Techniques with School-Aged Children

Sandra M. Chafouleas and

Ronald Dumont

In 1983, Goh and Fuller (1983) examined the considerable controversy concerning the value and adequacy of methods used in the assessment of personality and behavior. A central question regarded the ability of available methods (e.g., projective and self-report techniques) to measure underlying personality traits or characteristics. At that time, a more behaviorally oriented approach to assessment, which included rating scales and observation techniques, was emerging but not yet commonplace in practice. Although controversy regarding methods of personality and behavior assessment continues today (Mash & Terdal, 1997), the popularity and availability of more objective techniques of assessment have been increasing. Thus, the focus of personality and behavior assessment has been shifting toward the study of observable behaviors and emotions. This chapter focuses on the exploration of social and personal assessment methods considered direct. *Direct methods* are those that permit data gathering and analysis with minimal amounts of intermediate steps and subjective inference (Merrell, 1999), and allow for a conceptual problem-solving approach to assessment (Kratochwill & Shapiro, 2000).

Because great variability exists both between and within behavioral assessment measures, Cone (1978) developed the Behavioral Assessment Grid (BAG) to provide a system for classifying available direct behavioral measures. The BAG is a three-dimensional system that simultaneously considers the contents assessed, the methods used to assess, and the generalizability of scores. Although this system has existed for many years, it continues to offer a useful model for identifying and critiquing direct techniques. *Contents* refers to the areas of behavior to examine and can include cognitive, physiological, and motor skills. *Methods of assessment* include interviews, self-reports, ratings by others, self-observation, and direct observation. These methods of assessment can be placed on a continuum of directness depending on the extent to which the behavior of interest is measured at the time and place of its natural occurrence (Cone, 1978). Methods are considered indirect if they are rated by others or include a verbal representation of the behaviors and events surrounding the behaviors. Indirect methods include interviews, self-reports, or rating by others. In contrast, methods are direct if the rating occurs at the time of the actual behavior (Kratochwill, Sheridan, Carlson, & Lasecki, 1999). Examples of more direct methods include observation in the natural environment, analogue observation (observing behavior in a simulated situation), and self-monitoring (the individual observes and objectively records his or her own behavior).

The third consideration suggested by the BAG, *generalizability*, refers to the degree to which the results can be considered valid. They can be influenced by several factors: (a) the observer, (b) the observation setting and those in it (child, parent, teacher, etc.), (c) the observation system used, and (d) the multiple interactions among these factors.

Comparison of Direct Assessment and Projective Techniques

Given the relatively short history of direct assessment, it is not surprising that projective measures have traditionally ranked among the most frequently employed personality assessment techniques. In fact, Goh and Fuller (1983) found the use of projective techniques more common than self-report and behavior rating scales among practicing school psychologists. Almost 20 years after their investigation, projective techniques remain highly popular among clinicians (Merrell, 1999), despite increased knowledge and use of direct assessment technology. (See Chapter 7 for a thorough discussion of projective techniques.)

Merrell (1999) noted that there is limited similarity between the philosophy of direct and projective techniques. The premise behind projective techniques is that, when presented with ambiguous stimuli and asked to respond either verbally or in drawings, a person will project his or her unconscious motives, conflicts, or needs. In contrast, direct assessment techniques emphasize the study of observable behaviors and emotions. Situational or environmental variables play an important role in direct assessment and interpretation, yet tend to be de-emphasized in projective assessment (Kratochwill & Shapiro, 2000).

Despite the popularity of certain projective techniques, significant limitations to their use have been identified. In a review of the research concerning the use of human figure drawings, Motta, Little, and Tobin (1993) found evidence of weak psychometric properties, and no evidence that experts versus inexperienced psychologists could provide more accurate interpretation. In addition, it can be difficult to provide a specific definition of what the techniques are measuring. Further limitations of projective techniques include the lengthy amount of time needed for administration and scoring of many measures (e.g., Rorschach, TAT), and the utility of the personality descriptions in planning interventions.

In contrast, many direct assessment techniques involve fewer inferences. Given the emphasis on observable behaviors, direct assessment reduces errors brought by the clinician into the assessment process and diminishes bias due to overreliance on subjective judgment (Merrell, 1999). In addition, it often involves repeated measurement, which can be helpful when the goal includes monitoring behavior over time or across settings. Perhaps the greatest advantage offered by direct assessment techniques is the ease with which the assessment can be linked to treatment. In fact, one rationale for the development and use of direct assessment techniques was to demonstrate treatment utility, that is, whether the assessment resulted in helpful outcomes (Hayes, Nelson, & Jarrett, 1987). Because the primary purpose of assessment should be to provide information to change a problem, techniques such as direct assessment measures that allow a link to intervention present a clear benefit.

Types of Direct Assessment Techniques

Observation Techniques

Observation techniques provide information about behaviors that occur in the setting of interest. The selection of a particular observation technique depends on the behavior of interest. Behaviors can be categorized as having either meaningful duration (e.g., looking around, "on-task") or a sudden onset and offset (e.g., raising hand, kicking; Saudargas & Lentz, 1986). Not all observation techniques are equally appropriate for measuring behaviors. For example, simply counting the number of times a student is looking around may not provide clinically useful information. The information may become more meaningful if an observer calculates the percentage of time the behaviors occur throughout the observation period.

Tawney and Gast (1984) present three requirements that should be considered prior to selecting an observation technique. First, the target behavior must be identified in specific, clear, and complete terms. Clear definitions of the target behaviors aid in recognizing when those behaviors occur, and distinguishes them from other, related behaviors. Some behaviors are relatively easy to define and identify. For example, screaming can be defined as any vocal noise that can be heard throughout the room. A behavior such as "being cooperative" may be more difficult to define because it can be subject to many interpretations. Eliminating vague behavioral definitions, coupled with clear descriptors, helps define target behavior. Second, the objective for conducting the observation (e.g., intervention) must be determined. For example, although some behaviors may be considered as having both meaningful duration and a clear onset and offset, the observer must decide if one or both components are important to note. Suppose a teacher is concerned about a student who frequently seems to be out of his seat heading for the pencil sharpener. If the teacher is concerned about how long the student is out of his seat to sharpen his pencil, it may be important to observe both the number of times and the length of time it takes to sharpen the pencil. If the concern is to decrease the number of peer disruptions made through peer interactions, then it may be appropriate to record the number of times and number of peer interactions during the pencil-sharpening journey. Finally, the practical constraints of the environment in which the behavior is to be observed must be considered. For example, if a teacher or parent is going to conduct the observation, time constraints and simplicity of data recording would be important issues in the selection of an observation technique. In addition, if multiple behaviors are selected as observation targets, some methods of observation (e.g., momentary time sampling) more easily allow for the recording of multiple behaviors.

As with categorizing target behaviors, observation techniques fall under two types of recording systems: *event-based* or *time-based* (Wolery, Bailey, & Sugai, 1988). *Event-based* recording is used with behaviors that have a clear onset or offset. Data are recorded whenever the specified behavior occurs. *Event-based* recording techniques include narrative ABC (i.e., antecedents–behaviors–consequences) records, frequency counts, and whole and partial interval records. With these techniques, the unit of measure is simply the rate or number of times the specified behavior occurs. *Time-based* recording is employed when behaviors have a meaningful duration. Data are recorded according to specified time intervals. *Time-based* recording results in a measure that represents the percentage of intervals during which the behavior was observed.

Event-based recording.   Event-based observation techniques focus on documenting the occurrence of a specified behavior. These techniques are most useful when the selected behaviors are relatively discrete and have a clear onset and offset. When selecting an event-based observation technique, one should consider the use of appropriate counting procedures (e.g., occurrence, duration, latency), the gathering of data at the appropriate times (e.g., when the behavior is most likely to occur), the checking of the accuracy of counts, and the keeping of records for occurrence in relation to time (Wolery et al., 1988). There are three primary event-based recording techniques that will be considered here: narrative ABC record, frequency counts, and measures of duration and latency.

Narrative ABC records can take many forms, providing a global description of an event ("Kate left the room") to a more narrow description ("Kate, after getting into an argument with her teacher, left the room"). The narrative ABC record provides a description of the complete behavioral event, including what is occurring in the setting before (i.e., antecedents) and after the behavior occurs (i.e., consequences). This method is selected because it provides information using low inference. For example, the recording that "Kate slammed her book on the desk" would be considered to be low inference while recording that "Kate is frustrated" is not really a descriptor of the behavior, but rather a statement of high inference by the observer. In addition, because the complete behavioral event is described in an ABC record, information is available to determine why and when the behavior is occurring, which can be useful during intervention planning. Although it can be time-consuming to complete, summarize, and quantify information, it is actually quite easy to do. In addition, it has the advantage of providing detailed information about the setting that is not readily available with other event-based recording techniques, given its description of the complete behavioral event. For an example of a narrative ABC record, see Figure 5.1.

Frequency counts are very easy to use because the target behaviors are simply counted as they occur during the observation period. The number of times or the rate of the behavioral occurrence is summarized and can be easily graphed. Frequency counts are not well suited for behaviors that occur frequently. For example, if a student is swearing in an almost continuous manner, it can be difficult to obtain an accurate count. The information would probably not be very meaningful, other than noting that the swearing occurred frequently. The largest disadvantage with the use of frequency counts is that little information is provided about the duration and intensity of the behavior or about setting events.

Duration and latency techniques both involve measurement of time, either through recording the length of time the behavior occurs (duration) or recording the length of time between a signal and the response to the signal (latency). When using either of these techniques, it is essential that the starting and stopping points for the selected behavior be clearly identified. Correct latency recording can be difficult as

Child: Jeremy, first-grade student

Setting: Ms. Hall's classroom

Date/Time: 10 A.M. on Monday

Antecedents	Behaviors	Consequences
Teacher tells class to line up to go to gym class	Jeremy jumps up and pushes peer in order to be first in line.	Teacher tells Jeremy to go back to his seat.
	Jeremy refuses to go back to his seat, and kicks the wall.	Teacher moves Jeremy back to his seat.
	Jeremy yells "no" and "it's not fair" all the way across the room. Refuses to sit in seat.	Teacher tells Jeremy he must calm down immediately or he will miss gym class.
	Jeremy begins to cry and pound his fists on the desk.	Teacher calls principal's office to come pick him up.

FIGURE 5.1 *Example Narrative ABC Record*

the examiner must decide when the signal was provided and exactly when the behavior started or was completed (Alessi, 1988). Given the difficulty inherent with this criterion for many behaviors, these techniques are not as frequently used, and should be selected only when elapsed time is the primary concern. For example, latency recording is most commonly used when observing compliance issues, such as recording the time it takes for a child to turn off the television following a request by her mother.

Time-based recording.   Time-based recording techniques (sometimes referred to as *interval sampling*) involve observing the targeted child for a short period of time (interval) and then coding the observed behavior(s). Selection of these techniques is useful when target behaviors have more meaningful duration such as on-task behavior. When using these techniques, one should consider what behavior to observe, the length of observation interval, and when to code the behavior, depending on the technique selected (Wolery et al., 1988). Three types of time-based recording will be outlined here: whole interval, partial interval, and momentary time sampling.

When using *whole interval* recording, the behavior of interest is recorded only if it occurs continuously throughout the entire chosen interval. This method provides information regarding the number of whole intervals (time blocks) within which behavior was observed to occur. Thus, Johnny must display on-task behavior for 30 out of 30 seconds during an interval in order for it to be recorded as occurring. Determining the length of the interval is dependent on the frequency of the behavior. However, it is recommended that the length be of short to medium length, typically around 6 to 30 seconds (Alessi, 1988). Although more than one behavior can be observed at the same time with this technique, it is recommended that the behaviors to be observed during any single session be limited as the technique requires continuous observation. One caution related to the use of whole interval recording is that it can underestimate the true occurrence of the behavior because the behavior is only recorded if it occurs throughout the entire interval. For example, if only 2 seconds are left in the interval and the child stopped engaging in the target behavior, the behavior would not be recorded as occurring during that interval. Thus, it is not an appropriate method for observing behaviors with very short duration. In addition, it may not be appropriate for observing infrequently occurring behaviors, given the continuous time and attention required by the observer.

When using *partial interval* recording, the target behavior is recorded once if it occurs at any point during the recording interval. As with whole interval recording, the length of the observation interval is best determined by considering how often and under what conditions the behavior occurs. It is commonly selected when the behavior of interest is considered to be a low-frequency behavior (e.g., calling out). In contrast to whole interval recording, partial interval recording may overestimate the true occurrence of the behavior as the behavior is marked as occurring during the interval if it occurs at any time during the interval. Despite this caution, the technique can be useful for summarizing the consistency of the behavior.

Momentary time sampling involves coding behavior at specified interval marks, such as the beginning or end of each interval. Given that behavior is observed only at the interval mark, numerous behaviors can be simultaneously observed as the observer has ample opportunity to record while waiting for the next interval mark. For the same reason, it is easy to collect normative data (i.e., peer comparisons) when using this technique. The momentary time sampling method is especially helpful when the behavior of concern occurs at a moderate yet steady rate (e.g., vocal tics, thumbsucking). A review of available research on this technique suggests that it provides a more accurate estimate of the true occurrence of the behavior than whole or partial interval recording (Saudargas & Lentz, 1986). Figure 5.2 provides a comparison of information obtained using whole interval, partial interval, or momentary time sampling with out-of-seat behavior.

A number of readily available observation procedures and formats have been developed for research and commercial use. Each differs in the type of recording system (e.g., event-based, time-based), setting requirement (e.g., school, home, clinic), and behaviors to be observed (e.g., academic, behavioral). For review of various observation coding schemes available for school, home, and clinic use, the reader is referred to Merrell (1999). One example of an observational format that allows for the combination of both a time-based and event-based recording of multiple behaviors is the *Saudargas-Creed State-Event Classroom Observation System* (*SECOS*; Saudargas & Lentz, 1986). The *SECOS* uses a paper-and-pencil format, and provides operational definitions for the most commonly observed classroom behaviors (e.g., looking around, out of seat, playing with object). It allows the observer to code behaviors as states (i.e., meaningful duration), events (i.e., clear onset/cessation), or both. The 10-minute observation format allows the observer to record both time sampling (i.e., state behaviors) and frequency counting (i.e., event behaviors). In addition, both student and teacher behaviors can be observed, which can provide valuable information about interactions in the setting. At the beginning of each interval only, a mark is placed next to any ongoing state behaviors listed on the form. Throughout each of the 30–second intervals, the frequency of occurrence of each event behavior is recorded in the appropriate box. The *SECOS* is specifically a school-based coding scheme, and has been extensively field-tested.

Recently, the use of computer technology for conducting observations has begun to emerge and may be worth further consideration. Several computerized behavior observation programs are available for purchase. Among these are *!Observe* (Martin, 1998), *Behavior Observation Assistant* (*BOA*; Bunger Solutions, 1998), and the *Ecobehavioral Assessment System Software* (*EBASS*; Greenwood & Carta, 1994). These programs allow an observer to use various observation techniques to conduct systematic observations that employ a laptop or hand-held computer. Among the possibilities offered by the programs are calculation of reliability, data analyses, and individualization of the instrument settings. However, when selecting a computerized program with multiple data-collection possibilities, the user must understand the type of observation procedure he or she is using, particularly when comparing information across subjects or observations. The use of computer technology to conduct behavioral observations may be beneficial, given a few considerations. First, use of a laptop computer during observation may be obtrusive and could influence the target child's behavior, a problem known as *observer reactivity*. Second, useful-

Child:	Sarah, 12-year-old
Target Behavior:	Stereotypic rocking
Setting:	At home with caseworker
Date/Time:	Thursday at 3:30 P.M.

Actual Occurrence of Behavior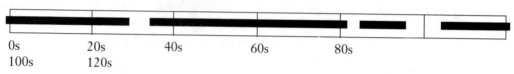

0s	20s	40s	60s	80s
100s	120s			

Momentary Time Sampling

Begin	Yes	Yes	Yes	Yes
No	Yes			

0s	20s	40s	60s	80s
100s	120s			

Observed Intervals: 5/6

Whole Interval

Yes	No	Yes	Yes	No	No

0s	20s	40s	60s	80s
100s	120s			

Observed Intervals: 3/6

Partial Interval

Yes	Yes	Yes	Yes	Yes	Yes

0s	20s	40s	60s	80s
100s	120s			

Observed Intervals: 6/6

FIGURE 5.2 *Comparison of momentary time sampling, whole interval, and partial interval recording using a 20s interval.*

Note: This example illustrates the potential over- or under-estimation of actual occurrence using various time-based recording techniques.

ness depends on the purpose of data collection and desired efficiency. For example, if the purpose of observation is to collect frequency counts of a behavior, it may be just as efficient to use paper and pencil as a computer. In contrast, for more complex data collection techniques such as momentary time sampling, use of computer software may facilitate accuracy of the collection and save time with data tabulation (Dumont & Chafouleas, 1999).

There have been relatively few investigations of the conventional psychometric properties of direct observation techniques (Kratochwill & Shapiro, 2000). It has been argued that there is limited need to establish psychometric properties as they present a paradigm that is different from traditional assessment instruments involving test construction. For example, it may be more relevant to establish a technique's sensitivity to behavior change rather than stability (Alessi, 1988). That is, does the selected observation technique detect any change in the target behavior? This is important because observation techniques often are used repeatedly to determine the problem and monitor effects of the intervention on behavior change. Because it is expected that the behavior will change, methods that are sensitive to these changes are desirable.

One area of reliability that has been addressed in the behavioral assessment literature is interrater (also known as interobserver) reliability, or the extent to which two observers agree that a particular behavior did or did not occur. In order to determine the consistency of the data, interobserver reliability should be 90% or greater (Wolery et al., 1988). If the reliability falls below 80%, the data should not be considered consistent. A simple formula for determining interval-by-interval percentage agreement among two or more observers is as follows: % agreement = number of agreements/(number of agreements + number of disagreements) x 100. Although calculation of percentage agreement does not correct for chance agreement, it can provide an easy check of the observation data. For a complete discussion of procedures for assessing reliability of observational coding systems, the reader is referred to Sattler (1992, pp. 510–518).

Wolery et al. (1988) identified a number of factors that influence the reliability of observational methods. First, the greater the complexity of the measurement system and the behaviors to be coded, the greater the possibility for error. Second, observer characteristics, such as expectancies or bias, carelessness, or observer drift, can be sources of error. Observer drift refers to a change over time in the way the definitions of the behavior are applied. Suggestions for reducing error and increasing reliability include training observers to a prespecified criterion prior to conducting observations, having two or more observers collect the data and conducting interobserver reliability checks with a specified criterion, standardizing observation codes, and withholding information from observers regarding intervention plans (Kratochwill et al., 1999). In addition, it is suggested that observations be conducted in an unobtrusive fashion in order to limit the observer's influence on the target's behavior.

Although traditional types of validity (i.e., content, concurrent, and construct) have not been typically examined with regard to observation techniques, one issue that has received attention relates to the generalizability of results. Unless specifically assessed, inferences regarding the generalization of observation data across settings, time, and behaviors cannot be made. A lack of social comparison data also can be a threat to the validity of the data. Consideration of normative behaviors in the observation setting will increase the appropriateness of the conclusions reached regarding the nature and severity of the target's behaviors. That is, do the target's behaviors differ significantly from others in the same setting? Including alternating observation of two or three nontarget participants with observation of the target would provide normative information, thus increasing the utility of conclusions. It has been recommended that multiple observations be conducted in order to limit threats to validity that exist when attempting to generalize beyond the situation that is specifically observed (Kratochwill et al., 1999).

Finally, it is important to determine the utility of using observation data in the development and implementation of an intervention plan. Similar to ecological validity, discussed by Wasserman and Bracken in Chapter 2, such an idea is closely related to treatment acceptability, or judgments about intervention procedures (Eckert & Hintze, 2000). Thus, when deciding a behavior needs to change, it is important to consider if the behavior change is important in the social environment, if the selected intervention is appropriate (i.e., least intrusive, ethical), and if the intervention procedures are relevant for the contexts in which they will be used. Obviously, behaviors that pose a threat to the child or someone else should receive attention first. However, when selecting among other types of behavior, there is leeway in deciding which behaviors are most important to change. For example, an observation might indicate off-task behavior during homework time would be a good target, yet a parent might indicate that completion of nighttime chores is more desirable. Thus, selecting completion of the chores may be a better choice and could increase the likelihood that the parent will help intervene to change the behavior. (See Chapter 4 for further guidelines regarding the selection of target behaviors.)

The following case study illustrates one use of a direct observation technique.

Case Study

Kristi is a 5-year-old kindergarten student who was referred by her mother because she frequently throws her toys across the room. When prompted, the mother indicated she thought the behavior was more likely to occur when Kristi was frustrated or when she was not receiving adult attention. In this case, a narrative ABC record was selected as the observation method in order to support information provided by the parent regarding which antecedents prompted the throwing behavior. Collecting information about the complete behavioral event was deemed important so that clarification of the factors most likely to elicit the behavior, as well as consequences for engaging in the behavior, could be determined. Then, this information could be conveyed to the parent to help her identify how she might best change the conditions surrounding the behavior.

Interview Techniques

Although the use of interviews historically has been influenced by psychodynamic theory, the influence of behavioral theory has changed the focus to more direct assessment (Beaver & Busse, 2000). Interviews are considered a less direct method of assessment because the information is removed, in time and place, from the actual behavior. Despite this, the usefulness of interviews has been well established and is often considered to be a critical component of certain assessments. For example, interviews can provide an overall frame of reference to guide assessment (Nuttall & Ivey, 1986), can allow for rapport building, which may benefit intervention implementation, and are a good first step to help determine what to do next in the assessment. In addition, it is relatively easy to obtain information through the flexible structure available in an interview (Gresham & Davis, 1988). That is, in contrast to the limited responses provided on a rating scale, an interviewer can probe for further, or more detailed, information about any area. Despite these advantages, cautions are necessary when interpreting the information obtained from interviews because it is based on indirect reports of behavior, and bias exists on the part of both the interviewer and interviewee.

Interviews are considered a unique method of assessment because they require direct contact and communication between the interviewer and interviewee, yet the direction of the interview must be purposeful and controlled by the interviewer. In addition, an interview can be conducted with the child, parent, or teacher in a variety of formats. These formats for interviewing include the use of diagnostic, behavioral, and structured or semistructured interviews. Deciding on the type of interview to use is dependent on the goals and objectives of the interview as well as the training and philosophy of the interviewer (Merrell, 1999).

Two areas that must be considered when conducting any method of interview include interpersonal communication and multiculturalism. First, the interviewer must attend to his or her verbal and nonverbal behaviors in order to enhance the interpersonal communication between him- or herself and the interviewee. These behaviors include effective attending, reflection and questioning, and proxemics (awareness of reactions to physical space maintained between individuals). For a review of general skills for enhancing interpersonal communication, the reader is referred to Kurpius and Rozecki (1993). Although all of these skills are necessary for successful communication, some may be more pertinent when an examiner utilizes an interview method. For example, when using a behavioral interview method, the style of questioning becomes essential. Interviewers must control questioning in a way that leads to specification of the problem and conditions surrounding the problem (i.e., "What does Johnny do that you consider disruptive?") (Gresham & Davis, 1988). Second, culture (i.e., ethnography, demographics, status, and affiliations) of both the interviewer and interviewee should be considered. In order to build culture-centered skills, Pedersen and Ivey (1993) recommend that the interviewer learn to recognize his or her culturally learned attitudes, opinions, and assumptions by comparing and contrasting his or her viewpoint with alternative viewpoints. By doing this, the interviewer can build knowledge (factual information) about particular cultures, and can increase his or her skills for interacting with different cultures.

Diagnostic interview.   When the goals of an interview include obtaining information, such as current presenting problems and developmental, school and family histories, the diagnostic or clinical interview is traditionally used. Given the detailed historical data required, this method most often is conducted with an adult caretaker or teacher, and can be supplemented with information from the child. The examiner might begin with questions related to general concerns, such as the reason for referral or the primary area of concern. Questions designed to elicit information about developmental history, family history, and school history are all important here. In addition, a number of published interview formats are available, such as the Structured Developmental History from the *Behavior Assessment System for Children* (*BASC*; Reynolds & Kamphaus, 1998). The diagnostic interview allows for open-ended questioning in a less structured and highly flexible format (Merrell, 1999). The main advantage of this format is the wide variety of issues and behaviors on which data can be gathered (Beaver & Busse, 2000). However, given the depth to which the interview might delve, it is not very time efficient. In addition, Gresham and Davis (1988) suggest that the phrasing of questions can draw attention to problems "within" the child (Johnny doesn't pay attention) rather than the situation (Johnny does not follow his father's instruction regarding cleaning his room). This may limit the breadth of interventions considered.

Behavioral interview.   The behavioral interview differs from other interview methods mainly in the level of structure provided to the interview process. Unlike other interview methods, the behavioral interview requires systematic problem solving to determine high specificity of problem definitions and identification of situational reasons as to why, or why not, the problem is occurring. That is, the interview process follows a step-by-step format to sequentially gather information, which is then used to solve a problem. This focus on a limited number of specified problem areas makes behavioral interviews more narrow in scope and focus than other interview formats. However, Gresham and Davis (1988) suggest that the detailed clarification is one advantage the behavioral interview holds over other methods with regard to the treatment utility of the assessment information. Given the careful analysis of behaviors and settings that should occur throughout a behavioral interview, this assessment can be easily linked to appropriate intervention strategies. While gathering information, the interviewer is able to assess the level of support needed by the interviewee to implement an intervention. The interviewer can then modify his or her verbal and nonverbal behaviors to provide the necessary support to determine a plan to change the problem behavior(s) that is acceptable to the interviewee (Erchul & Martens, 1997). The behavioral interview format can be used with a parent, teacher, or, if appropriate, the child. In addition, an adaptation of the behavioral interview process, Conjoint Behavioral Consultation, has been receiving greater attention and empirical support. Conjoint Behavioral Consultation involves a similar format, but parents and teachers work together in the interview to address behaviors occurring across contexts and settings (Kratochwill et al., 1999).

   The model for the behavioral interview includes three steps, each of which is accomplished in a separate interview: problem identification, problem analysis, and plan implementation/problem evaluation. Completing the goals set for each of the three steps brings the interview from the initial clarification of the problem through implementation of the intervention to intervention evaluation. In the problem identification stage, there are three primary goals: identifying and defining the problem behavior, obtaining estimates of frequency, intensity, and duration of the problem, and determining the methods and procedures for collecting data for use in intervention planning and evaluation (Erchul & Martens, 1997).

The main goals of the second step of the behavioral interview, problem analysis, include the use of the available data to establish goals for change, the development of a hypothesis about why the problem is occurring, and, finally, the planning and implementation of interventions to change the problem. The third step primarily involves the evaluation of the plan's effectiveness in achieving the goals. Questions to ask during the analysis stage include questions that help define the problem (e.g., what seems to be the problem?), determine the history of the target behavior, discuss the conditions surrounding the problem (i.e., the antecedents, sequences, and consequences), and analyze the patterns of behavior (i.e., deciding which hypotheses describe the occurrence of the behavior).

Because the information sought must be highly specific and clear, the interviewer must be careful to direct the behavioral interview process, and must be skilled at controlling and analyzing his or her own verbal and nonverbal behavior. For example, the interviewer must sort the information provided by the interviewee while the conversation is ongoing, and make the decisions about probing certain areas further while redirecting attention away from nonessential areas. In addition, because the interview is behavioral, the interviewer must possess skill related to applied behavior analysis or functional behavioral assessment. (For more specific information on conducting a functional behavioral assessment, the reader is referred to Chapter 4.)

Structured or semistructured interview. The creation of structured and semistructured interviews for assessing children has been prompted by the desire to have a clear and standardized format that is current with diagnostic criteria for mental disorders (Beaver & Busse, 2000). As such, most available measures were developed and validated in psychiatric settings; consequently, their utility in general settings is uncertain (Merrell, 1999). Structured interviews rely on specific wording, order, and coding of data, while semistructured formats provide more general and flexible guidelines (Edelbrock & Costello, 1988). The two formats differ in the degree of clinical inference required, with semistructured methods requiring greater inference and necessitating more intensive training for the interviewer. Examples of structured interview schedules that allow for assessment of more than one diagnosis include the *Diagnostic Interview for Children and Adolescents, Revised* (*DICA-R*; Reich, 1996) and the *NIMH Diagnostic Interview Schedule for Children* (*DISC 2.3*; Shaffer et al., 1996). An example of a semistructured interview that also assists in disorder diagnosis includes the various versions of the *Schedule for Affective Disorders and Schizophrenia for School-Aged Children* (see Kaufman et al., 1997, for a comparison of different versions).

No single structured or semistructured interview has been determined to be the best because all have demonstrated strengths and weaknesses (Edelbrock & Costello, 1988). However, it has been suggested that structured interview formats not be used when beginning an assessment as their more rigid structure may limit rapport building or may frustrate the parent. In addition, Beaver and Busse (2000) have suggested that interview formats focusing on *DSM-IV* diagnoses may have limited use in school settings. As such, measures that provide information that can be linked to school-related issues may be better choices. One example of a semistructured interview that can be useful in school settings is the *Vineland Adaptive Behavior Scales* (Sparrow, Balla, & Cicchetti, 1984). This semistructured interview is available in three different forms (Expanded, Survey, Classroom) and assesses several domains of personal and social skills.

The indirect nature of all interview methods poses a potential problem regarding the accuracy of information obtained. The best method would be to confirm the interview information with a more direct assessment method, but interviews can offer an excellent starting point and, in some cases, may be the only available method. Gresham and Davis (1988) have suggested that, if the purpose of assessment is for screening and classification, then it is necessary to demonstrate some traditional psychometric properties such as reliability, validity, and normative comparisons. Thus, the interviewer could examine available semistructured or structured options given the potential normative comparisons and the stronger evidence of traditional psychometric properties. In contrast, if the purpose of the assessment is intervention, demonstrating traditional psychometric properties may not be as essential. In this situation, it is important to have an accurate functional assessment and it may be necessary to include direct observation or self-monitoring, along with a behavioral interview. In summary, when selecting an interview method, the interviewer must consider the purpose of the assessment as well as the reliability and validity of each specified measure.

Another relevant issue regarding the reliability and validity of interview information stems from the child self-report literature (see McConaughy, 2000). The use of structured and semistructured interviews has produced more reliable diagnoses with older children (12 years of age or more) and parents. In addition, child interviews produce reliabilities that vary across different diagnostic categories, and scores on continuous or criterion scales produce higher reliabilities than categorical diagnoses. However, acceptable reliabilities for most diagnostic categories in clinical samples can be found with combined information from parent and child interviews. Given these findings, it is recommended that special consideration be given when interviewing a child due to developmental considerations in cognitive and socioemotional areas. A review of the literature suggests great age differences in how children perceive information about other people and describe or interpret interpersonal relationships (see Witt, Cavell, Heffer, Carey, & Martens, 1988). For example, younger children often use descriptive labels categorized as all or none (i.e., good or bad), and their behavior is described in simplistic terms. The burden of reducing error and collecting more accurate information falls to the examiner, who must have knowledge about development in cognitive and socioemotional areas. Witt et al. (1988) make three suggestions about how to improve the accuracy of child self-report information. The first involves modification of stimulus complexity, which includes monitoring the level of language, the "directness" of the questioning style, and the appropriateness of open-ended questions. Second, modification of response complexity should be considered. For example, the interviewer may decide to provide a limited number of response choices, using oral, written, or picture-selection formats. Finally, the interviewer should provide the child with appropriate expectations, which includes a clear explanation of the purpose of the assessment.

The case study below presents a situation in which an interview technique was included in the assessment.

Checklists and Rating Scales

Although the use of checklists and rating scales is becoming increasingly widespread in the evaluation of children and adults, their development is fairly new. Originally considered an observational method, the scales first began to appear in the early 1950s for use by nurses and other caretakers (Kamphaus & Frick, 1996). Today, checklists and rating scales are available in many forms. They can be either self-created, non-standardized forms (e.g., *School Self Report Scale* [*SSRS-R*]; Regional Services and Education Center, 1998) or commercially produced, standardized forms (e.g., *Behavior Assessment System for Children* [*BASC*]; Reynolds & Kamphaus, 1998). The *SSRS-R* was created for use as a self-report and provides the informant (child) with clear, contrasting statements about certain behaviors (e.g., sports, reading). The child needs only to evaluate his or her skills and circle a number on a 5-point scale. No normative data with which to compare the results are provided. The goal of this type of self-report is to provide data concerning the child's perceptions about how well he or she performs a certain task compared to how much he or she enjoys that same task. In contrast to these self-made scales are standardized scales sold commercially by various testing companies. These, too, can vary greatly in both the breadth and depth of what they assess, as well as in their psychometric properties.

Checklists and rating scales are used for a variety of purposes (e.g., screening, clinical diagnosis, program evaluation) as they provide a standardized format for obtaining summary judgments about a child's behavior (Merrell, 1999). Although often considered together, a checklist typically refers to a format involving a list of behav-

Case Study

Samantha is a 10–year-old female who was referred for assessment due to high levels of self-injurious behavior exhibited in the home. Because self-injurious behavior poses a threat to Samantha, her parent and caseworker wanted an assessment that would provide a concrete plan for changing the behavior. The evaluator elected to begin the assessment with a behavioral interview as it involves systematic problem solving to determine why and when the behavior is most likely to occur. This format provides specific information regarding setting events, allowing the evaluator, parent, and caseworker to decide how to change the behavior by manipulating the setting and to determine how to teach Samantha a more appropriate response. In this case, systematic problem solving was determined to be the most efficient way in order to quickly change a behavior causing harm to the individual.

iors that the rater marks as absent or present. The marked items are then summed. On the other hand, a rating scale allows the rater to estimate the degree to which each behavior is present, thus allowing for more precise measurement of frequency, intensity, or duration (Merrell, 1994). In contrast to direct observation techniques, which focus on specific and operationally defined behaviors, checklists and rating scales are often used to assess more global constructs of behavior (e.g., aggression, thought problems, somatic complaints). Although they provide yet another form of a direct assessment procedure, checklists and rating scales fall toward the indirect end of the continuum because the ratings are not done at the exact time a behavior occurs. Informant perceptions of behavior in a setting are assessed rather than collection of actual observation data. They can be more time- and cost-efficient than other techniques, however, given the relative ease of information collection across multiple dimensions, raters, and settings.

Checklists and rating scales vary widely in what they can do, thus, selection of a measure is dependent on the assessment goal. For example, the use of a specific academic rating scale (e.g., *Learning Disability Diagnostic Inventory* [*LDDI*]; Hammill, & Bryant, 1998) might be selected when the primary referral question has to do with educational, not behavioral, issues. When selecting a measure, it is important that the evaluator carefully examine how the instrument defines the area it purports to assess. Variability in interpretation of definitions (e.g., *aggression*) exists among measures, creating related but somewhat different scales (part of what is known as *instrument variance*) even among those scales that purport to measure the same construct. Thus, it is necessary to examine items incorporated in the scale for specificity and content to decide if the measure is appropriate for the situation.

The use of checklists and rating scales can offer a number of advantages. First, they provide a common frame of reference for comparing an individual to a cohort, and allow for multiple informants to provide information regarding common areas of concern. Second, they allow an informant to evaluate many aspects of behavior that might otherwise be ignored or missed, and provide a way to quantify certain qualitative aspects of behavior in a time-efficient and convenient manner. Despite these strengths, several disadvantages over other recording methods can be identified. First, some checklists and rating scales are not suited to recording important quantitative information, such as the frequency, duration, or intensity of behavior, or for recording antecedent and consequent events. In addition, most full-length norm-referenced rating scales are not designed for continuous monitoring of behavior, and do not adequately discriminate small changes in behavior. They are more commonly employed to assess behavior before and then after intervention. These limitations hinder their usefulness in designing and informing interventions.

Some checklists and rating scales are considered "unidimensional" while others are "multidimensional and multimethod" procedures. As the name implies, a unidimensional scale examines a single behavior (out-of-seat) or single domain (anxiety) as opposed to assessing a broad range of differing behaviors or domains. Examples of unidimensional scales include the *Reynolds Adolescent Depression Scale* (*RADS*; Reynolds, 1987) and the *Brown Attention-Deficit Disorder Scales* (*Brown ADD Scales*; Brown, 1996). Multidimensional procedures are designed to assess a number of relevant behaviors (anxiety, aggression, depression) rather than a single construct or dimension (attentional problems). Multimethod procedures are those in which multiple raters (e.g., parent, teacher, child self-report) provide information about a specific child. Examples of multidimensional and multimethod procedures include the *BASC* (Reynolds & Kamphaus, 1998), the *Achenbach System of Empirically Based Assessment* (*ASEBA*; Achenbach, 1997), and the *Conners' Rating Scale-Revised* (*CRS-R*; Conners, 1997).

The prime source of data in checklists and rating scales is the scale value (or number or score) on the particular rating scale. Scales can be designed to utilize many different forms of descriptive scaling. The user is typically asked to rate specific behavioral descriptions using a continuum on a descriptive scale. The simplest form may be a dichotomous (e.g., yes or no) rating while more complex ratings could include multiple descriptors (e.g., never seen, sometimes seen, always seen). Obviously, in comparison to a response format with multiple descriptors, a dichotomous rating cannot provide information regarding frequency, severity, or duration of behaviors (Edelbrock, 1983).

When using rating-form methods, an informant who knows the child rates the child's behavior. The reliability of results can be increased by ensuring the rater has known the child long enough to provide accurate assessment. Obviously, obtaining ratings of a child from a respondent who has only known that child tangentially or for a very short period of time (e.g., less than 1 month) would raise concern about the accuracy and reliability of the results. Although an appropriate length of time is difficult to specify, generally a 2- to 6-month period appears adequate (Edelbrock, 1983). Rating scales are typically designed so that the informant can indicate the degree to which a specific attribute has been observed (e.g., cooperativeness, aggression) or the attribute is perceived to be present in the child. These scales require that the informant not only be familiar with the child being rated, but also the degree to which the rated attributes are present. Again, this raises the issue of the appropriate selection of a measure in that the informant must be familiar with the setting to which the items are tied. For example, a teacher or counselor may find it difficult or impossible to answer items related to daily routines at home. In addition, Merrell (1999) cautions that clinicians must be aware of potential bias of response, such as rating a student positively or negatively due to another nonpertinent characteristic such as how the child looks (halo effect), providing an overly generous or critical response set (leniency or severity), or a tendency to select midpoint ratings (central tendency effects).

Another potential difficulty associated with checklist and rating scales is that informants vary in their interpretation of the scale positions. For example, if one were to use a rating scale requesting the informant to respond to descriptors such as *very often, sometimes,* and *often.* Does *very often* mean 99 to 100% of the time or 90 to 100% of the time? How would one differentiate between *sometimes* and *often?* Does *often* on a 4-point scale mean the same as it does on a 7-point scale? A scale that provides detailed examples of behaviors associated with each scale point can help informants apply consistent standards in interpreting scale values, and could enhance interobserver reliability. This is often accomplished by creating a clear definition of each level, such as anchoring the frequency descriptions to percentages of time. One way this can be done is: *very often* (86 to 100% of the time), *often* (66 to 85 percent of the time), *sometimes* (36 to 65% of the time), and *never or rarely* (0 to 35% of the time). Even though these percentages help to more precisely define the frequency descriptions ("very often" to "never"), raters still must estimate how often the behaviors in question occurred.

When using standardized rating scales, the issue of reliability and validity are often easily addressed. Traditional psychometric methods for computing reliability (test-retest, internal, interrater) should be found within the scale's manual. Additionally, studies addressing concurrent, construct, and criterion-related validity should be presented. Without published evidence for a scale's reliability and validity, users may be unsure as to what specific constructs have been measured by the chosen instrument, and unsure of how much credence can be placed in the findings. Although traditional psychometric properties are not typically available when using self-made or nonstandardized rating scales, these scales can be useful when examining behavior in a more descriptive rather than normative approach. Users of nonstandardized scales must acknowledge these limitations and be cautious about inferences made regarding the obtained results.

The case study below illustrates how a clinician might select a rating scale based on the needs of the specific situation.

Conclusion

Familiarity with the direct assessment techniques highlighted in this chapter should be considered a necessity for every clinician involved with the social and personal assessment of children and adolescents. Assessment of social and personal domains cannot be adequate without consideration of the conditions surrounding the behavior, and direct assessment techniques are linked most closely to rating behavior at the time and in the setting of occurrence. This direct data gathering involves fewer inferences and is unparalleled by other techniques. Perhaps even more importantly, the use of di-

Case Study

Juan, a 16-year-old male, has been referred for evaluation by his parents due to "a dramatic change in behavior." His parents reported that Juan has typically been a good student, active both in sports and extracurricular activities. Within the past two months, Juan has been reported to be failing three of his five subjects and, without explanation, quit the soccer team and dropped out of the drama production. Juan's parents believe that these behaviors began after his girlfriend broke off their relationship. In this case, the evaluator chose to begin the assessment with a behavior rating scale specifically designed to assess adolescent depression. Because Juan's behavior may be indicative of depression related to a specific event, a narrow-band instrument such as the *Reynolds Adolescent Depression Scale* was selected in order to more fully delve into issues related to depression.

rect assessment methods allows the evaluator to focus on specific referral questions and goals. The information gathered can then be easily and practically linked to intervention. Given the increasing demand on a clinician's time to provide appropriate services to greater numbers of clients, legislative demands for accountability in practice, and ethical requirements of clinical practice, efficient assessment practices that allow for generation and monitoring of intervention plans are essential. The variety of objective techniques described in this chapter, although varying in their strengths and weaknesses, helps the clinician meet these goals.

References

Achenbach, T. M. (1997). *Achenbach system of empirically based assessment.* Burlington, VT: University of Vermont.

Alessi, G. J. (1988). Direct observation methods for emotional/behavior problems. In E. S. Shapiro & T. R. Kratochwill (Eds.), *Behavioral assessment in schools: Conceptual foundations and practical applications* (pp. 14–75). New York: Guilford Press.

Beaver, B. R., & Busse, R. T. (2000). Informant reports: Conceptual and research bases of interviews with parents and teachers. In E. S. Shapiro & T. R. Kratochwill (Eds.), *Behavioral assessment in schools: Theory, research, and clinical foundations* (2nd ed., pp. 257–287). New York: Guilford Press.

Brown, T. T. (1996). *Brown Attention-Deficit Disorder Scales.* San Antonio, TX: The Psychological Corporation.

Bunger Solutions. (1998). *Behavior Observation Assistant.* Plano, TX: Bunger Solutions.

Cone, J. D. (1978). The behavioral assessment grid (BAG): A conceptual framework and a taxonomy. *Behavior Therapy, 9,* 882–888.

Conners, C. K. (1997). *Conner's Rating Scales-Revised Technical Manual.* Toronto: Multi-Health Systems.

Dumont, R., & Chafouleas, S. M. (1999, May). Conducting behavior observations: Some technical support? *Communiqué,* pp. 32–33.

Eckert, T. L., & Hintze, J. M. (2000). Behavioral conceptions and applications of acceptability: Issues related to service delivery and research methodology. *School Psychology Quarterly, 15,* 123–148.

Edelbrock, C. (1983). Problems and issues in using rating scales to assess child personality and psychopathology. *School Psychology Review, 12,* 293–299.

Edelbrock, C., & Costello, A. J. (1988). Structured psychiatric interviews for children. In M. Rutter, A. H. Tuma, & I. Lann (Eds.), *Assessment and diag-*nosis in child psychopathology (pp. 87–112). New York: Guilford Press.

Erchul, W. P., & Martens, B. K. (1997). *School consultation: Conceptual and empirical bases of practice.* New York: Plenum Press.

Goh, D. S., & Fuller, G. B. (1983). Current practices in the assessment of personality and behavior by school psychologists. *School Psychology Review, 12,* 240–243.

Greenwood, C. R., & Carta, J. J. (1994). *Ecobehavioral Assessment Systems Software.* Kansas City, KS: Juniper Gardens Children's Center.

Gresham, F. M., & Davis, C. J. (1988). Behavioral interviews with teachers and parents. In E. S. Shapiro & T. R. Kratochwill (Eds.), *Behavioral assessment in schools: Conceptual foundations and practical applications* (pp. 14–75). New York: Guilford Press.

Hammill, D. D., & Bryant, B. R. (1998) *Learning Disabilities Diagnostic Inventory.* Austin: TX: PRO-ED.

Hayes, S. C., Nelson, R. O., & Jarrett, R. B. (1987). The treatment utility of assessment: A functional approach to evaluating assessment quality. *American Psychologist, 42,* 963–974.

Kamphaus, R. W., & Frick, P. J. (1996) *Clinical assessment of child and adult personality and behavior.* Boston: Allyn and Bacon.

Kaufman, J., Birmaher, B., Brent, D., Rao, U., Flynn, C., Moreci, P., Williamson, D., & Ryan, N. (1997). Schedule for affective disorders and schizophrenia for school-age children—present and lifetime version (K-SADS-PL): Initial reliability and validity data. *Journal of the American Academy of Child and Adolescent Psychiatry, 36,* 980–988.

Kratochwill, T. R., & Shapiro, E. S. (2000). Conceptual foundations of behavioral assessment in schools. In E. S. Shapiro & T. R. Kratochwill (Eds.), *Behavioral assessment in schools: Theory, research, and clinical foundations* (2nd ed., pp. 3–18). New York: Guilford Press.

Kratochwill, T. R., Sheridan, S. M., Carlson, J., & Lasecki, K. L. (1999). Advances in behavioral assessment. In C. Reynolds & T. Gutkin (Eds.), *Handbook of school psychology* (3rd ed., pp. 350–382). New York: Wiley.

Kurpius, D. J., & Rozecki, T. G. (1993). Strategies for improving interpersonal communication. In J. Zins & T. Rozecki (Eds.), *Handbook of consultation services for children: Applications in educational and clinical settings*. San Francisco: Jossey-Bass.

Martin, S. (1998). *!Observe*. Corinth, TX: Psychsoft.

Mash, E. J., & Terdal, L. G. (1997). Assessment of child and family disturbance: A behavioral-systems approach. In E. Mash & L. Terdal (Eds.), *Assessment of childhood disorders* (3rd ed., pp. 3–68). New York: Guilford Press.

McConaughy, S. H. (2000). Self-reports: Theory and practice in interviewing children. In E. S. Shapiro & T. R. Kratochwill (Eds.), *Behavioral assessment in schools: Theory, research, and clinical foundations* (2nd ed., pp. 323–354). New York: Guilford Press.

Merrell, K. W. (1994). *Assessment of behavioral, social, and emotional problems: Direct and objective methods for use with children and adolescents*. White Plains, NY: Longman.

Merrell, K. W. (1999). *Behavioral, social, and emotional assessment of children and adolescents*. Mahwah, NJ: Erlbaum.

Motta, R. W., Little, S. G., & Tobin, M. I. (1993). The use and abuse of human figure drawings. *School Psychology Quarterly, 8*, 162–169.

Nuttall, E. V., & Ivey, A. E. (1986). The diagnostic interview process. In H. M. Knoff (Ed.), *The assessment of child and adolescent personality* (pp. 105–140). New York: Guilford Press.

Pedersen, P. B., & Ivey, A. (1993). *Culture-centered counseling and interviewing skills: A practical guide*. Wesport, CT: Praeger.

Regional Services and Education Center. (1998). *School Self-Rating Scale*. East Amherst, NH: Author.

Reich, W. (1996). *Diagnostic Interview for Children and Adolescents-Revised (DICA-R) 8.0*. St. Louis, MO: Washington University.

Reynolds, C. R., & Kamphaus, R. W. (1998). *Behavior Assessment System for Children*. Circle Pines, MN: American Guidance Service.

Reynolds, W. M. (1987). *Reynolds Adolescent Depression Scale*. Odessa, FL: Psychological Assessment Resources.

Sattler, J. M. (1992). *Assessment of children* (3rd ed.). San Diego: Jerome M. Sattler.

Saudargas, R. A., & Lentz, F. E. (1986). Estimating percent of time and rate via direct observation: A suggested observational procedure and format. *School Psychology Review, 15*, 36–48.

Shaffer, D., Fisher, P., Dulcan, M. K., Davies, M., Piacentini, J., Schwab-Stone, J. E., Lahey, B. B., Bourdan, K., Jensen, P. S., Bird, H. R., Canino, G., & Regier, D. (1996). The NIHM Diagnostic Interview Schedule for Children Version 2.3 (DISC-2.3): Description, acceptability, prevalence rates, and performance in the MECA study. *Journal of the American Academy of Child and Adolescent Psychiatry, 35*, 865–877.

Sparrow, S. S., Balla, D. A., & Cicchetti, D. V. (1984). *Vineland Adaptive Behavior Scales: Interview edition survey form manual*. Circle Pines, MN: American Guidance Service.

Tawney, J. W., & Gast, D. L. (1984). *Single subject research design in special education*. Columbus, OH: Bell & Howell.

Witt, J. C., Cavell, T. A., Heffer, R. W., Carey, M. P, & Martens, B. K. (1988). Child self-report: Interviewing techniques and rating scales. In E. S. Shapiro & T. R. Kratochwill (Eds.), *Behavioral assessment in schools: Conceptual foundations and practical applications* (pp. 14–75). New York: Guilford Press.

Wolery, M., Bailey, D. B., & Sugai, G. M. (1988). *Effective teaching: Principles and procedures of applied behavior analysis with exceptional students*. Boston: Allyn and Bacon.

Neuropsychological Assessment with School-Aged Children

Lawrence J. Lewandowski and
Jeremie R. Barlow

Psychologists who work with children, whether in schools, hospitals, agencies, or private practice, encounter youngsters with an array of cognitive, academic, social, and emotional difficulties. Some of these problems are the direct result of pre-, peri-, or postnatal brain dysfunction, or may be related to less than efficient brain organization and functioning. In many cases, the compromise of the central nervous system (CNS) creates challenges for the youngster that may ultimately affect his or her ability to communicate, learn, play, work, and get along with others. A compromise of the CNS can alter any human function from the most basic (i.e., eating, speaking) to the most sophisticated (i.e., writing, planning, problem solving). For these reasons, a specialty field emerged in the area of child (pediatric) neuropsychology aimed at the comprehensive assessment of child CNS problems and their effective management. This chapter attempts to equip the reader with a basic understanding of child neuropsychological assessment. We hope to inform the reader on what it is, why we do it, what it entails, how it is done, and what it can do for children with CNS dysfunction. The chapter concludes with a discussion of common pediatric disorders and their neurodevelopmental characteristics, followed by a case study that applies neuropsychological assessment to a child whose CNS compromise affected social and personality function domains, among others.

Neuropsychological Assessment: Definition and Rationale

Neuropsychological assessment (NA) is a process whereby one evaluates the psychological and behavioral manifestations of a neurological disturbance. That is, it attempts to determine the presence, nature, extent, location, and prognosis of a central nervous system dysfunction that affects sensory–motor, perceptual, cognitive, and affective functioning. Because the brain subserves all complex human behavior, and neuropsychological assessment attempts to assess the integrity of the entire brain, such assessment must be comprehensive and can be quite time-consuming. In a sense, NA describes a wide variety of human performances that reflect various aspects of CNS functioning and, collectively, the overall integrity of an individual's nervous system. By mapping the many functions of the brain via numerous general and discrete tests, such assessment determines what brain areas, regions, systems, and so forth are working or not working, and identifies the strengths and weaknesses of an individual both behaviorally and neurologically. Ultimately, this information is utilized to best manage, rehabilitate, and plan for a patient with any type of neurologic problem (Lezak, 1996).

To perform this assessment, the neuropsychologist must rely on a working knowledge of neuroanatomy and neurophysiology, familiarity with types of neuropathology and their characteristics, a theoretical understanding of brain organization and function, experience with neuropsychological testing of patients, and knowledge of the empirical literature on clinical research findings for any and all conditions. Clearly, this individual must be highly trained. However, the neuropsychologist is not alone in this endeavor.

Clinical neuropsychology is really a blend of disciplines, particularly neurology and psychology. The neuropsychological perspective fits nicely with the speech, occupational, and physical therapy fields, as well as nursing, education, rehabilitation, and others. In a sense, neuropsychology cuts across all of these areas and provides a uniting framework for communication about the function and dysfunction of an individual. Neuropsychology can forge a connection between the scientist and clinician, as well as the physician and educator, by providing an integrative perspective on brain and behavior.

A fundamental assumption of NA is that human performance, not easily attributed to environmental factors, must reflect the integrity of the nervous system. Specific and general problems in the nervous system reveal themselves in behavioral performance, sometimes in subtle and other times gross ways. By knowing what the normal nervous system is capable of, within a range of individual variation, the neuropsychologist has a template with which to compare test performances. Not only does this comparison allow a determination of good versus poor nervous system function, but it should provide information about the type of problem, its location, severity, velocity, and what can be done to maximize behavioral functioning despite a CNS problem.

A hallmark of NA is that it is a comprehensive form of human performance assessment. Unlike aptitude testing or educational assessment, which are focused on certain aspects of performance, neuropsychological assessment attempts to cast a wide net across all types of human behavior. Consequently, most neuropsychological approaches involve a large number of brief tests and tasks aimed at eliciting numerous behaviors that reflect the integrity of all aspects of the nervous system. Neuropsychological batteries are known for their breadth. A neuropsychologist will not spend a half-hour administering one test, but, rather, gives brief simple tasks to observe whether patients can or cannot perform them. Many of the tests are designed to yield dichotomous (i.e., impaired versus not impaired) rather than continuous data. In this way neuropsychologists can more efficiently address a wide array of human performances that correspond to our knowledge of brain structure and function.

Uses of Neuropsychological Assessment

Neuropsychological assessment is used in a wide variety of ways. In addition to clinical purposes, NA is frequently found in research settings. Assessment batteries are routinely given to patients in medical and research centers to build the empirical knowledge base, refine the tests and interpretations, and develop new and better techniques. Research contributes to neuropsychological descriptions of various clinical subgroups (i.e., attention-deficit hyperactivity disorder, traumatic brain injury, autoimmune deficiency syndrome, Tourette's syndrome, etc.). NA research, coupled with medical and neuroscience knowledge, forms a strong union of rapidly growing information about the organism and its behavioral repertoire. NA research also contributes to the overall effort to build a sound theoretical model of brain organization and function.

When it comes to clinical use, NA may be employed for a variety of reasons. In some cases, NA may be used for differential diagnosis or in supplementing a given diagnosis. As neuroradiologic devices improved, reliance on NA declined, particularly with respect to localizing lesions. Instead, NA has become useful in cases that do not have positive findings on imaging tests, yet may demonstrate behavioral changes (e.g., early Alzheimer's, mild head injury, learning disabilities, brain toxicity). NA appears to be sensitive to brain dysfunction that may result from genetic, chemical, or other abnormalities not routinely detectable by neurometric tests.

Besides diagnosis, NA provides a comprehensive description of an individual's human abilities. This quantified profile of human abilities can be used in a variety of ways. For example, one could use the profile as a baseline of function before treatment such as surgery or medication is initiated, and then compare that profile with one taken posttreatment. Another use of the profile would be an analysis of an individual's strengths and weaknesses. Such analysis would help with patient management, whether involving decisions about vocation, education, daily living, or emotional well-being. Clearly, there is more to neurologic diagnosis than discovering merely what or where the problem is. Neuropsychologists are interested particularly in patients' behavioral functioning regardless of their impairment and medical treatment. Many neuropsychologists favor a "strength" approach in which interventions and programming are geared toward healthy brain systems, thereby emphasizing what works for the individual rather than what is not working.

Strengths and Weaknesses of Neuropsychological Assessment

Neuropsychologists can use NA in the diagnosis and management of individual patients, whether in making preliminary diagnoses, referring to neurologists, assisting surgeons with brain–behavior information, or using a comprehensive profile for purposes of treatment management. Further, NA can be used to monitor patient progress after stroke, trauma or surgery, or over the course of treatment (i.e., medication or cognitive rehabilitation). NA information is, perhaps, best utilized by those seeking a thorough picture of a person's abilities as a reflection of one's neurological integrity.

Although NA has its benefits, it certainly is not useful or necessary for every child with a disorder. Among its shortcomings is the length of time that a comprehensive assessment takes, anywhere from three to eight hours of testing. Such an investment of professional time (and cost) is not always warranted and must be weighed for each potential referral. Another problem with NA is the shortage of qualified professionals to perform such assessment. Gradually, training programs have come closer to meeting the needs in most areas of the country, such that most families can get to a geographical location served by a psychologist with neuropsychological training.

Beyond these pragmatic considerations, there are problems associated with NA as an applied behavioral science. Any clinical work with patients is complicated by bias and error associated with the methods employed, individual variation of patients, and variability among clinicians. Many of the psychometric caveats and considerations described in Chapter 2 of this volume apply to NA, particularly the concerns about bias, error, validity, and reliability. A greater problem is that the state of the art in neuropsychology requires the clinician to make interpretations that are inferential and based on limited knowledge. The difficulty with validity in testing is made even more apparent when applying NA to children. In this case, test error is increased, knowledge is more limited, developmental variation is an added factor, and poor test performances are not unique to neurologic etiology as motivational, developmental, and situational factors may be responsible for observed behavioral disturbances.

Variation among subjects occurs not only in one's test performances on a given day, but also as a result of individual differences in brain structure and organization. Research demonstrates that these differences may be related to such factors as age, gender, handedness, intelligence, brain plasticity following an insult, as well as natural or genetic variation. Because every person has a slightly different brain structure and very different environmental experiences, the neuropsychologist cannot apply one set of assumptions about brain structure and function to all test takers. For example, not all persons have the same degree of left-hemisphere language specialization (Springer & Deutsch, 1989), and young children appear to be less functionally specialized and, perhaps, more functionally plastic than adults (Spreen, Tupper, Risser, Tuokko, & Edgell, 1984). These differences make it difficult and risky for neuropsychologists to make inferences from test data about the brain location(s) of impairment.

Components and Adjuncts of Neuropsychological Assessment

There is no single accepted method of neuropsychological assessment. NA is best viewed as a comprehensive assessment following a brain–behavior model. It involves some of the same ingredients as other assessment approaches, but it also has some unique features. The basic components of a neuropsychological assessment are listed below, along with some of the issues addressed by each component.

Referral.   Before one expends hours of time and effort, one should ensure NA is appropriate. Is there a likelihood or strong suspicion of CNS dysfunction? Could NA offer new information for treatment purposes? Ask why now, why is NA being sought at this time? Clarifying the referral question helps target the assessment and determines if it is necessary.

Record review.   Some assessment approaches do not thoroughly review birth, medical, and developmental background. Any medical or physical problems should be carefully examined. There may be a link between current functioning and prior health problems that are pertinent to the assessment. Also, if a child has longstanding CNS dysfunction, one would want to review functioning over that period of time. If a child has an acute disorder, the record review helps determine "premorbid" functioning.

Patient interview.   Interviews can be an excellent source of assessment information, as discussed more fully in Chapter 5. Those with CNS dysfunction may have apparent sensory or motor problems, as well as difficulties with language, memory, speed of processing, and interpersonal behavior. In addition to these observations at the interview, one can obtain the patient's own version of difficulties and ascertain their significance in the patient's everyday life.

Patient history.   A history is crucial to understanding a child's past and present functioning, particularly any significant changes in behavior related to brain trauma. Is the person engaged in age-appropriate activities, successful in chosen endeavors, able to maintain friendships, and meeting developmental milestones? Or, might the individual be delayed in some areas, impeded in some activities, less competent than peers, and showing a pattern of deficit consistent with CNS compromise?

Family interview.   Family members provide unique information and perspectives, especially for children. They may be able to render more accurate descriptions of a child's behavior and difficulties, and they can comment on the effects the child's condition may have on the family. Of course, family history can be critical in differential diagnosis for certain disorders.

Screening tests.   Rather than embark on a six-hour assessment, some psychologists prefer to begin with sensitive screening measures. These are usually very brief tests or tasks that indicate the likelihood of organic impairment or suggest the need for further neuropsychological assessment.

Neurologic soft sign testing.   This testing is generally the domain of the neurologist. Some trained neuropsychologists may test cranial nerve function informally, as well as neuromuscular integrity and basic cognitive functions. These test results can be helpful in diagnosis and deciding whether or not to refer to a neurologist. Such information gives the clinician a more global picture of the CNS, rather than just examining higher cortical functions.

Neuropsychological testing.   This is the crux of the assessment process. As will be discussed later, one can employ a fixed neuropsychological battery, supplement a fixed battery, or, essentially, design one's own test battery. The battery employed depends on the symptoms of each patient, as well as the testing preferences of the clinician. Consequently, neuropsychological assessments across patients are seldom comprised of identical test batteries.

Cognitive testing.   Typically the Wechsler scales are administered along with the test battery. Research has shown this series of tests to be useful in the delineation of cognitive strengths and weaknesses in persons with CNS compromise. Cognitive ability test profiles from Wechsler or other such tests are used in the overall interpretation to determine the presence, extent, and location of brain impairment, as well as the resources a person has for compensation.

Adjuncts.   Depending on the case and testing already available, an evaluation may include achievement, adaptive, or psychosocial testing. These areas of testing help determine how widespread the effects of CNS dysfunction are.

Most neuropsychological test batteries include a large number of separate psychological tests. These tests vary in nature and purpose, with the overall intent to sample as wide a variety as possible of human functioning, particularly as it reflects different parts of the nervous system. Some batteries of tests are predetermined and fixed so that the clinician does not deviate from the battery content or procedures unless to supplement the battery with certain preferred tests (e.g., Reitan approach). Other batteries are more flexible in that the clinician has tests available for assessing various functions generally and specifically (e.g., Luria approach). The clinician makes decisions about test usage as the assessment proceeds based on subject performance and the hypotheses formed by the examiner. The examiner continues to test hypotheses until a reasonably clear diagnostic impression emerges. In the selection of tests, neuropsychologists no longer necessarily look for the most sensitive tests of brain damage. Rather, they are interested in selecting tests that yield information about particular syndromes, brain structures, or functional systems (Luria, 1973). These and other approaches are described in more detail a bit later.

Neuropsychological tests are purposely varied with some assessing simple, discrete behaviors and others quite complex, some verbal and others nonverbal, some sensory–motor and others perceptual or cognitive. The purpose of so many diverse brief tests is to obtain broad coverage of neurological functioning, and then to determine whether a function is or is not working.

Neuropsychological Assessment of Children

The forms of adult neuropsychological assessment have changed over the past decade. With the rapid advances of medical technology, particularly computerized tomography and magnetic resonance imaging (MRI), the actual documentation of neuropathology has become much more accurate. Neurologists and neuroradiologists are better equipped to determine the presence and location of a brain lesion. Consequently the neuropsychologist plays a lesser role in "lesion hunting" and a greater role in patient management. It is the neuropsychologist's task to delineate the current functional profile of a patient so that the patient and family have a thorough understanding of what the patient can or cannot do and what rehabilitation should be considered. Of course, there are other issues the neuropsychologist may address, depending on the case, but this scenario is the most common.

Child NA, on the other hand, calls for a slightly different philosophy and approach. Many neurologically-based childhood disorders, such as autism, cerebral palsy, and dyslexia do not have a specified and documented site of brain damage. The neurological deficiency is inferred from a set of symptoms, neurological soft signs, and perhaps an abnormal electroencephalogram (EEG). The child neuropsychologist cannot usually talk in terms of the location or amount of brain damage incurred, and cannot reliably predict which parts of the brain are working efficiently. Instead, the child neuropsychologist must be able to compare children suspected of brain dysfunction with what he or she knows about normal development and about children known to be neurologically compromised who presented with the same symptom picture. In making these comparisons, the neuropsychologist attempts to describe the neuropsychological functioning of the child across all areas of performance and behavior (i.e., acquiring information, analyzing it, and acting on it). Thus, neuropsychological assessment of children involves a wide array of sensory, motor, perceptual, language, memory and problem-solving tests.

An attempt is made in this testing to examine comprehensively the child's neurological integrity as reflected in the child's behavior. Depending on the age of the child, this process may include: (a) a neurodevelopmental examination of reflexes, cranial nerves, gross sensory and motor abilities, balance and coordination, and so on; (b) a test of general mental functioning such as the *Wechsler Intelligence Scale for Children-III*; (c) tests of learning ability in reading, writing, math, and so forth; (d) tests of sensory and motor functioning such as manual speed and dexterity or discrimination of objects by touch; (e) tests of visual and auditory perception; (f) tests of language, memory, problem solving, and other higher level functions as appropriate; and (g) assessment of adaptive, social, and emotional behavior.

Neuropsychological assessment of children attempts to generate a comprehensive profile of a given child's functioning. Because there are some lawful neurological principles that apply to children, it is believed that NA is grounded in scientific reality. If approached from a point of view such as Luria's (1973), NA has theoretical guidelines for its use and application. Given this backdrop and a rich bank of research on the neuropsychological problems of children, NA is becoming a popular vehicle for better understanding the functioning of neurologically involved children.

Neurodevelopmental Issues

Based on present knowledge, it appears that the central nervous system develops in a systematic and even lawful manner for most individuals. We have been able to delineate the time course of CNS development in the fetus and are continuing to make progress in determining how the CNS unfolds after birth. Our knowledge of brain development is somewhat like an incomplete picture or puzzle. We have some of the pieces in place and then we mentally fill in the gaps and guess what the entire picture looks like. Even though early brain development is still much of a puzzle to everyone, let us attempt to draw a crude picture, which at least serves to spur critical thinking on this subject.

When children are born, their brains may be intact, but they are far from fully functioning. It takes time for maturation and experience to work their wonders and convert an infant into a talking, walking, functioning adult. During this time the brain changes, first rapidly, and later subtly and more slowly.

The specialization of pediatric neuropsychology is a relatively recent development. It came about due to the growing realization that adult and child neurobehavior differed in many significant ways, necessitating different methods of diagnosis and treatment. The issue of rapid and malleable brain development in children versus a less plastic, more specialized adult brain also made professionals reexamine the field of child neuropsychology as more than a downward extension of adult neuropsychology. Gradually, the need for a stronger developmental focus with children took hold, and with it came the need to determine brain–behavior relationships in children across ages and types of CNS disorders. Consequently, different testing procedures and separate databases were necessary for neuropsychological assessment of children (see Hynd & Willis, 1988; Tromontana & Hooper, 1989). Over the past 15 years these needs slowly have been addressed. Neuropsychological test batteries now exist for children, and numerous research studies on clinical subgroups of children have been performed (see Hynd & Willis, 1988; Rourke, 1989). Despite these clinical strides and advances in neuroscience and cognitive science, there is still an incomplete understanding of how the brain works in the able or disabled child.

Over the past ten years a better appreciation has developed for ways in which the young brain differs from the adult brain. The CNS of a child proceeds through active phases of maturation. The development of brain structures and organization over time means that brain function can evolve only in concert with the developing brain organ. In other words, behavioral functioning in children is limited by the rate of maturation of the neural equipment that subserves behavior and the environmental experiences needed to operate the equipment. Thus, insults of various types and degrees and at various times during development can cause a wide range of neuropsychological deficits. In children, the neuropathology most often encountered is congenital, diffuse, and static, as opposed to the acquired, often focal and progressive, forms of pathology sustained by adults (Spreen et al., 1984; Tromontana & Hooper, 1989). Because brain insults are present so early, the child is in a position to recover function after an injury in order to develop functions (i.e., motor, speech, and cognitive functions). Another feature of these early diffuse insults is that they may be genetic, biochemical, organizational, or even electrical in nature and leave no structural evidence of brain damage, such as the destroyed tissue found associated with many adult pathologies. Thus, with children who have soft neurological signs, EEG abnormalities, neuropsychological deficits, and learning problems, one might infer some type of brain "disturbance or dysfunction" rather than damage, disease, or injury per se (Spreen et al., 1984).

Another characteristic of early brain impairment is that the small and vulnerable brain encounters pervasive insults (i.e., anoxia, hemorrhage, hydrocephalus, etc.) rather than the localized pathology found more frequently in adults (i.e., stroke, tumor, Parkinson's Disease, etc.). These diffuse types of pathology in a brain that may be relatively plastic (less specialized) in function can result in a child with a potpourri of physical, behavioral, and neuropsychological symptoms that change with age and fit no particular pattern or syndrome. One cannot assume that a child with early brain compromise will have typical brain development and organization from that point onward. That is, the child may not be right-hand dominant or left-hemisphere specialized for language processes like most individuals. Any preprogrammed brain specialization (if there is such a blueprint) may be altered in its functional representation.

Clearly, the child's brain differs from the adult brain physically, developmentally, and functionally. Clinical research data on impaired and unimpaired groups of youngsters help the neuropsychologist make comparisons and tease out developmental, neurological, and psychological deviations from normality. Testing must be able to measure reliably these deviations and enable the clinician to build hypotheses as to the brain systems that are efficient and deficient. Knowledge of the characteristics and outcomes of different types of disorders helps the clinician interpret test information and develop a management plan for the child. Because the brain of the child is dynamic, plastic, and immature, long-term plans and predictions typically are not appropriate. Changes in function are monitored closely via repeated neuropsychological testing to assess the degree of change from baseline indications, as well as neurologic and radiologic examinations, if necessary. Treatment recommendations for children usually involve family and personal interventions as well as special educational programs. This is not only the case for children with learning disabilities, but for all children with CNS compromise.

There are certain developmental considerations worth mentioning specifically for children with learning disorders. Usually, these children have no known or proven form of brain pathology. Many people infer a brain etiology for learning disabilities and this is often supported by neuropsychological test results. Whether or not one believes with confidence in a brain explanation for learning disabilities, there are certain neuropsychological phenomena that have been observed repeatedly in this population (see Golden, 1981).

The child with subtle early CNS compromise has no apparent learning problems at birth or, perhaps, in preschool. However, if one examines large numbers of records from children with mild neurological impairments or learning disabilities, one finds the following manifestations of CNS compromise across development. During the infancy period, the reported problems consist of deviations in arousal, activity level, attention, temperament, sensory responsiveness, and muscle tone (Bayley, 1969; Gesell & Armatruda, 1941). Interestingly, these are the basic functions that the young nervous system is trying to regulate and master. The compromised CNS has difficulty mastering these somewhat elementary, yet developmentally important, functions. It is likely that less than complete mastery of these functions will hinder progress of the individual throughout the developmental period (Birch, 1964).

By the age of 6 to 24 months, motor activities and skills take on greater importance. The compromised children tend to have delayed motor milestones, inadequate neuromuscular integrity, and uncoordinated fine and gross motor function. Again, at a period when these functions (motor and physical mastery) are preeminent, the compromised child's nervous system seems overtaxed and unable to smoothly handle this phase of neurodevelopment (Gesell & Armatruda, 1941).

Between 2 and 4 years of age, the typical child is rapidly advancing in language skills. At this same age, psychologists and therapists receive reports on the compromised child concerning speech delay, articulation problems, phonologic disorders, dysfluency, and developmental language disorders. Once again, the functions that are developmentally most important are not performed well or easily automatized by the child with compromised CNS function. These may be related to underlying auditory processing problems (i.e., poor phonetic ability), a common accompaniment of learning disabilities (Blachman, 1997; Liberman & Shankweiler, 1985).

During the period between 4 and 6 years of age, there are increased reports of perceptual–motor problems (Ilg & Ames, 1965). This is not to say that the compromised child has overcome the problems mentioned earlier. In some children the various manifestations of poor CNS integrity are cumulative, whereas others may show only one or two manifestations. Therefore, the 5- or 6-year-old child may exhibit problems with attention, overactivity, speech delays, and now is unable to draw, build, cut on a line, print letters, or perform visual–motor tasks with ease. Because the child is often in a school setting by this time, there is usually someone who raises concern. It is no wonder that early explanations for learning disabilities were based on perceptual–motor difficulties observed initially in school (Hallahan & Cruickshank, 1973).

Between the ages of 7 and 12 years (the elementary school ages), children with compromised CNS functions experience academic and learning problems. These problems usually involve some deficient linguistic process and most often affect reading and writing (deHirsch, 1968; Orton, 1937). As the child advances in age, the academic and learning manifestations of the CNS compromise become most salient, while attentional, motor, and perceptual deficiencies become less pronounced or noticed. Frequently, the academic problems are joined by behavioral difficulties and social skill deficits that may render the compromised individual "at risk" for vocational, social, and psychological adjustment difficulties (see Ceci, 1986).

The manifestations of early CNS compromise are far different from the effects of brain disease in an older adult. This brief developmental overview highlights the changing manifestations of neurologic compromise in children. Neurodevelopmental patterns play a major role in helping professionals reach a clear understanding of learning disorders. Thus, the pediatric neuropsychologist needs to operate with a different knowledge base, different testing purposes and procedures, and an awareness of how neuropsychological information can assist the youngster with a compromised nervous system.

Brain-Based Pediatric Disorders

Many children suffer from brain-related disorders that are either congenital or acquired. Conditions such as cerebral palsy, epilepsy, encephalitis, pediatric autoimmune deficiency syndrome, brain tumors, hydrocephalus, traumatic brain injury, and many more place children at risk for cognitive, sensory, motor, academic, social, and emotional difficulties. In order to assess such a broad array of functions, and, at the same time, the integrity of the nervous system, a comprehensive neuropsychological assessment is warranted.

In addition to cases of known brain dysfunction, there are conditions considered to be "suspicious" with regard to nervous system dysfunction. Research has shown that childhood disorders such as autism, learning disabilities (LD), depression, and attention-deficit hyperactivity disorder (ADHD) have neurobiological bases. Behavioral symptomology associated with these disorders is frequently a result of dysfunction in the nervous system, resulting in a functional impairment of skills.

In many disorders of childhood, neuropsychological dysfunction manifests, in some form, throughout development. Research has shown that neurodevelopmental precursors often occur early in life in children with disorders such as cerebral palsy, LD, and autism. Individual variability exists across children and, in effect, common symptomology signaling specific pathological outcomes has been elusive. For example, despite the fact that children with learning disabilities have been found to exhibit a greater number of neurodevelopmental delays across domains, not all children with LD exhibit such impairment in early development. Additionally, the nature of the impairments identified in early development varies across children (Blumsack, Lewandowski, & Waterman, 1997). Thus, outcome prediction and classification based on early symptomology is not feasible for all disorders of childhood.

Just as the emergence of neurodevelopmental precursors varies from child to child, children with a specific disorder may exhibit impairment in more than one domain of functioning. An autistic child, for example, may have deficits in motor, language, social perception, and self-monitoring skills, or any combination of these areas. In order to diagnose effectively and treat childhood disorders, it is essential to conduct thorough assessments that yield information that is useful to design and implement individualized interventions. In addition to the variability in functional deficits across children with a common disorder, comorbidity often is associated with childhood disorders (e.g., LD, autism, ADHD). Thus, impairment may be more pervasive or more severe due to the presence of comorbid disorders. Given the potential for dysfunction across domains of functioning, neuropsychological assessment is best conducted across domains in order to assess the pervasiveness of dysfunction (as well as intact functioning) and describe children fully.

Recent advances in neuroimaging technology enable researchers to look farther into the origins of pathology than ever before. For the first time, functional as well as structural differences have been discovered in the brains of individuals with a variety of different disorders. To date, such technology has yielded only preliminary findings and currently offers severely limited utility as a diagnostic tool. Despite this lack of diagnostic utility per se, neuroimaging research provides insight into the biological roots of disorders and, in effect, informs some assessment and intervention practices.

Traumatic brain injury (TBI).   Each year a substantial number of children and adolescents suffer a head injury as the result of a vehicular accident, recreational activity, child abuse, and other causes. Consequently, there are millions of school-age students who have incurred mild to severe traumatic brain injuries. Some cases may show selective impairment based on the location and extent of brain injury. However, many TBIs involve general or diffuse brain dysfunction. Frequently, the injuries are followed by difficulties with attention and concentration, memory, speed of processing, and sustained mental effort on tasks. Typically, the brain reorganizes and functioning improves over time, an effect that is more pronounced among younger children. NA can be useful to document functional loss and return of function as well as targeting rehabilitation needs.

Attention-deficit hyperactivity disorder (ADHD).   A pattern of neuropsychological deficits has been identified in children with ADHD that implicates executive dysfunction as the primary impairment (Barkley, 1997; Farone & Beiderman, 1998; Tannock, 1998). Similar patterns of dysfunction occur in adults with frontal lobe lesions, indicating that ADHD may be due, in part, to structural or functional differences in frontal areas of the brain (Mattes, 1980). The relationship between frontal lobe dysfunction and ADHD was first proposed in the early 1970s (Satterfield & Dawson, 1971). Although the proposed relationship was theoretically sound, in the 1970s our ability to observe such neurologically-based dysfunction was severely limited. Studies designed to evaluate the action of stimulant medications provided further evidence for the involvement of the frontal system in ADHD. Preliminary neuroimaging studies found differences in fronto-striatal networks of the brain, thus corroborating previously speculative theory regarding frontal lobe dysfunction in ADHD

(Himelstein, Newcorn, & Halperin, 2000; Narbona-Garcia & Sanchez-Carpinter, 1999). Functional MRI research determined that these areas of the brain respond differently to stimulant medications in individuals with ADHD than do the brains of control subjects (Vaidya et al., 1998). Additionally, functional MRI studies revealed subnormal activation of the prefrontal systems of the brain responsible for higher-order motor control in ADHD adolescents (Rubia et al., 1999).

Behavioral ratings of symptoms indicative of executive dysfunction revealed differences between individuals with and without diagnoses of ADHD. Researchers suggested that the capacity to inhibit behavior, self-monitor, and to maintain a sense of self across time (Barkley, 1997) may be causal factors in the behavioral symptomatology associated with ADHD. Thus, assessment of children suspected of having ADHD must include measures of executive function as an integral component of the evaluation process. (Further discussion related to ADHD is provided in Chapter 15 of this volume.)

Learning disabilities (LD). Individuals with learning disabilities such as dyslexia and dyscalculia have been shown to differ in brain structure and function from nondisabled peers. Dyslexia and dyscalculia have been linked to lesions in the left and right hemisphere of the brain, respectively (Levin et al., 1996). These findings indicate that LD may be acquired following cerebral insult due to compensatory reorganization of neural systems. Approximately 93% of all adults are right-handed and a slightly higher percentage have language represented in the left hemisphere of the brain. Additionally, the brains of children with dyslexia were found to have reduced asymmetry in the left planum temporal (Hugdahl et al., 1998). Functional neuroimaging studies found that individuals with dyslexia show abnormally enhanced activation in the right hemisphere of the brain during reading tasks (Price et al., 1998). Similarly, brain-based differences emerged in persons with nonverbal learning disabilities. Neuroimaging research is ongoing in the field and continues to provide insight into the neurobiological basis of LD.

Autism. Although research into the neurobiology of autism has failed to locate conclusively the structural or functional abnormalities associated with the disorder, a number of studies have found isolated abnormalities in cerebral functioning. Functional MRI studies found an imbalance in interregional and interhemispheric blood flow as well as abnormality in the cingulate gyrus (Deb & Thompson, 1998). Additionally, structural abnormalities recently have been found to co-occur in the frontal lobe and cerebellum in a subset of autistic children (Carper & Courchesne, 2000). Despite the promising nature of the aforementioned findings, the body of evidence supporting the existence of a biological basis for autism is currently inconclusive.

Affective disorders. Positron emission tomography (PET) research has indicated abnormalities in the prefrontal, cingulate, and amygdala structures of the brain in individuals with mood disorders (Kennedy, Javanmard, & Vaccarino, 1997).

Neuroimaging research identified volumetric differences in the brains of depressed individuals (Dougherty & Rauch, 1997), as compared to nondepressed individuals. People with unipolar depression have been found to have a smaller frontal lobe, cerebellum, caudate, and putamen. Additionally, unipolar depression has been linked with an increased rate of white matter and periventricular hypertensities (Soares & Mann, 1997). Researchers also have found decreases in blood flow in the medial temporal lobes, left prefrontal cortex, and caudate with increasing severity of symptoms (Teneback et al., 1999). Individuals with bipolar disorder have been shown to have a larger third ventricle than controls, as well as a smaller cerebellum and temporal lobe (Soares & Mann, 1997). Similar functional abnormalities have been associated with anxiety disorders. For example, individuals who suffer from panic disorder have a high frequency of abnormal EEG and MRI scans (Dantendorfer et al., 1996). In conclusion, both structural and functional abnormalities have been linked to mood disorders and anxiety disorders.

Conclusion

The examples cited above indicate some of the neurobiological correlates of some common disorders often observed among school-aged children. There are many other childhood conditions that involve CNS dysfunction. These examples serve to illustrate the potential relevance of neuropsychology to the understanding of childhood disorders.

The remainder of this chapter presents a case study. The problems presented and the test batteries employed were selected in response to the symptomatology presented by this particular individual. The case includes brief background information, observations, and test performances that are explained and interpreted. Most importantly, there is an attempt to integrate the information such that the analysis reveals a thorough profile of the child's functioning from a neurobehavioral perspective. The recommendations offered illustrate the highly individualized nature of NA and its implications. It is crucial to bear in mind that there is no one standard set of tests to apply to children. Thus, the case study serves merely as one illustration, not as a prototype of neuropsychological deficits as generally observed and assessed among children. Those seeking information about specific neuropsychological children's batteries may wish to refer to specific authors for other case examples (e.g., Golden, 1981; Reitan & Wolfson 1985).

Case Study

Background. Jason is a 15-year-old adolescent who is experiencing academic and social difficulties. As a youngster he was diagnosed with "suspected" mild cerebral palsy, possible ADHD, and speech difficulties. In third grade he was tested by the school psychologist who found a Verbal IQ 40 points greater than the Performance IQ. Jason was designated as a student with a learning disability and he began receiving resource services for writing. Throughout school he has struggled with writing, some aspects of math, motor skills, and interpersonal relations. A neuropsychological evaluation was requested to get a more comprehensive picture of Jason's strengths and weaknesses.

Observations. Jason is a tall, soft-spoken young man who is polite and easy to test. He worked for long periods without wanting a break. Jason's speech was clear and articulate. He showed no signs of impulsiveness or hyperactivity, and displayed no unusual behavior. His dream is to play competitive basketball in high school and beyond, but he is considered a "project" by the coach because of his poor motor coordination. This was observed in the clinic as Jason stumbled and bumped into walls and objects as he walked.

Results.

Wechsler Intelligence Scale for Children-III

Verbal IQ	111
Performance IQ	71
Full Scale IQ	90

Wechsler Individual Achievement Test

Basic Reading	108
Math Reasoning	126
Spelling	114
Written Expression	73

Halstead Reitan Neuropsychological Battery

Category Test	*Poor performance*
Finger Tapping Test	*Low scores R & L hands*
Trail Making Test A	*Slow performance*
Trail Making Test B	*Within normal limits*
Tactual Performance Test	*LH slow performance*
Memory	*Poor*
Location	*Poor*
Embedded Figures Test	*Poor*
Benton Visual Retention Test	*Poor*
Hooper Visual Organization Test	*Poor*
Finger Agnosia	*Poor R & L*
Aphasia Battery	*Within normal limits*
Seashore Rhythm Test	*Within normal limits*
Grip Strength	*Within normal limits*

Recommendations. The results of the evaluation seem to fit the profile of a "nonverbal learning disability" (NLD). Jason experiences cognitive problems with visual–spatial tasks, such as those involving drawing, constructing, writing, organizing, and imaging. In addition, he has difficulty moving his body in space with efficiency. This could be related to his problems with visual–spatial analysis. Motor planning and fine motor control also are problematic for Jason. His biggest academic challenge is writing, both its organization and manual aspects. Reported difficulties in social relationships (i.e., misperceiving gestures and facial expressions, misreading situations) also contribute to a pattern consistent with NLD. The neuropsychological findings suggest that right cerebral hemisphere functions are relatively less efficient than left-hemisphere functions. A "strength approach" would suggest that academic and vocational decisions should capitalize on strengths in language and reading ability while compensating for problems with spatial analysis and motor coordination.

1. Jason continues to need resource support for written expression, and should retain his designation as a student with a learning disability.

(continued)

Case Study *continued*

2. Jason will benefit from test modifications and accommodations. The school should provide extended time for writing tasks and written exams (up to double time is sufficient). The use of bubble sheets should be avoided given Jason's problems with visual–spatial processing and poor eye–hand coordination.

3. Jason may find that for lengthy writing assignments "voice recognition" software is helpful to dictate essays to the computer. Studies show that dictation increases the output of students with LD and allows them to share their ideas more fully. The problem with such a system is the lack of accuracy of voice recognition and the need for editing.

4. Based on the test profile, it makes sense to rely on verbal and sequential approaches to instructional delivery. Teachers and specialists will need to provide learning strategies and curriculum modifications for tasks that involve visual imaging, construction, and spatial organization, such as art projects, geometry, physics, technology, and physical education.

5. Jason's involvement in sports seems to be good for his physical development and self-esteem. These and other efforts to increase fine and gross motor coordination should be continued.

6. It is suggested that Jason have a "walking IEP" that summarizes his learning strengths and weaknesses, curriculum modifications, and test accommodation needs for each class.

7. Jason is struggling with social development, self-esteem, and interpersonal relationships. His nonverbal learning disability and motor coordination impact his ability to be successful in some social situations, and that, in turn, affects his self-concept. Counseling may be useful at this time so that Jason better understands and copes with all aspects of his disability.

8. Next year, Jason and his family will give serious consideration to college and vocational school choices. Decisions about the type of school and educational program should be mindful of Jason's nonverbal learning disability and the pattern of strengths and weaknesses noted in the test profile.

References

Barkley, R. (1997). Behavioral inhibition, sustained attention, and executive functions: Constructing a unified theory of ADHD. *Psychological Bulletin, 121*, 65–94.

Bayley, N. (1969). *Bayley scales of infant development: Birth to two years.* San Antonio, TX: The Psychological Corporation.

Birch, H. G. (1964). *Brain damage in children.* Baltimore, MD: Williams and Wilkins.

Blachman, B. (1997). *Foundations of reading acquisition and dyslexia: Implications for early intervention.* Mahwah, NJ: Erlbaum.

Blumsack, J., Lewandowski, L., & Waterman, B. (1997). Neurodevelopmental precursors to learning disabilities: A preliminary report from a parent survey. *Journal of Learning Disabilities, 30*, 228–237.

Carper, R. A., & Courchesne, E. (2000). Inverse correlation between frontal lobe and cerebellum sizes in children with autism. *Brain, 123*, 836–844.

Ceci, S. J. (1986). *Handbook of cognitive, social, and neuropsychological aspects of learning disabilities* (Vol. 2). Hillsdale, NJ: Erlbaum.

Dantendorfer, K., Prayer, D., Kramer, J., Amering, M., Baischer, W., Schoder, M., Steinberger, K.,

Windhaber, J., Imhof, H., & Katschnig, H. (1996). High frequency of EEG and MRI brain abnormalities in panic disorder. *Psychiatry Research, 68,* 41–53.

Deb, S., & Thompson, B. (1998). Neuroimaging in autism. *British Journal of Psychiatry, 173,* 299–302.

deHirsch, K. (1968). Clinical spectrum of reading disabilities: Diagnosis and treatment. *Bulletin of the New York Academy of Medicine, Series 2, 44,* 470–477.

Dougherty, D., & Rauch, S. L. (1997). Neuroimaging and neurobiological models of depression. *Harvard Review of Psychiatry, 5,* 138–159.

Farone, S. V., & Biederman, J. (1998). Neurobiology of attention deficit hyperactivity disorder. *Biological Psychiatry, 44,* 951–958.

Gesell, A. (1940). *The first five years of life.* New York: Harper & Row.

Gesell, A., & Armatruda, C. S. (1941). *Developmental diagnosis.* New York: Hoeber.

Golden, C. J. (1981). The Luria Nebraska Children's Battery: Theory and formulation. In G. W. Hynd & J. E. Obrzut (Eds.), *Neuropsychological assessment in the school-age child* (pp. 277–302). New York: Grune & Stratton.

Hallahan, D. P., & Cruickshank, W. M. (1973). *Psychoeducational foundations of learning disabilities.* Englewood Cliffs, NJ: Prentice-Hall.

Himelstein, J., Newcorn, J. H., & Halperin, J. M. (2000). The neurobiology of ADHD. *Frontiers in Bioscience, 5,* 461–478.

Hugdahl, K., Heiervang, E., Nordby, H., Smievoll, A. I., Steinmetz, H., Stevenson, J., & Lund, A. (1998). Central auditory processing, MRI morphometry and brain laterality: Applications to dyslexia. *Scandinavian Audiology Supplement, 49,* 26–34.

Hynd, G. W., & Willis, W. G. (1988). *Pediatric neuropsychology.* New York: Grune & Stratton.

Ilg, L., & Ames, L. B. (1965). *School readiness: Behavior tests used at the Gesell Institute.* New York: Harper & Row.

Kennedy, S. H., Javanmard, M., & Vaccarino, F. J. (1997). A review of functional neuroimaging in mood disorders: Positron emission tomography and depression. *Canadian Journal of Psychiatry, 42,* D467–475.

Levin, H. S., Scheller, J., Rickard, T., Grafman, J., Martinowski, K., Winslow, M., & Mirvis, S. (1996). Dyscalculia and dyslexia after right hemisphere injury in infancy. *Archives of Neurology, 53,* 88–96.

Lezak, M. (1996). *Neuropsychological assessment.* New York: Oxford University Press.

Liberman, I. Y., & Shankweiler, D. (1985). Phonology and the problems of learning to read and write. *Remedial and Special Education, 6,* 8–17.

Luria, A. (1973). *The working brain.* New York: Basic Books.

Mattes, J. A. (1980). The role of frontal lobe dysfunction in childhood hyperkinesis. *Comprehensive Psychiatry, 21,* 358–369.

MTA Cooperative Group. (1999). A 14–month randomized clinical trial of treatment strategies for attention deficit hyperactivity disorder. *Archives of General Psychiatry, 56,* 1073–1086.

Narbona-Garcia, J., & Sanchez-Carpinter, O. R. (1999). The neurobiology of ADHD. *Review of Neurology, 28,* S160–164.

Orton, S. T. (1937). *Reading, writing, and speech problems in children.* New York: Norton.

Price, C. J., Howard, D., Patterson, K., Warburton, E. A., Friston, K. J., & Frackowiak, S. J. (1998). A functional neuroimaging description of two deep dyslexic patients. *Journal of Cognitive Neuroscience, 10,* 303–315.

Reitan, R. M., & Wolfson, D. (1985). *The Halstead Reitan Neuropsychological Test Battery: Theory and applications.* Tucson, AZ: Neuropsychology Press.

Rourke, B. P. (1989). *Nonverbal learning disabilities.* New York: Guilford Press.

Rubia, K., Overmeyer, S., Taylor, E., Brammer, M., Williams, S. C., Simmons, A., & Bullmore, E. T. (1999). Hypofrontality in attention deficit hyperactivity disorder during higher order motor control: A study with functional MRI. *American Journal of Psychiatry, 156,* 891–896.

Satterfield, J. H., & Dawson, M. E. (1971). Electrodermal correlates of hyperactivity in children. *Psychophysiology, 8,* 191–197.

Soares, J. C., & Mann, J. J. (1997). The anatomy of mood disorders—review of structural neuroimaging studies. *Biological Psychiatry, 41,* 86–106.

Solanto, M. V. (1998). Neuropsychopharmacological mechanisms of stimulant drug action in attention-deficit hyperactivity disorder: A review and integration. *Behavioural Brain Research, 94,* 127–152.

Spreen, O., Tupper, D., Risser, A., Tuokko, H., & Edgell, D. (1984). *Human developmental neuropsychology.* New York: Oxford University Press.

Springer, S. P., & Deutsch, G. (1989). *Left brain, right brain.* New York: W. H. Freeman.

Tannock, R. (1998). Attention deficit hyperactivity disorder: Advances in cognitive, neurobiological and genetic research. *Journal of Child Psychology and Psychiatry, 39,* 65–99.

Teeter, P. A., & Semrud-Clikeman, M. (1998). *Child neuropsychology: Assessment and intervention for neurodevelopmental disorders*. New York: Guilford Press.

Teneback, C. C., Nahas, Z., Speer, A. M., Molloy, M., Stallings, L. E., Spicer, K. M., Risch, S. C., & George, M. S. (1999). Changes in prefrontal cortex and paralimbic activity in depression following two weeks of daily left prefrontal TMS. *Journal of Neuropsychiatry and Clinical Neuroscience, 11*, 426–435.

Tromontana, M., & Hooper, S. (1989). Neuropsychology of child psychopathology. In C. R. Reynolds & E. Fletcher-Janzen (Eds.), *Handbook of clinical child neuropsychology* (pp. 87–106). New York: Plenum Press.

Vaidya, C. J., Austin, G., Kirkorian, G., Ridlehuber, H. W., Desmond, J. E., Glover, G. E., & Gabrieli, J. D. E. (1998). Selective effects of methylphenidate in attention deficit hyperactivity disorder: A functional magnetic resonance study. *Proceedings of the National Academy of Sciences, 95*, 14494–14499.

7

Use of Projective Techniques with School-Aged Children

Achilles N. Bardos,

Natalie Politikos, and

Sherri L. Gallagher

Many of the psychological assessments conducted with children involve referrals due to emotional or behavioral problems. In this chapter we will discuss the use of projective techniques in the personality assessment of young children and adolescents. The presentation is based on the assumption that projective techniques do not constitute the better method of conducting personality assessments, but complement the entire process of psychological evaluation, thus contributing to the comprehensive understanding of children's difficulties and effective treatment planning.

The use of projective techniques in psychological evaluations has been an area of controversy throughout the history of psychological testing and assessment. However, in all surveys conducted regarding the most frequently used tools, projective techniques have always appeared on, if not dominated, the lists of tests. In a national survey of school psychologists, Hutton, Dubes, and Muir (1992) reported that projective drawings were used the most to gather information about the social–emotional functioning of students referred for assessments.

The criticisms against the use of projective tests usually center on issues of standardization and psychometric properties (Joiner, Schimdt, & Barnett, 1996; Motta, Little, & Tobin, 1993). In extreme cases, some have even claimed that the inclusion of projective techniques might be unethical (Martin, 1983). A number of explanations can be offered for these criticisms, such as the decline in popularity of psychoanalytic theories, the complexity of many of these techniques, which are founded on principles of the psychoanalytic theory, insufficient to nonexistent training in graduate school programs, and difficulties in distinguishing the validity of a specific test or technique versus the validity of a decision-making process (Knoff, 1993). Arguments for and against the clinical utility of projective tests have been made numerous times on both practical and psychometric grounds (Bardos, 1993; Riethmiller & Handler, 1997), while Waehler (1997) stated that these differences in viewpoint are "a testament to the complexity of professional psychology" (p. 482).

Irrespective of the psychologist's theoretical orientation, the role of projective testing in the personality evaluation process is to facilitate the exchange of information between the child and the therapist; that is, projective tests and techniques are seen as a means of communication. It is for this reason that we use the terms *projective test* and *projective technique* interchangeably. Using projective techniques, the psychologist has the opportunity to interact with children in a primarily nonstructured environment, allowing the child to react to novel stimuli or utilize nonthreatening, familiar symbols as avenues of expressing feelings, emotions, reactions about their own lives and about others in their lives. Through the content of what is being communicated, as well as the style and cognitive structure of a child's thoughts, the psychologist learns about a child's motives, needs, and other aspects of his or her inner world that the child might not able to share in the clinical interview. In addition, some of this information could not be shared or observed through direct observation in a group, classroom, or self-report inventory. In other cases, especially with younger children who have not yet developed their expressive language skills, projective tests and drawings, in particular, serve as a means for childen to communicate with the examiner using their own symbols (drawings) or visual stimuli presented by the therapist. Groth-Marnat (1998) argued, "because many important aspects of personality are not available to conscious self-report, questionnaires and inventories are of limited value" (p. 499). Use of projective techniques, then, helps the psychologist form hypotheses that may assist in the understanding of a child's behavior. This information that can be used in the decision-making process of a differential diagnosis, and help determine the treatment action plans by answering questions that relate to the extent to which a child will benefit from planned interventions.

Human Figure Drawings

Psychologists have been using human figure drawings (HFD) for almost a century. A formal examination of HFDs, however, started with the work of Goodenough (1926) and the *Draw-A-Man* test.

Machover's (1949) approach has served as a foundation for incorporating projective drawings into personality assessments. She developed general guidelines for human figure drawings that could be applied to a person's drawings in order to obtain insight into that individual's personality. These qualitative guidelines (e.g., placement on the page, body part content, size, line quality, erasures) were used to identify specific aspects of an individual's drawings and were interpreted as signs of personality functioning. This has been termed the *body-image hypothesis*. For example, a large drawing was assumed to serve as a sign of an exaggerated self-concept, while a small drawing was assumed to indicate the presence of a low opinion of oneself.

Although Machover's approach has probably received most of the attention in the literature of HFDs, it was Koppitz (1968) who advanced their use through the development of a quantitative scoring system. Through this new actuarial scoring system, Koppitz discouraged the use of the specific items as signs of emotional disturbance and emphasized the examination of the entire figure for hypothesis generation. A number of new scoring systems have appeared in the recent literature, addressing some of the psychometric limitations of the early work with human figure drawings.

The Draw A Person: Screening Procedure for Emotional Disturbance

The *DAP:SPED* (Naglieri, McNeish, & Bardos, 1991) was developed as a screening tool for emotional difficulties in children ages 6–18. In the review of the literature, Naglieri et al., as had others, found that Machover's hypothesis of a one-to-one correspondence between a specific sign and a specific interpretation lacked empirical support. It was noted that many features or signs that Machover associated with emotional disturbance also appear in drawings of nondisturbed children. Koppitz's (1968) developmentally sensitive approach argued that the number of items found in a drawing is more important than the presence of any single item. However, despite the scoring improvements Koppitz's system offered, it failed the test of diagnostic validity. A major limitation of these frequently used approaches to the interpretation of HFD was the lack of objectivity in scoring, as scoring rules tended to be vague, lacked objectivity, and had low reliability. Finally, the literature clearly suggests that HFDs should be used as screening measures only.

Many of the hypotheses regarding links of specific signs of emotional disturbance in drawings were derived through drawings of children who were identified with emotional difficulties or a variety of psychiatric disorders, but very little was known about how typical, problem-free children drew. What is typical in a drawing of a child with no emotional difficulties? What is the frequency of occurrence of signs of emotional disturbance in the drawings of children who are in regular education classes and who are not receiving special education services? This second question was answered by the *DAP:SPED* through a carefully designed, nationally representative standardization sample of 2,260 children, ages 6–17 years old, who were asked to draw a picture of a man, woman, and self, resulting in a total of 6,780 drawings. The frequency of occurrence of 93 items reported in the literature during the past 75 years as potential emotional indicators across all drawings was examined and statistics were obtained for all 93 items across the 6,780 drawings. Only items that appeared in the drawings of fewer than 16% (one standard deviation) of the normative sample were selected to form the final list of items to be used in the determination of an atypical drawing. There were a total of 55 items selected, of which 47 were content items (e.g., legs together, transparency, eyes omitted), and 8 were measurement items (e.g., tall figure, top placement, right placement). By applying these criteria, the authors were able to describe the drawings of children free of formally identified emotional difficulties. The *DAP:SPED* offers gender-based norms because it was found that males had an overall higher number of signs in their drawings than females. In addition, the *DAP:SPED* norms were organized according to three age-specific groups of 6–8, 9–12, and 13–17 year-old children.

Administration and scoring.   The *DAP:SPED* requires a maximum of 15 minutes to administer (5 minutes for each drawing). Both the administrative directions and a scoring sheet are provided on the record form for each of the three drawings (i.e., Man, Woman, and Self) that children are asked to draw on three separate pages. Depending on the purpose of the testing, the *DAP:SPED* can be administered individually, as part of a referral, or in a group setting for screening purposes. There are numerous lists of questions that can be asked of the children for the three figures. Such questions ask the child to describe the drawing in terms of how the drawing thinks, feels, gets along with others, adults and children, among others. Many of these questions are formed on the basis of what is known about the child and the referral question.

Scoring the *DAP:SPED* requires about 3 to 5 minutes per drawing using the record form. Specific and detailed guidelines also are presented in the manual along with numerous examples and a learning-to-score chapter that includes materials used during the norming of the *DAP:SPED*. When scoring the *DAP:SPED*, the examiner determines the presence or absence of 55 items. To evaluate the measurement items, the examiner must use a set of age-specific scoring templates. For example, a template can be used to determine if a drawing is a big or a small drawing using the reference points provided by the standardization sample.

Psychometric properties.   The primary goal of the *DAP:SPED* is to offer a scoring system that is easy to apply, reduces subjectivity in scoring, and provides normative scores based on a standardization sample. A secondary goal was to develop a scoring procedure with good psychometric properties, a procedure that will yield a reliable score and provide evidence regarding its ability to differentiate between normal and clinical populations.

The *DAP:SPED* manual reports three types of reliability evidence. Internal consistency was determined to be adequate, given that the test is intended to serve as a screening tool for emotional difficulties. Alpha coefficients for ages 6–9, 9–12, and 13–17 were .76, .77, and .71, respectively. Test-retest reliability demonstrated the tool's consistency of scores over time, with stability coefficients of .67. Finally, inter-rater (.84) and intrarater (.83) reliability was established, an area that historically has been described as a major weakness of projective assessment techniques. These data suggest that improvements in new scoring systems such as the *DAP:SPED* can result in substantial improvements in the reliability of the scores offered by the test, and these reliabilities appear to be adequate for an instrument most often used as a screening procedure.

The *DAP:SPED* yields an overall *T*-score that leads to three decision-making levels. A standard score of less than 55 suggests that the drawing is typical of children this age; a score between 56–65 suggests that further evaluation is indicated; a standard score greater than 65 suggests that further evaluation is strongly indicated.

The *DAP:SPED* demonstrated its discriminant validity in studies using regular education and clinical groups of children, such as samples of children identified with emotional disturbance in residential (Andrews & Bardos, 1991) as well as in public school settings (Dwors, 1996; Dwors & Bardos, 1991), students with learning disabilities (Ryser, Lassiter, & Bardos, 1991), students who were sexually abused (Bruening, Wagner, & Johnson, 1997), students with hearing impairments (Bardos, 1993b, 1995), and studies with Native Americans (Helm-Yost, 1993). In these studies, the *DAP:SPED* was administered with other personality evaluation tools, such as measures of self-concept, behavior-rating scales, and self-report inventories.

House-Tree-Person

One of the most well-known projective tests, the *House-Tree-Person* (*HTP*), was developed in 1948 by Buck. It represents the author's position that, in addition to the HFD, two additional stimuli (a house and a tree) can elicit responses that relate to how individuals see themselves in relation to their home environment. The most recent manual and interpretive guide of the *HTP* was revised by Buck and Warren (1992). Similar to the drawing approaches discussed earlier, the *HTP* is primarily used as a rapport-building technique.

Administration of the *HTP* is somewhat similar to the *DAP*. The examinee is asked to draw a picture of a house, a tree, and a person (in this order) using three separate sheets of paper. There are numerous variations of the above with examiners using plain single sheets of paper or a formal scoring record form available through the publisher. The commercially available form facilitates the scoring process by providing guidance and suggestions for questioning. One administrative variation recommends the drawings of all three figures on a single sheet of paper. When requesting the drawing of a house only, the examiner rotates the paper so that its longer side is parallel to the subject. Although there is no time limit for the completion of the drawings, the examiner records the time interval between the administrative directions and the beginning of drawings, the time intervals between drawings, and the overall time. The examiner must follow closely and record the order of details drawn, pauses that occur while the examinee is drawing specific details, and any verbalizations that occur during the *HTP* session. Following the administration and completion of the three drawings, some clinicians request the drawing of another person of the opposite sex. The final step of the *HTP* administration includes the post-drawing inquiry, when the examinee is given the opportunity to describe each drawing and relate any feelings, thoughts, or ideas regarding the drawing or specific details. A set of questions is provided on the record form for each drawing, but the examiner is encouraged to follow up with additional questions when deemed necessary. Specific details that may not be clear or that may be avoided by the examinee's verbal description should be followed up with additional questions as well.

Scoring and interpretation. Despite the popularity of the technique among clinicians and those who use it in art therapy, limited research has been conducted with the tool, making it susceptible to criticism. Research studies in support of the *HTP* are primarily case studies conducted in the fifties and seventies. A number of case studies are presented in the 1992 edition of the *HTP* manual, but they also are quite dated. Additional studies examined the degree to which certain features or characteristics in drawings appear in certain clinical samples such as rapists, pedophiles, and those who are suffering from paranoia. These samples of adults produced drawings that appear to have some diagnostic significance. However, other studies found that these signs failed to discriminate among individuals with and without organic brain damage. Once again, however, the research quoted in 1992 is at least 30 or more years old.

Buck and Warren (1992) and many *HTP* advocates claim that the traditional experimental approach applied in these studies does not represent the entire spectrum of data gathered, especially the information gained during the post-drawing interview session. Many hypotheses are generated and tested during the interview, creating qualitative data that studies, as of today, have not considered. Given the advances in the methodology of qualitative research, and the fact that the *HTP* continues to be one of the most frequently used projective techniques in personality assessment, research studies with school-aged children both in clinical as well as in public school settings should be encouraged. This technique continues to have merit in the diagnostic process because it allows the psychologist to consider contextual variables in the drawings, information that, unfortunately, does not lead to data for empirical or psychometric analysis, but likely contributes to the understanding of a child's inner world and how he or she perceives and interprets the dynamics of surrounding people and events. As with the *DAP*, generation of hypotheses should always consider the age and cognitive ability of the child.

Draw A Family and Kinetic Family Drawings

An important consideration in personality assessment with children and adolescents is their view of the family structure, its dynamics, and the role played by the various members within this system (see Chapter 10 for more information on the importance of the family context to the developing child). The previously discussed drawing techniques require the child to draw pictures of individuals and objects in isolation. In the Draw A Family technique, and many of its variations, the child is asked to draw the figures of a family unit in action on a single page. The child is asked to "tell a story" about the picture. On completion of the drawings, the examiner follows the story and interjects, where appropriate, with questions. As with other techniques, size of figures, specific placement of individual drawings on the paper, and interactions among members all serve the purpose of generating or confirming the clinician's hypotheses formed as a result of the interview, referral question, or hypotheses derived from other more direct sources. The authors believed that, by asking the child to depict relationships in action, the child's perception of his or her position in the family unit can be more easily identified.

Prout and Phillips (1974) developed a similar technique, the *Kinetic School Drawing* (KSD). In the *KSD* the child is asked to draw human figures in action in a school setting. Knoff and Prout (1985) combined the *Kinetic Family Drawing* (KFD) and *KSD* techniques and developed the *Kinetic Drawing System* (KDS).

Psychometric properties.   There are no normative data for these techniques, and studies that examined their psychometric properties have produced mixed results.

Scoring and interpretation.   Scoring and interpretation of family drawings range from global, holistic evaluations to more objective scoring methods. The present state of research with the *KFD* and *KDS* is best summarized by Knoff and Prout (1985), who stated that research should take both a qualitative and a psychometric direction. Qualitatively, the *KFD* can assist with the identification of psychological issues and concerns that can be investigated or confirmed with additional personality measures. In this manner, the information gathered from the qualitative analyses of *KFD* might assist a therapist's selection regarding the most appropriate instrument or assessment approach to be followed. This function alone may explain the popularity of the instrument among clinicians. With properly designed studies, the contribution of the *KFD* to decision making in the evaluation process could be empirically examined.

Thematic Approaches

Despite the controversy surrounding them, thematic methods continue to thrive in clinical settings. Some of the controversy is related to their appropriate use and interpretation because the techniques require a sound theoretical background in psychodynamic theory, something that is less common in current training programs. These techniques attempt to identify the conscious and unconscious factors that influence the psychological functioning of the individual and the underlying dynamic factors (drives, needs, traits, or constructs) that form the personality (Knoff, 1986).

The most central assumption of thematic techniques is that an individual will reflect (or "project") her or his needs, desires, or conflicts when asked to impose meaning or order on an ambiguous stimulus. This hypothesis encompasses the notion that all behavior manifestations are expressions of an individual's personality (Knoff, 1986). Another key assumption suggests that the strengths of individuals' psychological needs are positively related to their direct or symbolic manifestation in thematic technique responses. Hence, the stronger the psychological need, the more likely it is that it will find expression in an individual's responses to projective techniques. The third central assumption is that there is a parallel between thematic technique behavior and the individual's behavior in the environment. In other words, research has shown (Kagan, 1956; Lesser, 1957; Murstein & Wolf, 1970; Mussen & Naylor, 1954) that those children who include aggression and lack of fear of punishment in their thematic responses tend to demonstrate similar behaviors in their everyday environment.

Thematic Apperception Test (TAT)

The *TAT* (Murray, 1943) is still listed as one of the most frequently used methods of assessment both in the United States and in other countries (Kroon, Goudena, & Rispens, 1998). Numerous instruments were developed along the same lines as the

TAT, in fact, "thematic apperception test" has come to specify a category of psychological instruments. Specific characteristics of thematic apperception tests include picture cards used to represent and suggest certain themes. Also, the cards usually portray people or figures with sufficiently human features to allow some degree of identification by the examinee.

Murray (1943) recommended that two sets of 10 cards be presented in separate sessions at least one day apart. Many clinicians, however, choose their own set of cards to use with individuals, and there is no general consensus on the choice of *TAT* cards for adult assessment (Kroon et al., 1998). According to the *TAT* manual, this instrument may be used with children from 4 years of age and up. However, only three cards are specifically for children, and only four *TAT* cards portray a scene that actually includes a child. There is much controversy over whether children can relate to the remaining cards and, hence, whether the *TAT* is an appropriate instrument for use with children. The manual gives no indication of the themes that the cards are likely to elicit in children.

Numerous scoring methods have appeared over the years, but most systems are very complex and time-consuming and are not widely used. Most clinicians use the *TAT* as an impressionistic method that is interpreted intuitively. It is important to note that none of the scoring methods developed were designed for scoring the *TAT* responses of children and adolescents (Kroon et al., 1998).

Knoff (1986) suggests that, with the content of stories in mind, the practitioner should analyze each story by identifying the hero, the motives, trends, and feelings of the hero, the forces within the hero's environment, the outcome of the stories, simple and complex themes, and interests and sentiments attributed to the hero. It is also important to observe the manner in which a child or adolescent tells a story, for it may reflect her or his cognitive style, expressive language, organization of thoughts, and ability to identify and elaborate on aspects of a *TAT* picture's plot.

Children's Apperception Test (CAT)

The *CAT* (Bellak & Bellak, 1991), first published in 1949, was developed specifically for use with young children aged 3 to 10 years. The 10 cards used depict animals rather than humans, on the assumption that certain animals are less threatening than humans for young children and that it would be easier for children to project unacceptable traits or emotions to animals. A parallel version with human figures (*CAT-H*; Bellak & Bellak, 1994) is available for older children.

The *CAT* administration and interpretation parallel those of the *TAT* in that the child is asked to tell what happens prior to the *CAT* picture, what is currently happening, and what will occur beyond the present activity. The *CAT* content is examined for the status of the hero and the primary conflict and outcome themes manifested in the stories. The *CAT* manual does not provide norms and the normative data that exist are outdated (from the 1960s).

Roberts Apperception Test for Children (RATC)

The *RATC* (McArthur & Roberts, 1982), a thematic apperception test for children aged 6 through 15 years, uses 16 black-and-white test cards that show fairly unambiguous scenes of people interacting in a contemporary setting as opposed to the dated pictures in the *TAT* and *CAT*. The *RATC* assumes that children identify more readily with realistic scenes, so that the projective response would be more related to the child's actual behavior (Kroon et al., 1998). Eleven cards depict parallel versions for girls and boys; the remaining cards are not gender-specific. The *RATC* goes beyond other thematic approaches by including cards depicting parental disagreement, the observation of nudity, parental affection, aggression situations, and school and peer relationships. The manual provides a brief description of each card but does not define the encompassing framework of developmental theory from which these themes have been derived (Kroon et al., 1998).

The *RATC* manual includes an explicit scoring system, which is one of the positive attributes of this thematic technique. The scoring system yields adaptive scales as well as five clinical scales. In addition to the adaptive and clinical scales, critical indicators such as atypical responses, maladaptive outcomes, and card rejections or refusals are also included in the scoring system (Knoff, 1986).

The *RATC* measures are clearly defined in the manual and satisfactory interrater agreement is reported for most of the measures. The *RATC* has been standardized on a sample of 200 "nonclinical" children and normative data are provided for four age groups. It is important to note that the *RATC* includes a set of cards for African American children. These cards differ only in the shaded skin color of the characters. No norms are available for this version of the *RATC*.

Tell-Me-A-Story (TEMAS)

The *TEMAS*'s (Costantino, Malgady, & Rogler, 1988) goal was to develop a culturally sensitive thematic apperception test for inner-city children. It emphasizes the perceptual–cognitive aspects of the projective response, is less psychodynamic than most of the other thematic apperception tests, and has incorporated various developmental and personality theories in its theoretical framework.

The *TEMAS* consists of 23 brightly colored drawings that depict contemporary inner-city scenes of family and peer interactions. A few cards have fantasy themes (i.e., dragons, dream scenes). A short form based on nine cards can also be used. There are 11 gender-specific cards, while the remaining cards are used with both genders. The parallel minority version portrays Hispanic or African American figures. The *TEMAS* administration is standardized, requiring specific instructions and elaborate questioning.

The *TEMAS* has normative data for 5- to 13-year-olds only. Investigation of the *TEMAS* psychometric properties presented moderate to high interrater reliabilities and variable consistency reliabilities in the .70s or below. Overall, the *TEMAS* has been received positively because of its clear, low-inference scoring system (Ritzler, 1993) and its good construct and discriminant validity (Kroon et al., 1998; Lang, 1992; Worchel & Dupree, 1990). Recent research indicates that the *TEMAS* test is a valid tool for multicultural assessment (Costantino & Malgady, 1996).

Children's Apperceptive Story-Telling Test (CAST)

The *CAST* (Schneider, 1989) was developed for use with children 6 to 13 years old. It has been hailed as a valid and reliable test unparalleled by other thematic appercep-tion tests (Aronow, 1995). "The *CAST* incorporates Adlerian theory, which centers on the view that individuals are social beings with goal-directed drives toward belonging" (Kroon et al., 1998, p. 107). Although Adlerian theory may not be endorsed by every test user, the emphasis on the individual's social functioning does have a general com-mon-sense appeal (Aronow, 1995).

The *CAST* consists of 17 color drawings that depict contemporary scenes with children from various ethnic groups in family, peer, and school situations. Fourteen cards have parallel male and female versions. There are standardized instructions and a series of five questions follows the presentation of each stimulus card. The responses are scored on three well-defined and clear indexes: Thematic Scales, Problem-Solving Scales, and various Thematic Indicators. Raw scores are obtained for the first two scales and then converted into *T*-scores.

The manual provides extensive information regarding test development and standardization based on a nationwide representative sample of 876 school children, aged 6 through 13 years. Interrater reliability was quite high for all 15 scales, and good internal consistency is reported for three out of four factors. The *CAST's* well-grounded theoretical framework and strong psychometric qualities make it one of the most exciting newer thematic apperception tests. In summary, the social setting of the test situation, examiner training and experience, children's shortened attention span, limited verbal skills, and their often spontaneous and revealing conversations are all factors that deserve special consideration when testing and interpreting thematic ap-perception tests.

Rorschach

The *Rorschach* is a test for personality analysis in which an individual is asked to de-scribe what he or she "sees" in a series of ten inkblot designs. Hermann Rorschach be-lieved that, by examining the strategies people use to formulate responses, the evaluator could describe how they are likely to handle a variety of real-world situa-tions (Exner, 1993). Five systematizers, Beck, Hertz, Klopfer, Piotrowski, and Rapaport, developed overlapping but independent systems to score and interpret the *Rorschach*. Exner combined the most useful components of the earlier five systems with his own research to develop the Comprehensive System (Exner, 1993). The Comprehensive System was normed on over 9,000 individuals (children, adolescents, and adults) and on 1,390 nonpatient children and adolescents (Exner & Weiner,

1995). Using the Exner System for scoring and interpretation makes the Rorschach more objective than other projective techniques, and provides objective information about the examinee. Exner (1993) believes that the *Rorschach* is more of a problem-solving task than a projective technique, a perceptual–cognitive task in which subjects respond to a series of problems consisting of ambiguous visual stimuli (Erdberg, 1996).

The *Rorschach* is applicable for students ages 5 through adulthood, but only as an additional test to provide added information concerning the personality of a subject. Of the current projective techniques, the *Rorschach* is probably the best instrument to provide hypotheses about the psychological operations, needs, styles, habits, problem-solving capacities, interpersonal functioning, and self-concept of an individual.

Administration

When testing a child, it is important to introduce the *Rorschach* with some brief and honest statements about the process. The examiner might say that there are ten inkblots or ask if the child has heard of the inkblot test. Because children tend to ask more questions than adults, it is important to answer their questions directly and honestly, which will also assist with rapport building. Before administering the *Rorschach*, the examiner should place the cards face down in the appropriate order out of the reach of the examinee. The examiner should be certain there is plenty of paper and an extra pen or pencil because responses are recorded verbatim. The examiner uses a Location Sheet during the inquiry stage. The examiner should be seated at the examinee's side to reduce body language communication during the administration and to give the examiner a better view of the inkblot features referred to by the individual. Administration time will range between 30-45 minutes, depending on the age of the child.

During the *response phase* the examinee is given each card and asked, "What might this be?" The examiner records the subject's answers verbatim. Silence by the examiner is generally the rule, interrupted only by the exchange of cards or when a nondirective comment is necessary.

After all ten cards are given, there is an *inquiry phase* during which where the examiner repeats the subject's answer to elicit what about the inkblot made the examinee give his or her response. The examiner rereads the responses given by the subject and asks him or her to demonstrate where on the blot he or she saw a particular percept (e.g., dancing bears) and what about the blot reminded the examiner of that percept. The subject explains his or her answer until the examiner sees the inkblot the way the subject sees it. The information obtained during the inquiry stage is later coded by the examiner (Exner, 1993).

Scoring

Scoring the *Rorschach* requires extensive training and is not an option in many graduate school programs, especially in school psychology. Each answer is scored by codes depending on many variables and this process is quite complex. Location of the percept often is the first element coded. Next, determinants are coded including characteristics such as apparent movement, use of color, shading, vista, texture, form, and lambda. In addition, the quality of the percept is given a code (form quality) that represents the extent to which the percept matches that actual stimulus. The examiner also codes the various ways the individual solved the *Rorschach* problem. After the answers are coded, the examiner completes the Structural Summary sheet, using separate codes to tabulate *various* summations, ratios, and constellations called *variables* (Barnett & Zucker, 1990). For an experienced examiner, the scoring and the Structural Summary will take between 30–60 minutes to complete.

Interpretation

During the first part of interpretation, known as the *propositional stage*, the examiner compares the child's Structural Summary with the age norms and summary provided by Exner and Weiner for children and adolescents. The data are addressed in groups of variables relating to specific characteristics of the personality. This process enables the examiner to arrive at initial hypotheses about the child while evaluating data from other sources (e.g., clinical interviews, observation, other assessment instruments).

In the second, *integration*, stage, the evaluator starts to create meaningful descriptions of the child. The interpreter goes beyond the data and uses his or her own clinical judgment, hypotheses and knowledge of human behavior and psychopathology to generate hypotheses. Because this stage involves clinical judgment, it is susceptible to errors resulting from limitations of the coding system (Barnett & Zucker, 1990).

The final stage in interpretation is the *final report stage* in which the clinician creates a report discussing the hypotheses and issues presented in the assessment. Included in the report will be issues of diagnosis, treatment planning, treatment evaluation, and recommendations.

Reliability and validity

Because of the dynamic developmental process in children, test-retest reliability is somewhat less than adequate for younger children, especially over long time periods. According to Exner and Weiner (1995), some variables are more stable than others. Sometime during adolescence, usually between 13 and 16, permanent personality styles usually take form and, with a few exceptions, do not change over time (Exner & Weiner, 1995). Accordingly, test-retest reliability is higher in adolescents. In a study in which retest data were compared between 7- and 15-year-old children, after a 9-month interval, only 5 of the 23 variables had retest correlations of .75 or higher for the younger group compared to 13 of the 23 variables for the older group. In terms of interrater reliability for the coding system, the *Rorschach* lacks ideal reliability (.75), especially for certain codes. According to many validity studies, people often solve the inkblots in the same manner that they use to deal with moderately ambiguous real-world situations (Erdberg, 1996).

Advantages and Drawbacks of the Rorschach

There are many advantages of using the *Rorschach* for personality assessment in school-aged children. First, the *Rorschach* allows the clinician to assess personality and social functioning that are difficult to assess in other ways (Barnett & Zucker, 1990). These include, but are not limited to, abstractness or concreteness of thinking, inner tensions, emotional expression and control, interest in social encounters, and situational stress. Another positive aspect is the use of an objective scoring system with substantial research on each variable and cluster of variables. Also, there are a multitude of documented validity studies for hypotheses generated from the Structural Summary. Finally, there are extensive normative data for subjects from age 5 through adulthood.

There are several disadvantages of the *Rorschach*. As with any projective technique, the *Rorschach's* interpretation process involves clinical judgment, which is susceptible to human error. In addition, to become a trained examiner, a semester-long course and clinical experience is required. The scoring system and interpretation are complex and require an extensive amount of practice and experience. Finally, the entire *Rorschach* assessment entails a lengthy administration, scoring, and interpretation process. These are some the reasons that the *Rorschach* might not be the choice of instrument for school psychologists, but may be appropriate in certain clinical applications.

Sentence Completion Tests

Among the oldest projective techniques are *Sentence Completion Tests* (*SCT*) which usually assess overall adjustment, interpersonal attitudes, personality styles, and other dynamically oriented information (Goldberg, 1965). *SCTs* are projective measures that leave open sentence stems for an examinee to complete with the first idea that comes to mind. Especially with children and adolescents, the examiner may also stress that there are no right or wrong answers. Most *SCTs* are written on a second- or third-grade reading level. Forty-item *SCTs* take approximately 10–25 minutes to administer to children. This measure is intended to convey the subjects' thoughts and feelings about their family, peer relationships, future, school, and employment.

The *Rotter's Incomplete Sentence Blank, Second Edition* (*RISB*; Rotter, Lah, & Rafferty, 1992) is one of the most widely used *SCTs*. The second edition includes sentence stems that take approximately 20–25 minutes to complete, has high school, college, and adult versions, and has included research on its reliability and validity. The *RISB* can be administered individually or in groups. Scoring criteria and examples are included in the manual and take about 15–20 minutes to score by an experienced scorer. The scoring system provides a numerical score that provides an Overall Adjustment Score. Sentences are grouped by content and each response is rated on a scale ranging from 0 (strong positive) to 6 (severe conflict). Scores for each of the 40 items are added together to obtain an Overall Adjustment Score, normally ranging from 80–205. The lower the overall score, the more well-adjusted the individual. The cutoff score of 145 may be used for adjustment and maladjustment and correctly classifies 40% to approximately 98% of individuals with both groups (Lah, 1989a).

The *RISB* reported interscorer, test-retest, and internal consistency reliability evidence with additional studies reporting favorable reliability estimates that ranged from .79 to .99 (Feher, Vandecreek, & Teglasi, 1983; Lah & Rotter, 1981; Vernallis, Shipper, Butler, & Tomlinson, 1970). In terms of validity, the *RISB* relies predominantly on face validity. The *RISB* appears to measure overall adjustment in high school students, college students, and adults. Norms are only provided for college students from the first edition of the *RISB* without normative data for the second edition. Norms for the High School and Adult Forms are absent. Psychologists should exercise caution when making inferences from data derived from the test.

The *Hart Sentence Completion Test for Children* (*HSCT*; Hart 1992) is another well-known sentence completion test. It consists of 40 items with sentence stems specifically designed for use with children. This assessment was created for school psychologists who needed an *SCT* sensitive to a child's development (Hart, Kehle, & Davies, 1983). Information is drawn from children on four dimensions of their world: Family, School, Social, and Self. The areas of assessment include: (a) External Environment (Perception of Family, Interaction with Family, Perception of Peers, Interaction with Peers, Perception of School, and Interaction with School); (b) Self-Perception (Need Orientation and Personal Evaluations); and (c) Intra-Personal Functioning measured with a ninth scale that synthesizes all scales (General Mental Health).

Administration of the *HSCT* is slightly different from the *RISB*. According to Hart et al. (1983), it is preferable to administer the *HSCT* verbally to the child and to record the responses verbatim. The verbal administration allows the psychologist to pursue unclear, contradictory or atypical, and out-of-context responses.

Two scoring systems, a scale rating system and item-by-item rating system, were developed to provide quantitative scores for each content area. On the scale rating system, the psychologist reads the items for a specific scale (e.g., school) and makes a single summary rating on a one to five, negative to positive continuum (1 = negative, 3 = neutral, 5 = positive). On the item-by-item rating system, a scoring template is used for each scale and then responses are rated as negative, neutral, or positive. A composite rating score is determined for each scale and the ratings from all eight scales are profiles for comparison and diagnostic purposes.

Interscorer reliability ranges from .50 to .86, depending on the specific scales (Hart et al., 1983). The scoring systems were found to have moderate (scale rating system) to high (item-by-item) interscorer reliability. In terms of validity, Robyak (1975) found that the scale rating system successfully distinguished between children with emotional disabilities and typical children on five of the eight scales across all ages. The item-by-item scoring system was evaluated by Swanson (1975), who found that interscorer reliabilities ranged from .90 to .99. Her results indicated that there were significant differences between children with emotional and learning disabilities and typical children. Overall, both scoring systems differentiated between children with emotional disabilities, learning disabilities, and nondisabled school-age children (Hart et al., 1983). One drawback of the *HSCT* is the lack of normative data.

Interpretation of SCTs

Although the *RISB* and *HSCT* have scoring systems, interpretation of the SCT is more informal and qualitative rather than quantitative. According to Lah (1989b), evaluators interpret sentence completions on three separate levels. The evaluator first examines what the subject has stated in his or her responses, looking for thoughts, feelings, and attitudes about the specific topics or persons in the sentence stems. The second level of interpretation involves exploring the language used in the responses, the length of the responses, and omissions. Finally, the examiner draws inferences from the examinee's responses. Here, the examiner takes note of how often information is mentioned, common or rare responses, patterns in word usage, emotions, behaviors, and traits. This information should be viewed as hypotheses about the subject and must be supported by other projective and objective information obtained about the individual (e.g., clinical interviews, observations, and other tests).

Advantages and Drawbacks of SCTs

SCTs are easy to administer and interpret, have semi-objective to objective scoring systems (Lah, 1989b), offer the best research evidence (other than that found in the Rorschach) to support their validity as projective measures, require less time to administer than other projective measures (e.g., *Rorschach* and *TAT*), can be administered individually or in groups, are available in many forms, and are affordable. On the down side, certain aspects of the scoring are time-consuming and it takes time to become a practiced interpreter of *SCTs*. In addition, because there is more structure in *SCTs* than other projective techniques, examinees can more easily control their responses. Responses may be easily distorted, hidden, or subjects may present themselves in a socially desirable manner (Lah, 1989b). Finally, *SCTs* may not be useful with lower-functioning individuals, due to the heavy emphasis on verbal skills.

Conclusion

Over the last twenty years there has been a decline in the use of projective techniques with children, primarily in school settings. In part this can be attributed to the lack of emphasis placed on projective techniques in training programs, the increased use of behavior rating scales, and criticisms that the projective techniques are falling short in terms of their psychometric properties. In spite of these factors, projective techniques continue to rank among the most frequently used tests in personality evaluations with children in surveys conducted during the last 10 to 20 years. It is interesting that school and clinical psychologists continue to use these measures, especially when direct assessment techniques have been promoted in the literature and many training programs have either significantly de-emphasized or completely abandoned teaching projective techniques.

Direct assessment techniques are usually presented as those measures needing the least amount of inference to understand and predict behavior, providing more "sound" information for treatment planning, as well as being the most time-efficient and psychometrically superior instruments. This discussion is not intended to fuel the polarization of approaches in personality assessment; rather, it is an attempt to conceptualize and assist in better understanding children, making useful diagnoses, and designing appropriate treatment plans. If we accept the assumption that behavior is a result of the interaction between the person and the environment, it will be easier to recognize that direct assessment and projective techniques complement each other. The role of the psychologist, then, becomes one in which, using a variety of tools, he or she comes to understand the contribution of both personality and environment in understanding why a behavior occurs. Some behaviors (e.g., "out-of-seat" behavior) can best be documented by direct classroom observations. Behavior modification interventions can be designed and implemented for this problematic behavior, thus providing the most effective and least intrusive assessment. In instances where behaviors are less easy to understand (e.g., difficulty making and maintaining friendships or aggressive attacks on others), however, it is the complexity of the underlying reasons for these behaviors that motivate the clinical or school psychologist to use a variety of measures, both objective and projective, in developing hypotheses and designing interventions.

The debate on the usefulness of projective techniques in personality evaluations will continue. It is our hope that the field will embrace Waehler's (1997) position that "it would be a mistake to do away with these procedures because we need more, not fewer, performance-based measures in our test batteries to compare and contrast with self-report measures" (p. 486). It is the responsibility of training programs to respond to the call by practitioners that these techniques have much to offer in the understanding of some children's behavior. Clinical and school psychologists cannot afford the utilization of limited techniques or approaches (behavior rating scales versus projective techniques) because a comprehensive personality assessment, especially with young children, requires the utilization of an array of techniques that complement each other.

References

Andrews, T., & Bardos, A. N. (1991, May). *Relationship of the Draw-A-Person: Screening Procedure for Emotional Disturbance and Self Concept ratings with a psychiatric sample.* Paper presented at the Spring conference of the Ohio School Psychologists Association.

Aronow, E. (1995). Review of the Children's Apperceptive Story-Telling Test. In J. C. Conoley and J. C. Impara (Eds.), *The twelft mental measurements yearbook* (pp. 180–183). Lincoln, NE: Buros Institute of Mental Measurements.

Bardos, A. N. (1993a). Human Figure Drawings: Abusing the abused. *School Psychology Quarterly, 8,* 177–181.

Bardos, A. N. (1993b, March). *Using the Draw A Person: Screening Procedure for Emotional Disturbance and the Devereux Behavior Rating Scale: School Form with hearing impaired students.* Paper presented at the annual Colorado State Symposium on Deafness, Colorado Springs, CO.

Bardos, A. N. (1995, February). *Emotional needs of children with hearing impairments.* Paper presented at the 1995 Courage to Risk conference, Colorado Springs, CO.

Barnett, D. W., & Zucker, K. B. (1990). *The personal and social assessment of children.* Boston: Allyn and Bacon.

Bellak, L., & Bellak, S. S. (1991). *Children's Apperception Test Manual (CAT)* (8th ed.). Larchmont, NY: C.P.S.

Bellak, L., & Bellak, S. S. (1994). *Children's Apperception Test Human Figures (CAT-H)* (11th ed.). Larchmont, NY: C.P.S.

Bruening, C. C., Wagner, W. G., & Johnson, J. T. (1997). Impact of rater knowledge on sexually abused and nonabused girls' scores on the Draw-A- Person: Screening Procedure for Emotional Disturbance (DAP:SPED). *Journal of Personality Assessment, 68,* 665–677.

Buck, J. N. (1948). The H-T-P technique: A qualitative and quantitative scoring manual. *Journal of Clinical Psychology, 4,* 317–396.

Buck, J. N., & Warren, W. L. (1992). *House-Tree-Person: Projective Drawing Technique.* Los Angeles: Western Psychological Services.

Burns, R., & Kaufman, S. (1970). *Kinetic Family Drawings (K-F-D): An introduction to understanding children through kinetic drawings.* New York: Brunner/Mazel.

Costantino, G., & Malgady, R. G. (1996). Development of TEMAS, a multicultural thematic apperception test: Psychometric properties and clinical utility. In G. R. Sodowsky & J. C. Impara (Eds.), *Multicultural assessment in counseling and clinical psychology.* Lincoln, NE: Buros Institute of Mental Measurements.

Costantino, G., Malgady, R. G., & Rogler, L. H. (1988). *Tell-Me-A-Story (TEMAS): Manual.* Los Angeles: Western Psychological Services.

Dwors, J. (1996). Differences in normal and seriously emotionally disturbed students on the Devereux Behavior Rating Scale-School Form, Draw A Person Screening Procedure for Emotional Disturbance, and the Millon Adolescent clinical inventory. Unpublished doctoral dissertation, University of Northern Colorado, Greeley, CO.

Dwors, J., & Bardos, A. N. (1991, May). *Relationship of children's drawings to self-concept and teacher rating scales.* Paper presented at the annual meeting of the Rocky Mountain Psychological Association, Denver, CO.

Erdberg, P. (1996). The Rorscach. In C. S. Newmark (Ed.), *Major psychological assessment instruments* (2nd ed., pp. 148–165). Boston: Allyn and Bacon.

Exner, J. E. (1993). *The Rorschach: A comprehensive system, volume 1: Basic foundations* (3rd ed.). New York: Wiley.

Exner, J. E., & Weiner, I. B. (1995). *The Rorschach: A comprehensive system, Volume 3: Assessment of children and adolescents* (2nd ed.). New York: Wiley.

Feher, E., Vandecreek, L., & Teglasi, H. (1983). The problem of art quality in the use of human figure drawing tests. *Journal of Clinical Psychology, 39,* 268–275.

Goldberg, P. A. (1965). A review of sentence completion methods in personality assessment. *Journal of Projective Techniques and Personality Assessment, 29,* 12–45.

Goodenough, F. L. (1926). *Measurement of intelligence in drawings.* New York: Harcourt Brace and World.

Groth-Marnat, G. (1998). *Handbook of psychological assessment* (2nd ed.). New York: Wiley.

Hart, D. H., (1992). *The Hart Sentence Completion Test for Children.* Unpublished Manuscript. Salt Lake City, IA: Educational Support Systems.

Hart, D. H., Kehle, T. J., & Davies, M. V. (1983). Effectiveness of sentence completion techniques: A review of the Hart Sentence Completion Test for Children. *School Psychology Review, 12,* 428–434.

Helm-Yost, D. (1993). The differentiation ability of the DAP:SPED with Navajo children when considering the variable of time. *Dissertation Abstracts International, 54*(3-A), 867.

Hutton, J. B., Dubes, R., & Muir, S. (1992). Assessment practices of school psychologists: Ten years later. *School Psychology Review, 21,* 271–284.

Joiner, T. E., Jr., Schmidt, K. L., & Barnett, J. (1996). Size, detail and line heaviness in children's drawings as correlates of emotional distress: (More) negative evidence. *Journal of Personality Assessment, 67,* 127–141.

Kagan, J. (1956). The measurement of overt aggression from fantasy. *Journal of Abnormal and Social Psychology, 52,* 390–393.

Knoff, H. M. (1986). *The assessment of child and adolescent personality.* New York: Guilford Press.

Knoff, H. M. (1993). The utility of human figure drawings in personality and intellectual assessment: Why ask why? *School Psychology Quarterly, 8,* 191–196.

Knoff, H. M., & Prout, L. (1985). *The Kinetic Drawing System: Family & School.* Los Angeles: Western Psychological Services.

Koppitz, E. (1968). *Psychological evaluation of children's human figure drawings.* New York: Grune & Stratton.

Kroon, N., Goudena, P., & Rispens, J. (1998). Thematic apperception tests for child and adolescent assessment: A practitioner's consumer guide. *Journal of Psychoeducational Assessment, 16,* 99–117.

Lah, M. I. (1989a). New validity, normative, and scoring data for the Rotter Incomplete Sentences Blank. *Journal of Personality Assessment, 53,* 607–620.

Lah, M. I. (1989b). Sentence completion tests. In C. S. Newmark (Ed.), *Major psychological assessment instruments* (Vol. 2, pp.133–163). Boston: Allyn and Bacon.

Lah, M. I., & Rotter, J. B. (1981). Changing college student norms on the Rotter Incomplete Sentences Blank. *Journal of Consulting and Clinical Psychology, 49*, 985.

Lang, W. S. (1992). Review of the TEMAS (Tell-Me-A-Story). In J. Kramer and J. Conoley (Eds.), *The eleventh mental measurements yearbook* (pp. 925–926). Lincoln, NE: Buros Institute of Mental Measurements.

Lesser, G. H. (1957). The relationship between overt and fantasy aggression as a function of maternal response to aggression. *Journal of Abnormal and Social Psychology, 55*, 218–221.

Machover, K. (1949). *Personality projection in the drawing of a human figure.* Springfield, IL: Charles C. Thomas.

Martin, R. (1983). The ethical issues in the use and interpretation of the Draw-A-Person test and other similar projective procedures. *The School Psychologist, 38*, 8.McArthur, D., & Roberts, G. E. (1982). *Roberts Apperception Test for Children manual.* Los Angeles: Western Psychological Services.

Motta, R. W., Little, S. G., & Tobin, M. I. (1993). The use and abuse of human figure drawings. *School Psychology Quarterly, 8*, 162–169.

Murray, H. A. (1943). *Thematic Apperception Test: Manual.* Cambridge, MA: Harvard University Press.

Murstein, B. I., & Wolf, S. R. (1970). Empirical test of the "levels" hypothesis with five projective techniques. *Journal of Abnormal Psychology, 75*, 38–44.

Mussen, P. H., & Naylor, K. (1954). The relationship between overt and fantasy aggression. *Journal of Abnormal and Social Psychology, 49*, 235–240.

Naglieri, J. A., McNeish, T. J., & Bardos, A. N. (1991). *Draw A Person: Screening procedure for emotional disturbance examiner's manual.* Austin. TX: PRO-ED.

Prout, H. T., & Phillips, P. D. (1974). A clinical note: The Kinetic School Drawing. *Psychology in the Schools, 11*, 303–306.

Riethmiller, R. J., & Handler, L. (1997). The great figure drawing controversy: The integration of research and clinical practice. *Journal of Personality Assessment, 69*, 488–496.

Ritzler, B. (1993). TEMAS (Tell-Me-A-Story): Review. *Journal of Psychoeducational Assessment, 11*, 381–389.

Rotter, J. B., Lah, M. I., & Rafferty, J. E. (1992). *Rotter Incomplete Sentences Blank manual, second edition.* New York: The Psychological Corporation.

Ryser, C., Lassiter, K., & Bardos, A. N. (1991, May). *Emotional indicators in the drawings of learning disabled children.* Paper presented at the annual conference of the Colorado Psychological Association, Denver, CO.

Schneider, M. F. (1989). *Children's Apperceptive Story-Telling Test.* Austin, TX: PRO-ED.

Swanson, C. H. (1975). *A validation study of the Hart Sentence Completion Test.* Unpublished master's thesis, University of Utah.

Vernallis, F. F., Shipper, J. C., Butler, D. C., & Tomlinson, T. M. (1970). Saturation group therapy in a weekend clinic: An outcome study. *Psychotherapy: Theory, Research & Practice, 7*, 144–152.

Waehler, C. A. (1997). Drawing bridges between science and practice. *Journal of Personality Assessment, 69*, 482–487.

Worchel, F., & Dupree, J. L. (1990). Projective story-telling techniques. In C. R. Reynolds and R. W. Kamphaus (Eds.), *Handbook of psychological and educational assessment of children: Personality, behavior and context* (pp. 70–88). New York: Guilford Press.

8

Information-Processing Perspectives in Understanding Social and Personal Behavior

Betsy B. Waterman

Some might wonder why there is a chapter on information-processing in a book about the social and personal assessment of children. In a sense, though, one might question how such a book could be developed without this discussion. Children, like all of us, are complex organisms whose worlds interconnect. Certainly critical to the development of a child's social and personal world is the integrity of the information-processing system. It is this system that allows the child to understand and interpret social events, link cause and effect, find solutions to a nearly endless number of problems, and identify, control, or express emotions. In short, it is the system on which all learning, including social and personal learning, depends.

Information-Processing Theory has its roots in the mid-1950s, when research from several different areas of inquiry began to converge. Chomsky (1956) startled a world still deeply influenced by the behaviorists' stimulus-response-reinforcement explanations for learning language by suggesting that the complex, syntactically accurate language of the two-year-old could not be developed in the linear way proposed by the behaviorists. He suggested that the young language learner stores a finite number of rules to guide language use that could then be applied in an infinite number of situations. Key to these ideas was the notion that the brain was able to store information that was not observable but that was critical to the learning process.

At the same time as Chomsky was completing his work, Miller's (1956) research related to the capacity of short-term memory and Newell and Simon's (1956) development of the first artificial intelligence program were also revealed to the psychological world. Behavioral theory was no longer powerful enough to explain how a person could remember, forget, or plan. Information-processing theory provided a model for understanding the ways children process or use the symbols of their environment, something that is critical to the assessment process and to the development of meaningful and specific interventions for children whose learning—academically, socially or personally—is somehow compromised.

The Information-Processing System

Although, certainly, there are many differences between the human mind and computer systems, the computer has provided a useful model from which to begin to understand the functioning of the human information-processing system (Bruer, 1993). Many architectural models (i.e., "the built-in mental features that allow our minds to build and execute programs," Bruer, 1993, p. 24) have been developed since the mid-1950s. Information-processing models that were developed needed to explain both verbal and nonverbal processing, memory for generic and specific information, and memory for unconsciously occurring procedures that guided skills such as those needed for motor, perceptual, or cognitive activities. As researchers began to test various models representing the human mind, it became clear that many fell short in explaining how the mind processed the nearly endless kinds of stimuli it encountered day-to-day.

Initially, memory was thought to consist of three essential parts: the Iconic or Sensory System Memory, which held information very briefly; Short-term memory, which temporarily stored current information until it was consolidated; long-term memory, where processed information was ultimately stored. Such a system, however, failed to provide adequate explanations for where and how the individual integrated information, or planned and evaluated incoming material. Newer models of information-processing evolved. These models included systems for briefly holding material, systems where new and old information is actively processed, systems that hold factual knowledge and skill-based information, and executive systems whose role is to guide the flow of information from one system to another.

The Sensory Memory System

The sensory memory system allows information to register for a very brief period. This brief registration of material is essential as it allows information that may quickly disappear to be held long enough to be perceived and, ultimately, to have some meaning attached to it. Information can enter the system through any of the sense receptors. Sensory registers are limited in what they can hold and information that is not attended to will quickly decay. Interestingly, information presented auditorily can be held up to 6 times longer than visual stimuli, with auditory information retained in its register for up to 3 seconds and visual information held for less than .5 seconds (Bruning, Schraw, & Ronning, 1999).

Incoming stimuli are initially perceived when attentional resources are allocated to them. These perceived stimuli are then associated with a known pattern and are "recognized" (Bruning et al., 1999). When stimuli have been perceived and recognized, they must then be processed in some way in short-term memory. Using the person's existing knowledge base, meaning is ultimately assigned. Recognition and the assignment of meaning depend on the nature of the stimuli, the knowledge the individual has about the stimuli, and the context within which the stimuli are introduced (Marr, 1982, 1985).

The Working Memory System

Initially, architectural models included rather simplistic models of short-term memory. These systems were seen as limited capacity stores where information was processed for meaning. More recently, researchers have begun to use the term *working memory* to capture a group of subsystems whose role is to perform the complex tasks associated with day-to-day learning. Baddeley and his colleagues (1974, 1986, 1998) and Bruer (1993) have proposed models of working memory. This memory system is seen as playing a support role in many complex activities such as reasoning, language comprehension, and long-term learning (Bruer, 1993; Gathercole & Baddeley, 1990).

According to Baddeley's model, working memory is a tri-part system consisting of the central executive and two subsystems, the articulatory loop and the visuo–spatial sketchpad. The latter two subsystems are each designed to process different kinds of information. According to Gathercole and Baddeley (1993), the articulatory loop is specialized for the maintenance and processing of verbal material. The visuo–spatial sketchpad, as its name suggests, is that area of the memory system where visual–spatial information is processed and maintained. The central executive, according to Baddeley (1983, 1986), is a limited capacity system that controls and manages information as it moves through the system. The articulatory loop is particularly critical in that it allows verbal information to be kept, through the use of rehearsal, without deleting resources from the central executive.

Baddeley and his colleagues make some assumptions as they relate to their model of working memory (Bruning et al., 1999). The first assumption is that each subsystem has individual attentional resources. This is important in that it allows one subsystem to process information without reducing the resources of another subsystem. Their model also assumes that, because the central executive regulates the processing of the two subsystems, the more deliberate and effective the central executive the more efficiently the subsystems will perform.

Bruer (1993) suggests a model of the cognitive architecture of the mind that also includes working memory as a key component of the information-processing system. In Bruer's model, information from the environment enters through the sensory system. Some of this information is moved to working memory where it can be actively processed. The working memory system, in Bruer's view, is that part of the cognitive architecture where strategies for planning, monitoring, and evaluating stimuli are applied. It is also the place where information held in long-term memory, such as metacognitive knowledge and skills, procedural knowledge (i.e., rules that help guide problem solving), and word and other basic knowledge, can be transferred and applied to new incoming information. Finally, working memory, according to Bruer, is the system responsible for the output phase of the information-processing system. This "output" of information may be seen behaviorally in terms of actions or verbalizations.

Working memory is further conceptualized by Bruer as a limited capacity store that both retains information and processes it simultaneously. In this way it differs from the traditional notion of short-term memory wherein the learner simply holds, but does not manipulate, information. An intact working memory system, then, is essential for the efficient and accurate storage, processing, and transfer of information.

Long-Term Memory System

Long-term memory, as suggested by Bruer, is a system where "chunks" of data are linked together in memory into networks of related information. Long-term memory holds networks of different kinds of information. Systems for storing specific events, general or generic information, and the unconscious, procedural memories needed to control motor, perceptual, and cognitive functioning, are all held within this system.

Many researchers and cognitive psychologists make distinctions between the types of knowledge that exist in the long-term memory system. *Declarative knowledge* refers to factual knowledge that is held in memory. *Procedural knowledge* is that information related to the "how" something is accomplished. Examples of declarative knowledge would be found in the knowledge a person has about history or what he or she did on a previous day. Information about how to ride a bike or fix a milkshake are both illustrations of procedural knowledge. The integration of declarative and procedural knowledge is important to learning. For example, for the individual to successfully make a milkshake, he or she must know the ingredients necessary (declarative knowledge) and the methods for completing the task (procedural knowledge). Procedural knowledge can be simple or complex and is often automatized (Bruning et al., 1999).

Declarative knowledge can be further divided into two subcategories: semantic memory and episodic memory. *Semantic memory* "refers to memory of general concepts and principles and their association" (Bruning, et al., 1999, p. 48). The knowledge in semantic memory represents networks of information that are stored in a way that allows for efficient and accurate retrieval. *Episodic memory*, on the other hand, is that memory each person has of personal or autobiographical experiences. Paivio (1986) has suggested that information in long-term memory can be represented in one of two ways, verbally or in images, with memory enhanced when information is coded in both manners.

Attentional Processes

It is important in understanding the information-processing system to describe attentional processes. Bruning et al., (1999) define *attention* as "a person's allocation of cognitive resources to the task at hand" (p. 30). Broadbent (1958) initially suggested that selection of what would be attended to occurred early in the information analysis process and that the individual could attend to only one stimulus at any given moment. Researchers, however, found that the simplistic model presented by Broadbent was not powerful enough to explain certain attentional phenomena.

One line of research that followed Broadbent's work suggested that multiple channels could be attended to, although one was attended to more completely or thoroughly than the other (Triesman, 1964, 1969). This model is referred to as the *attenuated processing model.* A second avenue of research suggested that attentional processes occurred after information was moved into memory rather than at earlier stages in the information analysis process. It further suggested that attention was generally automatic (Shriffrin, 1976; Shriffrin & Schneider, 1977). This model is called the *full processing model.* Current views of attention tend to suggest that both means of explaining the allocation of attentional resources may be correct, depending on the type of mental task the individual performs (Fischer, Duffy, Young, & Pollatsek, 1988).

Two basic types of tasks have been defined: resource-limited tasks and data-limited tasks (Nusbaum & Schwab, 1986). *Resource-limited tasks* improve when more attention is devoted to them. In contrast, *data-limited tasks* do not improve based on the amount of attention given to the task but, rather, on the quality of the information available to the learner. In the case of a resource-limited task, a person may comfortably work on a craft item and watch television simultaneously, but can allocate greater attentional resources to one or the other if performance or understanding requires it (e.g., a news bulletin breaks in warning of imminent severe weather or the stitches of a sweater a person is knitting fall off the needle). A data-limited task, for example, is listening and relistening to a voice message machine in an attempt to understand a garbled name spoken on the tape. No matter how much attentional energy is given to the task, the name may remain undecipherable.

It appears, at least generally, that a person must attend to something before this information can be moved to working memory. Attention is limited in capacity as we cannot attend to everything coming in through our sensory system simultaneously. Some of the factors that influence what a person may attend to include such features as size, intensity, novelty, incongruity, emotion, and personal significance (Ormrod, 1999).

Related to the notion of attentional resources is the concept of automaticity. Most researchers agree that automatic processes are acquired through extended practice and use little if any attention to complete (Bruning et al., 1999). Automatic processes allow the individual to complete tasks simultaneously leaving greater resources available for more complex tasks. For example, phonological (sound) encoding in the efficient learner, would be automatized, so that the student could give more attention to comprehension of the material he or she is reading.

The information-processing system, then, is made up of subsystems that allow for the sensory input of information, the allocation of appropriate attentional resources to perform the desired task, a working memory system where incoming and previously stored information can be actively processed, a long-term memory system for storing essentially limitless information over indefinite periods and mechanisms for guiding the entire system in planning, executing strategies, and maintaining and searching for already stored information. It is the complex interaction of these systems that is at the root of all learning whether it be academic material or social problem solving.

The Role of Memory in Learning and Social Development

According to Baddeley and his associates (1983, 1986, 1993, 1998), Bruer (1993), and other researchers and theorists, the working memory system is critical to the learning process. Both the models proposed by Bruer and Baddeley suggest a memory system where information is actively processed. It is a system where incoming information, either verbal or spatial, can be integrated with previously learned information, and where rules guiding problem solving, planning, or monitoring can be retrieved and applied to complete a task. People with poor phonological working memory would be expected to have poor long-term learning of verbal material, an essential component for the efficient acquisition of academic, social, and personal skills.

Working memory is an essential system but one that has limits. As Bruer (1993) wrote:

> Working memory can hold and process only a limited amount of information, and that for only short periods of time. We can quickly exceed its capacity, and when we do that any new information coming into working memory overwrites or obliterates what was previously there. Working-memory capacity is a limiting factor in our ability to process information. It is the bottleneck in our cognitive system. Skilled thinking, problem solving, and learning depend on how well we can manage this limited resource—on how efficiently we can store, process, and move information, into and out of working memory (p. 29).

The efficient learner, then, is the one who can effectively focus attention on the most essential information in his or her environment, who has achieved automaticity of basic subskills, who can efficiently select and apply appropriate strategies for a given task, and has access to multiple channels of information input (Bruning et al., 1999). If such abilities are missing, the student is likely to struggle as he or she simultaneously attempts to take in and hold incoming information, integrate old information, retrieved from long-term memory with newly entered information and, ultimately, store this information in a way that is readily retrievable.

Children learn when they are presented with a problem that cannot be solved using the "rules" they currently have available to them in long-term memory. They must modify the information held in long-term memory if they are to be successful in accomplishing the new task. This may be accomplished by the child spontaneously, or the new structures needed to complete the task may result from direct training (Bruer, 1993). Some children are able to engage independently in a strategy that leads to rule modification while others need step-by-step instruction that includes both direct teaching of the facts pertaining to the problem and the strategies needed to resolve the problem.

It is also the case that the learner can process only a certain amount of information at any given time. Sensory system capacity, attentional resources, and working memory capacity are limited. This means that learning can take place only at a certain pace and, for some students, it may, indeed, be a slow process. As Ormrod (1999) suggests, however, the limited nature of both attention and working memory in the analysis of information forces the system to organize, condense, and integrate data that makes long-term storage and retrieval more efficient.

Crick and Dodge (1994) have articulated a comprehensive social information-processing model that can help in understanding how children learn and act on social information. Their model assumes that each child brings a "set of biologically limited capabilities" (p. 76) and memories built from past experiences to each social situation. Each child then receives cues from the environment that he or she processes, ultimately resulting in a behavioral response. Crick and Dodge propose six processing steps in their social information-processing model: "(1) encoding of external and internal cues, (2) interpretation and mental representation of those cues, (3) clarification or selection of a goal, (4) response access or construction, (5) response decision, and (6) behavioral enactment" (p. 76). Steps 1 and 2 involve attentional resources directed to both external (situational) and internal experiences. Interpretation, Step 2, may involve the retrieval of personalized information already held in long-term memory, as well as causal analysis, inference about the experience of others in the situation, the individual's sense about his or her self-efficacy, and inferences about the evaluations of self and others. In Step 3, children clarify goals aimed at producing particular outcomes. This would require the simultaneous processing of many different types of information and most likely draws on the working memory system. Steps 4 and 5 appear to rely heavily on information from long-term memory to decide on a possible response and the evaluation of its possible outcome. Working memory and long-term memory are critical in Step 6, as children actually engage in the selected goal-directed behaviors. Crick and Dodge suggest that these processing steps occur in parallel (i.e., children are simultaneously encoding, interpreting, and accessing responses), something that requires intact working memory, and in sequence (i.e., one stimulus may trigger a specific response). (For an expanded treatment of this model, the reader is referred to Chapter 16, in which Cone relates these steps to models of interventions.)

Crick and Dodge propose that social information-processing (actual social skill) both influences and is influenced by social cognition (how and what the child thinks about him- or herself or social interaction) and social maladjustment. These authors also indicate that children who engage in more adaptive behavior are able to consider both instrumental (i.e., action-based responses) and relational (i.e., knowledge of how the action impacts others) cues. They hypothesize that much of social processing is automatic rather than conscious and reflective. This suggestion is particularly relevant given some recent findings by Rabiner, Lenhart, and Lochman (1990). These authors found that some socially maladjusted children responded adequately when information required reflective responses, but poorly when automatic processing was essential.

Dodge and Price (1994) suggested that a child's information-processing skill increases as a function of development: "when a child becomes confronted with increasing demands for behavioral performance by peers and teachers, that child responds over time with increasing skill in those aspects of social information processing that can enhance evaluations of behavioral competence" (p. 1395). The authors further suggest that such findings are consistent with the idea that a child's growth is related to cultural "demands and changes." Finally, researchers have found the amount of information that a child's sensory and working memory systems can handle increases with age (Bruning et al., 1999). This has implications for how much and in what way stimuli should be presented to children. Young children need to be presented with reduced amounts of information. They also benefit from the use of multiple modalities in instruction.

Crick and Dodge (1994) suggest that there is overwhelming evidence that social information-processing skill is related to social adjustment. It is their conclusion that a child must be able to accurately and efficiently encode social cues, correctly interpret them, search for appropriate responses to the social situation, make good decisions about which response is best, and then be able to actually execute the selected response. Problems experienced at any of these levels of social information-processing could negatively impact the child's social adjustment.

Evidence of Processing Deficits among Children with Poor Academic or Social Skills

We know that some students have greater difficulty in academic or social learning than others. Problems have been suggested at both the subsystem level, primarily in the articulatory loop, and in the central executive. Poor learners have been found to have a reduced memory span, particularly in the area of phonological encoding (Jorm, 1979). They also have been found to have difficulty in encoding familiar items such as digits (Torgesen & Houck, 1980) and letter sounds (Waterman & Lewandowski, 1993). Montgomery (1996) found that children with language impairments had reduced phonological working memory capacity, and Comier (1997) found that both phonological awareness and measures of working memory predicted reading and spelling achievement. All problems suggest possible difficulties in the articulatory loop subsystem that has been proposed by Baddeley and his colleagues.

Difficulties in central executive functioning have been suggested by Torgesen and Goldman (1977) and Swanson (1986, 1990, 1995). Students with learning difficulties have been found to use fewer verbal strategies, such as rehearsal, or mnemonic strategies (Torgesen & Goldman, 1977). Swanson (1990) found that children with learning disabilities showed worsening difficulties in processing as the demands of the memory task increased. He further suggested that at least some problems seen in comprehension were independent from deficits in phonological coding. Each of these researchers suggested that deficits in the working memory system, particularly in executive processing, may contribute to learning problems.

Others have suggested that problems in social development are related to deficits in social information-processing abilities. Problems interpreting nonverbal social cues (Pearl, 1986), remembering specific autobiographic information (Goodard, Dritschel, & Burton, 1997), or lack of automatization of basic social skills, such as interpreting tone of voice (Bye & Jussim, 1993), all may contribute to poor social performance.

Bryan, Sullivan-Burstein, and Mathur (1998) reviewed research findings as they related to the social information-processing model proposed by Crick and Dodge (1994) and students with learning problems. Students with learning disabilities were found to differ on many of the six steps included in Crick and Dodge's model (Tur-Kaspa & Bryan, 1994). Students with learning problems were found to have difficulties comprehending both nonverbal (Bryan, 1977) and verbal (Tur-Kaspa & Bryan, 1994) social information. They were also found to add extraneous information (Tur-Kaspa & Bryan, 1994). Each of these suggests problems at the encoding stage. Students with disabilities were also reported as having problems at the interpretation stage. They were found to have difficulty taking the perspective of others (Weiss, 1984) and in detecting lies (Wong & Wong, 1980), indicative of problems in mental representation and interpretation of social information. Oliva and LaGreca (1988) reported that boys with learning disabilities had difficulty developing goals, and Carlson (1987), Toro, Weissberg, Guare, and Liebenstein (1990), and Tur-Kaspa and Bryan (1994) all found that children with learning problems were poor social problem-solvers.

Moisan (1998) reviewed the literature related to learning disabilities and social deficits, and reported that 75% of children with learning problems have lowered levels of social competence and social status. She also found that these children are seen in a more negative light than their nondisabled peers. She suggested that children with learning problems have been found to be immature, possess poor problem-solving skills, have a lowered sense of self-esteem, and may be more aggressive or hostile.

Swanson (1996) and Swanson and Malone (1992) also reviewed research related to learning disabilities and social development. These authors suggested that children with learning disabilities were found to be more socially rejected than their nondisabled peers and engaged in or were the recipients of more hostile interactions. Verbal and nonverbal communication were found to be poorer among children with learning problems. Boys with learning problems were reported to have difficulty altering their "verbal style" when interacting with an adult rather than a peer. Children with learning problems also showed weaker empathy, had poor conflict resolution skills, frequently misinterpreted nonverbal messages, and were less tactful. Swanson and Malone, in their review of literature, reported that children with learning problems felt a greater sense of inadequacy and were more immature in their actions. Finally, students with learning problems were found to be less on-task, a behavior that these authors suggested was related to social status.

Studies completed at the University of Kansas Institute for Research for the Learning Disabled (Schumaker & Deshler, 1995) suggest that children who struggle in learning are both similar to and different from their peers socially and emotionally. The findings of these researchers suggest that students with learning disabilities are not as isolated socially as some educators have feared, and were reported to spend as much or more time with peers, talking on the telephone, and having as many good friends as their more typical age-mates. The University of Kansas Institute, however, found that students with learning disabilities engaged in fewer formal social activities, were less skilled problem solvers, and showed lower levels of social competence than children and adolescents without disabilities. In fact, adolescents with learning disabilities were found to possess social competence comparable to adolescents who were in the juvenile court system. On the positive side, students with learning disabilities were able to learn social skills. Techniques that appeared helpful in teaching social skills were modeling, verbal practice in naming behaviors, role-playing, and use of individual feedback.

Pearl (1986) reviewed research in areas of social functioning among children with learning problems, with specific emphasis on social perception, role-taking, and social knowledge. Her review suggested differences between children with and without learning disabilities in the first two areas of inquiry, but not in the third, as children with learning disabilities were less adept at social perception and role-taking. At the conclusion of her review, Pearl proposed that information-processing deficits, specifically difficulty processing nonverbal social cues, may explain social and emotional problems among youngsters with learning problems.

Nearly all theorists, educators, and researchers would acknowledge a connection between information-processing abilities, learning, and emotional and social development. The exact nature of this relationship, however, continues to be debated. Support can be found in the literature suggesting that information-processing deficits may be both the cause and the result of difficulties experienced in social and emotional development.

Emotions and Cognition

A relationship between emotions and learning is well documented. We know that, when people are successful in learning, they experience positive emotions such as pleasure or pride (Carver & Scheier, 1990; McLeod & Adams, 1989; Smith, 1991; Snow, Corno, & Jackson, 1996). When they fail at a task, they frequently experience negative feelings (Carver & Scheier, 1990; Stodolsky, Salk, & Glaessner, 1991).

Mood and memory also are clearly connected to each other. Bower (1994), Hertel (1994), Oatley and Nundy (1996), and Snow et al., (1996) all found that people were better able to attend to, remember, and retrieve information when they are happy. Bower (1994) also found that people could retrieve information from long-term memory more efficiently and accurately when emotions they experienced at the time of retrieval matched those felt when the information was stored originally. Researchers have found also that information that is emotionally charged is better attended to and processed (Bower, 1994; Edwards & Bryan, 1997; Heuer & Reisberg, 1990).

Crick and Dodge (1994) suggest that emotions and cognition interact across the stages of their proposed social information model, and that situations that elicit strong emotional responses may interfere with accurate and efficient encoding and interpretation of social information. These authors further propose that emotions may have a positive or negative impact on the child's motivation to set or seek social goals: "For example, feelings of anger toward a peer provocateur might serve as the impetus for a retaliatory goal, or feelings of anxiety might lead to the generalization of an avoidant goal (i.e., to remove oneself from the anxiety-provoking stimulus)" (p. 81).

Accessing and making decisions about particular responses, according to Crick and Dodge (1994), may also interact with emotion. They state that determining a particular behavior may change a child's emotional state (e.g., feeling relief) or affect the behavior he or she accesses (e.g., only thinking of extreme "all-or-nothing" behaviors such as running away). Finally, Crick and Dodge suggest that evaluation of a potential social action may be influenced by the child's prediction of the emotions that may be elicited from others if the child engages in a particular behavior. Anxiety also impacts cognition. This impact may be positive, as when tasks are easy and anxiety is high (Spielberger, 1966), or negative, when a task is difficult and anxiety is high (Dusek, 1980; Eccles & Wigfield, 1985; Eysenck & Keane, 1990).

Goldstein and Dundon (1986) suggest that emotional factors, such as the presence of depression, may reduce cognitive capacity and, thus, contribute to learning difficulties. Their research further indicates that children's performance improved when their affect improved. These researchers suggest that, at least for some children, negative emotions such as depression diminish the already limited capacity of attentional resources.

Goodard et al. (1997) considered the role of autobiographical memories in effective social problem solving and found that the students with the most effective and specific memories were the better social problem solvers. These findings, however, also revealed that the severity of depression a given student experienced also influenced his or her social problem-solving skill.

Derakshan and Eysenck (1998) studied the verbal reasoning performance of four groups of undergraduate students: high anxious/low defensive, high anxious/high defensive, low anxious/high defensive, and low anxious/low defensive. All groups were asked to complete both high and low memory demand tasks. These authors found a significantly slower rate of performance in both of the highly anxious groups. Reasoning speed was not affected for low anxious groups. This supports previous research that indicated that processing was negatively impacted by high levels of anxiety.

A connection, then, is clear between cognition and emotion. Emotions have been found to interfere with or enhance memory, determine what will be attended to, and divert or consolidate cognitive resources toward a given task or stimulus.

Social Knowledge, Social Performance, Cognition, and the Role of Environment

As with emotions and learning, the link between social knowledge, social performance, and processing abilities also has been established. At the very root of social skill development is the use of language (Goody, 1997). Goody suggests that language is an essential tool that allows for more effective and efficient storage of information and, as a result, more effective use of memory capacity. She further hypothesizes that effective language processing is essential in the development of "social intelligence." Problems in language processing, and the resulting memory difficulties, then, would be expected to interfere with social performance. In fact, many researchers have suggested that children with language-based learning disabilities, about 50–80% of those children with learning problems, exhibit poorer social, personal, and behavioral adjustment (Bender & Smith, 1990; Bryan et al.,1998; Crick & Dodge, 1994; Cummings, Vallance, & Brazil, 1992; Schachter, Pless, & Bruck, 1991; Vallance, Cummings, & Humphries, 1998). Vallance et al. (1998) suggest that impairments in the ability to effectively communicate thoughts and needs and a tendency to misinterpret the messages of others may contribute in significant ways to poor social skill development and, ultimately, to problem behaviors.

Kasik, Sabatino, and Spoentgen (1986), in a review of literature related to information-processing, learning problems, and social knowledge and performance, suggest that three factors must be considered in understanding research findings: (a) considering the child with a learning disability in relation to the demands of the task, (b) identifying the environmental factors that exist, and (c) understanding the expectations that teachers and others have for social competence. Their review of literature suggests that problems associated with activity levels, memory, and self-concept did not change much in response to environmental factors. They also suggest that interactions with parents and teachers were important to both academic and social performance. Such findings are consistent with the more recent work of Gross (1997).

Gross (1997) suggests that children who have difficulties learning often show signs of depression and a lowered sense of self-worth, and that such problems can interfere with the child's development of a healthy identity as a learner. Gross states that children learn to define themselves as a result of three factors—self-experience as it relates to mastering skills, information the child receives from others about him- or herself, and comparisons the child makes between his or her abilities and skill mastery versus the abilities of others. She suggested that the development of a child's identity as a learner begins early in the child's life and that the child's ability to compare him- or herself with others increases with age. The importance of feedback from the key figures in the child's life (i.e., parents, teachers) is seen as critical to the child's development as a learner (Gross, 1997; Kasik et al., 1986). Gross suggests that many of the messages children receive create conflicts for children who have learning problems (e.g., "why do I sometimes feel dumb and sometimes smart?"), which further complicates the child's development of a healthy identity as a learner. Younger children, according to Gross, tend to view themselves in very concrete, absolute ways. The student who struggles as he or she masters new skills is at-risk for viewing him or herself as a "poor" learner. As Gross (1997) wrote:

> Children who internalize a sense of being slow or poor learners are at considerable risk for failure. Lowered expectations have been shown to have a negative impact on how well children actually learn, and even on how willing they are to attempt tasks. Children with learning disabilities are vulnerable to paralyzing self-doubt, and often avoid learning in order to withdraw from further failure. The literature on learned helplessness is filled with examples of how children try to reduce their sense of failure and to avoid further experiences of incompetence. Labels such as 'slow,' 'stupid,' 'lazy,' and 'dumb' can have a devastating impact on motivation, curiosity and confidence and

are unfortunately all too frequently heard during the impressionable early school years (p. 2).

Gross further warns that a parent's view of his or her child's abilities easily can be unintentionally communicated to the child. Children who are unsure of their abilities may have fears that they are poor learners confirmed by a parent's overt anxiety or even gentle criticism. The development of a child who is a discouraged learner, then, is not surprising. One cost of a discouraged learner is the belief that action taken on the part of the learner has very little payoff. Such a belief is an essential element of an internalized sense of learned helplessness and results in passive learning.

Bye and Jussim (1993) suggest that the development of social knowledge, "what a person knows about human interaction, specifically the behavior expected and accepted in various social situations" (p. 144), and social performance, what the person actually does, is affected by a number of "filters." These authors posit an interaction of environmental factors, including cultural rules and roles, expectations and attractiveness, physiological factors, such as vision and hearing, and information-processing factors, such as attention (i.e., those aspects of their social world that children are attending to), arousal, encoding ability, retention, retrieval, abstraction, generalization, relational thinking, and reasoning all influence the development of social knowledge.

Social performance or behavior is, according to Bye and Jussim, influenced by the same environmental, physiological, and information-processing factors as the development of social knowledge. In addition to these three influencing factors are two others, social knowledge and motivation. The combination of these five filters determines one's social performance. These authors suggest that information-processing factors such as the ability to retrieve relevant social information from memory, the level of automatization of very basic social behaviors, such as information about proper tone of voice, facial expression, physical distance, and the ability to process cues from the environment, all influence the individual's social performance abilities. Attention to and retrieval of social information is affected by proximity, emotional interest, and personal relevance (Fiske & Taylor, 1991, as cited in Bye & Jussim, 1993). In addition, social information that is recent or has been experienced frequently is easier to recall.

Finally, Bye and Jussim suggest that beliefs, goals, and motivations influence social performance. Of particular importance to the current discussion is the notion that individuals' beliefs about their ability to be successful in a given situation affects their thoughts, emotions, and behavior (Meichenbaun, Butler, & Gruson, 1981, as cited in Bye & Jussim, 1993:

> Social performance is regulated by self-appraisal and goal setting; what people believe they can do affects what they will attempt (Fiske & Taylor, 1991) . . . People will strive only for a goal they believe is within reach; the stronger the belief, the harder they will work. Children who believe that their peers will accept them are more likely to risk initiating an interaction. There is evidence indicating that 'negative, self-referent ideation contributes to inadequate performance in a variety of situations' (Miechenbaum,

Butler, & Gruson, 1981, p. 40). If children continually regard themselves as socially in-adequate, it will have a detrimental effect on their social performance (pp. 154–155).

Conclusion

As Bye and Jussim (1993) and others suggest, social knowledge and skill development are most likely related to several interacting factors that involve environmental expe-riences, including the messages children receive from both peers and adults and their ability to process information about their social world accurately and efficiently. Children who have difficulty processing information, both verbally and nonverbally, are at risk for struggling socially and emotionally from several directions. First, the in-formation they receive about themselves as learners is often negative and creates a self-perception of being incompetent. This impacts what they are willing to try. Expectations held both by the children and the peers and adults in their lives are often low, reducing children's motivation or expectations that they can be successful socially. Second, the discouragement children with learning problems feel as a result of re-peated failures academically and socially also serves to diminish their levels of self-confidence and further impairs an already compromised information-processing system.

All of learning depends on the effective and efficient processing of information. This information gains access to the processing system by entering through one or more sensory modalities, is attended to and held in working memory while it is ana-lyzed, compared with previously learned material, or organized in some way. Finally, the information is stored for later retrieval. This information may be verbal or non-verbal in nature and it frequently involves information critical to the development of adequate social knowledge and skills. Problems in any area of the information-processing system can have a negative impact on the developing learner. Research suggests that children with learning disabilities sometimes possess problems in areas of information-processing including difficulties processing language, holding and processing information simultaneously, allocating attentional resources, interpreting social cues, developing social goals, and social problem solving. Determining if a child is struggling as he or she takes in, analyzes, stores, and retrieves information is a crit-ical but not always easy process. In most cases such a determination is made through a combination of inferences made from observations of the student's behavior, for-malized testing, and the ongoing evaluation of the effectiveness of the interventions that are attempted.

The child who loses critical information as he or she attempts to process it, who is misinterpreting verbal or nonverbal social cues, who has not automatized basic so-cial information, such as tone of voice, facial expression, or physical distance, or who attends to the wrong environmental stimuli is vulnerable emotionally and socially. He or she is more apt to show symptoms associated with depression, be a poor social problem solver, have a lowered sense of worth and competence, and be a less actively involved learner in general. In short, processing problems interfere with the acquisition of social knowledge, leaving affected children without critical information needed for social problem solving. Children with information-processing deficits are at risk for having reduced bases of social knowledge and awareness, which is made worse by an expectation, both from those around them and from themselves, for social failure. Interventions, then, must be aimed at helping them more effectively and efficiently acquire crucial social information and at the expectations they may have formed about their own social competence. Specific ideas for working with children who experience difficulties in learning and social development will be considered in further detail in Chapter 14 of this text. Understanding the importance of information-processing abilities and their impact on the development of social skills and emotional adjustment is essential as practitioners in both educational and clinical settings move toward developing and implementing effective interventions for children whose information-processing systems are impaired.

References

Baddeley, A. D. (1983). Working memory. *Philosophical Transactions of the Royal Society of London, B, 302,* 311–324.

Baddeley, A. D. (1986). *Working memory.* London: Oxford University Press.

Baddeley, A. D., Gathercole, S., & Papagno, C. (1998). The phonological loop as a language learning device. *Psychological Review, 105,* 158–173.

Baddeley, A. D., & Hitch, G. (1974). Working memory. In G. H. Bower (Ed.), *The psychology of learning and motivation* (Vol. 8, pp. 47–90). New York: Academic Press.

Bender, W. N., & Smith, J. K. (1990). Classroom behavior of children and adolescents with learning disabilities: A meta-analysis. *Journal of Learning Disabilities, 23,* 298–305.

Bower, G. H. (1994). Some relations between emotions and memory. In P. Ekman & R. J. Davidson (Eds.), *The nature of emotion: Fundamental questions* (pp. 303–306). New York: Oxford University Press.

Broadbent, D. E. (1958). *Perception and communication.* London: Pergamon.

Bruer, J. T. (1993). *Schools for thought: A science of learning in the classroom.* Cambridge, MA: MIT Press.

Bruning, R., Schraw, G., & Ronning, R. (1999). *Cognitive psychology and instruction.* Columbus, OH: Merrill.

Bryan, T. (1977). Learning disabled children's comprehension of nonverbal communication. *Journal of Learning Disabilities, 10,* 501–506.

Bryan, T., Sullivan-Burstein, K., & Mathur, S. (1998). The influence of affect on social-information-

processing. *Journal of Learning Disabilities, 31,* 418–126.

Bye, L., & Jussim, L. (1993). A proposed model for the acquisition of social knowledge and social competence. *Psychology in the Schools, 30,* 143–161.

Carlson, C. I. (1987). Social interaction goals and strategies of children with learning disabilities. *Journal of Learning Disabilities, 20,* 306–311.

Carver, C. S., & Scheier, M. E. (1990). Origins and functions of positive and negative affect: A control–process view. *Psychological Review, 97,* 19–35.

Chomsky, N. (1956). Three models for the description of language. *IRE Transactions of Information Theory, 2–3,* 113–124.

Comier, P. (1997). Distinctive patterns of relationship of phonological awareness and working memory with reading development. *Reading and Writing: An Interdisciplinary Journal, 9,* 193–206.

Crick, N. R., & Dodge, K. A. (1994). A review and reformulation of social information-processing mechanisms in children's social adjustment. *Psychological Bulletin, 115,* 74–101.

Cummings, R. L., Vallance, D. D., & Brazil, K. (1992). Prevalence and patterns of psychosocial disorders in children and youth with learning disabilities: A service provider's perspective. *Exceptionality Education Canada, 2,* 91–108.

Derakshan, N., & Eysenck, M. W. (1998). Working memory capacity in high trait-anxious and repressor groups. *Cognition and Emotion, 12,* 697–713.

Dodge, K. A., & Price, J. M. (1994). On the relation between social information-processing and socially competent behavior in early school-aged children. *Child Development, 65,* 1385–1397.

Dusek, J. B. (1980). The development of test anxiety in children. In I. G. Sarason (Ed.), *Test anxiety: Theory, research and applications* (pp. 87–110). Hillsdale, NJ: Erlbaum.

Eccles, J. S., & Wigfield, A. (1985). Teacher expectations and student motivation. In J. B. Dusek (Ed.), *Teacher expectancies* (pp. 185–226). Hillsdale, NJ: Erlbaum.

Edwards, K., & Bryan, T. S., (1997). Judgmental biases produced by instructions to disregard: The (paradoxical) case of emotional information. *Personality and Social Psychology Bulletin, 23,* 849–864.

Eysenck, M. W., & Keane, M. T. (1990). *Cognitive psychology: A student's handbook.* Hove, UK: Erlbaum.

Fischer, D. L., Duffy, S. A., Young, C., & Pollatsek, A. (1988). Understanding the central processing link in consistent-mapping visual search tasks. *Journal of Experimental Psychology: Human Perception and Performance, 14,* 253–266.

Fiske, S., & Taylor, S. (1991). *Social cognition* (2nd ed.). New York: McGraw-Hill.

Gathercole, S., & Baddeley, A. (1990). Phonological memory deficits in language disordered children: Is there a causal connection? *Journal of Memory and Language, 29,* 336–360.

Gathercole S., & Baddeley, A. (1993). *Working memory and language.* Hove, UK: Erlbaum.

Goldstein, D., & Dundon, W. D. (1986). Affect and cognition in learning disabilities. In S. J. Ceci (Ed.), *Handbook of cognitive, social, and neuropsychological aspects of learning disabilities* (pp. 233–250). Hillsdale, NJ: Erlbaum.

Goodard, L., Dritschel, B., & Burton, A. (1997). Social problem solving and autobiographical memory in non-clinical depression. *British Journal of Clinical Psychology, 36,* 449–451.

Goody, E. N. (1997). Social intelligence and language: Another Rubicon? In A. Whiten & R. W. Byrne (Eds.), *Machiavellian intelligence II: Extensions and evaluations* (pp. 364–396). Cambridge, England: Cambridge University Press.

Gross, A. H. (1997). Defining the self as a learner for children with LD. *National Center for Learning Disabilities* [On-line]. Available: www.Idonline.org/ld_indepth/self_esteem/defining_self.hfml

Hertel, P. T. (1994). Depression and memory: Are impairments remediable through attentional control? *Current Directions in Psychological Science, 3,* 190–193.

Heuer, F., & Reisberg, D. (1990). Vivid memories of emotional events: The accuracy of remembered minutiae. *Memory and Cognition, 18,* 496–506.

Jorm, A. F. (1979). The cognitive and neurological basis of developmental dyslexia: A theoretical framework and review. *Cognition, 7,* 19–33.

Kasik, M. M., Sabatino, D. A., & Spoentgen, P. (1986). Psychosocial aspects of learning disabilities. In S. J. Ceci (Ed.), *Handbook of cognitive, social, and neuropsychological aspects of learning disabilities* (pp. 251–272). Hillsdale, NJ: Erlbaum.

Marr, D. (1982). *Vision.* New York: Freeman Press.

Marr, D. (1985). Vision: The philosophy and the approach. In A. M. Aitkenhead (Ed.), *Issues in cognitive modeling* (pp. 26–61). Mahwah, NJ: Erlbaum.

McLeod, D. B., & Adams, V. M. (Eds.). (1989). *Affect and mathematical problem solving: A new perspective.* New York: Springe–Verlag.

Meichenbaum, D., Butler, L., & Gruson, L. (1981). Toward a conceptual model of social competence. In J. Wine & M. Smye (Eds.), *Social competence* (pp. 36–60). New York: Guilford Press.

Miller, G. A. (1956). Human memory and the storage of information. *IRE Transactions of Information Theory, 2–3* 129–137.

Moisan, T. A. (1998). *Identification and remediation of social skills deficits in learning disabled children.* Unpublished master's research paper. Chicago State University, Chicago, IL.

Montgomery, J. W. (1996). Sentence comprehension and working memory in children with specific language impairment. *Journal in Language Disorders, 17,* 19–32.

Newell, A., & Simon, H. A. (1956). The logic theory machine: A complex information-processing system. *IRE Transactions of Information Theory, 2–3,* 61–79.

Nusbaum, J. C., & Schwab, E. C. (1986). The role of attention and active processing in speech perception. In E. C. Schwab & H. C. Nusbaum (Eds.), *Pattern recognition by humans and machines* (pp. 113–157). San Diego, CA: Academic Press.

Oatley, K., & Nundy, S. (1996). Rethinking the role of emotions in education. In D. R. Olson & N. Torrance (Eds.), *The handbook of education and human development: New models of learning, teaching, and schooling* (pp. 257–274). Cambridge, MA: Blackwell.

Oliva, A. H., & LaGreca, A. M. (1988). Children with learning disabilities: Social goals and strategies. *Journal of Learning Disabilities, 21,* 301–306.

Ormrod, J. E. (1999). *Human learning.* Columbus, OH: Merrill.

Paivio, A. (1986). *Mental representations: A dual coding approach.* New York: Oxford University Press.

Pearl, R. (1986). Social cognitive factors in learning-disabled children's social problems. In S. J. Ceci (Ed.), *Handbook of cognitive, social, and neuropsychological aspects of learning disabilities* (pp. 273–294). Hillsdale, NJ: Erlbaum.

Rabiner, D. L., Lenhart, L., & Lochman, J. E. (1990). Automatic versus reflective social problem solving in relation to children's sociometric status. *Developmental Psychology, 26,* 1010–1016.

Schachter, D., Pless, I. B., & Bruck, M. (1991). The prevalence and correlates of behaviour problems in learning disabled children. *Canadian Journal of Psychiatry, 36,* 323–331.

Schumaker, J. B., & Deshler, D. D. (1995). Social skills and learning disabilities. *Learning Disabilities Association of America Newsbriefs.* [On-line]. Available: www.Idonline.org/Id_indepth/social_skills/socialskills_and_Id.html

Shriffrin, R. M. (1976). Capacity limitations in information-processing, attention, and memory. In W. K. Estes (Ed.), *Handbook of learning and cognitive processes* (pp. 64–92). Mahwah, NJ: Erlbaum.

Shriffrin, R. M., & Schneider, W. (1977). Controlled and automatic information-processing, II: Perceptual learning, automatic attending, and a general theory. *Psychological Review, 84,* 127–190.

Smith, E. L. (1991). A conceptual change model of learning science. In S. M. Glynn, R. H. Yeany, & B. K. Britton (Eds.), *The psychology of learning science* (pp. 43–64). Hillsdale, NJ: Erlbaum.

Snow, R. E., Corno, L., & Jackson, D., III. (1996). Individual differences in affective and cognitive functions. In D. C. Berliner & R. O. Calfee (Eds.), *Handbook of educational psychology* (pp. 243–310). New York: Macmillan.

Spielberger, C. D. (1966). The effects of anxiety on complex learning in academic achievement. In C. D. Spielberger (Ed.), *Anxiety and behavior* (pp. 361–398). New York: Academic Press.

Stodolsky, S. S., Salk, S., & Glaessner, B. (1991). Student views about learning math and social studies. *American Educational Research Journal, 28,* 89–116.

Swanson, H. L. (1986). Multiple coding processes in learning-disabled and skilled readers. In S. J. Ceci (Ed.), *Handbook of cognitive, social and neuropsychological aspects of learning disabilities* (pp. 203–228). Hillsdale, NJ: Erlbaum.

Swanson, H. L. (1990). Influence of metacognitive knowledge and aptitude on problem-solving. *Journal of Educational Psychology, 82,* 306–314.

Swanson, H. L. (1995). The role of working memory in skilled and less skilled readers' comprehension. *Intelligence, 21,* 83–108.

Swanson, H. L. (1996). Meta-analysis, replication, social skills, and learning disabilities. *Journal of Special Education, 30,* 213–221.

Swanson, H. L., & Malone, S. (1992). Social skills and learning disabilities: A meta-analysis of the literature. *School Psychology Review, 21,* 427–443.

Torgesen, J. K., & Goldman, T. (1977). Verbal rehearsal and short-term memory in reading-disabled children. *Child Development, 48,* 56–60.

Torgesen, J. K., & Houck, D. G. (1980). Processing deficiencies in children who perform poorly on the digit span test. *Journal of Educational Psychology, 72,* 141–160.

Toro, P. A., Weissberg, R. P., Guare, J., & Liebenstein, N. L. (1990). A comparison of children with and without learning disabilities on social problem-soving skills, school behavior, and family background. *Journal of Learning Disabilities, 23,* 115–120.

Triesman, A. M. (1964). Selective attention in man. *British Medical Journal, 20,* 12–16.

Triesman, A. M. (1969). Strategies and models of selective attention. *Psychological Review, 76,* 282–299.

Tur-Kaspa, H., & Bryan, T. (1994). Social information-processing of students with learning disabilities. *Journal of Learning Disabilities Research and Practice, 9,* 12–23.

Vallance, D. D., Cummings, R. L., & Humphries, T. (1998). Mediators of the risk for problem behavior in children with language learning disabilities. *Journal of Learning Disabilities, 31,* 160–171.

Waterman, B., & Lewandowski, L. (1993). Phonological and semantic processing in reading-disabled and nondisabled males at two age levels. *Journal of Experimental Child Psychology, 55,* 87–103.

Weiss, E. (1984). Learning disabled children's understanding of social interactions of peers. *Journal of Learning Disabilities, 17,* 612–615.

Wong, B. Y. L., & Wong, R. (1980). Role-taking in normal achieving and learning disabled children. *Learning Disability Quarterly, 3,* 11–18.

9

Understanding Teaching and Learning Preferences

Barbara A. Fischetti

The present chapter reviews ecological variables as they relate to the educational process. Variables helpful to academic achievement include task engagement, reinforcement schedules, feedback, and classroom practices. In spite of controlling for these conditions, some students continue to encounter academic difficulties and have, in point of fact, appeared unmotivated in the classroom. Ecological variables may not account for all of the differences in learning in the educational process.

The chapter poses personality variables or learning preferences as an influence in teaching and learning. The theory of psychological type is introduced and discussed as it relates to schools and learning. This theory posits that individual behavior is not random but based on how individuals use perception (sensing–intuition) and judgment (thinking–feeling) in conjunction with attitudes (extraversion–introversion and judging–perceiving). Personality type, measured by either the *Myers Briggs Type Indicator* (*MBTI*; Myers, McCaulley, Quenk, & Hammer, 1998) or the *Murphy Meisgeier Type Indicator for Children* (*MMTIC*; Meisgeier & Murphy, 1987), provides valuable information and intervention strategies for teaching and learning.

Studies relevant to personality type and education are presented and noted to be useful for both teachers and students. Classroom interventions based on psychological type are discussed and detail the many options for incorporating type in the classroom. Finally, type and teaching styles are used to review specific ways that a teacher leads with his or her own type preferences when teaching concepts in the classroom. Case studies provide illustrations of the theory discussed and its direct applicability to the teaching of students in the classroom.

Learning Variables

Environmental factors as they relate to academic achievement and classroom learning have been noted to improve or diminish educational outcomes. Lentz and Shapiro (1986) define these variables as time allotted for academic work, instructions, peer attention, and post-work contingencies. Likewise, they highlight teacher variables that are of prime importance to the teaching–learning process: goal setting and progress monitoring, direct questioning, performance feedback, appropriate instructional pacing, attending contingently to appropriate work, praising, prompting, contacting pattern during individual seatwork, and arranging contingencies for desirable academic engagement. Assessment of these important ecological variables was recommended as critical to identifying academic difficulties and designing appropriate academic interventions.

Gettinger (1995) and Rosenshine (1981) confirm the critical nature of academic engagement in the teaching–learning process. Of prime importance was not just the amount of time, but the nature and quality of instructional time actually spent with students (Walberg, 1988). In order to promote optimal student learning, academic engagement also must include interactive instruction between the student and the teacher. Lower teacher engagement time with students was found to result in smaller achievement gains (Stallings, 1980). It would appear that time devoted to discipline, grading papers, or completing additional administrative tasks such as cafeteria duty do not always translate to academic gains for students. Teacher behaviors and classroom practices can influence learning engagement time for students (Brophy & Good, 1986). Caldwell, Huitt, and Graeber (1982) found that academic achievement either leveled off or became negative when engagement time increased beyond a certain level. Students who already have mastered material may not gain academically from increased engagement time with a teacher.

The teaching profession has become more knowledgeable and proficient regarding ecological variables and their impact on the teaching-learning process. Research, theories, and synthesized work of the best practices in teaching are now available to assist teachers as they work to improve student acquisition of knowledge and its application. Hunter (1982) discussed effective teaching strategies for student academic success, and highlighted the importance of selecting appropriate instructional methods in the teaching–learning process. More recently, Saphier and Gower (1997) have explored the practice of pedagogy and detailed the best practices of teaching, noting that teaching is guided by three concepts: comprehensiveness, repertoire, and matching.

In spite of the research, some students continue to do poorly in school and report that schools do not adequately meet their needs. Teachers often say that students are unmotivated or undisciplined in their classrooms. Although ecological variables play a large role in the teaching–learning process, they do not account for all of the variability in the educational environment. Lewin (1976) notes that behavior is a function of the interaction between an individual's personality and ecological variables. Personality differences or learning preferences offer alternative models for developing interventions for students and teachers.

What other variables might assist teachers and students in the classroom? How do you reach the hard to teach? How can teachers improve their effectiveness for students? How can students begin to understand their learning preferences and convey this critical information to teachers? How does a psychologist assist students, teachers, and parents in their search for maximum learning and social–emotional growth?

Personality theory provides us with a framework for understanding individual cognitive processes as well as relationship style. This understanding improves our ability to match teaching instruction with learning preferences. It is clear that we need to understand individual preferences and apply this information to the teaching–learning process, especially when concepts are first introduced to students. In a study of styles of engagement of learning, Ainley (1993) notes that the characteristics students bring to the learning process influence and unite with their interpretation of the activity. Because student characteristics impact the learning strategy chosen and school achievement, it is important for teachers to understand student preferences as variables that impact the teaching–learning process.

The theory of psychological type offers us an understanding of cognitive processes and learning preferences. Most importantly, it provides us with an understanding of self and others that accepts and honors different approaches to the same task. Type is based on a theory of normal development that broadens our understanding of student and teacher behaviors and mental processing. Student differences are no longer maladaptive but, rather, an example of infinite learning potential. Communication improves when we understand learning preferences. Additionally, we can learn more effective ways of working with others, both individually and in groups.

Psychological Type

The theory of psychological type was first introduced by Carl Jung (1923) and extended by Isabel Briggs Myers (1980). The theory asserts that individual behavior is not random but based on how individuals prefer to use perception and judgment in combination with different attitudes. *Perception* involves how individuals become aware of, take in, or receive information. *Judgment* involves how individuals come to conclusions regarding the incoming information. Perception and judgment are mental functions. Jung referred to an individual's orientation of energy, extraversion and introversion, as *attitudes*. Katharine Briggs and Isabel Briggs Myers (1980) clarified a fourth preference, judging and perceiving, which was referred to as an attitude or orientation to the outside world. These attitudes denote which function is extraverted and assist in identifying the dominant and auxiliary functions of individuals.

The attitudes of extraversion (E) and introversion (I) comprise the first dichotomy of type preference. These are complimentary and indicate how individuals prefer to focus energy. With an extraverted preference, energy flows outward to people and the environment. Typical of this preference is the need to talk in order to think and the need for movement or activity. With an introverted preference, an individual is drawn to the inner world of thoughts and ideas. Typical of this preference is the need to think before talking and the need for solitude. It is important to note that a preference does not indicate that an individual relies solely on one to the exclusion of the other, only that the individual has more energy for the preferred attitude and less energy for the nonpreferred attitude.

The perceiving mental functions include sensing (S) and intuition (N). Those with a sensing preference take in information by way of the five senses. They rely on facts, details, and are practical and realistic. Individuals with an intuitive preference prefer to center on possibilities and relationships. Although they take in information by way of the five senses, they look for patterns to this information. They look toward what might be, in lieu of what is, and often view information in terms of the "big picture." Myers and McCaulley (1985) note that these preferences have the clearest relationship with occupational choice. Sensors tend to prefer occupations that rely on details and facts while intuitives prefer responsibilities that involve solving problems and imagining possibilities.

The judging preferences include thinking (T) and feeling (F). Those with a thinking preference make decisions based on logic and objective information. They may be viewed as impersonal and do not find conflict uncomfortable. Individuals with a feeling preference make decisions based on its impact on individuals. Information is looked at subjectively and decisions are reached based on values. Conflict is usually uncomfortable to those with a feeling preference and, for some, avoided at all costs. Myers (1980) identified these functions as the second most important preference for occupational choice. Feeling types enjoy jobs that rely on working and helping people while thinking types prefer work that involves ideas or theories that can be handled logically.

Judging (J) and perceiving (P) are the fourth type preference and define two ways of dealing with the outside environment. Those with a judging attitude prefer to live in an orderly and planned way. They value closure and enjoy organizing activities. An individual with a strong J preference also would tend to use the thinking–feeling function quickly, and would impress others as decisive. Individuals with a perceiving preference prefer to be spontaneous, flexible, and to leave their options open. Perceiving types are curious and open to what is new in their environment. A selection of P means individuals use the sensing–intuition function and delay making decisions while considering new data or new possibilities. The judging–perceiving preference is also utilized to determine the dominant and auxiliary function.

The four preferences together indicate a person's type (e.g., ENTJ). There are sixteen possible types that often are illustrated in a type table (Myers, 1980). Each type demonstrates particular characteristics that influence learning. Type preferences are not evenly distributed in the general population, with recent national normative figures demonstrating highest population percentages for ISFJ and ESFJ types (13.8% and 12.3%, respectively) and lowest percentages for INFJ and INTJ types (1.5% and 2.1%, respectively; Myers et al., 1998).

Developmental Aspects

Type develops throughout an individual's life (Jung, 1923). Type preferences are innate, yet the experience of a preference can be influenced by the environment. The attitudes of extraversion–introversion and judging–perceiving are noted to be present at birth and remain relatively stable throughout a person's life (Murphy, 1992). Smith (1997) identified attitude characteristics of babies as early as 2–3 months. The functions of sensing–intuition and thinking–feeling, however, develop throughout a person's life. In childhood, a preferred function emerges and becomes the dominant one. In adolescence, the second most preferred function or the auxiliary one emerges and is supportive to the dominant function (Murphy, 1992). It is important to understand that, if a dominant function is a judging function, then the auxiliary function is a perceiving function. Therefore, a dominant perceiving (sensing–intuition) function has an auxiliary judging (thinking–feeling) function. This provides balance in an individual.

The tertiary function, or the opposite of the auxiliary function, develops in early adulthood. Finally, in later adulthood, the inferior or the opposite of the dominant function develops in the personality. The inferior function is generally less mature and developed than the other functions. Behaviors associated with this function will, therefore, be less effective as it has less conscious energy available. The dominant function has the most conscious energy and determines the degree of consciousness of the other three (Myers et al., 1998). The auxiliary and tertiary are between the dominant and inferior in available energy.

Individuals are born with a predisposition to a preferred function. Jung (1923) hypothesized that the auxiliary, tertiary, and inferior functions are not all conscious. Children, therefore, are motivated to utilize their preferred function and this gives them greater competence with it. They also exert their auxiliary function. The environment can foster type development or discourage it by reinforcing activities contrary to type preferences. This can lead to *type falsification*.

A prime example of type falsification can occur when a child with an extraversion preference grows up with family members who have an introversion preference. This child may appear quiet and may not often discuss information with other family members. Once this child becomes involved with others with a similar preference at school, his or her natural preference for extraversion will become evident through his or her choices of classroom and playground activities. If assessed for type (as described later in this chapter), this child may respond based on the family experiences rather than his or her true type preference. This possibility emphasizes the importance of having type verified by the child.

The dominant function can be determined by first looking at the attitude of judging–perceiving. This attitude identifies which function of the individual is extraverted. If the individual prefers extraversion, this points to his or her dominant function. If an individual prefers introversion, then it is the opposite of this function that is the dominant function. This also indicates the direction of the flow of psychic energy. The auxiliary function, which is in the opposite attitude of extraversion or introversion, is the opposite mental function of perceiving or judging for balance. The tertiary function is the opposite function of the auxiliary and the inferior function is opposite the dominant function. Two examples follow:

	ENTJ	*ISFP*
Dominant	T	F
Auxiliary	N	S
Tertiary	S	N
Inferior	F	T

In terms of differentiation and development, the dominant function is the most differentiated; the inferior function is the least differentiated. Only one cognitive process or function can be in the control of consciousness at a time (Thompson, 1996). The inferior function, the least differentiated one, tends to manifest itself in a more primitive and archaic way when it reaches consciousness. This has been referred to as "being in the grip" (Quenk, 1996).

The sixteen combinations of four sets of preferences are each distinct in their characteristics. Each is the product of its dominant process and is modified by its auxiliary (Myers, 1980). It is important to remember that development and environment influence type, and that two people with the same type can behave differently. Additionally, all types have the inferior function, which can manifest itself in immature behavior. It is especially important to bear in mind that children are in the process of growth, which requires experiences that support type development. It is not unusual to see the attitudes early in a child's life; however, the functions develop during the lifetime from unconscious to conscious control. Children, therefore, may demonstrate their preferences with immature behaviors as they gain conscious control of their functions.

Measurement of Psychological Type

As noted at the outset of this chapter, the *MBTI* and the *MMTIC* are two instruments utilized for the assessment of psychological type. The *MBTI* was originally developed by Katharine Briggs and her daughter, Isabel Briggs Myers (1962). It is the most widely employed personality instrument in the world (Myers et al., 1998). The *MMTIC* was developed by Charles Meisgeier and Elizabeth Murphy (1987), and is currently under revision.

The *MBTI*, a personality inventory, is designed to measure personality type as posited by Jung and to make it understandable and useful to individuals in everyday life. The original version was based on the prediction ratio method and its present version is based on item response theory. The most recent version of the *MBTI* has a number of forms that include both self-scorable and computer versions. Form M is a 93–item version and the manual notes that it "contains the newest items, the most precise scoring procedure, and the most current standardization samples to produce scoring weights . . . [T]his form was designed to maximize precision of preference identification at the midpoint of each dichotomy and to eliminate the need for separate scoring keys for males and females" (Myers et al., 1998, p. 106).

The 1998 *MBTI* manual indicates that the tool can be administered to individuals above the age of 14. The Fry formula (Fry, 1977) produced a readability level of seventh grade. The manual notes high internal consistency (.90 and higher) based on split-half correlations and based on coefficient alpha (.91 and higher). No differences were found for males and females nor across age groups using coefficient alpha. Test-retest reliabilities were .94 on the extraversion–introversion scale, .90 on the sensing–intuition scale, .82 on the thinking–feeling scale, and .93 on the judging–perceiving scale, demonstrating consistency over time. With respect to validity, evidence is presented for the validity of the four preference scales and for the validity of whole types. The reader is referred to the test manual (Myers et al., 1998) for further discussion of the scale's psychometric properties.

The *MBTI* results are presented as a preference type for each of four scales. It is important to have the individual validate the results. In fact, individuals decide on the best fit even if it is in direct contrast to the *MBTI* results. The critical issue is to have the results explained and interpreted fully to a client. The *MBTI* also provides a description of the results and a preference clarity index and preference clarity category. These provide the client with an estimate of relative confidence that a preference has been identified correctly. It is extremely important that this information not be viewed as strength of preference or quality of the development of the preference.

The *MMTIC* was designed to assess type in children from grades two through eight. The Fry formula (Fry, 1977) produced a readability level of second grade. The authors (Meisgeier & Murphy, 1987) noted that the instrument can be read aloud to children with reading difficulties. The tool consists of 70 items and can be hand- or computer-scored. The *MMTIC* reports the psychological type of children, with one significant difference from the *MBTI*. Because children are developing, their responses on the *MMTIC* may not yield a clear preference. In these instances, the child's preference will be reported as undetermined (U). A child's reported preference could, therefore, have one or more U's. Murphy (1994) notes that it is unusual for a child to receive four U's. However, children who did were found to have lower self-esteem and achievement. Preference scale cutoffs were determined by discriminative analysis.

Reliability estimates for the *MMTIC* indicate that it is consistent across grade level, gender, and reading level. Internal consistency was computed using the Spearman-Brown method and found reliabilities of .62 for the extraversion–introversion scale, .68 for the sensing–intuition scale, .65 for the thinking–feeling scale, and .72 for the judging–perceiving scale. The authors acknowledge that reliability coefficients generally were less than those reported for the adult samples, but noted that the resultant magnitudes were comparable to student samples. The developmental nature of type would lead one to expect lower reliabilities among younger samples (Meisgeier & Murphy, 1987). Evidence for concurrent and content validity were presented in the manual. Twenty-one experts in the field of type rated the *MMTIC* by way of a five-point Likert scale relative to its content. The average mean rating was 4.1 and supported that the items accurately reflected the theory of psychological type. Murphy reported that there is unpublished reliability and validity data for students, grades 9 through 12 (Singer, 1996). Due to potential reading difficulties with the *MBTI* for some students, she suggests that students could be given the option to take the *MMTIC*.

Research on Type and Education

There have been numerous studies on type and education. These studies are summarized in the *MBTI* manual (Myers et. al., 1998) and by Hammer (1996). These studies investigated learning styles, cognitive styles, brain patterns, information-processing tasks, study methods, test taking, and decision making (Hammer, 1996). Several basic constructs have been confirmed (Beyler & Schmeck, 1992). A higher internal arousal state was noted for introverts, as well as greater cognitively related brain electrical activity patterns than extraverts (Wilson & Languis, 1989). As well, left hemispheric preferences correlated with sensing, thinking, and judging (Beyler & Schmeck, 1992), while right hemispheric functions were associated with greater preferences for intuition, feeling, and perceiving. A more recent review of literature (Power & Lundsten, 1997) on brain hemispheric preference confirmed that sensors favor the left hemisphere and intuitives favor the right hemisphere. Additionally, they noted that E, N, T, and P correlated more highly with a cerebral or abstract thought process and I, S, F, and J correlated more highly with a limbic or emotionally toned thought process.

DiTiberio (1996, 1998) conducted comprehensive reviews of research and found patterns of learning styles and cognitive processing based on type. Relevant to education is the finding that intuitive and introverted types score higher on the Scholastic Aptitude Test while judging types performed better on grade-point average (Schurr & Ruble, 1988). They also noted that, in abstract and theoretical courses, introverts and intuitives obtained higher grades, while extraverts and sensing types performed better in practical and applied courses. The reader is cautioned in interpreting this information to mean that one type performs better than another. Rather, one type may demonstrate a strength in relation to another type based on learning preferences, but this does not presuppose that a student cannot achieve but, rather, that a student may need to invest more energy to achieve at a desired level. Teaching that emphasizes all preferences can reduce the discrepancy of grades across types.

Other relevant studies on type and education identify aptitude and achievement levels, reading and language levels, writing studies, foreign language development, teacher types, gifted education, learning and behavior disorders, higher education attributes, behavioral tendencies of teachers, and learning preferences of students as they relate to type. Of particular interest for teaching was the summary of multiple studies (DiTiberio, 1996), which noted that matching teachers with learners based on type led to mixed results. Donovan (1994) noted that the developmental nature of type may well lead to students needing different kinds of instruction at different times during their schooling. This research highlights the need for diverse teaching strategies designed to improve student learning.

Classroom Interventions and Type Preferences

Research has provided educators with important information relative to the application of psychological type to the classroom. Studies investigating type and its application to teaching and learning have increased during the last decade. Lawrence (1997) discusses how the dominant function points to the basic motivation of students, and notes that understanding the dominant function and its motivation leads to making learning much more effective for students. Students with a dominant function of sensing want experiences that are real, practical, hands-on, and in the here and now. Students with an intuitive dominant function are more motivated when learning includes possibilities and imagination. Children with a dominant thinking function operate more effectively if there is logic and orderliness, either in the outside world or the inside world of ideas. Finally, students with a feeling dominant function need relationships in their lives that are positive and fulfilling. If a classroom is designed to provide all of these experiences, motivation will be stronger for learning.

Many other theorists (Bargar, Bargar, & Cano, 1994; Bayne, 1995; Fairhurst & Fairhurst, 1995; Golay, 1982; Lawrence, 1993; Meisgeier, Murphy, & Meisgeier, 1989; Murphy, 1992; VanSant & Payne, 1995) have applied type to the classroom and learning. Learning preferences based on the dominant function, temperament, the four pairs of preferences, and the combination of the four preferences have increased our knowledge of how to improve the teaching–learning process. All note that learning preferences need to be viewed in light of developmental level. Additionally, students need diverse experiences that require them to learn in a variety of ways. Finally, Bayne (1995) recommends that teachers begin with their own style and add activities and language that recognize other types.

Extraversion–Introversion Preferences

Children with an extraversion preference need to talk to think and enjoy action. They may demonstrate impulsivity and, at times, can become distracted by other activities in the classroom. Children with an extraversion preference may learn more quickly if they experience information first and then read about it. Classrooms helpful to children with an extraversion preference need to include small group work or peer teaming. Physical movement and work that involves talking are very useful to this learning preference. Students with this preference react more positively to verbal feedback, and young children with this preference may well need to learn to hold a thought in memory and to move mentally rather than physically. It is particularly helpful to this preference to have quiet when presented with extremely difficult tasks.

Children with an introversion preference need time to think and process information. The concept of wait time frequently discussed in education circles is critical to this preference. Often, it is helpful to this preference to give them notice before they are called upon in class, so that they have adequate wait time. Students with this preference typically prefer to be given time to reflect and complete their mental processing. It is critical for students with an introversion preference to be able to let their teacher know that they are continuing to think or need time to do so. Students with an introversion preference often lament that, as soon as they are ready to volunteer in class, the opportunity has passed and the class is on a new question or topic.

Murphy (1995) provides multiple suggestions for honoring extraversion–introversion preferences in the classroom. Conversation sticks (e.g., popsicle sticks, crayons, pennies, and tongue depressors) assist students when participating in group discussions. Each student receives two sticks and must use the sticks to offer verbal information to the group. Once a student has used the sticks, he or she must wait until all students have done so in order to get another chance to participate verbally in the conversation.

Other helpful activities offered include the mute button, "All Share or Share by Choice," increased wait time, advising extraverts that a message has been heard, seatwork signals (red and green cards), choice for discussion with peers or completing the assignment without discussion, and measuring participation by written methods. "All Share or Share by Choice" advises students prior to the completion of classwork whether or not their work will be shared with their classmates. Red and green cards help students advise their teacher when they require assistance by placing the card on their desk. These educational interventions honor type differences and also give students the opportunity to honor the type differences of their classmates.

Sensing–Intuitive Preferences

The sensing and intuitive preference helps the teacher understand how the children in their class take in information and process it. VanSant and Payne (1995) offer many practical and useful suggestions for teaching sensing and intuitive children. Their work shares lesson plans as well as motivating words and activities for this preference. They apply the theory of type and temperament theory to such concepts as time management, work habits, the learning environment, physical space, and type development.

Sensing children need to have hands-on learning experiences that are sequential and give them the facts. Sensing students want to know exactly what is expected of them prior to their beginning an assignment. It is helpful to the sensing student to have assistance in sorting details and with skimming while reading. These students may find it more difficult to find the main ideas. Assignments need to employ motivating words to elicit maximum effectiveness. Many teachers have utilized a process known as "verb swap" in their classes to help with motivating students. Verb swap encourages students to choose a verb that energizes them to complete an assignment (i.e., substituting *list* for *brainstorm*). A teacher may veto a verb swap if he or she is fostering type development of students by encouraging the use of their less-preferred ways of perceiving and judging.

Intuitive children need to start with the "big picture." They often are unaware of the details of projects as they are often found brainstorming the possibilities. Children with an intuitive preference may find it difficult to memorize or recall details, but often benefit from mnemonic devices for assistance. Intuitive children also can become frustrated as their products do not always match their visions. Reading that involves the understanding of abstract symbols is the natural advantage for the intuitive. An intuitive student might well choose to read about an assignment whereas a sensing student might well choose to work with the material of an assignment.

VanSant and Payne (1995) list activities and words that can be motivating for the sensing or intuitive child. Verbs motivating for the intuitive student include *dream, create, analyze, discuss, pretend, synthesize, determine,* and *critique.* Activities that can be motivating to the intuitive child are research, discussions, independent study, debates, role play, brain teasers, and reading. Verbs that have been noted to be helpful to the sensing child include, but are not limited to, *list, identify, show, choose, label, construct, make,* and *demonstrate.* Activities that can be motivating to the sensing child include adventures, contests, time lines, projects, manipulating materials, and data collection. The teacher can provide word and activity choices to students in order to best assess their knowledge and achievement.

Thinking–Feeling Preferences

After students take in and process information, they need to make decisions about it. The thinking and feeling preferences comprise the functions that influence how decisions are made by individuals. Children with a thinking preference choose to make decisions based on the logic and facts of the situation. These students often ask why rules are in effect and prefer logical subject matter and an orderly classroom. Competence is extremely important to this preference. Children with this preference may blame others when they encounter difficulty with subject matter. Thinking children often say what they think, which may cause them social difficulties. Reinforcement for this preference needs to be specific, fair, and tangible. Words of praise (i.e., "Good job!") that are not specific may be difficult to accept for this preference.

Feeling children make decisions based on relationships, value systems, and the human impact factor. They enjoy being appreciated by the teacher and prefer a warm, friendly classroom environment. Assignments that involve helping others and values are motivating for these students. Children with a feeling preference do not like conflict. They may have their feelings hurt by a thinking child or teacher who is just stating logical information. Children with a feeling preference may need to learn to take time for themselves and not to rely on others to evaluate their worth. Reinforcement for these children involves praise and appreciation. It is extremely helpful to children with a feeling preference to feel connected to others. Teacher acknowledgment helps them to feel welcomed in their classrooms. During inquiry, a teacher can honor type differences with this preference by asking students how they think or feel about a question or topic. This acknowledges both preferences and positively reinforces type differences.

Judging–Perceiving Preferences

The final preference scale, judging–perceiving, refers to the attitude of how an individual deals with the outside environment. Children with a judging preference like to plan ahead and generally are prepared for school. These students often finish projects well before the deadline and actually may find deadlines anxiety-producing. It is often helpful to these students to warn them that closure is imminent. They prefer teachers who are organized and have a schedule that is predictable. Children with a judging preference need to know the criteria by which their work will be evaluated and often must learn coping skills when they find themselves overscheduled in life. It is important for these children to learn to plan play time as well as school time. They take school very seriously and may become anxious if routines or assignments do not follow as anticipated or promised by the teacher.

Children with a perceiving preference are adaptable, curious, and flexible. In contrast to the judging student, perceiving students enjoy new and different experiences. They may demonstrate a difficulty with completion of assignments and may benefit from teacher assistance in this area. Deadlines are energizing to a perceiving child and they may often wait until the deadline is imminent to begin a project or assignment. This may be especially frustrating to a parent who is asked at 9:00 P.M. on a Sunday for school materials to begin a project that was assigned three weeks earlier and is due the next day. It can be helpful to this child to be taught the concept of backward chaining to assist with long-term assignments. Backward chaining and frequent deadlines help the child with long-term assignments (Murphy, 1995). The former asks students to move the deadline for an assignment from its due date back to the date that they must begin an assignment to be successful in completing it. The latter provides them with frequent deadlines to help with the pacing of assignments.

Children with a perceiving preference may find schedules, organization, and structure less helpful than students with a judging preference. It is particularly energizing to the perceiving student to have work that feels like play. In many instances, perceiving children will make work feel like play. The need for closure so important to the judging child is less important to the perceiving child. These children often move from one activity to another and demonstrate bursts of energy relative to learning.

Classroom Interventions and Personality Types

Research concerning the sixteen personality types identified particular characteristics associated with each type (Fairhurst & Fairhurst, 1995; Kiersey & Bates, 1984; Lawrence, 1993; McCaulley & Natter, 1996; Myers, 1980; Myers et al., 1998; Provost, 1992). Mamchur (1996) defines the characteristics of the sixteen types as they relate to students. These descriptions further the understanding of children in the classroom and as learners. As teachers become increasingly familiar with the strengths and areas of growth for various types, the classroom can represent an opportunity for students to foster their development of personality variables leading to greater achievement and satisfaction with the learning environment.

In keeping with temperament theory, Golay (1982) classifies four types of learners: the actual–spontaneous learner (SP), the actual–routine learner (SJ), the conceptual–specific learner (NT), and the conceptual–global learner (NF). He also identifies specific learning characteristics of these students. Golay emphasizes the importance of understanding each type of learner in order for teachers to more effectively meet their educational needs in the classroom. Kiersey and Bates (1984) identified the percentage of students for each learner in the classroom: 38% for the SP learner, 38% for the SJ learner, 12% for the NT learner, and 12% for the NF learner.

Actual–spontaneous (SP) learners are not particularly motivated by intellectual matters and prefer action and hands-on experiences. This learner can become bored easily and tends to dislike drill and routine. This student enjoys challenges and will do well with learning that is presented in a game-like fashion. Frequent variety and action best meet the need of this learner.

The *actual–routine* (SJ) learner tends to enjoy routine and generally demon-strates strong study habits. This student memorizes well and prefers material that is presented in a step-by-step fashion. Classroom rules are important to this learner and he or she expects everyone to follow them. Changes in routine can be stressful to this student. This pupil is often helpful to teachers by completing classroom jobs well.

The *conceptual–specific* (NT) learner is interested in theories and principles. This pupil is curious and enjoys experimenting. Classroom routine and memorizing details hold little interest for this student. These students can be viewed as cool and aloof by their classmates as they find it difficult to express their emotions, and they may feel lonely as communication with others may be terse and logical, which can cause them to be easily misunderstood by their classmates.

The *conceptual–global* (NF) learner is viewed by others as warm and friendly. This student is person–oriented and learns best when curriculum is related to them or other persons. These learners enjoy looking at possibilities about people. They are ex-cellent communicators and often do well academically. Students may look to them for help with personal problems as they exude personal warmth and concern for others. These pupils can become emotionally drained by others' problems and need to be en-couraged to take time for themselves. These students are also quite vulnerable to crit-icism. They avoid hurting others' feelings and will try to avoid conflict.

Teacher types have been found to differ significantly from their students. As ob-served by Lawrence (1993), there are more extraverted students than teachers at all levels, sensing types of teachers decrease in number as educational levels rise, SP types are absent from almost all teaching levels, feeling types outnumber thinking types up until the college level, and judging types outnumber perceiving types two to one. This illustrates the possibility that students could proceed through their education without experiencing a teacher who uses cognitive processes and relationship style similar to their own. The potential impact of this on their achievement and school satisfaction is noteworthy.

It is quite clear that type information, or knowledge thereof, can be exceedingly helpful for teaching students in the classroom. Recognition of the personal variables of students provides teachers with skills to enhance their relationships and to improve the educational performance of their students.

Teaching Styles and Type

Although it is clearly important for teachers to understand children in relation to type, it is equally important for them to understand themselves with respect to type as it in-fluences the way they teach in the classroom. Murphy (1992) asked teachers, based on dominant functions, to develop questions relative to a drug unit. She found that sens-ing teachers focused on details, intuitive teachers on broad essay questions, thinking teachers on reasons and punishments, and feeling teachers on the impact of drugs on people. She concluded that asking questions that honored type allowed students to more effectively demonstrate their knowledge and understanding of the content area.

Lawrence (1993) noted that classrooms of I, S, and J teachers were quiet and or-derly while the classrooms of E, N, and P teachers were noisier and demonstrated more movement. A student with opposite preferences might find a classroom difficult because of the way in which it is structured and taught due to type. He also reported the results from a dissertation completed by Thompson (1984, cited in Lawrence, 1993). This study investigated teachers' perceptions of their teaching. The results demonstrated differences in perceptions of planning, evaluating students, ideas for teaching, method of teaching, and teachers' perception of their success based on type functions.

Temperament theory provides further information regarding teaching style and type. Kiersey and Bates (1984) summarized the favorite instructional strategies and percentage of teachers based on temperament. The Traditionalist (SJ) teacher encompassed 56% of the teaching force. They prefer tests, drill, memorization, and demonstration as teaching techniques. The Change Agent (NF) makes up 32% of the teaching profession and utilizes group projects, discussion, simulations, and games as instructional techniques. The Achiever (NT) comprises 8% of the teaching profession and prefers lectures, tests, projects, and reports for teaching students. Finally, the Free Spirit (SP) includes 4% of teachers. This temperament enjoys projects, contests, shows, and games for teaching their classes.

As noted earlier, improving the learning of students and the satisfaction of teachers in schools will not be accomplished simply by grouping according to type. The developmental needs of students may best be met by a teacher who does not entirely match their type. Donovan (1994), in point of fact, noted that a teacher with an opposite type facilitated learning for students. In contrast, Boyd (1995) noted that pairing students with similar type teachers was favorable, although pairing students with a teacher with one different preference was better. Finally, greater satisfaction was noted by students when they were matched with teachers of similar type (Cooper & Miller, 1991; Lamphere, 1985).

Research supports the incorporation of type considerations in daily classroom management and instruction, as improved academic achievement, student satisfaction, and teacher satisfaction have been associated with these uses of psychological type. It has provided useful interventions for students. Type does not, however, excuse a person from accomplishing an activity. It does indicate that an activity may require more energy or assistance for completion, thus requiring a child to stretch and develop skills in a less preferred function or attitude. A prime example of this is the need for speaking a foreign language in school. A student with an introversion preference may need to exert more energy to accomplish this task or require more time to think in order to answer a teacher's questions. This does not preclude a student from meeting the class expectation. The student may do so in another way, such as by writing down three important points at the end of the discussion or participating verbally after an increase in wait time.

Conclusion

To be sure, ecological variables such as task engagement, reinforcement schedules, feedback, and classroom practices may affect academic achievement. Oftentimes, however, they seem to fall short of fully explaining motivational shortcomings displayed by some students. Differences in learning through the educational process may not be explicable using only ecological variables. Given the probable relationship between personality variables or learning preferences and actual learning or teaching, it is important to consider these additional dimensions while attempting to understand a child's struggles within the classroom.

As suggested in the foregoing pages, individual behavior is not random but derives from how individuals use perception and judgment, in conjunction with attitudes. Personality type, as assessed by either the *MBTI* or the *MMTIC*, provides valuable information that may lead to effective intervention strategies for teaching and learning.

The theory of type offers an excellent way to understand learning and teaching and to provide educational interventions to meet the needs of students. The present chapter presented personality type theory as a viable way to frame these educational processes. Using principles of type theory, specific classroom interventions were suggested, and specific case examples highlighted educational interventions as important

Case Studies

The following two brief examples demonstrate the potential effectiveness of incorporating type in an educational setting, and synthesize the previous information on type and its application to the classroom. Fischetti (1999) emphasizes the importance of teaching students self-awareness and understanding through type, and found that type was viewed as a prime vehicle for assisting students and teachers with the teaching–learning process.

Case 1

John, a 7-year-old boy, was noted to be distracted, have a short attention span, and was often not completing work in the classroom. During a lesson on foxes, John was animated during group discussion and evidenced high motor level. The teacher then directed the class to complete research and list three important concepts relative to foxes. John returned to his desk and within seconds jumped up and noted that he had to tell his best friend what he had learned from his research. The author, who was observing the class, however, leaned over and told John that it was currently quiet time and he needed to finish his assignment. It was suggested that he turn his paper over and write or draw the information on the back of his paper that he wanted to share with his friend. He was then assured that he would be given the opportunity to share this information

during group time. John quickly sat down and furiously followed the directions. He then completed the class assignment as directed by his teacher. During share time, John told his best friend the important information. John's teacher was clearly surprised by his behavior. The teacher asked to consult with the school psychologist to review educational interventions based on type. The teacher added this and other type suggestions to her repertoire for the classroom.

Case 2

Students in an eleventh-grade English class were introduced to the concept of type after taking the *MBTI*. The students who preferred introversion in this class expressed frustration as they never seemed to get a word in edgewise during class. The teacher and the class developed strategies for assuring that all students would have adequate wait time to participate in class. A "thumbs up" was an indication to the class that a student required more thinking time. The students also began to develop alternative assignments based on type with teacher input. Students designed test questions and began using the option of verb swapping. The students and teacher all reported that class was more interesting, more students were participating in class discussions, and class tests matched the students' learning preferences.

to teaching and illustrated improved student learning based on type preferences. Type theory offers an effective means by which to more fully understand school-aged children and may expand practitioners' repertoire of intervention techniques.

References

Ainley, M. D. (1993). Styles of engagement with learning multidimensional assessment of their relationship with strategy use and school achievement. *Journal of Educational Psychology, 85*, 395–405.

Barger, J. R., Bargar, R. R., & Cano, J. M. (1994). *Discovering learning differences in the classroom.* Columbus, OH: Ohio Agricultural Education Curriculum Materials Service, Ohio State University.

Bayne, R. (1995). *The Myers-Briggs Type Indicator: A critical review and practical guide.* London: Chapman & Hall.

Beyler, J., & Schmeck, R. R. (1992). Assessment of individual differences in preferences for holistic-analytic strategies: Evaluation of some commonly available instruments. *Educational and Psychological Measurement, 52*, 709–719.

Boyd, N. E. (1995). An examination of interpersonal relationships between student and cooperating teachers (Doctoral dissertation, University of Memphis). *Dissertation Abstracts International, 55A*, 3076.

Brophy, J. E., & Good, T. L. (1986). Teacher behavior and student achievement. In M. C. Wittrock (Ed.), *Handbook of research on teaching* (pp. 328–375). New York: Macmillan.

Caldwell, J. H., Huitt, W. G., & Graeber, A. O. (1982). Time spent in learning. *The Elementary School Journal, 82*, 371–480.

Cooper, S. E., & Miller, J. A. (1991). *MBTI* learning style-teaching style discongruencies. *Educational and Psychological Measurement, 51*, 699–706.

DiTiberio, J. K. (1996). Education, learning styles, and cognitive styles. In A. L. Hammer (Ed.), *MBTI applications: A decade of research on the Myers-Briggs Type Indicator* (pp. 123–166). Palo Alto, CA: Consulting Psychologists Press.

DiTiberio, J. K. (1998). Uses of type in education. In I. B. Myers, M. H. McCaulley, N. L. Quenk, & A. L. Hammer Eds.), *MBTI manual: A guide to the development and use of the Myers-Briggs Type Indicator* (3rd ed., pp. 253–284). Palo Alto, CA: Consulting Psychologists Press.

Donovan, A. J. (1994). The interaction of personality traits in applied music teaching (Doctoral dissertation, University of Southern Mississippi). *Dissertation Abstracts International, 55A*, 1499.

Fairhurst, A. M., & Fairhurst, L. L. (1995). *Effective teaching, effective learning: Making the personality connection in your classroom.* Palo Alto, CA: Davies-Black.

Fischetti, B. A. (1999). Type instruction for ninth graders: Self-understanding and awareness. *Bulletin of Psychological Type, 22*, 28–29.

Fry, E. (1977). Fry's readability graph: Clarification, validity, and extension. *Journal of Reading, 21*, 249.

Gettinger, M. (1995). Best practice for increasing academic learning time. In A. Thomas & J. Grimes (Eds.), *Best practices in school psychology–III* (pp. 943–954). Washington, DC: National Association of School Psychologists.

Golay, K. (1982). *Learning patterns and temperament styles: A systematic guide to maximizing student achievement.* Fullerton, CA: Manas-System.

Hammer, A. L. (Ed.). (1996). *MBTI applications: A decade of research on the Myers-Briggs Type Indicator.* Palo Alto, CA: Consulting Psychologists Press.

Hunter, M. (1982). *Master teaching.* El Segundo, CA: TIP.

Jung, C. G. (1923). *Psychological types.* New York: Harcourt Brace.

Kiersey, D., & Bates, M. (1984). *Please understand me.* Del Mar, CA: Promethesus Nemesis.

Lamphere, G. I. (1985). The relationship between teacher and student personality and its effect on teacher perception of students (Doctoral dissertation, United States International University). *Dissertation Abstracts International, 46A*, 1564.

Lawrence, G. (1993). *People types and tiger stripes.* Gainesville, FL: Center for Applications of Psychological Type.

Lawrence, G. (1997). *Looking at type and learning styles.* Gainesville, FL: Center for Applications of Psychological Type.

Lentz, F. E., & Shapiro, E. S. (1986). Functional assessment of the academic environment. *School Psychology Review, 25*, 346–357.

Lewin, K. (1976). *Field theory in social science*. Chicago: University of Chicago Press.

Mamchur, C. M. (1996). *Cognitive type theory and learning style*. Alexandria, VA: Association for Supervision and Curriculum Development.

McCaulley, M. H., & Natter, F. L. (1996). *Psychological type differences in education*. Gainesville, FL: Center for Applications of Psychological Type.

Meisgeier, C., & Murphy, E. (1987). *Murphy-Meisgeier Type Indicator for Children*. Palo Alto, CA: Consulting Psychologists Press.

Meisgeier, C., Murphy, E., & Meisgeier, C. (1989). *A teacher's guide to type: A new perspective on individual differences in the classroom*. Palo Alto, CA: Consulting Psychologists Press.

Murphy, E. (1992). *The developing child*. Palo Alto, CA: Davies-Black.

Murphy. E. (1994). On the brink of awareness. *Bulletin of Psychological Type, 17*, 1, 3.

Murphy, E. (1995). *Educational type tidbits*. Unpublished manuscript.

Myers, I. B. (1962). *Manual: The Myers-Briggs Type Indicator*. Princeton, NJ: Educational Testing Service.

Myers, I. B., with P. B. Myers. (1980). *Gifts differing: Understanding personality type*. Palo Alto, CA: Consulting Psychologists Press.

Myers, I. B., & McCaulley, M. H. (1985). *Manual: A guide to the development and use of the Myers-Briggs Type Indicator*. Palo Alto, CA: Consulting Psychologists Press.

Myers, I. B., McCaulley, M. H., Quenk, N. L., & Hammer, A. L. (1998). *MBTI manual: A guide to the development and use of the Myers-Briggs Type Indicator*. Palo Alto, CA: Consulting Psychologists Press.

Power, S. J., & Lundsten, L. L. (1997). Studies that compare type theory and left-brain/right-brain theory. *Journal of Psychological Type, 43*, 22–28.

Provost, J. A. (1992). *Strategies for success: Using type to excel in high school and college*. Gainesville, FL: Center for Applications of Psychological Type.

Quenk, N. L. (1996). *In the grip: Our hidden personality*. Palo Alto, CA: Consulting Psychologists Press.

Rosenshine, B. (1981). Academic engaged time, content covered, and direct instruction. *Journal of Education, 3*, 38–66.

Saphier, J., & Gower, R. (1997). *The skillful teacher* (5th ed.). Acton, MA: Research for Better Teaching.

Schurr, K. T., & Ruble, V. E. (1988). Psychological type and the second year of college achievement: Survival and the gravitation toward appropriate and manageable major fields. *Journal of Psychological Type, 14*, 57–59.

Singer, M. (1996). The nature and nurture of children: The *MMTIC* as a tool for understanding. *Bulletin of Psychological Type, 19*, 3–4.

Smith, D. (1997). Baby types: Early personality expression. *Bulletin of Psychological Type, 20*, 4–6.

Stallings, J. A. (1980). Allocated academic learning time revisited, or beyond time on task. *Educational Researcher, 9*, 11–16.

Thompson, H. L. (1996). *Jung's function-attitudes explained*. Watkinsville, GA: Wormhole.

VanSant, S., & Payne, D. (1995). *Psychological type in schools*. Gainesville, FL: Center for Applications of Psychological Type.

Walberg, H. J. (1988). Synthesis of research on time and learning. *Educational Researcher, 17*, 76–85.

Wilson, M. A., & Languis, M. L. (1989). Differences in brain electrical activity patterns between introverted and extraverted adults. *Journal of Psychological Type, 18*, 14–23.

10

Role and Influence of Family Functioning

Rona Preli

The family is the environment in which the individual grows and develops, and one cannot ignore the intimate context in which children spend the greatest part of each and every day. It makes inherent sense, therefore, to consider and address family functioning in assessing and understanding the social and emotional issues of the individual. This is of particular importance when considering problems in school-aged children. The principal task of any family is to provide for the development of its members (Carter & McGoldrick, 1980). The family is the primary context in which one learns to function in roles and relationships and is the primary source of learning about values, culture, traditions, and identity.

Systemic Theoretical Framework

The "systems" approach to understanding and treating family problems receives its name from General Systems Theory and the work of Ludwig von Bertanlaffy (1968). Broadly, the systems framework understands human functioning as embedded in and explained by the intimate context of the individual (Goldenberg & Goldenberg, 2000). This view differs from traditional psychology in that most theories of psychology seek to understand human functioning by looking for causal connections and etiology. The underlying assumption in traditional psychological theories is that the problem can be understood by asking "Why?" Such an approach is consistent with the medical model, which looks for a cause, thereby seeking to understand where a problem came from and, correspondingly, why it exists. The assumption is that the "cause" lies somewhere inside of the individual.

   As an example, consider the case of an eight-year-old who exhibits symptoms of a school phobia including anxiety over school attendance, an unwillingness to go to school in the morning, and somatic complaints when in school. The professional operating from a traditional theoretical framework or linear model might begin by wondering why the child is experiencing anxiety over school and what is going on inside of the child's psyche. This clinician would want to consider where this anxiety came from and what caused it. He or she might look at any trauma or troublesome experience suffered by the eight-year-old and how that child is emotionally or intellectually coping with these experiences. The assumption would be that, if the cause could be uncovered and the origins understood, then the problem could be treated. We will return later to this example to contrast how a clinician operating from a systemic framework might approach this same case.

Family therapy is a professional discipline in which the models of clinical practice share a common theoretical base often referred to as "system's theory" (Nichols & Schwartz, 1998). In truth, "system's theory" refers to both General Systems Theory and Cybernetics. Both are foundational theoretical works that underlie the models of practice in the field (Broderick & Schrader, 1981; Fishman & Rosman, 1986; Gurman & Kniskern, 1981).

General Systems Theory was developed by Ludwig von Bertanlaffy (1968), a prominent biologist. Von Bertanlaffy's intention was to articulate an approach to thinking about systems and phenomena across all disciplines. His model was an attempt to move away from reductionistic and mechanistic thinking. He believed that science had become too focused on studying phenomena in isolation and, thereby, missed the interaction between sciences and the larger view of phenomena in their natural context (Nichols & Schwartz, 1995).

The theory of *Cybernetics* was developed by Norbert Weiner (1948), a mathematician at MIT, and was initially developed during World War II to study machines. Cybernetics interested Gregory Bateson (1972), who applied the assumptions of the model to the conceptualization of family functioning. Bateson's work was groundbreaking in that it lead to a conceptual shift from thinking about psychopathology as caused by past events to something that is maintained in the present through a process of ongoing, circular feedback loops. From these fundamental theories, the family system's perspective retains several key assumptions and premises. These concepts form the theoretical basis of the field of family therapy.

Wholeness

The concept of "wholeness" suggests that the whole is greater than the simple sum of its parts. This assertion presumes that the individual in a family can best be understood as a component part of a complex and interacting system (Brown & Christensen, 1999). Wholeness also proposes that a family system is more complex than can be understood by viewing the individuals in isolation. For example, one could meet members of a family in different contexts, but to understand what the *family* is like, one needs to understand how the family relates together. In counseling couples, a therapist can hear one member's version of the problems and then the other member's version, yet the true complexity of the ways that they communicate and relate are only apparent when they are seen together.

To return for a moment to our case of the child with school phobia, the concept of wholeness would suggest that the child's behavior is a component part of the larger whole (the family) and can best be understood by comprehending the complexity of the family's interactions. The assumption is that the child's behaviors and symptoms are part of an ongoing interaction in the family and are unwittingly perpetuated and maintained by the family. To understand this, one needs to see how all members are involved and how they relate to each other and the behaviors exhibited by the child associated with the school phobia. To see the child and attempt to understand the child in isolation will only reveal a small part of the larger context, that the parents have, for example, been having marital conflict over the husband's loss of his job. Further evaluation of the family system reveals that the older sibling is a freshman in college. If the symptoms of the child are viewed in this way, one might discover that the family's finances are tight, the mother is having difficulty adjusting to the recent departure of her eldest, and the estrangement from her husband is making her particularly lonely. The father is also isolated, yet unable to demand more authority and attention in the family because he believes himself to be a failure, confirmed by his wife's hostility, disappointment, and withdrawal. He tries to approach his wife to address his isolation, but his approach is angry. Not surprisingly, his wife is angry in return and cannot understand why her husband has become so moody, angry, and unreachable. She distances from him in anger and confusion, and turns to her youngest son. The father also retreats in angry confusion, leaving his wife and son alone emotionally and physically. The son becomes his mother's confidant and greatest support. When he goes to school, he worries about her emotional well-being and fears that problems are erupting at home. The anxiety is manifest in stomachaches and headaches which, not surprisingly, work well in terms of allowing him to go home and be with his mother. She is both worried about him and is simultaneously glad for the diversion and for the opportunity to comfort and nurture her youngest. When the father hears of the child's problems, he is enraged that she "babies him," which only further exacerbates the marital split and the son's fears about his mother's well-being and his parent's marriage.

In a systemic approach, the concept of wholeness informs us that the child's symptomatic behavior and feelings of anxiety are part of far more complex issues. Using this theoretical approach, the options for intervening and addressing the issues of the whole family system are numerous, a point that is more fully developed later.

Structure and Sequences of Interaction

Systems are comprised of continually interacting parts that are patterned, recursive (repeating), and predictable. This simply means that members of a family system are constantly behaving and relating to one another. These ways of behaving and relating become patterned and routine over time and are, therefore, predictable. The repeating interactions form the "rules" that define roles and relationships among members of a family system. These "rules" are responsible for the maintenance of the system as a whole (Jackson, 1959). They define the structure of the system. The structure of a system refers to the way a system maintains boundaries that preserve the integrity and distinctness of the system from the environment (Goldenberg & Goldenberg, 2000).

These continuous and predictable ways of relating define the members of the family as distinct and different from other families, the community, and the larger social system of which they are a part. This further suggests that understanding an individual's behavior in isolation is insufficient. One must understand the sequences of interaction in which the behavior is embedded. In the case of the child with symptoms of school phobia, the symptom of school phobia would, therefore, be understood to be a part of an ongoing pattern of interaction among the members of the family. The symptomatic behavior does not occur in isolation, but, rather, is part of a larger interactional pattern among members of the family. The family both responds to the behaviors of the child and the child's behavior is a response to the behaviors of the other family members. This pattern of interaction does not occur once, but is ongoing over time and is predictable. The symptom is, therefore, not idiopathic in the family, but rather is part of the way the family relates and defines roles and relationships. In this example, the mother can maintain a role of nurturance and primacy in her child's life if the child continues to be symptomatic and in need of her help. The father remains on the periphery of their relationship as long as they continue to be bonded and united in their attempts to keep the father from coming between them. The marital relationship remains stressed and distant as long as the parents cannot reach accord on how to handle the parental demands being presented by their child. The child will likely remain anxious and fearful and will experience somatic problems as long as there is marital discord.

Organization

Systems are structured, such that change in any one part of the system will result in changes in the whole (Brown & Christensen, 1999). As parts of a system are in constant, mutual interaction, any change to one part will impact the entire system. A mobile is an example of this concept. A mobile is in constant fluctuation and this fluctuation varies according to how much force is applied from the environment. Wind will cause the mobile to fluctuate greatly. A relatively calm environment will result in little fluctuation of the parts of the mobile. However, even small changes are met with changes throughout the mobile. Each element moves in response to the movement of the other elements until the mobile regains a relatively static "resting" state, referred to as *homeostasis*. This organized movement functions to reestablish homeostasis, and is called *feedback*, the patterned response to stimulation from the environment within the system.

Again, this concept can be used to understand the child with symptoms of school phobia. The school can be understood to be an environmental stimulus that impacts on the child outside of the family system. When the child returns home to interact with the family, his behavior in response to the school is felt by the members of the family who, in turn, accommodate his behavior. Similarly, the father's work and corresponding loss of a job can be understood to be stimulation from the environment. The father's loss of a job not only affects him emotionally, but his emotional state requires accommodation from the other members of the family.

Similarly, the loss of a job is felt throughout the system as the other members react to compensate for the change. Perhaps the members have to alter their lifestyle in response to the loss of income. Perhaps the mother may need to go to work to compensate for the father's lost wages. The children must now adjust to the absence of the mother and, perhaps, the presence of the father. Chores done previously by the mother might now be assumed by other family members. Each member of the family responds to the change in an attempt to recalibrate the family system and return to a relative state of homeostasis. The family might refer to this state of homeostasis as "returning to normal."

If the child's symptoms are to be addressed successfully, one needs to be aware that any force applied from outside the system will be met with reactions from within the family system, which will seek to return the system to homeostasis. This virtually ensures that each attempt the school makes to "treat" the child will be met by what might appear to be an either subtle or overt counterattack on the part of a family member. This is not because the family wants the child to be symptomatic. Rather, the family is responding "instinctually" as a system does to changes felt from outside of the family. This response is an attempt to minimize the disturbance to the system and return to a state of homeostasis as quickly as possible. The family's response might appear to be an obvious reaction against the school's "interference" or might be far more covert. The "obvious" reactions might include refusing to have the child evaluated or seen by the professional staff. The family might claim that they can handle the child, or that the problem will "go away with time," or that the school is making too much of a little anxiety on the part of the child. The more subtle responses might manifest as overt agreement with the concern of the teacher and professional staff, yet involve little follow-through at home with the planned approach to treating the child. The family might claim that they forgot, or "don't have time." Instead of being firm with the child, the family might return to patterned responses. The mother may continue nurturing the child when he is fearful of school and the father may argue with the mother and retreat in disgust. To successfully treat the school phobia, the clinician must address the family's feedback cycles, which will function to counteract change imposed from the outside.

Systemic Models

The field of family therapy is comprised of models or schools of therapy, all of which share a common systemic base. Most models were created by pioneers in the field who established training centers to teach and practice their particular approach. Although each model focuses on family process, they differ in their approach to treatment. One model that is particularly useful in understanding families is the Structural Family Therapy model developed by Salvador Minuchin (1974). The model is widely used and sets forth a theory of family organization and structure, as it articulates a clear framework for assessment and treatment with great utility for both the novice and experienced clinician.

Structural Family Therapy

Structural Family Therapy is largely comprised of three primary constructs: structure, subsystems, and boundaries (Minuchin & Fishman, 1981). *Structure* refers to the organized pattern in which the family members interact. These patterns of behavior or patterns of interaction function to define roles and relationships among family members and, as such, allow for predictability. The structure of the family provides a set of "rules" that govern the ways in which family members relate. According to Structural Family Therapy, the structure of the family includes a hierarchy. The hierarchy of the family refers to the power structure and decision-making authority, or, simply, who is in charge. In Structural Family Therapy the assumption is that parents should have greater authority than children.

The family system, according to Structual Family Therapy, is comprised of a number of subsystems. A *subsystem* is a subunit of the family that comes together to fulfill a function. Within families there are commonly three subsystems. The first is the spousal or marital subsystem. The function of this subsystem is that of intimacy and companionship for the couple. The spousal subsystem is differentiated from the parental subsystem, whose function is the parenting, raising, nurturing, and disciplining of the children. The third subsystem is the sibling subsystem. The function of that system is socialization and building peer relationships among the children in the family. Within families it is common for family members to function in more than one subsystem. In an intact family unit, a man and woman may comprise both the marital subsystem and the parental subsystem. Despite the same membership, the functions of the subsystems are different, so each subsystem must be able to communicate without the interference of the other subsystems. As an example, if a husband and wife always talk about the children whenever they find a moment be together, it will be at the sacrifice of time to talk about each other and their relationship. Over time, the integrity of the marital subsystem will be so violated by the intrusion of the parental subsystem that the marital unit will cease to have an independent identity. In such a marriage, one day when the children have left home, the couple will find that they have drifted apart, no longer have anything in common, and have nothing to talk about.

Boundaries protect the integrity of subsystems. Boundaries are the invisible barriers that allow for both connectedness and autonomy in the family. Boundaries also function to protect the integrity of the family system from its environment. Boundaries vary from rigid to diffuse. A diffuse boundary has too little structure allowing for connectedness at the expense of autonomy. Too much information flows across a diffuse boundary. An example of a diffuse boundary might be a family in which the mother consults with and confides in her mother about all matters relating to the raising of the children and her relationship with her husband. The closeness between the daughter and her mother interferes with the ability of the daughter to form a cohesive and mutually supportive relationship with her spouse, who feels that the couple has no privacy. A rigid boundary has too little permeability, allowing for autonomy at the expense of connectedness as too little information can flow across it. An example of a rigid boundary might be a family in which a father works long hours and cannot find the time or energy to participate in child-rearing activities. His wife, therefore, assumes all responsibilities and independently makes all decisions concerning her children. The parental subsystem does not function cohesively as the father is left out of activities and the mother is central to and overinvolved in all activities.

Relationships characterized by diffuse boundaries are called enmeshed. Relationships characterized by rigid boundaries are called disengaged. In enmeshed relationships there is a heightened sense of support prohibiting independence and autonomy. In disengaged relationships, independence and autonomy prohibit support and involvement. Ideally, boundaries should be clear in relationships. This means that they should be neither rigid or diffuse, allowing for both connectedness and autonomy. Clear boundaries protect subsystems and individuals in the family, allowing them to function independently while maintaining sufficient connection.

Structural Family Therapy is based on a "normative" model of individual and family development (Brown & Christensen, 1999). Symptoms are not seen to be pathological, but an adaptation to normative or non-normative stressors encountered by the family. Normative stressors refer to those developmental stages and changes that all families encounter as a typical outcome of the passage of time and growth. For example, in early marriage, normative stressors would include accommodating and adapting as a couple, establishing mutual goals, dealing with extended family and in-laws. Non-normative stressors include those unexpected and off-time events that require adjustment and accommodation on the part of the family, such as an off-time death, loss of employment, a natural disaster, or a chronic or disabling illness. Symptoms occur as families are required to adapt and accommodate to these normative or non-normative stressors, yet lack the flexibility to create new patterns of relating and communicating as a system. Instead, the family resorts to old patterns of relating and communicating that are insufficient to address the changing circumstances. It is at this juncture that symptoms develop. Alleviation of the symptom, therefore, requires a change in the structure of the family system in the direction of more flexibility and adaptability.

Bevcar and Bevcar (1988) delineate six broad goals in Structural Family Therapy. First, there must be an effective hierarchical structure. Parents must be in charge. Thus, there must be a generation gap based on parental or executive authority. Second, there must be a parental/executive coalition. Parents must support and accommodate each other to present a united front to their children. Third, as the parental/executive coalition forms, the sibling subsystem becomes a system of peers. Fourth, if the family is disengaged, the goal is to increase the frequency of interaction and move toward clear, rather than rigid, boundaries. Fifth, if the family is enmeshed, the general goal would be to foster differentiation of individuals and subsystems. This would reflect a respect for age-appropriate experimentation with independent activity. Sixth, there must be a spousal subsystem established as an entity distinct from the parental subsystem.

To return to the child with symptoms of school phobia, the Structural Family therapist would be interested in obtaining information about the structure of the family, the hierarchy, the subsystems, the boundaries, the normative and non-normative stressors, and the patterns of interaction. The therapist may ask about the hierarchal structure of the family, the function of the subsystems, the presence of subsystems such as the marital, parental, and sibling subsystem, whether the subsystems can carry out their functions, and if the boundaries are sufficient to protect the integrity of the subsystems, allowing for both the autonomy and connectedness of the individuals in the family. The therapist also would determine if the parents were in charge and effective in their decision making and ability to both nurture and discipline, what stressors the family is currently experiencing, and whether the family's patterns of interaction and corresponding structure are adequately flexible to allow for the adaptation and accommodation to changes that are required of the family.

The Structural Family therapist, working with the family of the child with school phobia, would note that the hierarchy in the family is not clear. It is uncertain who has decision-making authority as the parents are not working together cohesively. The rules and consequences are not reinforced on a consistent basis. This is, in part, because the marital relationship is conflictual, resulting in rigid boundaries and a disengaged relationship between the spouses. Therefore, the marital subsystem is unable to fulfill its function of providing for the intimacy and companionship of the couple. In the absence of a functioning marital relationship, the wife is finding companionship with her youngest child. Correspondingly, the parental relationship also lacks cohesion. The marital conflict impacts the ability of the parental subsystem to work collaboratively. The parental subsystem's lack of cohesion creates an unclear hierarchy in which there are no clear rules or consequences for addressing the child's difficulties. The child's overly close or enmeshed relationship with his mother further interferes with the functioning of the parental subsystem as their closeness, or diffuse boundary, maintains the rigid boundaries between the parents. With the eldest child away at school, the sibling subsystem has gone through a substantial change. The youngest child is experiencing the normative transition that follows when an elder sibling leaves the family. The parents also are dealing with the changes resulting from the eldest child's move from home, both financially and emotionally. The father has experienced the non-normative stressor of a job loss and the corresponding adaptation of the family to the financial and emotional strain. The stressors the family is facing include both normative developmental changes and non-normative changes. The family currently lacks the flexibility to cope with the demands of these stressors and, correspondingly, a member is symptomatic. A number of changes, according to Structural Family Therapy, need to occur.

The hierarchy needs to be strengthened with the parents making conjoint, cohesive decisions about their children. Without the ability to work together, the parents will not be able to decide how to deal with the child's school phobia. The efforts of each parent will be undermined by the behavior of the other. For example, as the father tries to be firm with the child about remaining in school, the mother undercuts his efforts by nurturing and, in effect, rewarding him when he comes home. Inadvertently, the parents are reinforcing the school phobia with their inconsistency in terms of the differing ways they respond to the child.

The marital subsystem needs to be strengthened and the boundaries made more clear, allowing for increased connectedness. The marital discord and distance will encourage the overly close relationship between the mother and child. Their close relationship will prevent the child from adequately separating from his mother and successfully adjusting to the demands of school. The overly close relationship will effectively keep the father out and encourage the marital distance.

The boundary between the mother and child needs to be clearer, with more distance between the two. As the child is moved out of this overly close relationship with the mother, the parents will need to work together more closely. As the parents are closer, the child can worry less about his mother and leave the companionship responsibilities to his father.

Strategic Model

As was mentioned earlier, all models of family therapy share a common theoretical base in Systems Theory and Cybernetics, although they differ in terms of how they conceptualize family functioning. Other models of family therapy would be equally useful in understanding the dynamics of the family with the child experiencing symptoms of school phobia. As a comparison, consider the Strategic model of Jay Haley (1976) and Cloe Madanes (1982). This approach would emphasize the hierarchical configuration of the family, attending primarily to cross-generational coalitions. Cross-generational coalitions are the alliance of two members of a family system across generational lines against a third member. Typically, this involves a parent and child in an overly close relationship in an alignment against the other parent. According to the Strategic model, this dynamic in a family is indicative of an unclear structure that functions to maintain the symptom.

According to Jay Haley (1976), when an individual is symptomatic, the organization of the family has a hierarchical structure that is confused. He further states that an unclear hierarchy creates ambiguity in a family such that the members do not know who is a peer and who is a superior. A confused structure created by a cross-generational coalition violates the basic rules of organization in a family. When status positions are confused, Haley suggests that there will be a struggle to clarify the positions in the hierarchy. Therefore, a cross-generational coalition is also understood as functioning to balance power in families. In the family with the school phobic child, Strategic Family Therapy would observe that the alignment or cross-generational coalition of the mother and child functions to keep the father out of the decision-making loop. The closeness between the mother and child further functions to give her more influence in decisions relating to her child and disempowers her husband in terms of his ability to determine what happens. The child, simultaneously, has more power and influence in the daily routine and functioning of his family in that his symptoms organize the behavior of the other members of the family. The mother and father are, in effect, subject to the power of the symptom in terms of whether the child goes to school or stays home. As long as these family dynamics remain unchanged, the symptom will continue. This model of family therapy would focus primarily on first altering the sequences of interaction in the family to alleviate the symptom. Then the Strategic therapist would begin the process of restructuring the hierarchy. In this case, the professional working with the family would want to devise tasks or assignments that would get the child to go to school. The intervention would likely involve asking the parents to unite, thereby clarifying the hierarchy. Alternatively, the professional using this model might ask that the father be in charge of getting the child to go to school, thereby interrupting the cross-generational coalition and empowering the father to be instrumentally involved in dealing with the child's problem.

Natural Systems Model

Another model that is useful in assessing and understanding the functioning of the family with a school phobic child is the Natural Systems Model of Murray Bowen (1978). In this model of therapy, the therapist is most interested in triangles and "re-activity." This model proposes that, as stress builds in a dyad, a third member will be triangulated or pulled into that relationship in an attempt to alleviate the tension. When anxiety is increased beyond the level of tolerance of the dyad, a third person is sought to support the position of one member of the dyad against the other and the anxiety is lessened (Goldenberg & Goldenberg, 2000). Typically, in families it is a child who is pulled into the marital dyad as tension builds. Although triangulation is typical in relationships, it becomes dysfunctional when it is used repeatedly to avoid resolving problems in relationships. Triangles are created in an effort to achieve resolution of the problems of the dyad, but they actually tend to prevent resolution and the instability remains with more members participating in an escalating and increasingly unstable emotional field (Becvar & Becvar, 1996). Clearly, in the family with symptoms of school phobia triangulation is apparent. The therapist's concern would be in alleviating the stress and tension in the marital/parental dyad such that they could be freed to work out their relationships without the need to involve the child.

Interventions

One of the most basic and important considerations in planning therapeutic interventions is the role and function of the professional and the context in which one works (Pinsef & Wynne, 2000). For school-based professionals, that would involve understanding the limitations and restrictions on the extent of clinical involvement sanctioned by the school system. One would not want to begin working with a family therapeutically around issues of structural change if one's contact is limited to monthly meetings of the parents, teacher, and professional staff. The larger issues of structural change would be best referred to a practicing family therapist. This is not to imply, however, that clinicians functioning in a traditional school setting cannot use systems approaches therapeutically and have a systemic impact in their work with the family.

As suggested previously, models of family therapy are largely based on a non-pathological approach to understanding symptoms. This means that symptoms are seen as embedded in sequences of interaction and are, therefore, maintained and perpetuated by the family system as a whole. Systemic models, however, vary somewhat in their understanding of how symptoms arise and how they are treated. Many of the models perceive symptoms as arising when a family becomes stuck at a developmental transition point, that is, when a normative stressor occurs. The symptoms are also hypothesized to arise when families lack the flexibility to accommodate and adapt to non-normative stressors or crises. Again, the assumption is that families become stuck in sequences of interaction that are characteristic of their structure. That structure, however, is no longer adaptive. In order for the system to cope with stressors, the family needs to develop new patterns of relating and behaving. Once freed from the feedback cycles that return the family to homeostasis, the family needs to undergo a structural change, and the family will change in the direction of greater flexibility. These new, adaptive patterns of relating will become self-reinforcing and stabilizing.

All symptoms in school-aged children are, therefore, viewed similarly from this perspective. In this chapter, the example of the eight-year-old with symptoms of school phobia has been used. The symptoms could, however, be acting-out behaviors, attention-deficit or impulse control disorders, anxiety, depression, addiction, substance abuse, or eating disorders. Before continuing, it is vital to understand that the "nonpathological systems approach to treatment" does not rule out referral to other helping professionals for collaborative therapies. For example, depression can be effectively and successfully treated using a family therapy approach, yet the child may also benefit from pharmacotherapy as prescribed by a child psychiatrist (Kung, 2000; Shadish, Ragsdale, Glaser, & Montgomery, 1995). The fact that some symptoms may have a biological or physiological basis and will, therefore, respond to medical intervention does not preclude the fact that family systems become stabilized and organized around the existence of the biologically-based symptoms exactly as they would around the behavioral disorders. The family needs to change and modify their patterns of interacting to allow for structural change whether the symptom is school phobia or anorexia, the latter of which may require hospitalization to save the child's life.

Once the clinician has identified the symptom(s) and the symptomatic member(s), the first step in a systemic intervention is to obtain information from the parental/executive subsystem. This is imperative in order to get an accurate and clear understanding of the family's functioning, which can be assessed only by observing how members interact together and hearing what each has to say about how the family operates. Having both members of the parental/executive subsystem attend the meeting together is also important because it sets the precedent that the parents, together, are in charge of understanding and working to solve the child's problems. This message is transmitted by simply explaining how vital *both* of them are in addressing and solving the child's problem. This also begins the process of identifying the parents as an intact subsystem, clarifying the boundaries, and working toward cohesion in decision making. For many school-based professionals, having both parents attend a meeting might require a gargantuan effort. Many school psychologists and school-based clinical staff become complacent about the participation of parents and acclimate to working with whoever can come to meetings. If the clinician has as his or her therapeutic orientation that the participation of the entire family (including the father) is vital to successful systemic assessment and intervention, then he or she will begin the therapeutic relationship by aligning with the parents as a team and finding ways to express to them how important their help is in working with their child.

All school-based professionals have encountered the "resistant" parents who are angry or frightened because they believe they are being blamed by the professional staff for their child's problems. All parents feel a sense of responsibility, rationally or irrationally, that they are somehow to blame for their child's behavior. The more "blamed" they feel, the more "resistant" they will be to the intervention of the clinician as they will see it as an outside force to be dealt with rather than an internal corrective effort coming from themselves. The successful systemic clinician understands this and immediately works to establish a context that defines the parents' participation as helpful and vital and the relationship as a "team" approach rather than "all-knowing clinician versus irresponsible, underfunctioning parent." To ensure that the father participates, the clinician may want to call him personally and invite him. If there is marital/parental conflict, the mother may be unable to secure her husband's participation. If one parent is peripheral, it will be easy to get the enmeshed parent to come, but the peripheral one will remain uninvolved. Agreeing to work with the enmeshed parent alone only serves to perpetuate the enmeshment and the corresponding structural problems. The clinician can counteract these structural problems by simply addressing and calling each member personally to encourage, invite, and persuade them to participate. All too often, school-based professional staff work with the child alone. This functions to reinforce the power of the child and the helplessness of the parents in dealing with the child's problems. If the boundaries and hierarchy are to be clear, the parents have to be capable of successfully helping the child. The successful helping professional who has worked with the child alone has unwittingly reinforced the inadequacy of the parents to be helpful. This also may unwittingly perpetuate the notion that the problems are the child's fault and somehow reflect something wrong within the child rather than with the system.

Upon successfully securing the participation of both parents in the clinical meetings, the clinician has begun the essential work of reinforcing the parental/executive subsystem, clarifying boundaries, and moving to cohesive executive decision making. Next the clinician needs to begin to attend to the ways in which the family communicates to determine hierarchical structure, boundaries, and subsystem functioning. Some of this determination is aided by the collection of information. For example, it is helpful to find out when, where, how often, and how long the problem has existed. Also, one needs to know who is involved with the problem (for example, who responds directly to the symptomatic behavior), how the people in the family react and respond when the problem occurs, what and who makes the problem diminish, and what the other family members are doing throughout this period. At this point, the clinician is trying to determine the sequences of interaction around the symptom, attempting to understand who seems to be in charge (hierarchy), and how well the parents work as a team (cohesion), identifying what the boundaries are in terms of closeness and distance, and determining how well the subsystems function, such as the ability of the parents to take charge of children. Another important piece of information is the developmental data, including the normative and non-normative stressors.

This, again, will help to establish an understanding of the family's context and what they are attempting to respond to in their lives.

The clinician, at this point, is not just collecting data directly from the family's verbal report. The clinician is also observing the family's interaction. The clinician is looking to see how supportive one parent is of the other by watching their nonverbal communication. Do they agree? Is one involved while the other is uninvolved? Is there latent or overt conflict? Does the child sit closer to one parent than the other? Is the child physically placed between the parents and does he or she seem to be "holding them together?" Is there disagreement between the parents, and around what issues? Again, these questions are in the mind of the clinician as she or he watches the family interact and respond to questions. These questions will guide the clinician to a better understanding of the hierarchy, boundaries, and subsystem functioning.

If a child is symptomatic, one must assume that there is some lack of cohesion and clarity in the parental/executive subsystem. If this were not the case, the parents would have discovered a successful way to address the child's behavior (Haley, 1976). It also must be presumed that the family is stuck and needs to discover new ways of interacting and responding or the old patterns of response would have been successful. Once it has been established that there is conflict, disengagement, enmeshment, or an unclear hierarchy in the executive decision-making subsystem, the clinician begins restructuring. Again, it is unwise to undertake the task of providing family therapy if one is working in a traditional capacity in the school system. However, reinforcing parental/executive boundaries and working toward parental cohesion and clear plans of action are well within the capabilities of the school-based professional. One will want to acknowledge that her or his work will need, in all likelihood, to be followed up by an outside therapist if the family is receptive.

To reinforce the parental/executive subsystem, clarify the boundaries and work toward cohesion, the clinician can begin by supporting the efforts the parents have made, reinforcing those that have been successful. It is likely that the parents have tried many ways to address the problem and, perhaps, have been effective at some point. Certainly, the parents have ideas about what works in general with their child and what should and should not be done to address the problem. With the atmosphere of teamwork, mutual respect, and support of the parents' authority, the clinician can begin to move into the more difficult areas of creating a plan for intervention. The details of the plan for intervention are less important than the fact that the parents must create it together. It must put them in charge of the child, and they must cohesively see that it is carried out (Haley, 1976). Therefore, it is best to elicit their ideas about what they can do together to address the symptom. Agreeing to and conjointly sticking to a plan of action will challenge the structure of the family system and put the family's current way of interacting under stress. This will initiate the process of structural change and will likely inspire the family to seek more formal therapeutic intervention if the symptom is not quickly resolved.

As an example consider again the school-phobic child. If the parents conjointly create and stick to a plan ensuring that the child will go to school, only come home if he is verifiably ill, and make his father responsible for picking him up at school and staying with him if he is ill, all of the family's typical patterns of interaction will be challenged. The enmeshment between mother and child will be interrupted. The mother will be unable to find respite from her loneliness by dealing with her symptomatic child as the father will now have that job. The child will be removed from the mother's direct care and she will have a greater need for a relationship with her husband. This will clarify the marital boundary. The father will be more instrumentally involved and so will be a more functional member of the parental/executive subsystem. As the parental subsystem functions more effectively, the marital subsystem can begin to work more effectively as well. As the couple works together better, they will find ways to address the father's job loss and any financial difficulties. The parental cohesion will allow the child to worry less about his mother and will stop any unwitting reinforcement for his being sick and coming home. The child's attention will be redirected to coping with school and friends, which will help in establishing a peer subsystem to replace the sibling subsystem. If the school phobia alleviates quickly, the family will have successfully begun the process of structural change and will continue to move in the direction of more adaptive ways of interacting. If the school phobia persists, and the family members encounter substantial distress as they try to put the plan into effect, they could potentially be motivated to seek further therapeutic help. For example, if the parents of the child with school phobia find working together intolerable, they might then be more cognizant and receptive to the need for marital counseling. At this point, the school-based professional will want to function as a referral source.

As the clinician works with the parents to track how well the intervention plan is working, the parents may overtly or covertly evidence distress and discomfort (Haley, 1976). The clinician will want to watch carefully for signs of this distress. If the stress is overt, the parents might openly request advice, a referral, or suggestions for further therapeutic intervention. However, they might more subtly give "hints" that they are having difficulty. Often, at this juncture, school-based professionals might feel out of their area of expertise and try to ignore or simply not comment on the clues the family is offering. While this response is a courteous behavior in most social situations, it is counterproductive when working therapeutically with families. At this point, the clinician has the opportunity to encourage and facilitate change by identifying the family's discomfort, which will heighten, rather than dampen, their awareness of the need for change and will serve as an impetus toward the next step of accessing therapy. The tact and skill of the clinician will be pivotal in helping the family. The clinician may want to remain in a position of "team member" and be willing to note the family's difficulties. He or she may ask the members of the executive subsystem if they want to consider further therapy for the purpose of "helping them over a difficult period" or "helping them to be most effective in their efforts with their child." The clinician needs to find a balance between pushing and backing off. "Backing off," however, does not mean ceasing intervention. Rather, it means giving the family space and time to marshal resources and then gently pursuing further change once its members have had some respite from the stress. Too much respite will result in a return to structural homeostasis that will reinforce the symptom. Too little respite will alienate the family and result in their refusal to work with the professional staff. It is essential to collaborate with other professional staff members to compare observations and remain objective. It is also important to remain cognizant of the cultural issues that might be impacting on the therapeutic process.

Cultural Considerations

Culture influences every aspect of family functioning. According to McGoldrick (1982), culture influences the definition of family, family life-cycle phases, celebrations, occupation, and attitudes toward health, death, school, and therapy. *Culture* is a broad term and can include race, ethnicity, gender, socioeconomic status, religion, disability, education, or geographical area. From a family system's perspective, it is important to recognize that families can vary enormously in terms of the ways culture affects their patterns of communication, ways of behaving, relationships, values, rules, and roles. The philosophy among many schools of family therapy is: "If it's not broken, don't fix it." For some these variations may seem "abnormal," "undesirable," or "unhealthy," particularly when working with families that are culturally different from that of the helping professional. The true test of whether a family's structure and ways of relating are dysfunctional follows a determination of whether the family feels that it is troubled and in need of help, whether any members are symptomatic, and whether the family and its members are failing to move along developmental pathways (Goldenberg & Goldenberg, 2000). Conversely, if the family believes itself to be "doing O.K.," if no members are symptomatic, and if the family is supporting the "normal" developmental progress of its members, then the family is "functional" (Becvar & Becvar, 1996). If the family's patterns of interaction, including the hierarchy, executive subsystem, and boundaries are working according to the norms and expectations of that family, then it is "not broken and doesn't need to be fixed." All families will experience stress and disruption as they attempt to adjust to and master developmental tasks and cope with unexpected stressors (Goldenberg & Goldenberg, 2000). The process of adaptation is challenging and may create upheaval. One should not assume that the stress and anxiety that characterize developmental shifts are "pathological" or dysfunctional. The process of modifying family structure will be unique to each family. The manner in which the family responds will be impacted by their culture and may vary significantly from the coping characteristics of other cultural groups. For example, in some ethnic groups the expression of emotion and conflict is "normal." In these families, to cry and scream and argue is well within their comfortable range of functioning and serves as an effective method of communication and expression. In other families, stress is handled with silent strength. In these families, to express emotion is toxic and is outside of the family's comfortable range of functioning. Such expression of extreme emotion would be understood to be symptomatic. Again, as long as the family continues to make progress and the members remain symptom-free, the family is not to be considered in need of intervention.

Structural Family Therapy perceives "normal" families to be comprised of a clear hierarchical structure, clear boundaries, and effectively functioning subsystems. This does not presume, however, that only intact nuclear families are "normal." All family forms, such as single-parent families, extended family systems, and blended families are to be considered "normal" if they have clear boundaries, a clear hierarchy, and effectively functioning subsystems. It is the task of the clinician to be aware that families come in many forms. To discover the hierarchical structure of the family, one would not ask "who are the parents" and expect to obtain valuable information from all families. Caretaking functions and decision-making authority can be handled in many different ways. The clinician will want to know who cares for the child, how the care is shared, and how the caretakers communicate and agree on child rearing. The important issue to be assessed is whether the children have the security of a parental/executive subsystem that ensures that they are supported, nurtured, encouraged in their developmental stages, and given a clear structure within which to grow and experiment.

Conclusion

The literature in the field of marriage and family therapy reflects the importance of inclusion of the family system in the prevention, assessment, and treatment of psychosocial problems in children and adolescents. Prevention and early intervention has become a major focus in assessing and ameliorating early-onset symptoms in children such as aggression, drug use, delinquency, and violence before they mature into psychological disorders (Mrazek & Haggerty, 1994). Increasingly, models of prevention integrate factors associated with school, curriculum, and the family as they attempt to more effectively influence the lives of school-age children (Liddle & Hogue, 2000). For example, family therapy has been used successfully to provide in-home services for Head Start families (Leitch & Thomas, 1999; McDowell, 1999; Thomas, McCollum, & Snyder, 1999). Additionally, Barnes (1999) has written about clinical intervention with children of post-divorce families and the importance of support and collaboration with school personnel in aiding successful adjustment and adaptation. The importance of considering the family in the assessment of the social and emotional functioning of children cannot be ignored. Assessment and intervention by professionals within the school system can be enhanced by an understanding of systems theory and models of family therapy. Furthermore, collaborative work between the schools and family therapists can be an invaluable resource in the prevention and treatment of psychosocial problems in school-age children.

References

Barnes, G. G. (1999). Divorce transitions: Identifying risk and promoting resilience for children and their parental relationships. *Journal of Marital and Family Therapy, 25,* 425–442.

Bateson, G. (1972). *Steps to an ecology of mind.* New York: Ballantine.

Becvar, D. S., & Becvar, R. J. (1996). *Family therapy: A systemic integration.* Boston: Allyn and Bacon.

Bertanlaffy, L. von (1968). *General systems theory.* New York: George Braziller.

Bowen, M. (1978). *Family therapy in clinical practice.* New York: Jason Aronson.

Broderick, C. B., & Schrader, S. S. (1981). The history of professional marriage and family therapy. In A. S. Gurman & D. P Kniskern (Eds.), *Handbook of family therapy* (pp. 5–38). New York: Brunner/Mazel.

Brown, J. H., & Christensen, D. N. (1999). *Family therapy theory and practice*. Pacific Grove, CA: Brooks/Cole.

Carter, E.A., & McGoldrick, M. (Eds.). (1980). *The family life cycle: A framework for family therapy*. New York: Gardner Press.

Fishman, H. C., & Rosman, B. L. (1986). *Evolving models for family change*. New York: Guilford Press.

Goldenberg I., & Goldenberg, H. (2000). *Family therapy: An overview*. Pacific Grove, CA: Brooks/Cole.

Gurman, A. S., & Kniskern, D. P. (Eds). (1981). *Handbook of family therapy*. New York: Brunner/Mazel.

Haley, J. (1976). *Problem-solving therapy*. New York: Harper Colophon Books.

Jackson, D. D. (1959). Family interaction, family homeostasis, and some implications for conjoint family therapy. In J. Maserman (Ed.), *Individual and family dynamics*. New York: Grune & Stratton.

Kung, W. W. (2000). The intertwined relationship between depression and marital distress: Elements of marital therapy conducive to effective treatment outcome. *Journal of Marital and Family Therapy, 26*, 51–64.

Leitch, M. L., & Thomas, V. (1999). The AAMFT-Head Start training partnership project: Enhancing MFT capacities beyond the family system. *Journal of Marital and Family Therapy, 25*, 141–154.

Liddle, H. A., & Hogue, A. (2000) A family-based, developmental–ecological preventive intervention for high-risk adolescents. *Journal of Marital and Family Therapy, 26*, 265–280.

Madanes, C. (1982) *Strategic family therapy*. San Francisco: Jossey-Bass.

Madanes, C. (1984). *Behind the one-way mirror*. San Francisco: Jossey-Bass.

McDowell, T. (1999). Systems consultation and Head Start: An alternative to traditional family therapy. *Journal of Marital and Family Therapy, 26*, 155–168.

McGoldrick, M. (1982). *Ethnicity and family therapy*. New York: Guilford Press.

Minuchin, S. (1974). *Families & family therapy*. Cambridge, MA: Harvard University Press.

Minuchin, S., & Fishman, H. C. (1981). *Family therapy techniques*. Cambridge, MA: Harvard University Press.

Mrazek, P. J., & Haggerty, R. J. (Eds.). (1994). *Reducing risks for mental disorders: Frontiers of preventive intervention research*. Washington, DC: National Acamedy.

Nichols, M. P., & Schwartz, R. C. (1998). *Family therapy: Concepts and methods*. Boston: Allyn and Bacon.

Pinsof, W. M., & Wynne, L. (2000). Toward progress research: Closing the gap between family therapy practice and research. *Journal of Marital and Family Therapy, 26*, 1–8.

Price, S. J., McKenry, P. C., & Murphy, M. J. (2000). *Families across time: A life course perspective*. Los Angeles: Roxbury.

Shadish, W. R., Ragsdale, K., Glaser, R. R., & Montgomery, L. M. (1995). The efficacy and effectiveness of marital and family therapy: A perspective from meta-analysis. *Journal of Marital and Family Therapy, 21*, 345–360.

Thomas, V., McCollum, E. E., & Snyder, W. (1999). Beyond the clinic: In-home therapy with Head Start families. *Journal of Marital and Family Therapy, 25*, 177–190.

Watzlawick, P., Beavin, J. H., & Jackson, D. D. (1967). *Pragmatics of human communication*. New York: Norton.

Weiner, N. (1948). Cybernetics. *Scientific American, 179*, 14–18.

11

Assessment and Evaluation of Culturally Diverse Children: The Case of Latino Children

Roberto J. Vélasquez,

Jeanett Castellanos, and

Senaida Fernadez

To be effective, the diagnosis and treatment of mental illness must be tailored to all characteristics that shape a person's image and identity. The consequences of not understanding these influences can be profoundly deleterious. 'Culturally competent' services incorporate understanding of racial and ethnic groups, their histories, traditions, beliefs, and value systems (Satcher, 2000, p. 13).

As a practitioner (clinical or school psychologist), imagine yourself in one of the following scenarios: (a) You receive a referral from the Immigration and Naturalization Service to evaluate a Mexican-born five-year-old child who witnessed the death of his mother while crossing the Rio Grande River into the United States. The child is from Chiapas and primarily speaks an Indian dialect and very little Spanish. The child is placed with relatives in this country, but the father is asking that his son be returned to Mexico. The child claims to be hearing his mother's voice on a daily basis and he is convinced that she is nearby and looking out for him. The child's relatives are asking for asylum for the child because he is from a war-torn region of Mexico; (b) You are asked to evaluate a 16-year-old Salvadoran female who lives in a very tough barrio in

East Los Angeles. She is highly fearful of coming to school because female gang members who want her to join the gang are harassing and threatening her on a daily basis. She also complains of insomnia, depression, and nightmares. Unfortunately, her parents cannot understand her psychological complaints; (c) A 13-year-old Cuban American adolescent is brought by his parents to your private practice for psychotherapy. His parents complain that he does not want to speak Spanish at home and that he has become very *mal educado* (poorly socialized) by being disrespectful and defiant toward his grandparents and extended family. All of his friends are White and he prefers to identify as *Americano* instead of Cuban; (d) The mother of a 17-year-old *Nuyorrican* (a Puerto Rican who lives in New York) female brings her daughter for counseling to your community mental health center in the Bronx. The mother complains that her daughter does not want to return to Puerto Rico to live because she can no longer identify with the culture and she prefers to speak only English. The daughter states that she is very stressed by her mother, who views her as less than Puerto Rican because of how she identifies herself. The daughter reports many arguments with her mother, and has voiced a desire to run away from home; (e) A 16-year-old male, born in Tijuana, Baja California, Mexico, but raised in the United States since one year of age, is now facing deportation. He indicates to you that he is undocumented and quite worried about being deported to Mexico. He notes that he has no family in Mexico, and that he does not speak Spanish. He also tells you that he identifies as *Chicano* and not as *Mexicano;* (f) A 15-year-old Nicaraguan-born female whose nickname is "*huera*," because she is blond and blue-eyed and her features are European, or *gringo*, as her mother says, reports being confused and angry with respect to her ethnic identity. She says to you that she hates "looking White" and being treated differently by both Latinos and Whites at school. She also notes that she is highly distressed when her White peers and teachers do not acknowledge her cultural background.

Now, where or how do you begin to evaluate each of these distinct individuals? What issues must you definitely address in your evaluation? What assumptions do you test out in your evaluation of each person? Are there particular tests or measures that you might consider in evaluating each of these individuals? Do you simply refer each of these clients to a Latino/a practitioner? What if is there is no Latino/a practitioner in your community or city? To complicate each situation more, what if each of these potential clients' identity is changed to African American, Filipino American, Vietnamese, or a member of the Cherokee Nation? What if each of these people is either an immigrant or U.S.-born? What similar or different challenges do you now foresee in the evaluation and intervention processes?

The purpose of our chapter is threefold. First, to present a discussion on the importance of linking psychological assessment to interventions with culturally diverse children. We believe that many practitioners who have written in the past about the evaluation of culturally diverse or *minority children* have not linked assessment to the intervention process. We argue that success in the classification and treatment of culturally diverse children has to be anchored in the culturally competent assessment of the client. Clearly, psychological assessment and testing of children, irrespective of ethnicity or race, is here to stay (see Kamphaus, Petoskey, & Rowe, 2000). Second, we present some common misconceptions about the assessment of diverse children. For example, many practitioners are still under the false impression that the assessment of culturally diverse children is identical to the assessment of intellectual or cognitive functioning. We argue that such an assumption is not valid because the tools used to assess dysfunctional behavior are inherently different from cognitive measures. Third, we offer some practical recommendations for the assessment of culturally diverse children. These are based on our collective experiences of evaluating hundreds of culturally diverse children in many diverse settings ranging from refugee camps to community mental health clinics to day-treatment programs to public schools. We have also treated children with a variety of mental health issues, ranging from depression to schizophrenia to culturally-bound conditions like acculturation problems, *susto* (fright), intergenerational distress experienced by parents, and residual trauma due to racism or discrimination.

Although our points in this chapter are directed toward Latino children and adolescents, we believe that many of our comments, observations, and recommendations are generalizable to other ethnic or racial minority children in this country, including those from Puerto Rico. For example, it has been erroneously assumed that, unlike their Asian American and Latino counterparts, African Americans have not had to deal with issues of acculturation (Thompson, Anderson, & Bakeman, 2000). We also must recognize that the *experience* of not being a member of the majority culture, or of being a *minority*, is a unique experience for each child that is mediated by many factors, many of which have yet to be articulated in the literature. Although we acknowledge that a "shared minority status" experience can be a useful paradigm for understanding issues related to minority status, marginality, and exclusion, we also recognize that social, political, historical, and economic issues play a major role in the experience of each of these groups.

Linking Assessment and Treatment of Latino Children

The key to the successful treatment of Latino children in a variety of clinical, mental health, or school settings lies in the effective, accurate, and valid assessment of emotional, behavioral, or psychological problems (Chavez & Gonzales-Singh, 1980; Dana, 1993; Malgady, Rogler, & Constantino, 1987; Rivera & Cespedes, 1982; Vélasquez & Callahan, 1992). If the assessment is not geared toward the cultural, then the report is of little value to all parties concerned (Hays, 1996). In our experience, we have reviewed hundreds of evaluation reports on culturally diverse children. The useful reports typically reflect a strong desire on the part of the psychologist to answer culturally-based questions or hypotheses that have not been posed before, or that have been misinterpreted by other practitioners. Hays noted that "...effective intervention depends on an accurate assessment, and an accurate assessment requires both an awareness and knowledge of specific cultural influences on both clients and psychologists" (p. 193).

The assessment or evaluation, whether conducted in English or Spanish, or in both languages, serves as the foundation for the understanding and appreciation of Latino children's unique problems or concerns. In addition, the evaluation, if conducted from a culturally competent perspective, can be a potent first step in developing culturally responsive interventions on behalf of the Latino child (Cervantes & Acosta, 1992; Vélasquez, Ayala, & Mendoza, 1998). If conducted appropriately, the psychological evaluation of a Latino child should lead the practitioner to make well-informed decisions that are anchored in the child's identity, experience, language, culture, and worldview (Guarnaccia & Rodriguez, 1996; Vélasquez, 1995; Vélasquez & Callahan, 1992). At the same time, such an evaluation assists the practitioner in making sound and practical decisions about this child's treatment (e.g., identify or describe dysfunctional behavior, assist in diagnostic decision making, aid in treatment planning and selection, and evaluate treatment outcome).

Malgady et al. (1987), discussing the need to validly assess Latinos, including children, observe that a Latino client's "early contacts with a mental health agency are likely to be diagnostic in nature, whether the assessment performed is formal or informal, brief or intensive" (p. 228). They also note that "the procedure might include a mental status examination . . . psychological tests might be administered . . . and then a social history is taken to place test and interview data in proper [cultural] context. At the end of this process, a diagnosis is formulated, a disposition is rendered, and a treatment plan is developed" (pp. 228–229). Rivera and Cespedes (1982) noted that "valid psychological evaluations of . . . Latinos are important . . . and it may be that without these [evaluations] many [Latino] clients will be overlooked [by the mental health system] or misunderstood [by the psychologist]" (p. 58).

In evaluating Latino children, we always pose a series of questions, or hypotheses, that will allow us to design an evaluation that reflects cultural sensitivity. While we routinely ask questions related to psychosocial history (including nationality, family composition, discrimination experiences, etc.), mental health status, signs and symptoms of a particular problem or disorder, history of previous treatment, and family functioning, we also pose the following questions as a way of supporting the cultural validity of our evaluation.

1. What is the age of the child? We ask this because cultural milestones are very important in Latino culture. For example, recognition and acceptance of the familial hierarchy and role of the extended family is crucial to Latino children, and is taught and reinforced on a continuous basis. *Familism* is a concept with its own special meaning within Latino culture, and even varies from Latino subgroup to Latino subgroup, which implies a strong sense of solidarity, loyalty, pride, and cohesiveness (Cortes, 1995; Planos, Zayas, & Busch-Rossnagel, 1995; Rodriguez & Kosloski, 1998). Another concept that is taught to children is achievement, and its meaning within the context of the *familia* and community (Okagaki, Frensch, & Gordon, 1995).

2. What is the birth order of the child? The place of the child within the family constellation is very important, and, to a large extent, influences the rest of the Latino child's life. For example, oldest children are given significant responsi-

bility for younger siblings, and are expected to serve as parental figures under crisis situations. The first author recalls that, as early as age 7, his parents told him that if they died, he would be responsible for caring for the family for the rest of his life. Obviously, this message was overwhelming and scary, yet these messages reflect values of the culture. In this case, the meta-message was "No one can take care of our children but our oldest child."

3. Has the child served as a cultural broker or translator for the rest of the family? That is, has the child become parentified, out of practical necessity or survival because he or she is the most proficient in the English language or has studied in this country? This phenomenon is quite common among immigrant Latino families in which the burden of translating, not only language, but many aspects of U.S. culture falls to the Latino child (Buriel, Perez, DeMent, Chavez, & Moran, 1998; Tse, 1995). In evaluating adult clients who are also immigrants, it is not unusual for them to bring a child (sometimes as young as 6 years) to serve as a translator or interpreter. We have witnessed the pressure that comes with serving in such an important role, and the pseudo-parental responsibility given to the child. Perhaps, in some way, this is another way of reinforcing in the Latino child the need to take care of his or her parents later in life.

4. What is the ethnic identity of the child? How do they define themselves? Are they *Chicano, Mexicano, Cubano, Dominicano, Boriqua*, and so on? This is very important because a strong and crystallized ethnic identity has been linked to better mental health functioning and greater feelings of self-efficacy (see Niemann, Romero, Arredondo, & Rodriguez, 1999; Quintana & Vera, 1999). Also, a strong sense of ethnic identity has been viewed as part of a Latino child's resilience in the face of external or social stresses (Gordon, 1996). We view identity as the mechanism for displaying pride in and love for one's culture, or, if that identity is not crystallized, confusion, alienation, or disconnectedness toward one's culture, family, and community may result.

5. What is the emotional language of the child? Does the child feel more comfortable discussing his or her emotions or problems in English or Spanish, or in both languages? Past research on bilingualism and the expression of psychopathology suggests that Latinos who are proficient in Spanish and English not only express their problems differently, depending on the language in which they are interviewed, but their attributions of how they became ill or disabled and how they might become healthy again are different as a result of language (Bamford, 1991; Bradford & Munoz, 1993; Marcos, Alpert, Urcuyo, & Kesselman, 1973; Price & Cuellar, 1981).

  Also, language appears to regulate the extent to which emotions will or will not be expressed, or what types of nonverbal cues the child will emit. This also has been observed in the performance of bilingual Latinos on such tests as the Minnesota *Multiphasic Personality Inventory-2* (*MMPI-2*; Butcher, Dahlstrom, Graham, Tellegen, & Kaemmer, 1989) and its adolescent counterpart, the *Minnesota Multiphasic Personality Inventory-Adolescent* (*MMPI-A*; [Butcher et al., 1992]; see Vélasquez et al., 1997; Vélasquez et al., 2000;). We have observed numerous situations in which bilingual children perform very differently on clinical measures as a function of language when dealing with emotional issues or problems.

6. What are the idioms of distress, in either English or Spanish (or even in Spanglish, a slang blend of English and Spanish) that the Latino child uses to describe his or her emotional or psychological problems? For example, it is not unusual for Latino children to use *triste* ('sad') or *enojado* ('angry') to describe depression. In many ways, these idioms, grounded in Latino culture including spirituality, and religion, and influenced by the child's cultural subgroup, are better indicators of distress than traditional psychiatric jargon (see Aviera, 1996; Guarnaccia, Rivera, Franco, & Neighbors, 1996; Owen, 1998; Rogler, Cortes, & Malgady, 1994). For example, the term *deprimido*, which means 'depression,' has very little meaning in many Latino groups, and does not communicate severity or intensity the way words like *falta de fe* ('lack of faith'), *perdida de dignidad* ('loss of dignity'), or *encabronado* ('very, very angry') do. In one case, the first author worked with a Chicano youth from a barrio in San Diego, California. The youth, in the evaluation, kept saying that he was *locote*, or 'very crazy.' On further inquiry, the client defined the word as descriptive of his lack of personal control, cultural alienation, and feelings of marginality. More importantly, he used this term to refer to his condition of schizophrenia, in that he equated this lack of personal control, alienation, and feelings of marginality with being "very crazy."

7. Does the child come from a traditional or nontraditional family background? Most Latino families, in spite of acculturation toward mainstream culture, continue to hold traditional values that are largely defined by their community and religion. This traditionalism is seen in many aspects of family life including the adherence to sex roles, expression of emotions, morals and values, articulation of sexual themes, and the extent to which a person discloses problems to people outside of the household (see Flores, Eyre, & Millstein, 1998). Thus, it is often difficult to assess Latino youth because they are taught from the beginning that talking about problems outside of the home is not acceptable or can bring shame or embarrassment to the family (Santiago-Rivera, 1995).

8. What are the Latino child's beliefs about how people become mentally ill, problematic, or dysfunctional? This question is critical because health beliefs have been found to impact compliance with treatment and prognosis in both health and mental health settings for Latinos. Related to this question are additional issues including locus of control, fatalism, and beliefs in spiritual intervention. Obviously, when one is evaluating a child, it is very important to meet with the parent(s) or parental figure(s) to examine many issues related to the child's evaluation including the role of mental health beliefs (Guinn, 1998; Talavera, Elder, & Vélasquez, 1997).

9. What is the diagnostic history of this Latino child? In our work with Latino children, and children from other cultural groups, we are constantly frustrated with the problematic diagnostic histories of many children who have been in and out of a particular mental health care system. For example, it is very common to

find that a Latino child has numerous diagnoses, and that the majority are incorrect or inaccurate (Flaskerud, 1986; Johnson, 1993; Vélasquez, Johnson, & Brown-Cheatham, 1993). In one recent instance, the second author was asked to consult on a case in a public school in which a Latino child was so heavily medicated that he constantly fell asleep in class. Upon a review of the child's assessment history, she found that the child had been evaluated seven times and that each evaluation yielded a different diagnosis, ranging from dysthymia to schizophrenia. In the end, and after having the child examined by a physician, it was determined that the child's behavior was largely impacted by a rare diabetic condition that had never been identified. The psychiatric diagnosis of culturally diverse children, including Latinos, continues to be a major source of discussion in the profession (Canino, 1982; Chavez & Gonzales-Singh, 1980; Cuellar, 1982; Cuellar, Martinez, Jimenez, & Gonzalez, 1983).

10. What risk factors contribute to the psychological or emotional vulnerability of Latino children? Are any of these problems found in the child's life, now or in the past: poverty, parental absence, poor diet, a history of migration, gang affiliation, substance abuse, immigration, refugee status, medical illness, and so forth? According to the Federal Interagency Forum on Child and Family Statistics (1997), 66% of Latino children in female-headed households live in poverty, and 28% of Latino children in two-parent households live in poverty. Compared to 11% of White children, from either single or two-parent households, 39% of Latino children are living in poverty. An issue related to poverty is the lack of food security. In 1994, it was found that 8% of all children living at or below the poverty level sometimes or often did not have enough food to eat, compared to 1% of children living above the poverty level. Given the high number of Latino children living below the poverty level, one can only wonder about the deleterious effect of poor diet on academic achievement and physical development.

    In addition to poverty and poor diet, children also can be affected by the amount of prenatal care received by their mothers, as a lack of care can have a detrimental effect on subsequent development. In 1994, it was found that 69% of Latinas utilized early prenatal care as opposed to 83% of their White counterparts (Federal Interagency Forum on Child and Family Statistics, 1997).

    In adolescence, Latino youth face additional risk factors for psychological and emotional vulnerability. In 1997, 16% of Latino youth, ages 12–17, used cigarettes within a one-month period. Also, within this age group, 19% of Latino youth used alcohol, 8% used marijuana, and 1% used cocaine (National Center for Health Statistics, 1999). Additionally, among Latino adolescents, ages 15–17, the birth rates in 1997 were 68.2 per 1,000 young women (Ventura, Mathews, & Curtin, 1998). We have found that once risk factors are identified by the psychologist, assessment can become much more relevant because of the targeting of interventions (see Yin, Zapata, & Katims, 1995).

11. To what extent is the child or family affected by acculturative stress, or the stress to assimilate to mainstream culture? Acculturative stress has been found to impact many aspects of Latinos' functioning, including the level of risk for emo-

tional and health illnesses (Hovey, 2000; Saldana, 1994). There now exist many measures designed to evaluate some aspect of stress on Latino children and its impact on coping mechanisms, ethnic identity, and resilience (see Barona & Miller, 1994; Chavez, Moran, Reid, & Lopez, 1997; Colomba, Santiago, & Rossello, 1999; Cuellar, Arnold, & Maldonado, 1995; Norris, Ford, & Bova, 1996).

12. What factors contribute to the resilience of this child in spite of a multitude of stressors or risk factors? In other words, what are the buffers that serve to protect the Latino child from literally falling apart emotionally? Resilience can be composed of such factors as a strong family, caring and loving grandparents or *abuelitos*, strong *compadres*, religious or spiritual beliefs, *respeto* for others, and the ability to *improvisar* (improvise) in daily life situations that require problem solving. Other factors that contribute to resilience include a strong ethnic identity, maintenance of the Spanish language, familism, and *integridad cultural* (cultural integrity).

Common Misconceptions regarding the Assessment of Latino Children

Below are four common misconceptions regarding the assessment of Latino children. These misconceptions have been gleaned from past research, which has often portrayed Latinos in a deficient or negative light.

Misconception 1: Latino clients, especially children, are more difficult to assess or evaluate because they are not psychologically minded. This assumption, which echoes long-standing negative stereotypes of Latinos, is based on the belief that Latinos are not able to communicate to psychologists in the language or terminology that is used in clinical practice, or that Latino clients are somehow not as attuned or insightful about their emotional or psychological functioning as their White counterparts. In our experience, Latino clients, including children, are not deficient in their communication skills. In fact, from early childhood, a Latino child is taught to be highly competent within interpersonal relationships because social life, typically within the family and community, is such an important part of daily living. This concept is often referred to as *personalismo*.

Misconception 2: Problems in the clinical assessment of Latino clients, including children, are similar to those found in the intelligence/educational-testing field. This assumption is based on the belief that the issues (e.g., static versus dynamic nature of construct) found in the intelligence or cognitive testing of Latinos (usually in school settings) are identical or parallel to those found in the assessment or evaluation of Latinos in clinical settings. That is, intelligence is generally a static construct while mental illness and other issues, such as behavior problems or school performance, are subject to dramatic changes based on the intensity, frequency, and duration of a particular condition or disorder. When asked to serve on quality assurance panels, or to review child custody evaluations for the courts, the first author is often disheartened by the fact that many psychologists, especially those who work with minority clients, view the assessment of emotional problems in the same light as the evaluation of cognitive issues. That is, they assume that a mental health condition for Latino children is lifelong or long-term. Clearly, psychologists need to be more sensitive to the fact that these are separate, yet related, issues.

Although a child may consistently score within a certain range on tests of cognitive performance, it is inappropriate to assume that a child who is classified at one point as having emotional problems will continue to have problems throughout his or her lifetime. Once difficulties have been identified and an intervention has been set in motion, the probability increases that the problem will be ameliorated. By assuming that these problems and difficulties will follow a child throughout a lifetime, and ignoring the effect of a child's environment on behavior and emotional well-being, the practitioner does a disservice to the child being assessed.

Misconception 3: Psychological assessment devices, whether projective or objective, often misdiagnose or misclassify Latino clients. This assumption is based on the belief that, somehow, clinical measures are inherently biased, or that a test makes the ultimate decision about the diagnosis of a Latino child. Although there continues to be a vigorous debate about *etic* versus *emic* issues in the assessment of ethnic minorities, including Latinos (see Dana, 1993), and about appropriate test norms (see Cervantes & Acosta, 1992), psychological assessment instruments alone do not misclassify or misdiagnose a client. It is the psychologist who is most responsible for the misdiagnosis or misclassification of a Latino child because she or he interprets the data and makes decisions on many personal factors, including experience with a particular cultural group, be it Latinos, African Americans, or Asian Americans. For example, if the psychologist depends on only one instrument (e.g., the *Thematic Apperception Test*; Murray, 1943) or on a computerized interpretation of a particular test (e.g., the *MMPI-A*), then he or she is more likely to make diagnostic errors because she or he is limiting the database on the child.

Misconception 4: Issues in the psychological assessment of Latino youth are identical to those found in other ethnic minority groups, most notably African Americans. This assumption is based on the belief that basic issues in the assessment of Latino children are identical to those encountered in the assessment of other cultural groups, including African American children. Furthermore, this assumption presupposes that, because of a "shared minority status," which includes poverty, poor quality of education, high unemployment, and social marginalization, Latinos should perform similarly on a given measure, or that emotional problems experienced by Latinos are the same as those experienced by other minority groups. The reality is that the expression of psychological problems is largely defined by culture, with regard to symptomatology (which symptoms are displayed externally), idioms of distress to be used to describe the phenomena, availability of caregivers, healers, or psychologists, and beliefs in healing methods or procedures.

A salient, group-specific issue in assessment that arises when working with Latino youth is the issue of language. Differences in language can affect the way that children understand and respond to questions that are asked as well as the way in which they conceptualize and communicate their feelings to others. As previously discussed, many Latino groups have different terms for what is called *depression* in English. The issue of primary language and its effects on communication is not a variable that is shared across all ethnic minority groups. The misconception that issues in the assessment of minority groups are homogeneous, and the resulting assumption that treatments and interventions can be used interchangeably without modification, can have detrimental effects.

Practical Recommendations for Assessing and Evaluating Latino Children

The following practical recommendations, based on our experiences, are suggested for practitioners who will encounter a case in which they will need to assess a Latino child, and who are striving for valid cultural formulations.

Practitioners must recognize that the psychological assessment or evaluation of Latino children does not occur in a vacuum or independently of the client's sociohistorical background. Too often, well-intentioned practitioners fail by not acknowledging the client's unique experiences that define his or her worldview. These experiences include sex roles, socialization processes, acculturative stress, language barriers, immigration, and traumatic experiences of prejudice and discrimination. For example, the experiences of a third-generation U.S.-born Cuban, raised in an urban neighborhood outside of Miami, are quite different from those of a Cuban who recently arrived from his or her country. From the outset, practitioners must recognize that such important background variables do make a difference and need to be used in the interpretation of test data.

Psychologists must recognize that the psychological assessment of Latino children occurs within the context of a helping relationship. Practitioners are more likely to establish credibility, trust, and openness (i.e., self-disclosure) if the assessment relationship is viewed as comparable to a therapeutic relationship. Thus, Latino clients and their parents are more likely to participate or cooperate fully in the assessment process if they feel that the assessment is based on trust and mutual respect, and that the potential for a positive outcome exists. Also, practitioners should not be surprised or uncomfortable if Latino clients and their families "test" the practitioner because this can be part of the process of trust building. For example, a Latino family may come into a practitioner's office for an assessment of a child's scholastic aptitude for participation in a "gifted" program. The parents may ask a sarcastic question such as "Have you ever tested Mexican kids who are smart?" and watch for the practitioner's response. If the practitioner can recognize that the parent is using this question to test the practitioner's attitude toward ethnic minority children that he or she assesses, and is able to respond in an open, warm fashion, the family will begin to trust her or him.

Practitioners must recognize that the assessment or evaluation of Latino children is not a simple process that is mechanical or linear, or based on a specific formula (e.g., conduct a mental status examination, obtain a social history, administer a series of tests, and reach a diagnostic conclusion). Instead, the process is complex and requires the practitioner to be flexible, patient, and sensitive to alternative modes of assessment that are anchored in Latino culture. This includes assessing the belief systems that Latino children are socialized in regarding the origin and resolution of problems emanating from emotional, social, or personal domains.

Practitioners must recognize that the assessment of Latino children should have an educational component that allows the client to feel that he or she can benefit from the ultimate goal of assessment decision making that will lead to effective interventions. This is especially critical for Latino clients who have had limited or negative experiences in psychotherapy. Too often, practitioners present the evaluation process to Latino children in a rather secretive manner that implies an adversarial relationship between the psychologist and child. It is important to note that many children and their families may already have bad memories of previous evaluations, or of having to fight the system.

Practitioners must recognize the diversity or heterogeneity among Latino children. The long-standing image that "all Latino children are recent immigrants, monolingual, and have low socioeconomic status" is not true. Too often, practitioners depend on such a stereotype to make diagnostic or classification decisions, and even to determine what types of interventions might be most effective with Latino clients. Other stereotypes that are often voiced by practitioners include the belief that Latino children are not interested in treatment, that they are best treated with psychotropic medications rather than psychotherapy, or that they are not motivated to change their behaviors. Practitioners must recognize that many Latino clients have had negative experiences with prior assessment or testing. For example, it is common to work with parents who feel vulnerable or fearful about the assessment process because they were once misdiagnosed in academic settings. For these clients, it is important that the practitioner be open to discussing any reservations held by the client before the assessment or evaluation.

Practitioners must always recognize the role of sociocultural or moderator variables in the assessment of Latino children. These include age, identity, gender, language, nationality, acculturative stress, socioeconomic status, sex roles, folk beliefs, community standards, and ecological environment. For example, language or dialect is a powerful factor in defining and understanding the phenomenology of a Latino client's problems or concerns. Malgady et al. (1987) observe that "when the fact that bilingualism and language . . . is acknowledged, the following questions arise: In which language, English or Spanish, do bilinguals express greater psychopathology? And, of course, which language conveys the true nature and extent of pathology?" (p. 231).

Conclusion

The clinical or psychological assessment of culturally diverse or minority children is a complicated process that oftentimes requires more time and effort. It is also a process that is akin to psychotherapy in many ways, including the need to reach a level of intimacy that allows for trust and self-disclosure. It is a process that requires the psychologist to be aware of his or her beliefs about a particular cultural group, and to walk the thin line of hypothesis testing versus simply depending on cultural stereotypes or caricatures. In many ways, a practitioner never reaches full competence in the assessment of culturally diverse people because our world continues to become more and more diverse with respect to culture, language, and worldviews.

In this chapter, we have attempted to present our perspective on the assessment of children of Latino descent. We have only touched the tip of the iceberg by explaining our philosophy about what needs to be considered in the culturally competent assessment of Latino children. As we noted earlier, and as we have learned in the process of writing this chapter, culture is anything but static and continues to evolve in ways that we cannot yet envision. While our hope is not to overwhelm the reader, we must acknowledge the fact that we probably have. Yet, our dream continues to be that someday practitioners will find methodologies for attending to the role of culture in the manifestation of problems across and within cultures. Perhaps in the end, this is just one contribution to this dream that we hope is shared by others.

References

American Psychiatric Association. (1994). *Diagnostic and statistical manual of mental disorders* (4th ed.). Washington, DC: Author.

Aviera, A. (1996). "Dichos" therapy group: A therapeutic use of Spanish language proverbs with hospitalized Spanish-speaking psychiatric patients. *Cultural Diversity and Mental Health, 2,* 73–87.

Bamford, K. W. (1991). Bilingual issues in mental health assessment and treatment. *Hispanic Journal of Behavioral Sciences, 13,* 377–390.

Barona, A., & Miller, J. A. (1994). Short Acculturation Scale for Hispanic Youth (SASH-Y): A preliminary report. *Hispanic Journal of Behavioral Sciences, 16,* 155–162.

Bradford, D. T., & Munoz, A. (1993). Translation in bilingual psychotherapy. *Professional Psychology: Research and Practice, 24,* 52–61.

Buriel, R., Perez, W., DeMent, T. L., Chavez, D. V., & Moran, V. R. (1998). The relationship of language brokering to academic performance, biculturalism, and self-efficacy among Latino adolescents. *Hispanic Journal of Behavioral Sciences, 20,* 283–297.

Butcher, J. N., Dahlstrom, W. G., Graham, J. R., Tellegen, A., & Kaemmer, B. (1989). *Minnesota Multiphasic Personality Inventory-2 (MMPI-2): Manual for administration and scoring.* Minneapolis, MN: University of Minnesota Press.

Butcher, J. N., Williams, C. L., Graham, J. R., Archer, R. P., Tellegen, A., Ben-Porath, Y. S., & Kaemmer, B. (1992). *Minnesota Multiphasic Personality Inventory-Adolescent (MMPI-A): Manual for administration, scoring, and interpretation.* Minneapolis, MN: University of Minnesota Press.

Canino, G. (1982). The Latino woman: Sociocultural influences on diagnoses and treatment. In R. M. Becerra, M., Karno, & J. I. Escobar (Eds.), *Mental health and Latino Americans: Clinical perspectives* (pp. 117–138). New York: Grune & Stratton.

Cervantes, R. C., & Acosta, F. X. (1992). Psychological testing for Hispanic Americans. *Applied and Preventive Psychology, 1,* 209–219.

Cervantes, R. C., & Arroyo, W. (1994). *DSM-IV:* Implications for Hispanic children and adolescents. *Hispanic Journal of Behavioral Sciences, 16,* 8–27.

Chavez, D. V., Moran, V. R., Reid, S. L., & Lopez, M. (1997). Acculturative stress in children: A modification of the SAFE scale. *Hispanic Journal of Behavioral Sciences, 19,* 34–44.

Chavez, E. L., & Gonzales-Singh, E. (1980). Latino assessment: A case study. *Professional Psychology: Research and Practice, 11,* 163–168.

Colomba, M. V., Santiago, E. S., & Rossello, J. (1999). Coping strategies and depression in Puerto Rican adolescents: An exploratory study. *Cultural Diversity and Ethnic Minority Psychology, 5,* 65–75.

Cortes, D. E. (1995). Variations in familism in two generations of Puerto Ricans. *Hispanic Journal of Behavioral Sciences, 17,* 249–255.

Cuellar, I. (1982). The diagnosis and evaluation of schizophrenic disorders among Mexican Americans. In R. M. Becerra, M. Karno, & J. L. Escobar (Eds.), *Mental health and Latino Americans: Clinical perspectives* (pp. 61–81). San Diego: Grune & Stratton.

Cuellar, I., Arnold, B., & Maldonado, R. (1995). Acculturation rating scale for Mexican Americans-II: A revision of the original ARSMA scale. *Hispanic Journal of Behavioral Sciences, 17,* 275–304.

Cuellar, I., Martinez, C., Jimenez, R., & Gonzalez, R. (1983). Clinical psychiatric case presentation: Culturally responsive diagnostic formulation and treatment in an Hispanic client. *Hispanic Journal of Behavioral Sciences, 5,* 93–103.

Dana, R. H. (1993). *Multicultural assessment perspectives for professional psychology.* Boston: Allyn and Bacon.

Federal Interagency Forum on Child and Family Statistics. (1997). *America's children: Key national indicators of well-being.* Washington, DC: U.S. Government Printing Office.

Flaskerud, J. H. (1986). Diagnostic and treatment differences among five ethnic groups. *Psychological Reports, 58,* 219–235.

Flores, E., Eyre, S. L., & Millstein, S. G. (1998). Sociocultural beliefs related to sex among Mexican American adolescents. *Hispanic Journal of Behavioral Sciences, 20,* 60–82.

Gordon, K. A. (1996). Resilient Hispanic youth's self-concept and motivational patterns. *Hispanic Journal of Behavioral Sciences, 18,* 63–73.

Guarnaccia, P. J., Rivera, M., Franco, F., & Neighbors, C. (1996). The experiences of ataques de nervios: Towards an anthropology of emotions in Puerto Rico. *Culture, Medicine, and Psychiatry, 20,* 343–367.

Guarnaccia, P. J., & Rodriguez, O. (1996). Concepts of culture and their role in the development of culturally competent mental health services. *Hispanic Journal of Behavioral Sciences, 18,* 419–433.

Guinn, B. (1998). Acculturation and health locus of control among Mexican American adolescents. *Hispanic Journal of Behavioral Sciences, 20,* 492–499.

Hays, P. A. (1996). Culturally responsive assessment with diverse older adults. *Professional Psychology: Research and Practice, 27,* 188–193.

Hovey, J. D. (2000). Acculturative stress, depression, and suicidal ideation in Mexican immigrants. *Cultural Diversity and Ethnic Minority Psychology, 6,* 134–151.

Johnson, R. (1993). Clinical issues in the use of the *DSM-III-R* with African American children: A diagnostic paradigm. *Journal of Black Psychology, 19,* 447–460.

Kamphaus, R. W., Petoskey, M. D., & Rowe, E. W. (2000). Current trends in psychological testing of children. *Professional Psychology: Research and Practice, 31,* 155–164.

Malgady, R. G., Rogler, L. H., & Constantino, G. (1987). Ethnocultural and linguistic bias in mental health evaluation of Hispanics. *American Psychologist, 42,* 228–234.

Marcos, L. R., Alpert, M., Urcuyo, L., & Kesselman, M. (1973). The effect of interview language on the evaluation of psychopathology in Spanish-American schizophrenic patients. *American Journal of Psychiatry, 130,* 549–553.

Murray, H. A. (1943). *Thematic Apperception Test: Manual.* Cambridge, MA: Harvard University Press.

National Center for Health Statistics. (1999). *Health, United States, 1999. With health and aging chartbook.* Hyattsville, MD: National Center for Health Statistics.

Niemann, Y. F., Romero, A. J., Arredondo, J., & Rodriguez, V. (1999). What does it mean to be "Mexican"? Social construction of an ethnic identity. *Hispanic Journal of Behavioral Sciences, 21,* 47–60.

Norris, A. E., Ford, K., & Bova, C. A. (1996). Psychometrics of a brief acculturation scale for Hispanics in a probability sample of urban Hispanic adolescents and young adults. *Hispanic Journal of Behavioral Sciences, 18,* 29–38.

Okagaki, L., Frensch, P. A., & Gordon, E. W. (1995). Encouraging school achievement in Mexican American children. *Hispanic Journal of Behavioral Sciences, 17,* 160–179.

Owen, P. R. (1998). Fears of Hispanic and Anglo children: Real-world fears in the 1990s. *Hispanic Journal of Behavioral Sciences, 20,* 483–491.

Planos, R., Zayas, L. H., & Busch-Rossnagel, N. A. (1995). Acculturation and teaching behaviors of Dominican and Puerto Rican mothers. *Hispanic Journal of Behavioral Sciences, 17,* 225–236.

Price, C. S., & Cuellar, I. (1981). Effects of language and related variables on the expression of psychopathology in Mexican American psychiatric patients. *Hispanic Journal of Behavioral Sciences, 3,* 145–160.

Quintana, S. M., & Vera, E. M. (1999). Mexican American children's ethnic identity, understanding of ethnic prejudice, and parental ethnic socialization. *Hispanic Journal of Behavioral Sciences, 21,* 387–404.

Rivera, O. A., & Cespedes, R. (1982). *Rehabilitation of handicapped migrant and seasonal farmworkers.* Salt Lake City, UT: Institute of Human Resource Development.

Rodriguez, J. M., & Kosloski, K. (1998). The impact of acculturation on attitudinal familism in a community of Puerto Rican Americans. *Hispanic Journal of Behavioral Sciences, 20,* 375–390.

Rogler, L. H., Cortes, D. E., & Malgady, R. G. (1994). The mental health relevance of idioms of distress: Anger and perceptions of injustice among New York Puerto Ricans. *Journal of Nervous and Mental Disease, 182,* 327–331.

Saldana, D. H. (1994). Minority status and distress. *Hispanic Journal of Behavioral Sciences, 16,* 116–128.

Santiago-Rivera, A. L. (1995). Developing a culturally sensitive treatment modality for bilingual Spanish-speaking clients: Incorporating language and culture in counseling. *Journal of Counseling and Development, 74,* 12–17.

Satcher, D. (2000). Mental health: A report of the Surgeon General: Executive summary. *American Psychologist, 31,* 5–13.

Talavera, G. A., Elder, J. P., & Vélasquez, R. J. (1997). Latino health beliefs and locus of control: Implications for primary care and public health practitioners. *American Journal of Preventive Medicine, 13,* 408–410.

Thompson, C. P., Anderson, L. P., & Bakeman, R. A. (2000). Effects of racial socialization and racial identity on acculturative stress in African American college students. *Cultural Diversity & Ethnic Minority Psychology, 6,* 196–210.

Tse, L. (1995). Language brokering among Latino adolescents: Prevalence, attitudes, and school performance. *Hispanic Journal of Behavioral Sciences, 17,* 180–193.

Vélasquez, R. J. (1995). Personality assessment of Hispanic clients. In J. N. Butcher (Ed.), *Clinical personality assessment: Practical considerations* (pp. 120–139). New York: Oxford University Press.

Vélasquez, R. J., Ayala, G. X., & Mendoza, S. (1998). *Psychodiagnostic assessment of U.S. Latinos: MMPI, MMPI-2, and MMPI-A results: A comprehensive manual.* East Lansing, MI: Julian Samora Research Institute, Michigan State University.

Vélasquez, R. J., & Callahan, W. J. (1992). Psychological testing of Latino Americans in clinical settings: Overview and issues. In K. F. Geisinger (Ed.), *Psychological testing of Hispanics* (pp. 253–265). Washington. DC: American Psychological Association.

Vélasquez, R. J., Chavira, D. A., Karle, H. R., Callahan, W. J., Garcia, J. A., & Castellanos, J. (2000). Assessing bilingual and monolingual Latino students with translations of the MMPI-2: Initial data. *Cultural Diversity and Ethnic Minority Psychology, 6,* 65–72.

Vélasquez, R. J., Gonzales, M., Butcher, J. N., Castillo-Canez, I., Apodaca, J. X., & Chavira, D. (1997). Use of the MMPI-2 with Chicanos: Strategies for counselors. *Journal of Multicultural Counseling and Development, 25,* 107–120.

Vélasquez, R. J., Johnson, R., & Brown-Cheatham, M. (1993). Teaching counselors to use the *DSM-III-R* with ethnic minority clients: A paradigm. *Counselor Education and Supervision, 32,* 323–331.

Ventura, S. J., Mathews, T. J., & Curtin, S. C. (1998). Declines in teenage birth rates, 1991–97: National and state patterns. *National Vital Statistics Reports, 47,* no. 12. Hyattville, MD: National Center for Health Statistics.

Yin, Z., Zapata, J. T., & Katims, D. S. (1995). Risk factors for substance use among Mexican American school-age youth. *Hispanic Journal of Behavioral Sciences, 17,* 61–76.

12

Understanding the Social and Personal Needs of the Early School-Aged Child

Nancy J. Evangelista

Six-year-old Samuel is causing problems at school and at home. After attending a child-centered experiential kindergarten at his day-care center, he entered first grade full of energy, optimism, and self-confidence. But, as the months have passed, he has become disruptive and defiant. He fiddles with toys in his desk during instructional periods, shouts out his answers, rarely finishes assigned work, and his aggressive play has led to exclusion from the other boys. His teacher reports that Samuel is making poor progress in reading, and that he cares little about developing acceptable written products. Since his parent's separation six months ago, Samuel alternates between clinging to his mother and shouting at her in fits of temper. He cries both when he leaves for and returns home from weekend visits with his father. His mother seems frazzled with the demands of working, shuttling Samuel and his four-year-old sister to day care, and maintaining some semblance of household function as a single mother.

A brief discussion of Samuel's case with the adults who know him readily provides a variety of hypotheses that could guide an assessment of his social and personal functioning "He seems just like the boy I had last year with attention deficit disorder" claims his teacher. His day-care teacher dismisses any thought of problems, explaining, "Oh, boys are always behind in development—he just needs to mature." Meanwhile, Samuel's mother maintains that, "He's learned to act like that because of all the attention his father gives to him when he visits on weekends—he's spoiled and always wants to be the center of attention."

Samuel's case illustrates but a few of the perspectives for viewing social and personal behavior in young children that are likely to be espoused by the people who know and care about Samuel. This team of parents and professionals each offers a different lens through which Samuel's problem behaviors can be viewed, and each explanation for his behaviors can contribute to the methods and measures of assessment used and to the development of interventions. However, an appreciation of the unique aspects of emotional and social development and behavioral expression in the young school-age child is needed to set appropriate expectations for behavior, inform assessment questions, and, thus, to design the most appropriate intervention.

Developmental Considerations for Young School-Aged Children

Research on cognitive, social, and moral development has brought an increasing recognition that the interpersonal and emotional functioning of children as they enter school differs significantly from their older peers. Thus, advocates and policymakers advise that programs and services for young school-aged children be designed with their specific developmental needs and characteristics in mind.

Developmentally Appropriate Practice

The National Association for the Education of Young Children has been a leader in incorporating research on developmental needs of young children into guidelines for early childhood education. Their policy statement on *developmentally appropriate practices* (NAEYC, 1997) for educating children from birth through age eight emphasizes the interrelationship of the physical, social, emotional, and cognitive domains of development, the sequential building of skills and knowledge, and the influences of multiple social and cultural contexts on young children's learning. A heavy emphasis on social and personal skills is reflected in program guidelines that direct teachers and caregivers to: (a) recognize variations in development among children, (b) provide opportunities for active learning by allowing children to choose and plan their own activities, and (c) build social relationships between children through small group activities allowing negotiation and social problem solving. The guidelines specifically discourage teaching methods that are predominantly whole group and teacher-led, that emphasize paper-and-pencil activities at the expense of learning through active engagement with play and exploratory materials, and that create artificial divisions between the physical, emotional, social, linguistic, and cognitive aspects of the curriculum. Use of such methods is predicted to surface in complaints that young children are inattentive, unmotivated, or immature.

The NAEYC standards for developmentally appropriate practice have influenced educational policy for young children. For example, the New York State Education Department (1997) has published indicators of quality early elementary experiences, which draw heavily from developmentally appropriate practice guidelines. Research using low-income kindergarteners (Burts et al., 1993) and preschool and kindergarten children from low- and middle-income homes (Stipek, Feiler, Daniels, & Milburn, 1995) has been consistent in finding that developmentally-based methods were responsible for higher levels of self-esteem, while didactic teaching methods produced greater gains on academic measures.

Key Social and Personal Competencies

The research literature validates the importance of effective social and personal management skills as markers for success in the early grades (Meisels, 1998; Parker, Boak, Griffin, Ripple, & Peay, 1999). A detailed investigation of prerequisite skills valued by kindergarten teachers can be found in the work of Foulks and Morrow (1989). The critical survival skills identified by the teachers in their study clustered into three factors: (a) work habits, such as listening to directions and following classroom rules; (b) self-control, such as complying with teacher demands and making needs known in an appropriate manner; (c) absence of behaviors challenging teacher authority, such as verbal or physical aggression, tantrums, or disrupting the activities of others. It is interesting to note that Foulks and Morrow have described these skills as "academic survival skills," rather than "behavioral survival skills."

Developmental scales are often used to set goals and monitor progress toward desired competencies in young children, and social and personal skills are well represented on such scales. One example of a sequenced hierarchy of skills useful for gauging progress in young children is the Battelle Developmental Inventory (Newborg, Stock, Wnek, Guidibaldi, & Svinicki, 1988), a criterion-referenced scale extending from birth to age eight. The Personal–Social Domain is divided into six subdomains: Adult Interaction, Expression of Feelings/Affect, Self-Concept, Peer Interaction, Coping, and Social Role. Many of the target items for children from 5–8 years across these subdomains are consistent with the survival skills identified by Foulks and Morrow (1989).

The creation of a comprehensive system for measuring the development of children with disabilities from birth through age eight has been the goal of the research team at the Early Childhood Research Institute on Measuring Growth and Development (McConnell et al., 1998). They distilled literature on developmental milestones and curricula from a multitude of published sources, resulting in 17 key outcomes for children in the early elementary school years (ages five through eight). Of these 17 outcomes, two are categorized as social and emotional skills ("Child demonstrates social skills necessary to develop and maintain stable friendships" and "Child demonstrates ability to manage behavior in socially acceptable ways"). Additional outcomes from the domains of communication ("Child can use language to convey communicative and social intent [e.g., feelings, information, etc.]") and adaptive skills ("Child can state personal information and follow basic societal rules") are also key skills relevant to successful social and personal functioning.

A Model for the Development of Social and Personal Competencies

The expression of competence in the social and personal realm through interpersonally effective behavior is the result of many streams of influence impacting on the developing child. It is useful to build a conceptual model as a framework for unifying variables salient to the development of social and personal skills in young children

(Eisenberg, Fabes, & Guthrie, 1997). Although the model presented in Figure 12.1 has not been empirically tested, it incorporates major bodies of research on the development of emotional thinking, positive expression, and socially adept interactions.

At the core of interpersonal competence is a sequence of *developmental processes* that proceed to move children to more mature ways of thinking, through sequential increases in acquisition of knowledge, understanding of self, social cognition, moral reasoning, and coping behaviors. These developmental processes are drawn from theories of cognition and learning, and are conceived of as universal forces driving typical development (Gallagher & Reid, 1981). The *individual characteristics* of each child, such as temperament, intellectual capacity, language and communication skills, and impaired or intact information-processing systems, have innate biological and genetic roots and dictate the unfolding of developmental processes and resulting successes in acquiring knowledge and skills. The *socialization context*, comprised of environmental factors, serves either to enhance or detract from learning adaptive social skills. While individual characteristics are rooted in biological capacities, the socialization context shapes these characteristics as the child develops, and, to some extent, the child's characteristics may also impact on the socialization agents, such as parents and peers. Both forces influence the rate of growth and the mastery of each stage within the sequence of developmental processes. The resulting *social and personal competencies* are skills essential to successful functioning at home, in school, with friends, and in the community. It is these effective interpersonal skills, or alternatively, negative behaviors that denote failure to develop positive adaptive skills, that are often the focus of social and personal assessment. However, because child characteristics and the socialization context exert powerful influences on behavior, assessment of these factors is integral in an ecological model of adaptive and maladaptive behaviors. Interventions can then be

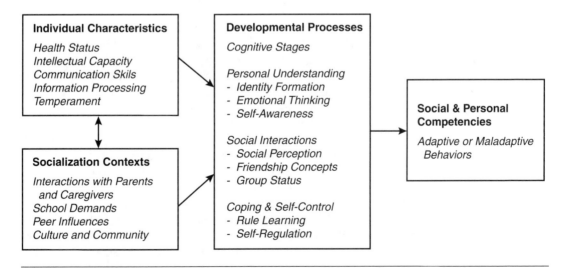

FIGURE 12.1. *A Model of Multiple Influences on Development of Social and Personal Competencies*

targeted at changing child competencies or changing aspects of the socialization context.

Individual Characteristics

At the heart of any discussion of competencies must be recognition of the unique characteristics of each individual child. Given the depth and breadth of this literature, this discussion will use broad strokes to review social and emotional sequelae of developmental problems and temperamental patterns commonly seen in young children.

Developmental Delays and Disorders.   Within the field of early childhood services for infants, toddlers, and preschoolers, the term *developmental delay* is used as a broad category for providing intervention services for children whose functioning within any of five developmental domains (cognition, communication, physical development, psychosocial development, and adaptive or self-care) lags behind chronological age norms. The passage of Public Law 99–457 in 1986 established this noncategorical definition in lieu of identification of specific disabilities for infants and toddlers, and the 1991 amendments to the federal special education law (Pub. L. 102-119) allowed states to use a noncategorical eligibility for preschoolers. The most recent reauthorization of the law (Individuals with Disabilities Education Act of 1997) now extends the option to use this definition for children from ages three through nine. The designation of developmental delay is often appropriate to describe young children who have a wide variety of problems affecting their development, ranging from transient delays due to health factors (such as complications of premature birth), to children who may eventually be identified with mental retardation or learning disabilities, to children whose primary problems are rooted in social and emotional causes.

As suggested in Chapter 8, social and communication skills are intertwined in their impact on the growing child's functioning. The ability to communicate ideas, information, and feelings (the pragmatic function of speech) lies at the heart of effective social relationships. Therefore, developmental delays in basic communication skills during early childhood are likely to manifest in problems with social skills and with handling stress and coping. The link between language competencies and behavior problems was underlined by Campbell (1995), who cites findings of poorer vocabulary and general language functioning in children with challenging behaviors who were identified by parents and teachers. Assessment and intervention for social and personal skills are especially important for children who have communication delays and disorders, or those who have communication disorders as part of a larger syndrome or disability (e.g., autism, motor impairment affecting speech).

The level of cognitive functioning is a profound individual difference affecting all areas of development. The presence of an intellectual impairment affects development of social and personal skills in several important ways. First, the child takes longer to master each stage of development, so that social and self-help skills are likely to be reflective of a younger child. Second, children with overall cognitive retardation do not learn as effectively through observation and incidental learning, which are critical learning routes for the subtleties of many social and interactive skills (Wood & Lazzari, 1997). Finally, children with mental retardation have higher levels of anxiety, depression, withdrawal, and aggression (Hodapp & Dykens, 1996), which detract from the ability to function effectively in the personal and social domains.

Early intervention services for young children have historically been designed to serve children with health problems, such as prematurity, that pose risks for subsequent developmental problems. Although the overall outcomes for children born at low birth weight (e.g., survival of the neonatal period, avoidance of major handicap) have improved, the impact of prematurity on neurodevelopmental functions may be manifested in more subtle problems, such as deficits in fine-motor skills, sensory processing, and emotional regulation (Goldson, 1996). Research conducted in early intervention programs for premature infants (Brooks-Gunn et al., 1994) has shown that children who participated in intervention services, such as direct therapies, supportive home visits, and play groups, had better behavioral functioning at kindergarten age than children who did not participate in intervention programming.

Subtle neurodevelopmental disorders may manifest as deficits in information processing. Problems with components of the information-processing system, such as perception, memory, attention, and inhibition, affect all areas of learning, including the social and emotional realm. A more thorough discussion of how disorders in components of the information-processing system translate into compromised social and personal functioning can be found in Waterman's Chapter 8 of this volume. Expanded coverage of neurodevelopmental consideration is provided by Lewandowski and Barlow in Chapter 6.

Temperament.   Temperament has been described as the "core" of personality and a stable pattern for organization of behavior (Teglasi, 1997). In their research review, Rothbart and Jones (1998) describe temperament as an inborn set of brain systems regulating emotional intensity, reactivity, and attentional focus. Their temperament scales and resulting factor-analytic work have yielded five distinct dimensions of temperament exhibited by school-age children: *fearfulness, irritability/frustration, approach/positive affect, attentional persistence, and activity level.* Temperamental characteristics are evident early in life, and longitudinal research has demonstrated the stability of behavioral patterns, such as negative emotional responses and activity level, throughout childhood and into adolescence (Shaffer, 1994).

As a building block for personality, temperamental style affects virtually all aspects of social and emotional functioning, such as the formation of parent–child relationships, mastery of self-regulation and self-control, and the development of friendships (Rothbart & Jones, 1998; Teglasi, 1997). Despite the robustness of temperament as an individual characteristic, interactions with parents and socializing experiences serve to moderate the extremity of temperamental characteristics. The concept of a "goodness of fit" was coined by Thomas and Chess (1977; as cited in Rothbart & Jones, 1998) to describe the degree to which parental responses are effective in moderating the child's temperament. However, in parent–child pairings with a poor fit, or when more extreme manifestations of temperament overshadow sensitive and responsive parenting, a difficult temperament may be the precursor to mental health disorders in childhood (Teglasi, 1997).

Socialization Contexts for Social and Personal Coping

The socialization of the growing child begins even before birth, as the family prepares for the arrival of a new member. Parental expectations, parent–child interactions, sibling relations, and extended family are all part of the home environment exerting influence on the child's development. School is the other primary socialization agent that influences the child through direct interaction. Cultural and community factors are well addressed in other sections of this book (e.g., see Chapters 11 and 17). Taken together, the ecological context offers a rich variety of factors that, woven together with individual characteristics, produces the fabric of each child's personality.

Family Influences.   It is difficult to conceive of child development in the absence of parental influence. As Greenspan observes: "It is in the context of relationships with important caregivers that babies and toddlers develop—and demonstrate—their cognitive, motor, and language skills, as well as intentionality and motivations" (1996, p. 232). Advocates for ecological assessment, therefore, promote assessment of the home environment, including parent–child relations, as an essential part of understanding and intervening, not only with infants and preschool children (Mott, 1997), but also with young school-age children (Pianta, Smith, & Reeve, 1991). Although other family factors, such as poverty, divorce and marital conflict, and child care, also exhibit pervasive influences on development, the literature reviewed here has been narrowed to a discussion of parental relationships and parenting styles.

The *attachment relationship* that an infant forms with a parent or primary caregiver is the foundation for subsequent learning about childhood relationships, including those with siblings, peers, teachers, and, to a lesser extent, adult relationships with lovers and life partners (Erwin, 1993). The quality of the attachment relationship impacts directly on early adaptation, and, as Lyons-Ruth, Zeanah, and Benoit (1996) note, serious disturbances in social relationships are likely outcomes if the infant is not cared for by stable, emotionally available caregivers. Research reveals four major patterns of infant attachments: (a) *secure*, seen in open parent–child communication, positive affect, and effective parental soothing; (b) *avoidant*, characterized by restricted communication and affect, few signals of distress, and the child's displacement of attention and anger away from the parent; (c) *ambivalent*, evidenced by heightened child distress, anger, combined with seeking contact with the parent, and failure of parental efforts to soothe the child; and (d) *disorganized*, in which the child may appear apprehensive, helpless, or disoriented, and vacillate between approach and avoidance of the parent (Lyons-Ruth et al., 1996).

Youngblade and Belsky (1995) hypothesize that attachment relationships are likely to impact peer relationships, especially relations with close friends. Their longitudinal research revealed that children who had secure attachment relationships with their parents at one year of age were found, at three years, to be more obedient, independent, and emotionally expressive than children with insecure attachments. At age five, these secure children had more positive peer interactions, such as shared fantasy play, sustained focus, and pleasurable affect, than children with anxious early attachments. The high level of congruence between mother–child and father–child relationships led the researchers to speculate that "stable environments breed stable relationships, and these stable relationships set the stage for later intimate relationships—via internalizations of expectations and skills—that are then generalized to other relationships" (Youngblade & Belsky, 1997, p. 52).

The longitudinal work of Lyons-Ruth, Easterbrooks, and Cibelli (1997) provides evidence of attachment patterns producing problematic functioning at school. Behavior ratings of children at 7 years of age, collected from mothers and teachers, all revealed that higher levels of internalizing behaviors (such as withdrawal, sadness, or worries) resulted from avoidant attachments recorded at 18 months. Externalizing behaviors (such as aggression, temper tantrums, or destructive actions) at age seven were highest among those toddlers who had displayed disorganized attachments, as opposed to stable patterns of attachment (even stable negative patterns such as avoidance). However, maternal depressive symptoms were a more potent predictor of both internalizing and externalizing problems exhibited at home and school.

In addition to attachment relationships, *parental styles* of discipline and nurturance have been another focus of research on family functioning. Shaffer (1994) provides a cogent review of Baumrind's pivotal work (1967, 1971; cited in Shaffer, 1994) on three distinctive parenting styles: (a) *authoritarian*, or controlling and detached parenting; (b) *authoritative*, or flexible, responsive, and nurturing parenting; and (c) *permissive*, characterized by warm but indulgent parenting with few rules and controls. Baumrind's own longitudinal work found that preschool children whose parents used an authoritative approach had the strongest cognitive competencies (creative thinking and achievement motivation), sociability, and group leadership skills in elementary school. Children of permissive parents were the least skilled in both cognitive and social domains, while children of authoritarian parents held a middle ground (Baumrind, 1977; cited in Shaffer, 1994).

Numerous other researchers have validated and expanded Baumrind's work with children from different cultures and ages. For example, the impact of parenting style on school readiness is seen in a recent study of Head Start children of Spanish-speaking immigrant mothers (Parker et al., 1999). Parker et al. (1999) found that parental strictness resulted in negative preschool behaviors, such as hostility. Children whose mothers interacted with them using warm, reciprocal interactions, coupled with direct and positive involvement with play materials, had higher ratings on measures of school readiness and social competence at the end of the Head Start year.

While research on parenting style has shown compelling effects on the child's behavior (Erwin, 1993; Shaffer, 1994), a more complex bidirectional picture has emerged from subsequent research, with child responses to parents serving to reinforce parental approaches. One of the first challenges for parents is the establishment of firm rules for the toddler who struggles with developmental issues of control and autonomy. Forehand and Wierson (1993) note that coercive and manipulative behavior by the child is likely to result when parents give authoritative directives, but eventually withdraw their requests in response to child defiance. The withdrawal of requests is reinforcing to the parents, as the child's defiance ends (temporarily) once parents have acquiesced to the child's demands. Campbell's (1995) extensive review of research on preschool behavior problems also documents the interactive cycle of parenting style and children's resulting problem behaviors, yet she cites substantial evidence that harsh and controlling patterns of parental behavior often precede negative child behaviors.

The influences of attachment, parenting style, and temperament on social competencies and maladaptive behaviors are integrated in the conceptual and empirical work of Rubin, Booth, Rose-Krasnor, and Mills (1995). These researchers identified differences in maternal–child play interactions for 4-year-olds who had insecure attachments at 20 months of age. The mothers attempted to redirect their children's activities to fit their own interests or desires, rather than following their children's play themes. In play interactions with age-peers, the insecurely attached children were observed to use dramatically higher levels of aggressive strategies.

Such findings led Rubin et al. (1995) to hypothesize about two distinct developmental pathways to social incompetence. The first path is postulated to begin with an irritable or difficult temperament, which may result in an insecure attachment. In reaction to the frustrations of dealing with difficult temperament, parents engage in patterns of insensitive and demanding parenting. Steeped in these stressful interactions, the child develops aggressive interactions with adults and peers, leading to eventual peer rejection. The second path begins with a fearful or anxious temperament and a resulting insecure attachment. This fearful temperament provokes parental patterns of overcontrol and insensitivity, and results in inhibited peer interactions, failure to utilize social skills, and, again, peer rejection.

This brief foray into the literature on family context reveals consistent findings that children's social and personal functioning builds on early attachment relationships and ensuing parenting styles, both of which are stable by the time children enter school. Preli's Chapter 10 in this volume provides a more advanced treatment of family dynamics—their complexity, their cyclicity, and their recalcitrance.

School Context.   As children enter formal schooling, the focus of education shifts from building prerequisite cognitive, social, and self-help skills to a stronger emphasis on achievement and independent functioning. The school context encompasses a myriad of factors ranging from broad macrosystem influences, such as pedagogy or current funding levels, to teacher training and experience, to the cultural background of the community. The discussion here will be limited to a narrower scope, focusing on factors influencing adjustment to school, and development of self-concept as a learner.

School adjustment has been defined as "the degree to which children become interested, engaged, comfortable, and successful in the school environment" (Ladd & Kochenderfer, 1996, p. 324). As previously discussed, kindergarten adjustment entails successfully meeting teachers' expectations for social and personal maturity, demonstrated through independent self-help skills, self-control and coping, and following teacher directives (Foulkes & Morrow, 1989).

Pianta, Smith, and Reeve (1991) explored the impact of parenting style on adjustment to school by designing a brief observation of parent–child interactions for use during the kindergarten screening process. Positive interaction ratings were related to positive teacher ratings of classroom adjustment in the fall of kindergarten, and added a small but significant improvement over child factors (e.g., cognitive and fine-motor abilities) in predicting first-grade adjustment.

The ability to form adaptive peer relations is another important ingredient in the adjustment process. Dunn (1993) reported that the presence of a familiar peer led to better adjustment among four-year-olds transitioning to new day-care settings. The security provided by familiarity appears to play a role in adjustment to school as well. Ladd and Kochenderfer's (1996) review of the literature linking friendship to school adjustment also found that initial adjustment to kindergarten was positively related to the presence of familiar peers, but that the reciprocal friendships were more important in continued social functioning.

Both internal and external changes combine to influence children's feelings of *self-worth and competence* and their beliefs about academic and social successes. Eccles (1999) noted three developmental forces that influence self-concept for young children: (a) cognitive changes related to reasoning skills, perspective-taking, and self-awareness; (b) a broadening of the child's world to include peers, teachers, and organized social groups (e.g., sports, scouts, etc.); and (c) the social comparison and competition that is inherent in classrooms and peer groups.

Because sophisticated social comparisons have yet to be mastered prior to kindergarten, children beginning school typically approach the prospect of this new step with excitement and confidence. Stipek and Ryan (1997) found that both low- and middle-income children approached kindergarten with a positive attitude, measured by high levels of self-confidence and expectations for success, but the low-income group scored significantly lower on cognitive measures. By the spring of the first-grade year, the advantaged children were achieving at higher levels, but also had higher levels of measured anxiety about performance. In contrast, the disadvantaged children were lower achievers, but still motivated and self-confident, leading the authors to speculate that, perhaps, their cognitive immaturity prevented them from making worrisome social comparisons (Stipek & Ryan, 1997). This work is especially interesting in light of the earlier work of Stipek et al. (1995), which found that low-income children in teacher-directed academically-oriented programs made greater academic gains, but these came at the loss of motivation that more child-centered developmentally-oriented programs preserved. More longitudinal research is needed to explore the impact of program emphasis on eventual academic and emotional outcomes for these vulnerable children.

A fascinating cross-cultural study of children's self-appraisals of academic competence provides information on changes across a greater age span. Little and Lopez (1997) found that second graders across the six different nations they studied universally endorsed both internal (effort, ability) and external causes (luck, teachers) as having equal effects on achievement. With advancing grade level, children increasingly ranked effort as the primary reason for success, followed by ability, and then teachers, while luck declined the most as a causal factor. Cultural factors also came into play, as German children, who are educated in an ability-tracked educational system, gave the highest endorsements for effort and ability. The Tokyo sample's low endorsement of teacher effects was viewed by the authors as reflecting the Japanese cultural emphasis on self-reliance (Little & Lopez, 1997).

Thus, socialization forces, such as parenting style, attachment relationships, and the cultural factors inherent in the school context, interact with individual child characteristics, such as cognitive level and temperament, in shaping the child's competence and adjustment to new social situations. But, in order to appreciate the unique aspects of the young school-age child's social and personal development, it is important to look more carefully at the developmental processes driving the child's understanding of feelings and relationships.

Developmental Processes Underlying Personal and Social Competencies

The early elementary school period is often viewed as a plateau of development, bridging the thinking of the preschooler to the more mature thinking of the preadolescent (Eccles, 1999). Thus, the developmental theories to be described here recognize shifts in thinking and reasoning at age five or six, with the next shifts generally occurring at age ten or twelve.

Cognitive Development.   In his analysis of Piagetian theory, Bjorklund (1989) emphasizes Piaget's assumptions about the very nature of learning, assumptions that are the foundation of many theories to follow. Among the most important foundational principles are: (a) the concept of stages of development, which are qualitatively different from those that precede and follow; (b) the constructivist perspective, which recognizes the child must act on the world in order to construct an understanding of it; and (c) the notion that understanding is the result of the child's adapting ideas for organizing the world to accommodate new perceptions.

Within the early elementary period, children's thinking falls between two stages. The earliest stage, involving understanding of perceptual inputs and appreciation of causes and effects (the *sensorimotor* stage), occurs during infancy. The *preoperational* or *representational* stage begins at approximately age two and extends through age six, encompassing the incredible growth of language, the ability to form mental images, and the use of symbols to represent thoughts that occur in the preschool years. The next stage, *concrete operations*, is characterized by logical thinking, such as understanding relationships among objects and the ability to predict actions and develop rules. Piaget (as cited in Bjorklund, 1989) targeted these skills as beginning at age seven and undergoing consolidation and expansion until age eleven. Thinking then moves to Piaget's last stage, *formal operations*, characterized by the ability to form abstractions and think about thinking itself. Thus, children in the early elementary grades are moving from the bounds of preoperational thinking into the logical thinking and prediction of the concrete operations stage.

Classroom teaching practices, such as those promoted by Gallagher and Reid (1981), are often targeted at science and mathematics curricula, and are designed to enhance children's construction of new levels of understanding through direct interactions with materials and with each other. Yet, the underlying changes in conceptual understanding also drive the construction of knowledge needed for social, emotional, and moral reasoning. The NAEYC's (1997) guidelines for developmentally appropriate practice thus stress how the young child's social contexts must be designed to promote development of social and emotional thinking.

Personal Understanding.   Erickson's theory of psychosocial development has provided a conceptual framework for considering the impact of societal influences on the emergence of self-concept and *identity formation*. Drawing from Piaget's stage theory for cognitive development, Erickson (1963) proposed that increasing cognitive capacity, mediated by social pressures, produces a series of challenges to the sense of identity. Mastery of each of the developmental stages, or "crises," as Erickson termed them, results in positive adaptation and sense of self. The toddler (ages 1–3) is learning consequences for behavior and struggling to assert herself; the crisis to be mastered is *autonomy versus shame and doubt* and the positive outcome is willpower. Once this crisis is mastered, the preschooler moves to trying out different adult roles and activities and feeling success at these attempts. The crisis of *initiative versus guilt* spans ages 3–6, with positive adaptation resulting in a sense of purpose. The entry into school, with the child's new role as a learner, is a pivotal societal force moving children to the next stage, the 7- to 11-year-old's crisis of *industry versus inferiority*. A sense of competence, the desired outcome for this stage, is developed based on feedback in meeting societal expectations.

Erickson's theory uses broad strokes to paint this impression of the child's developing identity. However, the developmental literature focuses on more specific aspects of feelings, self-awareness, and social comparisons, which offer depth and color to the child's self-portrait.

The building of *emotional thinking* is based on the recognition of emotions in others, recognition of emotions as they relate to self, and learning socially acceptable means of expressing emotion. Flavell, Miller, and Miller (1993) eloquently describe the impact of emotions on human behavior.

> It is difficult to imagine a socially competent human who did not possess an understanding of emotions and their relation to cognition and behavior. Children must acquire this knowledge to do effective 'social work,' such as identifying the feelings of other people toward them, anticipating whether their parents will be angry or pleased about their behavior, and hiding their socially inappropriate feelings (p. 189).

Research on infant development has documented the capacity of infants prior to their first birthday to respond to the emotions conveyed through the facial expressions of others (see Harris, 1989). Indeed, empathy, the emotion most closely linked to eventual moral behavior, has been readily identified in children at one year of age (Harris, 1989). The advent of symbolic language enables the child to label basic emotions in him- or herself (e.g., happy, sad, scared) by 24 months of age. Yet, observations of behavior suggest that children at this age are experiencing more complex emotions, such as shame, anxiety, and pride in response to parental feedback (Edwards, 1999).

As Harris (1989) explains, the most complex emotions, such as guilt, pride, and jealousy, involve appreciation for the sense of personal responsibility at the root of such feelings. Research findings compiled by Flavell et al. (1993) place emergence of these emotional states during the early school years. The child at age six assigns guilt according to outcome, so that an action that ends badly produces guilt, regardless of level of responsibility. In contrast, children at age 10 assign a heavier burden of guilt when intention to do wrong precedes the action.

In his writings on the origins of psychopathology, Greenspan (1981, 1996) speculates that young children must receive messages from caregivers that promote personal responsibility in order to learn to differentiate complex emotions (such as "You are frustrated because you can't make the toy work" and "You may not hit your sister when you are frustrated with toys"). Children who do not link emotions to personal responsibility may then be unable to differentiate emotions (such as anger and frustration) and may demonstrate constrictions in affect (the child responds with anger to many situations).

Along with the ability to identify emotions in self and others, children also learn societal rules for hiding emotions. Harris (1989) presents a fascinating discussion of his line of research on facial display rules for emotions. In a series of experiments involving stories in which characters might hide their emotions (e.g., not showing disappointment at receiving an undesirable gift), Harris and his colleagues found that, by age six, children could not only understand that the emotion conveyed might differ from the real feeling, but also appreciate that the surface behavior might actually mislead others. Harris's cross-cultural research revealed that, although Japanese children are specifically taught to keep a bland outward facial expression and to hide inner feelings at a younger age (three years), across cultures such control over emotional displays is in place by age six.

This research on the emotional roots for self-control meshes well with Piaget's placement of the beginning stage of operational thinking at age seven, as the formation of rules for appropriate emotional responses and expression are dependent on cognitive processes of rule formation and relationships among feelings and actions. In moving from simple to complex emotions, the young child has learned to take into account the feelings and expectations of others.

Edwards (1999) presents a series of pivotal questions about social and personal thinking from the young child's point of view. *Self-awareness* for the preschool child involves answers to questions such as, "What am I? What are you? What am I not? What will I become?" In contrast, the more sophisticated early elementary schooler wonders "What defines my identity? What can change? What stays the same?" A similar process of learning the definitions of family and friends is seen in the preschooler's growing awareness of kinship and social relations through questions such as, "Are you my relative? What are you called? Whom can I call friend?" The shift in cognitive understanding toward understanding rules and relationships among objects is reflected as the 6- to 8-year-old probes, "What is the connection between relatives? What is it that friends do for each other?" (Edwards, 1999). Comparison between self and others is the mechanism by which children begin to answer these questions.

The earliest sense of self-awareness is rooted in feedback from others. Flavell et al. (1993) describe how an infant comes to realize a sense of separateness from others through the sensorimotor feedback gained when exploring physical characteristics of self and others (e.g., touching faces and bodies). This rudimentary sense of self precedes self-recognition in mirrors or photos, which emerges at 18–24 months (Edwards, 1999). The toddler moves from integration of sensorimotor inputs defining self to learning verbal labels for name, gender, family status, and age that differentiate self from others.

Once constancy of understanding basic traits is established, the preschooler quickly learns to integrate evaluative messages given by others ("I am good" or "I am strong") into a stable sense of self. As Flavell et al. (1993) note, even three-year-olds display a stable pattern of self-descriptions of behavior (e.g., "I get mad a lot") that correlates with observed behavior and shows stability over periods of one month.

When the child moves from representational thinking into the categorical thinking of the concrete operations period, comparisons with others expand the construct of self. Social comparisons are evident by age four (Edwards, 1999) and are likely to take the form of comparison of concrete, readily observed characteristics (e.g., "I have curly hair and you don't"). Gradually, more psychologically-based characteristics are compared (e.g., "I'm smart"), yet the preschool child does not yet self-evaluate competencies in comparison to others, and generally takes on an expansive, optimistic view of his or her capabilities (Flavell et al., 1993). By elementary school, children have learned to incorporate feedback about their actual performance into their concept of self (e.g., "I'm not smart because I can't read like other kids in my class"). Thus, the process of evaluating personal characteristics in comparison to others builds on self-awareness and leads to the more complicated personal emotion of self-esteem, or level of satisfaction with self (Edwards, 1999).

Social Interactions.   The young child's skills in developing friendships and interacting within a group setting ranked high among the competencies expected for school success. Rather than solely an outcome of social competence, experience with friendships is, instead, viewed as a necessary precursor to further skill development.

In order for a child to interact successfully with peers and adults, the child must be able to think about others, including taking the perspective of another (*social perception*). Once again, consideration of Piagetian theory is helpful in reminding us of the capacity for social cognition at various stages in the young child's development. Children in the preoperational stage limit their focus to one aspect of a problem, and their tendency toward egocentricity limits that focus to their own perceptions. What the child sees and knows is presumed to be what others see and know.

The preoperational child's egocentric view is the first stage in Selman's theory of social perception (Selman & Yeates, 1987). Children entering kindergarten are solidly at this level, which roughly parallels Erickson's time frame for initiative versus guilt (ages 3–6), and which Selman labels as Level 0. Problem solving is accomplished by children impulsively taking what they want or asking powerful others (e.g., adults) to do so on their behalf (Flavell et al., 1993). Children then move to Level 1 (ages 6–9) where they are able to realize that the other person has a different point of view. If they do not hold this view, it is presumed to be incorrect. Problem-solving strategies are unilateral and directed toward achieving compliance with personal desires or correcting the view of another (Selman & Yeates, 1987). For example, at Level 1 a child desiring a toy might inform the other child (e.g., "I need that toy now") or use threats to coerce the peer to comply ("Give me the toy or I'll tell the teacher you won't share"). The child's ability to choose strategies selectively to persuade others, or to think of how others perceive him or her, marks Level 2. At this level a child might resolve the dilemma of the desired toy by suggesting swapping after a time period, or giving an alternative toy in an effort to appear generous. Problem solving based on Level 2 social perception is not solidly in the repertoire of most elementary children until ages 8–10 (Erwin, 1993).

The concrete thinking of the preoperational stage provides firm guidelines for *friendship* and who is a friend. Doll (1996) describes the circular theory that defines friends for preschoolers up through the kindergarten years. "Their friends are the children they play with, and playing with someone makes them a friend" (p. 167). Early friendships are formed readily among children who are exposed to each other, so that availability as a playmate (Doll, 1996), or provision of attractive toys to be shared (Flavell et al., 1993), are characteristics young children value in their friends. Personal characteristics are not highly valued, and friendships are a function of immediate circumstances, so that preschool and kindergarten children may appear rather fickle, with "best friend" status changing quickly.

With the advent of more sophisticated thinking about relationships among concepts comes a new appreciation for relationships among people. Newcomb and Bagwell's (1996) meta-analysis of cross-sectional research on age differences in friendship provides robust support for significant changes in the meaning of the relationship as children enter the school-age period. The early elementary-age child can now appreciate personal characteristics of friends, such as physical traits and appealing behaviors, and understands the contractual nature of friendship (Erwin, 1993; Flavell et al., 1993), borne out in interactions such as reciprocal helping and in admiration displayed by friends (Doll, 1996).

Yet the stability and commitment of young school-age playmates to each other is still fragile and largely self-centered. Doll (1996) cites research findings that only one third of friendships between first graders last more than one month. She then points out that the friendship strategies utilized by children this age can be accounted for by Selman's social perspective; children may try to bargain for friendships by doing favors, or threaten to withdraw their friendship if conflicts arise, so that relationships still may not be long-lived.

Young friends appear to take into account characteristics they share with their peers as a basis for early relationships. Aboud and Mendelson's (1996) review of research on the developmental determinants of friendship reveals that, beginning in preschool, children prefer playmates of their own age, gender, and race, even when opportunities to play in mixed groups are available. Beyond physical characteristics, children also seek out children whose functioning level matches their own. In a study conducted by Dunn and Cutting (1999), preschool children were observed playing with friends. The four-year-olds who shared personality characteristics, such as temperamental style, communicative abilities, and level of emotional expression, were found to engage in more pretend play and more communicative exchanges. Quarreling was a common theme in the boisterous play of many of these children, with active children and their similarly active friends involved most often in conflicts.

By mid-elementary school, children are aware enough to evaluate cognitive and social skills more closely, and growing commitment to the relationship aspects of friendship may be strong enough to support differences between friends on some characteristics. For example, cross-race friendships are found to increase throughout the early elementary years, and friends also demonstrate greater tolerance for differences in attitudes and opinions (Aboud & Mendelson, 1996). As with preschoolers, conflict between friends in early elementary school (e.g., arguments, teasing) still occurs frequently (Doll, 1996), but by age eight children are more committed to their relationships and better able to develop cognitive strategies for resolving conflicts (Newcomb & Bagwell, 1996).

Friendships offer important opportunities for mutual development of social skills. Ladd and Kochenderfer (1996) believe that the shared fantasy play that occupies preschool children helps in understanding and managing emotions, and, thus, in developing positive coping responses to stress. Research conducted by Newcomb and Bagwell (1996) has demonstrated that, while children are initially attracted to friends with similar social skill levels, their friendships provide opportunities for both partners to continue developing skills, and, thus, become more similar in social skill levels.

The process of forming groups and making decisions about acceptance and rejection (i.e., *social or group status*) begins at a young age. Dunn (1993) found that four-year-old children in her observational studies gossip about other children and make plans to exclude peers from their play. Yet, she also found that these children were likely to quickly change their minds about the attractiveness of many peers who offer an enticing toy or treat.

Children who are aggressive and noncompliant suffer more firmly entrenched social rejection, a trend that begins in preschool and continues throughout childhood and into adulthood (Erwin, 1993). Although there are clear distinctions between intimate relationships, such as friendships, and social status in groups (Aboud & Mendelson, 1996; Doll, 1996; Newcomb & Bagwell, 1996), many of the same characteristics that lead to attraction between pairs of friends also result in high ranking of social status (Aboud & Mendelson, 1996). High among the social skills associated with popularity in second and third grade are conflict resolution skills, such as explaining reasons for disagreements or adopting the point of view of another. In contrast, unpopular children are likely to be described by peers as bossy, bothersome, or noncompliant with rules for games and classroom behavior (Erwin, 1993).

In her discussion of rejected peers, Doll (1996) reports research demonstrating that unpopular children are not able to generate and act on solutions for the conflict inherent in social interactions; moreover, they attribute hostile intent to ambiguous situations, whereas accepted children have more benign attributions. In addition, a subgroup of rejected children includes temperamentally fragile children who are wary and inhibited in social situations leading to peers' perceptions of them as remote or disinterested in activities. In either case, rejected children are unlikely to develop the close relationships that buoy children through conflict or to develop further the very social skills that are so valued by peers and adults (Doll, 1996).

Coping and Self-Control.   As children move into the world of negotiated friendships and the world of school rules, they are expected to comply with rules and requests, control emotions and behaviors, and respond adaptively to stress (Newborg et al., 1984). Successful coping involves drawing from a multifaceted set of social and personal skills to meet stressful or challenging situations in socially appropriate ways. Williamson (1996) defines successful coping:

> Coping is the integration and application of developmental skills in the context of everyday living. It is the process of making adaptations in order to meet personal needs and to respond to the demands of the environment. The goal of coping is to increase feelings of well-being in situations interpreted as threatening or challenging. That is, children cope with situations in order to feel good about themselves and their place in the world (pp. 193–194).

Coping begins with *learning basic social rules* and eventually expands to understanding the *moral reasoning* behind these rules. Learning of social rules can be readily explained through a behavior-analytic approach, where the child's responses are shaped through imitation and maintained through contingent reinforcers or punishers. Behavior-analytic theory has been integrated with developmental tasks in Forehand and Wierson's (1993) comprehensive model for the development of noncompliant and disruptive behaviors. Their model stresses the toddler's developmental stage of seeking autonomy, when the child needs consistent reinforcement for compliant behavior, and lack of reinforcement for coercive, noncompliant behavior. The patterns of reinforcement adopted by parents shape the preschool child's development of continued patterns of compliance, eventual internalization of rules governing behavior, and generalization to other social situations, (e.g., peer and teacher relationships at school).

Learning to follow rules, however, can be differentiated from the meaning of rules; the literature on moral development illuminates these distinctions. Kohlberg's (1981) theory for the development of moral reasoning begins with the young child who has reached Piaget's concrete operational thinking level (approximately ages 6–7). Kohlberg considers this first level of rule learning to demonstrate "immature moralities," as Stage 1 reasoning is governed by the morality of authority. Children follow rules to avoid being punished, and believe that whoever makes the rules must be morally correct. Gibbs, Potter, and Goldstein (1995) have renamed Kohlberg's Stage 1 as "Might Makes Right." Children at this stage are more concerned about physical than psychological consequences for actions, and believe that actions that go undetected, and, therefore, unpunished, are morally correct (Gibbs et al., 1995; Kohlberg, 1981). Stage 2 is also mastered during the latter part of the concrete operational level and is still considered part of immature morality by Kohlberg. By this stage children are able to understand the reciprocity of relationships (recall Selman's levels of social reasoning) and believe that the exchange of favors and equal treatment constitutes moral behavior. Gibbs et al. (1995) use the phrase "You Scratch My Back, I'll Scratch Yours" to capture the thinking of children at Stage 2 reasoning. The preoccupation of first and second graders with fairness, insisting on equality in playing games or sharing treats, is evidence of this level of moral reasoning. Stage 3 reasoning, in which moral thinking is based on shared values and deeper commitment to relationships, is typically beyond the grasp of middle childhood and emerges in adolescence (Kohlberg, 1981).

Although the understanding of rules is essential for eventual autonomous coping, a growing body of research is uncovering the pivotal role of *self-regulation* in being able to follow those rules. Eisenberg's work on the role of regulation in coping with stress (Eisenberg et al., 1997) has enlightened our perspectives on the development of self-control. Eisenberg et al. (1997) view self-regulation as the appropriate selection of possible coping responses in response to activation of emotional states. Although much of the literature has examined responses to stress, self-regulation also encompasses coping responses to positive emotions as well. Coping responses have been categorized as falling within three categories: (a) changing or shifting the behavioral reaction, (b) changing or shifting the emotional reaction, and (c) changing the nature of the problem or stressful situation.

The ability to use any of these three coping responses is related to the child's cognitive level. A pivotal study conducted by Vaughn, Kopp, and Krakow (1984) found that children were able to delay gratification for several minutes at 24 months of age, coinciding with cognitive shifts at this developmental level. Children with more advanced language skills showed longer tolerance of delays. Eisenberg et al. (1997) summarized research on the strategies that children at different age levels (beyond preschool age) use for self-control. Younger children are better at marshaling strategies for changing their behavior than strategies for changing the problem itself. Strategies typically used for regulation at age five to six might include distraction with a material object, or leaving the table when challenged by a task. Such strategies help children to focus on a different emotion or reduce situational stress and, thus, feel better. By age eight, however, children begin to use cognitive strategies, such as concentrating on thinking about something else or using self-talk that will provide a comforting message, to regulate their emotions. Because younger children are limited in their ability to shift attention away from stressful aspects of a situation, they are more likely to become overwhelmed in situations where physical means of coping are not available or appropriate (Eisenberg et al., 1997).

In addition to developmental factors, coping responses are also linked to temperamentally-determined variables in response patterns. Eisenberg et al. (1997) apply the temperament construct to coping skills as a theoretical link between research on individual differences and regulation of emotional responses. Their empirical data from various studies have demonstrated that children who are high on dimensions of fear, irritability, or frustration easily become anxious or overaroused and have difficulty shifting to a more positive emotion. Children who are high on dimensions of approach, positive affect, and attentional control are better able to regulate emotional responses and to shift to more positive, adaptive feelings.

The remaining strategy in Eisenberg et al.'s (1997) coping model deals with the ability to change the situation and is, therefore, dependent on problem-solving skills. Requesting assistance is an example of a situationally focused problem solving strategy that is in the repertoire of toddlers, and continues to be useful throughout life. A simple model accounting for the process of problem solving used by very young children is offered by Williamson (1996.) His model begins with determining the meaning of an event, developing an action plan, implementing the coping effort, and self-evaluating the effectiveness of the outcome. Programs for developing sophisticated coping skills, such as the EQUIP program for peer mediation developed by Gibbs et al. (1995), are based on similar problem-solving models.

Drawing from the research base on information-processing systems (see Chapter 8 for a more comprehensive discussion), Dodge's social information-processing model (1986) provides a more comprehensive analysis of the various cognitive subskills utilized at each step of the problem-solving process. Dodge's ongoing program of research on social problem solving has identified age- and temperament-related characteristics that affect responding. For example, when given the opportunity to listen to audiotapes about a child prior to making a judgment about the intent of the child's behavior, 6-year-olds listened to one-third fewer cues than 10-year olds prior to making a judgment. This characteristic of curtailing opportunities for gathering data before responding also was shared by aggressive older boys (Dodge, 1986). Similar trends were found for increases in the ability to generate a variety of responses to hypothetical social problems, as aggressive and socially unsuccessful children demonstrated fewer and less mature responses than competent age-peers.

In viewing the coping literature with an eye turned specifically to the school domain, recall that Eisenberg et al. (1997) found that regulation of emotion and behavior were the predominant strategies used by children from preschool through age eight in coping with stress. Skinner and Wellborn (1997) point out that many strategies for emotional or behavioral regulation are off-limits in the classroom, such as screaming to vent emotions or leaving the classroom if frustrated. Therefore, children who are stressed may cope through oppositional behaviors, such as avoiding or refusing work, or by failure to pay attention, which can reduce the emotional stress engendered by challenging (or perhaps unchallenging) academic tasks. Skinner and Wellborn (1997) note that empirical findings validate a broad menu of strategies for coping that children use for meeting the demands of school. Positive strategies include behavioral responses, such as seeking assistance or cooperating with others, emotional responses, such as seeking comfort and familiarity, and cognitive responses, such as seeking information or resolving to work independently. The menu of maladaptive responses is similarly expansive, and includes behaviors, such as escape, perseveration or aggression, emotional responses, such as self-pity or self-blame, or cognitive distortions, such as feelings of abandonment, obsessions, or devaluation of tasks.

Thus, the capacity for young children to regulate emotions and behaviors, and to generate and apply solutions in stressful situations, appears to be linked to cognitive and representational capacities and to temperamental characteristics that are a poor match for the demands of coping with stress. In practical terms, those who work with young children must be mindful that problem behaviors that arise in meeting stressors, especially extreme stressors such as family divorce, abuse, or violence, may exceed volitional control (Eisenberg et al., 1997) and may be better viewed as the young child's attempts to marshal emerging capacities to cope.

Conclusion

The research on developmental processes reviewed here provides an overview of the complex and interrelated factors involved in the gradual building of social and personal skills in young school-age children. Skill development as an interactional process has been highlighted, recognizing that, as the child matures, primary socialization agents (family, peers, school) help to construct the child's understanding, which then influences the child's competence in meeting the challenges of the next stage. A coping perspective helps to appreciate the contributions of developmental stages, temperament, and prior experiences to the child's utilization of adaptive and maladpative strategies for dealing with the challenges of social interactions and stressful situations.

Throughout this review, the relationships of children with their primary caregivers—their parents—have emerged as a salient predictor of development and a variable that tempers future relationships and capacity to cope with stress and adjust to change. As children move into the new levels of social and personal understanding that characterize the early school years, they build on their previous positive experiences in forming their identity as learners and their image as socially competent and attractive friends. Prior negative experiences that reinforce aggressive or noncomplaint behaviors, or fail to develop the child's understanding of complex emotional responses and social messages, set up an interactive cycle of peer rejection and limited opportunities to further develop the adaptive coping skills needed for facing the social and academic demands of the school environment. Our efforts to provide assistance must be broad enough to encompass systemic elements that create and perpetuate stress in children, and yet specific enough to recognize each child's developmental level, individual characteristics, learned patterns of behavior, and the availability of supportive relationships in their lives. These elements are intimately linked to each young child's capacities not just to cope, but to thrive in today's complex world.

References

Aboud, F. E., & Mendelson, M. J. (1996). Determinants of friendship selection and quality: Developmental perspectives. In W. M. Bukowski, A. F. Newcomb, & W. W. Hartup (Eds.), *The company they keep: Friendships in childhood and adolescence* (pp. 87–112). Melbourne, Australia: Cambridge University Press.

Bjorklund, D. F. (1989). *Children's thinking: Developmental function and individual differences.* Pacific Grove, CA: Brooks/Cole.

Bredekamp, S., & Copple, C. (Eds.). (1997). *Developmentally appropriate practice in early childhood programs* (Rev. ed.). Washington, DC: National Association for the Education of Young Children.

Brooks-Gunn, J., McCarton, C. M., Casey, P. H., McCormick, M. C., Bauer, C. R., Bernbaum, J. C., Tyson, J., Swanson, M., Bennett, F. C., Scott, D. T., Tonascia, J., & Meinert, C. L. (1994). Early intervention in low-birth-weight premature infants: Results through age 5 years from the Infant Health and Development Program. *Journal of the American Medical Association, 272,* 1257–1262.

Burts, D. C., Hart, C. H., Charlesworth, R., DeWolf, D. M., Ray, J., Manuel, K., & Fleege, P. O. (1993). Developmental appropriateness of kindergarten programs and academic outcomes in first grade. *Journal of Research in Childhood Education, 8,* 23–31.

Campbell, S. (1995) Behavior problems in preschool children: A review of recent research. *Journal of Child Psychology and Psychiatry, 56,* 113–149.

Dodge, K. A. (1986). A social information processing model of social competence in children. In M. Perlmutter (Vol. Ed.), *Cognitive perspectives on children's social and behavioral development: Vol. 18. The Minnesota symposia on child psychology* (pp. 77–126). Hillsdale, NJ: Erlbaum.

Doll, B. (1996). Children without friends: Implications for practice and policy. *School Psychology Review, 25,* 165–183.

Dunn, J. (1993). *Young children's close relationships: Beyond attachment.* Newbury Park, CA: Sage.

Dunn, J., & Cutting, A. L. (1999). Understanding others, and individual differences in friendship interactions in young children. *Social Development, 8,* 201–219.

Eccles, J. S. (1999). The development of children ages 6 to 14. *The Future of Children, 9*(2), 30–44.

Education of the Handicapped Act Amendments of 1986, Pub. L. No. 99–457, 20 U. S. C. §1400 et. seq.

Edwards, C. P. (1999). Development in the preschool years: The typical path. In E. V. Nuttall, I. Romero, & J. Kalesnik (Eds.), *Assessing and screening preschoolers: Psychological and educational dimensions* (2nd ed., pp. 9–24). Boston: Allyn and Bacon.

Eisenberg, N., Fabes, R. A., & Guthrie, I. K. (1997). Coping with stress: The roles of regulation and development. In S. A. Wolchik & I. N. Sandler (Eds.), *Handbook of children's coping: Linking theory and intervention* (pp. 41–70). New York: Plenum Press.

Erickson, E. (1963). *Childhood and society* (2nd ed.). New York: Norton.

Erwin, P. (1993). *Friendship and peer relations in children.* Chichester, England: Wiley.

Flavell, J. H., Miller, P. H., & Miller, S. A. (1993). *Cognitive development* (3rd ed.). Englewood Cliffs, NJ: Prentice-Hall.

Forehand, R., & Wierson, M. (1993). The role of developmental factors in planning behavioral interventions for children: Disruptive behavior as an example. *Behavior Therapy, 24,* 117–141.

Foulks, B., & Morrow, R. D. (1989). Academic survival skills for the young child at risk for school failure. *Journal of Educational Research, 82,* 158–165.

Gallagher, J. M., & Reid, D. K. (1981). *The learning theory of Piaget and Inhelder.* Austin, TX: PRO-ED.

Gibbs, J. C., Potter, G. B., & Goldstein, A P. (1995). *The EQUIP Program: Teaching youth to think and act responsibly through a peer-helping approach.* Champaign, IL: Research Press.

Goldson, E. (1996). The micropremie: Infants with birth weight less than 800 grams. *Infants and Young Children, 8,* 1–10.

Greenspan, S. I. (1981). *Psychopathology and adaptation in infancy and early childhood: Principles of clinical diagnosis and preventive intervention.* New York: International Universities Press.

Greenspan, S. I. (1996). Assessing the emotional and social functioning of infants and young children. In S. J. Meisels & E. Fenichel (Eds.), *New visions for the developmental assessment of infants and young children* (pp. 231–266). Washington, DC: Zero to Three National Center for Infants, Toddlers and Families.

Harris, P. L. (1989). *Children and emotion: The development of psychological understanding.* Oxford, England: Blackwell.

Hodapp, R. M., & Dykens, E. M. (1996). Mental retardation. In E. J. Mash & R. A. Barkley (Eds.), *Child psychopathology* (pp. 362–390). New York: Guilford Press.

Individuals with Disabilities Education Act Amendments of 1991, Pub. L. No. 102–119, 20 U. S. C. §1400 et. seq.

Individuals with Disabilities Education Act Amendments of 1997, Pub. L. No. 105–17, 20 U. S. C. §1400 et. seq.

Kohlberg, L. (1981). *Essays on moral development, Vol. 1: The philosophy of moral development.* San Francisco: Harper & Row.

Ladd, G. W., & Kochenderfer, B. J. (1996). Linkages between friendship and adjustment during early school transitions. In W. M. Bukowski, A. F. Newcomb, & W. W. Hartup (Eds.), *The company they keep: Friendships in childhood and adolescence* (pp. 322–345). Melbourne, Australia: Cambridge University Press.

Little, T. D., & Lopez, D. F. (1997). Regularities in the development of children's causality beliefs about school performance across six sociocultural contexts. *Developmental Psychology, 33,* 165–175.

Lyons-Ruth, K., Easterbrooks, M. A., & Cibelli, C. D. (1997). Infant attachment strategies, infant mental lag, and maternal depressive symptoms: Predictors of internalizing and externalizing problems at age 7. *Developmental Psychology, 33,* 681–692.

Lyons-Ruth, K., Zeanah, C. H., & Benoit, D. (1996). Disorder and risk for disorder during infancy and toddlerhood. In E. J. Mash & R. A. Barkley (Eds.), *Child psychopathology* (pp. 457–491). New York: Guilford Press.

McConnell, S., McEvoy, M., Carta, J., Greenwood, C. R., Kaminski, R., Good, R. H., & Shinn, M. (1998). *Selection of general growth outcomes for children between birth and age eight.* (Technical Report #2). Minneapolis, MN: The Early Childhood Research Institute on Measuring Growth & Development.

Meisels, S. (1998). *Assessing readiness* (CIERA Report #3–002). Ann Arbor, MI: Center for the Improvement of Early Reading Achievement.

Mott, D. (1997). The home environment. In S. K. Thurman, J. R. Cornwell, & S. R. Gottwald, (Eds.) *Contexts of early intervention* (pp. 139–164). Baltimore, MD: Brookes.

New York State Education Department. (1997). *Early elementary resource guide to integrated learning.* Albany, NY. Author.

Newborg, J., Stock, J. R., Wnek, L., Guidubaldi, J., & Svinicki, J. (1988). *Battelle Developmental Inventory (BDI).* Allen, TX: DLM Teaching Resources.

Newcomb, A. F., & Bagwell, C. L. (1996). The developmental significance of children's friendship relations. In W. M. Bukowski, A. F. Newcomb, & W. W. Hartup (Eds.), *The company they keep: Friendships in childhood and adolescence* (pp. 289–321). Melbourne, Australia: Cambridge University Press.

Parker, F. L., Boak, A. Y., Griffin, K. W., Ripple, C., & Peay, L. (1999). Parent–child relationship, home learning environment, and school readiness. *School Psychology Review, 28,* 413–425.

Pianta, R. C., Smith, N., & Reeve, R. E. (1991). Observing mother and child behavior in a problem-solving situation at school entry: Relations with classroom adjustment. *School Psychology Quarterly, 6,* 1–15.

Pianta, R. C., & Walsh, D. J. (1998). Applying the construct of resilience in schools: Cautions from a developmental systems perspective. *School Psychology Review, 27,* 407–418.

Rothbart, M. K., & Jones, L. B. (1998). Temperament, self-regulation, and education. *School Psychology Review, 27,* 479–491.

Rubin, K. H., Booth, C., Rose-Krasnor, L., & Mills, R. S. L. (1995). Social relationships and social skills: A conceptual and empirical analysis. In S. Shulman (Ed.), *Close relationships and socioemotional development* (pp. 63–94). Norwood, NJ: Ablex.

Selman, R. L., & Yeates, K. O. (1987). Childhood social regulation of intimacy and autonomy: A developmental–constructionist perspective. In W. M. Kurtines & J. L. Gewirtz (Eds.), *Moral development through social interaction* (pp. 43–101). New York: Wiley.

Shaffer, D. (1994). *Social and personality development* (3rd ed.). Pacific Grove, CA: Brooks/Cole.

Skinner, E. A., & Wellborn, J. G. (1997). Children's coping in the academic domain. In S. A. Wolchik & I. N. Sandler (Eds.), *Handbook of children's coping: Linking theory and intervention* (pp. 387–422). New York: Plenum Press.

Stipek, D. J., Feiler, R., Daniels, D., & Milburn, S. (1995). Effects of different instructional approaches on young children's achievement and motivation. *Child Development, 66,* 209–223.

Stipek, D. J., & Ryan, R. H. (1997). Economically disadvantaged preschoolers: Ready to learn but further to go. *Developmental Psychology, 33,* 711–723.

Teglasi, H. (1997). Temperament. In G. G. Bear, K. M. Minke, & A. Thomas (Eds.), *Children's needs II: Development, problems, and alternatives.* Washington, DC: National Association of School Psychologists.

Vaughn, B. E., Kopp, C. B., & Krakow, J. B. (1984). The emergence and consolidation of self-control from eighteen to thirty months of age: Normative trends and individual differences. *Child Development, 55,* 990–1004.

Williamson, G. G. (1996). Assessment of adaptive competence. In S. J. Meisels & E. Fenichel (Eds.), *New visions for the developmental assessment of infants and young children* (pp. 193–206). Washington, DC: Zero to Three National Center for Infants, Toddlers and Families.

Wood, J. W., & Lazzari, A. M. (1997). *Exceeding the boundaries: Understanding exceptional lives.* Fort Worth, TX: Harcourt Brace.

Youngblade, L. M., & Belsky, J. (1995). From family to friend: Predicting positive dyadic interaction with a close friend at 5 years of age from early parent–child relations. In S. Shulman (Ed.), *Close relationships and socioemotional development* (pp. 35–61). Norwood, NJ: Ablex.

13

Reporting and Using Assessment Results

Virginia Smith Harvey

The ultimate purpose of psychological reports is to improve the functioning of the clients about whom they are written. They fulfill this purpose by increasing others' understanding of the client, and by communicating recommended interventions in such a way that they are understood, appreciated, and implemented by children, parents, and teachers, both now and in the future. Because reports answer referral questions by communicating assessment data, they serve as "a vehicle to convert the assessment data into faithfully designed and executed interventions that lead to improved student performance" (Surber, 1995, p. 161), and are "one of the most crucial parts of the evaluation process" (Nuttall, Devaney, Malatesta, & Hampel, 1999, p. 396). They help both the psychologist and the recipient interpret and synthesize results with other ecological and systemic data. In addition to serving these primary functions, reports provide documentation for legal and historical purposes (Ownby, 1997; Ownby & Wallbrown, 1986; Tallent, 1988; Teglasi, 1983).

Reports reflect the functioning of the author. If the majority of the psychologist's time is spent testing to determine special education eligibility, the report will convey such an approach. On the other hand, if the majority of the psychologist's time is spent in a consultative, problem-solving approach, the psychological report will graphically depict the recommendations, interventions, and ultimate outcomes for the student (Ownby, 1997; Surber, 1995). When appropriately embedded in a consultative approach, testing is preceded by problem definition and rapport building, and followed by intervention implementation and monitoring.

As discussed in other chapters of this volume, the assessment of behavior and personality has changed in the past few years. Projective techniques are viewed with less favor, behavioral assessment has been strengthened through psychometric advances in self-report and parent/teacher rating scales, structured and semistructured interview techniques are increasingly employed, and greater emphasis has been placed on analyzing the function of the child's behavior in the context in which it occurs (Kamphaus & Frick, 1996). (More advanced treatments of projective techniques, direct assessment techniques, and functional behavior analysis are provided in Chapters 7, 5, and 4, respectively.)

The assessment of behavior and personality is multifaceted, and encompasses the use of adaptive behavior scales, behavior observations, parent rating scales, projective techniques, self-report inventories, structured and semistructured interviews, teacher rating scales, the use of diagnostic criteria from the *Diagnostic and Statistical Manual of Mental Disorders (DSM-IV)* of the American Psychiatric Association (1994), behavioral diagnosis, and the assessment of school and family context. As the reader is aware, personality and behavioral assessment tools are based on various theories, ranging from psychoanalytic to behavioral. The psychologist must enable the report reader to be able to clearly differentiate test results and their respective theoretical bases.

To communicate interventions in such a way that they will be implemented by children and adults, psychologists must consider issues that affect treatment adherence. *Treatment adherence* is the degree to which individuals commit to and take actions to implement interventions (Meichenbaum & Turk, 1987), and is critical to produce successful student outcomes (Surber, 1995; Telzrow, 1995). An important aspect of treatment adherence is *treatment integrity*, or the planning and implementation of interventions with validity (Gresham, 1989).

Although psychologists presume that reports impact the treatment of clients, several studies have indicated that 50% or fewer reports directly alter the treatment of clients in psychiatric settings (Ownby, 1997). The manner in which reports are written can greatly affect the likelihood of treatment adherence, as they address several critical variables. To make it likely that treatments are adhered to, recipients of treatment recommendations must be persuaded that the situation is serious, that the treatment will be efficacious, that the benefits of treatment implementation are greater than the inconveniences, and that they have some control over treatment decisions. Additional variables that increase the likelihood of treatment recommendation implementation are the promptness of the response to the referral, good communication, and minimizing recommendations for treatments that are complex, lengthy, or require significant lifestyle changes (Meichenbaum & Turk, 1987).

If psychologists keep these variables in mind as they write reports, they facilitate the implementation of recommended interventions with integrity. Thus, to encourage treatment adherence, reports must be responsive, persuasive, prompt, communicative, and followed by monitoring the implementation recommendations.

Responsivity

Responsive psychological reports are broad-based and address the entire ecology of the clients. They also improve relationships between psychologists and report recipients and, thereby, increase the likelihood of obtaining positive, negative, and corrective feedback.

The most critical step in establishing responsivity is to answer the referral question(s) throughout the report. This requires defining the context of the referral problem. For example, problems vary according to the situation: they vary to the degree that they are manifested in group settings, to the degree that they are manifested in social or academic settings, and so forth. Information necessary to contextualize the referral problem includes the nature of the learning environment, the overall effectiveness of the curricula, and effectiveness of the curricula with other children of similar background. Additional necessary information includes the suitability of the present instruction to the child's learning style, program accommodations and modifications that have already been attempted, and the degree of success the program modifications have engendered.

Bersoff (1995) asserts that test results are affected by several variables, including the environment in which the test is given, the tendency of individuals to respond to testing based on their understanding of the testing situation, and the degree to which clients are included in the assessment process and planning. He believes that parents and students are capable and should be respected by being included in the assessment process. To obtain data that are not "obfuscated by mistrust, misunderstanding, and the inhibition of self-disclosure" (Bersoff, 1995, p. 286), it is imperative that psychologists include the child and parent in all aspects of the assessment planning process. When children and parents are not included in the assessment planning process, "it is possible that most of our test data and their subsequent interpretation may be of doubtful veracity" (p. 286).

According to Bersoff (1995), to obtain informed and ethical assessments, the psychologist should:

1. *Expand informed consent.* When obtaining informed consent, the psychologist discusses the source and reason for referral; the nature, advantages, and limitations of the recommended assessment methods; the information that will be included in the report; the dissemination of the report; and the purposes and possible consequences of the evaluation from the child's, parent's, and psychologist's perspective. The psychologist also obtains permission from both the child and the parent.

2. *Share impressions immediately.* Immediately after the administration of the assessment instruments, the psychologist verbally shares impressions with the child and parents. This provides opportunities for the child to hear how others perceive him or her, and for the psychologist to learn whether observed behaviors are evident in situations the parent observes.

3. *Critique written evaluation.* Before disseminating the report, the psychologist shows it to the parents and child and gives them the opportunity to add to, clarify, or disagree with the content. The report is then modified as appropriate.

St. George and Wulff (1998) have found that, when clients are involved in the assessment process, including the writing of the psychological report, reports serve as a therapeutic tool. When collaboration is started at the beginning of the client–psychologist relationship, the client helps shape both the treatment course and the report. This results in more realistic goals, increased client empowerment, and increased commitment toward goal completion. Although this study was conducted in a family therapy setting, the same results are likely when psychologists include children, parents, and teachers in school settings.

When a child's first language is not English, the responsive psychologist addresses the child's competency in both English and the native language, as well as the appropriateness of all assessment tools. Goupal-McNicol and Thomas-Presswood (1998) emphasize the importance of recognizing the impact of second language learning on assessment and applying an ecological approach in intellectual assessment. This involves following any traditional psychometric assessment with a psychometric potential assessment that includes: (a) testing the limits by suspending time restraints for timed tests, (b) contextualizing vocabulary words by asking the child to use them in a sentence, (c) permitting the child to use paper and pencil to solve arithmetic problems, and (d) a test-teach-retest format for items the child had not been exposed to prior to the testing.

A responsive psychologist describes the child's strengths and talents as well as areas of weakness. That is, the responsive psychologist focuses on the "whole" child rather than working from a deficiency or disability model. For example, the psychologist addresses all talents and forms of intelligence including musical, bodily kinesthetic, interpersonal, and intrapersonal. Although psychologists vary in the degree to which they have adopted an ecological perspective, they can steadfastly demonstrate responsivity by asserting the inappropriateness of administering tests in isolation. Even if other team members are officially designated as the individuals who perform classroom observations, achievement testing, and parent interviews, school psychologists can and should make it a practice to observe the student in a natural setting, interview the student, have the student complete some academic work in their presence, and meet with the student's parents.

Responsivity also is conveyed in the selection of treatment recommendations. Recommended treatments should be clearly responsive to the referral question. Those that are easy to implement are preferable to those that are difficult or disruptive to implement, although those that are more difficult may be required in order to gain effective results. Interventions should not require excessive involvement of the psychologist, should be built on existing structures or ideas, should include a maintenance plan, and should involve the child in monitoring the results. Implementations should be assessed by student outcome data (Surber, 1995).

Persuasion

To effect change, psychological reports must persuade the reader that the recommended treatments are appropriate and effective, and that their benefits will outweigh their inconveniences. To be persuasive, reports must focus on desired outcomes and help the readers connect the information they already have with the new information the psychologist presents. For example, the psychologist must connect the referral problem with the assessment results and the recommended interventions. This connective discourse occurs at the sentence and paragraph level as well as at the level of the entire report, a process discussed in greater detail by Ownby (1997).

Another essential aspect of persuasion is to describe recommendations and interventions in such a way that the reader is convinced not only that they are appropriate, but that they can be implemented without undue duress. This requires that the psychologist refrain from the temptation to accept canned recommendations from a computer program, textbook, or test manual without first exploring their appropriateness, a point described in greater detail by Carlson in Chapter 19. It further requires that psychologists research the community and school well enough to know that the recommendations are appropriate and available, and that the parents, teachers, and other school personnel have the skills, knowledge, and experience to implement them appropriately. Finally, it requires that psychologists include the child, parent, and teacher in the report writing process so that they have an opportunity to accept or refuse particular recommendations.

Communication

Finally, in order to facilitate treatment adherence, reports must clearly communicate assessment results and recommended interventions. This communication takes place in verbal conferences and written reports.

Verbal Communication

Graduate programs typically only address report writing, when the verbal form of communication also is essential. Students should be encouraged to practice verbal presentations in case presentations, role plays, and supervised case meetings. In addition to providing assessment results in written and oral form to professionals, psychologists must learn to communicate the assessment results to clients and their nonprofessional relatives. The traditional method of disseminating assessment results is to hold a conference in which the results are verbally described and then to distribute a written report either at the conference or later. Several modifications in these typical procedures will increase the probability of recommendation implementation and treatment adherence.

Generally, it is "neither advisable nor ethical to give the report prior to the verbal feedback" (Ritzler, 1998, p. 424). The best procedure is to have an informal meeting during which the psychologist gives a general interpretation of results and asks for feedback to ensure that accurate understanding and integration of the information has occurred. It is essential for the client, or his or her representative, to be an active participant in the conversation. This prevents overwhelming recipients with a barrage of information and enables them to share corrective information prior to the final meeting. This informal meeting and report revision is followed by the formal presentation. Although this process can be time-consuming, it is essential if there is to be the understanding necessary for the implementation of the recommendations.

As Kamphaus and Frick (1996) suggest, verbal communications of assessment results to children, parents, and teachers can be improved when psychologists are tactfully honest, use percentile ranks when reporting quantitative data, encourage parents' and teachers' opportunities to ask questions and provide corrective feedback, schedule sufficient time to process the results and reach closure, adjust their communication style to the recipient's level of education and sophistication, clearly define all terms, avoid making global or negative future predictions, and use good counseling skills, while being careful not to exceed their level of training and expertise. All of these suggestions are applicable to written reports as well as to verbal communications.

Written Reports

The information communicated in a written report reaches a much broader audience than the individuals in the child's life at the time of referral. Psychologists must take extreme care regarding what they put in writing, because records are circulated within schools, serve as legal records, and remain in the child's file past the age of majority (Nuttall et al., 1999). In addition, because reports are given to parents, psychologists must assume that eventually the client will read, and, hopefully, understand, the report.

To be effective communication agents, psychological reports must be prompt and clearly written. Otherwise, reports are in severe danger of being misunderstood and important recommendations ignored.

Promptness.   Research reviewed by Ailes (1988) indicates that 48 hours after a ten-minute oral presentation, only 25% of the information is retained, and less than 10% is retained after a period of a week. Because people have great difficulty processing and remembering information communicated orally, it is essential that written reports follow verbal communications as soon as possible. Otherwise, the results and recommendations are likely to be forgotten and incompletely implemented.

Despite the advantages of prompt report writing, psychologists often find report writing so onerous that they delay writing in favor of other activities, and postpone finishing the report until "after the interventions are in place, after the multidisciplinary conference, after the information has been verbally communicated and demonstrated to the referring teacher, and after eligibility and placement decisions have been made" (Ownby, 1997, p. 161). Unfortunately, this practice undermines the effectiveness of the report for two reasons. First, delayed report writing results in the psychologist attempting to write reports when he or she cannot remember details of the assessment process or even the child. This increases the time required to write the report and results in less vivid and accurate writing. Even more importantly, delayed delineation of interventions results in greatly reduced treatment adherence (Meichenbaum & Turk, 1987). Therefore, prompt report writing is both more efficient and more effective, and makes it much more likely that the interventions will be successfully implemented.

Readability.   Because parents and other nonpsychologists have access to psychological reports, it is essential that they be written intelligibly and use positive terms that are neither easily misunderstood nor frightening (Koocher & Keith-Spiegel, 1998; Nuttall et al., 1999). Authors of texts used in assessment courses commonly recommend that psychological reports be written in a readable manner (Kamphaus, 1993; Ownby, 1997; Sattler, 1992; Tallent, 1988). Psychologists are advised to write clearly and choose vocabulary that has common usage and a precise meaning. According to Nuttall et al. (1999), an important consideration is the audience: The language, content, tone, and recommendations vary according to who will receive the information and for what purposes. Yet, because normally only one version of a report is prepared, "plain English" should be used and technical terms defined.

Reports are criticized for excessive speculation, neglecting to include data, vagueness, ambiguity, and irresponsible interpretation (Harvey, 1997; Tallent, 1988). This lack of clarity exists even though recipients prefer clearly explained technical terms, understandable solutions, clear examples, and explanations (Cuarda & Albaugh, 1956; Pryzwansky & Hanania, 1986; Rucker, 1967; Shively & Smith, 1969; Tallent, 1988; Wiener, 1987).

It has become common practice for copies of psychological reports to be given to parents, which results in the likelihood that not only parents but also children will read them. Therefore, it is critical that psychological reports be understandable to the average person who reads at or below the twelfth-grade level. However, psychologists working in schools, clinics, and private practice often write reports at levels higher than the education level of their audience, including parents (Harvey, 1989, 1997; Wedig, 1984). It is notable that psychologists with different levels of training write reports at similar levels of difficulty regardless of work setting (Harvey, 1997). Even when cued in advance to write reports at a level understandable to the average parent, psychologists in training were able to reduce the reading difficulty of reports only by rewriting them.

Some computer programs and books designed to facilitate report writing suggest specific phrases for inclusion in reports (Zuckerman, 1995). However, psychologists must take extreme care when using these services lest they be led to include excessive jargon or inappropriate recommendations in their reports. When psychologists use jargon in reports, the reports are not understood and this reduces the credibility of the psychologist and results in considerable frustration on the part of the reader (Ownby, 1997; Surber, 1995). In Chapter 19 of this volume, Carlson discusses the benefits and liabilities of computer-based test interpretation and report generation, and readers are directed to her chapter for additional information on computer-generated reports.

To increase the readability of their psychological reports, psychologists can shorten sentence length, minimize the number of difficult words, reduce the use of jargon, reduce the use of acronyms, omit passive verbs, and increase the use of subheadings. However, practicing psychologists may need more than awareness of these methods to modify their writing style. Specific feedback about the readability of their own writing may be required. This could be obtained by peer review, soliciting consumer feedback (Ownby, 1997), regular calculation of reading level by hand, or using computer grammar checkers to calculate readability (Harvey, 1997). In addition, taking the role of a recipient while reading and editing the report can be very helpful. For example, Ritzler (1998) indicates that a useful tool in ensuring that reports are understandable is to have students revise them as though they are writing for their grandmothers, who are assumed to be "intelligent women who know little about psychology, but who can be sensitive and empathic when they understand someone's personality" (pp. 422–423).

Report Organization

There is some evidence that the traditional organization of psychological reports into sections (background information, assessment results, summary, and recommendations) is effective and preferred by consumers (Ownby, 1997). Reports should not be so short that they are restricted to reporting only tests scores and special education eligibility. Neither should they be so lengthy and all-inclusive that the reader is unable to discern the most significant information (Surber, 1995; Tallent, 1988).

Identifying information. Fundamental identifying information includes the child's name, date of birth, age at the time of testing, the dates of assessment, the date of the report, the name and credentials (including bilingual skills if relevant) of the psychologist, and the name and credentials of the supervisor, if applicable.

Reason for referral. In this paragraph the referral reasons are stated and clarified with information the psychologist obtained in parent, teacher, and child interviews. When a functional behavioral assessment (see Chapter 4) is included, the reason for referral also includes the definition of problem behavior in specific, measurable, and easily understood terms, acquired through observations of the child and interviews with the student, parents, and teachers. The entire psychological report serves to further clarify and respond to the referral questions through choice of assessment methods, the integration of information, and the selection of interventions.

Background information. Traditionally, background information is included at the beginning of the report. Most background information is obtained from file reviews and parent, teacher, and child interviews. The source of information always must be cited. Clearly, background information should be included only if the psychologist knows that it is accurate.

The child's educational, familial, cultural, linguistic, and medical background must be described well enough that the reader has a context in which to place the assessment information. It is important for parents and children to have a voice in what background information is included in the report (Bersoff, 1995; St. George & Wulff, 1998), and it is essential that psychologists are careful to avoid revealing information that the parents wish to remain private. When giving permission for inclusion of background information, parents should be aware of the purpose of the assessment, the intended use of the assessment information, and who will have access to the report, so that they can indicate which information they would prefer remain confidential.

Essential *educational background information* includes the extent of the child's exposure to formal education and past academic experiences including academic difficulties, grade retention, special education programming, remedial or transition programs, school attendance, number of schools attended, tendency to read or study at home, and, for children for whom English is a second language, years of instruction in native language and proficiency in reading and writing in the first language.

Relevant *familial and cultural background information* might be the family's perception of the problem; parental perceptions of the child's positive attributes, friends, level of independence, and interests; family composition, past and current; health of family members; educational levels and occupations of family members, here and in the country of origin; familial culture and customs, including gender roles and methods of discipline; extent of the child's acculturation; family attitude toward school, academic achievement, exceptionalities, emotional problems, special education, and mental health services; neighborhood factors; and the availability and use of community supports.

Linguistic background information is essential when a referred child's first language is not English to accurately determine the language in which assessment and instruction should be done. This involves determining the child's dominant language and English proficiency in four language domains: listening, speaking, reading, and writing. The assessment includes language skills both in school and at home; the language spoken at home between parents, siblings, parents and children, and others; the language in which stories are read to the child; and the language in which the child reads, writes, speaks in school, and watches TV. If the psychologist is not proficient in the child's dominant language, an interpreter will be required. Similarly, when parents are not fluent in English, interviews will require an interpreter. The ideal interpreter is knowledgeable regarding schools and educational programming, familiar with the community, and is acceptable to the family but is not a family member. Further discussion of language proficiency determination and ramifications for assessment professionals is provided by Geisinger in Chapter 20.

Relevant *medical background* includes the child's developmental and health history including serious illnesses, allergies, high fevers, accidents, injuries, developmental milestones, physical problems, and past and current medications and interventions. When appropriate, familial illnesses can be included. It also includes the history of vision and hearing acuity tests, previous ear infections, and current hearing and vision test results.

In many reports, *previous test results* are included in the background information when available and relevant. However, Ritzler (1998) prefers that background information be incorporated into the discussion of current assessment results, because he feels that, when previous test results are placed at the beginning of the report, they prejudice the reader's interpretation of subsequent informational and bias the reader toward accepting outdated results as most valid. Therefore, Ritzler suggests that previous test results are best integrated into the portion of the report addressing current assessment results.

Assessment procedures.   A primary task of a psychologist is to determine which qualities are "state" (relatively temporary) and which qualities are "trait" (relatively permanent). It is not possible to determine whether the results of any assessment tool in isolation indicate state or trait qualities. Thus, psychologists must include information from a variety of sources including file reviews, observations, parent and teacher interviews, as well as standardized and nonstandardized assessment tools. To orient the reader to the wide range of assessment methods used, psychologists often list assessment methods and sources of information at this point in the report.

Behavioral observations.   In this section, general behavioral observations, such as anxiety, trustfulness, attentiveness, persistence, and self-confidence displayed by the child, are usefully described, particularly when they vary from one instrument, subtest, or testing session to another. Specific, objective examples of behavior are helpful (Kamphaus, 1993).

The degree of rapport that the psychologist believes was established should also be described, and, if poor, the extent to which the psychologist believes this negatively affected test results. If rapport is not established, such that the results are not considered valid, the results should not be reported.

In this section, the psychologist also reports any modifications used during the testing, such as interpreters or testing of the limits. A statement of the probable reliability and validity of conclusions should be included, as well as a "comment about the appropriateness of the tests used for the particular child being tested" (Nuttall et al., 1999, p. 400). Specifically, the psychologist should address whether the child's ethnic group, disabilities, and level of English were included in the normative sample: if not, the psychologist "should caution the reader about the validity of the findings and focus more on qualitative rather than quantitative information" (p. 400).

In the past, it was common for psychologists to describe the child's physical appearance in this section of reports, and there are advantages and disadvantages to this practice. For example, Nuttall et al. (1999) indicate that the child's physical appearance and manner of dress should be described as indicators of the child's cultural background, care, and the family's economic condition. Ownby (1997), on the other hand, discourages this practice and describes it as archaic. If the psychologist decides to include a physical description because it is directly related to the child's issues, it is important to use objective language and refrain from using evaluative or judgmental terms. For example, a child's jeans can be described objectively as *torn*, but using the term *shabby* is judgmental.

Assessment results and interpretation.   The section on assessment results includes the findings from procedures employed by the psychologist, including observations, child interviews, and assessments with standardized and nonstandardized instruments. It also includes the results of trial implementations of functional behavioral interventions.

Assessment results should be organized by finding common themes or theories across tests and procedures rather than by specific tests (Nuttall et al., 1999; Ritzler,

1998; Sattler, 1992). That is, they should be organized within broad categories such as cognition, language, academic achievement, and social–emotional status. Within any categories employed, results should be organized by theme. For example, all of the observational, behavioral, child interview, self-report scale, teacher report, and parent interview data that suggest anxiety should be grouped together. In addition, the psychologist must do the work of reintegrating the "compartments" back into the integrated whole of a child within a context. When reading compartmentalized reports, the reader is forced to do the work of integrating the majority of the data and commonly reacts by reading only the integrative summary (Surber, 1995).

Rather than every report beginning with cognitive skills, Ritzler (1998) suggests that reports be organized such that the most salient elements are accorded first, or primary, place in the report. Thus, a report concerning a child whose primary issue is depression may begin with the section on intrapersonal and emotional development, and a report concerning a child whose primary issue is bullying may begin with the section on interpersonal and social skills. Additional information to address includes current mood and affect, degree and acuteness of disturbance, emotional lability, primary interpersonal and intrapersonal strengths and conflicts, coping strategies, and diagnostic impressions (Beutler, 1995).

Although this chapter focuses on reporting results from the emotional and social assessment of a child, every psychological report on a child should consider academic and cognitive functioning. Results of other assessments, including test scores when appropriate, should be reported and attributed. Even when the psychologist is not the individual completing academic testing, the report should address academic proficiency. Curriculum-based assessment of skills in math, language, reading, spelling, social studies, and science are critical elements of an effective psychological report. Similarly, cognitive skills are described and analyzed relevant to the child's social and emotional functioning, using an appropriately current theoretical framework (Flanagan, Genshaft, & Harrison, 1997).

Minimal quantitative data should be included in the body of reports, because it so frequently is misunderstood by readers. As indicated in the *Standards for Educational and Psychological Testing* (American Educational Research Association, American Psychological Association, & National Council on Measurement in Education, 1999), "Test scores, per se, are not readily interpreted without other information, such as norms or standards, indications of measurement error, and descriptions of test content. Just as a temperature of 50° in January is warm for Minnesota and cool for Florida, a test score of 50 is not meaningful without some context" (p. 62). Readily understandable interpretive information should be provided to any reader who is not a specialist, often in place of specific scores. Scores presented as standard scores should be accompanied by percentile scores and an explanation of percentile scores (e.g., "John's standard score of 100, which falls at the 50th percentile, indicates that out of a group of 100 children he would probably score higher than about 49 and lower than about 49"). When standard scores and scaled scores are presented, information should be included that enables the reader to readily understand them. Because of psychometric inadequacy, grade equivalent scores should not be reported. Furthermore, if test scores are thought to be invalid, because of a lack of rapport, insufficient linguistic proficiency, or some other problem, they should not be reported (Kamphaus & Frick, 1996).

Along with the emotional and behavioral assessment results, the psychologist reports on observations, preferably in more than one setting. Observations in class(es) in which a child experiences difficulty, unstructured settings such as recess, and settings in which the family interacts, such as a meal, are particularly helpful.

The report also can include the results of child interviews and address the child's perception of the problem, what the child likes and dislikes about school, and the child's perception of the school personnel's willingness to help. Additional helpful information includes the child's description of his or her special abilities, talents, interests, favored activities; friends and preferred academic work partners; tactfully described feelings about home, school, and relationships; what the child believes makes him or her happy, sad, angry; what the child does that makes others happy, sad, and angry; previous losses of significant persons; adjustment to a new culture; summer activities; and the child's future hopes, dreams, and vocational aspirations.

When psychologists effectively describe the results of functional behavioral assessments, their reports include the definition of problem behavior in specific, measurable, and easily understood terms, acquired through observations of the child and interviews with the student, parents, and teachers. They also include a description of the circumstances thought to maintain the problem behavior; a prioritization of problem behaviors, a clarification of which problem behavior will be addressed initially; and a description of testable hypotheses, including the context, setting events, antecedents, and consequences that are maintaining inappropriate behavior (Macklem, 1999). The report goes on to describe the results of methods used to test and eliminate hypotheses, such as additional interviews, observing the child in natural settings, documenting occurrences, setting events, triggering antecedents, applying consequences, and trying out interventions. Specific statements regarding these processes are included in the report, for example, "to test the hypothesis that assigned work was too hard, easier work was assigned but no change in work completion rate resulted." Finally, the narrative includes a description of the behavior support plan developed, including the delineation of strategies to alter antecedents or replace the defined problem behavior with desired behavior, results of the implementation of the behavior support plan for at least three weeks, and results of revisiting problem definition, regenerating hypotheses, and modifying the behavior support plan as appropriate.

Recommendations.   Recommendations should be specific and clear (Teglasi, 1983). As mentioned earlier, it is essential that psychologists investigate school, community, and personnel resources to ensure that recommendations are feasible. It is helpful for the psychologist to share informational handouts with parents and teachers (Kamphaus & Frick, 1996), although it is also important that the psychologist not overwhelm the recipients with unedited reams of paper.

When recommendations are specific, they are more likely to be implemented. Recommendations are best presented by providing an "action sentence which is underlined and preferably starts with a verb . . . and then discuss, why, how, and by whom these services should be provided" (Nuttall et al., 1999, p. 401). Several factors make recommendations more useful. Specific names of several potential therapists (taking into consideration resources available, including insurance), books, materials, parent training programs, treatment programs, and agencies (with verified sources and contact information) are extremely helpful.

Summary.   As the title of this section suggests, this section summarizes the body of the report and should provide no surprises to the reader. Ritzler (1998) suggests that no summary be provided, feeling that a four to seven page double-spaced report "is the briefest summary possible. Anything shorter would leave out critical information; many readers will go directly to the summary if one is available and will ignore the rest of the report" (p. 424). However, most reports do include summaries and readers appear to prefer this format (Ownby, 1997). Several methods can be used to increase the effectiveness of this section of the report.

In the summary, the psychologist specifically addresses how the assessment results clarify or answer the original referral questions, integrates the results of all observations and assessment procedures, and draws conclusions. As previously mentioned, the psychologist should never draw conclusions from the results of one instrument. Instead, conclusions should only be drawn when they are suggested by several different sources of information.

When working with children from nondominant cultures or for whom English is a second language, in writing the conclusions the psychologist must address language proficiency; indicate strengths, reasoning ability, and problem-solving skills; contextualize all scores and behavioral indicators; and consult with a person knowledgeable about the child's culture before drawing conclusions or making recommendations. The psychologist must also consider the student's culture in developing remediation strategies.

Often the summary includes diagnostic impressions, such as eligibility for special education services. In some jurisdictions, this diagnosis (or diagnosis exclusion) is included in the psychologist's report. Unfortunately, the lack of clarity around diagnoses can render this aspect of professional psychology extremely frustrating. Because every state (and in some states, every community) has latitude in the interpretation of disability eligibility, there is little consistency from one state, community, or school to another in designating a student as disabled.

The assessment of behavior and personality also highlights a difficulty in the intersection between education and psychology. Educators are under the auspices of the Individuals with Disabilities Education Act (IDEA). Psychologists are trained in the American Psychiatric Association's *Diagnostic and Statistical Manual of Mental Disorders (DSM-IV)*, and these two sets of criteria do not comfortably fit together. For example, in the IDEA, the definition of "severe emotional disturbance" excludes students who are "socially maladjusted" unless they also meet criteria for "emotional disturbance." This is frequently interpreted to mean that students with academic deficiencies who meet the *DSM-IV* definition for depressed, schizophrenic, or anxious, are also eligibile for special education programming, yet those who meet the *DSM-IV* criteria for conduct disorder or oppositional defiant disorder do not meet the criteria for special education services unless depression or anxiety is comorbid. Further, students can be identified as disabled yet not be eligible for special education services (Kamphaus & Frick, 1996). To psychologists working outside of schools, these distinctions appear arbitrary and are quite confusing, while psychologists working in schools are often frustrated in their quest for student eligibility for appropriate interventions. Similarly, the diagnosis of attention deficit disorder is highly controversial and students suffering from anxiety, post-traumatic stress disorder, or learning disabilities are often diagnosed with attention deficit disorder and prescribed medication rather than referred for appropriate educational or psychological services. (Expanded discussion of attentional difficulties experienced by school-age children is provided in Chapter 15 of this volume, together with some alternative strategies for intervention.)

Inclusion of Test Items and Test Protocols

Although parental inspection and review of records, including test protocols, is permitted under the Individuals with Disabilities Education Act (IDEA) and the Family Education Rights and Privacy Act (FERPA), psychologists can generally avoid actual inspection of protocols by providing enough fictitious examples to satisfy the curiosity of parents regarding the appropriateness of the test. Psychologists should vigorously avoid copying test protocols and giving them to parents as it is a violation of copyright law and test security. Supreme Court rulings (Detroit Edison Co. v. National Labor Relations Board, as cited in Koocher & Keith-Spiegel, 1998) have supported the right of a test developing company to retain test security. If a parent is unable to come to the school to meet with the school psychologist, psychologists may adhere to federal laws by sending a copy of the raw data along with the interpretation to another psychologist, who could then interpret the results for the parent.

Including photocopied test protocols with reports clearly violates the copyright held by the publishers of such instruments and is therefore illegal and unethical. Besides adherence to copyright law, the maintenance of test security is important to avoid compromising test validity and inaccurate interpretation by untrained individuals. Psychologists should not share actual test items or responses in forums that are potentially public, even situations such as professional list-serves. Psychologists should not supply copies of test protocols to parents because they are not trained to interpret the data and to do so violates test security (Koocher & Keith-Spiegel, 1998). Instead, the psychologist should interpret the results to the parents and provide them with an understandable report.

Follow-Up

As Salvia and Ysseldyke (1998) note, "there has been a dramatic shift from a focus on the process of serving students with disabilities to a focus on the outcomes or results of the services provided" (p. 740). Therefore, it is essential that psychologists not consider their work done when reports are completed. As Conoley and Gutkin (1986) suggest, "technical expertise in giving a test is no more important than technical expertise in disseminating results, planning intervention, and providing follow-up evaluation" (p. 459). All too often, psychologists have conducted assessments and made recommendations, but neglected to follow up on the implementation of these recommendations. As described previously, effective assessments are embedded in the consultation process and are followed by implementing, monitoring, and modifying recommendations. Psychologists should take a responsible and active role in these activities.

Conclusion

In order to elicit an appropriate degree of understanding and cooperation, written reports must be clearly and promptly written, logically organized, and comprehensive. To persuade readers to implement appropriate recommendations with integrity, reports must empower readers to connect previous impressions with the psychologist's new information and conclude that recommended treatments are appropriate, beneficial, and worth expending the effort to implement. To accomplish these goals, a number of issues need to be addressed. Training in graduate schools and at internship sites will need to reflect this orientation, and practicum and internship sites will need to reflect this practice. For example, psychologists in training will need to be taught how to expand informed consent, share results, and modify reports appropriately in response to parent, child, and teacher input while keeping the best interests of the child in mind.

Increasingly, psychologists will need to involve parents, children, and teachers in the assessment and report writing process. Doing so requires an investment of time, training in such involvement, and a willingness to abandon the expert's role for a collaborative and respectful role. Psychologists must adopt the practice of more frequently tailoring their assessment procedures to reflect the referral question, rather than using a standard battery. Similarly, psychologists will need to obtain and incorporate substantial contextual information to determine the appropriateness of the recommendations offered.

Finally, effective report writing affects the supervision of school psychologists. For example, in order to write effective reports, psychologists will need to reserve time in their schedules for report writing and rewriting. Writing reports well takes considerable time, and even more time is necessary when report writing is embedded in a consultative approach that starts with problem definition and ends with intervention monitoring. This often requires that psychologists educate supervisors about the time required. An effective tool to use in such education is data about the time expended in various cases, accompanied by the results of the assessment process, including the success of interventions and parental responses to questionnaires about their satisfaction with psychological services.

In order to fulfill their ultimate purpose, that of improving client functioning by influencing both current and future programming, psychological reports must be responsive, persuasive, communicative, and embedded in the consultation process.

Responsive reports clarify and address the referral question throughout the report, contextualize all assessment components, and involve all stakeholders in the report writing process. Both verbal and written communication are facilitated by tactful honesty, the use of percentile ranks when reporting quantitative data, encouraging parents and teachers to ask questions and provide corrective feedback, scheduling sufficient time to process the results, adjusting communication style to the recipients' level of education and sophistication, avoiding making global or negative future predictions, clearly defining all terms, and using good interpersonal skills. These procedures are necessary to ensure that psychological reports serve their ultimate purpose, that of improving the functioning of the clients about whom they are written.

References

Ailes, R. (1988). *You are the message.* Homewood, IL: Dow Jones-Irwin.

American Educational Research Association, American Psychological Association, & National Council on Measurement in Education. (1999). *Standards for educational and psychological testing.* Washington, DC: American Educational Research Association.

American Psychiatric Association. (1994). *Diagnostic and statistical manual of mental disorders* (4th ed.). Washington, DC: Author.

Bersoff, D. N. (1995). *Ethical conflicts in psychology.* Washington, DC: American Psychological Association.

Beutler, L. E. (1995). Integrating and communicating findings. In L. E. Beutler & M. R. Berrn (Eds.), *Integrative assessment of adult personality* (pp. 25–64). New York: Guilford Press.

Conoley, J. C., & Gutkin, T. B. (1986). Educating school psychologists for the real world. *School Psychology Review, 15,* 457–465.

Cuarda, C. A., & Albaugh, W. P. (1956). Sources of ambiguity in psychological reports. *Journal of Clinical Psychology, 12,* 267–272.

Family Education Rights and Privacy Act of 1974 (FERPA), Pub. Law No. 93-380, 20 U. S. C. A. § 1232g, 34 C. F. R. § Part 99 (1993).

Flanagan, D. P., Genshaft, J. L., & Harrison, P. L. (Eds.). (1997). *Contemporary intellectual assessment: Theories, tests, and issues.* New York: Guilford Press.

Goupal-McNicol, S., & Thomas-Presswood, T. (1998). *Working with linguistically and culturally different children.* Boston: Allyn and Bacon.

Gresham, F. M. (1989). Assessment of treatment integrity in school consultation and preferral inter-

vention. *School Psychology Review, 18,* 37–50.

Harvey, V. S. (1989, March). Eschew obfuscation: Support of clear writing. *Communiqué,* p. 12.

Harvey, V. S. (1997). Improving readability of psychological reports. *Professional Psychology: Research and Practice, 28,* 271–274.

Individuals with Disabilities Education Act. (IDEA of 1991), 20 U. S. C. Chapter 33; Department of Education Regulations for IDEA at 34 CFR 300 and 301 (September 29, 1992).

Kamphaus, R. W. (1993). *Clinical assessment of children's intelligence.* Boston: Allyn and Bacon.

Kamphaus, R. W., & Frick, P. J. (1996). *Clinical assessment of child and adolescent personality and behavior.* Boston: Allyn and Bacon.

Koocher, G. P., & Keith-Spiegel, P. (1998). *Ethics in psychology: Professional standards and cases* (2nd ed.). New York: Oxford University Press.

Macklem, G. (1999). *Functional assessment.* Unpublished manuscript.

Meichenbaum, D., & Turk, D. C. (1987). *Facilitating treatment adherence: A practitioner's guidebook.* New York: Plenum Press.

Nuttall, E. V., Devaney, J. L., Malatesta, N. A., & Hampel, A. (1999). Writing assessment results. In E. V. Nuttall, I. Romero, & J. Kalesnik (Eds.), *Assessing and screening preschoolers: Psychological and educational dimensions* (pp. 396–406). Boston: Allyn and Bacon.

Ownby, R. L. (1997). *Psychological reports: A guide to report writing in professional psychology* (3rd ed.). New York: Wiley.

Ownby, R. L., & Wallbrown, F. (1986). Improving report writing in school psychology. In T. R. Kratochwill (Ed.), *Advances in school psychology, Volume V* (pp. 7–50). Hillsdale, NJ: Erlbaum.

Pryzwansky, W. B., & Hanania, J. S. (1986). Applying problem solving approaches to school psychological reports. *Journal of School Psychology, 24,* 133–141.

Ritzler, B. A. (1998). Teaching and learning issues in an advanced course in personality assessment. In L. Handler & M. J. Hilsenroth (Eds.), *Teaching and learning personality assessment* (pp. 431–452). Mahwah, NJ: Erlbaum.

Rucker, C. M. (1967). Technical language in the school psychologist's report. *Psychology in the Schools, 4,* 146–150.

Salvia, J., & Ysseldyke, J. E. (1998). *Assessment* (7th ed.). New York: Houghton Mifflin.

Sattler, J. (1992). *Assessment of children, revised and updated third edition.* San Diego: Jerome M. Sattler.

Shively, J. J., & Smith, A. E. (1969). Understanding the psychological report. *Psychology in the Schools, 6,* 272–273.

St. George, S., & Wulff, D. (1998). Integrating the client's voice within case reports. *Journal of Systemic Therapies, 17*(4), 3–13.

Surber, J. M. (1995). Best practices in problem-solving approach to psychological report writing. In A. Thomas & J. Grimes (Eds.), *Best practices in school psychology–III* (pp. 161–169). Washington, DC: National Association of School Psychologists.

Tallent, N. (1988). *Psychological report writing* (3rd ed.). Englewood Cliffs, NJ: Prentice-Hall.

Teglasi, H. (1983). Report of a psychological assessment in a school setting. *Psychology in the Schools, 20,* 466–479.

Telzrow, C. F. (1995). Best practices in facilitating treatment adherence. In A. Thomas & J. Grimes (Eds.), *Best practices in school psychology–III* (pp. 501–510). Washington, DC: National Association of School Psychologists.

Wedig, R. R. (1984). Parental interpretation of psychoeducational reports. *Psychology in the Schools, 21,* 477–481.

Wiener, J. (1987). Factors affecting educators' comprehension of psychological reports. *Psychology in the Schools, 24,* 116–126.

Zuckerman, E. L. (1995). *Clinician's thesaurus: The guidebook for writing psychological reports* (4th ed.). New York: Guilford Press.

Author Note

This chapter discusses reports written to address the psychological and educational progress of children. Forensic reports, which address the culpability of alleged offenders, have additional requirements. For information, the reader may consult the following works.

Hess, A. K., & Weiner, I. B. (Eds.). (1999). *The handbook of forensic psychology* (2nd ed.). New York: Wiley.

Hoghughi, M. S., Bhate, S. R., & Graham, F. (1997). *Working with sexually abusive adolescents.* Thousand Oaks, CA: Sage.

Melton, G. B., Petrila, J., Poythress, N. G., & Slobogin, C. (1987). *Psychological evaluations for the courts: A handbook for mental health professionals and lawyers.* New York: Guilford Press.

Developing Interventions for Use with Children Who Experience Learning and Social Challenges

Betsy B. Waterman

Information-processing abilities both influence and are influenced by the child's social and emotional abilities and experiences. Information-processing deficits clearly impact a child's ability to succeed academically. When children fail in school, there is an indirect cost to these children in terms of self-esteem, self-efficacy, sense of competence, and degree of social acceptance (Swanson & Malone, 1992). Cognitive abilities also may be directly related to the child's social and emotional functioning. As suggested in Chapter 8, the child's ability to correctly encode social information, interpret and represent this information in memory, select goals and responses in differing social situations, and act on his or her social decisions are all dependent on intact social information-processing abilities (Crick & Dodge, 1994) and language competence (Tur-Kaspa & Bryan, 1994).

Children whose learning is deficient often exhibit difficulties in social functioning. These children have been found to be more rejected by peers than their nondisabled counterparts, to possess poorer social problem-solving and conflict resolution skills, to engage in and be recipients of more hostile interactions with others, and have greater difficulty altering their verbal style to match the age of the person with whom they are communicating (Swanson & Malone, 1992). Children with learning problems also were found to have difficulties comprehending nonverbal social information, lack automatization of basic social skills (e.g., interpretation of the tone of voice of another), add inaccurate information to that which actually was presented in a given social situation, be poor perspective-takers, have difficulty selecting reachable and appropriate goals, and have problems engaging in appropriate social problem solutions.

Developing a Model for Assessment and Intervention of Social Deficits

Bye and Jussim (1993) and Crick and Dodge (1994) offer useful models from which appropriate interventions can be developed. Bye and Jussim suggest at least two general areas to be considered in understanding and modifying social behaviors, social knowledge and social performance. Bye and Jussim define *social knowledge* as "what a person knows about human interaction, specifically the behaviors expected and accepted in various social situations" (p. 144). Social knowledge was viewed by these authors as that information that one has about self and others, the attributions one makes about cause and effect, and the procedural knowledge the person holds in memory that reflects information about what behavior is expected in any given situation. In other words, social knowledge refers to what a person knows about his or her social world. *Social performance*, according to these writers, refers to the actual behavior in which the person engages. The quality of this performance is seen in the child's level of social skill and competence. Bye and Jussim suggest that social knowledge is essential to the development of social performance but is not, in itself, necessarily sufficient for adequate social action. A child, then, who has adequate social knowledge available to him or her, will not necessarily engage in appropriate social behavior. These authors suggest that three "filters" influence the development of social knowledge: environmental factors, physiological factors, and information-processing factors. The child's social knowledge, coupled with motivational factors, according to Bye and Jussim, then influence the person's actual social performance or actions.

Crick and Dodge suggest a six-process model for understanding social information processing. These six processes are the encoding process, representation process, response search process, clarification and selection of a goal process, response decision process, and enactment process. Each must be considered in reviewing or designing research that looks at social development. These authors further suggest that these processes can be taught to children, and, therefore, are important in the development of interventions for children with social deficits.

If one considers both Bye and Jussim's model and Crick and Dodge's Social Information Processing model in identifying areas for assessment and intervention, the following domains might be considered as target areas of intervention: personal factors, environmental factors, information-processing factors, and physiological factors.

Developing an understanding of the child's personal being is important as professionals who work with the child identify and engage in interventions. Low self-esteem, expectations for failure in social situations, attributions for social success, and the expected evaluations from self and others could influence the manner in which a child acquires and maintains a social information and knowledge base and the proficiency with which the child ultimately performs in social situations (Crick & Dodge, 1994; Lavoie, 1994; Schwab Foundation for Learning, 1996).

Similarly, environmental factors, such as low social status (Moisan, 1998), high levels of stress (Rubenzer, 1996), or cultural variables could affect social information and knowledge as well as social performance. Environmental factors also influence the amount of information to which the child is exposed (Bye & Jussim, 1993).

Information about the specific social situation also can be essential in understanding and intervening with a child's behavioral response in a given situation.

The acquisition of both social information and social knowledge requires accurate encoding, interpretation, and integration of social information (Bye & Jussim, 1993; Crick & Dodge, 1994). Intact verbal and nonverbal language, the ability to accurately perceive social data, the ability to consider simultaneously multiple pieces of social information, and the ability to efficiently and accurately recall past social information are essential abilities for a child striving to develop the social information and knowledge base on which social action is predicated.

Finally, gathering information about physical factors related to the child is essential as these, too, influence social development. Each person is unique in terms of his or her temperament, level of stamina, levels of arousal, and his or her ability to attend (Bye & Jussim, 1993). Some children have greater difficulty than others in focusing and sustaining attention, responding reflectively, and controlling their moods. Understanding something about the child in relation to physiological differences is one area that is often overlooked but offers important information on which effective interventions can be based.

Areas of Assessment

Personal Factors

Attributions for success or failure and motivation.   Arnold (1997) suggests that children with learning disabilities are more apt to attribute both success and failure to factors outside of themselves, such as luck. Because external explanations for behavior reduce the feelings of control the child has over a given situation, it is not surprising that children with learning problems show less motivation and persistence on tasks. Unfortunately, these attributes simply serve to further reduce the child's sense of personal control and he or she may become even more discouraged and disengaged academically and socially. How the child makes attributions is related directly to the evaluations the child expects to receive from him- or herself and from others. Crick and Dodge (1994) suggested that the expectations children hold about their own evaluations and the evaluations of others are part of what is stored in memory. These memories are derived from the collection of past responses received from others. For example, a child may attempt to enter a group of children and be turned away repeatedly. In Crick and Dodge's words, "perceived peer disapproval (the interpretation of the peer response) may lead to decreases in feelings of social competence" (p. 86). A pattern of disapproval, then, results in a molar view of themselves that affects their own expected self-evaluation and the evaluation of their social behavior that they expect from others.

Assessment of the way in which a child makes attributions and develops expectations for social evaluation may involve use of direct assessment techniques (e.g., observation, teacher rating systems, use of rating and interview scales), projective measures (see Chapters 5 and 6 for more detailed discussions), functional analyses of behavior (see Chapter 4), and the use of self-reports and developmental inventories, depending on the nature of the suspected difficulties (for further elaboration on this topic see Vitulano, Carlson, and Holmberg in Chapter 3).

Observations allow the assessor to view the child in a variety of settings using highly structured or less structured observational measures. Generally, structured observational checklists or code strategies focus on small clusters of similar behaviors (e.g., level of cooperation) and determine how often such behaviors are demonstrated in certain situations and at certain times.

Teacher rating systems ask the teacher to observe and record a targeted child's number of social interactions with peers. Behavior-rating scales may be completed by parents, teachers, or the child and are more indirect measures of social attitudes. These scales typically assess a child's skill and actual performance levels in a variety of situations and environments. Like behavior-rating scales, interviews may be conducted with parents, teachers, or the targeted child. These can provide anecdotal information about the child's perceived status within a group.

Projective measures typically ask the child to draw or tell stories about ambiguous stimuli. The assumption is that the stimuli presented tap into the child's less conscious thinking. Finally, asking direct questions such as, "Why do you think this event happened?" or "Why do you think Bobby did that to you?" may offer useful information about the attributions the child may be making about his or her role in a given social situation or the intent of the behavior of others.

Self-awareness.   Bye and Jussim (1993) define self-awareness as the knowledge the person has about him or herself. This includes the child's awareness of his or her strengths and limitations and knowledge of his or her personal history. Assessment of a child's self-knowledge might include gathering data about the child's early history and important events in the child's life from both the child and a parent or caregiver. It also may involve a comparison of the child's own perceived strengths and weaknesses with the perception of the child's strengths and weaknesses held by pertinent adults in the child's life. Finally, the use of sociometric measures may offer information about how the child views his or her own interpersonal relationships or strengths and weaknesses. It also can offer information about the perceptions that the child's peers hold about the targeted child's social relationships and perceived competencies. Sociometric instruments measure a child's "acceptableness" within a particular social group (e.g., a classroom). Typically these involve asking each child within a group to rank their peers according to a certain criterion, such as level of cooperation, popularity, or skill.

Emotional state.   Emotional states such as loneliness (Cassidy & Asher, 1992; Crick & Ladd, 1993), anxiety (Derakshan & Eysenck, 1998), anger (Crick & Dodge, 1994), and depression (Crick & Dodge, 1994) impact processing ability and, ultimately, social development. Crick and Dodge also suggest that situations that are negative and highly emotional may result in rapid, "without thinking" social problem solving. Numerous formal rating scales exist for measuring single constructs such as anxiety and depression and may be useful in determining the emotional state of the child as well as rating scales that consider multiple constructs. (Additional information about the assessment and treatment of depression, anxiety, and attentional disorders can be found in Chapter 3. In Chapter 15, Cushman amplifies the discussion of attentional difficulties and offers suggestions for understanding and intervening on behalf of children who struggle with attentional issues.)

Environmental Factors

Assessment of stress levels.   An indirect cost to children with learning or processing difficulties may be high levels of stress. It has long been recognized that stress can inhibit learning. Rubenzer (1996) states that,

> School-related stress is the most prevalent, untreated cause of academic failure in our schools. It is believed to afflict an alarming 6 to 10 million children a year. In a classroom of 25 students, between one and three students are at high risk for developing stress-related problems which would probably interfere with learning . . ." (p. 1).

Stress has been defined as "the physiological and emotional reaction to psychological events" (Rubenzer, 1996, p. 1). Although all people experience stress as an ongoing part of their lives, children with learning and social disorders have an increased risk of experiencing overwhelming levels of stress. Insensitivity of others, low self-esteem, dependency on special education teachers, labels, and difficulty using language to express their needs all contribute to heightened levels of stress among this group of individuals (Rubenzer, 1996). Stress, then, is both a response to a disability and can heighten or increase the effects of the disability. In an effort to escape from an anxiety-producing task a child may respond impulsively, thereby further diminishing his or her performance. Some of the behaviors that may be seen in school that signal high levels of stress include changes in effort in school, irritability, impulsive responding, emotional outbursts, distractibility, frequent attentional shifts, somatic symptoms, such as headaches or stomachaches, sleeping problems, difficulty concentrating, being accident prone, eating problems, and depression.

Assessment of social status.   Social status has been found to be an important factor in a child's social development (Gross, 1997; Swanson & Malone, 1992). In fact, Crick and Dodge (1994) state:

> peer status has the most potential for influencing a child's future social information processing (and subsequent social adjustment). The reason is that peer status (i.e., liking or disliking for the child) is often reflected in the peer's behavior toward the child (e.g., rejection, acceptance, annoyance, or approval). Thus perceived peer disapproval (the interpretation of the peer response) may lead to decreases in feelings of social competence (p. 86).

Social status also was found to be negatively affected among children with learning problems (Moisan, 1998), placing these children at risk for social difficulties.

Assessing a child's social status, then, may offer useful information when developing interventions. There are a number of techniques that may be useful in assessing social status: sociometric devices, teacher ranking systems, behavior-rating scales, interviews, and observation checklists or codes.

Experience with social situations.   Although many researchers have indicated that intact social processing leads to better social adjustment (Crick & Dodge, 1994), others have suggested that a reciprocal effect with social adjustment, and the resulting social experiences, enhances social cognitions or processing (Coie, 1990). Crick and Dodge suggest that the experiences that children have impact what they understand about themselves and others, and indicate that social experience can affect self-concept, the understanding of cause–effect relationships, and the establishment of self-perceptions. Some of the assessment questions that might be considered in assessing the child's social experience base include: What information does this child have about social outcomes of behavior, awareness of available goals, causes of social events, and information about what behavior is seen as "good" or "bad" behavior by others? What is the speed with which the child can respond to a social situation? Is the child able to detect subtle but important social cues such as facial changes, social distances, and gestures?

Information-Processing Variables

Language abilities.   Level of language competence appears to be related to the development of social knowledge and performance. Assessing the integrity of the child's language abilities, then, is one area to consider before developing interventions.

Language consists of several subskill areas: speech articulation and speech production, receptive language, expressive language, and social or pragmatic language. The child must be able to articulate the sounds of language clearly. This skill requires the child to coordinate the oral–motor movements necessary to produce and combine speech sounds to form syllables and words. The child also must be able to receive language such that he or she can follow verbal directions, develop an adequate vocabulary, and gather information about the world efficiently and accurately. Receptive language exists in both oral and written (i.e., reading) forms. The child also must be able to put together words to formulate thoughts that then are spoken or written. This requires the efficient and accurate retrieval of specific words on demand, the ability to name items, as well as the ability to apply rules of syntax (grammar), morphology (changes in word beginnings and endings), and semantics (word meaning). Language provides the means for placing information into memory in efficient ways, linked to conceptual "headings" that allow for accurate, speedy retrieval.

Pragmatic language is language that is used in social situations and is functional in nature. It allows the child to make his or her own needs known, to express ideas that are personally important, to ask questions, to greet others, and to learn about how others feel or think. Language is adaptive in that the child can learn to apply language knowledge in a variety of everyday situations or change his or her language in similar but different circumstances (e.g., when talking with a peer rather than an adult).

Language allows the child to tell a story or converse with others about a variety of topics. Language provides a means for the individual to encode incoming social information, interpret these cues, and identify and evaluate possible social goals. Language is also the mediator for social problem solving.

Assessment of language often is conducted by a speech and language practitioner and may involve a number of formal evaluation measures. Observations by parents, teachers, or other individuals also may provide information about the integrity of the child's language systems. For example, does the child have difficulty naming objects, tend to "talk around a subject," or exchange words that share similar sounds or meaning?

Although the language discussed so far is verbal in nature, it is not the only kind of language. The understanding and interpretation of nonverbal language is crucial to the development of an adequate social information and knowledge base and, ultimately, to social performance. Siegel (1998) suggests that there are several similarities between verbal and nonverbal language that are relevant to the issue of assessment. Both types of language are organized systems that are essential for communication; both are learned; both involve receptive and expressive elements. Siegel also outlines a number of differences between verbal and nonverbal language. She describes verbal language as discrete, conscious, and able to be stopped at will, while much of nonverbal language is unconscious and not easily stopped on demand. Siegel points out that children who break nonverbal language rules almost always create a "negative emotional impact on the receiving person" (p. 1). Such negative interactions are costly to the child emotionally and socially.

Siegel suggests that nonverbal language is comprised of four components: facial expression, paralinguistic features (prosody), body movements, and gestures. In assessing nonverbal language, the child's rhythm—the rate of the child's walking, talking, or eating should be reviewed. The child's recognition and ability to follow the rules of personal space also is important. Siegel points out that the appropriate distance for personal space is up to 18 inches, 18 inches to 4 feet for interactive space, 4 to 12 feet for social space, and 12 feet or more for public space. The ability to engage and accept appropriate social touch, recognize facial expressions, gestures, or postures, and interpret the meaning behind a certain tone of voice are all areas that Siegel sees as important in the assessment of nonverbal language.

Memory.   Language skill and memory are intricately linked. Language deficits may cause significant problems as a child attempts to place new information in memory, integrate old information with new information, and organize information in long-term memory so that it can be retrieved on demand.

There are a number of behaviors that are frequently observed in an academic setting that may signal possible working memory problems. These include a high dependence on teacher and peer input when following directions (e.g., looking at peers to see what task they are beginning to do or failure to begin a task without direct contact with the teacher), repeating questions, blurting out answers, difficulty persisting in a task, completing the wrong task or ignoring certain aspects of a task (e.g., circling instead of underlining an answer), answering the wrong question, answering a question several seconds or minutes after it was asked, distractibility, careless errors, apparent impulsive responding, seeking frequent reassurance, passive learning, trouble organizing tasks, and responding at very concrete levels.

From a functional and behavioral assessment perspective (see Chapter 4), one might determine that a child engages in a problem behavior to obtain or avoid an outcome, such as failure, by not trying. If the child, however, suffers from deficits within the information-processing system, educators also must consider if the behaviors are attempts to compensate for or camouflage memory difficulties. If the latter is true, then interventions that help change the demands on memory are more apt to be effective than interventions designed to directly increase effort. Proceeding in this way may mean changing the way in which information is presented, increasing opportunities for practice, and shortening the amount of output requested at any given point.

As an example, consider the following. The child may hear the teacher's request to take out a specific book and complete specific questions but lose this information as he or she opens the desk to retrieve the book. A natural response by this individual might be to look or speak to another child in order to reclaim the information lost from memory. Particularly if the educator believes the function of the behavior is to avoid work, this method of coping with disappearing information is likely to annoy the teacher and result in an intervention (e.g., a verbal correction) that diminishes the child's spirit and does nothing to help child regain the information he or she needs to begin the task.

High levels of dependence and passive responding are both predictable outcomes for the child if the amount of effort the child puts into a task does not consistently (or perhaps ever!) result in a significantly improved product or when the child recognizes that his or her peers produce higher quality work with much less effort. It is not difficult to understand the potential costs to the child emotionally and socially as his or her sense of competence, worth, and personal power are chronically undermined.

An inability to move toward more abstract responding could be associated with problems in the working memory system as well. Abstractions require the simultaneous consideration of multiple aspects or rules associated with a concept or concepts. As the child has more and more experience with an idea, ultimately broader, less observable, understandings of the concept are acquired. If the child has difficulty holding enough consistent information such that he or she can make comparisons or contrast information, then moving to more abstract levels of thinking is difficult. Problems in understanding cause–effect relationships, identifying goals, and evaluating social goals and behaviors all depend on more complex social processes associated with abstract reasoning abilities (Bye & Jussim, 1993; Crick & Dodge, 1994).

Evidence of problems in the retrieval of information from long-term memory also may reflect difficulties at the integration or processing stage (i.e., working memory). The assumption here is that information that is "coded" incorrectly or poorly integrated with already existing information will be more difficult to retrieve from memory. Some of the behaviors that may signal problems in the organization of information in long-term memory include interchanging items or terms that are part of the same larger category without regard to their specific differences (e.g., confusing

Magellan and Columbus, or Edison and Franklin), interchanging terms that share phonological elements (e.g., the words *migrate* and *migraine*), word-finding problems, saying "I forgot" rather than "I don't know," and slow, laborious responding.

If information is not integrated effectively in memory, then retrieval will be less efficient and more energy-consuming. In a sense, what is happening to such children is somewhat analogous to the experience that people have when they go into a room to get something but, upon arriving, realize that they have forgotten what they had gone after. On retracing their steps, something triggers their memory and they can complete the task successfully. For the typical person this happens only occasionally and is annoying but not debilitating. For some children, however, it is a much more pervasive problem. They have difficulty taking in new information and holding it in memory accurately while processing it in some way (e.g., comparing the new information with other things they have learned, or executing multiple processes such as those required in writing). The child must, in a sense, "refire" memories repeatedly in order to accomplish a task.

A slow, systematic approach to tasks appears to be one strategy on which some individuals rely to aid in recall. Difficulties keeping certain memories "alive" while they process them seems to be an issue here and a slow, deliberate processing approach may allow them time to refind or reactivate information such that they ultimately can "capture" at least a part of the information they are seeking. They also appear to be attempting to attend to as many small details as they can. This may be helpful to them but also results in a higher likelihood of overwhelming their processing systems and losing sight of the "big picture." They may rely also on contextual information and feedback from those around them as they struggle to remember incoming information.

Problems in memory function clearly could interfere with the child's social information processing at all stages of Crick and Dodge's model. The encoding, interpreting, and retrieval of social experiences may be flawed. In fact, Crick and Dodge and others suggest that children with learning disabilities have been found to add details as they recalled certain social situations (Tur-Kaspa & Bryan, 1994). This could disrupt the association between cause and effect and make goal selection and evaluation flawed at best. Problems in memory may make it difficult for the child to develop accurate perceptions of his or her own social experiences and to understand the perspectives of others. Indeed, Weiss (1984) reports that children with learning problems have difficulty in perspective-taking and Oliva and LaGreca (1988) suggest that these children have difficulty developing goals and are poor problem solvers (Toro, Weissberg, Guare, & Liebenstein, 1990; Tur-Kaspa & Bryan, 1994).

A secondary outcome of memory deficits is the emotional cost to the child. A child with learning problems may possess lowered self-worth, expectations for failure, and lowered motivation. Children with learning problems often are more socially rejected and have a greater sense of inadequacy than their peers (Moisan, 1998; Swanson & Malone, 1992). Such experiences impact their social interrelationships. Some may withdraw, while others become more aggressive. Social status is affected in either case.

Formalized memory tests, observation of classroom behaviors, teacher and student checklists, and tests of cognitive functioning may provide valuable information about the integrity of the information-processing system. If children struggle in learning, whether the cause is primarily the result of deficits in information processing or interference from a negative emotional state, it is likely that memory is somehow being negatively impacted. Interventions, then, that reduce memory demands may help the child, whatever the source of the learning problems.

Physiological Variables

Stamina and persistence, attentional factors, and the integrity of sensory systems are three physiological variables that warrant evaluation. Each child varies in the level of stamina or persistence that he or she brings to a task (Bye & Jussim, 1993). Understanding the child's individual ability to sustain energy toward a given task would be relevant as one identifies possible interventions. Assessment of stamina and persistence could be completed using observational techniques and rating and interview scales. Medical assessments may be appropriate as well.

Bye and Jussim (1993) suggest that children with attentional deficits may miss important information that is essential in building social knowledge. These authors state:

> [S]ome social knowledge is explicitly taught, such as saying 'please' and 'thank you' and getting to school on time. However, much social knowledge is not explicitly taught and must be acquired through astute observation of others' behavior. Children with ADHD often have difficulty attending to the most important elements in the vast array of environmental stimuli. A child with untreated ADHD may miss feedback and subtle social information from models (p. 149).

These authors further suggest that many mental health problems experienced by children, such as depression, may interfere with the child's ability to adequately attend and should be considered as a possible source of inattention. (Other sources of inattention are described in some detail in Chapter 15).

Determining the child's ability to initiate and attend to relevant stimuli, then, is important as appropriate interventions are designed. There are a number of rating scales that measure attentional factors, and they can be used in conjunction with observational techniques and scales that measure specific mental health problems such as depression or anxiety (see Chapter 3).

Finally, the sensory integrity of each child must be considered. Children who have sensory losses, particularly in vision and hearing, are at risk for missing important social information. Although screening in these areas can be completed by school medical staff, more comprehensive assessments are typically done by vision and hearing specialists.

Developing Interventions

Appropriate, comprehensive, and ongoing assessment of children who demonstrate learning or social problems is essential in developing effective interventions. Although pharmacological interventions may be appropriate in some cases, these are not considered here. Most interventions outlined here are behavioral or cognitive in nature and may involve changes in the way instruction occurs, differences in how a teacher or other significant adult approaches the child, strategies for learning, or activities that may be included in counseling or other therapeutic settings. Interventions aimed at reducing the negative effects of personal, environmental, information-processing, and physiological deficits are outlined below.

Personal Factors

Interventions for improving self-efficacy, motivation, and persistence.   Given the importance of self-efficacy, motivation, and persistence to the process of social and emotional learning, interventions in this area need to be considered. The development of a child's sense of his or her own personal power and desire to seek and sustain energy toward a specific goal are related to the child's belief that he or she can actually succeed in any given situation. This belief is affected by the child's past experience and the skill the child actually possesses. At least four key factors, as they relate to intervention, should be considered: the establishment of opportunities for success, the encouragement of active participation on the part of the child, the provision of adequate structure, and effective, instructive communication.

It is critical that all children be provided with multiple, ongoing situations in which they can be successful both academically and socially. This means that coursework needs to be well within the ability levels of the child at any given point and that activities be broken down into small, manageable units with frequent verbal feedback provided. Goals need to be realistic and highly competitive situations should be avoided.

Children who experience multiple learning and social failures often become passive participants in their environment, further diminishing their learning. Interventions designed to increase the child's active role in day-to-day academic and social functioning are important. Well-designed cooperative learning activities, opportunities to tutor others, and learning methods for self-monitoring can increase the level of active involvement on the part of the student.

The provision of adequate structure also is important for the child who struggles in learning. A child who can predict adequately what will occur in the future has reduced levels of anxiety and is more likely to become actively engaged in the learning process. Rules and outcomes for breaking such rules need to be established jointly by the adult and the child and should be applied consistently. Such structure may take the form of well-designed activities in which the goal of the activity is clear and the methods for reaching the goal are understood by the child. Outlining the day's events and the order in which these events may occur is another method of providing structure for a child.

Finally, clear, effective communication with the child is essential. The messages that are given can encourage or defeat the child. Statements that separate behavior from the child (e.g., saying, "I don't like what you did" rather than "You are a bad boy"), use of frequent feedback, telling the child what to do rather than what not to do, and the use of pictorial displays or graphs for sharing information may all be helpful in communicating effectively with a child.

Interventions for building self-awareness. Self-awareness is a critical building block for the development of social knowledge and skill. Feedback plays a central role here, as it does in the promotion of self-efficacy, motivation, and persistence. Feedback can be received from others, from oneself, or from a situation. Information about one's strengths or weaknesses, for example, can help in building self-awareness. Learning to monitor one's own emotions, thoughts, or actions is also vital to self-awareness. Involvement in an activity such as therapeutic horseback riding can provide both physical (improvements in balance and body movements) and psychological benefits (improvements in one's sense of competence).

A second important area for building self-awareness is related to the knowledge of family and cultural factors that the child holds. Knowing about and understanding the family's history and cultural background can be important to the development of self-awareness. Developing cultural awareness throughout the year, having the child interview an "elder" member of the family, or developing a pictorial or anecdotal family tree may be useful interventions to consider.

Environmental Factors

Two environmental factors that impact social and personal development include the amount of stress the child experiences and his or her level of social status. Stress, while an unavoidable aspect of life, can interfere with social and personal learning. Both physical and cognitive methods for managing stress can be effective. Relaxation training, meditation, breathing exercises, physical exercise, and good nutrition may all help reduce the negative impact of stress. Cognitive interventions include teaching positive "self-talk," goal setting, how to define wants and needs, and time management.

A second environmental variable that may affect social and personal learning is that of social status. Research has suggested that a child's social and academic development impacts and is impacted by that child's perceived level of social status. Children who have difficulty remaining on-task often have low social status. Helping improve the child's ability to sustain task performance, then, is one important area to consider in designing interventions. It also has been suggested that teacher-directed instruction of social skills may be helpful in improving social problem solving and social status.

Information-Processing Factors

A third general area that should be targeted for intervention is that of information-processing skill and development. Language, memory abilities, and skills in encoding, interpreting, taking social action, and evaluating such action are all important areas for intervention. Skills in both academic and social areas are dependent on direct teaching and opportunities for practice.

There are many published language programs available and these typically are part of the services provided by speech and language therapists. Reading to the child, making talking fun and safe, responding to the child's intended message without correcting grammar or pronunciation, and modeling appropriate social messages, such as greeting, making requests for help, and sharing information, may be useful in improving and encouraging language development.

Walker, McConnell, Holmes, Todis, Walker, & Golden (1983) suggest a method for improving the encoding and interpretation of social information known as the ACCEPTS program. The steps in this program include defining the skill and including guided discussion of examples, modeling a skill being done correctly, modeling a skill being done incorrectly, reviewing and discussing the targeted skill, using and discussing a model of a second example of the skill, modeling a range of examples, combining the skill with hypothetical practice opportunities, modeling a skill again being done correctly (if needed), role-playing the skill, and getting an informal commitment from the student to try the new skill in a naturally occurring setting.

When the problem appears to be related to motivational issues (i.e., the child knows the skill but does not use it consistently), the use of Applied Behavior Analysis in developing appropriate and effective interventions may be helpful. If it appears that the child is having difficulty knowing when to apply a given social skill, it is essential to help the child learn to recognize the important social cues on which to base social action. Lavoie (1994) suggests an approach known as the "social autopsy." This involves helping the child analyze the situation in which he or she may have made a social error and discussing alternative methods for "fixing" the error. The technique involves immediate feedback, discussion of the action taken, and identifying reasons why the action may have had negative outcomes.

Finally, Bos and Vaughn (1994) suggest a strategy designed to aid the child in looking at problems and evaluating goals for behavior. The program teaches the child ways of identifying problems he or she may encounter in everyday social situations, methods of finding solutions among a number of alternatives, steps for evaluating possible solutions, and ways to engage in the solution selected.

Conclusion

The development of adequate social knowledge and skills is critical as children grow into effective, well-adjusted, productive adults. Not infrequently, practitioners are being asked to develop, monitor, and evaluate interventions in ways that are measurable by the courts, committees on special education, parents, and school personnel. Recognizing the areas of social knowledge that the child must possess and understanding the specific skills and subskills that are necessary for social competence is essential for all practitioners who work with children who struggle academically, socially, and behaviorally. Models and means of assessing these variables are improving, as are the methods for intervening in effective ways. Technological advances exist today that may serve to reduce the memory demands made on a child in the areas of reading and writing. In addition, technological programs that will act to cue children's behavior as they encounter certain social situations or experience certain levels of emotional response may be on the horizon. In any case, it is clear that the practitioner must address a broad range of personal, environmental, information-processing, and physical factors for intervention in order to be most effective in helping children improve their social and emotional functioning. Perhaps, most important of all, is the recognition that "blaming" a child for school failure or social misbehaviors does little to improve that child's performance. Increasing opportunities for successful academic and social experiences, making the child's world predictable and safe, reducing memory demands, providing direct social instruction, and building self-awareness and empathy among groups of children are effective in changing children's negative behaviors.

References

Arnold, N. (1996/1997). Learned helplessness and attribution for success and failure in LD students. *Their world.* New York: National Center for Learning Disabilities.

Bos, C. S., & Vaughn, S. (1994). *Strategies for teaching students with learning and behavior problems* (3rd ed.). Boston: Allyn and Bacon.

Bye, L., & Jussim, L. (1993). A proposed model for the acquisition of social knowledge and social competence. *Psychology in the Schools, 30,* 143–161.

Cassidy, J., & Asher, S. R. (1992). Loneliness and peer relations in young children. *Child Development, 63,* 350–365.

Coie, J. D. (1990). Toward a theory of peer rejection. In S. R. Asher & J. D. Coie (Eds.), *Peer rejection in childhood* (pp. 365–401). Cambridge, England: Cambridge University Press.

Crick, N. R., & Dodge, K. A. (1994). A review and reformulation of social information-processing mechanisms in children's social adjustment. *Psychological Bulletin, 115,* 74–101.

Crick, N. R. & Ladd, G. W. (1993). Children's perceptions of their own experiences: Attributions, loneliness, social anxiety, and social avoidance. *Developmental Psychology, 29,* 244–254.

Derakshan, N., & Eysenck, M. W. (1998). Working memory capacity in high trait-anxious and repressor groups. *Cognition and Emotion, 12,* 697–713.

Deshler, D. D., & Schumaker, J. B. (1993). Strategy mastery by at-risk students: Not a simple matter. *The Elementary School Journal, 94,* 153–165.

Gross, A. H. (1997). Defining the self as a learner for children with LD. *Their World.* New York: National Center for Learning Disabilities.

Lavoie, R. D. (1994). Learning disabilities and social skills with Richard Lavoie: Last one picked . . . first one picked on [Video and Teacher's Guide]. Available from PBS Video, 1320 Braddock Place, Alexandria, VA 22314–1698.

Moisan, T. A. (1998). Identification and remediation of social skills deficits in learning disabled children. Unpublished master's thesis, University of Chicago, Chicago, IL.

Oliva, A. H., & LaGreca, A. M. (1988). Children with learning disabilities: Social goals and strategies. *Journal of Learning Disabilities, 21,* 301–306.

Prater, M. A., Bruhl, S., & Serna, L. A. (1998). Acquiring social skills through cooperative learning and teacher-directed instruction. *Remedial and Special Education, 19,* 160–172.

Rubenzer, R. L. (1996). Stress management for the learning disabled. *ERIC Digest #452.* Reston, VA: ERIC Clearinghouse on Handicapped and Gifted Children.

Schwab Foundation for Learning. (1996). *Building self-esteem and dealing with disappointments at school.* [On-line]. Available: *www.schwableaarning.org/html/resource/resources*

Siegel, A. (1998). Learning the language of relationships. *Newbriefs:* Learning Disabilities Association of America.

Smith, J. O. (Fall, 1995). *Behavior management: Getting to the bottom of social skills deficits.* Paper presented at the LD Forum-Council for Learning Disabilities. Purdue University-Calumet, Hammond, IN.

Swanson, H. L., & Malone, S. (1992). Social skills and learning disabilities: A meta-analysis of the literature. *School Psychology Review, 21,* 427–443.

Toro, P. A., Weissberg, R. P., Guare, J., & Liebenstein, N. L. (1990). A comparison of children with and without learning disabilities on social problem-solving skills, school behavior, and family background. *Journal of Learning Disabilities, 23,* 115–120.

Tur-Kaspa, H., & Bryan, T. (1994). Social information processing of students with learning disabilities. *Journal of Learning Disabilities Research and Practice, 9,* 12–23.

Walker, H. M., McConnell, S., Holmes, D., Todis, B., Walker, J., & Golden, N. (1983). *The Walker social skills curriculum: The ACCEPTS program.* Austin, TX: PRO-ED.

Weiss, E. (1984). Learning disabled children's understanding of social interactions of peers. *Journal of Learning Disabilities, 17,* 612–615.

15

Understanding and Assisting Children and Adolescents with Attentional Difficulties

Thomas P. Cushman

Attention-deficit hyperactivity disorder (ADHD), as a source of inattention, has become the most commonly diagnosed and most studied of the childhood disorders (Reid, Vasa, Maag, & Wright, 1994). In 1989, approximately 41% of all visits to physicians when mental health was the concern were for reasons of attentional problems, and that figure rose to almost 60% by 1996 (Hoagwood, Kelleher, Feil, & Comer, 2000). Severe problems of attention are reported to be as high as 44% of children who receive special education services, yet only half of those students received targeted interventions for their attentional problems (Bussing, Zima, Perwien, Belin, & Widowski, 1998). Only half of the children designated as ADHD received services in 1995, yet public schools spent over $3 billion in attempts to help children with attentional problems (National Institutes of Health [NIH], 1998).

It is likely that there are multiple sources of inattention (Biederman et al., 1995; Cantwell, 1996; Cushman & Johnson, 2000; Jensen, 1998; Jensen et al., 1997). Attentional problems are associated with increased risks for low academic achievement, grade-level retention, poor peer and family relations, conduct problems, and early experimentation with alcohol or drugs (Barkley, 1997; Elia, Ambrosini, & Rapoport, 1999). Zentall (1993) reported that more than 80% of eleven-year-old children classified as ADHD were found to be at least two years behind in reading, spelling, math, or written language. Task orientation has been found to be important in the success of very young children as early as kindergarten (Schoen & Nagle, 1994).

As noted in Chapter 3, problems with inattention occur in as many as 5% of children, perhaps more (Cantwell, 1996), with the highest rates of incidence observed among males. Males are diagnosed with ADHD up to nine times as often as females in clinical populations (Barkley, 1998; Cantwell, 1996), and up to four times as often in epidemiological studies. Cantwell suggests that males are referred

261

more commonly than girls because boys with the disorder tend to be more aggressive and impulsive, whereas girls tend to be inattentive. Although Barkley (1998) speculates that the reason for the increased incidence among males is due to their genetic vulnerability, Pollack (1998) suggests that the higher incidence of attentional problems in males may be related to our cultural expectations and the socialization process. Barkley (1990) points out, however, that the true rates of incidence cannot be determined accurately because the disorder cannot be strictly defined or precisely measured.

Definitions

The Diagnostic and Statistical Manual of Mental Disorders: Fourth Edition (*DSM-IV*; (American Psychiatric Association, 1994) defines attention-deficit hyperactivity disorder as "a persistent pattern of inattention and/or hyperactivity–impulsivity that is more frequent and severe than is typically observed in individuals at a comparable level of development" (p. 78). Three subtypes of ADHD are conceptualized in the *DSM-IV*: combined type, predominantly inattentive type, and predominantly hyperactive–impulsive type. Each of the subtypes comes with a set of criteria such as "often fails to give close attention to details" or "makes careless mistakes in schoolwork, work or other activities" (p. 83), and "often does not seem to listen when spoken to directly" (p. 84). Criteria for ADHD also include the notion that some symptoms appear before the age of seven, that some degree of impairment has been identified in at least two settings, and that there is evidence of impairment in social, academic, or occupational performance.

Cantwell (1996) states that there is a general consensus that the core symptoms of ADHD consist of an inattention domain and a hyperactivity domain. Sabatino and Vance (1994) found that hyperactive and impulsive children are more likely to have serious conduct disorders, whereas children with attention deficits are more likely to display anxiety, depression, and shyness. Lahey and Carlson (1991) conclude, by way of a review of factor-analytic studies, that a distinct disorder of ADD without hyperactivity does exist, but little is known about essential characteristics and treatment strategies for this subtype of ADD. Lahey and Carlson also conclude that those of the "inattentive type" have fewer conduct problems, are more socially withdrawn, more likely to be depressed or anxious, and tend to be less rejected by their peers than children with the predominantly hyperactive–impulsive type. As is evident from the foregoing, there continues to be considerable controversy and lack of clarity around the definition of ADHD and related terminology.

Although there are professional differences of opinion, Barkley (1990) and Jensen (2000) agree that there is a problem in establishing the cutoff point to determine that a particular ADHD symptom is developmentally inappropriate. Jensen states that ". . . it remains unclear whether ADHD is best conceptualized as the far end of a normal continuum (such as reflecting a more extreme manifestation of a set of temperamental characteristics) or whether it reflects a qualitatively different behavioral syndrome" (p. 195). Sabatino and Vance (1994) observe that the symptoms of

ADHD are subjective, and even contradictory at times. Any system of nomenclature (labeling) must have a common set of characteristics in order to be useful. In a review of 39 sources, Goodman and Poillion (1992) found 69 characteristics as descriptive of ADD and there was little agreement among the researchers as to what were the key characteristics. Goodman and Poillion also conclude that many of the characteristics described were subjective in nature. They go on to state that "studies examining attentional factors failed to find significant differences between children with and without ADD" (p. 51), and conclude by questioning the validity and reliability of the ADD diagnosis. Although it was stated at the NIH Consensus Conference (NIH, 1998) that further research is needed in order to validate the disorder, the group concluded that ADHD is a valid diagnosis that defines a maladaptive cluster of characteristics.

Etiology

There is general agreement that the etiology of ADHD remains unknown (Barkley, 1998; Goodman & Poillion, 1992), and it is unlikely that a single etiological factor can account for the variety of symptoms associated with ADHD (Cantwell, 1996). Goodman and Poillion (1992) reviewed 25 papers on the etiology of ADHD and found 38 possible causes for the disorder. "Little agreement was found among authors regarding the numerous and diverse causes addressed, and little empirical validation was found to support any of the causes" (p. 51).

Biological Factors

Shelton and Barkley (1999) and Barkley (1998) have attempted to determine an etiology for ADHD. They state that ADHD is likely to have a genetic or biological cause, and report studies that suggest a decreased cerebral blood flow, frontal lobe deficits on neurological tests (see also Chapter 6), and various psychophysiological findings that suggest the role of some central nervous system mechanism. Further attempts to support a genetic or biological etiology for ADD were made by Zametkin et al. (1990). These authors completed a study of adults with ADD who had an ADD child, using positron emission tomography (PET). The ADD adults appeared to have lower rates of cerebral glucose metabolism than adults without ADD, but the authors cautioned readers about the study's lack of reproducibility and possible subjective interpretation by the radiologist.

Jensen (2000) states that the biological explanation is consistent with neuropsychological, electrophysiological, and neuroimaging studies that show "fairly consistent differences in prefrontal cortical, parietal, and basal ganglia functioning associated with ADHD . . ." (p. 195). Jensen acknowledges, however, that we know little about the etiology of ADHD and that the biological explanation may be insufficient, ". . . given the number of children who show significant remission (20–40%) over the course of development" (p. 195). Thus, the call by NIMH (1998) for more research in this area appears more than warranted.

Comorbid Conditions

The American Association of Child and Adolescent Psychiatry (AACAP; 1997) states that a number of disorders or comorbid conditions could be mistaken for ADHD, and suggests that a number of inattentive children may be struggling with anxiety, realistic fears, depression, or the results of abuse or neglect. The AACAP also notes that children with symptoms often associated with ADHD simply may be at the higher end of the normal range of activity or that such children may be of a temperament that is a mismatch for their parents.

According to Perrin and Last (1996), ADHD and anxiety may be related etiologically and they share common risk factors. As evidence, they indicate that roughly one third of ADHD children have a history of anxiety disorder and that ADHD with comorbid anxiety presents a different clinical profile than ADHD alone. Anxious ADHD children tend to be less impulsive, have fewer conduct problems, and tend to do more poorly on memory tasks than ADHD children without comorbid anxiety. Jensen, Martin, and Cantwell (1997) observe that anxiety is so common among children classified as ADHD that two new subclassifications should be delineated: anxious and aggressive subtypes. The internalizing disorders of depression and anxiety are almost as common among ADHD children as the externalizing disorders. Anxiety and depression are found in between one third and one half of children diagnosed with ADHD (Pfiffner et al., 1999), supporting the conclusion of Angold and Costello (1993) that there are significant associations between ADD and depression.

Conduct disorders and oppositional defiant disorders, which are considered externalizing disorders, are comorbid with ADHD in about half of all children identified as ADHD (Pfiffner et al., 1999). When externalizing disorders are comorbid with ADHD, the child or adolescent is more likely to be in a context of severe family conflict and is at greater risk for school failure and delinquency than children or adolescents without comorbid externalizing disorders.

Other disorders that are commonly associated with ADHD include language and communication disorders, chronic tics, and Tourette's Syndrome (Cantwell, 1996). Cantwell concludes that "assessment and treatment of the comorbid disorder is often equally as important as assessing and treating the ADD symptomatology" (p. 981), and that is especially the case given that so little is known about the relationship between the comorbid disorders and the symptoms of inattentiveness and hyperactivity (NIH, 1998). The comorbid disorders may be the source of the inattentiveness, or they may be the result of the symptoms of the disorder or there may be some more complex relationship between the ADHD symptoms and the comorbid conditions yet to be determined.

Environmental Factors

Cantwell, referring to a study by Goodman and Stevenson (1989), states that genetic factors have been implicated in the transmission of ADHD for 25 years, pointing to relatively high concordance rates (51%) in monozygotic twins and significant concordance rates (33%) among dizygotic twins. On the other hand, Biederman et al. (1995) say that "many disorders run in families because of environmental—not genetic—factors" (p. 1495). The authors conclude that there is a clinically meaningful relationship between adversity in the family environment and ADHD. The specific risk factors include chronic conflict, decreased family cohesion, and exposure to parental psychopathology. Biederman et al. stress the importance of developing interventions that can reduce such adverse factors within a family system.

For some children, ADHD symptoms may well represent adaptive responses to environmental contexts (Jensen et al., 1997). For example, increased motor activity can be useful in stimulating the development of muscles and motor skills. Jensen et al. point out that well-focused attention actually can be quite maladaptive in either highly threatening or highly novel contexts because something important can be missed. If a child is in a threatening environment early in life, he or she may adapt by constantly scanning the environment for sources of potential threat. Later in life, in school, the child may be asked to sit attentively and screen out contextual stimulation while remaining attentive to the task at hand. The same authors further indicate that impulsivity can be highly adaptive in a hostile environment where there is little time to think about a response. In such situations, a delayed response could be catastrophic.

Jensen (2000) expresses concern that ADHD has been reified as a "thing" or "true entity" rather than as a working hypothesis. In the absence of a known etiology (Cantwell, 1996; Carey, 1999b; Goodman & Poillion, 1992; Jensen, 2000; NIH, 1998), the relative lack of agreement regarding the descriptive characteristics of ADHD (Goodman & Poillion, 1992; Sabatino & Vance, 1994) or knowledge of the relationship between ADHD and comorbid disorders (Manassis, Tannock, & Barbosa, 2000; NIH, 1998), the process of identifying children who need help for attentional problems runs the risk of being subjective and represents a special challenge. Assessment for intervention becomes critical because the current state of affairs suggests that attentional problems are related to, associated with, or may even stem from a variety of sources. At a minimum, sources of inattentiveness likely include temperament characteristics (Carey, 1999a; Jensen, 2000), anxiety (Jensen et al., 1997; Manassis et al., 2000; Passarallo, Hintze, Owen, & Gable, 1999; Perrin & Last, 1996; Pfiffner et al., 1999; Taghavi, Neshat-Doost, Morodi, Yule, & Dalgleish, 1999), trauma (Ford et al., 1999; Jensen, 1998), depression (AACAP, 1997; Angold & Costello, 1993; Cotugnol, 1993; Pfiffner et al., 1999), abuse or neglect (AACAP, 1997), adversity in the family (Biederman et al.,1995; Pfiffner et al., 1999), adaptive responding to certain contextual demands (Jensen et al., 1997), and biological or genetic sources (Barkley, 1998; NIH, 1998). A comprehensive assessment process that identifies any of the myriad of possibilities is the first step toward developing a helpful and meaningful set of interventions to serve the child or adolescent and his or her family.

Assessment

As with most, if not all psychological conditions, there is no test or set of tests that can be used to make a definitive diagnosis of ADHD (AACA, 1997; Barkley, 1990; Cantwell, 1996). It is a clinical decision and a variety of assessment procedures may be used to facilitate the process of making that judgment. Assessment of ADHD typically means that the practitioner assesses the degree of symptomatology including inattentiveness, hyperactivity, or both. To be successful in developing effective interventions, one must also work to determine the possible sources of the inattentiveness or hyperactivity and any related comorbid conditions as treatment outcomes are more favorable when these procedures are followed (Landau & Burchman, 1995). For example, in the common case, in which ADHD and depression are both present, interventions must be developed to address the problems associated with inattentiveness and with the depressed affect.

Functional Behavioral Assessment

Landau and Burchman (1995) suggest that school-based assessments of children with attention problems need not use diagnostic criteria for ADHD. They suggest, instead, that the objective of the assessment process is to determine the extent to which attentional problems interfere with the child's academic, affective, and social development so that specific interventions can be developed in the context of a problem-solving process. Similarly, McDougal, in Chapter 4, points out that most behaviors have a function or serve a particular purpose for the child or adolescent. The core components of functional assessment are to clearly and operationally define the target behavior, identify the variables in the environment that sustain or discourage the target behavior, identify the purpose or function of the behavior, and identify the child's strengths to be used in developing interventions. By identifying the function or reason for inattentive behavior, and by identifying the contingencies that maintain it, or environmental conditions that play a role in sustaining the inattentive behavior, interventions can be tailored to the child. Assessment and intervention become individualized processes of problem solving that minimize the need to label and increase the probability of effective outcomes (Dawson, 1995; Landau & Burchman, 1995).

Parent Interview

The AACAP (1997) refers to the parent interview as the core of the assessment process in determining the source or sources of attentional problems. The interview should include full developmental and medical histories, family history, psychosocial history and a history, of the attentional problems and associated outcomes of concern (Cantwell, 1996). The symptoms of attentional problems, as described by the parent or primary caregiver, are viewed as "diagnostic" of ADHD only if they exceed what would be expected of a child at that particular developmental stage (Cantwell, 1996). Schweibert, Sealander, and Tollerud (1995) and McKinney, Montague, and Hocutt (1993) refer to a number of structured interviews that can be used to collect information regarding attentional and related problems.

Child Interview

Cantwell (1996) suggests that a developmentally appropriate interview be conducted with the child or adolescent in order to obtain his or her perspective on the symptoms and the impact of those symptoms. The AACAP suggests that even standardized interviews with children are less useful in assessment of ADHD than interviews of primary caregivers, but that they can be useful in determining related or comorbid conditions or in determining contingencies that may be involved in sustaining the behavior. The interview also can provide information regarding the child's interests and strengths to be used to develop interventions. As part of the interview process with children, structured checklists and questionnaires can be used in order to obtain diverse information to further determine what related or comorbid conditions might be at play or to help give information on the purpose or function of the inattentiveness. For example, the *Piers-Harris Children's Self-Concept Scale* (Piers, 1996) has subscales that provide information related to both internalizing and externalizing problems or disorders. Other scales can be given on a follow-up basis such as the *Revised Children's Manifest Anxiety Scale* (Reynolds & Richmond, 1994) or the *Children's Depression Inventory* (Kovacs, 1992) in order to gain information relevant to comorbid conditions or function of behaviors before developing intervention strategies.

Behavior Rating Scales

When used with an appropriate degree of caution, behavior rating scales can provide a good deal of useful information efficiently (Goldman, Genel, Bezman, & Slanetz, 1998; McKinney et al., 1993). Broad-based behavioral scales, such as the home and school versions of the *Behavior Evaluation Scales-2* (McCarney, 1994), can help determine the potential sources of inattention or comorbid disorders that, as noted earlier, are important in developing appropriate interventions (Landau & Burchman, 1995). Other behavior rating scales that are commonly used include the *Child Behavior Checklist* (Achenbach, 1991) and the ADD-H: *Comprehensive Teacher Rating Scale* (ACTeRs; Ullman, Sleator, & Sprague, 1985).

Barkley (1990) provides information summarizing the psychometric properties of a number of scales, and Dykman, Raney, and Ackerman (1993) discuss over 40 rating scales that have been used in the assessment of attentional problems. Although behavior rating scales are helpful in the assessment process, one must proceed with some degree of caution because they are vulnerable to rater bias. For example, Abikoff, Courtney, Pelham, and Koplewicz (1993) found that children who defy the wishes of their teacher are more likely to be rated as hyperactive or inattentive, regardless of the level of inattention as determined by trained observers. Reid and Maag (1994) express concern that, because behavior rating scales have the appearance of being objective, practitioners can be misled and draw conclusions prematurely. Again, Reid and Maag stress the need for a broad-based assessment process so that the child's academic progress is monitored, too, and the *Academic Performance Scale* (DuPaul, Rapport, & Perriello, 1991) is suggested for this use.

Observations

In order to assist clinical decision making regarding the developmental appropriateness of a child's attentiveness and activity level, observations of the child in several contexts is suggested (AACAP, 1997). Observations across contexts also can provide information on environmental conditions and antecedent/consequent conditions that may sustain the behavior. Observations can give information regarding the purpose of the behavior as well. Structured systems of observation have also been developed for use in the classroom, playground, and lunchroom (Gadow, Sprafkin, & Nolan, 1996).

Continuous Performance Tests

Continuous performance tests (CPTs) are computer-based, gamelike tasks that require a child to sustain attention and also to inhibit responses (Gordon & Mettleman, 1988). Gordon and Mettleman report that their system has good reliability and they provide extensive normative information. Although children diagnosed with ADHD have been found to have significantly more difficulty with CPTs than those without attention problems (Losier, McGrath, & Klein, 1996), the correspondence between impulsive errors on CPTs and impulsive behavior has not been established (Abikoff & Klein, 1992), and there is a general consensus that continuous performance tests are not diagnostic of attention problems or ADHD (DuPaul, Anastopoulos, Shelton, Guevremont, & Metivia, 1992; Goldman et al., 1998).

Medical Evaluation

A complete medical evaluation is an important part of the assessment process in order to screen for any health or neurological problems that may cause or exacerbate the problems of inattention (Goldman et al., 1998). AACAP (1997) reports that the data are insufficient to support the usefulness of electroencephalograms or neuroimaging studies in the assessment of ADHD. However, such tools appear to have considerable promise for research purposes and possible future assessment applications.

Pychoeducational Assessment

Because the incidence of learning and academic problems among those with attentional problems ranges from 10 to 25% (Richters et al., 1995), intellectual and standardized achievement tests need to be provided for children with attentional problems (Goldman et al., 1998). A comprehensive process of assessment should include a comprehensive interview with the child's or adolescent's primary caregiver, an interview with the child or adolescent, behavior rating scales that are both broad-based and more specific to attentional issues, observations of the child or adolescent across several contexts, a medical evaluation, and an assessment of academic performance and cognitive functioning. The multimodal assessment can enhance the likelihood of determining the level of inattentiveness, possible information about the function of the child's behavior, and, perhaps, the source or sources of the symptoms as well as related comorbid conditions, so that individualized interventions can be developed to serve that specific child's needs.

Interventions

Use of Stimulants

When children's and adolescent's attentional problems are determined to be due to ADHD, stimulant medication has been the first line of intervention. The use of stimulants has been encouraged by numerous studies that indicate that the symptoms of restlessness and inattentiveness are reduced, at least in the short term (Angold, Erkanli, Egger, & Costello, 2000; Elia et al., 1999; Forness & Kavale, 1988). Approximately 90% of children diagnosed with ADHD receive methylphenidate (LeFever, Dawson & Morrow, 1999; Wolraich et al., 1990), while others receive dextroamphetamine or pemoline (Elia et al., 1999). Methylphenidate and dextroamphetamine are class II (controlled) substances (Elia et al., 1999), and, consequently, vulnerable to improper use and addiction (Sweeney, Forness, Kavale, & Levitt, 1997).

LeFever, Dawson, and Morrow (1999) agree that the short-term benefits of stimulant medications have been well studied, but noted that there remains a dearth of evidence demonstrating long-term benefits on school achievement, peer relationships, or problem behavior in adolescents. They also indicate that the unexplained racial and socioeconomic differences in ADHD treatment and the steady rise in the use of stimulants have become important public health issues. In a recent study, it was found that the majority of those receiving methylphenidate did not meet the criteria for being designated as ADHD, and it was concluded that, in the community studied, medication was being used in a manner that is inconsistent with diagnostic guidelines (Angold et al., 2000).

Pemoline is a psychostimulant that is not a class II drug and has low abuse potential. As such, it has been prescribed for children or adolescents at risk for substance abuse problems (Riggs, Laetitia, Mikulich, Whitmore, & Crowley, 1996). However, pemoline causes toxic liver problems in about 2% of those who ingest it and the problems are sometimes fatal or require liver transplantation (Elia, Ambrosini, & Rapoport, 1999). Consequently, methylphenidate and dextroamphetamine are often referred to as the drugs of choice because of their well-documented effectiveness in reducing symptoms of inattention, at least in the short term, without the potential hazards associated with pemoline. Still, all psychostimulants have side effects. Common side effects of psychostimulants include insomnia, decreased appetite, gastrointestinal pain, irritability, and an increase in heart rate and blood pressure (Elia et al., 1999; Sweeney et al., 1997). Early weight loss is a side effect of stimulants, but the long-term effect on weight is reported as being minimal (Elia et al., 1999).

Although short-term behavior changes with the use of psychostimulants are well documented, the effects on classroom performance and academic skill development have been mixed. Forness et al. (1992) report slight adverse effects of methylphenidate on reading measures, yet Elia et al. (1999) report some improvements in academic performance. Sweeney et al. (1997) question whether the decreases in classroom performance among some children treated with stimulants are worth the relative gains made in behavior. Forness et al. conclude that one should proceed very cautiously with methylphenidate if the goal is to enhance basic academic skills or acquisition of new material. They go on to state that children's response to the stimulants is variable and outcomes depend on what is measured. For example, the effects of methylphenidate tend to be stronger for measures of behavioral outcomes than for measures of academic performance (Lloyd, Forness, & Kavale, 1998).

Behavioral Interventions

The second most commonly employed type of intervention for children with attentional problems is behavioral intervention (Cantwell, 1996). Behavioral interventions include antecedent and consequent manipulations (Gardill, DuPaul, & Kyle, 1996). Antecedent manipulations are changes made to the learning environment in order to enhance attention or reduce behavior problems before they begin. Gardill et al. suggest that classroom structure be established by providing students with a schedule and by posting rules so that expectations are clear. Seating students in close proximity to the teacher has been demonstrated to enhance attentiveness, and academic tasks should be brief and be followed up with immediate feedback. Short verbal cues may need to be given on a regular basis and it can help to have someone in the class repeat directions to the group. Peer tutoring also has been demonstrated to increase the time on-task of ADHD children.

Consequent manipulations include teacher feedback, reinforcement, and response cost systems. Pfiffner and Barkley (1990) found that feedback regarding behavior is most constructive when delivered near the onset of the target behavior and when it is firm, brief, and consistent. Frequent positive feedback (positive reinforcement) immediately following the desired behavior has been demonstrated to reduce the targeted behavior problems (Martens & Kelly, 1993) and response cost procedures and the use of tangible reinforcements have been found to be effective in reducing disruptive behavior even in preschool children (McGoey & DuPaul, 2000).

Incentive systems should be developed with the child or adolescent being a full partner in the process so that she or he can give input regarding target behaviors, help in setting realistic goals, and provide feedback on the most appealing reinforcers (Dawson, 1995). In addition, if the system needs to be revised, Dawson points out that the student can provide valuable insights. When built into the development and implementation of the incentive system, the student learns valuable skills in task analysis, goal setting, self-monitoring, and self-evaluation, according to Dawson, as well as lessons in collaboration.

It is important to determine the child or adolescent's positive, prosocial, and adaptive behaviors so that such strengths can be used to develop interventions. For example, if an inattentive child is a strong reader and focuses well in that particular context, free reading time could be used to positively reinforce appropriate behavior.

Because immediate feedback is important in working with inattentive children, tokens or points, which provide the child with information about his or her performance, can be used when the child engages in the appropriate behavior. The tokens or points accumulate and the child can turn them in when the goal is reached, in order to receive the reinforcement. A response cost system is when tokens or points are withdrawn for targeted, inappropriate behavior.

Cognitive behavioral interventions include self-monitoring, self-instructional strategies, and self-evaluation. Miranda and Presentacion (2000) used the "Stop and Think" program developed by Kendall, Padever, and Zupan (1980), which includes the use of self-instruction, self-monitoring, problem solving, and the use of contingent reinforcers to enhance behavioral outcomes. They concluded that positive effects were demonstrated on the symptoms of inattentiveness and hyperactivity. Just as importantly, however, school problems and antisocial behaviors were reduced, even in the population of aggressive children. Dawson (1995) points out that one downside to cognitive behavioral interventions is that they can be labor-intensive to implement.

Parent Involvement

Parent training for families with a child who has been designated as ADHD is often highly effective (AACAP, 1997; Cantwell, 1996; Diller, 1998). Parents can make significant gains in working with their children by learning to give clear instructions and to use contingency management techniques.

Home–school communication systems are useful because they enable teachers and parents to collaborate and it increases the number of reinforcers that are available to the child because parents can provide particularly meaningful reinforcers (Dawson, 1995). Such a system should specify target behaviors and a simple rating scale can be developed in order to indicate the child's degree of success in meeting the mutually developed goals. A list of reinforcers should be developed that the child can receive at home and, at the end of the school day, the student and teacher review the behavior and the report is sent home with the child, to the parents (Dawson, 1995).

Family conflict and parental psychopathology are two adverse conditions that have been associated with an increased risk of attentional problems or ADHD (Biederman et al., 1995; Carlson, Jacobvitz, & Stroufe, 1995). When such conditions are revealed in the assessment process, the practitioner can suggest parent or family consultation with qualified professionals (see Chapter 10 for information on working with families).

Certainly, comparisons of different interventions must be viewed with caution due to methodological problems inherent in such studies (Whalen & Henker, 1991). Lloyd et al. (1998), however, found formative evaluation (curriculum-based measurement), cognitive–behavioral strategies, direct academic instruction, and mnemonic training to be among the most effective interventions in classroom settings, and all were found to be stronger in their effects than the use of psychostimulants.

The research in the treatment of attentional problems generally has not taken into account comorbid conditions or etiological sources of inattention (Jensen, Martin, & Cantwell, 1997), yet treatment outcomes would be enhanced by connecting interventions to the source or sources of inattentiveness and by addressing the comorbid conditions (Cantwell, 1996). Outcomes would be enhanced when the function of the behavior is addressed and changes are made in the contingencies and environment that have been determined to play a role in sustaining the inattentive behavior.

Integrative Perspectives: A Call for Research

Meditation and Relaxation Training

Garber, Garber, and Spizman (1996) state that the symptoms of ADHD can be reduced by training children and adolescents in the use of progressive muscle relaxation training and that problems associated with both externalizing (aggression) and internalizing (mood) disorders also can be reduced by such training. Gant (1999) refers to attending behavior as a learnable skill and suggests that attention can be enhanced by learning skills such as meditation. By inducing the relaxation response through relaxation training or meditation, oxygen consumption, heart and respiratory rate, and blood pressure are all decreased (Benson, 1996). Meditation and relaxation training appear to have the potential to help children learn to focus and to concurrently address the common comorbid condition of anxiety. When anxious, scanning behavior increases and children become alert to everything that is happening around them because such responsiveness is highly adaptive in threatening contexts (Hannaford, 1995; Jensen et al., 1997). Chronic and severe stress in infancy and early childhood seem to be particularly disabling. When stress is high, the stress hormones and neurochemical transmitters prepare the child to respond in an impulsive and action-oriented manner and to scan the environment for sources of threat (Jensen, 1998; Jensen et al., 1997). Meanwhile, unused neural connections important for academic learning may be pruned away (Jensen, 1998; Kotulak, 1997), and the child may not be ready for the calm and settled approach usually required of children at school.

Greenberg and Deckro (1998), of the Mind/Body Medical Institute at Harvard, have developed an education initiative aimed specifically at helping children and adolescents in educational contexts. The primary objective of the training they provide is to help students and teachers to develop skills designed to decrease the physical, emotional, and behavioral outcomes of anxiety by eliciting the relaxation response through simple meditative exercises. There has been a dearth of empirical research in this area but one study (Kratter & Hogan, 1982) asked children to focus on a sound for just a few minutes, each day, and their attentiveness improved. A good deal of research, however, is needed.

Temperament

Temperament researchers agree that individual differences in behavioral tendencies can be identified; they are present very early in life and they tend to be stable over time and across variable situations (Martin, 1994). The temperament characteristics most related to school achievement include activity level, distractibility, and task persistence. Those children who are high in activity level and distractibility and low in task persistence "by nature," tend to be seen as having an attention deficit in the context of school (Carey, 1998; Martin, 1994). Temperament predispositions toward high levels of activity and distractibility can make a child less responsive to positive reinforcers or other environmental contingencies (Martin, 1994) and, consequently, the child may need contextual adaptations in school such as a fast moving instructional pace, opportunities to move about, frequent breaks, and increased levels of novelty. Temperament information can be gathered in interviews with primary caregivers and there are several instruments available (Carey, 1999a; Martin, 1988). The *Murphy-Meisgeier Type Indicator for Children* (*MMTIC*; Meisgeier & Murphy, 1987) is a scale that provides a four-letter code that is descriptive of temperament or "psychological type," and some suggest that particular profiles on the *MMTIC* put a child at risk for being misdiagnosed with ADHD (Johnson, 1998; Lawrence, 1997). For a more comprehensive discussion of this topic the reader is referred to Chapter 9 by Fischetti. This is an area that is ripe for research and the tools for such research are readily available.

Conclusion

Issues related to problems of inattention are likely to remain controversial well into the foreseeable future. Educators, parents, and medical personnel will continue to search for ways to reduce the problems associated with inattentiveness, impulsivity, and distractibility. Because there is such a wide range and variety of sources for inattentiveness, and, perhaps, for ADHD, the assessment process needs to be comprehensive in scope and focused on the maladaptive nature of the behaviors rather than on making a diagnostic statement. The objective of the evaluation process is to gather information regarding the potential sources of the inattentiveness, the function of such behaviors, contingencies and environmental conditions sustaining the behaviors, the individual's interests and strengths, and any comorbid or related conditions that play a role in the problem behaviors.

Once such information has been acquired, developing interventions takes the form of a problem-solving process. Changes may be made in the environment or structure of the setting, behavioral contingencies may be altered, collaboration with primary caregivers should be initiated and maintained, and cognitive behavioral interventions may be developed. The National Association of School Psychologists (NASP; 1998) suggests that psychostimulants should be considered for use only after attempting the less invasive treatments noted above, and that a decision to use medication should rest exclusively with the parents.

Clearly, more research is needed in the area of the etiology of ADHD and the effectiveness of medical, behavioral, and other psychosocial treatments for problems of inattention. Research is called for in the use of relaxation training methods and the role of temperament in attentional problems as well.

References

Abikoff, H., Courtney, M., Pelham, W. E., & Koplewicz, H. S. (1993). Teachers' ratings of disruptive behaviors: The influence of halo effects. *Journal of Abnormal Child Psychology, 21,* 519–533.

Abikoff, H., & Klein, R. G. (1992). Attention-deficit hyperactivity and conduct disorder: Comorbidity and implications for treatment. *Journal of Consulting and Clinical Psychology, 60,* 881–892.

Achenbach, T. M. (1991). *Integrative guide for the 1991 CBCL/4–18 YSR, and TRF profile.* Burlington, VT: University of Vermont Department of Psychiatry.

American Association of Child and Adolescent Psychiatry. (1997). Practice parameters for the assessment and treatment of children, adolescents, and adults with attention-deficit/hyperactivity disorder. *Journal of the American Academy of Child and Adolescent Psychiatry, 36*, supplement, 85s-121s.

American Psychiatric Association. (1994). *Diagnostic and statistical manual of mental disorders* (4th ed.). Washington, DC: Author.

Angold, A., & Costello, E. J. (1993). Depressive comorbidity in children and adolescents: Empirical, theoretical and methodological issues. *American Journal of Psychiatry, 150,* 1779–1791.

Angold, A., Erkanli, A., Egger, H. L., & Costello, E. J. (2000). Stimulant treatment for children: A community perspective. *Journal of the American Academy of Child and Adolescent Psychiatry, 39,* 975–984.

Barkley, R. A. (1990). *Attention deficit hyperactivity disorder: A handbook for diagnosis and treatment.* New York: Guilford Press.

Barkley, R. A. (Ed.). (1995). *Taking charge of ADHD: The complete, authoritative guide for parents.* New York: Guilford Press.

Barkley, R. A. (1997). Behavioral inhibition, sustained attention, and executive functions: Constructing a unifying theory of ADHD. *Psychological Bulletin, 121,* 65–94.

Barkley, R. A. (1998). Attention-deficit hyperactivity disorder. *Scientific American, 279,* 66–71.

Benson, H. (1996). *Timeless healing.* New York: Scribner.

Biederman, J., Milberger, S., Faraone, S. V., Kiely, K., Guite, J., Mick, E., Ablon, J. S., Warburton, R., Reed, E., & Davis, S. G. (1995). Impact of adversity on functioning and comorbidity in children with attention-deficit hyperactivity disorder. *Journal of the American Academy of Child and Adolescent Psychiatry, 34,* 1495–1503.

Bussing, R., Zima, B.T., Perwien, A.R., Belin, T.R., & Widawski, M. (1998.) Children in special education : Attention deficit hyperactivity disorder, use of services, and unmet needs. *American Journal of Public Health, 88,* 1–7.

Cantwell, D. P. (1996). Attention deficit disorder: A review of the past 10 years. *Journal of the American Academy of Child & Adolescent Psychiatry, 35,* 978–987.

Carey, W.B. (1998) *Understanding your child's temperament.* New York: MacMillan.

Carey, W. B. (1999a). *The Carey Temperament Scales.* Westchester, PA: Temperametrics.

Carey, W. B. (1999b). Commentary: Problems in diagnosing attention and activity. *Pediatrics, 103,* 664–666.

Carlson, E. A., Jacobvitz, D., & Stroufe, L. A. (1995). A developmental investigation of inattentiveness and hyperactivity. *Child Development, 66,* 37–54.

Carlton, R. M., Ente, G., Blum, L., Heyman, N., Davis, W., & Ambrosino, S. (2000). Rational dosages of nutrients have prolonged effect on learning disabilities. *Alternative Therapies, 6,* 85–91.

Cotugnol, A.J. (1993). The diagnosis of attention deficit hyperactivity disorder (ADHD) in community mental health centers: Where and when. *Psychology in the schools, 30,* 338–344.

Cushman, T. P., & Johnson, T. B. (2000, January). Attention, trauma and anxiety. *Communiqué, 29,* pp. 16–17.

Dawson, M. M. (1995). Best practices in planning interventions for students with attention disorders. In A. Thomas & J. Grimes (Eds.), *Best practices in school psychology-III* (pp. 987–998). Washington, DC: National Association of School Psychologists.

Diller, L. (1998). *Running on Ritalin.* New York: Bantam Books.

DuPaul, G. J., Anastopoulos, A. D., Shelton, T. L., Guevremont, D. C., & Metivia, L. (1992). Multimodal assessment of attention-deficit hyperactivity disorder: The diagnostic utility of clinic-based tests. *Journal of Clinical Child Psychology, 21,* 194–402.

DuPaul, G. J., Rapport, M. D., & Perriello, L. M. (1991). Teacher ratings of academic skills: The development of the Academic Performance Rating Scale. *School Psychology Review, 20,* 284–300.

Dykman, R. A., Raney, T. J., & Ackerman, P. T. (1993). *Forum report: Review of assessment tools.* Washington, DC: Office of Special Education Programs, U.S. Department of Education: National ADD Forum.

Elia, J., Ambrosini, P. J., & Rapoport, J. L. (1999). Treatment of attention-deficit hyperactivity disorder. *New England Journal of Medicine, 340,* 780–788.

Ford, J. D., Thomas, J., Racusin, R., Davis, W. B., Ellis, C. G., Rogers, K., Reiser, J., Schiffman, J., & Sengupta, A. (1999). Trauma exposure among children with oppositional defiant disorder and attention deficit-hyperactivity disorder. *Journal of Consulting and Clinical Psychology, 67,* 786–789.

Forness, S. R., & Kavale, K. A. (1988). Psychopharmacologic treatment: A note on classroom effects. *Journal of Learning Disabilities, 21,* 144–147.

Forness, S. R., Swanson, J. M., Cantwell, D. P., Guthrie, D., & Sena, R. (1992). Response to stimulant medication across six measures of school-related performance in children with ADHD and disruptive behavior. *Behavioral Disorders, 18,* 42–53.

Gadow, K. D., Sprafkin, J., & Nolan, E. E. (1996). *ADHD School Observation Code*. Stony Brook, NY: Checkmate Plus.

Gant, C. (1999). *ADD and ADHD: Complementary medicine solutions*. Syracuse, NY: MindMender.

Garber, S. W., Garber, M. D., & Spizman, R. F. (1996). *Beyond Ritalin*. New York: Random House.

Gardill, M. C., DuPaul, G. J., & Kyle, K. E. (1996). Classroom strategies for managing students with attention deficit hyperactivity disorder. *Intervention in School and Clinic, 32*, 89–94.

Goldman, L. S., Genel, M., Bezman, R. J., & Slanetz, P. J. (1998). Council report: Diagnosis and treatment of attention deficit hyperactivity disorder in children and adolescents. *Journal of the American Medical Association, 279*, 1100–1107.

Goldstein, S. (1997). *Managing attention and learning disorders in late adolescence and adulthood*. New York: Wiley.

Goodman, G., & Poillion, M. J. (1992). ADD: An acronym for any dysfunction or difficulty. *The Journal of Special Education, 26*, 37–56.

Goodman, R., & Stevenson, J. (1989). A twin study of hyperactivity: II. The aetiologic role of genes, family relationships, and perinatal adversity. *Journal of Child Psychology and Psychiatry, 30*, 691–709.

Gordon, M., & Mettleman, B. B. (1988). The assessment of attention: 1. Standardization and reliability of a behavior based measure. *Journal of Clinical Psychology, 44*, 682–690.

Greenberg, B., & Deckro, G. (1998). *Mind/Body Medical Institute Education Initiative: Teacher training materials*. Cambridge, MA: Harvard University.

Hannaford, C. (1995). *Smart moves: Why learning is not all in your head*. Arlington, VA: Great Ocean.

Hoagwood, K., Kelleher, K. J., Feil, M., & Comer, D. M. (2000). Treatment services for children with ADHD: A national perspective. *Journal of the American Academy of Child and Adolescent Psychiatry, 39*, 198–206.

Jensen, E. (1998). *Teaching with the brain in mind*. Alexandria, VA: American Association of Counseling and Development.

Jensen, P. S. (2000). Commentary: The NIH ADHD consensus statement: Win, lose or draw? *Journal of the American Academy of Child and Adolescent Psychiatry, 39*, 194–197.

Jensen, P. S., Martin, D., & Cantwell, D. P. (1997). Comorbidity in ADHD: Implications for research, practice, and *DSM-IV. Journal of the American Association of Child and Adolescent Psychiatry, 36*, 1065–1079.

Jensen, P. S., Mrazek, D., Knapp, P. K., Steinberg, L., Pfeffer, C., Schowalter, J., & Shapiro, T. (1997). Evolution and revolution in child psychiatry: ADHD as a disorder of adaptation. *Journal of the American Association of Child and Adolescent Psychiatry, 36*, 1672–1679.

Johnson, T. B. (1998, May). Psychological type/learning styles research: An alternative view to ADD/ADHD diagnosis. *Communiqué, 26*, pp. 12–14.

Kendall, P. C., Padever, W., & Zupan, B. (1980). *Developing self-control in children: A manual of cognitive–behavioral strategies*. Minneapolis, MN: University of Minnesota.

Kotulak, R. (1997). *Inside the brain*. Kansas City, MO: Andrews McMeel.

Kovacs, M. (1992). *Children's Depression Inventory*. North Tonowanda, NY: Multi-Health Systems.

Kratter, J., & Hogan, J. D. (1982). The use of meditation in the treatment of attention deficit disorder with hyperactivity. (ERIC Document Reproduction Service NO. ED 232–787).

Lahey, B. B., & Carlson, C. L. (1991). Validity of the diagnostic category of attention-deficit disorder without hyperactivity: A review of the literature. *Journal of Learning Disabilities, 24*, 110–120.

Landau, S., & Burchman, B. G. (1995). Best practices in the assessment of children with attention disorders. In A. Thomas & J. Grimes (Eds.), *Best practices in school psychology* (pp. 817–829). Washington, DC: National Association of School Psychologists.

Lawrence, G. (1997). *Looking at type and learning styles*. Gainesville, FL: Center of Applications of Psychological Type.

LeFever, G. B., Dawson, K. V., & Morrow, A. L. (1999). The extent of drug therapy for attention-deficit hyperactivity disorder among children in public schools. *American Journal of Public Health, 89*, 1359–1364.

Lloyd, J. W., Forness, S. R., & Kavale, K. A. (1998). Some methods are more effective than others. *Intervention in School and Clinic, 33*, 195–200.

Losier, B. J., McGrath, P. J., & Klein, R. M. (1996). Error patterns on Continuous Performance Test in non-medicated and medicated samples of children with and without ADHD: A meta-analysis review. *Journal of Child Psychology and Psychiatry and Allied Disciplines, 37*, 971–987.

Manassis, K., Tannock, R., & Barbosa, J. (2000). Dichotic listening and response inhibition in children with comorbid anxiety disorder and ADHD. *Journal of the American Academy of Child and Adolescent Psychiatry, 39*, 1152–1159.

Martens, B. K., & Kelly, S. Q. (1993). A behavioral analysis of effective school teaching. *School Psychology Quarterly, 8,* 10–26.

Martin, R. P. (1988). *Temperament Assessment Battery for Children–Manual.* Brandon, VT: Clinical Psychology.

Martin, R. P. (1994). Child temperament and common problems: Hypotheses about causal connections. *Journal of School Psychology, 32,* 119–134.

McCarney, S. B. (1994). *Behavior Evaluation Scale–2: Home/School Version.* Columbia, MO: Hawthorne Educational Services.

McGoey, K. E., & DuPaul, G. J. (2000). Token reinforcement and response cost procedures: Reducing the disruptive behavior of preschool children with attention-deficit hyperactivity disorder. *School Psychology Quarterly, 15,* 330–343.

McKinney, J. D., Montague, M., & Hocutt, A. M. (1993). Educational assessment of students with attention deficit disorder. *Exceptional Children, 60,* 125–131.

Meisgeier, C., & Murphy, E. (1987). *The Murphy-Meisgeier Type Indicator for Children: Manual.* Palo Alto, CA: Consulting Psychologists Press.

Miranda, A., & Presentacion, M. J. (2000). Efficacy of cognitive–behavioral therapy in the treatment of children with ADHD, with and without aggressiveness. *Psychology in the Schools, 37,* 169–182.

National Association of School Psychologists. (1998). *Position statement: Students with attention problems.* Bethesda, MD: Author..

National Institutes of Health (1998). *National Institutes of Health consensus development conference statement.* Silver Spring, MD: Prospect Associates.

Passarello, D. J., Hintze, J. M., Owen, S. V., & Gable, R. K. (1999). Exploratory factor analysis of parent ratings of child and adolescent anxiety: A preliminary investigation. *Psychology in the Schools, 36,* 89–102.

Perrin, S., & Last, C. G. (1996). Relationship between ADHD and anxiety in boys: Results from a family study. *Journal of the American Academy of Child and Adolescent Psychiatry, 35,* 988–996.

Pfiffner, L. J., & Barkley, R. A. (1990). Educational placement and classroom management. In R. A. Barkley (Ed.), *Attention-deficit hyperactivity disorder: A handbook for diagnosis and treatment.* New York: Guilford Press.

Pfiffner, L. J., McBurnett, K., Lahey, B. B., Loeber, R., Green, S., Frick, P. J., & Rathouz, P. J. (1999). Association of parental psychopathology to the comorbid disorders of boys with attention-deficit hyperactivity disorder. *Journal of Consulting and Clinical Psychology, 67,* 881–893.

Piers, E., & Harris, D. (1996). *Piers-Harris Children's Self-Concept Scale.* Los Angeles: Western Psychological Services.

Pollack, W. (1998). *Real boys.* New York: Holt & Company.

Reid, R., & Maag, J. W. (1994). How many fidgets in a pretty much: A critique of behavior rating scales for identifying students with ADHD. *Journal of School Psychology, 32,* 339–354.

Reid, R., Vasa, S. F., Maag, J. W., & Wright, G. (1994). An analysis of teachers' perceptions of attention deficit hyperactivity disorder. *Journal of Research and Development in Education, 27,* 195–202.

Reynolds, C., & Richmond, B. (1994). *Revised Children's Manifest Anxiety Scale.* Los Angeles: Western Psychological Services.

Riccio, C. A., Hynd, G. W., Cohen, M. J., & Gonzalez, J. J. (1993). Neurological basis of attention deficit hyperactivity disorder. *Exceptional Children, 60,* 118–124.

Richters, J. E., Arnold, L. E., Jensen, P. S., Abikoff, H., Connors, C. K., Greenhill, L. L., Hechtman, L., Hinshaw, S. P., Pelham, W. E., & Swanson, J. M. (1995). NIMH collaborative multisite, multimodal treatment study of children with ADHD: I. Background and rationale. *Journal of the American Academy of Child and Adolescent Psychiatry, 34,* 987–1000.

Riggs, P. D., Laetitia, T. L., Mikulich, S. K., Whitmore, E. A., & Crowley, T. J. (1996). An open trial of pemoline in drug dependent delinquents with attention deficit hyperactivity disorder. *Journal of the American Academy of Child and Adolescent Psychiatry, 35,* 1018–1024.

Sabatino, D. A., & Vance, H. B. (1994). Is the diagnosis of ADHD disorder meaningful? *Psychology in the Schools, 31,* 188–196.

Schweibert, V. L., Sealander, K. A., & Tollerud, T. R. (1995). Attention deficit hyperactivity disorder: An overview for school counselors. *Elementary School Guidance and Counseling, 29,* 249–259.

Schoen, M. J., & Nagle, R. J. (1994). Prediction of school readiness from kindergarten temperament scores. *Journal of School Psychology, 32,* 135–147.

Shelton, T. L., & Barkley, R. A. (1999). The assessment and treatment of attention deficit/hyperactivity disorder in children. In J. A. Incorvaia, B. S. Mark-Goldstein, D. Tessmer (Eds.), *Understanding, diagnosing and treating ADHD in children and adolescents: An integrated approach.* (pp. 27–68). Northvale, NJ: J. Aronson.

Smith, B. H., Pelham, W. E., Gnagy, E., Molina, B., & Evans, S. (2000). The reliability, validity, and unique contributions of self-report by adolescents receiving treatment for attention-deficit hyperactivity disorder. *Journal of Consulting and Clinical Psychology, 68,* 489–499.

Sweeney, D. P., Forness, S. R., Kavale, K. A., & Levitt, J. G. (1997). An update on psychopharmacologic medication: What teachers, clinicians and parents need to know. *Intervention in School and Clinic, 33,* 4–21, 25.

Taghavi, M. R., Neshat-Doost, H. T., Morodi, A. R., Yule, W., & Dalgleish, T. (1999). Biases in visual attention in children and adolescents with clinical anxiety and mixed anxiety-depression. *Journal of Abnormal Child Psychology, 27,* 215–223.

Ullman, R. K., Sleator, E. K., & Sprague, R. L. (1985). Introduction to the use of ACTeRs. *Psychopharmacological Bulletin, 21,* 915–919.

Wang, G. J., Volkow, N., Fowler, J., Ferrieri, R., Schlyer, D., Alexoff, D., Pappas, N., Lieberman, J., King, P., Warner, D., Wong, C., Hitzemann, R., & Wolf, A. (1994). Methylphenidate decreases regional cerebral blood flow in normal human subjects. *Life Sciences, 54,* 143–146.

Whalen, C. K., & Henker, B. (1991). Therapies for hyperactive children: Comparisons, combinations and compromises. *Journal of Consulting and Clinical Psychology, 59,* 126–137.

Wolraich, M. L., Lindgren, S., Stromquist, A., Milich, R., Davis, C., & Watson, D. (1990). Stimulant medication use by primary care physicians in the treatment of attention-deficit hyperactivity disorder. *Pediatrics, 86,* 95–101.

Zametkin, A. J., Nordahl, T. E., Gross, M., King, C., Semple, W. E., Rumsey, J., Hamburger, S., & Cohen, R. M. (1990). Cerebral glucose metabolism in adults with hyperactivity of childhood onset. *New England Journal of Medicine, 323,* 1361–1366.

Zentall, S. S. (1993). Research on the educational implications of Attention Deficit Hyperactivity Disorder. *Exceptional Children, 60,* 143–153.

End Note

I wish to thank Dr. Thomas Johnson for his input and support in the development of this chapter.

Developing Interventions for Use with Children Who Demonstrate Behavioral and Emotional Difficulties

Scott L. Cone

Behavioral and emotional difficulties among school-age children can be framed effectively in ecological terms. The discussion presented in this chapter includes a brief review of some popular comprehensive theories of problem behavior in youth. The contributing elements of this ecological perspective—individual, family, school, and peer variables—are reviewed next. Examples of the interdependence of these separate elements in understanding behavioral and emotional difficulties are provided.

The second main section covers three intervention approaches—peer group interventions, strength-based and solution-focused interventions, and life-space interventions—that are well suited for a social understanding of problem behavior in school-age children. The unique contribution of each intervention, as well as examples of the synergistic potential of combining these approaches, are reviewed. Notably, these interventions are applicable to community, clinic, and school settings for a diverse range of behavioral and emotional difficulties.

Kazdin (1993a) broadly defines mental health as the "absence of dysfunction in psychological, emotional, behavioral, and social spheres . . . [and] . . . optimal functioning or well-being in psychological and emotional domains" (p. 128). This definition makes obvious the distinction between interventions geared toward treatment (i.e., addressing the "dysfunction") and those geared toward prevention (i.e., promoting "optimal functioning"). Debates pitting these two approaches against each other (Cowen, 1997) advanced thinking on several fronts and has resulted in a realization that the distinction between treatment and prevention is not entirely clear (Kazdin,

1993a). The interventions reviewed herein address dysfunctional patterns of behavior and work to promote optimal functioning.

The predominant referral issue in clinical settings for children and adolescents is some variant of disruptive behavior such as attention-deficit hyperactivity disorder (ADHD), conduct disorder, or oppositional defiant disorder (Kazdin, 1993b). Similarly, within school settings, disruptive behavior in the classroom is considered a primary contributor to academic underachievement (Hinshaw, 1992). Therefore, the applicability of the following interventions to manage disruptive behavior is emphasized.

In a review of interventions for children and adolescents, Kazdin (1988) identifies over 230 treatment methods, making the current discussion far from comprehensive. The intervention approaches discussed have clear roots in traditional theories of psychotherapy, but have been adapted by practitioners to fit real-world demands in both educational and clinical settings. Space constraints prohibit a comprehensive review of these theories. Interested readers are directed to reviews of traditional approaches to treatment such as behavior modification (Hersen, Eisler, & Miller, 1990; Kazdin, 1989), cognitive or cognitive–behavioral approaches (Beck, 1995; Murphy, 1989), or psychodynamic therapies (Barber & Lane, 1995; Wallerstein, 1995).

Theories of Behavioral and Emotional Difficulties

As used herein, the term *behavioral and emotional difficulties* is intentionally broad for three reasons. First, in keeping with the overall theme of this book, the chapter focuses on developing interventions based on the personal and social functioning of the child, rather than the treatment of a particular diagnosable disorder. Second, youth in need of intervention frequently present with clusters of problem behavior, rather than fit a single diagnosis. Finally, many youth who do not fit a clinical or educational taxonomy still may be in need of psychological assistance, a point made earlier by the authors of Chapter 3.

The need to consider the broader social context of community, school, family, and peers when attempting to understand youth with behavioral and emotional difficulties is increasingly apparent. In three separate prominent journals with special sections devoted to adolescence, the introductory articles highlighted the need for "a developmental approach that . . . considers how context interacts with individual proclivities" (Tolan, Guerra, & Kendall, 1995b, p. 516), "an integrative perspective . . . [that] takes into account multiple contexts and domains of functioning and locates these in interaction with the adolescent's development" (Liddle, 1996, p. 4), and an appreciation of "the essential partnership of pivotal socializing institutions in the lives of adolescents and the powerful influences of these combined institutions—families, schools, media, and peers" (Takanishi, 1993, p. 87). Unidirectional theories have been discarded in favor of attempts to identify the underlying processes that contribute to academic failure and behavior problems (Hinshaw, 1992) and that emphasize the need to understand behavior in children within the contextual setting and in reference to the youth's developmental level (Tolan, Guerra, & Kendall, 1995a).

Patterson, DeBaryshe, and Ramsey (1989) propose a developmental theory of antisocial behavior that involves the role of family, school, and peers. Initially, parenting characteristics such as inconsistent discipline, minimal positive parental involvement, and inadequate supervision inadvertently train and reinforce a pattern of coercive behaviors by the child. When interacting with adults and peers in the neighborhood and school environments, the coercive child's behaviors are met with peer rejection and academic failure. Deviant peer group membership follows and provides the youth with training and encouragement for further delinquent behaviors.

A similarly comprehensive approach is problem-behavior theory (Jessor & Jessor, 1977). Problem-behavior theory is a social–psychological analysis focused on the contribution and interrelationship among the three systems of personality, perceived environment, and behavior. Personality relates to motivation, beliefs, and personal control. For example, understanding personality involves identifying salient motivating goals for adolescence such as academic achievement, independence from adults, and peer affection. The second system, perceived environment, relates to the notion of life-space (Lewin, 1951), although Jessor and Jessor emphasize the individual's perception of the environment. The peer group is a major component of the perceived environment and serves both as a model and as a support for behavior. The behavior system incorporates two opposing structures of problem and conventional behavior. With respect to problem behavior, Jessor and Jessor suggest a more comprehensive approach by demonstrating intercorrelations among deviant behaviors that were previously conceptualized as independent actions. Hypotheses about problem behavior are generated by the study of the interplay of forces within and among the three systems.

Jessor (1993) describes a conceptual model of adolescence based on a developmental behavioral science paradigm. In this model, the adolescent is understood in the overlapping contexts of family, school, and neighborhood. Similar to problem-behavior theory, the influence of the peer group is understood within the community contexts of school and neighborhood. These three contexts are subsumed within the larger social structure including economic, political, and cultural systems. In addition to the contextual, ecological perspective, the model is viewed as variable along a continuum of adolescent development.

Theories such as those reviewed briefly here epitomize the need to understand youth with behavioral and emotional difficulties within a broad social and developmental context. Within this broad conceptualization, three areas—family, school, and peers—are regarded consistently as critical components in understanding youth with behavioral and emotional difficulties. Given the importance of these systems when developing interventions, an overview of the theoretical importance of these broad contextual areas is provided following the discussion of individual variables.

Individual Variables

A thorough understanding of children's emotional and behavioral difficulties includes the surrounding context of family, school, and peers, along with discussion of individual variables within the child. Of particular interest is how children process social information and the subsequent influence on behavior and social adjustment. Crick and Dodge (1994) propose a six-step model of social information processing based on a review of the literature. In Steps 1 and 2, the child encodes and interprets the social situation. This process is influenced by factors such as the history of individual experiences, recent events, and the social context. Children with social histories of peer rejection and higher rates of aggression were found to differ in how they interpret ambiguous social situations. For example, researchers demonstrated an attributional bias in aggressive youth who interpret the intent of a peer's behavior as hostile, compared to interpretations rendered by their nonaggressive counterparts (Dodge & Coie, 1987).

Based on the interpretation of the social situation, the third step involves formulating and clarifying a goal. With socially maladjusted youth, the goal frequently involves attaining social acceptance. In the fourth step, the child considers various responses that could be used to attain the goal established in Step 3. Of interest is the number of response options accessed or constructed, the content of the response, such as friendly or aggressive, and the order of the accessed responses. A history of hostile and aggressive experiences may result in the increased accessibility of an aggressive response construct (Graham & Hudley, 1994). Response decision is the fifth step and this step relates to an evaluation of the impact of the response (i.e., will it be effective) and the outcome expectation (i.e., the consequences of engaging in this response). Following these considerations, the final step of behavioral enactment occurs.

Crick and Dodge's (1994) model of social information processing is particularly relevant given the importance of the social context in which the child operates. Children's family history, peer relationships, and school experiences shape how they process social information. In turn, these cognitive processes impact how children relate to their social environment. Effective interventions need to consider the interactive nature of these various factors.

Family Variables

Researchers who examine family variables in relation to childhood behavioral and emotional difficulties have focused primarily on family structure and parenting practices. Griffin, Botvin, Scheier, Diaz, and Miller (2000) examine the role of both family structure and parenting practices on problem behavior, including substance abuse, delinquency, and aggression. Although problem behaviors occur with greater frequency in single-parent families compared to two-parent families, the results identified parental monitoring as the strongest protective factor. A similar pattern was observed in studies of adolescent depression. Family cohesiveness, not structure per se, was identified as a protective factor against adolescent depression (Cumsille & Epstein, 1994). Interestingly, and in relation to individual variables discussed earlier, the adolescent's cognitive appraisal of family functioning was the strongest predictor of adolescent depression.

These two studies demonstrate a beneficial effect of parenting practices on adolescent adjustment. Other researchers suggest that some aspects of parenting may have a detrimental impact. For example, in an examination of the intergenerational relationship of antisocial behavior, the likelihood of antisocial behavior in children increased incrementally depending on the presence of no antisocial parent, one antisocial parent, or two antisocial parents (Robins & Earls, 1985). Parental discipline practices have been suggested as key factors determining the presence of antisocial behavior in children of antisocial parents (Patterson et al., 1989). Specifically, parenting practices such as inconsistent applications of discipline, failure to encourage prosocial behaviors, and insufficient monitoring of children's activities all have been associated with increased problem behavior in children.

In an examination of factors that influence adolescent substance abuse, peer influences were identified as the strongest predictor, although this relationship was weaker in homes with a father or stepfather present (Farrell & White, 1998). Further, in homes headed by single mothers, a strong parent–adolescent relationship buffered the impact of negative peers. Cooper, Peirce, and Tidwell (1995) identify a similar moderating effect of parenting practices. In addition to family structure (single or blended family), multiple family factors such as strained maternal–adolescent relationship and family-related stress levels were related to adolescent substance abuse. This research supports the need for an interactive model to understand adolescent substance abuse and that incorporates family structure, parenting practices, and peer influences.

Academic and School Variables

Given that school performance is the primary functional task for children, this is a key criterion in identifying youth with behavioral and emotional difficulties. An association between problem behavior and academic failure has been observed consistently (Hinshaw, 1992; Jessor & Jessor, 1977; O'Donnell, Hawkins, & Abbott, 1995; Patterson et al., 1989), although the mechanissm underlying this association are not well understood. Theories have implicated familial variables (Patterson et al., 1989), peer group affiliation (Oetting & Beauvais, 1987), and the school environment (Eccles et al., 1993).

Patterson et al. (1989) suggest that coercive behavior patterns established from ineffective parenting practices may contribute to difficulties in the academic setting. More specifically, these children may spend less time on school tasks, be deficient in the skills necessary for academic success, such as attending to and answering questions, and failing to complete regular homework assignments. In addition to contributing to poor academic skills, such ineffective parenting practices are unlikely to correct effectively any early signs of academic failure. However, there is some indication that interventions geared toward improving school attendance and academic performance may mediate the relationship between maltreatment and delinquency (Zingraff, Leiter, Johnsen, & Myers, 1994).

Oetting and Beauvais (1986) propose peer cluster theory to better understand problem behavior in youth. Rather than problem behavior, such as drug use, being viewed as a contributor to academic failure, peer cluster theory views such behavior as a result of peer group membership prompted by academic failure. Using path analysis to establish support for this theory, Oetting and Beauvais (1987) argue that school failure and a dislike of school result in membership in a peer group that encourages drug use. Another examination of the relationship among problem behaviors such as drug use, violence, victimization, and academic standing provides additional support for peer cluster theory (Beauvais et al., 1996). Youth in good academic standing showed less problem behavior than students doing less well academically. This pattern followed for youth who dropped out of school showing the highest rates of all problem behavior. Beauvais et al. argue that academic problems contribute to the development of deviant peer clusters that model and support problem behavior.

The school environment also may relate to problem behavior in early adolescence. Using a stage–environment fit model, Eccles et al. (1993) provided evidence that the structure of some schools may not be most suitable for the evolving developmental tasks of young adolescents. For example, as the need for autonomy and influence in decision making increased, some middle school environments became more restrictive. As a result, student's motivation and self-perceptions regarding school performance and academic success declined. A similar mismatch between the student's developmental needs and the family environment also was found.

Peer Relationship Variables

Perhaps the most persuasive argument regarding the importance of the peer group on children's development is offered by group socialization theory (Harris, 1995). Harris demonstrated that the process of socialization is a highly context-dependent form of learning with the peer group as the predominant context for children and adolescents. Results from group behavior research, such as in-group favoritism (Billig & Tajfel, 1973), out-group hostility (Zimbardo, 1972), and within-group assimilation (Asch, 1952/1987; Sherif, Harvey, White, Hood, & Sherif, 1961), were used by Harris to demonstrate the powerful socializing impact of the group process. More specifically, group socialization theory posits that children are motivated to identify with a group. As a function of group affiliation and in relation to the broader social context, the individual assimilates the major group norms in order to promote identification with the primary peer group as distinct from other groups. Within the peer group, youth attempt to differentiate from others in order to build status in the group and promote their own individual differences. It is through this process of peer group affiliation that the most powerful socializing force on youth is produced.

Membership in a peer group that models and supports problem behavior theoretically increases such behavior (Jessor & Jessor, 1977). Empirical support of this trend has been well demonstrated (Dishion & Andrews, 1995; Dishion, McCord, & Poulin, 1999; Gold, 1970; Patterson, 1993). Dishion et al. label this process "deviancy training" in their investigation of the role of the peer group in problem behavior. Using videotapes of peer interactions, delinquent youth displayed more positive reactions to rule-breaking discussions compared to nondelinquent youth.

The peer group is, arguably, the primary socializing force for all youth. Young people having trouble in school or subjected to ineffective or abusive parenting practices have difficulty relating well to peers and, thus, seek out a similarly troubled peer group. Problem behaviors have been suggested to be encouraged in such deviant peer groups, making this a key focus for interventions.

The ability of children to build relationships with their peers appears to be related to some parenting practices. Physically maltreated children were rated consistently with lower social preference scores by peers, as more unpopular by teachers, and as more withdrawn by mothers (Dodge, Pettit, & Bates, 1994). Patterson et al. (1989) identified family coercive practices that inadvertently taught children maladaptive ways of relating that lead to rejection from their peers. As a result, such youth seek deviant peer group membership.

Although discussed under separate headings, the interrelationships among the developmental influences of family, school, peers, and the individual child are obvious. Family practices have been shown to impact peer relations and academic performance. School setting and academic performance influence adolescent behavior and peer-group affiliation. Peer group affiliation is a major socializing force for young people, which, in turn, influences school performance and social behavior. In relation to these findings, the following section describes three intervention approaches designed to assist youth within the overlapping contexts of family, school, and peer groups. For illustrative purposes, practices employed by a specific residential facility for children and adolescents are used throughout the discussion.

Interventions

The following interventions are used regularly at Edwin Gould Academy, a coeducational residential school for children and adolescents in the foster care and juvenile justice systems. As a residential program emphasizing education 24 hours a day and striving, in most cases, for reunification of the child with his or her family, the treatment of the individual is inherently context-specific. Effective treatment involves the development of a therapeutic atmosphere within the individual's residence, classroom, and the larger campus community. Prior to discharge, strengthening family support and building community resources are essential. The treatment modality at Edwin Gould Academy is a peer-group intervention called Positive Peer Culture (Vorrath & Brendtro, 1985). In addition to Positive Peer Culture, an increased emphasis on students' strengths has developed in the program and within similar peer group interventions across the United States. The renaming of the organization National Association of Peer Group Agencies (NAPGA) to Strength Based Services International (SBSI) reflects the nationwide paradigm shift in peer group agencies. In addition, life-space interventions, particularly for students in crisis, are incorporated in the training repertoire of many specialists who work with youth.

Peer Group Interventions

Peer group interventions address problematic behavior in youth by influencing the values and behaviors of the peer group. Positive Peer Culture is one of a variety of peer group interventions used in schools and residential treatment centers across the United States and the world (Vorrath & Brendtro, 1985). Similar programs, such as Guided Group Interaction (GGI), Peer Group Counseling (PGC), Peer Culture Development (PCD), and Equipping Youth to Help One Another (EQUIP), are all based on a similar program philosophy (Giacobbe, Traynelis-Yurek, & Laursen, 1999). Although the primary setting for peer group interventions has been residential programs, such as treatment centers and juvenile justice facilities, this treatment approach is increasingly applied to the behavioral and emotional difficulties among students within school settings (e.g., Resolving Conflict Creatively Program, RCCP; Lantieri & Patti, 1997). Studies assessing the potential benefits of peer group interventions have demonstrated positive results (Gibbs, Potter, & Goldstein, 1995; Gold & Osgood, 1992). Gold and Osgood assessed over 300 delinquent boys from four different peer group intervention programs from intake to 6 months following discharge. The boys demonstrated improvement on a variety of measures of behaviors, values, and feelings.

Researchers have long recognized the capacity for negative youth subcultures to develop and exacerbate the antisocial tendencies of its individual members (Gold, 1970; Gold & Osgood, 1992), particularly in residential settings for juvenile delinquents (Brendtro, 1999). Dishion et al. (1999) caution that this process of deviancy training in congregate care settings may have iatrogenic effects for young people labeled as antisocial. Though their research adeptly identifies deviancy training among troubled youth, these researches have yet to examine with equal vigor the potential for these young people to redirect their energy toward caring for and helping their peers. It is the firm belief in this positive potential in young people, especially those who demonstrate disruptive, antisocial behaviors, that has been the impetus for Positive Peer Culture programs since the late 1960s.

In a review of peer group interventions, Brendtro, Brokenleg, and Van Bockern (1990) identify four essential qualities of successful programs: attachment, achievement, autonomy, and altruism. Note that these qualities resemble the motivating goals—academic achievement, independence, and peer affection—within the personality construct of problem-behavior theory (Jessor & Jessor, 1977). A brief description of each quality, the rationale for its importance, and an example of how it is implemented in a Positive Peer Culture (PPC) program follows.

Attachment refers to a sense of connectedness and belonging. Although positive adult attachments are critical, adolescence is a time when group identification and affiliation are paramount (Harris, 1995). The importance of attachment in a peer group intervention was illustrated in a study of successful and unsuccessful adolescents in a PPC program (Lee, 1996). Boys deemed unsuccessful by program standards scored lower on an assessment of their desire for inclusion and affection from others as compared to boys considered to be successful. Whether these lower scores were a cause or a consequence of being unsuccessful was not clear, although these results highlight the importance of attachment in a PPC program.

A PPC program is designed by congregating youth into separate groups of 9 to 12 young people. Group cohesion is promoted by keeping the group together as much as possible. Many residential programs have the advantage of being able to keep a group together throughout the day. Obviously, a sense of connectedness and belonging will not develop among group members who do not have significant contact with each other. At a minimum, the group should meet five times per week to conduct group meetings.

Once formed and together, the staff promotes group reliance by providing opportunities for the group to depend on one another. Activities such as Outward Bound or ropes courses challenge youth and encourage group members to cooperate. Such experiences help form positive attachments among group members and build group cohesiveness.

A central tenet of a PPC program involves directing youth to engage in helpful behavior with each other. Such altruistic behavior, discussed more fully below, promotes attachment by connecting youth during the helping process. Much like the positive attachment that occurs in a therapeutic alliance, youth build sincere, caring friendships when they help each other. Unlike serendipitous friendships that evolve from the opportunity to help a stranger, staff employing a peer group intervention actively fosters such relationships among group members.

Achievement, the second quality of an effective peer group intervention, refers to opportunities for positive accomplishments. Many youth with behavioral and emotional difficulties have histories of personal and academic failure (Hinshaw, 1992). An effective PPC program continually strives to provide groups with the opportunity to experience success. Three specific examples include academic achievement, service learning projects, and achieving success by helping others.

A major feature of the innovative approach at Edwin Gould Academy is the joining of a residential treatment center and a New York State Special Act Public School under a unifying PPC program philosophy (Thompson, 1998). Among the many advantages of this approach is the ability to promote a sense of pride and achievement within groups around academic success. Rather than punish individual students who fail to complete homework assignments or prepare for a test, teachers and residential staff work collaboratively to challenge the group to help and support their peers. Consistent with the research of Zingraff et al. (1994), academic achievement has the additional benefit of reducing emotional and behavioral difficulties.

Service learning projects are group-oriented volunteer activities that provide youth an opportunity to experience the esteem-building benefit gained from giving to others (Vorrath & Brendtro, 1985). In addition to these altruistic benefits, successful projects provide youth with a sense of accomplishment and demonstrate the potential value and worth of a cohesive group. For example, a group of young men recently volunteered at a day-care center for young children between 5 and 7 years of age during a summer service learning project. This courageous role reversal put those in the role of receiving care into the role of providing care, resulting in a powerful, positive, therapeutic experience for all the young people involved.

Perhaps the most celebrated example of achievement for students in a PPC program occurs when a group member graduates from the program. In a traditional PPC program within a residential setting, the group provides input about the readiness of their peer for discharge based on that student's history of giving and receiving help. During a graduation ceremony, the group is celebrated for their role in the treatment success. Here, the sense of pride, accomplishment, and achievement usually enjoyed solely by adult treatment practitioners is shared with—in fact, centered on—the group.

Autonomy is the third quality of an effective peer group intervention. As most practitioners know, it is a misguided effort to attempt to control youth presenting with behavior problems. Eccles et al. (1993) note that some adolescent environments provide less opportunity for decision making even though the developmental need of the adolescent is for increased autonomy. Opportunities for autonomy can occur in a structured, group-oriented, residential program and a typical high school classroom provided the focus is self-government.

By providing PPC groups an opportunity to make decisions in all areas that impact their lives, workers help shape prosocial, caring, and helpful values within the group. Within a residential setting, group members provide input regarding weekly home visits, weekend activities, chores assignments, and the day-to-day routine. In a typical setting, staff makes such decisions in meetings independent from group members, frequently under direction from supervisors or program administrators. A PPC program, in contrast, strives to operate from the group members up, rather than administration down—*bottom up* versus *top down* models, respectively. Staff challenges the underlying values of group decision making in order to promote responsible, autonomous action from the young people who comprise the group.

Altruism, the final element of an effective peer group intervention, refers to being of value to others. In a PPC program, youth are entrusted with the responsibility to help and care for one's peers, thereby learning about and experiencing their own intrinsic worth. Central to an effective PPC program, and the primary opportunity for youth to be of value to others, is the group meeting. All group members are expected to attend a 90–minute meeting led by a trained adult. The meeting format involves a problem statement, awarding the meeting, problem solving, and summary (Vorrath & Brendtro, 1985). The meeting encourages youth to openly discuss problem behaviors with each other. The group leader functions to assist the group in becoming effective helpers. In the beginning of the meeting, all students disclose recent problem behavior. The group then focuses on helping one group member. The meeting provides a prime opportunity to shape group norms and values and teach youth to be effective helpers. Once functioning, this meeting serves as a powerful forum for youth to challenge antisocial behaviors demonstrated by peer members, empathize with others who share similar tragic life stories, and provide support for those in need.

Staff extends the helping behavior nurtured in the group meeting throughout the day by enlisting the group to manage problem behavior. When confronted with oppositional or disruptive behaviors, staff encourages other group members to help their struggling peer. Such an intervention is not intended to encourage a group to bully or coerce a peer into compliant behavior. In fact, program initiators have taken great care to document potential misuses of peer interventions (Brendtro & Ness, 1982) and articulate the philosophy around peer-assisted behavior management (Brendtro & Ness, 1991). The goal is to develop a caring and therapeutic culture in which the peer group functions to assist its members in managing daily conflicts and problems in living.

Strength-Based and Solution-Focused Approaches

Recognition of the need to address the qualities and characteristics of youth from a point of strength has grown (Jessor, 1993). In a lead article in a special issue of *American Psychologist* on adolescence, Takanishi (1993) stresses a new focus that promotes behaviors that enhance health in youth rather than the treatment of single problems. This approach reflects a paradigm shift in intervention philosophy that impacts work with youth, families, peer groups, and schools. As mentioned earlier, PPC is based on a belief that young people have the capacity to help one another. A similar framework has been increasingly applied to youth in classrooms and families. Two approaches that seek to promote resiliency when working with youth are strength-based and solution-focused interventions.

Strength-based practices were developed in response to an overemphasis by treatment professionals on what is wrong with the youth and families that come to our attention. Terms such as *deficit* (what's lacking?), *dysfunction* (what's not working?), and *disability* (what cannot be done?) all emphasize weaknesses in the individual. Strength-based practices seek to help people by pointing out the positive qualities the individual or family may have in abundance, what is working well, and areas in which they are capable or most capable. Further, inherent in many perceived weaknesses are underlying strengths that are susceptible to intervention when recognized and nurtured. This practice does not ignore problems or merely "look on the bright side," but works to enhance areas of known strength and enlighten youth and families about unrecognized strength.

Wolin, Desetta, and Hefner (2000) identify seven resiliencies in a working model of strength-based practice: insight, independence, relationships, initiative, creativity, humor, and morality. An accompanying book (Desetta & Wolin, 2000) provides examples of these resiliencies with true stories written by teens who have overcome adversity. One story highlights a girl's struggle to accept that her family does not meet her idealized vision of what a family should be like. Her capacity for insight about the reality of her situation has increased her ability to accept the loss related to this unfulfilled hope.

Another example of a strength-based intervention is illustrative. A child who functions as a negative leader in a group (e.g., Polsky, 1962) is frequently identified as particularly problematic. In a group care or classroom setting, this young person may be feared by other students, workers, and teachers for his or her ability to mislead the whole group, promoting chaos. Though the behavior is disruptive in this context, at least some of the underlying qualities in the youth can be framed as definite strengths such as charisma, leadership skills, capacity to influence others, and ability to build relationships. Whether the outcome is anti- or prosocial, using one's skills and talents is inherently satisfying and, thus, reinforcing. Rather than attempt to thwart the youth's capacity to lead, a strength-based approach works to redirect these energies to function in an adaptive, positive manner. Perhaps this young person could coordinate a class project, lead the group during a work project or school play, or even run for a position in student government. Experiences of prosocial leadership may satisfy this student's need to lead and redirect heretofore negative energies in a positive direction.

Solution-focused therapy developed in the mid-1980s as a brief therapy in response to managed care demands (De Shazer, 1985). This approach increased in popularity during the 1990s and has been applied with parents and families (Berg, 1994; Lee, 1997; Zimmerman, Jacobsen, MacIntyre, & Watson, 1996), adolescent group work (Banks, 1999; LaFountain, Garner, & Boldosser, 1995), and in schools (Downing & Harrison, 1992; Murphy, 1996; Murphy & Duncan, 1997). In addition, many solution-focused practitioners link strength-based concepts in their work (Corcoran, 1997; De Jong & Miller, 1995; Green, Lee, Trask, & Rheinscheld, 1996).

Murphy (1996) describes two assumptions of a solution-focused brief therapy approach used in schools. The first parallels the strength-based perspective: "[S]tudents, teachers and parents have the resources and strengths to resolve school problems" (p. 184). This paradigm shift toward strengths, successful functioning, and competencies allows the practitioner to direct the intervention—including the student, family, and school personnel—toward solution opportunities. The second assumption is that a "small change in any aspect of the problem situation can initiate a solution" (p. 185). Inherent in this assumption is the ecological perspective mentioned throughout this chapter and elsewhere in this volume. Given the interrelationship of problem behavior and the broader social system, it follows that a minor adjustment by the individual may produce a magnified effect via changes in how the system operates.

Elaboration of some of the specific techniques used by solution-focused therapists may serve to illuminate these assumptions and clarify this approach. Three techniques to be reviewed include the Miracle Question, the Exception Finding Question, and the Scaling Question. These techniques are a sample of the hallmarks of a solution-focused approach (Berg, 1994).

When using the *Miracle Question,* the clinician asks the client to describe what life would be like in behavioral terms if a miracle occurred and his or her problem were solved. More than just a question, this process is used to gather assessment data and to encourage the client to develop behavioral goals. The process also acts to shift the client to a more positive perspective.

The clinician uses the *Exception Finding Question* to highlight the absence of the problem situation based on the client's experience. This technique has been used following the Miracle Question to focus the client on past or present occurrences of the desired behavioral goal. For example, a youth who expresses frustration based on conflict with a parent can be questioned about past times that were conflict-free. A focus on the client's behavior in these scenarios is essential. This process can identify past behaviors that have produced the desired result.

The clinician can gather information about progress toward goals by using the *Scaling Question.* Using a numeric scale from one to ten, clients are asked to rate a variety of subjective experiences such as current satisfaction or belief in their own ability to change. Following this, the therapist probes for specific behaviors or "what would need to happen" to improve on the subjective experience scale. The Scaling Question can then be applied to a query about the likelihood that the client will engage in this behavior. This process guides the client to break down seemingly overwhelming situations into smaller, more manageable behaviors that are steps toward a solution.

Life-Space Interventions

Working with troubled youth in congregate care facilities, the need for on-the-spot interventions was apparent. This work led Redl and others in the 1950s to the development of life-space interventions (LSI). Borrowing from life-space concepts put forth by Lewin (1951) and psychoanalytic concepts in the treatment of wayward youth advanced by Aichorn (1935), Redl and his associates developed usable techniques for those working directly with troubled youth. Nicholas Long worked under Redl in the mid-1950s and 1960s and expanded the clinical utility of the LSI. Mary Wood incorporated LSI into her developmental therapy curriculum, further demonstrating the utility of this intervention in schools for seriously emotionally disturbed youth. Many years later, this work culminated in a how-to text about LSI (Wood & Long, 1991).

Children vary in their capacity to deal effectively with the emotional demands of everyday life. Competing expectations from adults, individual frustration tolerance, peer group affiliations, and academic demands are among the many struggles faced by youth. Although youth with behavioral and emotional difficulties characteristically deal less effectively with these demands, most children and adolescents require some help or support at a time of challenge. For this reason, LSI has been widely used in residential and academic programs to help youth work through crisis situations (Beck & Dolce-Maule, 1998; Wood & Long, 1991).

The term *life-space* refers to the individual within a social context. Redl (1966) stressed understanding children's behavior within the context of their "direct life experience." When a child is in crisis, it is the role of the youth counselor, clinician, or teacher to function as a mediator among the forces in the young person's life-space. In order to convey the major concepts used, the six steps of a LSI, including the five common therapeutic goals, are reviewed next, based on the more detailed description by Wood and Long (1991). The first three steps of a LSI focus on the problem. Steps 4 through 6 comprise the solution.

Step 1, *Focus on the Incident*, directs the student to the event that gave rise to the crisis. The challenge of this first step depends on the child's capacity to cope with the emotions that result from the incident. Commonly, anger is displaced toward the worker. Supporting a student and allowing for an "emotional drain off" builds rapport, eventually opening the door to an opportunity to direct the student to begin describing the incident.

Step 2, *Students in Crisis Need to Talk*, is an interactive process wherein the practitioner walks the student through a time line of events. Unlike an interrogation, the practitioner uses detailed questions to encourage disclosure from the student and helps the individual organize and process what just happened. Active listening and reflection encourage the flow of information by assuring the student that he or she has been heard.

After sufficient information has been gathered, the practitioner moves to Step 3, *Find the Central Issue and Select a Therapeutic Goal*. The central issue may be directly related to the incident, such as when a child responds inappropriately to frustration or provocation. In other cases, the incident may serve merely to provide an opportunity for a child to express indirectly an underlying anxiety, such as feelings of alienation or a recent conflict with parents. When the central issue has been identified, an assessment of the student's motivation to change or gain insight about his or her behavior is assessed. Depending on the identified central issue and assessment of the student's perception and motivation to change, the practitioner selects a therapeutic goal. Before discussing solution steps, a brief review of the five therapeutic goals—Organize Reality, Confront Unacceptable Behavior, Build Values to Strengthen Self-Control, Teach New Social Skills, and Expose Exploitation—is provided to facilitate the understanding of the latter three steps.

The Organize Reality goal is used to help expand a student's understanding of an incident. This goal is applicable when helping aggressive youth interpret the intent of a peer's actions in an ambiguous situation. This scenario frequently results when an aggressive youth perceives a peer's actions as having a hostile intent (Dodge & Coie, 1987). When confronted with this situation, the intervention goal is to organize reality by helping the student explore other possible motives for the behavior.

Some students may have adopted an antisocial value system that condones deviant behavior. The goal in this situation is to Benignly Confront Unacceptable Behavior. By refocusing the student's perspective from his or her behavior to the perspective of the impact of the behavior on others, the practitioner promotes insight by the student about his or her actions. Modifying a narcissistic perspective to a more empathic viewpoint takes time and skill and is unlikely to occur in a single LSI. When used in conjunction with peer group interventions, the practitioner can encourage this shift in perspective to be addressed by the peer group. Even in moderately positive peer cultures, the group can be highly effective in conveying unflattering admonitions about behavior. This approach is particularly salient when intended gratification of the behavior is anticipated from the peer group.

The third goal strives to Build Values to Strengthen Self-Control. This goal is appropriate when a student has an organized, realistic picture of what happened and a clear sense of remorse and regret about the action, yet lacks an inner expectation of self-control. The presence of regret is key because it suggests the capacity for the child to make the right choice based on an existing value system. Unfortunately, sequencing is a problem in that the inner uncomfortable state associated with the behavior occurred after the behavior rather than serving a self-control function. This goal relates to strength-based and solution-focused philosophies. For example, the Exception Question could be used to prompt the student for times when he or she used a positive value system to exert self-control in a tempting situation. Highlighting these instances serves to build the student's internal expectation regarding the capacity for self-control.

Some crisis situations come about as a result of inept or inefficient social practices. Here, the practitioner is directed toward the fourth goal, Teach New Social Skills. A student engaged in disruptive behavior while attempting to impress someone to whom he or she is attracted or in an effort to build new relationships in a foreign peer group are common examples. The role of the practitioner in such a scenario is to affirm the student's intentions and provide alternative behavioral options that may better meet the individual's needs. Take notice of how such an approach differs from a more disciplinary, judgmental response or from the actions one would take if the therapeutic goal were to Confront Unacceptable Behavior. All too often when work-ing with youth with behavioral and emotional difficulties, the response by staff is harsh and based solely on overt behavior without consideration of intent. Such a re-sponse fails to provide children with the necessary tools to meet their needs and may further ostracize them from adults and peers.

A final goal as presented by Redl (1959) and Wood and Long (1991) is to Expose Exploitation. Some students find themselves in troublesome situations following ma-nipulation by more sophisticated students. Usually under the guise of friendship, such relationships are commonplace when examining group dynamics (Polsky, 1962). The role of the practitioner is to demonstrate the self-serving behavior of the manipulator while sensitively pointing out how the behavior of the other was a form of exploita-tion. In addition to dealing with this situation in a LSI, this scenario lends itself to both strength-based and peer group interventions. The qualities of both students that underlie their behaviors can be reframed as strengths. The manipulator has the ca-pacity to influence others, show initiative, and demonstrate leadership ability. The ex-ploited student may be cooperative, dedicated, loyal, and value relationships. The fact that these strengths were misused in this scenario to produce an undesirable outcome can be challenged while also recognizing both students' capacity to redirect their skills to accomplish greater things. By pointing out the misguided application of potentially useful, advantageous qualities, the practitioner conveys a sense of hope and optimism to both students.

In terms of a peer group intervention in the Expose Exploitation scenario, the practitioner could conduct the LSI with the entire group and lead them to the dis-covery of this manipulation. This process can serve to challenge the value system of the manipulator, provide social support to the exploited, and highlight the potential for success in both students by focusing on their underlying strengths.

Step 4, *Choose a Solution Based on Values*, follows selection of a therapeutic goal. Ideally, the choice comes from the student following a process of exploring various al-ternatives. After a solution has been selected and agreed on, it is time for Step 5, *Plan for Success*. To maximize the likelihood that the insight gained and the solution selected are translated into actual change, the practitioner and student rehearse the solution and explore possible consequences. In a sense, Step 5 concludes the discussion of the event and the solution. In the final step, the practitioner helps the student *Get Ready to Resume the Activity*. Anticipated issues are explored and concrete steps are provided to ensure a smooth transition.

Conclusion

In developing interventions for children with behavioral and emotional difficulties, this chapter has encouraged a shift from more traditional psychotherapy models to in-terventions that are readily applied in school and community settings. Three specific advantages are noteworthy. First, progress in research and practice has redirected the focus of interventions from the individual to the system or context. With adolescents, the primary focus is the peer group context. Second, rather than directing interventions only at deficits, there are clear benefits to building on children's and families' strengths and working with a focus on problem solutions. Finally, although the set hour-per-week pattern of traditional individual psychotherapy has advantages of consistency and regularity, long interludes between sessions may miss the moment, especially for children and adolescents. A life-space intervention approach, on the contrary, has the advantage of helping youth when it may be most needed and can provide maximum benefit.

The interventions discussed illustrate the blurred distinction between treatment and prevention orientations. Although used in many residential treatment centers for pronounced emotional and behavioral difficulties, the interventions reviewed are adaptable to virtually all youth in schools, community programs, and clinics. The encouragement of prosocial peer networks, the development of strengths in young people, and building therapeutic response skills among adults working with youth has universal applicability.

References

Aichorn, A. (1935). *Wayward youth*. New York: Viking.

Asch, S. E. (1987). *Social psychology*. Oxford, England: Oxford University Press. (Original work published 1952).

Banks, V. (1999). A solution focused approach to adolescent groupwork. *Australian & New Zealand Journal of Family Therapy, 20*, 78–82.

Barber, S., & Lane, R. C. (1995). Efficacy research in psychodynamic therapy: A critical review of the literature. *Psychotherapy in Private Practice, 14*(3), 43–69.

Beauvais, F., Chavez, E., L., Oetting, E. R., Deffenbacher, J. L., & Cornell, G. R. (1996). Drug use, violence, and victimization among White Americans, Mexican Americans and American Indian dropouts, students with academic problems, and students in good academic standing. *Journal of Counseling Psychology, 43*, 292–299.

Beck, A. T. (1995). Cognitive therapy: Past, present, and future. In M. J. Mahoney (Ed.), *Cognitive and constructive psychotherapies: Theories, research, and practice* (pp. 29–40). New York: Springer.

Beck, M., & Dolce-Maule, D. (1998). The development of a quality school: A four year journey. *International Journal of Reality Therapy, 18*(1), 23–28.

Berg, I. K. (1994). *Family-based services: A solution-focused approach*. New York: Norton.

Billig, M., & Tajfel, H. (1973). Social categorization and similarity in intergroup behavior. *European Journal of Social Psychology, 3*, 27–52.

Brendtro, L. K. (1999). Positive peer culture: Enlisting youth in reclaiming youth. In G. A. Giacobbe, E.

Traynelis-Yurek, & E. K. Laursen (Eds.), *Strengths based strategies for children and youth: An annotated bibliography* (pp. ii-ix). Richmond, VA: G & T.

Brendtro, L., Brokenleg, M., & Van Bockern, S. (1990). *Reclaiming youth at risk: Our hope for the future*. Bloomington, IN: National Educational Services.

Brendtro, L. K., & Ness, A. E. (1982). Perspectives on peer group treatment: The use and abuse of Guided Group Interaction/Positive Peer Culture. *Children and Youth Services Review, 4*, 307–324.

Brendtro, L. K., & Ness, A. E. (1991). Extreme interventions for extreme behavior: Peer-assisted behavior management in group treatment programs. *Child and Youth Care Forum, 20*, 171–181.

Cooper, M. L., Peirce, R. S., Tidwell, M. O. (1995). Parental drinking problems and adolescent offspring substance use: Moderating effects of demographic and familial factors. *Psychology of Addictive Behaviors, 9*, 36–52.

Corcoran, J. (1997). A solution-oriented approach to working with juvenile offenders. *Child & Adolescent Social Work Journal, 14*, 277–288.

Cowen, E. L. (1997). The coming of age of primary prevention: Comments on Durlak and Well's meta-analysis. *American Journal of Community Psychology, 25*(2), 153–167.

Crick, N. R., & Dodge, K. A. (1994). A review and reformulation of social information-processing mechanisms in children's social adjustment. *Psychological Bulletin, 115*, 74–101.

Cumsille, P. E., & Epstein, N. (1994). Family cohesion, family adaptability, social support, and adolescent depressive symptoms in outpatient clinic families. *Journal of Family Psychology, 8*, 202–214.

De Jong, P., & Miller, S. D. (1995). How to interview for client strengths. *Social Work, 40*, 729–736.

Desetta, A., & Wolin, S. (Eds.). (2000). *The struggle to be strong: True stories by teens about overcoming tough times.* Minneapolis, MN: Free Spirit.

De Shazer, S. (1985). *Keys to solution in brief therapy.* New York: Norton.

Dishion, T. J., & Andrews, D. W. (1995). Preventing escalation in problem behaviors with high-risk young adolescents: Immediate and 1–year outcomes. *Journal of Consulting and Clinical Psychology, 63*, 538–548.

Dishion, T. J., McCord, J., & Poulin, F. (1999). When interventions harm: Peer groups and problem behavior. *American Psychologist, 54*, 755–764.

Dodge, K. A., & Coie, J. D. (1987). Social information-processing factors in reactive and proactive aggression in children's playgrounds. *Journal of Personality and Social Psychology, 53*, 1146–1158.

Dodge, K. A., Pettit, G. S., & Bates, J. E. (1994). Effects of physical maltreatment on the development of peer relations. *Development and Psychopathology, 6*, 43–55.

Downing, J., & Harrison, T. (1992). Solutions and school counseling. *School Counselor, 39*, 327–332.

Eccles, J. S., Midgley, C., Wigfield, A., Buchanan, C. M., Reuman, D., Flanagan, C., & Mac Iver, D. (1993). Development during adolescence: The impact of stage–environment fit on young adolescents' experiences in schools and in families. *American Psychologist, 48*, 90–101.

Farrell, A. D., & White, K. S. (1998). Peer influences and drug use among urban adolescents: Family structure and parent–adolescent relationship as protective factors. *Journal of Consulting and Clinical Psychology, 66*, 248–258.

Giacobbe, G. A., Traynelis-Yurek, E., & Laursen, E. K. (1999). *Strengths based strategies for children and youth: An annotated bibliography.* Richmond, VA: G & T.

Gibbs, J., Potter, G., & Goldstein, A. (1995). *The EQUIP program.* Champaign, IL: Research Press.

Gold, M. (1970). *Delinquent behavior in an American city.* San Francisco: Brooks and Coleman.

Gold, M., & Osgood, D. (1992). *Personality and peer influence in juvenile corrections.* Westport, CT: Greenwood Press.

Graham, S., & Hudley, C. (1994). Attributions of aggressive and nonaggressive African-American male early adolescents: A study of construct accessibility. *Developmental Psychology, 30*, 365–373.

Green, G. J., Lee, M., Trask, R., & Rheinscheld, J. (1996). Client strengths and crisis intervention: A solution-focused approach. *Crisis Intervention & Time-Limited Treatment, 3*, 43–63.

Griffin, K. W., Botvin, G. J., Scheier, L. M., Diaz, T., & Miller, N. L. (2000). Parenting practices as predictors of substance use, delinquency, and aggression among urban minority youth: Moderating effects of family structure and gender. *Psychology of Addictive Behaviors, 14*, 174–184.

Harris, J. R. (1995). Where is the child's environment? A group socialization theory of development. *Psychological Review, 102*, 458–489.

Hersen, M., Eisler, R. M., & Miller, P. M. (Eds.). (1990). *Progress in behavior modification* (Vol. 26). Newbury Park, CA: Sage.

Hinshaw, S. P. (1992). Academic underachievement, attention deficits, and aggression comorbidity and implications for interventions. *Journal of Consulting and Clinical Psychology, 60*, 893–903.

Jessor, R. (1993). Successful adolescent development among youth in high-risk settings. *American Psychologist, 48*, 117–126.

Jessor, R., & Jessor, S. L. (1977). *Problem behavior and psychosocial development: A longitudinal study of youth.* New York: Academic Press.

Kazdin, A. E. (1988). *Child psychotherapy: Developing and identifying effective treatments.* Elmsford, NY: Pergamon Press.

Kazdin, A. E. (1989). *Behavior modification in applied settings* (4th ed.). Pacific Grove, CA: Brooks/Cole.

Kazdin, A. E. (1993a). Adolescent mental health: Prevention and treatment programs. *American Psychologist, 48*, 127–141.

Kazdin, A. E. (1993b). Psychotherapy for children and adolescents: Current progress and future research directions. *American Psychologist, 48*, 644–657.

LaFountain, R., Garner, N., & Boldosser, S. (1995). Solution-focused counseling groups for children and adolescents. *Journal of Systemic Therapies, 14*(4), 39–51.

Lantieri, L., & Patti, P. (1997). *Waging peace in our schools.* Boston: Beacon Press.

Lee, M. (1997). A study of solution-focused brief family therapy: Outcomes and issues. *American Journal of Family Therapy, 25*, 3–17.

Lee, R. E. (1996). FIRO-B scores and success in a positive peer-culture residential treatment program. *Psychological Reports, 78*, 215–220.

Lewin, K. (1951). *Field theory in social science: Selected the-*

oretical papers. (D. Cartwright, Ed.). New York: Harper & Row.

Liddle, H. A. (1996). Family-based treatment for adolescent problem behaviors: Overview of contemporary developments and introduction to the special section. *Journal of Family Psychology, 10,* 3–11.

Murphy, G. E. (1989). Cognitive therapy: A review. In J. G. Howells (Ed.), *Modern perspectives in the psychiatry of neuroses* (pp. 260–285). New York: Brunner/Mazel.

Murphy, J. J. (1996). Solution-focused brief therapy in the school. In S. D. Miller, M. A. Hubble, & B. L. Duncan (Eds.), *Handbook of solution-focused brief therapy* (pp. 184–204). San Francisco: Jossey-Bass.

Murphy, J. J., & Duncan, B. L. (1997). *Brief interventions for school problems: Collaborating for practical solutions.* New York: Guilford Press.

O'Donnell, J., Hawkins, J. D., & Abbott, R. D. (1995). Predicting serious delinquency and substance use among aggressive boys. *Journal of Consulting and Clinical Psychology, 63,* 529–537.

Oetting, E. R., & Beauvais, F. (1986). Peer cluster theory: Drugs and the adolescent. *Journal of Counseling and Development, 65,* 17–22.

Oetting, E. R., & Beauvais, F. (1987). Peer cluster theory, socialization characteristics, and adolescent drug use: A path analysis. *Journal of Counseling Psychology, 34,* 205–213.

Patterson, G. R. (1993). Orderly change in a stable world: The antisocial trait as a chimera. *Journal of Consulting and Clinical Psychology, 61,* 911–919.

Patterson, G. R., DeBaryshe, B. D., & Ramsey, E. (1989). A developmental perspective on antisocial behavior. *American Psychologist, 44,* 329–335.

Polsky, H. (1962). *Cottage six.* New York: Russell Sage.

Redl, F. (1959). The concept of a therapeutic milieu. *American Journal of Orthopsychiatry, 29,* 721–736.

Redl, F. (1966). *When we deal with children.* New York: Free Press.

Robins, L. N., & Earls, F. (1985). A program for preventing antisocial behavior for high-risk infants and preschoolers: A research prospectus. In R. L. Hough, P. A. Gongia, V. B. Brown, & S. E. Goldston (Eds.), *Psychiatric epidemiology and prevention: The possibilities* (pp. 73–84). Los Angeles: Neuropsychiatric Institute.

Sherif, M., Harvey, O. J., White, B. J., Hood, W. R., & Sherif, C. W. (1961). *Intergroup cooperation and competition: The Robber's Cave experiment.* Norman, OK: University Book Exchange.

Takanishi, R. (1993). The opportunities of adolescence—research, interventions, and policy: Introduction to the special issue. *American Psychologist, 48,* 85–87.

Thompson, G. (1998, December 9). School takes on others' failures: Teaching the delinquent and abandoned with success. *New York Times,* pp. B1, B5.

Tolan, P. H., Guerra, N. G., & Kendall, P. C. (1995a). A developmental–ecological perspective on antisocial behavior in children and adolescents: Toward a unified risk and intervention framework. *Journal of Consulting and Clinical Psychology, 63,* 579–584.

Tolan, P. H., Guerra, N. G., & Kendall, P. C. (1995b). Introduction to special section: Prediction and prevention of antisocial behavior in children and adolescents. *Journal of Consulting and Clinical Psychology, 63,* 515–517.

Vorrath, H. H., & Brendtro, L. K. (1985). *Positive peer culture* (2nd ed.). New York: Aldine De Gruyter.

Wallerstein, R. S. (1995). Research in psychodynamic therapy. In H. J. Schwartz, E. Bleiberg, & S. H. Weissman (Eds.), *Psychodynamic concepts in general psychiatry* (pp. 431–456). Washington, DC: American Psychiatric Press.

Wolin, S., Desetta, A., & Hefner, K. (2000). *A leader's guide to The Struggle To Be Strong: How to foster resilience in teens.* Minneapolis, MN: Free Spirit.

Wood, M. M., & Long, N. J. (1991). *Life-space intervention: Talking with children and youth in crisis.* Austin, TX: PRO-ED.

Zimbardo, P. G. (1972). Pathology of imprisonment. *Society, 9,* 4–8.

Zimmerman, T. S., Jacobsen, R. B., MacIntyre, M., & Watson, C. (1996). Solution-focused parenting groups: An empirical study. *Journal of Systemic Therapies, 15*(4), 12–25.

Zingraff, M. T., Leiter, J., Johnsen, M. C., & Myers, K. A. (1994). The mediating effect of good school performance on the maltreatment–delinquency relationship. *Journal of Research in Crime and Delinquency, 31,* 62–91.

17

Community-Based Interventions for Urban and Minority Youth

Gerald Porter and
Lawrence A. Vitulano

Traditionally, in our society, services of all kinds have been provided to children and their families in specialized and isolated venues. Education was provided by schools but children's other needs, in areas such as health care, social services, or criminal justice, were typically offered in geographically diverse locations by specialized agencies with little regard for client problems that fell outside their purview. Usually, services would be provided only if a child's parents or other advocates actively pursued assistance, or, in the case of the juvenile or criminal justice system, whether as perpetrators or victims, they were thrust into the system. Often, providers did not appreciate how their interventions might unintentionally create new problems for highly stressed or marginalized children and families. For example, the family of a father who is incarcerated might be impoverished or need counseling to cope with their loss. The stress that such an event might generate in a child could result in academic failure or social withdrawal in school. Depression in the mother in reaction to the father's incarceration could result in child neglect or an inability to follow through with referrals for needed services.

Over the years, service providers to children and their families noticed that a small, but perhaps growing, segment of the population required interventions from multiple agencies. Often the individuals and families with the most difficult and seemly intransigent problems were those who most needed services from more than one provider. Similarly, educators increasingly observed that the children who were the most likely to fail or become serious behavior problems came from the same families that needed multiple services within the community (Chesapeake Institute, 1994; Northwest Regional Educational Laboratory, 1991a, 1991b).

Two of the groups most likely to need these multiple services were poor youth in urban areas and children (and their families) of color including African Americans, Latinos, and Native Americans. Poor urban youth and children of color are two groups that overlap, but perhaps this overlap population is the most at-risk for academic failure, serious emotional disturbance, inadequate health care, and entanglements in the criminal justice system (Chesapeake Institute, 1994; Northwest Regional Educational Laboratory, 1991a, 1991b; McPartland & Slavin, 1990).

Existing services have been shown consistently to be inadequate to meet the needs of children and adolescents with serious emotional or behavioral problems (Chesapeake Institute, 1994; Northwest Regional Educational Laboratory, 1991b; Morley & Rossman, 1997). Cotton (Northwest Regional Educational Laboratory, 1991b) reports a long list of inadequacies with traditional services. A few of the most common problems include cultural insensitivity, conflicting eligibility requirements, services delivered in a dehumanizing and excessively bureaucratic manner, the absence of needed service providers in the locality, and the limited availability of services due to client time constraints or geographical distance.

Researchers and policymakers began to formulate strategies for serving these children and families with complex multifaceted problems. Usually the strategies proposed involved bringing together divergent service providers into a single shared location that was readily accessible to this hardcore underserved population, and some form of case management to coordinate services and to make certain families could successfully navigate the system to get what they need (Chesapeake Institute,1994; Morley & Rossman, 1997). Schools, in theory, might be the ideal location for the provision of comprehensive, integrated services for a variety of reasons. Schools already are located in neighborhoods throughout the city and are readily accessible to residents of every neighborhood. Often, children from the most disturbed families are first identified in the classroom, and so teachers frequently are the first to realize that a child and its family have serious difficulties. Identifying a child at school or in a preschool screening can result in early intervention, a more cost-effective way to produce greater developmental and psychological gains. Early intervention with appropriate developmental supports might break the transmission of maladaptive behavior from one generation to the next (Chesapeake Institute, 1994).

What is Community-Based Intervention?

There is no single simple answer to the question posed in this section heading. Community-based intervention means different things from different institutional perspectives. From the vantage point of education, community-based intervention implies a broader sense of mission than conventional schooling has assumed. From a community-based perspective, the goal of education is not merely the acquisition of a prescribed set of academic skills presumed to be necessary for success in the world. Community-based intervention implies a more developmental, ecological, and learner-centered approach to education. Academic success and the facilitation of the natural developmental process is not likely to occur unless the child, as a complete person, is nurtured and given the necessary attention. Such an approach implies that schools need to do more, but simultaneously need to recognize their limitations. It is the dual acknowledgment of the necessity to provide for the needs of the whole child, combined with the knowledge of what they cannot do, that has encouraged schools to enter into partnership with other service providers in the community.

In order to remove the barriers to academic success, foster personal growth, and prepare children to be productive citizens, the schools, in partnership with other providers in the community, must address whatever problems interfere with the realization of these goals. Any kind of social–emotional difficulty in the child's environment, such as parental psychiatric or marital problems or sibling conflict, must be addressed. Problems in accessing health care or mental health services, difficulties with the courts or the justice system, the use of excessive physical punishment or sexual abuse, and the effects of poverty, including overt consequences, such as poor diet and nutrition, or covert effects, such as inadequate cognitive stimulation or demoralization, all must be acknowledged and addressed. Chronic or life-threatening disease in a child, parent, or sibling must be considered in the form of appropriate treatment and to ameliorate the psychoemotional stress that inevitably arises as a result of such experiences. Schools cannot deal with such problems alone but, in collaborative arrangements with other providers, schools can be valuable contributors to a comprehensive, integrated response to such difficulties.

Each child is a unique individual, and this is particularly evident among children who themselves, or in combination with their families, have complex, multifaceted difficulties. For such children and their families, the concept of integrated services implies that the treatment plan for each child is actively designed to meet the particular needs of the individual child and her or his family. The child cannot be adequately served if the disruptive, debilitating family issues in the child's environment are not also being considered. This coordination of services implies facilitating the availability of services by removing barriers such as lack of transportation, the need for child care, lack of respite care, or lack of health insurance (Morley & Rossman, 1997). A community-based approach also implies a preference for early intervention, a commitment to the least restrictive interventions, and preventive activities before remedial services are needed.

From an educational perspective, community-based intervention (CBI) is defined as any of a variety of integrated, coordinated services designed to prevent or remediate any problem that interferes with the academic success of a child. It is assumed that services conventionally available in a school constitute only one component of the variety of services available within a community. In addition, it assumes that these services will be coordinated so that they meet the particular multifaceted needs of individuals.

CBIs also can be designed to target particular populations or problems of a given community that might involve as few as two cooperating agencies or as many as necessary to address a large-scale need in underserved populations. Whether narrow in scope and mission or broad and comprehensive in composition, CBIs usually embrace the kind of collaborative, idiographic, inclusive philosophy of service described above.

Varieties of Community-Based Interventions

CBI programs can vary dramatically in scope and in the type of services emphasized. At the more modest end of the spectrum, there are collaborations between two agencies to address some specific deficit recognized, but not adequately addressed, by both parties. These dual agency partnerships might target a particular problem or class of clients that neither agency could serve effectively alone. One example of such a partnership is the Child Development–Community Policing Program of New Haven, Connecticut. The program involves the cooperation of two agencies that might typically have little or no direct contact.

The Child Development–Community Policing Program

When children and adults witness, or are direct victims of violence, basic psychological functioning is undermined and the lines between fantasy and reality are blurred as the individual's most powerful and potentially frightening fantasies about bodily damage, loss of relationships, and loss of impulse control are enacted in a most immediate way. Symptoms that may follow often involve disruptions in patterns of sleeping, eating, toileting, attention, and relating as well as experiences of generalized fearfulness and possible flashbacks of the violent event. When a child is exposed to the dangers of violence on a regular basis, symptoms may develop into a chronic syndrome in which physiological, cognitive, and affective regulatory capacities are severely compromised.

Due to increasing concerns about the particular burden that violence places on children's development, the Child Development–Community Policing Program (CD–CP) was developed in New Haven, Connecticut. Based on the application of sound developmental principles, the program began in 1991 as a collaboration between the Yale Child Study Center and the New Haven Department of Police Services (Marans et al., 1995). It is the natural outgrowth of several early meetings among clinicians and police about shared concerns for children surrounded by violence. The CD–CP attempts to reorient police officers in their interactions with children and, consequently, helps them to better utilize their psychological role as providers of a sense of security and as models of benign figures of authority. Similarly, this collaboration allows mental health clinicians an opportunity to play a more significant role in the lives of children and families exposed to violence in the community, home, and schools. Although police officers come in daily contact with children who are victims, witnesses, and perpetrators of violence, they generally have neither the professional training, sufficient time, nor other resources necessary to meet these children's psychological needs. Conversely, clinic-based mental health professionals may be professionally equipped to respond to children's psychological distress, but have little opportunity to do so. Too often, traumatized children are rarely seen in outpatient clinics until months or years later, if at all, when chronic symptoms or maladaptive behavior brings them to the attention of parents, teachers, or juvenile courts. Valuable opportunities are, therefore, lost. Intervening at the moment when professional contact could be most useful may provide both immediate stabilization and a bridge to a variety of helping services.

Currently, the CD–CP provides a range of training and consultation services in the community, including a 24–hour on-call senior clinician available to officers, children and families who are directly involved in violent incidents. In addition, cases are reviewed at a weekly case conference cochaired by police officers and clinicians. At this meeting, cases are presented, information shared, and treatment plans developed. The conference is regularly attended by senior clinicians and police, staff from probation and protective services, and other individuals who can contribute to the care and planning of a specific case under discussion. This might include, for example, the beat officer and the child's former therapist. In addition, clinicians meet weekly for discussion and supervision of this intense collaborative work that often requires immediate action and involvement in horrific traumatic situations. Over the years, it has been found that this work cannot be accomplished by a single entity. It necessarily takes an interdisciplinary approach, with team members who are mutually supportive and available to work together on a moment's notice. Also, the nature of this work often results in more than one or two clinicians being involved in the treatment of a family with multiple children.

The training for the CD–CP approach is necessarily collaborative. Police train clinicians and clinicians train police in their respective procedures, responsibilities, and interventions, with "the best interests of the child" guiding the work. Police spend hours taking clinicians on ride-alongs with them on their tours of duty, explaining and showing how they work. This experience is counterbalanced by just as many hours in the classroom teaching clinicians about policing administration, procedures, tactics, and other essential matters. Concomitantly, clinicians offer police an introduction to the theories of development that guide their work, with an emphasis on practical approaches to understanding and helping children and families. For instance, police officers often find it quite helpful to understand why babies frequently cry when separated from their caregivers or why adolescents are so challenging on the streets in the presence of their peers.

The CD–CP model has been replicated in several cities across the United States and Europe. In the past four years alone, the New Haven police have referred over 1,000 children and their families who have experienced violence, as well as hundreds of children who have committed serious violent offenses. These children often have received clinical services within minutes of the police response to scenes of violence and tragedy, such as murders, stabbings, beatings, fires, drownings, and gunfire. The children and their families have been seen individually and as part of larger groups. Settings for these services have been in their homes, at police stations, at schools, in their neighborhoods, and within the Child Study Center. As part of the CD–CP model, specialized outreach teams have now been established for victims and child witnesses of domestic violence and for juveniles placed in detention. Specialized outreach programs have been instituted for high-risk children. Programs have been developed in the schools for children exposed to gang and other related forms of violence and in the courts for gateway delinquents who, as first-time offenders, are at risk of developing more chronic patterns of antisocial or other maladaptive forms of adjustment.

Overstimulation and excessive levels of stress often threaten a child's newly consolidated and most recently attained developmental capacities. The regression that can follow is especially compromising for children whose development already is fragile. However, it is essential that the assumptions about a child's possible traumatization not be determined solely by the facts associated with the violent event but, rather, by the meaning the child attributes to the event. If we can determine the best interventions, then we must learn about the *child's* experience of the external events in the context of her or his inner life. Above all else, clinicians must continue to be good and careful listeners. Children's exposure to violence may precipitate a host of responses that reflect the powerful convergence of internal and external dangers. These are derived from both the past and the present and are mediated by the degree of support and availability of the family. Unfortunately for far too many children in this country, the violent horrors that originally belonged only to the world of the child's most primitive fears and terrors materialize in real-life experiences. As a result, basic feelings of safety and security, essential to the child's developing sense of competence and mastery, are severely undermined. However, in addition to the symptomatology that may follow, the traumatic experiences can introduce a small window of opportunity for informed proximate interventions that can help identify and untangle the various webs of danger and, consequently, help a child return to a more normal path of development.

This model was recently found helpful for a 13-year-old girl who refused to return to school after several physical altercations with her classmates. One evening, the on-call clinician was summoned after this adolescent was assaulted at the corner bus stop near her home. She was even more upset after being questioned by the police, who were trying to get a description of the suspect. After an hour interview, the young girl revealed to the clinician that the assault was especially upsetting because the perpetrator reminded her of other men who used to do bad things to her. In fact, a family caretaker had been molesting her, but she was afraid to reveal the situation previously because of family allegiances and threats of retaliation from the perpetrator. Together, this girl, her clinician, and her community police officer determined how to approach her family and eventually prosecute the perpetrator, to everyone's satisfaction and great relief. In the acute phase of the treatment, picture drawings helped the adolescent describe and remember the horrific events of the past. Later, in twice-weekly psychotherapy for the following six months, she was able to reestablish trusting relationships with her mother and regain her previously high level of functioning at school, both academically and on the athletic field. The community police officer continues to be available to the family and thus helps to ensure a sense of safety and provide a source of available authority for this girl.

Comprehensive Community Initiatives as Large-Scale Community Based Interventions

The CD–CP program is an example of a small, localized collaboration. At the other end of the size and scope scale, there are comprehensive community-based systems of care. Weiss (The Aspen Institute, 1999) called such large-scale efforts comprehensive community initiatives (CCIs). She explained that CCIs "aim to reform human service and collateral systems in geographically bounded communities. They work across functional areas—such as social services, health care, the schools, and economical and physical redevelopment—in an effort to launch a comprehensive attack on the social and economic constraints that lock poor children and their families in poverty. They bring local residents into positions of authority in the local program, along with leaders of the larger community, public officials, and service providers" (p. 1).

CCIs targeting mental health services for children and their families have been initiated by various states, the federal government, and private foundations. In an effort to foster reform in services to children with serious emotional disturbance, the federal government, in 1986, instituted the Child and Adolescent Service System Program (CASSP). The goal was to reduce the utilization of costly and restrictive inpatient intervention and to encourage outpatient treatment in the local community. The CASSP also hoped to reduce treatment costs by funding the creation of a comprehensive system of care that would function as a large-scale CCI, bringing together schools, child welfare agencies, and mental health providers. It was envisioned that, working in collaboration, seriously emotionally disturbed children and their families would be provided with individualized services from multiple agencies that would constructively involve parents and maintain child clients in their home schools and community (Northwest Regional Educational Laboratory, 1991a; Robert Wood Johnson Foundation, 1998).

Attempting to expand this type of large-scale system of care for underserved children, adolescents, and their families, the Robert Wood Johnson Foundation initiated a national demonstration project in 1998 called the Mental Health Services Program for Youth (MHSPY). The program was started with an initial investment of $20 million. The MHSPY was conducted in eight communities across the United States, including the entire state of Vermont. The MHSPY shared essentially the same philosophy and goals as the CASSP. Saxe and Cross (Robert Wood Johnson Foundation, 1998, p. 5) write that the "MHSPY's most important idea may not be coordinated systems of care but the idea that services must be designed specifically around the needs of children and families."

Policy analysts and government officials, to a lesser extent, have long advocated CCIs, but, until relatively recently, few such initiatives actually have been implemented. This may be because such large-scale efforts demand an enormous reorganization of service delivery systems, funding arrangements, personnel utilization, and geographic location of programs. Such efforts are costly and it has not been unambiguously demonstrated that the investment produces sufficient rewards.

Youth Community Service Programs

Another variant of CBIs are youth community service programs. Youth community service programs provide young people with opportunities to make meaningful contributions to the neighborhoods where they live or to the greater community. Community service may take many forms and can be directed to such concerns as environmental cleanup and ecological management, crime prevention, housing restoration, tutoring and academic remediation, and peer counseling. Some of the most innovative community service programs enable youth to identify the problems they, as a group, are most concerned about, formulate interventions, and then carry out their plans. Lewis (1992) believed that community service programs give urban youth the chance to develop important vocational and life skills. Participants can observe directly how their actions improve the welfare of the community. As a result, Lewis asserts that community service promotes academic achievement, builds self-confidence and self-esteem, cultivates empathy for others, builds problem-solving skills, provides the opportunity for youth to work cooperatively with peers and adults, and gives young people the responsibility for the completion of socially valued tasks. These kinds of experiences cultivate a sense of personal responsibility as well as a sense of place based on the assumption of a valued role within their community. It should be mentioned that the philosophy behind these kinds of activities is very much in keeping with those described by Cone (Chapter 16) as peer group interventions.

Ianni (1992, p. 1) claims that every community has an implicit youth charter that consists of an "unwritten set of expectations and standards" for young people. This implicit youth charter defines what is considered acceptable, appropriate behavior and the attitudes that community members are expected to hold. Community service provides young people with a context in which to measure themselves against the standards of the charter. Youth learn about the society and about the roles they might take within it. Ianni also argues that the nature and quality of our relationships is dependent on place. He calls for community-based interventions for youth that institutionalize behavior based on demands imposed by mutually acknowledged shared needs rather than intervention that focuses on changing individual behavior in isolation.

The community can be a social support system for youth that can compensate for emotional and material deficits in family life. Ianni (1992) argues that caring, supportive community involvement can overcome the debilitating effects of an uncaring family. Positive youth development interventions are thought to increase competence in five major areas: social, emotional, cognitive, behavioral, and moral competencies (Catalano, Berglund, Ryan, Lonczak, & Hawkins, 1998).

Guidelines for Starting a Successful Community-Based Intervention

Whatever the scope or focus of CBIs, these interagency collaborations offer schools and participating providers a number of advantages. Successful CBIs are likely to share a number of characteristics according to Sheridan (1995).

Effective CBIs are both top-down and bottom-up in their organizational structure. The intellectual capital and management expertise coming from school and agency-based professionals must constantly be balanced with the insights and personal investment of members of the community. This means that children and their parents, as well as other interested community members, should be involved in the planning and operation of a CBI from the onset (National Clearinghouse on Families and Youth, 1996; Northwest Regional Educational Laboratory, 1991b). If the initiative for a CBI comes from a school, Sheridan (1995) warns that schools must assume a collaborative role and not try to assume control. The particular configuration of services must be determined by the needs of the community and the availability of resources. For this reason, the planning and development phase of establishing a CBI is necessarily inclusive and creative. The program must meet the needs that community members find meaningful and formulate service delivery systems that are easily accessible (Chesapeake Institute, 1994). Planners need to be creative not only in where they locate services, or in the formulation of particular strategies, but in finding ways to fund interventions without becoming bogged down in the usual interagency turf wars.

Sheridan (1995) notes that successful CBIs are client-centered and take a problem-solving approach. Prevention and interventions that foster development need to be emphasized. School and other agency administrators need to allocate time for staff involvement in the collaboration process. In addition, staff may need training because it is likely that they will be required to perform new tasks and to assume unfamiliar roles. Administrators, as part of their inclusive efforts, must hire staff who live in and are visible members of the community being served. Finally, the evaluation phase of establishing a successful CBI involves designing program measures that are sensitive to the collaborative structures and arrangements that comprise the program (Ascher, 1990; Sheridan, 1995).

The Advantages of School Participation in Community-Based Interventions

The development and implementation of a CBI is a substantial undertaking. Sheridan (1995) identified four reasons schools might want to make that effort. First, by sharing and pooling resources with other agencies, schools can do more to help underserved students that can be done in isolation. By addressing student needs outside the traditional academic skills mandate, schools ultimately can better accomplish their primary mission. Secondly, the shared context between two or more service providers not only increases the available resources for treatment, but encourages the development of new and innovative interventions that a school or single agency might not have been able to launch independently. School/community partnerships also create new opportunities for the professional development of staff and foster innovation in the delivery of services (Ascher,1990). Finally, Sheridan concluded that CBIs result in better and increased instructional services to all students. By attending to student needs that traditionally were referred out or went unaddressed, schools, in partnership with other agencies, can direct more time and attention to instruction because the student problems that interfered with learning are now being treated.

Characteristics of Good Community-Based Interventions

There are a number of characteristics that most successful CBIs exhibit. Most take a problem-solving approach to the identification of goals and interventions (Sheridan, 1995). The process of defining the problem should be inclusive, in that parents and other stakeholders in the community, along with the professional and management staff of the participating agencies, all participate in the process. Planners should try to determine who is not getting the services they need, where these services might be provided, and who is going to directly intervene with the clients. Building a shared consensus is challenging because the ability to come up with collaborative strategies is dependent on agreeing on the nature of the problem(s) and on the rationale for proposed solutions. Staff from participating agencies need to be honest about their limitations and shortcomings. For example, the police in the CD–CP Program described earlier had frequent contact with children and families who were victimized by violence but had little expertise in meeting the psychological needs of victims. Similarly, mental health clinicians could help the victims of violence cope with their psychological distress, but lacked the ability to intervene swiftly before maladaptive coping responses become chronic. Working together, both agencies could compensate for limitations in their traditional modes of service delivery. If parents and community members are involved in consensus-building, they will see firsthand that the problems are not clear-cut, and be challenged to take responsibility in more constructive ways.

Successful CBIs are likely to take an ecological approach (Morley & Rossman, 1997; Sheridan, 1995). This means that, during the problem definition and intervention formulation stages of collaboration, all the factors that contribute to the inadequate service to specific groups of children and families must be considered. Any of the social, economic, political, interpersonal, psychiatric, or legal issues that have bearing on the well-being of the child need to be considered and, ultimately, addressed. The inclusion of all the potential stakeholders is a good way to make sure the analysis will be ecological.

The National Association of State Boards of Education (1992) advocates that CBIs develop a formal management plan that spells out all the responsibilities and strategies that need to be followed for successful implementation. Good planning and management are essential (Hahn, 1992), and these activities must include the least powerful stakeholders, such as poor and minority parents, in all phases of CBI implementation. Collaborative program development and implementation implies that no stakeholder group or agency can dominate or take control of the process. In the example of the CD–CP, both the police and mental health professionals respected each other's expertise in their respective domains, and both police and clinicians devoted a considerable amount of time to learning each other's policies and procedures.

Once the program is underway, it is essential to determine if it really works. Both formative and summative evaluation strategies need to be developed and the data obtained should be used to revise the implementation of interventions when appropriate. The complex, and often qualitatively complex interactions embedded within a CBI, may necessitate some alternative approaches to evaluation, a possibility discussed later in this chapter.

Barriers to Building Community Based Interventions

The barriers that prevent the building of new CBIs or impair the performance of existing CBIs have two sources, agencies and clients. Agency-based barriers are those imposed by the providers themselves, and usually boil down to institutional resistance to change in one guise or another. The management and staff of an agency may lack the motivation to collaborate for any number of reasons—fear of losing influence, clients, or funding. At a more basic level, the sense of mission at an agency may be too narrow to allow the kinds of changes and collaborative arrangements implied by CBIs.

The funding of agencies, especially government or United Way agencies, has often been based on the number of clients served in the previous fiscal year, or on the perceived uniqueness or necessity of the services offered. Sharing clients or acknowledging agency limitations might in some cases result in a loss of funding, or require new models of funding to preserve existing levels or allow for expansion to a community-based format. Another agency-based barrier to forming CBIs is simply a lack of staff knowledge about how to go about it. Agencies also may suffer from inertia. Sometimes this inertia might come from satisfaction with the status quo despite the fact that some clients may not be adequately served. As well, inertia can result from burnout or the demoralization that can sometimes infect providers, resulting in a loss of confidence in the agency's ability to address entrenched problems.

Client-based barriers to building CBIs generally revolve around the difficulty and complexity of the problems hard-to-serve clients pose to agencies. Client barriers are typically of two types: lack of access and client needs that interfere with the ability to use services. Lack of access includes problems such as the services are too costly, the location is too far from a client's home, clients are overwhelmed by the number of places they are expected to go within a short period of time, lack of child care, or lack of transportation to provider locations. Some client barriers originate with the client's problems such as mental disorders (e.g., schizophrenia, anxiety disorders, depression, etc.) or general medical conditions (e.g., life-threatening illnesses such as cancer, AIDS, etc.).

For clients, the referral process traditionally has been problematic. Clients often had to seek services outside their immediate community and lacked the transportation to get there, or faced other obstacles involving child care or the availability of services during off-work hours. The simple fact that the referred service was in an unfamiliar part of town might be sufficiently daunting to a client already conflicted about pursuing services. Even though no single barrier might prevent a client from pursuing services, the accumulation of minor hurdles can be an effective deterrent. Clients might also be shunted back and forth from one agency to another without getting what they need, and without any consideration that the nature of the problem may undermine their ability to access services independently. Clients may have serious problems communicating with multiple providers, and agencies also may fail to effectively communicate vital information essential to appropriate care to the client or other service providers.

Ascher (1990) recommends that CBIs establish an accessible community location (often schools are ideal) from which case managers can coordinate the provision of integrated services. Case managers with access to a good information systems that links participating agencies can be more effective and reduce client runarounds.

Interagency partnerships often are designed to overcome limitations of the component providers. Typically, these problems involve difficulty with client access and poor coordination with other essential services. In their efforts to overcome past limitations, the developers of CBIs confront a number of barriers. In the example of the CD–CP, a 24-hour hotline staffed by a senior clinician was made available to increase access to mental health expertise. In addition, police and senior clinicians from the Yale Child Study Center held weekly case conferences that often brought in other agencies or interested parties to tailor a collaborative response to particular problems.

Participating agencies need to be committed to overcoming traditional turf claims over clients and resources. Restrictive funding policies should be replaced with creative financing that permits clients to access multiple services simultaneously (Ascher, 1990; Sheridan, 1995). Cotton (Northwest Regional Educational Laboratory, 1991b) reports that bringing professionals together from various cooperating agencies to brainstorm on a particular shared problem can be a particularly effective way to overcome funding difficulties. Bringing professionals together provides an effective way to improve treatment. In the CD–CP, when the interdisciplinary treatment planning group recognized particular community-based needs, specialized outreach teams were formed to deal with victims of domestic violence and with children at risk for antisocial behavior close to where the problems occurred.

Often, professionals do not have the skills to work collaboratively, so training programs in collaboration for staff across agencies can cultivate new knowledge, expertise, and commitment to cooperation. For example, both police and mental health workers in the CD–CP build mutual respect with reciprocal training. The program also enables police officers to better fulfill their original mission by teaching them how to better instill community members with a sense of security and benign authority concerning the police.

Evaluating Community-Based Interventions

CBIs pose evaluators a unique, and often inadequately considered, challenge. Weiss (The Aspen Institute, 1999) and others (White & Wehlage, 1995) suggest that conventional quantitative evaluative procedures are inadequate to capture the complex interactions of collaborative service arrangements. Difficulties in adequate evaluation can be illustrated by the example of an evaluation of a successful career exploration program for economically disadvantaged youth. The New York State Adolescent Vocational Exploration Program (AVE) was a collaboration between the New York State Department of Labor, the State Education Department, urban community-based organizations, local educational agencies, and local workforce preparation units funded under the Job Training Partnership Act. The AVE program was conducted in various forms for a number of years in the 1980s and served thousands of youth in their local communities. A private contractor, MAGI Educational Services, evaluated the program for the state. MAGI's annual evaluations were textbook examples of conventional methods focusing on a variety of outcome measures. An array of specific outcome measures in three broad domains were examined, including participant performance, program performance, and staff evaluation. The AVE program was judged a great success based on its performance in each of these three domains.

However, none of these evaluation measures directly tested the efficacy of the assumptions implicit in the AVE program's theory of change. The AVE program assumed that urban youth, especially children of color, have difficulty getting and retaining jobs because they lack sufficient knowledge of the workplace to be successful. This was an unproven assumption. The very thorough and rigorous assessment of program outcomes never really evaluated the implicit assumption that was at the foundation of AVE's various interventions. Measurement of the assumptions that the program was built on would be essential in order for judgments about the soundness of the program concept to be made.

Weiss (The Aspen Institute, 1999) advocates theory-based evaluation to analyze the truth of program theory. Weiss believes that an evaluation focus on theoretical assumptions ultimately results in findings that make clearer and more constructive contributions to the general body of knowledge. Evaluation that corroborates program theory provides a useful theoretical toolbox for building more empirically justified public policy, program development, and informed public opinion.

Weiss (The Aspen Institute, 1999) also argues that appropriate evaluation of CBIs necessarily requires that the specific assumptions of collaborative arrangements be assessed. What distinguishes CBIs from conventional interventions is their collaborative character. Evaluation of a CBI should measure whether or not the cooperative working together of agencies is actually a factor in client outcomes. Part of such an evaluation would involve assessing the functionality of the interagency links themselves. Do CBIs with higher levels of cooperation produce better client outcomes than poorly integrated CBIs?

In the early 1990s, the Department of Defense and the National Institute of Mental Health conducted the Fort Bragg Demonstration Project over a five-year period. They evaluated the value of a CBI-type model of care for emotionally and behaviorally disordered children in comparison to a more traditional disjointed, limited access model. The Fort Bragg model was a comprehensive, integrated system of care that provided clients with individualized case-managed service. In contrast, the comparison sites provided a traditional model of care. It was hoped that the Fort Bragg model would provide children and their families more quality care for less money because inpatient services would be avoided in favor of outpatient community-based interventions.

No clinically significant outcomes were found for children in the two models. In fact, the Fort Bragg model turned out to be 1.5 times more expensive than the cost of traditional services in the comparison sites. Saxe and Cross (Robert Wood Johnson Foundation, 1998) explain, however, that the Fort Bragg Demonstration Project "served three times the number of children, far more than were served at the two comparison sites. . .Children in the demonstration were less likely to go to the hospital and residential treatment but more likely to use intermediate services. They also had significantly more therapy visits and longer time in treatment" (p. 6).

Although it seems clear that the Fort Bragg model provided better quality care, the evaluation study might have produced fewer counterintuitive results if the theoretical assumptions of the model had been assessed at various levels. For example, there seems to have been an implicit assumption that parent involvement would improve treatment outcomes. However, there were no specific analyses to test this notion. It may be that parent involvement plays a role, but in a more complex and qualitatively rich way than was detected in the outcomes-focused evaluation analyses.

CBIs present evaluators with new challenges, just as CBIs present program planners and developers with new challenges in how services will be coordinated and delivered. The collaboration of agencies seems intuitively obvious to most clinicians, but we are not yet at the point that we know this intuition to be true, at least for large-scale comprehensive systems of care. On a smaller scale, interagency partnerships, as shown with the CD–CP in New Haven, clearly do fill gaps in the delivery of services that benefit children and their families, as well as enhance the realization of the participating agencies' primary mission. In the CD–CP, the police came to be seen more positively by the community, and mental health professionals were able to intervene with victims of violence in a more timely fashion. Perhaps in the world of interagency collaboration small is beautiful. At least at our current level of understanding of the relationship between the scale of interagency collaboration and the theories of treatment, smaller-scale CBIs are less costly and offer clearer benefits to clients.

At the current stage in the evolution of CBIs, evaluation, especially theory-based evaluation, is extremely important. Program developers need to test the many unproven theoretical assumptions that inform many of the most common intervention practices. These kinds of evaluative data can inform not only the refinement of future program development but can help to clarify the elements of effective CBIs.

Conclusion

Providers have long observed and lamented that there is a subset of the population that requires a mix of multiple services from multiple agencies. This hard-to-serve population, disproportionately poor and minority, suffers from a complex web of interrelated problems that would seem to require a coordinated attack on multiple fronts simultaneously in order to make a meaningful difference. The emergence of CBIs has come about to address this perceived deficit of integrated, comprehensive, and coordinated services.

Schools can be particularly important partners in CBIs. Schools are distributed throughout communities, and are accessible where other institutional service providers are not because the schools are conveniently located in or near the neighborhoods where people live. Schools also are well-situated to screen and identify at-risk children and their families. Early identification can facilitate early intervention, which is widely acknowledged as the most clinically productive and cost-effective time to provide treatment. Schools within a given community provide a locus of highly trained professionals who can offer direct service, provide consultation to parents and other providers, as well as assist in the design of innovative programs.

School psychologists, in particular, bring to the schools and collaborative community arrangements a unique set of skills for serving children, adolescents, and their families. School psychologists have expertise in development, assessment, consultation, and direct intervention, and, consequently, can play a valuable role in the development of new interagency relationships and in the services such arrangements ultimately offer clients.

The logic of CBIs implies a new paradigm of human services. The traditional model of service provision was conceived as autonomous agencies offering a limited set of institutionally defined services to isolated individual clients who had to initiate access to these services from wherever they happened to be located. There was a tendency for the services to be crisis-oriented and to focus on those clients with the greatest difficulties. This traditional model has been particularly inadequate at serving the poor and persons of color.

The new model of service implicit in CBIs, and in their large-scale counterparts, CCIs, has arisen to respond to the needs of those who fell between the cracks of the old system of isolated providers. The new paradigm strives to bring services directly to clients and actively strives to overcome barriers that might interfere with a client's ability to access needed services. Clients are not necessarily conceived as isolated individuals but as a nexus of interdependent individuals who function collectively as a system (articulated in greater detail by Preli in Chapter 10). The problems of one individual that pull them into the system of services may be compensatory reactions to the actions and situations created by other individuals within a family system. The services offered within this new paradigm are tailored to the particular needs of clients and their family system, and it is presumed that early intervention, given closer to home or at the source of the problem, is not only more clinically effective but more economical, at least in the long run. The new paradigm assumes that multiple services will be delivered from multiple providers, and that this multifaceted treatment will be coordinated by some form of case management based on a firsthand and intimate knowledge of clients and the barriers they face in accessing appropriate services.

The paradigm implicit in CBIs reflects the commitment of human service professionals, policymakers, and government to do what has not been done adequately in the past. The CBI paradigm is inspired by the desire to effectively serve the poor, people of color, and the many people of all descriptions who simply fell between the cracks of the old system. The emergence of this new model of service is merely the latest installment in the long tradition in Western societies of social reform.

References

Ascher, C. (1990, February). Linking schools with human service agencies. *ERIC Digest, 62.* (ERIC Document Reproduction Service No. ED 319877).

The Aspen Institute. (1999). *Nothing as practical as good theory: Exploring theory-based evaluation for comprehensive community initiatives for children and families.* New York: Author.

Catalano, R., Berglund, M., Ryan, J., Lonczak, H., & Hawkins, J. (1998, November). *Positive youth development in the United States: Research findings on the evaluations of positive youth development programs.* (NICHD Publication). Washington, DC: U.S. Department of Health and Human Services.

Chesapeake Institute. (1994, September). *National agenda for achieving better results for children and youth with serious emotional disturbance.* Washington, DC: U.S. Department of Education.

Hahn, A. J., (1992). Education is education, but not when it's public affairs education (some further notes on education vs. advocacy). *Adult Learning, 3* (7), 29–31.

Ianni, F. (1992). Meeting youth needs with community programs. *ERIC Clearinghouse on Urban Education Digest, 86,* Office of Education Research and Improvement. (ERIC Document Reproduction Service No. ED 356291)

Lewis, A. (1992). Urban youth in community service: Becoming part of the solution. *ERIC Clearinghouse on Urban Education Digest, 81,* Office of Educational Research and Improvement. (ERIC Document Reproduction Service No. ED 351425)

Marans, S., Adnopoz, J., Berkman, M., Esserman, D., MacDonald, D., Nagler, S., Randall, R., Schaefer, M., & Wearing, M. (1995). *The Police-Mental Health Partnership: A community-based response to urban violence.* New Haven, CT: Yale University Press.

McPartland, J., & Slavin, R. (1990). Increasing achievement of at-risk students at each grade level. *Policy Perspectives Series.* Washington, DC: U.S. Department of Education.

Morley, E., & Rossman, S. (1997). *Helping at-risk youth: Lessons from community-based initiatives.* Washington, DC: U.S. Department of Justice.

National Association of State Boards of Education. (1992). *Partners in educational improvement: Schools, parents, and the community.* Alexandria, VA: Author.

National Clearinghouse on Families and Youth. (1996, July). *Reconnecting youth and community: A youth development approach.* Washington, DC: U.S. Department of Health and Human Services.

Northwest Regional Educational Laboratory. (1991a, March). *Educating urban minority youth: Research on effective practices.* Portland, OR: Author.

Northwest Regional Educational Laboratory. (1991b, November). *School-community collaboration to improve the quality of life for urban youth and their families.* Portland, OR: Author.

Robert Wood Johnson Foundation. (1998). *National Program Report: 1998–1999 Anthology, Chapter 9, National Health Services Program for Youth.* Princeton, NJ: Author.

Sheridan, S. (1995). Best practices in fostering school community relationships. In A. Thomas & J. Grimes (Eds.), *Best practices in school psychology-III* (pp. 203–212). Washington, DC: National Association of School Psychologists.

White, J., & Wehlage, G. (1995). Community collaboration: If it is such a good idea why is it so hard to do? *Educational Evaluation and Policy Analysis, 17,* 23–38.

18

Play Therapy Interventions for Early School-Aged Children

Jay Cerio

Play therapy is a child psychotherapy approach that has been in use for over 80 years. Originally rooted in psychoanalytic ideas (Hug-Hellmuth, 1921), play therapy developed into a broad field that incorporated elements of humanistic, developmental, and behavioral approaches (O'Connor, 1991). Play therapy has been used with a variety of child problems, including oppositional behavior (Barlow, Strother, & Landreth, 1986), aggressive behavior (Sloan, 1997; Willock, 1983), bereavement (LeVieux, 1994), anxiety (Milos & Reiss, 1982), physical and sexual abuse (Mann & McDermott, 1983), and compulsive hair pulling (Barlow, Strother, & Landreth, 1985). Yet, play therapy remains a controversial approach because of limited empirical support and difficulty in identifying the mechanisms that drive change in the therapy. What is play therapy? What is the goal of using such an approach? With what types of clients is it used? Does it work? The purpose of this chapter is to attempt to answer these questions and provide the reader with the basic knowledge necessary for using play therapy.

The term *play therapy* is usually applied to a cluster of theoretical models for using play as a method of counseling children. Within this context, professionals typically have in mind a particular way of using play, that is, an underlying philosophical framework. However, despite one's theoretical leanings, the use of play media is as much a modality for counseling children as talking is a modality for counseling adults. The play therapy counseling modality incorporates the use of toys, art materials, games, and activities common to the experience of children. Through these activities children communicate their feelings, thoughts, and needs, and counselors develop an understanding of the internal experiences of children.

Play therapy is also a method for approaching children on their phenomenological level. When counselors use play with children, they are operating in the territory of childhood. This provides them with the opportunity to see the world as children see it and to understand the impact of the adult world on children. Play is the child's natural way of operating, just as speaking is with adults (Axline, 1947). Play therapy provides a means for building a therapeutic relationship with a child. Through the play therapy process, counselors establish the necessary relationship conditions that serve as the basis for therapeutic change (Rogers, 1957). Once these conditions are firmly established, change may occur either through direct intervention or the use of nondirective techniques.

The use of play as a counseling method assumes an underlying belief that play is an essential activity for children. Through play, children behave and interact in a developmentally appropriate manner, practicing, modeling, communicating, and discharging feelings (Bettelheim, 1987; Erikson, 1963; Landreth, 1991). Thus, a counselor's use of play therapy is a way of conveying respect for the child's world and the belief that children are capable of using play effectively to deal with their internal experiences.

There are many types of play therapies that offer counselors philosophical foundations on which to base their practice. The four main groups of play therapies are humanistic, developmental, psychodynamic, and behavioral. *Humanistic play therapies* focus more on relationship variables that enhance children's natural tendencies toward growth. *Developmental play therapies* are grounded in principles of child development and can be more directive and therapist-driven. *Psychodynamic play therapies* have descended from the earliest attempts to counsel children within a play framework and are rooted in psychoanalytic theory. *Behavioral play therapies* use play more for initial rapport-building and progress to standard behavior modification techniques (O'Connor, 1991).

Although pioneers in the field did not state firm age guidelines for the use of play therapy, it appears from early writings that this approach was originally intended for use with children who were approximately three to eight years of age (Axline, 1947; Moustakas, 1959), consistent with the developmental stages reviewed by Evangelista in Chapter 12. Children younger than three are in transition from the prelanguage to the preoperational stages of cognitive development, while children up to age eight are shifting from preoperational to concrete operational thinking (Piaget, 1962). Children in the preoperational stage use language concretely and are not able to think abstractly. Therefore, they are not good candidates for traditional insight-oriented talking therapy. Play serves as a more natural, nonlanguage-based means for children to communicate their feelings and conflicts (Axline, 1947).

During the past 20 years, views of the functions of play have broadened, as has the age range in which play therapy is used. Even though children older than eight years may be functioning above the preoperational stage and able to use language more skillfully, play still is an important part of their everyday experience. Play is also a less direct avenue to children's internal lives (Erikson, 1963) and, therefore, a convenient means for circumventing defensiveness. Finally, play allows older children to regress to an earlier developmental level if they need to do so in order to confront or avoid problematic issues.

It is now not unusual to see play therapy approaches used with older adolescents and young adults (Landreth, 1991). The play activities chosen might be different from those used with younger children, but the underlying principles are still the same. The most typical age range for play therapy is ages three to eleven. However, various play therapy approaches have been used with children as young as 18 months and as old as seventeen years (Cerio, 2000). Because this chapter is concerned with interventions for young school-age children, the focus of the discussion will be on the traditional age groups of children with whom play therapy has been used.

Research on Play Therapy

Play therapy suffers from the problem of not being a rigorous, research-based psychotherapy approach. Thus, it has earned the reputation of being some sort of mystical, "touchy-feely" activity for which there is little evidence to validate its use as a viable form of psychotherapy. It is unfair, then, to proceed with any discussion regarding the use of play therapy without attending to empirical research in this area.

Actual research on play therapy has been sparse, the designs problematic, and the findings inconclusive, providing further fuel for naysayers to assert that play therapy is not a real form of psychotherapy. This problem is related to overreliance on anecdotal case studies and faith in the theoretical or philosophical perspectives of "experts" who assert their *beliefs* in the efficacy of this approach, but fail to provide conclusive evidence to back their claims. Problems with research in play therapy involve problems in methodology, which includes research designs, measures, and treatment integrity, as well as conceptual biases and the relevance of the outcomes measured.

Research Design

Play therapy studies typically have failed to incorporate control groups or alternative interventions into their designs (Axline, 1947; Griffiths, 1971). This has made it nearly impossible to conclude that positive outcomes of play therapy are the result of anything more than spontaneous remission. Proponents of play therapy contend that improvement in client functioning after the introduction of play therapy interventions provides evidence of effectiveness. Critics assert that this argument holds no *empirical* weight. This does not mean that play therapy has no effect in ameliorating children's problems. Without a "no treatment" control group, it is impossible to form a valid conclusion in this respect. Related to this is the failure to include alternative intervention or placebo groups in play therapy studies. The lack of these comparison groups makes it difficult to determine whether or not play therapy is essentially different from play, and whether simply paying attention to children yields similar outcomes as play therapy.

Measurement Issues

Dependent measures that have been used in the past to assess the impact of play therapy were clearly deficient. The collection of relevant and objective data has been limited (White & Allers, 1994). Many case studies simply incorporate a therapist's report of improvement as the primary "measure." Other studies use nonstandardized symptom checklists and client self-reports of improvement. Typically, only one source of data has been used, be it client, parent, teacher, or therapist. These methods of measuring outcomes increases the potential for placebo effects that affect findings, as individuals may perceive improvement simply because they know they are being studied, whether actual change has occurred or not (Gay, 1976). This measurement problem has been a major criticism of play therapy outcome research, contributing to the perception that play therapy is nothing more than a placebo with no real therapeutic benefits. Obviously, but unfortunately, this diminishes the validity of using play therapy when it actually might be helpful.

Treatment Integrity

Insuring the standard application of interventions—that is, the integrity of the treatment being used—is not only a problem in play therapy research, but in most nonbehavioral psychotherapy research as well. Treatment integrity allows researchers to evaluate whether or not a technique or method is effective, and helps to control for such factors as therapists' personal styles. Past play therapy studies typically have not established that methods have been used in standard ways across therapists and clients (Griffiths, 1971; Swartz & Swartz, 1985). Only recently have studies incorporated some combination of manualized interventions and manipulation checks (Boehm-Morelli, 1999; Kaplewicz, 1999; Sloan, 1997). When these types of checks are used, differences between play therapy and play become easier to recognize, and comparisons among interventions become more clear.

Conceptual Biases and Outcomes

Conceptual biases run rampant in play therapy research. This appears to be related to the powerful influences of nondirective, humanistic play therapy approaches (Axline, 1947; Moustakas, 1959) that were developed after World War II. These models, which emphasize the importance of client self-direction and self-esteem in client functioning (Landreth, 1991), have impacted the way in which play therapy research is conducted and the interpretation of research results. For instance, in her classic study of remedial readers, Axline (1947) concludes that reading improvement was related to the development of congruence between ideal and real self, a person-centered theory concept, and basically ignores the impact of reading instruction. It is probable that this same conceptual bias led to the acceptance of anecdotal case studies, presented within strict theoretical frameworks (Barlow et al., 1985; Nystul, 1980), as demonstrations of play therapy efficacy. Finally, there has been an overemphasis on investigating the influence of play therapy on self-esteem or self-concept (Crow, 1994; Elliott & Pumfrey, 1972; Griffiths, 1971), without much regard as to whether these areas influence other areas of functioning.

Phillips (1985), in a research review article, suggests that one of the most frequently occurring problems with play therapy outcome studies involves the objective measurement of meaningful outcomes. The first part of this statement, the need for more objective and comprehensive measures, was addressed above. The second part, the need to examine outcomes that are more meaningful, will require a shift from theoretically-based to behaviorally-based outcomes using assessment practices that are appropriately matched to the problem at hand (e.g., see Chapters 3, 4, 5, and 15 for related discussions). Specifically, research needs to focus on outcomes that clearly demonstrate improvement in client functioning. Thus, rather than simply measuring the effects of play therapy on self-concept, research needs to determine whether self-concept is causally linked to specific areas of client functioning. Research also needs to investigate the efficacy of play therapy with specific types of problems, such as depression, anxiety, trauma, bereavement, aggression and anger management, and effects of divorce. By incorporating improvements in research design, measures, and treatment integrity, and utilizing state-of-the-art statistical techniques, researchers should be able to more clearly assess therapeutic outcomes of play therapy.

Findings of Play Therapy Research

Given all the reservations discussed above, what does the play therapy research tell us? Play therapy appears to have some effect on enhancing children's global self-esteem or self-concept (Crow, 1994; Griffiths, 1971; Swartz & Swartz, 1985). However, the value of this outcome relative to specific problems is questionable. Early research by Axline (1947) and Bills (1950) suggested that play therapy enhanced interventions with remedial readers by positively impacting self-concept. Results of later research by Elliott and Pumfrey (1972) were less conclusive, suggesting a connection between a play therapy intervention and improvement in reading achievement of poor readers, but no concomitant improvement in self-esteem. These studies were plagued by many of the methodological problems previously described. Recent research using methodology that addresses these problems (Boehm-Morelli, 1999; Kaplewicz, 1999) found no effect of nondirective play therapy on either reading achievement or reading self-concepts of remedial readers who participated in individual or group play therapy interventions. Boehm-Morelli used a state-of-the-art measure of reading self-concept, but both she and Kaplewicz failed to incorporate general self-concept measures. This leaves us with the conclusion that play therapy seems to have a positive effect on global self-concept or self-esteem, but does not appear to impact self-concept related to reading and, subsequently, reading performance. Thus, it appears that the early findings of Axline and Bills have not found clear support in later studies.

There is research that suggests that play therapy has a positive effect on specific types of problems. Barlow et al. (1986) found this approach to be effective in ameliorating the symptoms of a 5-year-old selectively mute male. These same authors, in another case study (1985) of a 4-year-old female, found that her habitual hair pulling was alleviated after participating in play therapy. A study by Mann and McDermott (1983) found that a group of abused and neglected children showed improvement in self-esteem, academic performance, social relationships, and impulse control after being involved in play therapy. Mendell (1983) cites cases in which the effects of the "developmental interference" of parental divorce have been ameliorated through play therapy. Young children experiencing separation anxiety were noted to have lower posttest anxiety scores after three play therapy sessions (Milos & Reiss, 1982). Play therapy also has shown some effectiveness in reducing physical and verbal aggression with children referred specifically for problems with aggression (Sloan, 1997; Willock, 1983).

Most of the above findings suffer from the limitation of being individual case studies that failed to use any type of control comparison. However, Boehm-Morelli's (1999), Kaplewicz's (1999), and Sloan's (1997) studies are particularly important because their designs addressed shortcomings of previous research. Boehm-Morelli and Kaplewicz included both placebo and control groups in their studies of remedial readers, which allowed them to conduct comparative analyses in order to arrive at their conclusions. Sloan incorporated two different play therapy conditions, used standardized instruments for assessing outcomes, and collected outcome data from multiple sources (teachers, parents, peers, clients, independent raters). This provided corroborative data across reporters and settings that validated the findings.

Is play therapy useful? The smattering of studies that constitute the body of research in this area suggests that there is potential for the effectiveness of this approach to be validated for use with specific types of problems, but until better-designed studies are conducted to investigate outcomes, its use will continue to be based more on anecdotal information and faith. Interestingly, national surveys of training program directors conducted by Cerio, Taggart, and Costa (1997, 1999), showed that 55 percent of school counseling programs and 43 percent of school psychology programs reported offering training in play therapy. Further, 80% of school counseling and 60% of school psychology program directors felt that training in play therapy should be included in the preparation of individuals entering these professions. So, despite the limited evidence supporting this approach, experts in the field seem to believe that it is a useful modality for counseling children.

Using Play Therapy with Young School-Aged Children

A General Framework

All this being said, what is a reasonable approach for utilizing play therapy with children? The human technology approach of Carkhuff and Berenson (1977), a proven adult model of psychotherapy, provides a relevant guide for using play therapy. This approach views psychotherapy as a process that incorporates elements of person-centered, psychodymanic, and behavioral approaches (Aspy, Aspy, Russel, & Wedel, 2000), in a sequential progression that leads to problem resolution.

Carkhuff and Berenson (1977) identify three stages: exploration, understanding, and action. The first stage, or downward phase, is characterized by development of the therapeutic alliance and clients telling their stories. At the beginning of the stage, clients tend to be vague and general, with the counselor's job being to clarify and help the client become more specific and focused. As this occurs, the client develops a clearer understanding of issues, conflicts, feelings, behaviors, and thoughts, and the connections among them. At this point, the client has entered the stage of understanding, or the bottom phase of counseling. Once clients develop a clear understanding of issues, they can then move on to think about options for dealing with them. By the end of this stage, the client has narrowed these options and focuses on specific courses of action. The counseling process then progresses to the action stage, or upward phase. This stage is characterized by the client choosing and implementing options in order to effect change. Carkhuff and Berenson do not think of counseling as a seamless process that moves sequentially from one stage to the next. They see the process more as a series of miniprocesses in which the client moves from exploring to understanding to action regarding one problem, which in turn leads to exploring, understanding, and action in a related area, and so forth.

A simple extrapolation of this model to children does not require a quantum leap in thinking. Early in the play therapy process, children play in an exploratory manner, trying out various toys and moving from theme to theme before they settle on more focused play with consistent themes. During this time, the counselor uses descriptive responses and gradually moves to labeling of feelings. As the child's play becomes more focused, the counselor's responses become more specific, characterized by more feeling responses. The child usually begins to repeat particular scenarios with consistent themes, a sign that he or she is progressing to the stage of understanding. For example, a 4-year-old female was referred because she was exhibiting symptoms of anxiety related to physical abuse committed by her stepfather. In the first few sessions, her play was diffuse, and she moved from one toy to another without focus. Then, she developed a scenario in which she was the mother and the therapist was the child, and she protected the therapist from the mean father. This scenario became a regular ritual in her play, signaling that this was a central issue with which she was dealing.

The term *understanding*, used within a context of counseling children, does not have the same meaning as it does with adult clients. With children, *understanding* means that themes begin to emerge in the play that allow the counselor to understand the child's experience or perception of the issues in her or his life. Once these become clear, then the process can progress to the action stage.

The term *action* applied to children also differs somewhat from the definition used with adults. *Action*, here, really refers to a number of possibilities ranging from unstructured, nondirective play to very specific behavioral interventions. Some children who have entered the action stage may be simply working on issues in their play through recurring rituals and themes of their play. This would be more commonly observed with such problems as trauma related to disasters or child abuse. In these cases, the counselor continues using descriptive and feeling responses, and moves in the direction of helping the child use the metaphor. For instance, a 7-year-old girl who was sexually abused replays a scenario over several sessions in which she makes snakes out of Play-Doh and has them surround and attack mother and baby family figures. The counselor labels feelings for the child, specifically the family's fear and helplessness in the face of the snake attacks. Then the counselor intervenes by asking the client if there is any way the family members can protect themselves. Through open-ended questioning and gentle prodding, the counselor empowers the client to extend the metaphor to include the family successfully protecting itself from, and finally defeating, the snakes.

Other action stage interventions are more structured and behaviorally oriented. For instance, it becomes clear to a counselor that a child who expresses and exhibits anxiety in the play situation would benefit from learning simple relaxation techniques. This requires that the counselor teach the child a skill, and that the child practice the skill outside of the counseling session. Depending on the developmental level of the child, this might mean that the counselor will use play media in teaching this skill, or simply suspend the play session and use direct instruction and practice with the child. In this situation, the counselor uses intervention responses almost exclusively.

Toy Selection and Room Structure

Toys should be selected based on whether or not they are useful in facilitating self-expression (Axline, 1947; Landreth, 1991; O'Connor, 1991). While most types of toys are appropriate, there are some basic categories of toys that tend to facilitate therapeutic play. Real-life toys include such things as dollhouses, family figures, dolls, baby bottles, doctor kits, cars, farm animals, and telephones. These generally serve as templates for direct metaphors, particularly regarding interpersonal conflicts. Acting out or aggressive toys are useful for expression of anger, and include such items as guns, handcuffs, hammers, toy soldiers, cowboys, pirates, and comeback dolls. Expressive media—finger paints, crayons, markers, Play-Doh, puppets, sand, blocks, Legos—are less structured and facilitate the release of a wide range of emotions and expression of less direct metaphors (Landreth, 1987). Finally, competitive or rule-oriented toys allow for indirect expressions of conflict with adults (Schaefer & Reid, 1986). These include board games such as Trouble, Sorry, and checkers, and athletic equipment such as whiffle ball, Nerf basketball and football, and velcro darts.

It is not necessary to have a large number of toys, although greater variety allows for more choice. However, it is recommended that some toys in each category be available, as well as toys designed for children of different developmental levels. Providing older children access to toys designed for younger children allows older children to regress, which is sometimes both necessary and permissible in the context of the therapy.

The next ingredient necessary for getting started in play therapy is a play area. A large playroom (about half the size of a classroom) is ideal, but usually not a possibility in most counseling settings. Any reasonably-sized office is acceptable. Children are very competent at figuring out how to use the space, be it a closet or a classroom. The important element needed is an enclosed, private space that protects children's confidentiality and allows them to feel safe within the permissive atmosphere of the playroom (Landreth, 1991).

The organization of the playroom is dependent on whether the therapist practices a more or less structured approach to play therapy. If one's approach is more nondirective, then one should avoid organizing toys in a way that directs the child toward specific toys. If one is more directive, then the counselor might choose toys that he or she feels are relevant to the child's issues. Aside from considering one's approach, toys can be arranged in whatever way is convenient within the context of the space being used. It is sometimes easier to confine expressive media, such as clay and paint, to a table in order to provide a stable surface on which to work, and to place games on a shelf for easier accessibility. It is also important to have the playroom arranged the same way every time the child has a session. The predictability of the play setting provides a sense of security for the child. This is critical for the development of trust between child and counselor (Donovan & McIntyre, 1990).

Finally, providing a modicum of structure within the playroom is necessary for creating an emotionally safe environment for the child (Donovan & McIntyre, 1990; Gil, 1991; O'Connor, 1991). This includes clearly stating time limits when the child enters the room ("We have 30 minutes today" or "You'll be here until the big hand is on the six") and establishing some basic rules. The common rules of the playroom are necessary for: (a) giving the child a sense of control within the playroom ("You can play with anything in the room, talk, do both or do nothing. It's up to you"); (b) insuring physical safety ("You may not hurt yourself or me, or mess up yourself or me on purpose"); (c) providing a means of establishing the necessary atmosphere of permissiveness ("You don't have to clean up after yourself unless you want to, or unless you are told to do so"); and (d) protecting the physical integrity of the play area ("You may not break toys on purpose") (Axline, 1947; Landreth, 1991).

Basic Therapeutic Skills

The cross-theoretical approach to play therapy presented here relies on the substantial body of microskills research with adults produced by Carkhuff, Truax, Berenson, and Ivey (Carkhuff & Berenson, 1977; Ivey & Ivey, 1999; Truax & Carkhuff, 1967). This research has identified behaviors that tend to facilitate client communication in counseling. Although the research is generic, it does support the earlier research and principles of the person-centered approach developed by Rogers (Rogers, 1961). Ideas regarding effective responding are downward extrapolations of this research. Hence, there is a mild bias toward the more nondirective type of responding, at least during the early stages of the therapeutic process.

The critical idea to understand when using play therapy is that, when children play, they may or may not be talking. Talking is useful, but not essential to play therapy. Even if a child talks during therapy, this comprises only a small portion of the message. What the child is doing—nonverbal cues and actions—is much more important to understanding the child's frame of reference. Thus, counselors' responses to children in play therapy should address their actions as much or more than their verbalizations.

Attending Behaviors.   Egan (1998) has taken the research on attending skills and formulated a general model for facilitative behavior in adult counseling situations, which he summarized in the acronym, SOLER:

S = Face the client squarely

O = Open posture

L = Lean toward the client

E = Make eye contact

R = Relax

These behaviors are ones that have been shown to increase verbal output and, thus, are seen as facilitative when conducting talking therapy with adults.

In play therapy, these attending behaviors can be extrapolated downward and defined as behaviors that communicate interest in and attention to what children do as they play. These play therapy attending behaviors may be easily remembered by using the acronym S-K-I-L-L-E-D.

S = SIT in close proximity to the child, while allowing the child to
       determine the comfort zone

K = Place yourself physically on the KID'S level

I = Show INTEREST by giving your undivided attention

L = LOOK at what the child is doing

L = LISTEN to what the child is saying

E = Convey EMPATHY for the child

D = DESCRIBE what you see as well as what you hear

The SKILLED behaviors provide the counselor with a method for conveying to the client that he or she is receiving the counselor's undivided attention, that the counselor is interested in what the child is doing, and that the counselor is trying to understand the child's perspective. This is a foundation for conveying empathy to the child, a critical variable in the therapeutic process (Rogers, 1975).

Facilitative conditions.   In addition to attending behaviors, there is a cluster of therapeutic conditions that have been identified as enhancing the therapeutic relationship. These conditions—unconditional positive regard, empathy, genuineness, and specificity of response—first identified by Rogers (1957), have been shown to be critical predictors of positive therapeutic outcomes in some 50-plus years of clinical research (Lambert & Bergin, 1994).

Empathy, in particular, has been shown to be critical to therapeutic progress *across counseling approaches* (Butler & Strupp, 1986). Thus, even when using strict behavioral interventions, counselors need to develop and convey empathy to the client if they are going to be effective therapists. This is extremely important when working with children because adult frames of reference are so different from those of children. Adults need to develop empathy for a child in order to understand the child's experiences. The way to do this is by entering into the child's world on his or her own level. Play becomes the vehicle for doing this.

Responding to Children in Play Therapy

Facilitative responding is the means for conveying the facilitative conditions. In this type of responding, the counselor gives the child his or her *undivided* attention and conveys interest in and understanding of what the child is doing. The counselor needs to do this both nonverbally (getting down on the child's level, watching the child) and verbally (describing the play, labeling feelings that are observed). There is no research-based system for effective responding in play therapy as there is with traditional adult talking therapy (Carkhuff & Berenson, 1977). Landreth (1991) provided excellent and extensive guidelines for responding facilitatively in play therapy, but his analysis of what constitutes an appropriate response is based largely on his theoretical orientation. A more general framework for analyzing whether or not a response is facilitative is provided below.

The response typology described here is based on a few simple assumptions. First, there is a range of appropriate facilitative responses. When counseling children, it is more important for counselors to be accurate and to show children that the counselor is within the realm of understanding, than to be precise and pick the best possible responses. Second, children are fairly open and willing to give counselors immediate feedback regarding whether or not their responses are accurate. The feedback may be verbal, such as telling counselors outright that they are wrong, or nonverbal, such as withdrawing or making a sudden change in play activity. Third, most children are relatively resilient. Hence, one particular inaccurate response by a counselor neither destroys the relationship nor the child.

Given these assumptions, what constitutes a facilitative response in play therapy is based more on the function of a response than on determining effectiveness. First, responses can be classified as either facilitative or nonfacilitative. The facilitative play therapy responses are subdivided into four categories: descriptive, feeling, nondirective intervention, and directive intervention responses.

Descriptive responses are straightforward feedback to the child regarding his or her observable behavior. For example, a counselor might respond, "Those dolls are really hitting each other," to a scenario in which the client depicts two dolls fighting. The purpose of this type of response is to communicate to the child that the counselor is paying attention to and understanding the child's play. With *feeling responses*, the counselor focuses on the emotion that is evident in the child's play and labels it. An example of this would be a counselor responding, "It looks like this doll is really mad at that one," to the scenario described above. The purpose of this type of response is to help clients become aware of their feelings and provide them with the opportunity to discharge these feelings and feel understood.

The purpose of *nondirective intervention* and *directive intervention* responses is to aid the child in problem-solving, teach the child coping strategies, and help the child attain closure on an issue. These responses are more action-oriented and, as indicated by the labels, can be open-ended or specific. Extending the scenario described above, the child identifies the two dolls that are fighting as mother and father and introduces a third doll, identified as the daughter who is watching. One possible nondirective intervention response would be, "It looks like the parents are really mad at each other.

What is something the daughter could do?" If the client replied, "The daughter could get in between them and stop them," the counselor might then use a directive intervention response such as, "That wouldn't be very safe for the daughter. What is something the daughter could do that would be safe?"

Placing these responses within the Carkhuff and Berenson (1977) framework, certain types of responses are more useful during certain stages of the counseling process. Descriptive and feeling responses are used during the exploration and understanding stages because these types of responses are more open-ended, facilitating spontaneity and disclosure in the child's play. Nondirective and directive intervention responses are used in the action phase of counseling when the client is problem solving and working toward closure with specific issues. However, it is important to keep in mind that counseling is not a lockstep activity; thus, any of these responses may be used at any stage of counseling. This model is simply meant to serve as a conceptual framework for understanding responding in relation to the counseling process.

Case Study

Presenting problems

Jenna was a 4-year-old girl who was referred for counseling because she was having tantrums, was clingy and demanding with her mother, and had begun soiling herself after having been toilet trained for almost two years. Jenna's mother reported that this behavior had been occurring for approximately three months. Jenna's parents had been separated for one year, and her mother, younger brother, and she had relocated to the town in which the maternal grandparents lived, leaving Jenna's father eight hours away. Jenna's mother reported that the separation was acrimonious, and that Jenna had been exposed to much conflict between her parents. Jenna had also overheard unpleasant phone conversations between her mother and father since the move took place. Physical problems and sexual abuse were ruled out as factors contributing to the symptoms.

Course of Treatment

Early sessions. The first three sessions were quite problematic for Jenna. She had difficulty separating from her mother, crying quite persistently during the early parts of these sessions. The therapist decided to use a soft, furry monkey puppet as a transitional ob-

ject for Jenna, but remained insistent that she enter the playroom. The therapist brought the puppet to the waiting room at the beginning of the session, and began interacting with Jenna through the puppet at that point. Jenna was allowed to hold the puppet as she walked to and entered the playroom, and usually elected to keep the puppet nearby during the early sessions. Generally, her crying continued for five or ten minutes and then stopped.

Jenna's play behaviors during the early sessions were predictably exploratory (Nordling & Guerney, 1999), with little focus on specific toys or themes. She would move from drawing to Play-Doh, to sand play, to the dollhouse, trying out various materials but not staying with one particular toy or scenario for more than a few minutes.

Middle sessions. With the fourth session, Jenna began separating easily from her mother, taking the puppet from the therapist and then moving immediately to the playroom. Her play became more focused and thematic by the sixth session, as was evident in a scenario that became a focal point of therapy. During this session, Jenna was walking past the outstretched feet of the therapist when she stopped and began kicking the sole of one of the therapist's

(continued)

Case Study (continued)

feet and yelling, "You're a very bad father," at the foot. She then would say to the foot, "Go away!" The therapist cooperated with the instruction and withdrew his foot. Jenna then said, "Come back," and repeated the scenario. This would be repeated three or four times, followed by a shift in Jenna's play from using unstructured media to playing a board game, a much more structured type of activity.

Jenna repeated the "bad father" pretend for several sessions, until another important shift occurred in her play. After kicking the therapist's foot and stating, "You're a very bad father," she turned to the other foot and, kicking it, yelled, "And you're a very bad mother." Immediately after making this statement, she asked the therapist to read a story to her, choosing a book about divorce from the bookshelf. She sat quietly and listened for a few minutes, and then moved on to playing a board game with the therapist. This scenario was repeated for several more sessions, with Jenna spending more time admonishing the "mother" as she replayed the scenario.

Later sessions. Jenna eventually moved on from the "bad father/bad mother" scenario, one day asking the therapist to tell her a story, while she was playing in the sandbox. The therapist asked Jenna what she would like the story to be about and Jenna replied that she wanted it to be about a king, a queen, and a princess. The therapist made a decision to use this story as a metaphor for Jenna's situation. The therapist began the story, "Once upon a time, there was a king, a queen and a princess," and then allowed Jenna to direct the plot of the story. She instructed the therapist to build three castles in the sand, which she said were the king's, queen's, and princess's castles. Jenna started the story with the family living together, then having the king and queen begin fighting. She then had the queen and princess move to the queen's castle together, and finally had the princess move to her own castle because she was angry with the king and queen. Jenna would repeatedly destroy the king's and queen's castles, and have the therapist build in-

creasingly smaller castles for them. The story would end with the king and queen living in their own tiny castles, and the princess living in her own huge castle.

At this point, the therapist elected to implement a structured intervention directed at the situation and feelings Jenna was expressing in her story. Jenna had constructed a clear picture of her perceptions of her family situation through her sandbox story. She had expressed her feelings of anger and disappointment with both parents through her repeated destroying of the castles and rebuilding of smaller castles. The princess always ended up triumphant but not satisfied in her story. Based on this conceptualization of the play, the therapist decided to use the story to introduce coping strategies to Jenna.

As Jenna retold the story in subsequent sessions, the therapist began using directive and nondirective intervention responses to begin challenging Jenna and providing ideas regarding age-appropriate coping behaviors. Nondirective intervention responses included the following questions: "What does the princess really want?" "What will really make her happy?" "What else could the princess do besides wrecking the castles?" "How can the princess let the king and queen know that she is mad without destroying their castles?" Directive intervention responses included statements such as: "The king and queen aren't going to live together again." "The princess could let the king and queen know that she doesn't want them to argue in front of her." "The princess can have her own safe place in the queen's castle that she can go to when she doesn't want to be with the king and queen." "The princess can let the king and queen know that she loves both of them, but is still mad."

In the final sessions, time was devoted to having Jenna practice a few coping strategies directly, then moving to unstructured play time. Her play at this point became more of the relationship type, in which she sought out opportunities for interactive play with the therapist. No new themes emerged, and she became less focused once again, moving from activity to activity.

Concurrent parent counseling. Children do not exist in a vacuum; their everyday lives are influenced by the adults around them. Jenna was no exception to this, particularly in light of the connection between her presenting problems and her family situation. Because of this, the therapist met with Jenna's mother approximately every two sessions to help her understand and respond appropriately to Jenna's behavior. As Jenna progressed to learning coping strategies, the therapist prepared her mother by coaching her on ways she could support and reinforce Jenna's use of such strategies. Most importantly in this case, as is necessary in most divorce situtations involving children, was the therapist's emphasis on helping the mother separate adult–couple issues from parent–child issues.

Commentary

Jenna's case is a good example of the Carkhuff and Berenson (1977) model as it applies to play therapy. Her play activities and verbalizations are typical for children in the 4- to 7-year-old age range (approximately kindergarten through second grade). The exploratory stage of therapy was characterized by more child-centered, nondirective play therapy. Jenna's "bad father/bad mother" metaphor illustrates how exploration within a play therapy context allows a child to communicate an issue and the feelings related to it (anger at both parents about their separation), just as an adult might do using words. But Jenna did not have the words to express this. What she did have was a child's natural skills to play. The therapist's job, however, was the same as it would have been with an adult who was in the exploration stage: to reflect and label feelings in order to clarify the client's experience. With Jenna, the therapist made statements like, "You are very mad at the father," and "You are so mad, you want the mother to go away." What should be noted is that the therapist did not say "your father" or "your mother." This was because Jenna did not identify the characters as

her father or mother, just as "the father." The therapist, then, showed respect for Jenna's frame of reference by *not* interpreting the characters to be Jenna's parents, which would impose the therapist's frame of reference.

As Jenna moved to the king–queen–princess scenario, she progressed to a more advanced metaphor in which she communicated understanding of the situation. During this stage of understanding, she symbolically described the separate living situation of her parents and her desire to punish them for failing her. While this, in effect, was an action, it was not a reality-based, constructive action, hence was not really part of the action stage. It simply signaled that the client wanted to do something. Another sign that Jenna had progressed beyond just discharging feelings was that her symptoms began to abate during this stage. She stopped soiling herself and having tantrums. She was less clingy and demanding. And she began helping with her younger brother, assuming the role of an older sibling.

The therapist viewed the repetition of the king–queen–princess story as a sign that Jenna was ready to move on to concrete action. The therapist decided to use more concrete, behaviorally-based interventions, to which he transitioned through the metaphor that Jenna had created. This, again, was a way to respect Jenna's experience while introducing new skills that would help her in the future. It was also a way to circumvent resistance, because the strategies were presented in the client's language. Once introduced in the metaphor, the therapist moved to direct instruction and practice, which Jenna accepted as part of the therapeutic interaction. If Jenna had not cooperated with this direct approach, the therapist would have remained with the less direct use of Jenna's story as the template for skill enhancement.

How long did all this take? Jenna's case involved 21 sessions of counseling with Jenna, and 9 parent sessions, over a period of six months. While there are no tried and true guidelines for duration of treatment in play therapy, experienced play therapists would

(continued)

Case Study (continued)

consider the number of sessions required for symptom remission in this case as falling within the norm for less directive approaches that are typically used with young children. It should be noted, however, that there has been a move toward developing brief models of play therapy intervention. This is a relatively recent phenomenon that is likely to change the way play therapy is conducted with children.

Future Developments in Play Therapy

Research

Where is the play therapy field going from here? Given the popularity of this approach, even in light of the problems with the research in this area, it would certainly make sense for there to be thorough examination of what works and what does not work. Well-constructed studies such as Sloan's (1997), Boehm-Morelli's (1999), and Kaplewicz's (1999) are steps in this direction. However, there is much more work to do in this respect. Again, using improved research methods and tools, it should be possible to produce more definitive conclusions in many of these areas.

Therapeutic effectiveness. Clearly, research needs to investigate the efficacy of play therapy in remediating childhood social–emotional problems. Any such research needs to focus on examining specific play therapy techniques used with specific types of children, and measure specific outcomes. Again, Sloan's (1997) research provides a good model for such studies.

Play therapy process. There are a number of conceptualizations of the therapeutic process in play therapy, such as Nordling's and Guerney's (1999), that are based on clinical observations and specific theoretical models. Research that has been conducted on play therapy processes (Hendricks, 1971) has been constrained by small sample sizes and rather antiquated research techniques. Future research using larger samples and up-to-date observation systems should help illuminate common phenomena that occur at specific points of the play therapy process, independent of any particular theoretical framework.

Microskills. What constitutes an effective facilitative response in play therapy? What limit-setting techniques are most effective? These are examples of the many questions that need to be answered regarding the therapist–client interactions in play therapy. As with other areas in this field, ideas about therapeutic technique are based on theoretical viewpoints. Whether or not any of the current literature on therapeutic responding and limit setting is valid remains to be proven.

Play therapy training.   Cerio et al. (1999) found that training in play therapy is becoming more widespread, but the type and depth of training varies considerably. Research needs to examine such topics as training practices for the various helping professions that provide counseling to children (for example, school psychologists and social workers), and the type of training that prepares individuals to use play therapy effectively.

Multicultural issues.   Research on the use of play therapy with diverse populations of children is almost nonexistent (Landreth, Homeyer, Bratton, & Kale, 1995). Future studies need to investigate such areas as cultural differences in children's play, the effects of using culture-specific toys, and differential reactions to therapist–client interactions that may be culturally based.

Physical effects of play.   Is there a biological basis for the use of play therapy? We have known for years that exercise stimulates the release of compounds produced by the body, such as endorphins, that help alleviate pain and mitigate the effects of stress (Ray & Ksir, 1990). Is it possible that play might produce similar effects with children? This may prove to be an interesting avenue of research, particularly during this era when many psychological disorders have been connected to brain dysfunction (see, for instance, Lewandowski and Barlow's discussion in Chapter 6).

Practice

Play therapy practice has been steadily evolving beyond the constraints of traditional child-centered and psychodynamic models. Approaches like strategic family play therapy (Ariel, 1997) and filial family play therapy (Guerney, 1997) have expanded into more family-focused interventions. These types of approaches emphasize the dynamics of family relationships, involving both parents and children in therapeutic interactions ranging from nondirective play to structured interventions. Depending on the particular theoretical framework, the goals of these approaches may vary from relationship enhancement (Guerney) to specific reconstitution of family dynamics to allow for more functional family interactions (Ariel). The reader is referred to Preli's description of family dynamics in Chapter 10 for an expanded treatment of family systems and implications for intervention practices. Filial therapy, in particular, has been demonstrated as an effective approach for strengthening parents' acceptance of and empathy for their children (Sensue, 1982; Sywulak, 1978). Other techniques, such as the Family Puppet Interview (Gil, 1994) simply help involve children in the family therapy process (Giudici & Cerio, 1999).

Experts in the field (Kaduson & Schaefer, 1999; O'Connor, 1997) have also been actively developing more structured therapy models that are compatible with practice in a managed-care environment. These short-term approaches combine elements of traditional relationship-focused therapies with structured techniques as a means of decreasing the length of the therapeutic process. Overall, the field is becoming "eclecticized," evolving into a more mature, practical application of play therapy with children.

Conclusion

It is doubtful that play therapy, like many other forms of psychotherapy, will ever attain the stature of science. This may not even be a desired goal for, as Jerome Frank reminds us, a primary function of psychotherapy is to understand the *meaning* of behavior, that is, the subjective experience of the client (Holland & Guerra, 1998). Thus, it may make more sense to think of play therapy as a *scientific art;* that is, an art that puts science at its service. Although this perspective might eschew the rigor of a physical science, it is probably a more realistic view of psychotherapy.

Conducting psychotherapy with young children has been a constant challenge since the time of "Little Hans" (Freud, 1909/1955). While behavioral approaches seem to be more appropriate with children for whom problems are clearly externally evident, such interventions neither acknowledge nor address behaviors and symptoms that are generated by internally directed issues, such as depression. Play therapy provides a reasonable alternative for allowing children to deal with such problems on their level using one of their primary skills, play. It is not the only alternative, but should at least be among the alternatives available to counselors who work with children.

References

Ariel, S. (1997). Strategic family play therapy. In K. O'Connor & L. Braverman (Eds.), *Play therapy theory and practice: A comparative presentation* (pp. 368–396). New York: Wiley.

Aspy, D., Aspy, C., Russel, G., & Wedel, M. (2000). Carkhuff's human technology: A verification and extension of Kelly's (1997) suggestion to integrate the humanistic and technical components of counseling. *Journal of Counseling and Development, 78,* 29–37.

Axline, V. (1947). *Play therapy: The inner dynamics of childhood.* Boston: Houghton Mifflin.

Barlow, K., Strother, J., & Landreth, G. (1985). Child-centered play therapy: Nancy from baldness to curls. *The School Counselor, 32,* 347–356.

Barlow, K., Strother, J., & Landreth, G. (1986). Sibling group play therapy: An effective alternative with an elective mute child. *The School Counselor, 34,* 44–50.

Bettelheim, B. (1987, March). The importance of play. *Atlantic Monthly,* 35–46.

Bills, R. E. (1950). Play therapy with well-adjusted readers. *Journal of Consulting Psychology, 14,* 246–249.

Boehm-Morelli, H. (1999). *Reading self-concept and reading achievement as a function of play and nondirective play therapy.* Unpublished dissertation, Alfred University, Alfred, NY.

Butler, S., & Strupp H. (1986). Specific and nonspecific factors in psychotherapy: A problematic paradigm for psychotherapy research. *Psychotherapy, 23,* 30–39.

Carkhuff, R., & Berenson, B. (1977). *Beyond counseling and therapy* (2nd ed.). New York: Holt, Rinehart and Winston.

Cerio, J. (2000). *Play therapy: A do-it-yourself guide for practitioners.* Alfred, NY: Alfred University Press.

Cerio, J., Taggart, T., & Costa, L. (1997, November). *Play therapy training practices for school psychologists: Results of a national study.* Poster session presented at the annual meeting of the New York State Association of School Psychologists, White Plains, NY.

Cerio, J., Taggart, T., & Costa, L. (1999). Play therapy training practices for school counselors: Results of a national study. *Journal for the Professional Counselor, 14,* 55–65.

Crow, J. (1994). *Play therapy with low achievers in reading.* Louisville, KY: University of Louisville. (ERIC Document Reproduction Service No. ED 375–358)

Donovan, D., & McIntyre, D. (1990). *Healing the hurt child.* New York: Norton.

Egan, G. (1998). *The skilled helper: A problem management approach to helping* (6th ed.). Pacific Grove, CA: Brooks/Cole.

Elliott, C., & Pumfrey, P., (1972). The effects of play therapy on some maladjusted boys. *Educational Research, 14*, 157–163.

Erikson, E. (1963). *Childhood and society* (2nd ed.). New York: Norton.

Freud, S. (1909/1955). *The case of "Little Hans" and the "Rat Man."* London: Hogarth Press.

Gay, L. (1976). *Educational research: Competencies for analysis and application.* Columbus, OH: Charles C. Merrill.

Gil, E. (1991). *The healing power of play.* New York: Guilford Press.

Gil, E. (1994). *Play in family therapy.* New York: Guilford Press.

Giudici, K., & Cerio, J. (1999). A comparison of the effects of two family play therapy activities on child participation, comfort, and activity preference in family therapy. *Journal for the Professional Counselor, 14*, 69–80.

Griffiths, A. (1971). Self-concept in remedial work with dyslexic children. *Academic Therapy, 2*, 125–133.

Guerney, L. (1997). Filial therapy. In K. O'Connor & L. Braverman (Eds.), *Play therapy theory and practice: A comparative presentation* (pp. 131–159). New York: Wiley.

Hendricks, S. (1971). *A descriptive analysis of the process of client-centered play therapy.* (DAI 32/07A). Unpublished doctoral dissertation, University of North Texas, Denton, TX.

Holland, H., & Guerra, P. (1998, August). A conversation with Jerome Frank. *Counseling Today, 40*, 1–14.

Hug-Hellmuth, H. (1921). On the technique of child analysis. *International Journal of Psychoanalysis, 2*, 287.

Ivey, A., & Ivey, M. (1999). *Intentional interviewing & counseling: Facilitating client development in a multicultural society* (4th ed.). Pacific Grove, CA: Brooks/Cole.

Kaduson, H., & Schaefer, C. (Eds.). (1999). *Short-term play therapy for children.* New York: Guilford Press.

Kaplewicz, N. L. (1999). *Effects of group play therapy on reading achievement and emotional symptoms among remedial readers.* Unpublished doctoral dissertation, Alfred University, Alfred, NY.

Lambert, M., & Bergin, A. (1994). The effectiveness of psychotherapy. In A. Bergin & S. Garfield (Eds.), *Handbook of psychotherapy and behavior change* (4th ed., pp. 143–189). New York: Wiley.

Landreth, G. (1987). Play therapy: Facilitative use of child's play in elementary school counseling. *Elementary School Guidance & Counseling, 22*, 253–261.

Landreth, G. (1991). *Play therapy: The art of the relationship.* Muncie, IN: Accelerated Development.

Landreth, G., Homeyer, L., Bratton, S., & Kale, A. (1995). *The world of play therapy literature.* Denton, TX: Center for Play Therapy.

Lebitz-Giudici, K., & Cerio, J. (1999). A comparison of the effects of two family play therapy activities on preference, comfort, and satisfaction in family therapy. *Journal for the Professional Counselor, 14*, 69–80.

LeVieux, J. (1994). Terminal illness and death of father: Case of Celeste, age 51/2. In N. B. Webb (Ed.), *Helping bereaved children: A handbook for practitioners* (pp. 81–95). New York: Guilford Press.

Mann, E., & McDermott, J. (1983). Play therapy for victims of child abuse and neglect. In C. Schaefer & K. O'Connor (Eds.), *Handbook of play therapy* (pp. 283–307). New York: Wiley.

Mendell, A. (1983). Play therapy with children of divorced parents. In C. Schaefer & K. O'Connor (Eds.), *Handbook of play therapy* (pp. 320–354). New York: Wiley.

Milos, M., & Reiss, S. (1982). Effects of three play conditions on separation anxiety in young children. *Journal of Consulting and Clinical Psychology, 50*, 389–395.

Moustakas, C. (1959). *Psychotherapy with children.* New York: Harper & Row.

Nordling, W., & Guerney, L. (1999). Typical stages in the child-centered play therapy process. *Journal for the Professional Counselor, 14*, 16–22.

Nystul, M. (1980). Nystulian play therapy: Applications of Adlerian psychology. *Elementary School Guidance & Counseling, 15*, 22–30.

O'Connor, K. (1991). *The play therapy primer.* New York: Wiley.

O'Connor, K. (1997). Ecosystemic play therapy. In K. O'Connor & L. Braverman (Eds.), *Play therapy theory and practice: A comparative presentation* (pp. 234–284). New York: Wiley.

Phillips, R. (1985). Whistling in the dark? A review of play therapy research. *Psychotherapy, 22*, 752–760.

Piaget, J. (1962). *Play, dreams and imitation in childhood.* New York: Norton.

Ray, O., & Ksir, C. (1990). *Drugs, society, & human behavior* (5th ed.). St. Louis, MO: Times Mirror/Mosby.

Rogers, C. (1957). The necessary and sufficient conditions for therapeutic personality change. *Journal of Consulting Psychology, 25*, 95–103.

Rogers, C. (1961). *On becoming a person.* Boston: Houghton Mifflin.

Rogers, C. (1975). Empathic: An unappreciated way of being. *The Counseling Psychologist, 5*, 2–10.

Schaefer, C., & Reid, S. (Eds.). (1986). *Game play: Therapeutic use of childhood games*. New York: Wiley.

Sensue, M. (1982). Filial therapy follow-up study: Effects of parental acceptance and child adjustment. (Doctoral dissertation, The Pennsylvania State University). *Dissertation Abstracts International, 42*, 148A.

Sloan, S. (1997). *Effects of therapeutic aggressive play: Does it increase or diminish spontaneous aggression?* Unpublished doctoral dissertation. Alfred University, Alfred, NY.

Swartz, S., & Swartz, J. (1985). *Counseling the disabled reader.* Paper presented at the Annual Meeting of the Illinois Council of Exceptional Children. (ERIC Document Reproduction Service No. ED 265689)

Sywulak, A. (1978). The effect of filial therapy on parental acceptance and child adjustment. (Doctoral dissertation, The Pennsylvania State University). *Dissertation Abstracts International, 38*, 6180B.

Truax, C., & Carkhuff, R. (1967). *Toward effective counseling and psychotherapy*. Chicago: Aldine.

White, J., & Allers, C. (1994). Play therapy with abused children: A review of the literature. *Journal of Counseling and Development, 72*, 390–394.

Willock, B. (1983). Play therapy with the aggressive, acting out child. In C. Schaefer & K. O'Connor (Eds.), *Handbook of play therapy* (pp.387–411). New York: Wiley.

19

Computer-Based Test Interpretation and Report Generation

Janet F. Carlson

The ubiquity of computers and related technology has influenced the assessment process substantially for several decades now, both in terms of computer-adaptive or computer-assisted administration and in software applications that score, interpret, and sometimes generate narrative test reports. Some discussions of computer uses in testing manage to cover both administration and interpretation issues (e.g., Butcher, Perry, & Atlis, 2000; Kramer & Gutkin, 1990; Moreland, 1985a). The scope of this chapter is restricted, however, to the use of computers or computer software in attaching meaning to test takers' performance, as this aspect of technology has the greatest relevance to practitioners, including those in training. Thus, the use of computers in scoring, interpretation, and report generation comprise the primary focus of the discussion that follows. Due consideration is given to current uses and professional perspectives concerning applications of available computer technology. Readers are encouraged to review Harvey's recommendations in Chapter 13 about effective report writing generally, as the principles enumerated therein maintain their relevance in the present context as well.

Historical Context

The use of computers to score tests is far from a recent phenomenon, as computers were put to this purpose in the early 1930s when Strong's *Vocational Interest Blank* (Strong, 1927) was subjected routinely to machine scoring. Computerized test interpretation for personality measures began to appear somewhat later, as computer assisted test interpretation systems for the *Minnesota Multiphasic Personality Inventory* (*MMPI*; Hathaway & McKinley, 1943) appeared in the mid-1960s (Moreland, 1992). Since then, many more computerized interpretive systems assessing a wide variety of human functions have followed, including additional systems for tests in vocational and personality domains, as well as a large number in the areas of cognitive ability, achievement, and many other functions and domains. Murphy (1998) estimated that over 400 computer-based test interpretation systems and services are available commercially at present. Computer interpretive systems for tests used with children that assess domains beyond cognitive ability and academic achievement may be somewhat more scarce, but computer-administered versions of several personality and behavioral measures are readily available. For example, the *Children's Depression Inventory* (Kovacs, 1992), *Children's State-Trait Anxiety Inventory* (Spielberger, 1973), Conners' *Continuous Performance Test* for attentional problems (Conners, 1994), *Children's Personality Questionnaire* (Porter & Cattell, 1985), *Diagnostic Interview for Children and Adolescents* (Reich, Herjanic, Welner, & Gandhy, 1982), and *Conners' Rating Scales* (Conners & Barkley, 1985) are among the measures available with computerized options, either in administration, scoring, interpretation, report generation, or all of the foregoing (Sturges, 1998).

Initially, the use of computers to score and interpret tests was held in check by the lack of widespread availability of the hardware needed to do so. Practitioners who opted to use computers in their assessment practices generally mailed completed response forms to central processing locations where they were machine scored, perhaps interpreted, and mailed back. The stilted narratives and mechanistic prose (Baker, 1989) that sometimes accompanied the scores in the earliest days of these programs were of limited value and use. Many computerized interpretive programs today continue to use the system of mailing response forms to a central location for processing, but many accompanying narratives are considerably more polished. In fact, by the mid-1980s the quality of the written narratives had improved and at least some could be described as "highly detailed, well-written, empirical-sounding" interpretations even "for tests for which validity data are practically nonexistent" (Moreland, 1985b, p. 816). But interpretive statements offered were frequently unrelated to each other, as they derived from item clusters or scaled scores related to specific dimensions of personality, for example (Moreland, 1992). The independence of interpretive statements was especially apparent when the report format presented interpretations as a simple string of sentences listed (and sometimes numbered) in a column, or when one interpretive statement seemed to contradict another, as occasionally happened. Even with improvements in narrative prose, computer-generated reports—more often than hand-generated ones—need to include disclaimers about apparent contradictions from sentence to sentence or section to section of the report.

The proliferation of "personal" computers added a new dimension to test scoring and interpretation options, heretofore impractical due to size, cost, portability, and power constraints. The burgeoning availability and affordability of desktops, laptops, palmtops, dockables, and so forth brought this type of technology and its regular application into the everyday lives of psychologists beginning in the early to middle part of the 1980s, continuing through this day, and, undoubtedly, extending well into the future.

Such options were and are inherently appealing to many psychologists in applied settings who continue to be key assessment experts and major users of tests. Surveys of school psychologists, for instance, consistently demonstrate the prominence of assessment activities in their professional roles (Fisher, Jenkins, & Crumbley, 1986; Reschly & Wilson, 1995; Smith, 1984). Estimates indicate that assessment activities consume more than 50% of school psychologists' time (Eyde, 1996), despite a concomitant recognition of the need for greater diversity of services to be offered by school psychologists (Kramer & Epps, 1991). Comprehensive psychoeducational assessments take considerable time to complete; one recent estimate reported median values of more than 12 hours. The authors (Lichtenstein & Fischetti, 1998) hasten to point out that their data were highly variable, however, and report that more than one quarter of the psychoeducational evaluations in their study required in excess of 15 hours to complete. Given these time requirements, potentially time-saving computer applications (Finger & Ones, 1999; Maddux & Johnson, 1993) would allow practitioners to reallocate time to other demands. But there are other benefits as well, including a very high level of reliability as computer interpretations produce the same results time after time, using the same set of scores (Butcher, 1995).

Kamphaus (1993) identifies and summarizes numerous benefits of computer-based test scoring and interpretation, citing advantages in data storage and retrieval, computational efficiency, accuracy of computed scores, scoring flexibility, and various processing benefits such as error trapping, whereby impossible values are flagged as such, password protection, and word-processing capabilities. Interpretive advantages described by Kamphaus include the potential for computer-based test interpretation software to enhance divergent thinking and hypothesis generation. Hypotheses developed in this way can then be considered, confirmed, or discarded in light of additional data obtained from other sources. These benefits can act to enrich the assessment process by promoting a wider variety of possibilities to evaluate and help to effect a truly comprehensive understanding of the individual child.

There are important drawbacks corresponding to each of these advantages, however. Storing data electronically creates additional issues with respect to maintaining confidentiality (McMinn, Buchanan, Ellens, & Ryan, 1999; Reed, McLaughlin, & Milholland, 2000). Data-entry errors may or may not be flagged by error trapping features built into many software programs, because most of the traps detect impossible values and not all erroneous values are also impossible. From the recent rash of computer viruses and "hacking" incidents, a number of which have been global in scale and some of which have penetrated data systems thought to be highly secure, it almost goes without saying that password protections are limited in their worth as far as ensuring the security of data.

The comfort that can accompany computer scoring and test interpretation may be unwarranted, given the fallibility of humans, even those who qualify as testing experts, whose knowledge may be used to construct algorithms, and those whose technical expertise is used to translate experts' knowledge into computer languages (Sundberg, 1985). Of course, there is always the possibility of data-entry errors committed by the individual test user who enters individual test takers' responses or scores. The resultant sense of security, therefore, may be false and may contribute to professionals extending their competence beyond real limits because it is so very easy to do so (e.g., see Jacob-Timm & Hartshorne, 1998). For quite some time and continuing somewhat even today, computers were regarded as invincible, never tiring or making careless errors as do people (Maddux & Johnson, 1993). However, it is equally important to remember that computers cannot think or use judgment as people do, weighing alternatives simultaneously in light of vast amounts of data, quantitative and qualitative. Even highly sophisticated state-of-the-art hardware and software cannot act entirely in place of the professional's own thoughtful and reflective processes. Ultimately, the golden rule of thumb is that if one cannot perform a task without computer assistance, one should not perform that task with computer assistance.

The foregoing benefits and liabilities all may have serious implications, although one could argue that the well-informed, cautious professional can work in ways that mitigate the potentially harmful effects of these concerns. More difficult to surmount are the somewhat broader issues discussed next that are vexing in their nature because they have been, and continue to be, problematic aspects of computer-based interpretive systems. Among the more intractable concerns are ethical issues, validity questions, and context considerations, discussed in turn in the following sections.

Considerations and Limitations of Use

Ethics, Testing, and Computers

During the 1980s, when personal computers first began to gain widespread use and application software started to keep pace with advancements in hardware (Matarazzo, 1985) later in the decade, there was an initial flurry of concerns and specific guidelines about appropriate uses of such software, given what were perceived to be almost boundless possibilities (American Psychological Association Committee on Professional Standards and Committee on Psychological Testing and Assessment, 1986; Burke & Normand, 1987; Kramer, 1988; Moreland, 1985b). Some writers cautioned against blanket acceptance of computerized test interpretations or reports, noting that the appearance of absolute accuracy, precision, and freedom from human error was misleading (Maddux & Johnson, 1993; Matarazzo, 1985). Matarazzo (1986) also criticized reports generated by computers for failing to recognize individual test taker's uniqueness and for presenting interpretations that were unsigned, presumably in order to leave no one actually accountable for the content of the report (Butcher et al., 2000). Moreland (1985a, 1985b) encouraged prospective users of computer-based test interpretation software to evaluate the programs and related research in terms of validity concerns such as small sample sizes, questionable external criterion measures, failure to consider base-rate accuracies, and other problems.

Since the mid-1980s, many professional associations have developed well-thought-out guidelines for responsible or ethical use of various emerging technologies, such as computerized test interpretation, or have embedded appropriate caveats in their wider spectrum of ethics codes and so on. For example, the *Ethical Principles of Psychologists and Code of Conduct* (American Psychological Association [APA], 1992) clarified psychologists' responsibilities as far as computer applications in assessment processes, including using computerized administration and scoring services, as well as interpretive and report-generation services or software. The National Association of School Psychologists (NASP) also addressed appropriate uses of computers and other technology in its *Professional Conduct Manual* (1997). Both APA and NASP explicitly note that using such available technologies does not diminish the individual psychologist's responsibility in assessment practices such as test selection, accuracy of scoring, or the validity and reliability of instruments, scores, interpretations, and so forth. Essentially, computer-based test interpretations are viewed as a form of professional communication. Although changes to ethics codes and professional conduct manuals clarified some very important matters, some debate continues (e.g., Jacob-Timm & Hartshorne, 1998), at least with regard to the use of narratives produced by a computer program. Practitioners need to bear in mind that some may question a decision to use computer-generated prose in a professional report.

The most recent edition of the *Standards for Educational and Psychological Testing* (American Educational Research Association, American Psychological Association, & National Council on Measurement in Education, 1999; hereafter referred to as the *Standards*) incorporated concerns about computer-generated interpretations in several related standards, such as those related to test administration, scoring, and reporting; supporting documentation for tests; responsibilities of test users; and psychological testing and assessment applications. Standard 11.21 succinctly specifies that test users should not use computer applications to perform functions that the test user him- or herself could not do: "Test users should not rely on computer-generated interpretations of test results unless they have the expertise to consider the appropriateness of these interpretations in individual cases" (p. 118). This standard is consistent with the views of many others who made similar assertions, recommending that computer-based test interpretations be used in addition to, but not in place of, expert judgment (Anastasi & Urbina, 1997; Butcher et al., 2000; Jacob-Timm & Hartshorne, 1998; Moreland, 1985a, 1992). As Sturges (1998, p. 187) aptly noted, "[w]hen psychological test interpretation is done by unqualified persons, the same principles apply regardless of whether the measures are paper-and-pencil or computer-assisted."

With regard to the prevalence of use of computerized test interpretation software, McMinn et al. (1999) surveyed 420 psychologists in independent practice about both their use of various technologies and their ethical beliefs about practices associated with these technologies. Among the survey items were several that concerned computerized testing. Rather surprisingly, McMinn et al. note the relatively modest rate of use of computer applications, despite some earlier predictions about the proliferation and expanded use of computer technology that would characterize the future (e.g., Johnson, 1979; Madsen, 1986). A number of individual practitioners surveyed in 1987 (Jacob & Brantley, 1987) reported that they expected to use computer-based test interpretation software in the future, although they reported they did not use it currently. Some of those surveyed probably have ended up using such technology, but the predicted rampant escalation of computer applications in testing simply has not materialized. Computerized test scoring and interpretation systems have found a seemingly comfortable niche within the assessment market, but they certainly do not dominate it.

With regard specifically to the use of computerized test interpretation software, nearly half of the respondents to McMinn et al.'s (1999) survey indicated that they never used such technology. Only about 20% reported that they used this kind of technology "fairly" or "very" often, which the authors note represented a slight decline from a decade earlier, when Farrell (1989) and Jacob and Brantley (1987) conducted similar surveys. Farrell found that 29% of psychologists in independent practice used this kind of technology routinely, while 33% of the school psychologists in Jacob and Brantley's study responded similarly. As for the probity of using computerized test interpretation software, a substantial majority of respondents (more than 78%) indicated that they regarded computer-based test interpretation as an ethical practice "under many circumstances" or "unquestionably" (McMinn et al., 1999). So it seems that psychologists believe this kind of technology can be used ethically and responsibly, but—for whatever reasons—most of them do not use it regularly.

Over the years that computer-based test interpretation systems have been readily available, there has been greater opportunity for circumspection, informed discussion, and consideration of benefits and risks by individual psychologists as well as by professional organizations. On balance, the field seems to have moved away from brash predictions implying that all testing—administration, scoring, interpretation, and report writing—would be completed by computers by the turn of the century. Too, psychologists have arrived at a more balanced view of computer applications, not only for what they can do, but for what they cannot do. Some recent reviews (e.g., Butcher, 1995; Butcher et al., 2000) suggest that computerized test interpretation represents accepted, appropriate practice. Others (e.g., Murphy, 1998) hold that controversy about this method of interpretation exists and will continue.

Validity Concerns

As suggested earlier, the reliability of computer-based test interpretations is virtually perfect (Butcher, 1995). However, the same cannot be said for their validity. Among the major concerns raised during the time when computer-based test interpretation began to gain widespread use was the issue of validity. Cogent commentaries by Matarazzo (1986), Moreland (1985a, 1985b, 1992), and others (e.g., Burke & Normand, 1987), urged prospective users to investigate the worth of these programs in a manner parallel to that used for selecting individual tests as far as validity and related concerns (e.g., see related discussion by Wasserman and Bracken in Chapter 2). One complication in attempting to do so, however, relates to psychologists' lack of training and ability to evaluate computerized interpretation programs. As a rule, psychologists receive explicit training as part of their doctoral work in testing, including instruction in how to evaluate the psychometric properties of tests and how to determine appropriate uses of tests. But few will have the technical expertise needed to evaluate the development of software used to score or interpret tests, or to construct narrative reports based on test data. Exacerbating this situation, the documentation that accompanies the software rarely provides sufficient information on which to make such determinations.

Moreland (1985a, 1985b) offers guidelines for practitioners to follow as they assess the utility of computer-based test interpretation systems. First, prospective users of such programs, should consider and investigate the credentials of the individual who authored the program, with particular attention to whether the author has a scholarly record involving the instrument in question. Moreland also recommended that prospective users examine the published documentation that accompanies the software, being certain to evaluate the integrity of the reference citations and the validity evidence provided in the written documentation. Test users were encouraged further to search for published reviews of the software that might appear in such journals as *Computers in Human Behavior, Social Science Microcomputer Review,* and the *Journal of Personality Assessment.* These reviews serve a purpose similar to those provided for tests themselves in compendia such as the *Mental Measurements Yearbook,* originally edited by O. K. Buros and published most recently by the University of Nebraska at Lincoln, and the *Test Critiques* series, published by PRO-ED.

Programming strategies for the development of computerized test interpretation systems generally involve one of two approaches. *Actuarial approaches* are based on statistical correlations between test data and interpretive statements that have been empirically demonstrated (Butcher et al., 2000). Computerized interpretive programs using an actuarial approach often are developed concurrently with a particular test. Ergo, they often yield high validity coefficients, at least for the population on whom the test and its corresponding interpretive system were developed (Moreland, 1985b). However, these populations sometimes are rather small, calling into question the generality of the findings, such that concerns emanating from actuarial prediction are less related to test validity than to generality.

Clinical approaches to the development of computerized test interpretation software depend mostly or even exclusively on clinical expertise that is incorporated into the linkage algorithms (Butcher et al., 2000). These kinds of programs base interpretive conclusions on the work of one or more clinicians whose knowledge of published research and clinical expertise are used to interpret test data. Validation efforts in this case often involve comparisons between findings rendered in computer-generated reports and those generated by hand (Moreland, 1992). Validity coefficients derived in this way are questionable, in that the hand-generated reports used for comparison may themselves be of questionable validity. On a more positive note, computer-based test interpretation programs constructed using experts' knowledge and expertise to develop the algorithms that comprise the programs ultimately provide the test user access to the knowledge base of expert consultants beyond those to whom he or she normally has access (Moreland, 1992). It is tantamount to accessing a virtual consultant or even a team of experts with each case one encounters.

A recent review by Butcher et al. (2000) concerning the validity of computer-based test interpretation systems indicates that computer-generated narrative reports for personality assessment yield interpretive statements comparable to those generated by individual clinicians. Their findings confirm those of Andrews and Gutkin (1991), completed almost a decade earlier, who examined consumers' views of a report they believed was authored either by a computer or by a clinician. Consumers regarded the reports similarly on dimensions such as credibility, overall quality, and level of confidence they placed in the report's findings. Butcher et al. affirm previous suggestions (e.g., Jacob-Timm & Hartshorne, 1998) that computerized test interpretation programs may serve as useful adjuncts to clinical judgment, but reports generated via computer should not be regarded as replacements for those written by a skilled and properly trained clinician.

Butcher et al. (2000) further caution that computer-based test interpretation procedures that have been validated in certain settings cannot be assumed valid in alternative settings. This caveat parallels validity discussions related to specific instruments, wherein it is noted that tests validated for specific uses are not necessarily valid for other uses. Of particular concern in this regard are instances in which computerized test interpretation procedures are used for individual test takers from so-called mainstream situations and—based on valid outcomes produced within those confines, followed by good decision making within those confines—the outcomes prompt wider use of the computerized system. Extending the application to settings and contexts well beyond those in which its validity was demonstrated to be adequate stretches credulity. This concern relates to what are generically considered "context" issues, which are discussed more fully in the section immediately following this one.

Waterman and Carlson (Chapter 1) note that the ultimate goal of assessment is to develop interventions to help a child overcome problems or obstacles that interfere with his or her optimal functioning. In Chapter 2, Wasserman and Bracken specify that a critical consideration in assessment is the extent to which evaluation procedures lead to treatments and interventions that will benefit the examinee, a feature of tests or assessment processes known as *treatment validity* or *treatment utility* (Hayes, Nelson, & Jarrett, 1987). A parallel concern, discussed by Kramer and his associates (Kramer, 1988; Kramer & Gutkin, 1990) regards computer-based test interpretation software. These authors point out that the treatment validity of any particular interpretive package can be no better than the treatment validity of the particular test or tests in question and the interpretive algorithms that undergird the computer program. Kramer and Gutkin express great skepticism about the treatment utility of computerized interpretations, questioning the extent to which treatment efforts can be enhanced by such systems. They also note, however, that this shortcoming is not specific to computerization, so much as to the limits of the tests and the interpretive systems themselves.

Context Considerations

Ultimately, assessment is a human endeavor, the end goal of which is to communicate effectively about individuals, often a single individual in the caseloads of school and clinical psychologists. A lingering and major question concerning the probity of computer-based test interpretation practices relates to their shortcomings in producing truly integrated and useful reports. Some software programs claim to offer integrated reports based on input data from several measures. However, many times the tests included in these packages are published by the same company and, therefore, may not reflect what practitioners tend to use in their test batteries. Given that the available couplings may be more a matter of convenience for test developers, software developers, and publishers, test users and users of computer-based test interpretation systems should be certain to choose wisely, if at all.

Another concern relates to that portion of the report commonly called the "Behavioral Observations" section, traditionally included in reports to provide a narrative description of the test taker that characterizes a large array of potentially meaningful aspects of behavior (Harvey, 1997; Ownby, 1997; Tallent, 1988). As summarized earlier by Harvey (Chapter 13), a test taker's level of motivation, ability to engage in the purposes of testing, confidence, persistence in the face of both success and failure, degree of attentiveness, and so on should be addressed in a well-written report. These behavioral elements, aptly observed and documented, may become quite important in attaching meaning to test results. Some computerized interpretive systems allow for comments on some or most of these elements, sometimes in the form of sentences or phrases, but also in what amounts to a fill-in-the-blank operation. Sentences are then assembled using appropriate algorithms, and strung together in a predetermined order to make a paragraph, the contents of which sometimes can be altered considerably via strategic editing. The computer-generated report may use a heading, such as "Behavioral Observations," to summarize the qualitative data that were entered, but the programs simply cannot use or integrate this information later in making interpretations in light of such aspects of behavior. In the end, it seems unlikely that these kinds of machinations accurately capture the essence of the individual child being evaluated. As well, the unique characteristics of the individual test taker cannot be brought to bear later on test findings in order to ascertain more fully the meaning of particular scores, or to develop interventions with these considerations in mind.

The poignancy of these shortcomings was summarized early on by Sundberg (1985), who suggested that computer-based test interpretations are largely dependent on "statements used by the computer [that] are based on clinical lore and expert impressions . . . It is important that the user . . . know something about . . . the limitations of blind computer printouts" (pp. 1010–1011). The case history and any special circumstances about the setting or the referral are not considered and there is no opportunity for exchanges of information between the referring party and the computerized program. Other writers (e.g., Maddux & Johnson, 1993) express similar concerns, noting the computer's limits as far as scoring subjective responses or detecting potentially important subjective cues given by a test taker. Maddux and Johnson are opposed especially to the use of computers in interpreting test results. They note that, typically, the problems that bring about a referral for testing represent complex human difficulties and need to be addressed on human terms, using what traditionally is termed "clinical judgment" or "professional expertise." It is not possible to vest computer programs with these uniquely human skills, in that their development in people remains enigmatic and difficult to reduce to discrete, discernible steps.

Butcher et al. (2000) note that the power and flexibility of computers have been underutilized in the area of psychological test interpretations, as most programs function to "look up and list out" (p. 15) possibilities. In most instances, this reality leaves much to be desired as narrative reports are intended to capture the three-dimensional essence of the test taker, based on the set of structured human interactions and related data gathering that comprise the assessment process. Likewise, Kramer (1988) criticizes the current practice of clinging to norm-based instruments and interpretations that follow from this model, versus developing technologically driven innovations that foster more effective linkages between assessments and treatments.

The foregoing problem is compounded by the fact that the storage capacity of personal computer systems is quite large, meaning that the number of elements provided in a given list of possible interpretations or suggested interventions can become unwieldy and impractical. Responsible test givers must recognize the need for professional judgment, for example, in identifying interventions that are best suited for the particular child for whom they are developing a plan. In such considerations, it is imperative to weigh individual circumstances such as those described elsewhere in this volume related to cultural (Chapter 11), community (Chapters 16 and 17), and familial (Chapter 10) features of the individual's life. The *Standards* (1999) speak directly to this issue, stating in the comment section of Standard 5.11 that computer-based interpretations "may not be able to take into consideration the context of the individual's circumstances . . . [and] . . . should be used with care in diagnostic settings, because they may not take into account other information about the individual test taker, such as age, gender, education, prior employment, and medical history, that provide context for test results" (p. 65).

Narrative reports generated by a computer should not be used to substitute for one written by a psychologist (Eyde et al., 1993). In working with computer-generated narratives as preliminary drafts, responsible practitioners will be sure to integrate results from computer printouts with additional information obtained from other sources. It is especially important to recognize statements that are overly general and could be applicable to almost any test taker, a phenomenon known as the *Barnum effect*, which acts to homogenize information appearing in the narrative report, making individual test takers less and less distinct. This drawback has been regarded as commonplace in many computer-generated reports (Butcher et al., 2000; Moreland, 1992). Matarazzo (1985), for instance, notes, with reference to a specific computer-generated interpretive report for the *MMPI*, at least half of the interpretive statements provided apply to virtually anyone. In an effort to reduce Barnum effects, it is incumbent on responsible test users to detect and reject "errors of overstatements in English narrative produced by computer software" (Eyde et al., 1993, p. 214).

Future Directions

Despite some genuine attractions, computer-based test interpretation systems are similar to other interpretive systems—imperfect. They do apply decision rules more consistently, have greater storage capacities, and conduct analyses more rapidly (Kamphaus, 1993; Kramer, 1988). The aura of precision and heightened accuracy that accompanies them may be undeserved, however, and even misleading. It is vital to bear in mind that a report that comes from a computer is not inherently better or more valid than one that develops by a clinician's hand. Responsible use of computerized interpretation upholds earlier guidelines that regard such programs as adjunctive or preliminary measures. Until and unless computers can be vested with human qualities and programmed in ways that more closely mimic the integrative analysis, interpretation of test session behavior, quantitative and qualitative, and, ultimately, the synthesis of results, the current status of computerized test interpretation is unlikely to change dramatically in the near future.

One benefit of the ongoing presence, if not rapid expansion, of computers and related technology in the professional lives of clinical and school psychologists is that the increase in electronic capabilities will continue to bring to the fore important assessment-related issues. The advent of computerized test interpretation software that could run on personal computers has prompted closer scrutiny about technology's influence on responsible and ethical practices, generally within professional associations such as APA and NASP, as well as within individual psychologist's practices as demonstrated in recently published works (McMinn et al., 1999; Reed et al., 2000). Ultimately, this kind of attention helps to keep practitioners current and attuned to important developments that affect their practices and their clients' well-being.

Professional psychologists as well as individuals in training for the profession should continue to look to their respective professional associations for guidance on assessment matters such as those deriving from computer technology. As well, it is worthwhile to stay abreast of various interdisciplinary efforts that relate to testing practices, such as the recently published *Standards* (1999) and *Responsible Test Use* (Eyde et al., 1993). The latter work presents several dozen case studies, amassed from real cases solicited via the critical incident technique. This approach is especially effective in illuminating the complexities of circumstances and helping psychologists and other professionals who use tests to develop an appreciation of the myriad ways in which assessment issues manifest in the "real" world. Several apt illustrations and commentaries concerning factors involved with computer applications of tests and test interpretations are provided, and a number of the 86 elements of competent test use provided relate specifically to computer-based test interpretation practices.

The judicious application of computer technology may facilitate more comprehensive efforts in screening for potential difficulties among school-age children. Time and financial constraints frequently prohibit large-scale assessments that delineate who within a given population is at risk for low base-rate disorders or events, such as suicide. For example, screening instruments for depression or suicide that have an option for computer administration and interpretation permit screening on a much wider, more cost-effective basis than is possible otherwise. These kinds of applications may become even more important in the future, for low base-rate events with serious—even irreversible—outcomes, such as suicide among the young, which, as noted by Vitulano, Carlson, and Holmberg in Chapter 3, has seen an increased rate over recent years.

Throughout this volume, the problems a child may experience—rather than his or her educational classification or clinical diagnosis—were to be at the center of attention. A major drawback of computer-generated reports is that they do not automatically link findings or interpretations to the "reason for referral." It remains the responsibility of the individual test giver to relate interpretations to presenting problems, and to show how the results answer the referral questions and indicate effective interventions. Indeed, the major point of collecting and interpreting data is to bring the resultant interpretations to bear on problems the child experiences in order to promote interventions that improve his or her circumstances. Although Matarazzo's (1985) words no longer can be considered recent, they continue to apply to assessment practices today. He stressed that an interpretive report must be able to build a cohesive theory of the individual while, at the same time, remaining flexible in order to accommodate special cases, such as may occur as a function of various contextual considerations (cultural, ethnic, or linguistic background, for instance). Data are interpreted differently in the context of unique features of the individual test taker. For example, imagine that a given test taker completes a 4-hour assessment battery in a single afternoon. The extent to which one regards this as an accomplishment depends on many factors, not the least of which is the test taker's age and the presenting problems. If the child is 6 years old and was referred because of attentional difficulties evidenced within a classroom setting, the examiner probably has a large number of new hypotheses to explore, based less on test scores and more on the unique attributes of this particular test taker.

Conclusion

In the words of Matarazzo (1985), "psychological assessment is a clinical art built upon a still accumulating but less than adequate scientific base" (p. 249). This astute characterization holds true to this day. Practitioners can expect improvements in the adequacy of the scientific base on which the art of assessment is built but, in the end, the essential nature of the assessment process is unlikely to change dramatically in the foreseeable future. As a human endeavor, assessment practices must continue to allow for some degree of human nature to influence the process. The challenge for the present and the future is to restrict unwanted human elements (e.g., bias) from obscuring the true nature of the problems experienced by children, while continuing to permit ample opportunity for the test taker to demonstrate his or her "best" abilities, "best" meaning most accurate.

Computer technology is here to stay and will continue to extend its influence and permeate more and more aspects of both our personal and professional lives. With regard to technology and the assessment process, psychologists have covered much territory and established important guiding principles concerning the use of technology—whether computer or otherwise—especially with respect to how using technology affects one's professional practices and responsibilities. The need to do so originally was hastened by the onslaught of personal computerization during the 1980s, and the continued need to monitor and include these aspects of assessment practices will be sustained by the omnipresence of this technology. Individual practitioners need to make informed choices about whether and how to use technological innovations to best serve their constituents. As demonstrated in the foregoing discussion, computer-based test interpretations are not, themselves, a panacea. More realistically, they involve very real gains, coupled with very real concerns.

References

American Educational Research Association, American Psychological Association, & National Council on Measurement in Education. (1999). *Standards for educational and psychological testing.* Washington, DC: American Educational Research Association.

American Psychological Association. (1992). Ethical principles of psychologists and code of conduct. *American Psychologist, 47,* 1597–1611.

American Psychological Association Committee on Professional Standards and Committee on Psychological Testing and Assessment. (1986). *Guidelines for computer-based tests and interpretations.* Washington, DC: American Psychological Association.

Anastasi, A., & Urbina, S. (1997). *Psychological testing.* Upper Saddle River, NJ: Prentice-Hall.

Andrews, L. W., & Gutkin, T. B. (1991). The effects of human versus computer authorship on consumers' perceptions of psychological reports. *Computers in Human Behavior, 7,* 311–317.

Baker, F. B. (1989). Computer technology in test construction and processing. In R. L. Linn (Ed.), *Educational measurement* (3rd ed., pp. 409–428). New York: Macmillan.

Burke, M. J., & Normand, J. (1987). Computerized psychological testing: Overview and critique. *Professional Psychology: Research and Practice, 18,* 42–51.

Butcher, J. N. (1995). How to use computer-based reports. In J. N. Butcher (Ed.), *Clinical personality assessment: Practical approaches* (pp. 78–94). New York: Oxford University Press.

Butcher, J. N., Perry, J. N., & Atlis, M. M. (2000). Validity and utility of computer-based test interpretation. *Psychological Assessment, 12,* 6–18.

Conners, C. K. (1994). *Conners' Continuous Performance Test.* Toronto, Canada: MHS.

Conners, C. K., & Barkley, R. A. (1985). Rating scales and checklists for child psychopharmacology. *Psychopharmacology Bulletin, 21,* 809–843.

Eyde, L. D. (1996, August). Ethical use of tests in school settings. In P. L. Harrison (Chair), *Use and misuses of tests in school settings.* Symposium conducted at the meeting of the American Psychological Association Convention, Toronto, Canada.

Eyde, L. D., Robertson, G. J., Krug, S. E., Moreland, K. L., Robertson, A. G., Shewan, C. M., Harrison, P. L., Porch, B. E., Hammer, A. L., & Primoff, E. S. (1993). *Responsible test use: Case studies for assessing human behavior.* Washington, DC: American Psychological Association.

Farrell, A. D. (1989). Impact of computers on professional practice: A survey of current practices and attitudes. *Professional Psychology: Research and Practice, 20,* 172–178.

Finger, M. S., & Ones, D. S. (1999). Psychometric equivalence of the computer and booklet forms of the MMPI: A meta-analysis. *Psychological Assessment, 11,* 58–66.

Fisher, G. L., Jenkins, S. J., & Crumbley, J. D. (1986). A replication of a survey of school psychologists: Congruence between training, practice, preferred role, and competence. *Psychology in the Schools, 23,* 271–279.

Harvey, V. S. (1997). Improving readability of psychological reports. *Professional Psychology: Research and Practice, 28,* 271–274.

Hathaway, S. R., & McKinley, J. C. (1943). *The Minnesota Multiphasic Personality Inventory* (Rev. ed.). Minneapolis, MN: University of Minnesota Press.

Hayes, S. C., Nelson, R. O., & Jarrett, R. B. (1987). The treatment utility of assessment: A functional approach to evaluating assessment quality. *American Psychologist, 42,* 963–974.

Jacob, S., & Brantley, J. C. (1987). Ethical–legal problems with computer use and suggestions for best practices: A national survey. *School Psychology Review, 16,* 69–77.

Jacob-Timm, S., & Hartshorne, T. S. (1998). *Ethics and law for school psychologists* (3rd ed.). New York: Wiley.

Johnson, J. (1979). Technology. In T. Williams & J. Johnson (Eds.), *Mental health in the 21st century* (pp. 7–9). Lexington, MA: D. C. Heath.

Kamphaus, R. W. (1993). *Clinical assessment of children's intelligence: A handbook for professional practice.* Boston: Allyn and Bacon.

Kovacs, M. (1992). *Children's Depression Inventory.* Toronto, Canada: MHS.

Kramer, J. J. (1988). Computer-based test interpretation in psychoeducational assessment: An initial appraisal. *Journal of School Psychology, 26,* 143–153.

Kramer, J. J., & Epps, S. (1991). Expanding professional opportunities and improving the quality of training: A look toward the next generation of school psychologists. *School Psychology Review, 20,* 452–461.

Kramer, J. J., & Gutkin, T. B. (1990). School psychology, assessment, and computers: An analysis of current relationships and future potential. In T. R. Kratochwill (Ed.), *Advances in school psychology* (pp. 131–150). Hillsdale, NJ: Erlbaum.

Lichtenstein, R., & Fischetti, B. A. (1998). How long does a psychoeducational evaluation take? An urban Connecticut study. *Professional Psychology: Research and Practice, 29,* 144–148.

Maddux, C. D., & Johnson, L. (1993). Best practices in computer-assisted assessment. In H. B. Vance (Ed.), *Best practices in assessment for school and clinical settings* (pp. 177–200). Brandon, VT: Clinical Psychology Publishing.

Madsen, D. H. (1986, April). Computer-assisted testing and assessment in counseling: Computer applications for test administration and scoring. *Measurement and Evaluation in Counseling and Development, 1,* 6–14.

Matarazzo, J. D. (1985). Clinical psychological test interpretations by computer: Hardware outpaces software. *Computers in Human Behavior, 1,* 235–253.

Matarazzo, J. D. (1986). Computerized clinical psychological interpretations: Unvalidated plus all mean and no sigma. *American Psychologist, 41,* 14–24.

McMinn, M. R., Buchanan, T., Ellens, B. M., & Ryan, M. K. (1999). Technology, professional practice, and ethics: Survey findings and implications. *Professional Psychology: Research and Practice, 30,* 165–172.

Moreland, K. L. (1985a). Computer-assisted psychological assessment in 1986: A practical guide. *Computers in Human Behavior, 1,* 221–233.

Moreland, K. L. (1985b). Validation of computer-based test interpretations: Problems and prospects. *Journal of Consulting and Clinical Psychology, 53,* 816–825.

Moreland, K. L. (1992). Computer-assisted psychological assessment. In M. Zeidner & R. Most (Eds.), *Psychological testing: An inside view* (pp. 343–376). Palo Alto, CA: Consulting Psychologists Press.

Murphy, K. R. (1998). *Psychological testing: Principles and applications* (4th ed.). Upper Saddle River, NJ: Prentice-Hall.

National Association of School Psychologists. (1997). *Professional conduct manual.* Washington, DC: Author.

Ownby, R. L. (1997). *Psychological reports: A guide to report writing in professional psychology* (3rd ed.). New York: Wiley.

Porter, R. B., & Cattell, R. B. (1985). *Children's Personality Questionnaire.* Champaign, IL: Institute for Personality and Ability Testing.

Reed, G. M., McLaughlin, C. J., & Milholland, K. (2000). Ten interdisciplinary principles for professional practice in telehealth: Implications for psychology. *Professional Psychology: Research and Practice, 31,* 170–178.

Reich, W., Herjanic, B., Welner, Z., & Gandhy, P. R. (1982). Development of a structured psychiatric interview for children: Agreement on diagnosis comparing child and parent interviews. *Journal of Abnormal Child Psychology, 10,* 325–336.

Reschly, D. J., & Wilson, M. S. (1995). School psychology practitioners and faculty: 1986 to 1991–92 trends in demographics, roles, satisfaction, and system reform. *School Psychology Review, 24,* 62–80.

Smith, D. K. (1984). Practicing school psychologists: Their characteristics, activities, and populations served. *Professional Psychology: Research and Practice, 15,* 798–810.

Spielberger, C. D. (1973). *Manual for the State–Trait Anxiety Inventory for Children.* Palo Alto, CA: Consulting Psychologists Press.

Strong, E. K. (1927). *Vocational Interest Blank.* Stanford, CA: Stanford University Press.

Sturges, J. W. (1998). Practical use of technology in professional practice. *Professional Psychology: Research and Practice, 29,* 183–188.

Sundberg, N. D. (1985). [Re: Behaviordyne Psycho-diagnostic Laboratory Service for the Minnesota Multiphasic Personality Inventory (a computer-based test interpretation)]. In J. V. Mitchell, Jr. (Ed.), *The ninth mental measurements yearbook* (pp. 1010–1011). Lincoln, NE: Buros Institute of Mental Measurements.

Tallent, N. (1988). *Psychological report writing* (3rd ed.). Englewood Cliffs, NJ: Prentice-Hall.

20

Testing the Members of an Increasingly Diverse Society

Kurt F. Geisinger

Perhaps the most notable change in U.S. society in the last several decades is that our society is becoming increasingly diverse and this diversity itself is changing many aspects of society. Imagine the following situation. One night in 1971, a psychologist working for a particular school district falls asleep and awakens some 30 years later and returns to work as a Rip Van Winkle–type school psychologist in the year 2001. Although this example is obviously fictional, try to imagine what changes a school psychologist in 2001 would encounter that would not have been present, or at least as prevalent, in 1971 (or some other time in the relatively recent history of applied psychology). Many of the tests that school and clinical psychologists use today are strikingly similar to those of an earlier time; they may even carry the same names! They would certainly contain a number of identical or very similar test questions. Many of the therapeutic approaches also are remarkably unchanged. Technology, too, of course, has affected the educational process, but not yet in as many structured ways as will someday be likely. I suggest that the greatest single change in the United States that has affected education is in the composition of the society in general and of schoolchildren in particular. These changes have an extraordinary impact on the work of psychologists dealing with school-age children and adolescents. This chapter focuses on the use of tests with specific members of this changing population. As such, the chapter describes first some of these populations changes, and then addresses how these alterations impact tests and the psychologists who use them.

Changing Population Trends

The Census Department of the United States (U.S. Census Bureau, August 25, 2000) provides considerable information both of a factual, current basis and of a prognostic,

346

future-oriented population trend basis. As of July 1, 2000, the population of the United States was estimated to be approximately 275 million; it has grown from a July 1, 1995 estimate of approximately 263 million. The Census Bureau also categorizes the population into demographic groupings. Of the 275 million number, approximately 70.4% is White, not Hispanic; 12.8% is African American,[1] not Hispanic; 11.8% is Hispanic; 4.1% is Asian American and Pacific Islanders; 0.9% is Native American. Population changes occur in two primary ways: (a) immigration and emigration, and (b) birth and death rates. Each of these is considered in turn.

The population of our country is both growing and changing rapidly. The U.S. Census Department (January 14, 2000) expects that the population in the United States will approximate 300 million people in the year 2010, only ten years from the time this chapter is being written, and projects that it will be 338 million in the year 2025, a more than 28% increase from 1995. Of this total, in 2010, some 202 million (67.3%) are likely to be White, non-Hispanic; 43.7 million (14.6%) will be Hispanic; 40 million (13.3%) will be Black; 15.3 million (5.1%) will be Asian and Pacific Islander; 2.8 million (0.9%) will be Native American. Clearly, in the next decade, the White, not Hispanic percentage of the population is declining and the Hispanic, African American, and Asian populations are increasing, with the Hispanic population becoming the largest of the so-called minority groups. Estimates of future population of the United States by the U.S. Census Department are available in five-year intervals to the year 2100. By the year 2025, the population of the United States is expected to be approximately 338 million, of which the White, not Hispanic proportion will be 62%; Hispanic, 18.2%; African American, 13.9%; and Asian, 6.5%. What should be clear from these estimated data is that the percentage of the population that is Hispanic is increasing and the percentage that is White, not Hispanic is decreasing. The African American, Asian, and Native American populations are not increasing proportionally to a major extent, although it may be noted that the Asian population is expected to increase over the next 25 years and then to decrease.

A snapshot from the recent past demonstrates the impact of immigration. From July 1, 1995 until July 1, 1999, a period of four years, the foreign-born resident population in the United States increased 12.4% from approximately 23 million to 25.8 million (U.S. Census Bureau, April 11, 2000). The largest proportion of this increase was with Hispanics (43%), followed by White, not Hispanic (25%), Asian (24.5%), and Black, not Hispanic (7%). Much of the increase in the White, not Hispanic grouping was from Eastern Europe and Asia. These immigrants are individuals who generally come to the United States as language minorities. Most of the White, not Hispanic group presently is coming from Eastern Europe. Little increase in the Native American population, which is, of course, indigenous, occurred during this period. Clearly, the largest groups coming to the United States through immigration are those who are likely to be cultural and language minorities.

Sandoval (1998b) reviewed many of the demographic changes that we can expect in the coming century. According to Sandoval, "over the next 30 years, the U.S. population is expected to increase by 72 million to 335 million in 2025.[2] Forty-four million of that increase (61% of the population growth) will come from Hispanic and Asian groups, who together will increase from 14% to 24% of the national population" (pp. 387–388). The percentage of European Americans in our population will decline, as the percentages of African Americans, Native Americans, and other non-White groups will increase proportionally (Sandoval, 1998b). Sandoval also expects that these changes in the population, perhaps coupled with decreasing social distances among the various demographic groups, will likely lead to "more intermarriage and blending of cultures" (p. 388). Some immigrant groups will choose to assimilate into the mainstream culture, "such as Irish, Italians, and Jews, for example, over succeeding generations have become part of the majority population, at least for test interpretation purposes" (p. 388). Some groups will choose to remain as a subculture, at least in part.

Various ethnic populations are often not evenly spread throughout the country. Ten states in the union have consistently high concentrations of Hispanics, for example (Fernandez, 1995). Thus, those test users whose work is geographically limited (as is the case with most clinicians) need to have special knowledge of the populations who reside in the areas of their practice.

The proportional growth is especially notable among youth, who are the primary focus of this volume. Dehne (2000) estimates that, in 2005, 50% of the 18-year-old people in the United States will be people of color. This proportion, of course, is higher than the proportion of the total population that are people of color (now or in 2005), but this difference reflects differences in birthrates. This change also indicates transformations that are occurring in our society and the need for our concern with diversity, especially when considering psychological issues related to youth.

As we move to considering how to assess all of the individuals who compose our rapidly changing society, we must focus on the most important questions: the issues of language and culture (Frisby, 1998; Geisinger, 1998; Sandoval & Durán, 1998).

Limited-English-Proficient (LEP) Students

One of the institutions in which the testing of ethnic and language minorities has faced the loudest criticisms is in the educational system. Criticisms are pervasive and intense. Malgady (1996) suggests that examples of test misuse with cultural and language minority group members are so common that one should assume that even widely accepted and validated psychological measures are not valid for members of underrrepresented groups, until evidence proves otherwise.

The 1990 U.S. Census found that approximately 14% of schoolchildren lived in homes where the primary language was not English. Students whose English-language ability is relatively weak and whose education in U.S. schools suffers on this account are often referred to as Limited-English-Proficient (LEP) students. Fleischman and Hopstock (1993) found that the vast majority (approximately three quarters) of LEP students are Spanish speaking, with about 20%–25% of the LEP students not being Spanish-language students. About one half of this remaining fourth constitutes Asian language groups (e.g., Chinese, Vietnamese) with the residual half coming from all other groups, primarily European, Native American, and other backgrounds. Professionals who use tests in schools or clinical settings are most likely to encounter these individuals who face educational diagnosis and treatment planning decisions to disproportional degrees, perhaps, at least in part, because of their difficulty in the English language. That language minority children are a higher proportion of those needing such decisions in the schools and mental health settings should not be surprising. Those who use tests, it should be clear, need to know how to assess ethnic and language minority children, in part because these groups appear to be growing, in part because they are already large, and in part because they often face decisions requiring the use of tests. The understanding of a number of psychometric concepts is critical to proper test use with these individuals.

Important Psychometric Characteristics in Tests for a Diverse Society

The primary criticisms concerning the use of psychological tests with members of ethnic and language minority groups have focused on the use of cognitive tests, such as intelligence tests, especially in educational and industrial settings, in which group differences are frequently present and litigation often results from such test use that leads to differential assignment to preferred outcomes (e.g., acceptance at the college of one's choice, the offer of a job).

> That tests reflect cultural differences should not be startling. Much of the concern centers on the lowering of test scores by cultural conditions that may have affected the development of aptitudes, interests, motivation, attitudes and other psychological characteristics of minority group members . . . Differences in the experiential backgrounds of such groups or individuals are inevitably manifested in test performance. Every psychological test measures a behavioral sample. Insofar as culture affects behavior, its influence will and should be detected by tests. If we could rule out all cultural differentials from a test, we might thereby lower its validity as a measure of the behavioral domain it was designed to assess. In that case, the test would fail to provide the kind of information needed to correct the very conditions that impaired performance (Anastasi & Urbina, 1997, p. 545).

Amplification of these contentious matters would be beyond the nature and length of the present chapter, but may be found in a dizzying array of sources, some of which have been remarkably controversial and well publicized (e.g., Herrnstein & Murray, 1994; Kamin, 1974; Samuda, 1975).

There are several important junctures when test users must use their professional talents in making decisions about test use and test interpretation in a multicultural society. First, test users must decide what tests to use to make an assessment, in the case of a single individual and in the case of groups, whatever their size. Second, test users must decide how to administer selected instruments, or whether to administer an instrument to specific individuals, when it was identified for use with all test takers.[3] An example of making this kind of exception would be in the use of a nonverbal self-concept scale rather than one heavily dependent on English reading ability when assessing a Spanish-speaking youth whose reading ability in English is quite limited. Third and finally, a professional test user must interpret the results of an assessment. Each of these concerns is discussed in the remainder of this chapter.

Test Selection

Those professionals who use psychological tests with their clients must first decide what tests to use. Traditionally, psychologists and other professionals have been trained to select tests (or to develop a test themselves) that provide the most appropriate information for whatever the decision to be made, whether the decision be high stakes (e.g., college admission), for classroom decision making, or those used in counseling or diagnostic decision making (e.g., Anastasi & Urbina, 1997). Test users are generally encouraged to consider information provided in test manuals and other repositories (e.g., the Mental Measurements Yearbook series) of such information to evaluate critically the reliability and validity of a testing instrument. Test users are urged to use tests that are valid and appropriate for the use in question. Tests are not valid universally regardless of the nature of the test use. It is improper to discuss specific tests as valid or invalid without defining the nature of the use to which the scores are to be put. (See Chapter 2 by Wasserman and Bracken for elaboration of these concepts.)

For purposes of the present chapter, test reliability refers to the consistency of measurement, whether that consistency is over time, over test forms of the same instrument, over test administrators and scorers, or over an entire pool of possible test questions. A bathroom scale is reliable if it consistently yields the same or very similar weights for an individual whose weight is not changing. That a scale is consistent does not mean that the scale yields valid, or true, weights, however. Many individuals have bathroom scales that are consistently inaccurate. (In fact, many of us enjoy the benefits of just such instruments!) It is necessary that a test is reliable if it is to be valid, but reliability never insures validity.

An assessment is valid, however, if it provides information that is both correct and that is intentionally sought. Instruments sometimes provide correct information that is not what is deliberately sought. Consider the following example. A custody hearing is being held in which the divorcing father and mother must both complete psychological inventories as requested by the court's psychologist. Both father and mother seek custody of the child and both are extremely anxious when completing the inventory. It is possible, depending on the items involved, that the results might be an accurate reflection of the anxiety that is felt rather than the variable that the inventory is intended to measure. In such an instance, the instrument may reflect anxiety accurately, but because that is not the construct that the inventory is designed to assess, it does not yield a valid measurement, in this case because the extreme anxiety confounds the assessment. Anastasi and Urbina (1997) provide a more complete description of procedures used to estimate the reliability and validity of an instrument in a given population.

In a diverse society, test users must evaluate tests and assessment devices using criteria in addition to reliability and validity. Test users also must evaluate the appropriateness of the instrument to the population(s) that they serve. That is, tests need to be evaluated against criteria in different groups. The results of such studies inform the potential test user whether the tests are suitable for the specific population to be assessed. Once again, potential test users are encouraged to review test manuals, research reports, and other critical reviews in making informed judgments as to the aptness of a given measure for the individual or groups to be assessed. Geisinger (1998) provides a list of questions that test users should ask when making this determination; these questions were adapted slightly for this chapter to focus more on diversity from a multicultural perspective. The issues underlying these questions follow and include the composition of the group to be tested, the appropriateness of specific tests for members of those groups, and whether adaptations of the instrument are available or likely to be constructed.

The composition of those to be tested. First, a test user, whether considering the assessment of a single individual or of a larger group (e.g., a school district), must determine the nature of the characteristic(s) to be assessed and the influence of language and culture on that characteristic. In the case of a group, one must consider the entire composition of those to be tested from this same perspective. While this concern is seemingly simpleminded, it is nevertheless critical. Let us first consider a small, well-defined population as might be found in a school district. The test selector needs to know the ethnic, cultural, and language background of the entire population. With regard to culture, the test user needs to be informed about the degree to which any individuals who have come to the country recently are acculturated. If there are those in the district who reside geographically or in some other manner in a subculture (e.g., an apartment complex inhabited by Russian immigrants), this factor, too, must be considered. With regard to language, the test user needs to know the extent to which the individuals are able to communicate in a complex, generally highly verbal undertaking, that is, to respond to questions on a psychological measure in the language in which the testing may be performed, which in the United States is most typically English. One also needs to know how many other languages are prevalent in the group. These issues are discussed later in this chapter.

Appropriateness of the instrument. Second, the test user needs to know the extent to which the assessment instrument can be administered to all of the members of the group. This discernment may not be a simple one. This judgment likely should be based on an assessment of whether members of various groups to be tested were included in the norm and validation samples in which the test was originally constructed and evaluated, respectively, and whether the instrument has been evaluated empirically for fairness and bias. A debated topic is whether minority groups (by definition, relatively small in number) should be represented accurately in norm or validation samples or whether they should be overrepresented, given their importance in our society and, in many cases, for testing professionals. A professional decision on this concern must be made at the time a test is selected (or developed). If groups relevant for a specific use of a measure are not adequately represented in norm and validity samples, subsequent research of this type could justify using an assessment instrument with a given subpopulation. Ultimately, a professional test user is responsible for selecting, administering, and interpreting an instrument. If he or she decides to use an instrument with a member of a group that was not included in the original norm or validation samples, and on which there are not data to justify the use, the professional judgment appears to be highly questionable. Local research is often one way to rectify such absences, but such research does take time and can be rather costly. Given the small numbers of members of underrepresented groups, empirical research with these groups may even be impossible or virtually impossible in local settings. Use of an instrument with individuals for whom the measure is not intended is highly problematic.

If members of the ethnic minority group in question have been included in the norm and validation samples and if the test appears to be valid for the ethnic minority group, an additional question must be answered: Is the test fair for the members of this group? This question addresses the issues of fairness and bias. (Sometimes the words *bias* and *fairness* are used as virtual opposites; others use the term *bias* as a narrowly psychometric concept, and the word *fairness* to refer to the nature of the actual use. An excellent reference on this topic is van de Vijver & Tanzer, 1998. Tests must be evaluated for their appropriateness for use with varying groups. It must be documented that a test is not only valid, but that it is equally valid in the sense that the results of testing are equally meaningful for various individuals independently of their group membership. This issue is the technical question of bias and has been discussed widely in the discipline of psychological testing. Appropriate summaries may be found in Berk (1982), Geisinger (1992), and van de Vijver (2000). In general, part of the validation process must be a determination that the psychological instrument is valid for members of all groups with whom the test is likely to be used and that its use is fair. Bias is a source of test invalidity; technically, bias is a source of test variance that is related to group membership rather than the construct being measured per se and is, thus, a source of test invalidity. That such information is considered as part of the validation process is clearly seen in the negative. If a test is not fair, then group membership is a source of invalidity; that is, group membership interferes with the ability of test users to make proper interpretations. Such conclusions can be made only after empirical research. Panels are sometimes convened to assess the perceived appropriateness and fairness of the questions on an instrument. In such cases, panels may well be able to identify inappropriate or offensive word choices and even to predict that wording may contribute to confusions among some segments of society. However, research has generally not shown that such panels can target those items on which different groups in our society will differ appreciably (Tittle, 1982).

In addition to determining that a test as a whole is appropriate for use with a particular ethnic minority group, a test user should inspect the process through which the instrument was constructed. Proper procedures call for an analysis as part of test development, referred to as "differential item functioning" or "DIF" analyses. Such investigations are generally performed as part of the test construction process to see that members of differing groups respond to individual items similarly. Only items that do not show DIF should remain on a published instrument. (For additional information on studies of this type, see Berk, 1982; Crocker & Algina, 1986; or Embretson & Reise, 2000. Readers may refer to the related discussion provided by

Wasserman and Bracken in Chapter 2.) After 20 years of research, however, the psychometric literature has not coalesced around a single statistical approach to identify inappropriate or unfair questions. A number of different analyses are available.

When a test user is making a decision about test use with a single individual, the judgment is perhaps easier than when considering a large and diverse group. In such an instance, it is appropriate to gather much information about the individual, his or her background, and educational and personal skills, abilities, and other personal characteristics to consider whether the person can be appropriately assessed with the instrument.

Adaptations of the instrument.   When testing a member of a so-called minority group, and especially when testing an individual whose dominant language is not English, one must decide whether it is more appropriate to perform the assessment in English or some other language. This decision should be based on three primary factors: the nature of the assessment, the relative strengths of the test taker in both languages, and the availability of the assessment or a reasonable alternative in the client's primary language. It should not be based on the test administrator's ability in that language. If the judgment is that the individual should be tested in another language, a referral may need to be made.

Some assessments need to be performed in English; a test of English-language writing ability for placement in the proper English class would be a simple case in point. Individuals who are bilingual should be tested in their primary language, or in the second language if it is sufficiently strong (Pennock-Román, 1992). If the client's English language ability is weak, the lack of language facility often interferes with proper responding on the part of the test taker. Imagine a LEP student completing a multidimensional self-concept scale so that a school psychologist will have a more complete understanding of the student. If the student does not understand the language, indeed, even the nuances of the language, his or her responses and, hence, scores are likely to be affected, with the scores being invalid, at least to some extent. Finally, the psychologist must ascertain whether the instrument or one comparable to it is available in the desired language.

One can inspect the test manual pertaining to a measure to see whether different language versions are available. Furthermore, even if the publisher has not produced a translated or adapted version of the test, one can check the professional literature or contact the test publisher to see if certain additional language forms are available. (In many cases doctoral students and other researchers have translated an instrument for research purposes. Of course, it is incumbent on the test user to determine whether the adapted instrument meets professional standards to the extent that the original measure did. (See Geisinger, 1994, for an elaboration of this process.) Reviewing the literature for this purpose has become increasingly easier with the advent of electronic literature databases. In many cases states contract with a test publisher to construct an educational test for a given purpose. In such an instance, it is common for a state to require that several different language versions be constructed to serve the needs of those who speak, understand, read, and write the more common languages present in the state.

Some adaptations or translations of tests are formal and are performed by the test author, publisher, or their colleagues. In other cases, especially in the case of many noncognitive instruments, the measure may be constructed for use in a single research study, such as a dissertation. In such an instance, the test may be adequately translated, but it is unlikely that more than scant psychometric data have been collected to judge the reliability, validity, and bias of the instrument, to develop norms, or to equate scores on the newly translated form to the original version. It is critical that the psychometric characteristics of translated test forms be studied carefully so that it is clear that the test measures the same characteristic in both languages, that the construct measured by the instrument is (equally) meaningful in both languages and cultures and for both culturally different populations,[4] and that specific scores convey the same meaning in both language forms. These criteria are not often met. It should be noted that, when measures are translated for research purposes only, they do not need to meet the professional standards normally required of professional tests (American Educational Research Association, American Psychological Association, & National Council on Measurement in Education, 1999) that instruments used in "guiding decisions" about individuals are presumed to have. Tests used for high-stakes decisions require still higher standards.

The translation of tests and assessment devices is one appropriately referred to as *test adaptation* because the process is more complex than a simple translation. Sometimes concepts or activities (e.g., ice skating or making a snowman [sic]) that are mentioned in the items on an instrument are not transferable to other cultures (e.g., the Caribbean), even if the wording may be directly translated. The wording of items may intentionally change the meaning, perhaps in subtle ways. One technique that has sometimes been used to insure the quality of a translation is called *back translation*. In this procedure, the instrument is initially translated to the target language by a first translator and then translated back to the original language by a second, independent translator. The original author of the measure (not the initial translator) then can compare the back-translated version against the original instrument. If differences appear, the quality of the translation becomes suspect. The inherent weakness of this procedure, however, is that, if the original translators know that their work will be evaluated by this technique, they choose wordings that are most likely to result in a back-translated instrument consonant with the original measure. Such a translation may not be the one that best leads to an accurate representation of the construct in the target language and culture.

Adapting[5] a test to a new language is a difficult process that, if done competently, will involve multiple test translators, tryouts, investigations to norm and equate the new form to the English-language version, reliability and validity studies, and studies of fairness or bias. All of the above are not necessarily needed when adapting a test for research purposes, but if the test is to be used operationally with test takers, regardless of the stakes involved, the above steps in the adaptation process are all required.

Many of the examples in this section relate almost solely to language differences. However, cultural differences may require adaptation as well. Consider the following example. An English-language interest inventory is developed in Australia with a target population of high school-age students. In one item, students are asked whether they like Cricket, a sport that is played and followed closely in Australia. If this measure enjoys success in Australia, some psychologists would undoubtedly wish to use it with appropriate individuals in the United States. Clearly, few people in the United States understand the sport, and some might even think it relates to the hobby of insect collection.

Test Administration

Language issues.   Pennock-Román (1992) has studied the validity of various high-stakes cognitive tests used for admission to U.S. higher education programs with language minorities, including both Hispanics and individuals from other countries. Such tests are normally justified with the use of predictive validity, where it is determined how well the tests predict future criteria of academic success. Her findings can be summarized with the following generalizations. She demonstrated that the use of these tests with language minorities might or might not be valid in predicting future scholastic criteria. The primary factor that influences whether the test will yield valid predictions is the developed English-language ability of the test taker. If students have strong English ability, the test is relatively likely to provide valid scores, scores appropriate to their future success; if their English skill is not strong, the test will not generally provide useful information.

Such results have not been clearly established using noncognitive (affective) measures to date, but it certainly appears reasonable that test results using an English-language measure are not likely to be valid if administered to individuals whose English-language skills do not permit them to comprehend the questions adequately. The results of Pennock-Román suggest the necessity of assessing English-language skills prior to performing the actual assessment, especially if the stakes of the assessment are high. Only those individuals whose English language ability at least matches that minimally required by the instrument should be assessed with it.[6] Otherwise, the user risks an invalid assessment that could lead to improper advice and decisions. Thus, prior to any assessment, English-language ability should be ascertained first, formally or informally. If the English-language assessment indicates significant strength, the measure, presuming no cultural limitations in the instrument, can probably be given with confidence. If the English-language assessment is not strong, or if it does not meet that required by the target assessment, then alternate procedures should probably be undertaken. Such alternate procedures include using an adapted form or a different assessment instrument altogether.

Test users should never administer an instrument in a manner that differs from those procedures specified in the manual (American Educational Research Association et al., 1999). Specifically, test users should never adapt, translate or employ measures in actual use if those involved are not willing to engage in the extensive validation and other research that would justify use of the measures operationally. Translating an instrument for a single individual (or a group), administering it in its new form, and making interpretations based on the original norms, validation, and reliability results is test misuse that is simply unacceptable.

Test administrator issues.   Anastasi and Urbina (1997) refer to assessments in which the test administrator and test taker represent different cultural groups as *transcultural contacts*. Numerous studies have been performed assessing the impact of such test administrator effects on test results. The vast majority of these studies have been performed using intellectual assessments as the type of measurement instrument and using Black and White test administrators and Black and White test takers, respectively. Essentially, an interaction is proposed (that Black test takers would do better when tested with Black test administrators and that White test takers would perform better with racially similar examiners). The hypothesis that Black examinees would perform in an enhanced manner with Black examiners has been found in some instances (e.g., Katz, Roberts, & Robinson, 1965), but general conclusions are that such results are not typically found (Shuey, 1966). Some summaries of these conclusions suggest that the jury remains out (Samuda, 1975). Jensen (1980), on the other hand, found that much of the research in this area was experimentally flawed and concluded: "Viewing the results of all these studies together, it seems safe to conclude that the evidence lends no support to the popular notion that the race of the examiner is an important source of variance between whites and blacks on tests of mental ability" (pp. 602–603). While little variance overall may be assigned to this interaction, it is not impossible to imagine that such findings might be present in the cases on certain individuals, such as those for whom race is a particularly poignant variable.

Less research using affective measures and these same examiner variables has been performed, however, and what has been performed has generally used projective techniques. Gibby, Miller, and Walker (1953) suggest that such findings would be likely in projective personality assessments. Samuda suggests that the complex social interactions between test administrators and test takers in the case of individualized assessments may confuse test-taking behavior and, hence, the test results. As racial and ethnic groups in our society become more integrated, however, it is plausible that the potential for such interactions will be reduced. At present, the best advice to clinicians is to be aware that such a test taker–test administrator interaction effect, while unlikely, is not impossible and that clinicians should consider the possibility of its existence when considering the effects of the testing environment on the test administration when interpreting test results.

Test Interpretation

Sandoval (1998a) reviews some of the factors test users should consider in making decisions using test results with members of culturally diverse groups (or simply interpreting the assessments of such individuals). Sandoval considers this type of judgment as "critical thinking in test interpretation." Beginning with a reminder of the groundbreaking work of Meehl and his colleagues (e.g., Dawes, Faust, & Meehl, 1989), Sandoval categorizes some of the kinds of decisions that test users make and then mentions a few cognitive biases, cognitive processes that unintentionally influence the way we consider and combine data such as test scores. Sandoval reminds us that decisions using (valid) test data are more likely to be valid than those not employing such information. He suggests considering a number of factors that will help those who work with diverse individuals avoid mistakes in test interpretation and decision making. These issues include the base rates of the occurrence of diagnoses, adequately sampling behavior (and not using a single test score), avoiding inferences of causality between behaviors and diagnoses, avoiding confirmatory biases (very close to stereotypes), and not being overly influenced by recent or vividly recalled events.

Guidelines for interpreting test results.   Those who administer, interpret, and use psychological assessments need to understand the characteristics being assessed, know the instrument and critical interpretive concerns regarding it, and have an in-depth understanding of the individuals themselves. The Office of Ethnic Minority Affairs (1993) of the American Psychological Association has issued guidelines to those who provide psychological services to members of ethnic, linguistic, and culturally diverse populations. In part, these guidelines state:

> Psychological service providers need a sociocultural framework to consider diversity of values, interactional styles and cultural expectations in a systematic fashion. They need knowledge and skills for multicultural assessment and intervention, including abilities to
>
> - recognize cultural diversity;
> - understand the role that culture and ethnicity/race play in the sociopsychological and economic development of ethnic and culturally diverse populations;
> - understand that socioeconomic and political factors significantly impact the psychosocial, political, and economic development of ethnic and culturally diverse populations; . . . and
> - understand the interaction of culture, gender, and sexual orientation on behavior and needs (p. 45).

Two specific guidelines in this document are especially appropriate for consideration. Guideline 2 states, "Psychologists are cognizant of relevant research and practice issues as related to the population being served" (p. 46). Guideline 2d emphasizes the assessment aspects: "Psychologists consider the validity of a given instrument or procedure and interpret resulting data, keeping in mind the cultural and linguistic characteristics of the person being assessed. Psychologists are aware of the test's reference population and possible limitations of such instruments with other populations" (p. 46). Thus, psychologists should perform assessments of the culturally diverse if the psychologist has expertise both in the area of the characteristic (i.e., the construct to be measured by the instrument) and the culture or ethnicity involved. Interpretations must be culturally sensitive and may need to be culture-specific. Language is one component of culture.

Assessing whether students have requisite language skills to complete an assessment in a meaningful manner is a comparatively easy judgment relative to judgments pertinent to acculturation. Specifically, whether a test taker who is not fully acculturated to the predominant U.S. culture should be given a particular assessment developed in and for that culture is a much more complex judgment. Such decisions should generally be made carefully, and after consulting information about the assessment in particular and the professional literature regarding the assessment of individuals from the culture from which the test taker came. In most cases, in considering the acculturation of test takers, test users will need to engage in a process akin to interpreting test results. This process is exactly what Sandoval (1998a) has referred to as "critical thinking in test interpretation," as noted above.

The Limited-English-Proficient population within U.S. schools has received considerable attention in recent years. Nevertheless, judgments about how to assess such individuals are rarely easy and depend, in many cases, on careful assessments of the students' language skills: expressive and interpretive, written and oral. Culture, however, is a particularly difficult matter in assessing affective characteristics, whether personality, attitude, or other aspects of individuality. Therefore, it is important to assess the extent to which a test taker who has immigrated to the United States has become acculturated to the country. It also may be appropriate to perform such an assessment when the individual appears to be completely or almost completely grounded within a subculture in the United States.

Supportive data on adapted forms of the assessment instrument.   If a test has been translated or adapted to a target language, and a test user would like to use the target language version of the instrument, the test user must first evaluate the quality of the revised instrument. This evaluation would be performed just as one would for a new instrument. One must consider whether its reliability and validity are not only acceptable, but are also similar to the form in the original language. Furthermore, one must see if procedures have been performed so that the test user knows whether he or she can interpret scores in a similar manner as scores from the original form. The experimental and statistical procedures that would permit such a determination are beyond the scope of the present chapter but may be found in Geisinger (1994) or Sireci (1997, in press).

Some New and Important Skills for Professional Test Users in a Diverse Society

As stated previously, test users must be competent in the characteristic(s) assessed by the test to be used, the developmental psychology of children in the age range to be tested, and the traditional concepts for interpreting test results for children that age. Test users in a multicultural society also must be familiar with various measures (and their interpretation) that can be administered in a manner to determine whether it is appropriate to assess the individual with a desired test. These measures assess acculturation and language capability.

Assessment of acculturation.   Personality, behavior, and culture are closely intertwined. Cuéllar (2000) has described culture as a moderator variable between personality and behavior. That is, culture influences the strength of relationship between personality and behavior that personality attempts to predict. Culture plays a central role in understanding behavior; with culture defined as "learned behavior transmitted from one generation to the next" (Cuéllar, p. 115). Behavior is influenced by culture in complex, interactive, and, sometimes, changing ways.

When an individual leaves one culture and joins a second, the transition is generally slow. "Most psychological research defines the construct of acculturation as the product of learning due to contacts between the members of two or more groups" (Marín, 1992, p. 345). Such contacts do not generally change an individual quickly. In general, acculturation occurs when individuals reside in multicultural societies or come into contact with a new culture. Acculturation involves different and hierarchical levels: (a) learning the facts related to the history and traditions of the new culture, including changing patterns of eating and information acquisition; (b) changing more central behaviors in an individual's social life, of which language preference and skill may be one of the most central; and (c) changing one's values, norms, worldview, and interaction patterns (Marín, 1992). Given the influence of acculturation on characteristics and behavior, clearly psychologists working with clients who have entered the United States and culture need to understand the extent to which the people have acculturated.

The measurement of acculturation, then, is the assessment of the degree to which individuals adapt and acclimatize themselves to the new culture, generally the United States. Measurement should include assessments of each of the three levels of acculturation mentioned above. Of course, not all individuals fully assimilate to their new culture. Many keep or even decide to keep certain aspects of their earlier culture; such individuals are sometimes considered bicultural (Marín, 1992). "Berry (1980) suggested that there are six areas of psychological functioning where acculturation has a direct effect: language, cognitive styles, personality, identity, attitudes, and acculturative stress" (Marín, 1992, p. 241). Acculturation changes may occur in some of these areas or domains and not in others, and change is likely to be uneven across these different domains. Stress is an effect of acculturation as well; it is stressful to be in a new culture and it is also stressful to adapt to the new culture (or perhaps to relinquish aspects of one's previous culture). Psychologists working with diverse clients need to consider this form of stress in formulating diagnoses and treatment plans.

Cuéllar presents a list of approximately 30 measures of acculturation. Many measures of acculturation were developed from the 1970s through the 1990s. Some measures are quite limited, and focus primarily, or even solely, on language acquisition or the acquisition of rudimentary cultural facts, for example. Cuéllar also describes some of the relations between personality and acculturation. Given the kinds of assessment that many applied psychologists perform and the influence of acculturation, knowledge of the influence of acculturation on the specific characteristics of interest is critical when working with diverse clients.

Marín identifies a number of problems with the measurement of acculturation. Most measures are unidimensional, while it is clear that acculturation is a multidimensional phenomenon. Not all measures have been studied psychometrically. The measures are frequently too heavily weighted toward language skill and language preference because of the ease of its assessment. Many of the measures have been developed primarily for research purposes. Clearly, it is important for applied psychologists to consider the acculturation of individuals with whom they are working, but the science of assessing acculturation is not yet as advanced as one would hope for psychological applications with individuals.

Assessment of language proficiency.   As noted in the previous section, the assessment of acculturation often includes some aspects of language acquisition and language preference. It already has been noted that assessments may need to be performed in a language other than English.

The assessment of language skills and ability is itself an assessment of a highly complex ability. One of the most basic ways that a psychologist can "assess" language preference and proficiency is self-report; that is, clients may be asked about their language preference and given the opportunity to choose the language in which they will be assessed.

Cummins (1983) suggests a distinction between two related levels of language proficiency, cognitive academic language proficiency (CALP) and basic interpersonal communicative skills (BICS).

> A student that gets along satisfactorily on the playground, where cognitive demands are presumably lessened by the immediacy of physical and social context, may encounter difficulty in the classroom when it comes to reading, writing, solving word and math problems, and generally acting on a more abstract level. The student may have adequate BICS without sufficient CALP (Oller & Damico, 1991, p. 100).

To respond to a paper-and-pencil psychological inventory will require CALP, which some believe requires six to eight years of education in the language to develop.

Over the past decade a movement toward the holistic measurement of language has been occurring (Oller, 1992). In part, this means that multiple assessments and types of assessments are essential when a careful evaluation of language skills is needed. That is, one needs assessments that are norm-referenced and those that are criterion-referenced; one needs assessments of oral language and of written language; within oral language, one needs assessments of hearing and speaking; and within written language, one needs assessments of reading and writing. If a psychologist desires a comprehensive assessment of an individual whose primary language is not English, all of the above may be needed. If, on the other hand, a psychologist needs to know if an individual has adequate English-language proficiency to read and respond to an objective attitude scale or personality inventory, a test of reading alone may suffice. Sandoval and Durán (1998) suggest that most commercial language proficiency tests used in schools, clinical settings, and job settings generally involve the predominant use of relatively objective test items. Others have responded that such tests are too limited and suggest using newer tests that assess language in a more complex and authentic manner. A relatively limited-in-scope, but widely available test of English-language proficiency generally does not require more than an hour. Many instruments assess primarily receptive skills (reading and oral comprehension) using the multiple-choice format. More complete descriptions of language assessment may be found in Oller and Damico (1991) or Sandoval and Durán (1998). A comprehensive assessment of language proficiency should be composed of information from numerous sources, some of which are tests and others are observations. Observations should provide those being assessed with "rich and engaging contexts" (Oller & Damico, 1991, p. 105). For example, a test administrator may wish to observe a child interacting orally with her peers in a play setting or a classroom. Whether such an instrument is needed is an important judgment for the psychologist or test user.

Training Issues

All psychologists and other professionals who use tests must first and foremost be qualified to use the tests. They must understand the concepts of reliability, validity, test bias, test standardization, norms, and test interpretation (Geisinger & Carlson, 1998). They should have been exposed to the *Standards for Educational and Psychological Testing* (American Educational Research Association et al., 1999). In addition to knowing the basics of testing, testing professionals should learn, while in graduate school, about the use of tests, including common examples of test misuse. Test users also need to learn to read test manuals critically and carefully (Geisinger & Carlson, 1998), because much of the information to be reviewed by test users may be found there. Aiken et al. (1990) performed a very large survey of doctoral psychology training programs and, unfortunately, found that measurement courses were offered by less than one half of the training programs studied. Only about one quarter of the programs self-reported that their students were competent in methods of reliability and validity assessment. Clearly, change is needed in this basic regard.

Anastasi and Urbina (1997) have called for the training of test administrators to include cultural training so that examiners have knowledge of one or more dissimilar cultures "with special attention to the likely cultural effects on the behavioral development of individuals" (p. 345). It has been mentioned throughout this chapter that those performing assessments with culturally diverse clients need to have training and experience in working with members of the ethnic and cultural groups in question.

Conclusion

Our society is growing rather rapidly and changing in composition. The increase in underrepresented groups in our society is certain, and the increase in language minorities, especially Hispanics and, to a lesser extent, Asians, is notable. The importance of psychological testing in U.S. society is clear and it is critical that we test members of underrepresented groups validly, and that we interpret the results of these testings appropriately and fairly.

This chapter has described in general terms some of the most central issues that must be considered in test selection or development, test administration, and in interpreting the results of an assessment. The primary concerns are those of language and acculturation. Tests in English are likely to be valid and appropriate for some members of underrepresented groups, especially if their English-language proficiency is strong. Strong English-language skills, however, should not be interpreted as complete acculturation. Instruments used with the predominant population may not be appropriate for all members of U.S. society. Psychological instruments can be adapted for both language and culture. While such adaptations are always imperfect, they can, nevertheless, be quite useful and informative. Assessments of acculturation and language proficiency may be needed to decide what measures to administer, to adapt specific measures, or to interpret the findings of an assessment.

Test users are always responsible for their actions. Therefore, we all need to learn about the ethnic and cultural groups to which our clients belong. Our findings must be interpreted in terms of the backgrounds of our clients. Perhaps, if we apply these general rules to the interpretation of test results from members of underrepresented groups, we will find them so helpful that they will inform the way we test majority group members, too.

References

Aiken, L. S., West, S. G., Sechrest, L., Reno, R. R., Roediger, H. L., III, Scarr, S., Kazdin, A. E., & Sherman, S. J. (1990). Graduate training in statistics, methodology, and measurement in psychology: A survey of Ph.D. programs in North America. *American Psychologist, 45,* 721–734.

American Educational Research Association, American Psychological Association, & National Council on Measurement in Education. (1999). *Standards for educational and psychological testing.* Washington, DC: American Educational Research Association.

Anastasi, A., & Urbina, S. (1997). *Psychological testing* (7th ed.). Upper Saddle River, NJ: Prentice-Hall.

Berk, R. A. (Ed.). (1982). *Handbook of methods for detecting test bias.* Baltimore, MD: Johns Hopkins University Press.

Berry, J. (1980). Acculturation as varieties of adaptation. In A. M Padilla (Ed.), *Acculturation: Theory, models, and some new findings* (pp. 9–25). Boulder, CO: Westview Press.

Crocker, L., & Algina, J. (1986). *Introduction to classical and modern test theory.* New York: Holt, Rinehart and Winston.

Cuéllar, I. (2000). Acculturation as a moderator of personality and psychological assessment. In R. H. Dana (Ed.), *Handbook of cross-cultural and multicultural personality assessment* (pp. 113–130). Mahwah, NJ: Erlbaum.

Cummins, J. (1983). Language proficiency and academic achievement. In J. W. Oller, Jr. (Ed.), *Issues in language testing research* (pp. 108–130). Rowley, MA: Newbury House.

Dawes, R. M., Faust, D., & Meehl, P. E. (1989). Clinical vs. actuarial judgment. *Science, 243,* 1668–1674.

Dehne, G. (2000, November). *The future of independent higher education.* Paper presented at the 28th Annual National Conference for the Chief Academic Officers of Independent Colleges and Universities, Tampa, FL.

Embretson, S. E., & Reise, S. P. (2000). *Item response theory for psychologists.* Mahwah, NJ: Erlbaum.

Fernandez, E. W. (1995, May). *Using analytic techniques to evaluate the 1990 Census coverage of young Hispanics.* Population Division, U.S. Bureau of the Census, Washington, DC. Technical Working Paper No. 11.

Fleischman, H. L., & Hopstock, P. J. (1993). *Descriptive study of services to Limited English Proficient students, Volume 1: Summary of findings and conclusions.* Arlington, VA: Development Associates.

Frisby, C. L. (1998). Culture and cultural differences. In J. Sandoval, C. L. Frisby, K. F. Geisinger, J. C. Scheuneman, & J. Ramos Grenier (Eds.), *Test interpretation and diversity: Achieving equity in assessment* (pp. 51–73). Washington, DC: American Psychological Association.

Geisinger, K. F. (1992). Fairness and selected psychometric issues in the psychological testing of Hispanics. In K. F. Geisinger (Ed.), *Psychological testing of Hispanics* (pp. 17–42). Washington, DC: American Psychological Association.

Geisinger, K. F. (1994). Cross-cultural normative assessment: Translation and adaptation issues influencing the normative interpretation of assessment instruments. *Psychological Assessment, 6,* 304–312.

Geisinger, K. F. (1998). Psychometric issues in test interpretation. In J. Sandoval, C. L. Frisby, K. F. Geisinger, J. C. Scheuneman, & J. Ramos Grenier (Eds.), *Test interpretation and diversity: Achieving equity in assessment* (pp. 17–30).

Washington, DC: American Psychological Association.

Geisinger, K. F., & Carlson, J. F. (1998). Training psychologists to assess members of a diverse society. In J. Sandoval, C. L. Frisby, K. F. Geisinger, J. C. Scheuneman, & J. Ramos Grenier (Eds.), *Test interpretation and diversity: Achieving equity in assessment* (pp. 375–386). Washington, DC: American Psychological Association.

Gibby, R. G., Miller, D. B., & Walker, E. I. (1953). The examiner's influence on the Rorschach protocol. *Journal of Consulting Psychology, 17,* 425–428.

Herrnstein, R. J., & Murray, C. (1994). *The bell curve: Intelligence and class structure in American life.* New York: Free Press.

Jensen, A. R. (1980). *Bias in mental testing.* New York: Free Press.

Kamin, L. J. (1974). *The science and politics of I.Q.* Mahwah, NJ: Erlbaum.

Katz, I., Roberts, S. D., & Robinson, J. M. (1965). Effects of difficulty, race of administrator and instructions on Negro digit-symbol performance. *Journal of Personality and Social Psychology, 70,* 53–59.

Malgady, R. G. (1996). The question of cultural bias in assessment and diagnosis of ethnic minority clients: Let's reject the null hypothesis. *Professional Psychology: Research and Practice, 27,* 73–33.

Marín, G. (1992). Issues in the measurement of acculturation among Hispanics. In K. F. Geisinger (Ed.), *Psychological testing of Hispanics* (235–251). Washington, DC: American Psychological Association.

Office of Ethnic Minority Affairs of the American Psychological Association. (1993). Guidelines for providers of psychological services to ethnic, linguistic, and culturally diverse populations. *American Psychologist, 48,* 45–48.

Oller, J. W., Jr. (1992). Language testing research: Lessons applied to LEP students and programs. In *Focus on Evaluation and Measurement: Proceedings of the second National Research Symposium on Limited English Proficient Student Issues* (pp. 43–123). Washington, DC: Office of Bilingual Education and Minority Language Affairs, U.S. Department of Education.

Oller, J. W., Jr., & Damico, J. S. (1991). Theoretical considerations in the assessment of LEP students. In E. V. Hamayan & J. S. Damico (Eds.), *Limiting bias in the assessment of bilingual students* (pp. 77–110). Austin, TX: PRO-ED.

Pennock-Román, M. (1992). Interpreting test performance in selective admissions for Hispanic students. In K. F. Geisinger (Ed.), *The psychological testing of Hispanics* (pp. 99–136). Washington, DC: American Psychological Association.

Samuda, R. J. (1975). *Psychological testing of American minorities: Issues and consequences.* New York: Dodd, Mead.

Sandoval, J. (1998a). Critical thinking in test interpretation. In J. Sandoval, C. L. Frisby, K. F. Geisinger, J. C. Scheuneman, & J. Ramos Grenier (Eds.), *Test interpretation and diversity: Achieving equity in assessment* (pp. 31–49). Washington, DC: American Psychological Association.

Sandoval, J. (1998b). Test interpretation in a diverse future. In J. Sandoval, C. L. Frisby, K. F. Geisinger, J. C. Scheuneman, & J. Ramos Grenier (Eds.), *Test interpretation and diversity: Achieving equity in assessment* (pp. 387–402). Washington, DC: American Psychological Association.

Sandoval, J., & Durán, R. P. (1998). Language. In J. Sandoval, C. L. Frisby, K. F. Geisinger, J. C. Scheuneman, & J. Ramos Grenier (Eds.), *Test interpretation and diversity: Achieving equity in assessment* (pp. 3–16). Washington, DC: American Psychological Association.

Shuey, A. M. (1966). *The testing of Negro intelligence* (2nd ed.). New York: Social Sciences Press.

Sireci, S. G. (1997). Problems and issues in linking tests across languages. *Educational Measurement: Issues and Practice, 16* (1), 12–19.

Sireci, S. G. (in press). Evaluating cross-lingual test comparability using bilingual research designs. In R. K. Hambleton, P. Merenda, & C. Spielberger (Eds.), *Adapting educational and psychological tests for cross-cultural assessment.* Hillsdale, NJ: Erlbaum.

Tittle, C. K. (1982). Use of judgmental methods in item bias studies. In R. A. Berk (Ed.), *Handbook of methods for detecting test bias* (pp. 31–63). Baltimore, MD: Johns Hopkins University Press.

U.S. Census Bureau, Population Estimates Program, Population Division. (April 11, 2000). *Foreign-born resident population estimates of the United States by sex, race, and Hispanic origin: April 1, 1990 to July 1, 1999.*

U.S. Census Bureau, Population Estimates Program, Population Division. (August 25, 2000). *Resident population estimates of the United States by sex, race, and Hispanic origin: April 1, 1990 to July 1, 1999, with short-term projection to July 1, 2000.*

Van de Vijver, F. (2000). The nature of bias. In R. H. Dana (Ed.), *Handbook of cross-cultural and multicultural personality assessment* (pp. 87–106). Mahwah, NJ: Erlbaum.

Van de Vijver, F., & Tanzer, N. K. (1998). Bias and equivalence in cross-cultural assessment: An overview. *European Review of Applied Psychology, 47,* 263–279.

End Notes

1. The term used by the U.S. Census Department is *Black;* the terms *Black* and *African American,* the preference of the writer, are used interchangeably in this section.

2. Note that current U.S. Census estimates are now approximately 338 million in 2025, up some 3 million from the date when Sandoval employed the 335 million figure.

3. While many of the examples in this chapter deal with students who are also members of language minority groups, these same points are appropriate for children who are members of traditionally underserved groups, such as African Americans, even if they are English native speakers. A test that has not included African Americans in the norm or validation samples, for example, would likely be inappropriate for their use, even if they could read the questions on the instrument appropriately. In such an instance, it is not clear that the interpretation of scores that result from it would still be appropriate.

4. That is, one population for each different language form of the test.

5. The word *adaptation* is preferred to *translation* because the work is generally more than a translation. Adapting a test to a new language (and culture) will generally involve changing the concepts in some of the test items so that the content is appropriate to test takers from the new culture. See Geisinger (1994) for a more complete description of this process.

6. It is increasingly clear, because of our multilingual society, that professionally developed tests should indicate the level of English required to validly complete the instrument.

21

The Shape of Things to Come

Jane S. Halonen and

Harriet C. Cobb

The year is 2015.

Miguel, a 10-year-old, has just moved into the school district and shows many signs of not getting along well.

The first person to suspect that there might be a problem was the physical health specialist. When she scanned the microchip embedded in Miguel's upper arm, she was dismayed by some of the data she saw. His health data in his early years were scanty. He had been treated for listlessness, anemia, and stomachaches several times before his family moved away from Detroit. His record showed no unusual injuries, but the irregular contact with doctors revealed in the data scan suggested that Miguel's health care was inconsistent at best. His small stature also signaled potential poor nutrition. She suspected that his teeth would need some attention and made a note to keep track of his academic progress.

When the health technician scanned the report on Miguel's family background, she was not surprised by what she saw. Miguel moved from Detroit with his family when his mother lost a good factory job. His father is unemployed and appears to contribute very little to the family's financial support. Case records indicate that he has been treated twice for substance abuse. Miguel has two older brothers. His oldest brother stayed in Detroit when the family moved. Miguel's mother didn't know how he planned to support himself. At 13, the middle brother was eager to come to a new city to join the soccer team. Miguel's mother reported that this brother was a good athlete, a strong student, and had quite a few friends in Detroit. She was confident that he would make the transition well. But she was most worried about her youngest son, Miguel, who had always seemed a bit fragile, but had withdrawn even more ever since the move had taken place.

Miguel drew the school shift that entailed Internet-based remote classes in the morning and group socialization classes in school centers in the afternoon. Population demands forced nearly year-round use of the school building, with children receiving education in shifts. The

Education Planning Commission established remote computer sites in central locations in the neighborhood with the labs overseen by minimally trained computer technicians. From the outset, Miguel transmitted homework irregularly. The only subject area that he seemed genuinely interested in was Geography, especially anything having to do with oceans and rivers. He rarely made eye contact with the computer camera when linked with his teacher. He never generated questions to link with other students in the cluster. The family made no attempt to explain his lackluster performance.

During socialization afternoons, Miguel didn't fare any better. His small stature prompted a great deal of teasing from his new classmates, who seemed to be especially hard on him. His social skills clearly were underdeveloped compared to his peers. At times during recess and physical education, Miguel would retire to the corner of the room and quietly cry. Despite diversity tolerance training sessions, Miguel's classmates seemed to relish picking on the child, whose minimal resources seemed to be dwindling.

The school bus driver initiated the referral for comprehensive assessment and evaluation. Trained in small group dynamics, the driver noted that Miguel always sat at the back of the bus, staring out the window. Although he prevented the other children from picking on Miguel through a carefully designed behavior-modification plan, he recognized that Miguel definitely needed a different level of intervention.

A community case manager pulled together preliminary reports from all of the school personnel who had interacted with Miguel, as well as from his mother and from other people in the community who had interacted with Miguel. She also decided which specialists would constitute the assessment/intervention team.

She contracted with a diagnostic specialist to do the psychoeducational evaluation. Some of the testing could be completed remotely. With minimal supervision by the computer technician, many dimensions of Miguel's performance could be assessed, evaluated, and compared to national norms with the touch of a button. With a bit more work, his responses could be contrasted with the ethnic and gender subgroup norms to arrive at more finely tuned predictions. Local norms, collected by school, neighborhood, and individual classrooms, also were in the database, so that Miguel's performance could be compared with other students served by the school. However, some aspects of the evaluation would have to be conducted face-to-face. She arranged for private transportation to bring Miguel during school hours to complete the testing and selected the practitioner who had the most experience with Hispanic and Latino children.

The case manager would arrange for a blood test to evaluate Miguel's nutritional status and tap his genome profile. This way she could determine if his short stature and poor nutritional development would interact with specific genetic weaknesses that might require gene therapy. She would have to check to see if she had the proper clearance to gain access to the genome information.

The case manager next assigned a community resource specialist to determine other kinds of contacts that might help support the family. At the very least, a family caseworker could assess the strain the move had caused the family. Perhaps Miguel would turn out to be a good candidate to have a foster grandparent in the evenings. Ever since the robust economy had allowed wealthy baby boomers to retire early, the foster grandparent program had become a huge social movement. The movement provided a great opportunity for retirees who needed to find spiritual investment. The community resource specialist might also be able to offer connections to contacts in Detroit to ease the family's anxieties about their oldest son's activities. Job placement and drug screening also might be possible to help the family get back on its feet.

Predicting the future is a high-risk business. Readers may not agree with all of the changes we predicted in the fictional case of Miguel. However, chances are good that you will agree that the next 15-year period is likely to produce some significant changes in how the art, science, and business of mental health practice with school-age children gets accomplished.

Who could have predicted the dramatic changes in assessment and in intervention that would transpire in the years following Lightner Witmer's creation of the first clinic devoted to caring for school-related problems in children (Viney & King, 1998)? Witmer's introduction of the mental health clinic in 1896 was schema-altering in several ways. It acknowledged that the learning problems of children were significant in their own right. It provided an interruption of business as usual for families and schools. And it produced new kinds of practitioners to assist families with developmental challenges posed by their children.

When the profession of child psychology emerged, the problem-solving strategies were distinctly linear. The child's symptoms were seen as signals of significant distress. The parents, probably together in a first-time, enduring marriage, presented the child so the practitioner could fix the problem through kind words and good advice. Early assessment focused on careful observation and interviewing of interested parties, resulting in a straightforward prescription that was perhaps more common sense than science based.

Approximately one century later, the most salient characteristic of practice is complexity. Paying attention to the whole child means conducting an ecological analysis of all the factors that might impinge from a dizzying array of possibilities. For example, the elements that may impinge on any pattern of success or failure listed even in this single volume include the following: genetics, temperament, neurobiology, ethnic heritage, socioeconomic traditions and resources, birth order, gender, language facility, emotional sturdiness, learning preferences, information-processing skills, family relations, peer relations, self-esteem, and so forth. Conducting a comprehensive assessment simply involves many more domains than Lightner Witmer could have imagined.

Models such as the Referral Question Consultation (RQC) process, emphasize an ecological problem-solving model that serves to explain why a referral problem is occurring (Batsche & Knoff, 1995). As suggested in Chapter 4 by McDougal and Chafouleas, it is essential to understand not only *what* behavior occurs, but *why* it occurs. This protocol guides the development of a more specific, yet multifaceted intervention, one that addresses the problems and strengths of a child. Solutions are not merely changes in classroom placement, but a constellation of assistance for students such as Miguel and for the significant others (teachers, family members, and community specialists) who are in a position to reach him, as further elaborated by Cone's discussion in Chapter 16 concerning peer group and strength-based intervention models, and by Porter and Vitulano's description of community-based interventions in Chapter 17.

Possible Changes on the Horizon

Our purpose in writing this chapter is to highlight some of the important directions that we believe will characterize mental health practice in the future. We provide the following predictions, some of which were illustrated by Miguel's story:

Increased reliance on school-based assessment and intervention in community-linked teams. The complexity of assessment and intervention processes argues against a solitary expert attempting to solve problems in an expert but disconnected manner. Emerging assessment technologies that bring together a targeted group of professionals may produce a more economic and efficient means of identifying critical concerns. Not every kind of educational and health professional is required for every case. Therefore, a generalist case manager who can coordinate the diverse findings of more specialized individuals may become a critical new role for the mental health care professional. Multiple Child Resource Teams at each school may provide the best coverage.

The notion of "full-service schools" (Adler & Gardner, 1994) encourages alliances between schools and community health and human services, with the school serving as the base for a comprehensive care system to children and families. Adelman (1996) goes further in describing an "enabling component" as a guide for policy, research, and practice. In this model, an extensive array of school-based interventions are integrated with community-based interventions to produce a "comprehensive and integrated continuum of enabling activity" (p. 435). This approach is aimed specifically at students whose families are of limited means. The clusters of activities include:

- Classroom-focused programs such as tutoring, research-based instructional strategies, and so on
- Student and faculty mental health and social services
- Crisis assistance and prevention
- Support for transitions from grade-to-grade, school-to-school, and school-to-work
- Home involvement to support families in helping their children succeed in school
- Community outreach to both the private and public sectors for support, with a focus on volunteers.

Increased depth of data regarding brain integrity. We recognize that we are at the brink of a remarkable period of discovery and invention regarding direct assessment of brain function. Functional magnetic resonance imaging (MRI) techniques, computerized transaxial tomography (CAT) scans, and positron emission technology (PET) scans already have opened up new vistas in understanding how the brain works and when it fails, as articulated more fully by Lewandowski and Barlow in Chapter 6. Use of electroencaphalogram (EEG) data and neurochemical analyses to aid in diagnosis and to monitor intervention (e.g., of attention-deficit/hyperactivity disorder, Cushman's cautions in Chapter 15 notwithstanding) appear to be only a few years away. Many of the neurological and psychological tests that we currently use may become as outmoded as a mercury-based thermometer, still useful but replaced by more efficient and reliable methods with greater ecological integrity than seen heretofore. Although we cannot predict if a one-stop brain scan will produce all the information we need to understand the role of brain integrity in a child's difficulties, the promise is clear. Knowledge of the normal development of brain structure will enable diagnosticians to recognize subtle deviations as the measurement techniques become increasingly sensitive (Lyon & Rumsey, 1996). As links between differences in brain morphology and learning behavioral disorders are established, components of interventions can be more tailor-made.

Improved access to genetic history.   One of the most exciting aspects of science at the close of the 20th century was the announcement that new secrets are being unveiled through the Human Genome Project. As we decode the basic genetic sites for an array of diseases, the relationship between assessment and intervention becomes more clear. Where a dysfunctional gene contributes to a child's problem, gene therapy may provide a part of the solution. Genetic scientists are focusing primarily on genetically linked diseases. However, we may discover how genes influence other aspects of behavior, both functional and not, as well. This likely prospect is exhilarating from the standpoint of how much might be remediated directly through the genes, but it does not come without a cost. In addition, gene therapy will not work in isolation. Even problems that are predominantly genetic concerns are likely to require interdisciplinary teams and referral networks for assisting families with genetic disorders (Peters, Djurdjinovic, & Baker, 1999). Historically, genetic counseling has been offered at the time of heightened prenatal probability or diagnosis of a birth defect. As a result of an accumulation of massive research efforts, knowledge of all genetic information that exists in human cells is emerging. Child and family mental health providers in the future will consider applications of genetic information to interventions. Such interventions include assisting the family in understanding the implications of the medical condition, choosing among options for coping with adjustment to the condition, the risk of recurrence with regard to care, and knowledge of a family member's medical future. Correcting genetic defects at conception or even in utero may well become possible within the next decade.

Increased concerns about access to protected information.   The prospect of cracking the genetic code is an exciting one, but not without threat to some basic values. For example, the easy distribution of confidential information through electronic means places that information at risk. Certainly it will be helpful for legitimate care providers to have access to the information that will allow them to address the complexity of a child's circumstances; however, unrestricted access to private information poses a grave challenge to our values (Freedman, 1998). We speculate that there will be different kinds of clearances that may be granted to maximize the protection of privacy, but that, nonetheless, facilitate communication that will help solve children's problems.

Determining evaluations will be less focused on diagnosis, and more on determining individual needs.   Old models would attempt to determine Miguel's "intelligence," his achievement on nationally developed and normed tests, and his information-processing deficits with little effort devoted to formulating effective, individualized interventions based on these findings. The outcome typically would be that Miguel might be labeled as mentally retarded, learning disabled, or something else. The intervention would be that Miguel would be removed from the classroom and instructed in a different environment, often using a different curriculum. He would be retested once a year, using the same nationally developed and normed achievement tests, to see if he had made progress. Every third year the entire testing and eligibility evaluation process would recur. In the future, the gap between special education and "individualized regular education" will continue to narrow, as educational, social, and emotional interventions are developed based on an assessment of the child's competencies and needs, rather than from a diagnostic label that does not directly translate to planning interventions (see Chapter 14 for related discussion by Waterman).

We see an increasing emphasis on multidimensional evaluation that is linked directly to intervention. Curriculum-based or "authentic" assessment models are the best known of these approaches. A child is tested, usually in the classroom environment, over material that has just been taught. If results indicate sufficient mastery, the teacher or instructional technologist knows that the child is ready to move to the next curricular activity. If the child has not learned the content, that signals the need to re-teach the material, perhaps in a somewhat different format. There is no time lapse between teaching and testing. Monitoring of progress is simple, direct, and easy to demonstrate to the student, to parents, and to other stakeholders in the educational process (Shapiro & Elliot, 1999). A major current trend in assessment is this move away from testing merely to determine eligibility for entitlement programs (i.e., special education, gifted, remedial education, etc.), and toward "authentic" assessment. As a consequence, labels may be de-emphasized.

Personalized instruction will become standard practice.   Effective instructional strategies such as teaching mnemonic techniques will help Miguel, no matter where he is "placed" for instruction (Kavale & Forness, 1999). For Miguel, more personalized instruction (not necessarily remedial in nature) will be integrated with his computer-based learning tasks. There may be an inaccurate assumption that Miguel is more of a self-regulated learner than he is at this time. Intervention that is supported by research means that effective versus ineffective methods will be more quickly identified and his progress tracked (e.g., with curriculum-based assessment procedure). Rather than being placed in a special education classroom, Miguel's teacher and Miguel will receive instructional consultation from a special education teacher, a reading specialist, or a school-based psychologist. They might assess Miguel's competencies in areas such as how he uses strategies when he confronts unfamiliar material in various academic areas. Their work can be applied and reinforced by his new foster grandparent, who could help add that personal touch that makes Miguel believe in his abilities.

Increased reliance on smaller community units.   In 15 years, our population will be substantially larger, particularly in urban areas. Although we cannot predict how important investment in education will be, it is clear that substantial changes will be necessary for the system to handle all the customers. We think dwindling energy supplies will have a direct impact on how best to deliver education. The emphasis will be on moving greater proportions of activity to home-based or neighborhood-based approaches. In Miguel's story, we created a neighborhood-based computer center in which many traditional subject areas might be delivered electronically via interactive learning strategies. Innovations in education will be developed at the grassroots level, rather than from top-down, rule-driven, or legislative changes (Grimes & Tilly, 1996).

Expanded use of educational volunteers.   Although we may not presume that the economy will continue to provide significant early retirements, the sheer numbers of people who will have reached retirement may provide a new pool of potential helpers who will be looking for ways to add meaning to their lives. Such individuals could comprise a superb corps of educational volunteers to provide assistance to children in need of caring extended families. School volunteers can provide myriad services, such as assistance with screening, tutoring, and supervision (Sheridan, 1995). Population trends suggest that traditional nuclear families may be significant minorities. Mobility also diminishes the degree of extended family contact a child might receive. Increasingly, communities may endorse the development of "families of choice," individuals selected by families to provide the functions that real family members cannot provide. Or, case workers may attempt to convene such networks of support.

Engagement of parents will be personalized.   Parental involvement in improving a child's circumstances is the ideal. However, trends suggest that family units will be more loosely defined and perhaps parents, struggling with providing for the family, may be less emotionally available to engage in programs for change. We anticipate that effective engagement of a family unit will involve resource development for parents as well as children. For example, in Miguel's case, effective intervention strategies may require drug-abuse intervention for his father and job retraining for both parents. To promote engagement, support professionals will stay networked or will purposefully and regularly maintain evening office hours. The school may offer regular parent enrichment classes and develop incentives for participation that are attractive to overcome or avoid participation stigma.

Miguel's mother needs emotional support to address her own feelings of being overwhelmed. A parent support group (perhaps at Miguel's school, short-term, with in-home follow-up) may relieve some of her stress and provide her with targeted techniques to cope with her personal and family situation. In this case, Miguel's aunt is willing to visit regularly to bolster her sister's morale, and to accompany her to Al-Anon meetings. Such increased emphasis on school-based family interventions is a critical component of our future scenario (Vickers & Minke, 1997).

High-achieving families will continue to seek private refuge.   Setting a single standard for all also is harmful to high-achieving children. Many are capable of learning much more than what is embodied in various statewide or national curricula; yet school personnel feel they must not teach beyond the set curriculum because doing so would take time away from less able students who have not learned this minimum. Instructional time is at a premium and, as a result, many schools are decreasing elective courses and enrichment opportunities. Already, many parents from both low- and high-income brackets are moving their bright and capable students to private schools that do not fall under such statewide mandates in order to get a broader and deeper curriculum for their children. In an unintended, but predictable, outcome, the exodus of these children (and their families) from public schools actually will make it harder for the schools to attain the prescribed standard on a school-wide basis. Although this trend seems to be gathering momentum, we suggest that the great divide between the "haves" and "have-nots" eventually will force some reorganization. The child and school psychology literature only briefly acknowledges the trends of charter schools or increasing *partial* privatization of schools (Franklin, 1996). Psychologists who know the literature on effective schools can play a major role in matching alternatives in schooling for children like Miguel.

High-stakes testing will diminish.   The current emphasis on using "high-stakes" testing has a limited life span. Already it is clear that the children who do not pass are either channeled into special education or are retained, with the predictable consequence of markedly greater risk of becoming dropouts. While politicians and the public continue to misunderstand the role of norm-referenced and criterion-referenced testing in providing a quality education, lower-achieving children will become increasingly marginalized. If, as is predictable, the "losers" in high-stakes testing turn out to be low-income or minority students or both, the result will be a further widening of the gap among socioeconomic groups and among ethnic and racial groups in our society. Surely, that outcome is not acceptable to most citizens of the United States (Kohn, 2000).

Availability of targeted and current reference group information.   In place of the challenge to compare results of a child's performance to normative information that may not be a proper match, instruments that will compete successfully for use in the marketplace will have to provide specialized norms—likely in addition to national ones—that allow appropriate comparisons. Test viability will depend on the ease and meaningfulness of comparisons. If this prediction holds, test developers and publishers will need to be increasingly responsive to these marketplace demands by, for instance, offering guidelines about how to develop local norms for a particular instrument.

Report writing will become more focused and tailored.   In view of what we understand about information processing, comprehensive assessment reports may become a thing of the past. As Harvey points out in Chapter 13 of this volume, we need to organize conclusions in a way that promotes the greatest adherence to recommendations. It may be possible to subject the results of an assessment battery to a writing support program that will help the writer order the components of the test in terms of predicted adherence, an innovation that could mitigate some of the liabilities of computer applications in report writing (discussed by Carlson in Chapter 19).

Children's overall programs will be increasingly specialized with the use of technology.   Teachers may become educational systems managers through technology. As we continue to develop greater expertise about the delicate mix of factors that determines learning effectiveness, we may be able to provide individualized programming for children that takes into account attention span, reinforcement preference, and preferred video display styles, among other variables. In situations where children present with learning difficulties, computer-based programs might be able to provide compensation or adjustment. Because our knowledge of children's skills and deficits can be assessed more thoroughly and quickly, we also may see greater credence given to specialty schools that will provide a greater motivational incentive to children through programming and special features (Tennyson & Morrison, 1999).

Collaborative projects will emphasize building resilience.   To the dismay of some traditionalists in education, school experiences have expanded to include training for life well beyond the basics of reading, writing, and 'rithmetic. Because of the growing complexity of life beyond the classroom, we would expect educational designers to build in more formal opportunities for children to develop emotional resilience and social competence (Miller, Brehm, & Whitehouse, 1998). In Miguel's scenario, his mornings would be spent at a computer terminal and his afternoons in affective learning circumstances with other children. Those situations might be derived from careful functional analysis that takes into account his social deficits, emotional needs, and his interests.

Redefinition of professional care providers' time to include more professional development.   The rate of change in the Information Age is dizzying. School and mental health administrators will have to make more purposeful spaces in the work life of the professional, paraprofessional, and volunteers to stay current. There is presently a large chasm between theory and practice. If helpful information continues to be ignored, we simply stay mired on both sides. Well-planned staff development can foster enthusiasm for innovation as well as develop needed competence for enhancing students' learning. Green (1995) delineates a best practice model for staff development that increases the chances for effective programs in the future. If we are truly serious about the promotion of healthy families, then early and comprehensive intervention will require the emergence of new and committed professionals. For example, imagine the following training opportunities: cafeteria workers with social skills training, bus drivers with behavior-modification certificates, bachelor-level trained psychological technicians to work with teachers, information technicians to work on design and delivery of educational systems, information digesters. Given the magnitude of the task ahead, the employment future for well-trained practitioners could be bright indeed.

Conclusion

Future assessment and intervention approaches will become increasingly integrated. We know that children's problems have many causes including, but not limited to, temperament, cognitive characteristics, family interactions and parenting styles, reaction to trauma, and so forth (McConaughy & Achenbach, 1999). Given the complexity of causes, assessment must include information from multiple sources, including direct assessment of the child's physical characteristics, cognitive, educational, socioemotional functioning and health, and less direct information gathering regarding the child's environment (tapping sources of information including parents or caretakers and teachers). Advances in developmental psychopathology emphasize the complexity of the diagnostic process, and provide us with clearer directions for intervention. Further, our knowledge of the relationship between risk and resilience factors mandates a systematic plan and a multisystemic intervention that is meaningfully linked to the assessment.

Interventions that focus on assisting the child in accomplishing developmental tasks, such as academic competence, social–interpersonal skills, emotional intelligence, and self-regulated behavior, are critical. Assessment and intervention, seen as complex and meaningfully intertwined, are squarely at the center of our conceptualization of the future of psychological services to children.

References

Adelman, H. S. (1996). Restructuring education support services and integrating community resources: Beyond the full service school model. *School Psychology Review, 25,* 431–445.

Adler, L., & Gardner, S. (Eds.). (1994). *The politics of linking schools and social services.* Washington, DC: Falmer Press.

Batsche, G. M., & Knoff, H. M. (1995). Linking assessment to intervention. In A. Thomas & J. Grimes (Eds.), *Best practices in school psychology-III* (pp. 569–586). Washington, DC: National Association of School Psychologists.

Dryfoos, J. G. (1994). *Full-service schools: A revolution in health and social services for children, youth, and families.* San Francisco: Jossey-Bass.

Franklin, M. (1996). A practitioner's view of school reform: Does it really matter? *School Psychology Review, 25,* 512–516.

Freedman, T. (1998). Genetic susceptibility testing: Ethical and social quandaries. *Health and Social Work, 23,* 214–222.

Green, S. K. (1995). Implementing a staff development program. In A. Thomas & J. Grimes (Eds.), *Best practices in school psychology-III* (pp. 123–134). Washington, DC: National Association of School Psychologists.

Grimes, J., & Tilly, W. D. (1996). Policy and process: Means to lasting educational change. *School Psychology Review, 25,* 465–476.

Kavale, K. A., & Forness, S. R. (1999). Effectiveness of special education. In C. R. Reynolds & T. B. Gutkin (Eds.), *Handbook of school psychology* (3rd ed., pp. 984–1024). New York: Wiley.

Kohn, A. (2000). *The case against standardized testing.* Portsmouth, NH: Heinemann.

Lyon, G. R., & Rumsey, J. M. (1996). Neuroimaging and developmental disorders: Comments and future directions. In G. R. Lyon & J. M. Rumsey (Eds.), *Neuroimaging: A window to the neurological foundations of learning behavior in children* (pp. 227–236). Baltimore, MD: Paul H. Brooks.

McConaughy, S. H., & Achenbach, T. M. (1999). Contributions of developmental psychopathology. In C. R. Reynolds & T. B. Gutkin (Eds.), *The handbook of school psychology* (3rd ed., pp. 247–270). New York: Wiley.

Miller, G. E., Brehm, K., & Whitehouse, S. (1998). Reconceptualizing school-based prevention for antisocial behavior within a resiliency framework. *School Psychology Review, 27,* 364–379.

Peters, S. A., Djurdjinovic, L., & Baker, D. (1999). The genetic self: The human genome project, genetic counseling, and family therapy. *Families, Systems, and Health, 17,* 5–25.

Shapiro, E. S., & Elliot, S. N. (1999). Curriculum-based assessment and other performance-based assessment strategies. In C. R. Reynolds & T. B. Gutkin (Eds.), *Handbook of school psychology* (3rd ed., pp. 383–408). New York: Wiley.

Sheridan, S. (1995). Best practices in fostering school/community relationships in best practices in school psychology. In A. Thomas & J. Grimes (Eds.), *Best practices in school psychology-III* (pp. 203–212). Washington, DC: National Association of School Psychologists.

Tennyson, R. D., & Morrison, D. (1999). Computers in education and school psychology: The existing and emerging technology knowledge base supporting interventions with children. In C. R. Reynolds & T. B. Gutkin (Eds.), *Handbook of school psychology* (3rd ed., pp. 885–906). New York: Wiley.

Vickers, H. S., & Minke, K. M. (1997). Family systems and the family–school connection in children's needs. In G. G. Bear, K. M. Minke, & A. Thomas (Eds.), *Children's needs II* (pp. 547–558). Bethesda, MD: National Association of School Psychologists.

Viney, W., & King, D. B. (1998). *A history of psychology: Ideas and context.* Boston: Allyn and Bacon.

End Note

The authors wish to express gratitude for the assistance of our graduate students, Alice Bontempo and Kevin Szmejterowicz.

Author Index

376

Subject Index